Sentence Basics

Diction, Usage,
and Mechanics

Sentence Basics

Diction, Usage, and Mechanics

Elliott L. Smith
Ferris State University

Blythe M. Smith

St. Martin's Press   NEW YORK

Senior editor: Karen Allanson
Manager, publishing services: Emily Berleth
Publishing services associate: Kalea Chapman
Project management: Omega Publishing Services, Inc.
Art director: Sheree Goodman
Cover design: Carolyn Joseph
Cover art: Private Collection

For information, write:
St. Martin's Press, Inc.
175 Fifth Avenue
New York, NY 10010

ISBN: 0-312-06560-4

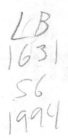

To the Instructor

The goal of *Sentence Basics: Diction, Usage, and Mechanics* is to provide students with a "user-friendly" resource that will instruct and assist them—particularly at the drafting, revising, and editing stages of the writing process—in a variety of items that may broadly be categorized under the label of *usage*. And, of course, an equal goal of the text is to provide composition instructors with an effective teaching tool for an entry-level composition course.

Sentence Basics is divided into four parts comprising ten chapters:

Part One: "Diction and Usage"
Part Two: "Sentence Mechanics"
Part Three: "Sentence Editing"
· Part Four: "The Writing Process"

Part One includes four chapters. Chapter 1, "Introduction to Diction and Usage," presents the term *diction* as it is used throughout the text, and includes three self-checking pretests to be taken in turn before the student begins each of the next three chapters. Chapters 2, 3, and 4 each present a series of four-page instructional sequences that explain (with the help of work exercises) various issues of diction and usage. Chapter 2, "Nonstandard or Inappropriate Expressions," examines some common deviations along with their more standard counterparts (e.g., *alot / a lot; alright / all right; could of / could have; on account of / because; kind of* or *sort of / mildly*). Chapter 3, "Words That Sound Alike," explains usage differences between pairs or sets of similar-sounding words (e.g., *addition / edition; cite / sight / site; complement / compliment; medal / meddle / metal / mettle*). Chapter 4, "Important Distinctions," points out necessary distinctions between pairs or sets of terms that are commonly confused and imprecisely used (e.g., *adapt / adopt; agree to / agree with / agree on;*

among/between; number of/amount of). Each of these three chapters concludes with a review exercise, and the Instructor's Manual provides quizzes that may be used at regular intervals within the sequences.

Part Two of *Sentence Basics* includes three chapters. Chapter 5, "Introduction to Sentence Mechanics," defines *sentence mechanics* or *mechanical conventions* and presents two self-checking pretests to be taken in turn before the student begins each of the next two chapters. Three "minor" marks of punctuation—brackets, slashes, and the ellipsis mark—are treated here, principally as a matter of emphasis. Chapter 6, "Current Conventions of Punctuation," considers the comma, semicolon, colon, period, question mark, exclamation point, dash, parentheses, apostrophe, and quotation marks. Each section and subsection includes explanatory material, elaborate sets of examples, and a variety of exercise quizzes. Chapter 7, "Additional Mechanical Conventions," considers the use of capitals, abbreviations, numbers, italics (underlining), and hyphens. Both of these chapters conclude with comprehensive review exercises, and answers to all of the exercises are provided in the Instructor's Manual.

Part Three of *Sentence Basics* includes two chapters. Chapter 8, "Commonly Occurring Sentence Problems," begins with a self-checking pretest that covers all ten of the sentence problems treated in this chapter and Chapter 9. The errors covered here are the (1) sentence fragment, (2) run-on sentence, (3) comma splice, (4) subject-verb agreement error, and (5) pronoun case error. Chapter 9, "Commonly Occurring Sentence Problems Continued," carries on with the (6) pronoun-antecedent error, (7) misplaced modifier, (8) dangling modifier, (9) faulty parallelism, and (10) faulty verb form. The emphasis throughout these two chapters is upon error recognition and editing. Each of these chapters concludes with a set of five review exercises, and the Instructor's Manual includes answers to these, along with a set of ten additional quizzes (with answers) on all ten sentence errors.

Part Four of *Sentence Basics,* "The Writing Process," features Chapter 10, "Introduction to the Writing Process." The chapter has three main parts: (1) Pre-Writing, (2) Drafting, and (3) Revising. Intended to provide beginning students with an introductory framework for thinking about the writing process, the chapter also features discussions of purpose, audience, free association, brainstorming, mapping, the working thesis and the thesis statement, editing, and proofreading. The drafting section presents appropriate introductory discussions of the traditional organizational strategies: (1) narration, (2) description, (3) exemplification, (4) comparison, (5) analogy, (6) classification, (7) analysis, (8) process, (9) cause/effect, and (10) definition.

Sentence Basics: Diction, Usage, and Mechanics is a very fundamental and focused text growing out of many years in the classroom. Although it is accessible to most students, it does not in any way patronize anyone; it does not assume—as many texts today seem to—that current students are incapable of learning something simply because they have not learned it in the past. To the contrary, the text assumes that virtually all can, and will, learn everything here. The method of instruction throughout is that of instructional examples followed by practical exercises—a redundancy of instructional examples followed by a redundancy of practical exercises.

We are grateful to the reviewers who assisted us in the development of this book: Vivian Brown, Laredo Junior College; Paul Devlin, Ferris State University; Osborne Robinson, Jr., Catonsville Community College; and Elizabeth Wahlquist, Brigham Young University.

Elliott L. Smith
Blythe M. Smith

Contents

Sentence Basics

*Diction, Usage,
and Mechanics*

PART ONE
DICTION AND USAGE

Chapter 1

Introduction to Diction and Usage

To be able to write well, you must possess a number of important skills. Some textbooks call them competencies. One of the most important of these skills—one that is often overlooked or neglected even in writing classes—has to do with word selection. *Diction,* an important word in the title of this book, as well as in the title of this introductory chapter, can be defined as "the choice of words, or groups of words, that one uses to say or write something." Thus, an incorrect, inaccurate, inappropriate, or imprecise word choice is an error in diction. For example, if you write *accidently* for *accidentally, heartrendering* for *heartrending,* or *publically* for *publicly,* you have made an error in diction. Similarly, if you inadvertently write *coarse* when you mean *course, feudal* when you mean *futile,* or *trader* when you mean *traitor,* you have made an error in diction. A diction error also occurs when the expression *all the farther* is substituted for *as far as,* when *owing to the fact that* is substituted for *because,* or when *viable alternative* is substituted for *good choice.* Finally, diction errors occur when writers are not careful about maintaining important distinctions between words and expressions that have related meanings. This carelessness often results in confusion between such pairs as *affect* and *effect, comprise* and *compose, disinterested* and *uninterested,* and *envious* and *enviable.*

The purpose of this chapter is to introduce you to the range of potential diction problems that student writers—and indeed writers of any type—have to contend with day to day. To begin, read the following twenty sentences and fill in the blanks.

1

1. Many adults look back on the period of their own (*adolescence / adolescents*) _____

    _____ with mixed emotions.

2. They slept for (*a while / awhile*) _____ and then drove for another eight hours.

3. Once again, we were (*flustrated / frustrated*) _____ in our effort to get a Whammo Burger franchise.

4. No matter where I looked, I could find no one who would (*lend / loan*) _____

    _____ me any money.

5. Not everyone can (*bare / bear*) _____ all the stress that this position engenders.

6. A (*bunch / group*) _____ of rowdies showed up at the party looking for a fight.

7. What was the young man's (*principal / principle*) _____ means of supporting himself?

8. (*Due to / Because of*) _____ your previous experience, the company is considering offering you the position.

9. I drove (*passed / past*) _____ the house several times before going in.

10. Amos and Buffy say they have been in love with (*each other / one another*) _____

    _____ since grade school.

11. In my opinion, there is no such thing as a (*minuscule / miniscule*) _____ amount of leaking radioactive material.

12. By the middle of August, the children are usually (*anxious / eager*) _____

    _____ to get back to school.

13. From the surrounding mountains, the sweet (*cent / scent / sent*) _____ of honeysuckle embraced the village.

14. Most of the students performed (*exceedingly / excessively*) _____ well on the national examination.

15. Clearly, the building was (*burglarized / burgled*) _____ by amateurs.

16. The Antiquity Society is looking for (*historic / historical*) _____ evidence that the Red Paint tribes actually lived in the region.

17. The cheese and crackers will (*complement / compliment*) _____ the spicy vegetable soup quite nicely.

18. Many humans seem to have a fundamental (*disability / inability*) _____ to imagine a life different from their own.

19. A major (*hinderance / hindrance*) _____ to improving public education is public apathy.

20. Cadwallader has decided to move even (*farther / further*) _____ north of the border—up, he says, where virtue still lives.

The answers to the odd-numbered sentences are not difficult, if you know them—that is, they are not arguable: (1) *adolescence*, (3) *frustrated*, (5) *bear*, (7) *principal*, (9) *past*, (11) *minuscule*, (13) *scent*, (15) *burglarized*, (17) *complement*, and (19) *hindrance*. However, because language usage is not an exact science, not all knowledgeable people—including composition instructors—will agree that all the distinctions called for in the even-numbered sentences are equally important or necessary. Nevertheless, the intended answers are: (2) *a while*, (4) *lend*, (6) *group*, (8) *Because of*, (10) *each other*, (12) *eager*, (14) *exceedingly*, (16) *historical*, (18) *inability*, and (20) *farther*.

In sentence 2, *awhile*, being an adverb, is an inappropriate object of the preposition *for*. In sentence 4, *lend* is a better choice because it is always a verb, and the sentence clearly calls for a verb. In sentence 6, *group* is a better choice because *bunch* tends to refer to things that are fastened together. *Because of* is a better choice in sentence 8 because *due to* is a pretentious substitute for *because of*, meaning "on account of." In sentence 10, *each other* is preferable because *one another* can be more precisely used to refer to more than two of something. *Eager* is the better response in sentence 12 because *anxious* means "worried" or "filled with anxiety," not simply "in a hurry." In sentence 14, *exceedingly* is the better choice because *excessively* is a negative term meaning "too much." *Historical* is the more precise usage in sentence 16 because *historic* does not mean "established by history," the meaning needed. In sentence 18, *inability* is the better choice because it means "a fundamental incapacity." And *farther* is a better choice than *further* in sentence 20 because distance is the key consideration, not amount or degree.

The goal of diction study is accurate, appropriate, and precise usage. This goal should not be misunderstood as a preference for pretentiousness, for hairsplitting, or for verbal stuffiness. To the contrary, it is sloppy and imprecise diction that so often gives rise to pretentious, "nice," or stuffy writing, resulting in such inappropriate substitutions as *share with* for *tell*, *impact negatively* for *harm*, *interact verbally* for *talk*, *opted for* for *chose*, *being as how* for *because*, or *in regard to* for *about*.

Because the study of diction includes a substantial amount of material, we have broken this material down into three parts and devoted the next three chapters to these parts. Chapter 2 is entitled "Nonstandard or Inappropriate Expressions"; Chapter 3 is entitled "Words That Sound Alike"; and Chapter 4 is entitled "Important Distinctions." Each of these chapters begins with an introduction that carefully explains the material to be presented, the exercises to be worked, and the quizzes that your instructor will likely give. The remainder of this chapter (Chapter 1) includes three self-scoring pretest exercises, one for each of the subsequent three chapters. You should do the first pretest exercise *after* reading the introductory material to Chapter 2 but *before* beginning to work the instructional exercises in the chapter. Then follow the same procedure for the second and third pretests.

To work these pretest exercises, simply encircle or underline the correct italicized word within the parens of each numbered sentence. If the first choice is the correct one, put an *A* in the blank in front of the number. If the second choice is the correct one, put a *B* in the blank. Sometimes there will be third and fourth choices. Be sure to use the appropriate letter in the blank. Please keep in mind that you are not expected to get high scores on these pretests; they are designed to demonstrate to you what you will need to learn as you are doing the instructional exercises in the chapters.

SELF-CHECKING PRETEST EXERCISE 1
Nonstandard or Inappropriate Expressions

_____ 1. There was (*a lot / alot*) of confusion at the planning session.

_____ 2. We finally reached a consensus (*about / as to*) what should be done next.

_____ 3. The wrong oil was (*accidently / accidentally*) put into the truck.

_____ 4. Few thought the film was (*all that / particularly*) entertaining.

_____ 5. We must do an (*analysis / analysation*) of each proposal.

_____ 6. This is (*all the farther / as far as*) the party will go in supporting the bill.

_____ 7. Please (*ask / state*) the question as clearly as you can.

_____ 8. What (*aspect / area*) of law enforcement are you interested in?

_____ 9. (*Be sure and / Be sure to*) contact your advisor at least once each month.

_____ 10. (*Because / Being as*) there was so little time left, we declined the invitations.

_____ 11. The store had been (*burglarized / burgled*) four times within a single year.

_____ 12. One cannot help (*but wonder / wondering*) who discovered the truth.

_____ 13. The cause of the breakdown (*was / was due to*) a faulty electric cable.

_____ 14. The quarrel (*centered on / centered around*) who would head the new division.

_____ 15. Elizabeth (*claimed / insisted*) that she had never been a member of the Communist party.

_____ 16. (*Many / Considerable*) proposals were presented at the conference.

_____ 17. The revised motion was substantially (*different from / different than*) the original one.

_____ 18. Speedy Motors is (*doubtful if / doubtful that*) it can continue to absorb such losses.

_____ 19. Not everyone is (*enthusiastic / enthused*) about the prospect of going to Scandinavia.

_____ 20. The less expensive models were (*equally as / just as*) reliable as the more expensive ones.

_____ 21. Germaine's (*expertise / competence*) at handling angry customers is amazing.

_____ 22. Most of the (*women* / *females*) on the committee supported the motion.

_____ 23. Once again, we were (*flustrated* / *frustrated*) in our efforts to win the championship.

_____ 24. The class had many (*fun* / *enjoyable*) afternoons in the park.

_____ 25. This university (*has got to* / *must*) improve its image across the state.

_____ 26. The audience was not prepared for such a (*heartrending* / *heartrendering*) story.

_____ 27. Noise can be a great (*hindrance* / *hinderance*) to concentration.

_____ 28. We must (*hone in on* / *focus on*) the problems that are causing us the most trouble.

_____ 29. Lack of regular exercise can (*impact negatively* / *affect*) one's general well-being.

_____ 30. I have just read an (*in-depth* / *exhaustive*) account of the Bay of Pigs fiasco.

_____ 31. People should (*talk* / *interact verbally*) with their neighbors as often as possible.

_____ 32. The cat spent the afternoon looking for (*its* / *it's* / *its'*) slippers.

_____ 33. A few people were (*kind of* / *somewhat*) offended by the officer's remarks.

_____ 34. Jacqueline is a (*forceful* / *loquacious*) and disarming apologist for women's rights.

_____ 35. Conrad spends (*a majority* / *most*) of his free time in the computer lab.

_____ 36. Julian's only (*memento* / *momento*) of the trip is a book of poetry purchased in Inverness.

_____ 37. Our profits have been (*miniscule* / *minuscule*) compared to those of our competitors.

_____ 38. Most of the (*negatory* / *negative*) mail came from out of town.

_____ 39. Acme Corporation lost the contract (*on account of* / *because*) it submitted a late bid.

_____ 40. Douglas Manufacturing has (*chosen* / *opted*) to discontinue its retail product lines.

_____ 41. It takes awhile to (*orientate* / *orient*) oneself to living in a foreign country.

_____ 42. The heating bill is high (*because* / *due to the fact that*) the house is inadequately insulated.

_____ 43. Benjamin becomes (*paranoid* / *uneasy*) every time a storm is in the forecast.

_____ 44. These two have been (*partners* / *pardners*) in the car wash business for two decades.

_____ 45. Can you remember (*the point in time* / *when*) Silver Bridge fell into the Ohio River?

_____ 46. Prepare yourselves; the king will arrive (*presently* / *soon*).

_____ 47. What (*preventive* / *preventative*) measures are now available?

_____ 48. The president of the union stated (*publicly* / *publically*) that the pension fund was sound.

_____ 49. Please explain the (*reasons why* / *reasons that*) we are losing our foreign markets.

_____ 50. (*Regardless* / *Irregardless*) of public opinion, this is what must be done.

_____ 51. The residents of the valley were (*taken away* / *evacuated*) only minutes before the avalanche.

_____ 52. You will (*seldom ever* / *almost never*) see an indigo bunting within the sanctuary.

_____ 53. Students are (*supposed to* / *suppose to*) document their sources on this assignment.

_____ 54. We must (*try to* / *try and*) present ourselves as responsible members of the community.

_____ 55. How often does the average student (*utilize* / *use*) the library?

_____ 56. The board is looking for a (*viable* / *workable*) plan to downsize the university.

_____ 57. Exactly when the exchange (*transpired* / *occurred*) is not a matter of public record.

_____ 58. Not only were the meetings (*infrequent* / *unfrequent*), but they were also brief.

_____ 59. Was the customer satisfied (*with the paint* / *paintwise*)?

_____ 60. The (*lady* / *woman*) who lives in the upstairs apartment teaches mathematics at the university.

Answers: 1–A, 2–A, 3–B, 4–B, 5–A, 6–B, 7–B, 8–B, 9–B, 10–A, 11–A, 12–B, 13–A, 14–A, 15–B, 16–A, 17–A, 18–B, 19–A, 20–B, 21–B, 22–A, 23–B, 24–B, 25–B, 26–A, 27–A, 28–B, 29–B, 30–B, 31–A, 32–A, 33–B, 34–A, 35–B, 36–A, 37–B, 38–B, 39–B, 40–A, 41–B, 42–A, 43–B, 44–A, 45–B, 46–B, 47–A, 48–A, 49–B, 50–A, 51–A, 52–B, 53–A, 54–A, 55–B, 56–B, 57–B, 58–A, 59–A, 60–A.

SELF-CHECKING PRETEST EXERCISE 2
Words That Sound Alike

_____ 1. Christian monks usually live (*acetic* / *ascetic*) lives.

_____ 2. Many (*adolescence* / *adolescents*) are unsure about what they want to do in life.

_____ 3. It is difficult to make an (*allusion* / *elusion* / *illusion*) to a literary work that one has not read.

_____ 4. Ned wants to become a systems (*analyst* / *annalist*).

_____ 5. Is there an effective (*anecdote* / *antidote*) for the venom of a mamba?

_____ 6. The (*ascent* / *assent*) of the hot-air balloons was quite impressive.

_____ 7. Regular (*attendance* / *attendants*) is compulsory in all these classes.

_____ 8. The current reduction in applications does not (*auger* / *augur*) well for the university.

_____ 9. Mercedes occasionally wears (*bazaar* / *bizarre*) costumes to class.

_____ 10. Who could (*bear* / *bare*) to live such a monotonous life?

_____ 11. The senior citizen (*bloc* / *block*) undid the senator's campaign to gain the nomination.

_____ 12. If you have the skill to remove it, there is a fine sculpture hiding within that (*bolder* / *boulder*).

_____ 13. That miser has a fortune in gold (*bouillon* / *bullion*) buried in the cellar.

_____ 14. Perhaps you should (*bridle* / *bridal*) your temper a bit.

_____ 15. What a (*callous* / *callus*) disposition the old man has.

_____ 16. The caviar (*canapé* / *canopy*) was quite tasty.

_____ 17. The primary (*cannon* / *canon*) of militant capitalism is that the rich shall inherit the earth.

_____ 18. We must (*canvass* / *canvas*) the delegation before voting.

_____ 19. Was the (*capital* / *capitol*) building burned to the ground during the Civil War?

_____ 20. Because the motion (*sensor* / *censor*) malfunctioned, the burglers were not caught.

_____ 21. The dogs were unable to pick up the (*cent* / *scent* / *sent*) of the wily fox.

_____ 22. This is the (*cite* / *sight* / *site*) where the new hockey arena would have been built.

_____ 23. The Bulldogs (*clinched* / *clenched*) the league championship without having to play another game.

_____ 24. There may be only a fine line between (*complacence* / *complaisance*) and graciousness.

_____ 25. The grade given me by the instructor was a sufficient (*complement* / *compliment*) for my efforts.

_____ 26. Once again, the (*courier* / *currier*) service has lost an important package.

_____ 27. Everyone stood in a (*cue* / *queue*) waiting for the tour buses to arrive.

_____ 28. Only the (*currant* / *current*) issue of *Newsweek* carried the story.

_____ 29. During the long winter months, sunlight (*deprivation* / *depravation*) can affect one's disposition.

_____ 30. The company's (*descent* / *dissent*) into bankruptcy seemed inevitable.

_____ 31. Each company within the conglomerate is a (*discreet* / *discrete*) operation.

_____ 32. Such expert stroking will no doubt (*elicit* / *illicit*) a favorable response.

_____ 33. All afternoon the storm seemed (*eminent* / *imminent*).

_____ 34. Only once did anyone hear a (*faint* / *feint*) tapping sound on the pipe.

_____ 35. Because our efforts to raise capital proved (*feudal* / *futile*), we closed the business.

_____ 36. Not until midsummer do the gardens achieve full (*florescence* / *fluorescence*).

_____ 37. You must move (*foreword* / *forward*) at once on this project.

_____ 38. The (*fowl* / *foul*) odor coming from the oven was that of an overdone turkey.

_____ 39. You should know by now that life is a (*gamble* / *gambol*); there are no guarantees.

_____ 40. The (*gorilla* / *guerrilla*) forces had obviously been trained in the jungle.

_____ 41. Such fabricated meat is too (*grisly* / *gristly* / *grizzly*) to enjoy.

_____ 42. A (*hail* / *hale*) of bullets kept the squad pinned to the ground.

_____ 43. These cookies were (*handmade* / *handmaid*) by students studying for degrees in home economics.

_____ 44. These shirt (*hangars* / *hangers*) were made in Bath, England, in the nineteenth century.

_____ 45. The Lapps are a (*hardy* / *hearty*) people, accustomed to the frigid Arctic winters.

_____ 46. Naomi sees herself as a (*heroin* / *heroine*) to life in general.

_____ 47. Each day the peasants visit the (*holey* / *holy* / *wholly*) shrine and pray for a miracle.

_____ 48. This course is supposed to provide some (*incite* / *insight*) into how the physical universe operates.

_____ 49. It takes a (*knave* / *nave*) and a scoundrel to steal money from the collection plate.

_____ 50. Climbing the (*ladder* / *latter*) of success is a task that cannot be accomplished overnight.

_____ 51. Only (*lean* / *lien*) meat should be used in this stew.

_____ 52. About midnight, (*lightening* / *lightning*) struck the barn and then the water tower.

_____ 53. A stronger (*magnate* / *magnet*) is needed to turn the second vane.

_____ 54. The old lion had a magnificent (*maize* / *maze*)-hued (*main* / *mane*).

_____ 55. What (*manner* / *manor*) of man would sell his own family into slavery?

_____ 56. A military (*medal* / *meddle* / *metal* / *mettle*) is hardly adequate recompense for the loss of a son or a daughter.

_____ 57. Today it takes a certain stubborn (*medal* / *meddle* / *metal* / *mettle*) for a person to enter a public school classroom in the role of teacher.

_____ 58. I prefer chocolate (*moose* / *mousse*) to a Canadian (*moose* / *mousse*).

_____ 59. The class sat (*moot* / *mute*) as the instructor repeated his request for (*assistants* / *assistance*).

_____ 60. Mrs. Mercedes Vanderoften, (*nay* / *nee* / *neigh*) Vanderseldom, rose to present her case.

_____ 61. A city (*ordinance* / *ordnance*) prohibiting mimes from performing in public buildings was approved unanimously.

_____ 62. Your chronic fatigue suggests that you should (*pair* / *pare* / *pear*) your activities by about half.

_____ 63. No one wants to (*parish* / *perish*) in a shark-infested sea.

_____ 64. Tourism long ago (*passed* / *past*) manufacturing as the barometer of the local economy.

_____ 65. You can't (*pedal* / *peddle* / *petal*) communism to people who are well fed and well clothed.

_____ 66. The new (*peer* / *pier*) extends much farther into the bay than the old one did.

_____ 67. A quarter (*penance* / *pennants*) doesn't make up for a ten-dollar wrong.

_____ 68. The first of the (*plodders* / *plotters*) to be charged denied any knowledge of the coup.

_____ 69. Why (*pore* / *pour* / *poor*) over your notes every night when the exam is weeks away?

_____ 70. Alas, the (*premiere* / *premier*) showing of the film resulted in riots all over town.

_____ 71. Isn't the first (*principle* / *principal*) of Christianity supposed to be "love one another"?

_____ 72. We come here (*quiet* / *quite*) often, but not too often.

_____ 73. How long can the duke expect to (*rain* / *reign* / *rein*) over his restive fiefdom?

_____ 74. The University Players are doing a (*review* / *revue*) featuring skits from old television comedy shows.

_____ 75. We (*road* / *rode* / *rowed*) home in the back of a '58 Chevy pickup.

_____ 76. You can't get away with talking such (*rot* / *wrought*) to people who have been around the block once or twice.

_____ 77. The local art (*salon* / *saloon* / *solon*) is currently featuring a collection of minimalist watercolors.

_____ 78. In those lean times we ate meat (*shear* / *sheer*) enough to read the newspaper through.

_____ 79. One cannot help (*shudder* / *shutter*) at the dangers that today await the growing child.

_____ 80. Old Cadwallader is the (*sole* / *soul*) survivor of his high school Parcheesi team.

_____ 81. Like Bartleby, I prefer to remain (*stationery* / *stationary*) at the moment.

_____ 82. During the cold winter, we often dream of (*summary* / *summery*) afternoons just like this one.

_____ 83. With (*their* / *there* / *they're*) arms held high, the prisoners marched out of the courtroom.

_____ 84. Will (*their* / *there* / *they're*) be time enough after lunch to visit the alligator farm?

_____ 85. Once upon a time, a (*trader* / *traitor*) like you would have been quickly executed.

_____ 86. (*Undue* / *Undo*) pressure is being put on these children to succeed.

_____ 87. Steadman is a (*voracious* / *veracious*) consumer of trivia games.

_____ 88. It was a (*virile* / *viral*) infection that had weakened the distance runners.

_____ 89. How much toxic (*waist* / *waste*) can one landfill accommodate?

_____ 90. At this time of year the (*weather* / *whether*) can be quite unpredictable.

Answers: 1–B, 2–B, 3–A, 4–A, 5–B, 6–A, 7–A, 8–B, 9–B, 10–A, 11–A, 12–B, 13–B, 14–A, 15–A, 16–A, 17–B, 18–A, 19–B, 20–A, 21–B, 22–C, 23–A, 24–B, 25–B, 26–A, 27–B, 28–B, 29–A, 30–A, 31–B, 32–A, 33–B, 34–A, 35–B, 36–A, 37–B, 38–B, 39–A, 40–B, 41–B, 42–A, 43–A, 44–B, 45–A, 46–B, 47–B, 48–B, 49–A, 50–A, 51–A, 52–B, 53–B, 54–A;–B, 55–A, 56–A, 57–D, 58–B;–A, 59–B;–B, 60–B, 61–A, 62–B, 63–B, 64–A, 65–B, 66–B, 67–A, 68–B, 69–A, 70–B, 71–A, 72–B, 73–B, 74–B, 75–B, 76–A, 77–A, 78–B, 79–A, 80–A, 81–B, 82–B, 83–A, 84–B, 85–B, 86–A, 87–A, 88–B, 89–B, 90–A.

SELF-CHECKING PRETEST EXERCISE 3
Important Distinctions

_____ 1. Is (*a* / *an*) ounce of prevention still worth a pound of cure?

_____ 2. Currently there is an (*excess* / *access*) of college graduates in the field of criminal justice.

_____ 3. Montague has been (*accused of* / *charged with*) making insensitive remarks on occasion.

_____ 4. Gretchen has long been a(n) (*addicted* / *devoted*) supporter of the Hinterland Light Opera Society.

_____ 5. Isn't it too late to (*affect* / *effect*) a change in the party platform?

_____ 6. (*All* / *All of*) the fruit had been contaminated by a chemical spray.

_____ 7. Doesn't anyone have an (*alternate* / *alternative*) proposal to offer?

_____ 8. (*Although* / *Though*) the climate here is pleasant enough, it rains too much.

_____ 9. Elizabeth is in (*always* / *all ways*) an outstanding student.

_____ 10. Today there is a pervasive distrust of government (*among* / *between*) the common people.

_____ 11. Everyone was (*anxious* / *eager*) to finish packing and leave for the lake.

_____ 12. The local department stores do not have sales clerks (*anymore* / *any more*).

_____ 13. Hadn't the chief been (*appraised* / *apprised*) of the fact that the prisoner had escaped?

_____ 14. You should (*assure* / *ensure* / *insure*) your house and its contents for full replacement value.

_____ 15. The lecture sessions at these conferences are (*particularly* / *awfully*) interesting.

_____ 16. They worked in the yard for (*awhile* / *a while*), then cleaned the garage.

_____ 17. You are the (*benefactor* / *beneficiary*) of having had the opportunity to attend a good university.

_____ 18. It was a (*benign* / *malign*) wind that brought the crippled ship safely to port.

_____ 19. Our (*biennial* / *biannual*) conventions always occur in odd-numbered years.

_____ 20. Alas, poor Cadwallader has been (*bit / bitten*) by the desire to live a life of public service.

_____ 21. A malfunctioning valve was the (*cause of / reason for*) the explosion.

_____ 22. (*Censor / Censure*) by one's peers can sometimes be more embarrassing than traditional punishment.

_____ 23. Genevieve is the most (*ceremonial / ceremonious*) individual I have ever known.

_____ 24. Don't buy a(n) (*cheap / inexpensive*) car; it will cost you a fortune over time.

_____ 25. Temper tantrums seem a bit (*childish / childlike*) for a psychology professor who writes books about human behavior.

_____ 26. There is nothing wrong with the real estate business that a few more paying (*clients / customers*) wouldn't cure.

_____ 27. As one drives north from Florida in the early spring, the (*climatic / climactic*) differences can be dramatic.

_____ 28. The new league will be (*comprised of / composed of*) twelve teams.

_____ 29. You must present yourself more (*confidently / confidentially*) if you want others to have faith in you.

_____ 30. When she eats, Jessica plays with her food (*consistently / constantly*).

_____ 31. Try not to be so openly (*contemptuous / contemptible*) of other people.

_____ 32. A (*continual / continuous*) line of cars encircled the entire city.

_____ 33. Although the story was (*credible / creditable*), it wouldn't have been had it been told by anyone else.

_____ 34. The analysis was quite (*decisive / incisive*); it cut straight to the issues in question.

_____ 35. Every unit that was produced in 1990 had (*defective / deficient*) gaskets and thus had to be recalled.

_____ 36. Once this car becomes an antique, it will no longer (*deprecate / depreciate*) in value.

_____ 37. More and more people seem (*uninterested / disinterested*) in watching professional football on television.

_____ 38. In basketball, tall players have a (*distinct / distinctive*) advantage over short ones.

_____ 39. We were declared ineligible (*due to / because of*) a recent change in the rules.

_____ 40. After the game, all the players shook hands with (*each other / one another*).

_____ 41. Which fuel is more (*economic / economical*), natural gas or electricity?

_____ 42. So far, the cure for the common cold has remained (*elusive / illusive*).

_____ 43. Miriam found herself in the (*enviable / envious*) position of having four scholarship offers from which to choose.

_____ 44. "Nothing succeeds like success" seemed to be the (*epigram / epigraph / epithet / epitaph*) most appropriate to the situation.

_____ 45. Emotional extremes seem to be a characteristic (*epidemic / endemic / pandemic*) to the adolescent state of mind.

_____ 46. A seventy-thirty split in assets doesn't seem (*equable / equitable*) to me.

_____ 47. Dunstan buys a new car (*ever so often / every so often*), four or five just this year.

_____ 48. Everyone agreed that the judgment was (*exceedingly / excessively*) fair and reasonable.

_____ 49. We spent an (*exhaustive / exhausting*) weekend putting new siding on the house.

_____ 50. The regular exchange of personal letters has today become something of an (*exotic / erotic / esoteric*) means of social intercourse, engaged in by only a few.

_____ 51. Today many people travel (*farther / further*) to go to work than a medieval peasant traveled in a lifetime.

_____ 52. No (*fewer / less*) than three hundred people showed up for the demonstration.

_____ 53. Poor Boris is likely to (*founder / flounder*) from job to job for the rest of his life.

_____ 54. Don't risk even a (*glance / glimpse*) directly into the flame of the larger furnaces.

_____ 55. How (*good / well*) did the class do on the placement tests?

_____ 56. The families were (*gratified / grateful*) to learn that none of the victims had suffered.

_____ 57. It seemed a bit ironic that the thief was (*hanged / hung*) for stealing a rope.

_____ 58. (*He / Him / Himself*) and Bruno always went fishing on Sunday morning.

_____ 59. Actually, there is no (*historic / historical*) evidence that the incident ever occurred.

_____ 60. Are these people (*hypercritical / hypocritical*), or do they really think they are perfect?

_____ 61. The incident was (*illustrative / illustrious*) of the magnitude of human folly.

_____ 62. A creative society requires large numbers of (*imaginary / imaginative*) people.

_____ 63. Cadwallader is (*incapable of / unable to*) pay(ing) his bills at the moment; he hasn't received his inheritance.

_____ 64. What an (*incredible / incredulous*) season the Rhinos had, fourteen wins without a loss.

_____ 65. This is one of those (*ingenious / ingenuous*) inventions that will require a dozen additional ones to make the first one necessary.

_____ 66. Slowly and (*insidiously / invidiously*) the ever-warming planet extinguished all human life.

_____ 67. You can't (*integrate / segregate*) the parts of your life into absolutely discrete segments.

_____ 68. Although your goals are (*laudable / laudatory*), your behavior is reprehensible.

_____ 69. We can't just (*lie / lay*) down and die; we must fight.

_____ 70. Quentin can't play a recorder, (*leave alone / let alone*) a fluegelhorn.

_____ 71. No one would (*lend / loan*) the poor man a dollar.

_____ 72. With your cholesterol level and high blood pressure, you're (*liable / apt / likely*) to have a stroke at any time.

_____ 73. The tournament continued (*as / like*) it had begun, with the seeded players being eliminated.

_____ 74. Try not to (*lose / loose*) control of yourself when the going gets tough.

_____ 75. Leslie's cousin is a (*waiter / waitress / waitperson / server / dining attendant*) at the Hoof and Claw.

_____ 76. The time (*maybe / may be*) right to raise the entrance requirements.

_____ 77. Even though there was a war on, the national (*morale / moral*) could hardly have been higher.

_____ 78. Vivian became (*nauseous / nauseated*) after eating the cream sauce.

_____ 79. The patient's improvement was (*negligent / negligible*) at best, hardly noticeable.

_____ 80. (*A large number of / A large amount of / Many*) guests arrived at the reunion in a state less casual than sobriety.

_____ 81. The chargé insisted that he was on (*official / officious*) business.

_____ 82. We found ourselves in a (*pendant / pendent*) state; we didn't know what to say or what to do.

_____ 83. What (*percent / percentage*) of our students go on to graduate school?

_____ 84. Isolation of the individual, especially the elderly, is an unfortunate (*parameter / perimeter*) of urban life.

_____ 85. Hindsight usually provides a better (*perspective / prospective*) than does foresight.

_____ 86. Seymour has the (*physiology* / *physiognomy*) of a philosopher; he never smiles.

_____ 87. County politics (*is* / *are*) controlled by neither Republicans nor Democrats.

_____ 88. Let us (*precede* / *proceed*) to the drawing room before the guests arrive.

_____ 89. You can expect the doctor to (*proscribe* / *prescribe*) the continued consumption of alcoholic beverages.

_____ 90. For the evening's entertainment, why not (*prophecy* / *prophesy*) a little something that will scare the bejesus out of the servants.

_____ 91. Weakened from hunger, the lad fell (*prostrate* / *prostate*) on the floor.

_____ 92. Will you never get that (*quote* / *quotation*) right?

_____ 93. Because Andrew apologized with (*regretful* / *regrettable*) eyes, Phoebe believed him.

_____ 94. I spent a (*restful* / *restive*) hour or two dozing in the afternoon sun.

_____ 95. Although Siegfried didn't graduate first in his class, he did perform (*respectfully* / *respectively* / *respectably*).

_____ 96. I didn't realize what hard work (*sculpture* / *sculptor*) could be.

_____ 97. To avoid the mosquitoes, let's (*set* / *sit*) in the car and watch the fireworks.

_____ 98. (*Since* / *Because*) Bruce had once had the same operation, he knew what Vivian was going through.

_____ 99. We expect to be in North America (*sometime* / *some time*) in August of 1992.

_____ 100. The house wasn't as (*spatial* / *spacious*) as it appeared to be from the road.

_____ 101. Humans are the only (*specie* / *species*) that composes sick and cruel jokes.

_____ 102. Who would ever (*suspect* / *suspicion*) an English instructor of being a professional assassin on the side?

_____ 103. Soccer is an older sport (*than* / *then*) either American football or baseball.

_____ 104. This is the painting (*which* / *that*) has been stolen from three galleries.

_____ 105. Considering the current data, we (*think* / *feel* / *believe*) we should reduce the price on the airbrush unit.

_____ 106. The children got a (*thrashing* / *threshing*) for misbehaving at the opera.

_____ 107. The artist's use of acrylics on Masonite was quite (*unique* / *unusual*).

_____ 108. Did your uncle (*used to* / *use to*) play major league baseball?

_____ 109. No one really knows (*whether* / *if*) the painting will sell or not.

_____ 110. Does anyone know (*who's* / *whose*) books these are or (*who's* / *whose*) winning the match?

Answers: 1–B, 2–A, 3–A, 4–B, 5–B, 6–A, 7–B, 8–A, 9–B, 10–A, 11–B, 12–A, 13–B, 14–C, 15–A, 16–B, 17–B, 18–A, 19–A, 20–B, 21–A, 22–B, 23–B, 24–A, 25–A, 26–B, 27–A, 28–B, 29–A, 30–B, 31–A, 32–A, 33–A, 34–B, 35–A, 36–B, 37–A, 38–A, 39–B, 40–B, 41–B, 42–A, 43–A, 44–A, 45–A, 46–B, 47–A, 48–A, 49–B, 50–C, 51–A, 52–A, 53–B, 54–A, 55–B, 56–A, 57–A, 58–A, 59–B, 60–B, 61–A, 62–B, 63–B, 64–A, 65–A, 66–A, 67–B, 68–A, 69–A, 70–B, 71–A, 72–C, 73–A, 74–A, 75–E, 76–B, 77–A, 78–B, 79–B, 80–C, 81–A, 82–B, 83–B, 84–A, 85–A, 86–B, 87–A, 88–B, 89–A, 90–B, 91–A, 92–B, 93–A, 94–A, 95–C, 96–A, 97–B, 98–B, 99–A, 100–B, 101–B, 102–A, 103–A, 104–B, 105–A, 106–A, 107–B, 108–B, 109–A, 110–B;–A.

Chapter 2

Nonstandard or Inappropriate Expressions

The purpose of this chapter is to acquaint you with diction errors that occur as a result of misspellings, nonstandard word constructions, and expressions that in formal writing situations are considered inappropriate for one reason or another.

If we take a quick look at the first exercise sequence of the chapter (page 21 through 24), we can see examples of each of these diction errors. For example, *alot* is a common misspelling of *a lot*. Similarly, *accidently* is a common misspelling of *accidentally*. And *alright* is a commonly occurring misspelling of *all right*. The nonstandard word constructions *acrost* and *acrossed* are incorrect substitutions for the preposition/adverb *across*. Similarly, the construction *ain't* is a nonstandard substitute for *am not, is not, are not, has not,* and *have not.* Finally, *around* is an inappropriate substitute for *about* in such expressions as "*about* noon" or "*about* ten years old"; *as to* is an inappropriate substitute for *about* in such expressions as "questioned *about* his voting record" or "some doubt *about* your meaning"; *all that* is an inappropriate substitute for *very* or *particularly* in such expressions as "not *very* funny" or "not *particularly* informative"; and *allow* is an inappropriate substitute for *admit* or *consider* in such expressions as "will never *admit* that he made a mistake" or "wouldn't even *consider* the possibility of such a thing."

The chapter contains fifteen instructional sequences. Each sequence is composed of four pages, two pages that explain the usage errors under consideration one by one and two pages that allow you to check your understanding of the explanations by completing the sentence fill-in exercise. You simply write the correct response in the blank provided within each sentence. If your instructor is using the Instructor's Manual that accompanies the text, you will probably be asked to work the sequences in sets of three; the Instructor's Manual provides quizzes at intervals of every three sequences: 1–3, 4–6, 7–9, 10–12, and 13–15. At the conclusion of the chapter is a review exercise that includes one hundred items. Your instructor may want to give this as a test.

Before beginning the first instructional sequence, don't forget to turn back to page 5 in Chapter 1 and work through the pretest exercise for the chapter. The specific instructions for doing the pretest are on page 3.

Nonstandard or Inappropriate Expressions (1)

a lot/alot: *Alot* is a common misspelling of *a lot*. (Everyone had *a lot* [not *alot*] of fun at the party. John had *a lot of* problems with inorganic chemistry.) In the second example, *many, several,* or *a number of* would be a further improvement on *a lot of*. Similarly, *a lot* should not be used to mean "often" or "frequently." (Jan goes to the theater *frequently* [not *a lot*].)

about/around: When you have an apparent choice between these two words, with the intended meaning of "nearly" or "approximately," choose *about*. (The missing child was *about* [not *around*] seven years old. The train left the station at *about* [not *around*] midnight.) Do not use *around about* together. (The family lived in Denver *about* [not *around about*] ten years ago.)

about/as to: Avoid substituting *as to, in reference to,* or *in regard to* for the preposition *about*. All three are pretentious and will characterize your writing as such. (The senators were questioned *about* [not *as to*] their positions on the new foreign aid bill. Langston left no question *about* [not *in regard to*] his political preferences. Your statements *about* [not *in reference to*] affirmative action were obscure at best.)

accidentally/accidently: *Accidently* is a common misspelling of *accidentally*. (The cat maintains that she swallowed the canary *accidentally* [not *accidently*].)

accused/alleged/suspected: Avoid using these words in such expressions as *accused arsonist, alleged rapist,* or *suspected embezzler*. Instead, say *the person accused of arson, the man alleged to have committed the rape, the clerk suspected of embezzlement,* or something similarly appropriate. Calling someone a *suspected embezzler* labels the person an embezzler from the outset.

Achilles' heel/Achilles tendon: The first of these means "one's vulnerable or susceptible spot," the spot where Paris fatally wounded Achilles. The second is the tendon that connects the back of the heel to the muscles of the calf of the leg. Athletes today often stretch or tear it. The common error is that writers use the latter when they mean the former. (In his campaign for the Senate, the young candidate's inexperience at massaging fragile egos proved to be his *Achilles' heel* [not *Achilles tendon*].)

acrost/acrossed: Both of these are nonstandard substitutes for *across*. (The group of young children calmly walked *across* [not *acrossed*] the busy street. A tree had fallen *across* [not *acrost*] the driveway during the storm.)

ain't: Although in the eighteenth century a standard contraction for *am not*, today *ain't* is nonstandard for *am not* as well as for *is not, are not, has not,* and *have not*. Its use, except in colloquial or humorous contexts, is generally viewed as a sign of poor language sophistication and will likely call into question the user's educational and socioeconomic background. (Poor Alfons *is not* [not *ain't*] the man he used to be.)

alibi: Avoid using *alibi* to mean either "an excuse" or "any type of defense." Use *excuse* or whatever other expression may be needed. (The swimmers offered no *excuse* [not *alibi*] for their mediocre performance. If you did the best job you could, there is no reason to *apologize* [not *alibi*].) Reserve *alibi* to mean "a plea of, or the fact of, having been elsewhere when the crime was committed." (The defendant had an airtight *alibi;* he was undergoing open-heart surgery at the time of the robbery.)

all right/alright: *All right* means "satisfactory," "adequate," "unhurt," "safe," or "entirely correct." *Alright* is a common misspelling and should be avoided. (The tour was *all right* [not *alright*], although nothing spectacular. Jeanette's answers were *all right,* whereas Baxter's were *all wrong*.)

all that: Avoid using the phrase *all that* in place of *very* or *particularly*. (The story wasn't *very* [not *all that*] funny. The film wasn't *particularly* [not *all that*] entertaining.)

allow: Avoid using *allow* to mean "to admit," "to concede," "to think," "to suppose," "to consider," "to say," "to assert," or a combination of these meanings. (The dean *admitted* [not *allowed*] that our complaint had some merit. Tod was willing to *concede* [not *allow*] that Elizabeth was a better tennis player than he. My uncle *thought* [not *allowed*] that all foreigners should be carefully watched. The visiting prince *said* [not *allowed as how*] he liked America very much.)

almost/like to have: Do not use the phrase *like to have* as a substitute for *almost* or *nearly*. (The puppy *almost* [not *like to have*] drowned trying to swim across the swollen creek to its master. We *nearly* [not *like to have*] died from the heat.)

SENTENCE FILL-IN

1. The mayor was repeatedly questioned (*about / as to*) _____ her connections with subversive organizations.

2. This fight (*ain't / isn't*) _____ likely to last very long.

3. Professor Swain's lectures are not (*all that / particularly*) _____ interesting, but his tests are fair enough.

4. The (*accused rapist / man accused of rape*) _____ claimed to be suffering from amnesia.

5. It takes (*a lot / alot*) _____ of ability and practice to become a professional athlete.

6. A gaggle of geese flew (*acrost / acrossed / across*) _____ the sky just at sunset.

7. Three of the race cars (*nearly / like to have*) _____ skidded into the canal.

8. The older children swam (*about / around*) _____ an hour, then went to dinner at the canteen.

9. I will (*allow / admit*) _____ that we might have done better had we had any idea of the level of the competition.

10. Once again, Glenna (*accidentally / accidently*) _____ erased the program from her disk.

11. Excessive self-regard has been the (*Achilles tendon / Achilles' heel*) _____

    _____ of more than one aspiring politician.

12. It is not (*all right / alright*) _____ to take advantage of defenseless people.

13. The company has discovered (*a lot of / a number of*) _____ glitches in the new software.

14. You don't have to (*apologize / alibi*) _____ for not being able to foretell the future.

15. Ted lost (*around / about*) _____ fifty pounds during the time he worked as a lumberjack.

16. The (*accused arsonist / woman accused of arson*) _____ seemed almost indifferent about the charges.

17. In spite of a high position in the community, the family wasn't (*all that / very*)_____

    _____ well off.

18. My cousins swim (*across / acrossed / acrost*) _____ the lake once in the morning and once each afternoon.

19. Alison (*almost / like to have*) _____ passed out from dehydration.

20. During the summer months, the family goes to the lake quite (*a lot / often*) _____

_____ .

21. Shoes like those (*ain't / aren't*) _____ easy to find in a small town.

22. Winston (*accidentally / accidently*) _____ pressed the accelerator rather than the brake.

23. We were not in agreement (*about / in reference to*) _____ what should be done next.

24. A torn (*Achilles' heel / Achilles tendon*) _____ has put more than one NFL wide receiver out for a season.

25. It isn't (*particularly / all that*) _____ unusual to find insects encased in chunks of amber.

26. Not studying is an unacceptable (*alibi / excuse*) _____ for failing the examination.

27. We thought everything would be (*all right / alright*) _____ once our plane landed in the United States.

28. There was (*a lot / alot*) _____ of serious debate after the formal meeting had ended.

29. Many of my older students (*allow / contend*) _____ that the future isn't as bright as it once was.

30. The Court's decision (*about / in regard to*) _____ the constitutionality of affirmative action quotas is still unclear.

Nonstandard or Inappropriate
Expressions (2)

a.m./p.m.: Avoid the expressions *in the a.m.* and *in the p.m.* (The party finally broke up at four o'clock *in the morning* [not *in the a.m.*]. Not until about seven o'clock *in the evening* [not *in the p.m.*] did the plane land.)

analysis/analyzation: Avoid the awkward construction *analyzation* as a pretentious substitute for *analysis*. (The class read a very thorough *analysis* [not *analyzation*] of John Cheever's short story "The Swimmer.")

and/or: In most contexts, *and/or* should be avoided in favor of saying more precisely what you mean—*and* or *or*. (The accused may be convicted *or* [not *and/or*] acquitted. Is she a relative *or* [not *and/or*] a friend of the family? I would like whole wheat toast *and* [not *and/or*] marmalade.)

anyplace/someplace: As adverbs, *anywhere* and *somewhere* are better choices than *anyplace* and *someplace*. (Before coming to college, Alfred had not traveled *anywhere* [not *anyplace*] in particular. The child was lost *somewhere* [not *someplace*] in the mountains.) As nouns, *anyplace* and *someplace* are standard. (The stranger wasn't from *anyplace* I had heard of. We were only looking for *someplace* to lay our weary heads.)

anyway/anyways: *Anyways* is nonstandard for *anyway,* which is an adverb meaning "nevertheless" or "regardless." (We will get the job done *anyway* [not *anyways*]. I am coming home *anyway* [not *anyways*], no matter how bad the weather is.) *Any way* is a phrase indicating any direction or course. (The commission couldn't see *any way* [not *anyway*] to save the project.)

anywhere/anywheres: *Anywheres* is nonstandard for *anywhere.* (The third applicant said that she was willing to go *anywhere* [not *anywheres*] the company wanted to send her.)

as far as/all the farther: The second phrase is an inappropriate and awkward substitute for the first. (Columbus is *as far as* [not *all the farther*] we intend to go on this leg of our odyssey.) Similarly, *all the faster* should be avoided as a substitute for *as fast as.* (You were warned; this is *as fast as* [not *all the faster*] the old units can operate.)

ascared: This is a nonstandard blending of *afraid* and *scared.* Use either of these when appropriate, but not the blend. (Are you still *afraid* [not *ascared*] of the dark? Ellen said that she was *scared* [not *ascared*] to within an inch of her life by the screaming monkeys.)

ask a question: Because *ask* means "to put a question to" or "to inquire," the *question* part of this expression is almost always unnecessary. (Several students *asked* [not *asked ques-*

tions] about the decline of dinosaurs. Several others *presented questions* [not *asked questions*] about the probability of intelligent life on other planets. Don't *inquire* [not *ask a question*] about the old man's estranged family.)

aspect: The word *aspect* is derived from the Latin root *spec,* meaning "to look." Thus, it means "the way something looks from a particular vantage point." (The castle is seen in its most awesome *aspect* from the west at sunset. This latest information allows us to view the problem in a whole new *aspect.*) Avoid using *aspect* to mean such things as "part," "feature," "element," and so on. (The proposal has three important *parts* [not *aspects*]. Her most imposing *feature* [not *aspect*] is her nose.)

author: When tempted to use *author* as a verb, substitute *write, compose, create,* or something similar—although you will also want to avoid any form of *do.* (We met an author who had *written* [not *authored* and not *done*] more than fifty books. While on her tour of the Greek islands, Helen *composed* [not *authored* and not *did*] her now famous sonnet sequence.)

awesome: Limit the use of *awesome* to describe something that inspires intense feelings of reverence, fear, and wonder by displays sublime, sacred, or majestic. (The 1980 eruption of Mount St. Helens was *awesome* indeed, even on television. An *awesome* trail of fire and mechanical thunder followed the rocket toward its window into outer space.) Do not exaggerate *awesome* with such expressions as *totally awesome* or *mega-awesome.* Events and occurrences that are less than *awesome* should be so described. (The final quarter of the game was *exciting* [not *awesome*]. Our minister occasionally preaches an *inspirational* [not *awesome*] sermon. An *impressive* [not *awesome*] number of students showed up for the concert.)

SENTENCE FILL-IN

1. Most people lose their naiveté (*somewhere / someplace*) _____ between thirty-five and fifty.

2. Nigel maintains that he has always been (*ascared / afraid*) _____ of bats and crabs.

3. In our house, no one liked cooking very much (*anyway / anyways*) _____.

4. Isaac Asimov has (*authored / written*) _____ more books than most people have read.

5. Forty miles is (*all the farther / as far as*) _____ the troop walked in a single day.

6. No one expected such an (*impressive / awesome*) _____ display of erudition from one so young.

7. Owen's first class meets at seven-thirty (*in the a.m. / in the morning*) _____, the second not until noon.

8. Isabel (*posed / asked*) _____ the question so beautifully that her instructor was dumbstruck.

9. The band of vagabonds said that they weren't going (*anywhere / anywheres*) _____ in particular.

10. Alas, this is (*all the happier / as happy as*) _____ most people ever expect to be.

11. Helen's most charming (*aspect / trait*) _____ is an evenness of temperament.

12. Your (*analysis / analyzation*) _____ of the situation was both clever and incisive.

13. The children ran into the woods because they were (*ascared / scared*) _____.

14. Professor Rand has become Gwendolyn's friend (*and* or *and / or*) _____ mentor.

15. The refugees survived (*any way / anyway / anyways*) _____ they could.

16. I haven't made up my mind whether I want breakfast (*or* or *and / or*) _____ lunch.

27

17. How many sonnets did Shakespeare (*do / compose*) _____ ?

18. So far, we have not found (*any way / anyway*) _____ to repeat the experiment.

19. The most appealing (*aspect / feature*) _____ of the tax proposal is that it affects everyone equally.

20. Devil's Rock is now (*as far as / all the farther*) _____ the road goes.

21. The necklace might have been lost (*anyplace / anywhere*) _____ between the airport and the office building.

22. Don't (*inquire / ask questions*) _____ about the skeletons in the family closet.

23. The performance was (*awesome / exciting*) _____ from beginning to end.

24. Because he works at night, Mitchell eats breakfast about eight o'clock (*in the p.m. / in the evening*) _____ .

25. Good scouts can locate food almost (*anywhere / anywheres*) _____ they go.

26. Eighty miles per hour was (*all the faster / as fast as*) _____ the old MG roadster would travel.

27. The new process has three (*aspects / steps*) _____ , and each one is equally vital.

28. In advanced composition class, we have to write an (*analysis / analyzation*) _____ of a major work of literature.

29. Imogene is no longer (*ascared / fearful*) _____ of being carried off in the night by hideous gargoyles.

30. Stored (*somewhere / someplace*) _____ in the recesses of our minds are all the experiences of childhood.

Nonstandard or Inappropriate Expressions (3)

balance: Except in situations dealing with money or bookkeeping, *balance* is an inappropriate substitute for *rest* or *remainder*. (For the *rest* [not *balance*] of the trip, they ate in less expensive restaurants. After studying for an hour, we spent the *remainder* [not *balance*] of the afternoon driving golf balls into the neighbor's swimming pool.)

be sure to/be sure and: The second expression is an inappropriate substitute for the first. (One must *be sure to* [not *be sure and*] eat wholesome meals while away at college. The instructor said that we should *be sure to* [not *be sure and*] clean our brushes after each class.)

being as/being that: Avoid using either of these expressions as substitutions for *because,* which is a subordinating conjunction indicating causation. (*Because* [not *Being as*] they were carefully prepared, the students did well on the examination. *Because* [not *Being that*] the HIV virus has contaminated the blood supply in some places, scientists are working to develop synthetic blood.) *Being as how* is an equally inappropriate substitute for *because.* (The instructor thought that *because* [not *being as how*] you had already taken two years of German you would be able to answer the questions.)

better had: This is a nonstandard substitute for *should, must,* or *ought to.* (I knew that I *should* [not *better had*] tell my parents before going to Florida during spring break.) The reverse expression, *had better,* is appropriately used in giving advice or issuing a mild threat. (My advisor told me that I *had better* [not *better had*] spend more time in the library.)

bored: If *bored* is followed by a preposition, it should be *by, with,* or *from*—never *of*. (The children were *bored by* [not *bored of*] the classroom puppet shows. Everyone was *bored from* [not *bored of*] lack of mental exercise. The campers quickly became *bored with* [not *bored of*] swimming every afternoon.)

boughten: *Boughten* is a nonstandard adjective formed from the verb *bought*. It means "purchased," as at a store, or "not homemade." *Store-bought* is an appropriate correction for the expression because it retains the historical or rural tone. (My grandmother said that she got her first *store-bought* [not *boughten*] dress at the age of sixteen. Uncle Eben wore his *store-bought* [not *boughten*] hair only to church.) Other corrections are also possible. (Such *acquired* [not *boughten*] elegance cost him thirty years of imitating his superiors.)

broke: Do not use *broke* as a substitute for *broken,* the past participle form of the verb *break*. (The power belt was *broken* [not *broke*] when the unit arrived. The bird's neck was *broken* [not *broke*] when the little fellow crashed into the living room window.)

burglarize/burgle: When you have an apparent choice between these two verbs, unless you are writing something intended to be humorous, *burglarize* is the better choice. (The house was *burglarized* [not *burgled*] sometime between midnight and two o'clock in the morning.)

burst/bust: *Burst* is a verb whose past and past participle forms are also *burst*. *Bust*, a verb with a past and past participle form of *busted*, is an inappropriate substitute for *burst*. (Soon after the dam *burst* [not *busted*], the village was inundated by a wall of water. I thought my heart would *burst* [not *bust*] when the child finally found her mother.) Nor is *burst* an appropriate substitute for *bust*. (Estelle imagined what a pleasure it would be to *bust* [not *burst*] the bully in the mouth.)

but that/but what: Do not use either of these as a substitute for the word *that* in clauses following an expression of doubt. (She doesn't doubt *that* [not *but that*] the contest will be a close one. No one questions *that* [not *but what*] the men were real heroes.)

but yet/still yet: Avoid these (nonstandard) two-word connectors in favor of either word used alone. (Dr. Morrison is quite gruff with his students, *yet* [not *but yet*] most of them insist that they like him. The sauce was spicy *but* [not *but yet*] mild. The community surrounding the lake has grown in recent years; *still* [not *still yet*] it is a nice place to spend the summer.)

cannot (can't) help but: The *but* added to the *not* makes this expression twice negative. Thus, the *but* should be removed. (I cannot help *thinking* [not *but think*] that I have met you somewhere before. I cannot help *recalling* [not *but recall*] the time you swam all the way across the bay.)

SENTENCE FILL-IN

1. Everyone was in a light mood (*because / being that*) _____ we were on holiday.

2. Just a few minutes after midnight, the officer (*burst / busted*) _____ into the theater and shouted, "Fire!"

3. I am (*bored of / bored with*) _____ watching television for several hours each evening.

4. The trip was a bit too long, (*still yet / yet*) _____ we had an enjoyable time.

5. Garments (*bought / broughten*) _____ from a catalog were a great treasure to us when we were children.

6. The lads could not help (*but laugh / laughing*) _____ about the predicament they were in.

7. For the (*balance / rest*) _____ of the term, the class grew steadily smaller and less pleasant.

8. Why would anyone (*burglarize / burgle*) _____ the houses of such poor people?

9. The gears on my bicycle have been (*broke / broken*) _____ for several weeks now.

10. No one doubts (*that / but that*) _____ the tuition to state universities will continue to increase for the near future.

11. The last thing my mother told me before I left for college was to (*be sure to / be sure and*)

    _____ brush my teeth regularly.

12. The theater was greatly overcrowded, (*but / but yet*) _____ the film was worth the discomfort.

13. (*Being as / Because*) _____ Margaret is a professional, she should do well in the local tournament.

14. When visiting a foreign country, (*be sure to / be sure and*) _____ conduct yourself like something other than an ugly American.

15. You (*better had / had better*) _____ pay more attention to where your children are spending their afternoons.

16. (*Because / Being that*) _____ the exploitation of migrant workers is immoral, something should be done about it.

17. Alas, Uncle Gifford is a man (*broke / broken*) _____ by a life overly punctuated with disappointments.

31

18. Whoever is the last to leave should (*be sure to* / *be sure and*) _____ turn out the lights.

19. All those who passed the examination could not help (*but realize* / *realizing*) _____ _____ how fortunate they were.

20. The candidate knew that he (*should* / *better had*) _____ tell his constituents about his less than exemplary past.

21. Few of our friends questioned (*that* / *but what*) _____ we would be exonerated in the end.

22. Students often become (*bored from* / *bored of*) _____ a monotonous regimen of attending class and studying.

23. The elementary school on the next street was (*burgled* / *burglarized*) _____ _____ three times over the summer.

24. No one enjoyed the (*remainder* / *balance*) _____ of the safari; each person was limited to only one meal a day.

25. Her students are not as advanced as they once were; (*still yet* / *still*) _____ _____, Professor Winters enjoys the mental exercise of teaching.

26. The caravan left early (*being as how* / *because*) _____ the weather was supposed to deteriorate later in the day.

27. Our dream of riches (*burst* / *busted*) _____ when we learned the truth about our investments.

28. Our neighbors preferred original Christmas cards to (*boughten* / *store-bought*)_____ _____ ones.

29. They could not help (*thinking* / *but think*) _____ that they had heard all this before.

30. For his own sake, Grant (*better had* / *must*) _____ be absolutely certain that all of his information is accurate.

32

Nonstandard or Inappropriate Expressions (4)

can't hardly: Because *hardly* is a negative, this expression is a double negative—that is, it says "no" twice. To correct the problem, simply omit the *not* part of the contraction. (Because she is agoraphobic, Melissa *can hardly* [not *can't hardly*] force herself to leave the house. The committee *can hardly* [not *can't hardly*] persuade anyone to accept the position of secretary.)

cause . . . is (was) due to: Avoid this double cause expression by using simpler statements. (The *cause* of your indigestion *was* [not *was due to*] too much rich food. The *cause* of the breakup *was* [not *was due to*] incompatibility in matters of the pocketbook. For a time, no one realized that the *cause* of the explosion *was* [not *was due to*] faulty wiring.)

center on/center around: *Center around,* a contradictory idiomatic expression, should not be used as a substitute for *center on* or *center upon.* (As usual, the debate *centered on* [not *centered around*] how the delegates were to be selected.) Another alternative is to replace *center* with *revolve.* (Our all-night discussions usually *revolved around* [not *centered around*] what we thought we wanted to do with our lives.)

claim: *Claim* is an inappropriate general substitute for *say, assert, state,* or *declare.* (The advertisement *says* [not *claims*] that the new models get fifty miles to the gallon.) *Claim* should be reserved for use when some legal right is involved. (The defendant *claimed* that he was entitled to face his accusers.)

class: Avoid using *class* as a substitute for *style, very good, outstanding, quality, innovative,* and so on. (The final set of dancers certainly had *style* [not *class*]. This corporation has a *very good* [not *class*] retraining policy for displaced employees.) Above all, avoid the currently ubiquitous expression *world-class.* (We intend to field an *internationally competitive* [not *a world-class*] soccer team.)

coleslaw/cold slaw: *Cold slaw* is a nonstandard substitute for *coleslaw.* (All of us wanted mustard, ketchup, and *coleslaw* [not *cold slaw*] on our hot dogs.)

commentate: Radio and television commentators *comment;* they do not *commentate,* no matter how much they talk or how clever what they say may be. They *describe, analyze, narrate, explain, clarify, encapsulate, review,* or whatever; but they do not *commentate.*

complexioned/complected: *Complexioned* is an adjective meaning "having a specific skin coloration or an overall skin texture and appearance." (Many fair-*complexioned* people have to limit the time they spend in bright sunlight. The young lass was as softly *complexioned* as a lullaby hummed in the twilight.) *Complected* is nonstandard for *complexioned.*

conference: A *conference* is a meeting, often formal, of several people held for the purpose of discussing matters of common interest. The jargonish use of *conference* as a verb, meaning "to confer with," "to meet," "to talk," "to discuss," "to advise," "to commiserate," and other similar things, should be avoided. (Fewer and fewer instructors *meet* [not *conference*] with their students outside the classroom. The program committees *talked* [not *conferenced*] most of the afternoon. They have already *talked* [not *conferenced*] the problem to death.) Equally inappropriate, and off-putting to careful users of language, is the construction *conferencing* used as a substitute for the noun *conference*. (The delegates to the National Convention of Troublemakers and Evildoers spent most of the week *in conferences* [not *conferencing*].)

considerable: Avoid using *considerable* in connection with countable items. (*Many* [not *Considerable*] choices were presented to us. A *large* [not *considerable*] number of delegates left the hall.)

could have/could of: *Could of* is nonstandard for *could have*. (Although we *could have* [not *could of*] driven all the way home in one day, we took two.)

couple of: Avoid using *couple of* to mean "a few" or "several." (I made only *a few* [not *a couple of*] new friends during my summer in Europe. The group visited *several* [not *a couple of*] private galleries.) If you mean two, say two. (There are at least *two* [not *a couple of*] good reasons not to eat eggs.)

cute: Because the word *cute* is used to mean many things, avoid it except perhaps to mean "childishly attractive." (The performance was *a bit artificial* [not *cute*]; it bordered on the melodramatic. What a *clever* [not *cute*] little brain you have; think what it might be if it ever grows up.)

SENTENCE FILL-IN

1. The bombing raids (*centered around* / *centered on*) _____ the regional capitals of the ancient nation.

2. Worldwide, white- (*complexioned* / *complected*) _____ people are a minority of the human race.

3. A good plow horse (*could of* / *could have*) _____ beaten either one of those sorry thoroughbreds.

4. The (*coleslaw* / *cold slaw*) _____ was too tart for my taste.

5. Jennifer located at least (*a couple of* / *two*) _____ dress shops on Michigan Avenue that she liked.

6. Like many of the other players, Herman (*can hardly* / *can't hardly*) _____ _____ walk the day after a match.

7. Please don't be (*smart* / *cute*) _____; people often never recover from first impressions.

8. The sportscaster (*commentated* / *described*) _____ the game in elaborate, perhaps exhaustive, detail.

9. We (*talked* / *conferenced*) _____ on the telephone rather than taking the time for a face-to-face meeting.

10. The cause of Morton's repeated tardiness (*was due to* / *was*) _____ poor local bus service.

11. Like my entire family, I (*can hardly* / *can't hardly*) _____ tolerate the smell of burning potpourri.

12. Jeannette (*asserts* / *claims*) _____ that the instructor told her the paper would receive a high mark.

13. Constant exposure to the elements hardens the softly (*complected* / *complexioned*) _____ skin of youth.

14. You have had (*many* / *considerable*) _____ opportunities to discuss the situation with your advisor.

15. The university has developed a (*world-class* / *quality*) _____ program in plastics engineering.

16. As is usual at the beginning of a quarter, management spent most mornings (*in conferences* / *conferencing*) _____.

17. Only now do we know that the real disagreement (*centered around / revolved around*) _____ the authority to make decisions.

18. The play included a (*cute / clever*) _____ reversal at the very end.

19. This is a(n) (*innovative / class*) _____ little company; it holds no less than a hundred patents.

20. Although Arnold asked for (*cold slaw / coleslaw*) _____, the waitress brought him a tossed salad.

21. Everyone has agreed that you (*can hardly / can't hardly*) _____ expect the opposition to support you without a reason.

22. Twenty years ago no one (*could have / could of*) _____ anticipated such a thing as the AIDS pandemic.

23. Julian (*claims / says*) _____ that literary agents have stolen three manuscripts of novels from him and sold them to famous writers.

24. Parents should (*talk / conference*) _____ with their children at every opportunity.

25. The cause of the poor crop (*was / was due to*) _____ almost continuous rain throughout April and part of May.

26. There were (*considerable / several*) _____ scenes in the film that I thought were needlessly violent.

27. After (*a couple of / quite a few*) _____ drinks, they decided to swim across Lake Michigan to Milwaukee.

28. Most of the students' complaints (*centered on / centered around*) _____ the rising cost of going to college.

29. As usual, Terence (*claimed / insisted*) _____ that the Celts of ancient Ireland, or Eire, discovered America.

30. The provost declined to (*comment / commentate*) _____ on the recent controversial decisions made by the president of the university.

Nonstandard or Inappropriate
Expressions (5)

different from/different than: *Different than* should not be used as a substitute for *different from,* even when using *different from* may result in an added *how, what,* or *that which*. (Although your account of the incident was *different from* [not *different than*] Susan's, you accused the same people that she accused. Mostly it is the little things that make life so *different from how* [not *different than*] it used to be. The problem turned out to be *different from what* [not *different than*] we had originally thought it was. This is a philosophy greatly *different from that which* [not *different than*] I was taught to follow as a child.)

direct opposite: Because *opposite* means "antithetical," "contrary," or "different in every way," *direct opposite,* and its close relatives *exact opposite* and *precise opposite,* are overstatements or redundancies and should be avoided. (Good is the *opposite* [not *direct opposite*] of evil. Poverty is the *opposite* [not *exact opposite*] of affluence. Your statements are *contrary to* [not *the precise opposite of*] your behavior.)

disremember: Avoid this nonstandard construction, meaning "to forget," in favor of *forget, fail to remember,* or *cannot remember*. (We often *forget* [not *disremember*] the lessons learned in youth. My aging aunt *cannot remember* [not *disremembers*] where she was born.)

don't think/doesn't think: When these expressions appear in such statements as "I *don't think* I should go to graduate school just now" and "Ted's sister *doesn't think* joining the air force is a good idea," they don't really make sense. Not thinking isn't what is being talked about. Appropriate revisions might read as follows: "I *have decided* not to go to graduate school just now" and "Ted's sister *thinks* joining the air force is a bad idea."

doubt if/doubtful if: The first of these expressions is an inappropriate substitute for *doubt that* or *doubt whether*. (I *doubt that* [not *doubt if*] we will leave before spring. Many people *doubt whether* [not *doubt if*] there will ever be a cure for AIDS.) The second is an inappropriate substitute for *doubtful that* or *doubtful whether*. (Can you any longer be *doubtful that* [not *doubtful if*] you were misrepresented? It is *doubtful whether* [not *doubtful if*] any of them will recover.) Because the distinctions between the use of *doubt that* and *doubt whether* as well as between *doubtful that* and *doubtful whether* are so fine, a good strategy is to use *doubt that* and *doubtful that* in all situations except when awkwardness results. Generally, *whether* is used when doubt and uncertainty are genuine or sincere.

drowned/drownded: *Drownded* is a nonstandard substitute for *drowned,* the past tense form of the verb *drown*. (Someone *drowned* [not *drownded*] a snake in the birdbath.)

enthusiastic/enthused: *Enthused* is an inappropriate substitute for *enthusiastic,* which means "having or showing enthusiasm," "ardent," or "eager." (Alas, not everyone on the planet was *enthusiastic* [not *enthused*] about the prospect of a visit by a colony of aliens.)

equally as: In combination, these two words are a bit redundant and should be replaced by *just as, equally* used alone, or *as* used alone. (The second speech was *just as* [not *equally as*] significant as the first one. Intelligence and perseverance are *equally* [not *equally as*] important for the serious student. My sister is *as* [not *equally as*] clever as my father at board games.)

escape/excape: *Excape* is a nonstandard spelling (also suggesting a mispronunciation) of *escape*. (No prisoner has *escaped* [not *excaped*] from this dungeon in more than five hundred years.)

even though/eventhough: The second is an incorrect (one-word) arrangement of the first. (*Even though* [not *Eventhough*] they were teammates for more than ten years, Tim and Andrew never became close friends.)

everywhere/everywheres: *Everywheres* is nonstandard for *everywhere*. (There were little red bugs *everywhere* [not *everywheres*] the children wanted to play.)

exact same: Use either of these words, but not both together. (This is the *same* [not *exact same*] recipe that my grandmother used on the farm. Those are the *exact* [not *exact same*] orders that the captain gave us before the battle began.)

except: *Except* is accurately used as a preposition meaning "excluding" or "but." (Dr. Thompson was responsible for everything *except* the tickets.) Avoid using *except* as a conjunction meaning "but" or "were it not that." (We would have quit *were it not that* [not *except*] we needed letters of recommendation from the foreman. Dustin wanted the job, *but* [not *except*] he was reluctant to leave home.)

SENTENCE FILL-IN

1. Mason (*doesn't think he wants / has decided not*) _____ to work on the farm this summer.

2. I find the artist (*equally / equally as*) _____ competent with oils and acrylics.

3. Luke and Melissa were (*doubtful whether / doubtful if*) _____ they should try to make it home or stay at school.

4. The new departmental secretary seems a bit too (*enthused / enthusiastic*) _____

   _____ about his work to suit me.

5. Occasionally, my forgetful uncle (*cannot remember / disremembers*) _____ his own name.

6. No one has (*drownded / drowned*) _____ in this lake for more than a half century.

7. If we could (*escape / excape*) _____ today, we might make it home for Christmas.

8. The climate of Western Michigan is not too (*different than / different from*) _____

   _____ the climate of the Scottish Highlands.

9. (*Even though / Eventhough*) _____ she was too young for the part, Paula delivered a creditable performance.

10. The writer's tenth novel was (*equally as / just as*) _____ intriguing as the first.

11. Your idea of success in life is (*contrary to / the direct opposite of*) _____ what I have been taught.

12. Those are the (*exact same / same*) _____ words my father said to me when I left home to live on my own.

13. The resolution of the problem was not greatly (*different than / different from what*) _____

   _____ we had hoped it would be.

14. We would have enjoyed ourselves (*except / were it not that*) _____ we didn't have enough money.

15. Myrna (*doubts that / doubts if*) _____ the university will continue to field a women's lacrosse team.

16. Alas, the company has finally (*drowned / drownded*) _____ in a sea of red ink.

17. Thadeus has been working on the (*same* / *exact same*) _____ job for more than thirty years.

18. Vernon had enough ability to be a professional, (*except* / *but*) _____ he was unwilling to train properly.

19. The doctors (*don't recommend* / *don't think*) _____ that you (*should*) participate in strenuous exercise just yet.

20. On Friday Beth said the (*exact opposite* / *opposite*) _____ of what she had said on Monday.

21. As one grows older, there is no (*excaping* / *escaping*) _____ the message delivered by a good mirror.

22. Your notions about a good marriage are substantially (*different from* / *different than*)

    _____ my own.

23. I will always love you, (*even though* / *eventhough*) _____ you have never loved me.

24. Alas, we often (*disremember* / *forget*) _____ those lessons that we didn't want to be taught in the first place.

25. Edmund says that he finds the exercise (*as* / *equally as*) _____ energizing in the morning as it is relaxing at night.

26. Because of the level of competition, I (*doubt if* / *doubt whether*) _____ any team can now go undefeated for an entire season.

27. Almost no one seemed very (*enthused* / *enthusiastic*) _____ about the beginning of the new term.

28. The victory was achieved in a way fundamentally (*different than* / *different from how*)

    _____ they had wanted to accomplish their goal.

29. Despite stiffer prison sentences, violent crime seems to be increasing (*everywhere* /

    everywheres) _____ .

30. Few commentators (*doubted that* / *doubted if*) _____ the senator would be reelected for a third term.

Nonstandard or Inappropriate Expressions (6)

expertise: Because the word *expertise* has been so widely used as a synonym or substitute for many other words—e.g., *skill, experience, knowledge, talent, ability, know-how, competence, familiarity*—a good practice is to avoid its use in favor of one of these words. (Two of the art instructors at the university possess great *skill* [not *expertise*] at woodcarving.)

factor: Because *factor* is such an overused word, avoid using it as a general replacement for such words as *item, consideration, point, reason, ingredient, component, element, part, circumstance, quality, characteristic*, and *situation*. (Money was the most important *consideration* [not *factor*] in her not taking the position. Mutual respect is one of the more important *ingredients* [not *factors*] of a successful marriage.) Because a *factor* is an element contributing to a result, resist the impulse to use the expression *contributing factor;* drop *contributing*. (The investigators ignored several *factors* [not *contributing factors*] during their examination of the causes of the explosion.)

fantasy/fantasize: The better choice of a verb form for the noun *fantasy* is *fantasy*, not the pop psychology term *fantasize*. (Virtually all normal children *fantasy* [not *fantasize*] about the future.)

female/woman: Except in scientific contexts, avoid using *female* to refer to a human being. *Woman* is an acceptable correction when it fits the situation of the sentence. (Several *women* [not *females*] opposed the plan to convert their dormitory into a campus office building. Madeline is the first *woman* [not *female*] to be elected president of the Student Government Association.)

figure/calculate: Avoid using either of these as a substitute for *think, suppose, expect*, or *judge*. (Few fans *thought* [not *figured*] the series would be a close one. We *thought* [not *calculated*] that the leaves would be off the trees by the middle of October. I *expect* [not *figure*] the train will be an hour late; it always is.)

finalize: *Finalize* is a pretentious substitute for *close, conclude, end*, or *finish*. (They *closed* [not *finalized*] the deal with a handshake. The agreement was *concluded* [not *finalized*] at four o'clock in the morning.)

flustrated: This is a nonstandard expression created from a confused combining of *flustered*, meaning "nervous," "confused," or "befuddled," and *frustrated*, meaning "disappointed," "foiled," or "defeated." (Once again, we were *frustrated* [not *flustrated*] in our efforts to gain admittance to the convention. High-strung individuals are sometimes more easily *flustered* [not *flustrated*] than the rest of us.)

for nothing/for free: The second expression is an inappropriate substitute for the first and for *at no cost, at no charge*, and *without charge*. (Breakfast at the Grand was provided *without charge* [not *for free*]. Last weekend student volunteers worked *for nothing* [not *for free*] at the shelter.) *Free* used alone can also work in some situations. (Breakfast at the Grand was *free*.)

free gift: Because *free* means "with no charge," this expression is redundant. Use one word or the other, but not both. (The battery was *free* [not *a free gift*]. Jan received a *gift* [not *free gift*] from her ex-employer.)

free gratis: Because *gratis* means "without charge," "for nothing," or "free," the expression *free gratis* is a bit overdone. Use *free* or *gratis*, but not both. (Both breakfast and lunch were *free* [not *free gratis*]. It is unusual for such a service to be provided *gratis* [not *free gratis*].)

fun: Do not use *fun* as an adjective in such expressions as *fun time, fun game,* or *fun afternoon*. (To our surprise, we had a *good* [not *fun*] time at the amusement park.) *Fun* used alone is fine. (To our surprise, we had *fun* at the amusement park.)

function/functionality: Although it is not possible to deny the existence of the word *functionality* any more than it is possible to deny the existence of pompous people, it is, nevertheless, sound advice to avoid both when possible. Do not use *functionality* as a substitute for the noun *function*. (Each part of the organization performs its own discrete *function* [not *functionality*], and all parts are necessary to make things run smoothly.)

funny: An overused word generally, *funny* should not be employed as a substitute for such words as *strange, odd, curious, unusual, extraordinary, bizarre, uncommon, eccentric, peculiar,* and the like. (Our tour guide had a *peculiar* [not *funny*] mannerism of blinking his eyes one after the other.)

SENTENCE FILL-IN

1. My freshman year in college was a (*fun / carefree*) _____ time; then I came to my senses.

2. You are not the first (*woman / female*) _____ to leave this company out of frustration at the lack of opportunity for advancement.

3. The champagne was (*free gratis / gratis*) _____ to all diners.

4. Surprisingly, the treaty was (*concluded / finalized*) _____ in a matter of weeks.

5. The lieutenant's (*expertise / skill*) _____ at finding obscure clues is well known.

6. If you work (*for nothing / for free*) _____, you put too low a value on your labor.

7. We must determine the (*function / functionality*) _____ of this mechanism before we can understand anything.

8. The clinic is looking for a (*female / woman*) _____ surgeon to work in the emergency room.

9. One of the most important (*factors / elements*) _____ of a good murder mystery is suspense.

10. The computer was (*free / a free gift*) _____, but the software cost a small fortune.

11. When you were a child, did you ever (*fantasy / fantasize*) _____ about being able to fly?

12. Estelle has a (*funny / bizarre*) _____ sense of humor; in fact, it borders on the grotesque.

13. No one (*thought / figured*) _____ that you would be able to grow trees on such barren ground.

14. We played three (*fun / invigorating*) _____ sets of tennis before going to the reunion.

15. My psychology instructor sometimes becomes (*flustered / flustrated*) _____ when several bright students press her for specific examples to support her theories.

16. I would (*calculate / judge*) _____ the only important difference between the two teams to be experience.

17. Success is seldom a (*free gift / gift*) _____; it must be paid for with time and effort.

18. We cannot (*finalize / complete*) _____ the plans for the tournament until we know how many teams will compete.

19. This set of encyclopedias was given to me (*gratis / free gratis*) _____ by my mentor.

20. (*Competence / Expertise*) _____ at handling people is a commodity for which many companies will pay handsomely.

21. The first (*circumstance / factor*) _____ in your loss of credibility was your use of a phony name.

22. Every semester I have been (*flustrated / frustrated*) _____ in attaining my goal of earning a perfect four-point grade average.

23. Because of his scholarship, August is able to go to college (*at no cost / for free*)_____

   _____.

24. A necessary (*component / factor*) _____ in the maintenance of a partnership is compatibility.

25. Clarice's aunts and uncles have lived in some (*funny / unusual*) _____ parts of the world.

26. Without the ability to (*fantasize / fantasy*) _____, we would be stuck with an unrelenting diet of reality.

27. We passed a (*nostalgic / fun*) _____ afternoon, floating down Elk River in a canoe and remembering when we were young and madly in love with each other.

28. This is the (*female / woman*) _____ who jumped into the canal and saved the drowning infant.

29. What is the true (*function / functionality*) _____ of ritual in the life of ordinary people?

30. In truth, almost everyone (*expected / figured*) _____ that youth would be served in the end; but it wasn't.

Nonstandard or Inappropriate
Expressions (7)

gal/girl: As a matter of discretion if for no other reason, avoid using *gal* or *girl* to refer to a woman. In many instances, *person* can be a further refinement on *woman*. (The company now employs three *women* [not *gals*] in the research division. Many of the *women* [not *girls*] in the senior seminar are unhappy with the instructor's grading system. Mother Teresa is a *person* [not *woman*] of enormous compassion.)

got to: Avoid using *got to, have got to,* or *has got to* to denote an obligation or necessity. Better choices are *have to, has to,* and *must.* (You *must* [not *got to*] do better than a fifth place finish. They *have to* [not *have got to*] be home by dark. The federal government *has to* [not *has got to*] develop some form of a national health program soon.)

guess: *Guess* is an inappropriate substitute for *suppose.* (I *suppose* [not *guess*] we had better look for another source of entertainment. I *suppose* [not *guess*] that most of the staff will take the week off between Christmas and New Year's.)

had better: Take care not to drop *had* from this expression. (This nation *had better* [not just *better*] get on with the task of improving its educational system. Thomas *had better* [not just *better*] apologize for the oversight.)

had ought/hadn't ought: The first is a nonstandard substitute for *should,* and the second for *shouldn't;* avoid both. (We agreed that we *should* [not *had ought to*] leave before the police arrived. A person of high principles *shouldn't* [not *hadn't ought to*] go into politics.)

heap/heaps: Do not use either of these as a substitute for *large amount, many, much, very much,* or *greatly.* (The company made a *large amount* [not *heap*] of money on the dam project. We anticipated *many* [not *heaps of*] problems with the design of the new model. It pleases us *greatly* [not *a heap*] that you graduated first in your class.)

heartrending/heartrendering: The second expression is a confusion of the first, which means "causing significant grief or anguish." The bad joke in this error is that fat is rendered, not hearts. (Losing one's parents at such an early age can be a *heartrending* [not *heartrendering*] experience.)

height/heighth: *Heighth* is a not uncommon misspelling of *height,* which is pronounced to rhyme with *fight.* (These trees can be expected to reach a *height* [not *heighth*] of sixty feet.)

hike: *Hike,* either as a noun or verb, is an inappropriate substitute for *increase* and *raise.* (The landlord is looking for any reason to *increase* [not *hike*] the rent. This is the third postal rate *increase* [not *hike*] in five years. Tell me how we can *raise* [not *hike*] our prices when the competition is already underselling us.)

himself/hisself: *Himself* is a reflexive or intensive pronoun for which *hisself* is a non-standard substitute. (The cook wounded *himself* [not *hisself*] while mistreating the food processor. Andrew *himself* [not *hisself*] is to be blamed for the cash shortage, not one of the assistants.)

hindrance/hinderance: *Hinderance* is a common misspelling of *hindrance*. (Today computer phobia can be a great *hindrance* [not *hinderance*] to one's education.)

hold/ahold: *Ahold* is an inappropriate substitute for *hold,* as is the variant *aholt.* (The swimmers were instructed to grab *hold* [not *ahold*] of the rope and not let go. Once the young man got *hold* [not *aholt*] of a new idea, he used it at every opportunity.)

home in on/hone in on: The second of these phrases is a confusion of the first, which is probably derived from the activities of homing pigeons and means "to target," "to focus on," "to select," or "to describe." (Triangulation allowed us to *home in on* the illegal broadcast.) Discreet usage, however, is to avoid both phrases in favor of more familiar expressions. (The panel wanted to *focus on* [not *home / hone in on*] only one problem at a time. The third chapter *described* [not *homed / honed in on*] the massacre with elaborate detail.)

hopefully: *Hopefully* should be used to mean "in a hopeful manner" or "filled with hope." (The old man prayed *hopefully*. John watched the stock market report *hopefully*.) Do not write "*Hopefully,* Ted will do well on the test." (*I hope* Ted will do well on the test. Ted *hopes* he will do well on the test.)

SENTENCE FILL-IN

1. It makes no sense to (*raise / hike*) _____ the price of American cars when they are already too expensive.

2. The team (*better / had better*) _____ continue to practice until a day or two before the tournament.

3. Marlon taught (*himself / hisself*) _____ French in preparation for taking a trip to France.

4. Alas, we received (*heaps of / many*) _____ complaints about the radical design of the new model.

5. It was a (*heartrending / heartrendering*) _____ tale that the child told about her family.

6. The instructor repeatedly told the students to take (*ahold / hold*) _____ of the clay with both hands.

7. If you want to graduate in four years, you (*got to / have to*) _____ take more than twelve hours per semester.

8. The captain was (*himself / hisself*) _____ on the bridge when the explosion occurred.

9. The (*gals / women*) _____ usually take their break in the nonsmoking lounge.

10. Careful research helped the task force (*hone in on / home in on*) _____ the source of the problem.

11. I (*suppose / guess*) _____ we shouldn't expect every student to be a potential genius.

12. The team had an average (*height / heighth*) _____ of almost six feet.

13. (*Hopefully / We hope*) _____ both Lorraine and Ingrid can pass the physical for flight school.

14. If a serious disagreement occurs, you (*should / had ought to*) _____ leave at once.

15. Few would question that racial prejudice is a (*hindrance / hinderance*) _____ _____ to the formation of a kinder, gentler society.

16. Austin sometimes takes (*himself / hisself*) _____ too seriously in matters of the heart.

17. The president of the university is a very competent (*woman / person*) _____ _____ as well as a cheerful soul.

47

18. The patrol took (*aholt / hold*) _____ of the child's hand as the pair crossed the street.

19. We (*had better / better*) _____ sterilize all the big pots before cooking for the banquet.

20. (*Hopefully / I hope*) _____ the two sides will stop quibbling and get down to business.

21. It pleases us (*greatly / a heap*) _____ that all our grandchildren have graduated from college.

22. The child is expected to grow to a (*heighth / height*) _____ somewhere between that of his mother and father.

23. For most people, noise is a (*hindrance / hinderance*) _____ to productive study.

24. The doctor said that you (*must / have got to*) _____ include more quality protein in your diet.

25. This is the fifth consecutive year in which we have experienced (*hikes / increases*)

_____ in our property taxes.

26. With chilling precision, the final speaker (*described / honed in on*) _____ the scene of the battle.

27. I (*guess / suppose*) _____ you thought the ill-mannered guest was (*funny /

humorous*) _____ .

28. Norton argues with (*hisself / himself*) _____ about everything, including whether or not he is argumentative.

29. Few things are more (*heartrending / heartrendering*) _____ than stories of unrequited love.

30. No one (*hadn't ought to / should*) _____ talk to his parents in such a disrespectful manner.

Nonstandard or Inappropriate
Expressions (8)

impact: As a noun, *impact* means "violent contact," "a forceful collision," or "the force of a collision." (The *impact* of the crash was so great that the two vehicles were virtually welded together.) As a verb, *impact* means "to force tightly together" or "to pack." (The teeth had become *impacted* to the point that they had to be removed.) Avoid using impact as a verb vaguely meaning "to affect" or "to hit." (Chronic exposure to loud noise can *harm* [not *impact*] one's hearing. A regular diet will likely *improve* [not *impact*] your health. Lack of sleep can *reduce* [not *impact*] one's effectiveness on the job. The missile *hit* [not *impacted*] the ground a few hundred yards short of the target.) Take particular care to avoid such expressions as *positive impact, negative impact, impacted positively, impacted negatively, impacted on,* and the like; they characterize your writing as jargonish.

in case: Avoid using *in case* as a substitute for the subordinating conjunction *if*. (*If* [not *In case*] the rains come, the picnic will be held inside. *If* [not *In case*] you do not like the product, the company will refund your money.) *In case* is also an inappropriate substitute for *in the event.* (We were told to watch the old house for several days *in the event* [not *in case*] the thief returned to collect the rest of the loot.)

in color: Avoid following a noun naming a color with the phrase *in color*. Such constructions are double indications of color and thus redundant. (After the storm, the sunset was bright *orange* [not *orange in color*].)

incidentally/incidently: *Incidently* is a common misspelling of *incidentally*. (Claire mentioned only *incidentally* [not *incidently*] that she had not read the book she was criticizing.)

in-depth: Avoid substituting this overused telejournalistic expression for such words as *comprehensive, thorough, detailed, exhaustive, extensive, profound,* and so on. (Several students indicated that they wanted to write *a detailed* [not *an in-depth*] analysis of how converting to semesters would affect the university.)

interact with: This expression means "to do something that involves another person in some way." It is an affected expression that should be avoided in favor of more specific word selection indicating reciprocal action. (Verbal people like to *talk to* [not *interact vocally with*] other people. Small children must be taught how to *get along with* [not *interact with*] other kids. When they were brought together, it became clear that the old hermits had no idea how to *communicate with* [not *interact with*] one another.)

interface with: This is a pretentious expression derived from computer jargon and meaning "to communicate," "to discuss," "to connect," "to act together," and so on. It should be avoided in favor of more specific word selection indicating what you intend to say. (A better way is needed whereby Congress and the president can *communicate with* [not *interface with*] each other. It is in the area of research that academia and industry most often *work together* [not *interface with each other*]. Alas, students and teachers do not *socialize* [not *interface socially*] much at this university.)

into: Avoid using *into* as a substitute for *interested in, concerned with, dedicated to, occupied with,* and so on. (Edmund is really *dedicated to* [not *into*] his daily exercise regimen. Joan is greatly *concerned about* [not *into*] starving people.)

is when/is where: Do not use either of these expressions between a naming element (the subject of a sentence) and a following clause that says something about that naming element. Do *not* write "A comma splice *is when* only a comma is used between two independent clauses." Instead, write "A comma splice *occurs when* only a comma is used between two independent clauses." Do *not* write "Illiteracy *is where* a person cannot read or write." Instead, write "Illiteracy *is* the inability to read and write." Of course, such statements as "Charleston, West Virginia, *is where* I was born" and "Summer *is* a time *when* few think of the blizzards of February" are perfectly correct.

its/it's/its': *Its* is the standard possessive form of the personal pronoun *it.* (By this time of year the mountain ash has usually lost *its* berries. This wine is past *its* peak.) *It's* is the contraction of *it is* or *it has.* (Once again, *it's* about time for the tornado season. *It's* always been one of Susan's dreams to visit Austria.) *Its'* is a nonstandard possessive, an attempt to make possessive what is already possessive. (Every dog has *its* [not *its'*] day. Even for an accountant, life has *its* [not *its'*] little pleasures.)

SENTENCE FILL-IN

1. Although the book is generally dull, it does have (*its / it's / its'*) _____ moments, especially in the third and ninth chapters.

2. Is it true that men and women sometimes have difficulty (*interacting with / communicating with*) _____ each other?

3. The challenge was to take a(n) (*thorough / in-depth*) _____ look at our own prejudices.

4. Georgiana is no longer (*into / concerned about*) _____ the political theories of extraterrestrials.

5. Watching too much television may (*negatively impact / diminish*)_____ one's thought processes.

6. The arts and the sciences should (*interface / work together*) _____ to produce fully educated students.

7. Sibling rivalry (*is the phenomenon wherein / is when*) _____ brothers and sisters compete for parental approval.

8. The jacket was sunset (*orange in color / orange*) _____ and made of the most expensive wool.

9. We will know when (*it's / its / its'*) _____ time to end the meeting; everyone will become restless and irritable.

10. Oswald maintains that he has learned to (*interact verbally with / talk to*) _____ _____ the animals.

11. The missile (*hit / impacted*) _____ the unguarded carrier only minutes after war had been declared.

12. When he goes shopping, Charles is only (*incidentally / incidently*) _____ interested in saving money.

13. Since retiring, Professor Heath has (*gotten into / became interested in*) _____ _____ restoring antique furniture.

14. (*If / In case*) _____ you do not like the class, you can always drop out.

15. Plagiarism (*occurs when / is where*) _____ you take the work of another and present it as your own.

16. (*Its / It's / Its'*) _____ not one of this company's practices to hire unqualified people.

17. Ambrose is deeply (*concerned about / into*) _____ the rights of the powerless.

18. Yes, son, your father will always be available (*if / in case*) _____ you need him.

19. The speaker maintained that the recent successes of feminism have greatly (*impacted / hurt*) _____ public education; fewer intelligent women are willing to become teachers.

20. We were required to write a(n) (*detailed / in-depth*) _____ narrative of a poet's life.

21. How often do poets and engineers (*communicate with / interact vocally with / interface with*) _____ each other?

22. Anemia (*is when / occurs when*) _____ there is a reduction in the number of red blood cells.

23. Although the meadow appeared to be dark (*green / green in color*) _____, the aroma of clover blossoms was everywhere.

24. Be sure to take a heavy jacket (*in case / in the event*) _____ the weather turns cold.

25. Wide reading over a period of time (*broadens / impacts positively*) _____ one's view of the world.

26. Professor Gulliver is more than (*incidently / incidentally*) _____ concerned about the welfare of his colleagues.

27. The kitten meowed when it misplaced one of (*it's / its' / its*) _____ computer mice.

28. How do we learn to (*get along with / interact with*) _____ people we have not trusted in the past?

29. Smog (*is where / is created when*) _____ noxious smoke and fog are mixed together.

30. One can only guess how additional foreign competition will (*impact / affect*) _____ _____ our pricing structure.

Nonstandard or Inappropriate Expressions (9)

-ize: Although the use of the verb-forming suffix *-ize* is perfectly standard in such words as *civilize, legalize, jeopardize, deputize, pasteurize, dramatize,* and many others, you should, nevertheless, use judgment in avoiding awkward and pretentious constructions such as *accessorize, permanentize, sloganize, incentivize, prioritize,* or *colorize.* (We have decided not to *use slogans in* [not *sloganize*] our spring promotions. What will it cost to *insulate* [not *quietize*] the house?)

kind of/sort of: Avoid using either *kind of* or *sort of* as a substitute for *rather, somewhat, a bit, mildly, slightly,* and the like. (By mid-afternoon most workers are *a bit* [not *kind of*] hungry. Her remarks were *mildly* [not *sort of*] humorous. Aren't you being *rather* [not *kind of*] presumptuous in questioning such a well-known expert?)

knots per hour: Never use the redundant *knots per hour,* or its close kin in nautical ignorance *knots an hour;* a *knot* is "one nautical mile (6,076.12 feet) per hour." (Doing an easy *twenty knots* [not *twenty knots per hour*], the huge ocean liner moved quietly through the night.)

like for: When tempted to use this expression, drop the *for.* (Mother would *like* [not *like for*] everyone to come home for the holidays. I don't *like* [not *like for*] my children to have to live such hard lives.)

literally: *Literally* means "actually," "really," or "word for word," and is used to stress the truthfulness of a statement that might be read as figurative or metaphorical. (Working all summer with a construction crew *literally* drained me of any desire to become a contractor.) *Literally* should not be used as a general intensifier in a statement that is obviously figurative or metaphorical. (We were, *in a manner of speaking,* [not *literally*] dead on our feet. If this is true, it will, *as they say,* [not *literally*] stand the world on its ear. Maggie cried until her heart *seemed to break* [not *literally broke*].)

loquacious: Avoid the error of using *loquacious* to mean "fluent," "eloquent," or "forceful with words"; it means "fond of talking" or "given to excessive talking." (My European history professor is a very *powerful* [not *loquacious*] lecturer; he keeps the members of the class riveted to their seats.)

majority: A *majority* is more than half, as of those voting in an election. It contrasts with *minority,* which means "less than half of a (countable) total." Avoid using *majority* as a general substitute for *many, much,* or *most.* (*Most* [not *A majority*] of my time is spent studying. *Much* [not *A majority*] of the criticism came from unemployed professional people. We passed *many* [not *a majority*] of our afternoons strolling beside the river.)

male: Except in scientific contexts, avoid using *male* as a noun to refer to a human being. (The contention that every *man* [not *male*] on the planet harbors latent desires to kill and plunder is extreme. When Ted was young, he went to a private school for *boys* [not *males*].)

man/gentleman: Today the word *gentleman* means "a courteous and gracious man who possesses a strong sense of personal honor," and its use should be limited to such a notion. Do not use it as a general substitute or synonym for *man;* such usage leads to incongruity. (After shouting obscenities at the usher, the *man* [not *gentleman*] left the theater. The *man* [not *gentleman*] was convicted on nine counts of rape.)

may have/may of: *May of* is nonstandard for *may have*. (Nancy *may have* [not *may of*] answered all the questions on the quiz correctly.)

meaningful: Except as an antonym for *meaningless, meaningful* is a vague, pretentious, and overused word to be avoided in favor of more specific choices. (*Serious* [not *Meaningful*] negotiations were delayed for a month. Alice made her point in a very *persuasive* [not *meaningful*] manner. Color can be used in *symbolic* [not *meaningful*] ways in portraiture.) Such expressions as *meaningful dialogue, meaningful experience,* and *meaningful relationship* should be avoided because their use tends to stereotype the writer in the minds of educated readers.

memento/momento: *Momento* is a common misspelling of *memento*. (Gillian has a carved Dala horse as a *memento* [not *momento*] of her trip to Sweden.]

might have/might of: *Might of* is nonstandard for *might have*. (If conditions had been only slightly better, the team *might have* [not *might of*] launched the rocket.)

SENTENCE FILL-IN

1. Twenty-five (*knots / knots per hour*) _____ is a good speed for a vessel this size.

2. The class would (*like for / like*) _____ you to perform the very first piece you composed.

3. One-third of those tested (*may have / may of*) _____ misunderstood the directions.

4. The third (*male / man / gentleman*) _____ to the left was about two centuries tardy in his attire.

5. Jerome (*literally / almost*) _____ died with every stride during the last three miles of the marathon.

6. Alas, my father and I never had a (*meaningful / serious*) _____ talk about anything.

7. On Saturday we spent (*most / a majority*) _____ of the day walking through antique malls.

8. It can be a difficult task to (*incentivize / motivate*) _____ poorly paid employees.

9. The only (*momento / memento*) _____ I have of my years at Charleston High School is a pen and ink sketch of the now razed building.

10. Bernice is (*loquacious / fluent*) _____ in no less than seven languages.

11. Young (*boys / males*) _____ are as inquisitive about the world around them

    as are young (*girls / females*) _____ .

12. When I was lost and alone in the jungle, I (*may have / may of*) _____ eaten a grub or two.

13. Isn't it (*kind of / rather*) _____ unusual for all the golfers to par the course?

14. Each of us (*might have / might of*) _____ done more to help make the exchange students feel less homesick.

15. As expected, (*a majority / most*) _____ of the opposition came from people who already had good hospitalization.

16. Uncle Hobart could (*in a manner of speaking / literally*) _____ eat his weight in shrimp once a day.

17. The day (*could have / could of*) _____ gone worse; we (*might have / might of*) _____ lost our boat as well.

18. How does one (*muffle / quietize*) _____ the exhaust of such a powerful engine?

19. In those days, (*a majority / most*) _____ of Joan's little friends had never heard of anatomically correct dolls.

20. Franklin has a way of saying things in a particularly (*meaningful / persuasive*)

_____ manner.

21. Our parents always (*like / like for*) _____ us to bring the grandchildren to the lake in July.

22. Stiff joints from old injuries are the principal (*momentos / mementos*) _____

_____ of an adolescence spent on the practice field.

23. Richard Burton was the most (*eloquent / loquacious*) _____ popular actor I ever saw on stage.

24. We have received a proposal to (*fountainize / install fountains in*) _____ the city parks.

25. Roxanne maintains, only half in jest, that in his heart every (*male / man*) _____

_____ wants to ride a horse and rope cows.

26. Constance (*may have / may of*) _____ been no more than nine when she won her first tournament.

27. Everyone was (*mildly / sort of*) _____ bored by the postured melancholy that dominated the poet's manner as he spoke.

28. In such ancient rituals, each object or action is (*meaningful / symbolic*) _____

_____ for those who understand.

29. How many (*knots / nautical miles*) _____ is it from New York to Cherbourg, France?

30. The first (*man / gentleman*) _____ struck the second a solid blow to the side of the head; then they both commenced to biting each other about the ears.

Nonstandard or Inappropriate Expressions (10)

minuscule/miniscule: *Miniscule* is a nonstandard spelling of *minuscule*. (One would hardly call the damage *minuscule* [not *miniscule*] when half the factory went up in flames.)

more better: Because *better* means "more desirable," drop the *more*. (Albert's plan was *better* [not *more better*] than all the others. Almost everyone likes summer *better* [not *more better*] than winter.)

more preferable: Because *preferable* means "more desirable," drop the *more*. (Wealth is *preferable* to poverty.) Notice that *preferable* is followed by *to*, not *than*, which tempts the incongruous construction *more preferable than*. (Companionship is *preferable to* [not *more preferable than*] loneliness.)

more than/above: In almost all situations, *above* is an inappropriate substitute for *more than*. (Professor Anderson has *more than* [not *above*] a thousand volumes in her collection of out-of-print usage textbooks. The report said that *more than* [not *above*] seven hundred warriors fell in the battle.)

must have/must of: *Must of* is nonstandard for *must have*. (The village officials *must have* [not *must of*] thought the bridge had been completed.)

myself: Do not use this intensive/reflexive pronoun as a substitute for either *I* or *me*. (My wife and *I* [not *myself*] have been married for twenty-five years. The letter was addressed neither to Blythe nor to *me* [not *myself*].)

negative/negatory: *Negatory* is a nonstandard substitute for *negative*. (No one anticipated such a *negative* [not *negatory*] response to the new requirements for full professor.)

nice: Because it is used to mean virtually anything, try to avoid *nice* altogether. (Margaret has a very *agreeable* [not *nice*] personality. What a *kind* [not *nice*] gesture the gift turned out to be. Thomas did a *thorough* [not *nice*] job on the lab project.) The one exception to this caveat is *nice* used to mean "carefully delineated." (The third chapter makes a *nice* distinction between euthanasia and mercy killing.)

night/nite: *Nite* is a nonstandard spelling of *night*. (Alice sometimes spends the entire *night* [not *nite*] reading a book.)

nowhere/nowheres: *Nowheres* is nonstandard for *nowhere*. (The dogs, usually ready for the hunt, were *nowhere* [not *nowheres*] in sight.)

off/off of/off from: Generally, neither *off of* or *off from* should be used as substitutes for *off*. (They were told to keep *off* [not *off of*] the playing field until Friday. The escaped convicts were injured when they fell *off* [not *off from*] a moving train.) Occasionally, however, *off from* is necessary to express a specifically intended meaning. (Because of his own bad behavior, my uncle has been cut *off from* the rest of the family. The story was that the children simply wandered *off from* the day-care center.) Both *off* and *off of* are nonstandard when used as a substitute for *from,* indicating a source. (John borrowed the tuxedo *from* [not *off of*] his cousin. Vincent usually gets his tuition money *from* [not *off*] his stepfather.)

old-fashioned/old-fashion: The second is a misspelling of the first. (As one grows older, many so-called *old-fashioned* [not *old-fashion*] ideas don't seem as quaint or out-of-date as they once did.)

on account of: *On account of* is an inappropriate substitute for *because* or *because of.* (Sidney will not graduate in the spring *because* [not *on account of*] he failed chemistry. The annual picnic was postponed *because of* [not *on account of*] bad weather. *Because of* [not *On account of*] one complaint, the entire program was dropped.)

open/open up: *Open up* is an inappropriate substitute for *open.* (When Shannon *opened* [not *opened up*] the door to the mysterious cottage, a gaggle of ghosts drifted out into the yard.)

opt: *Opt* and its various varieties—*opted, opting, opting to, opt(ed) for, opt(ed) out,* and *opt(ed) out of*—were all at one time vogue usages suggesting a choice or the idea of choosing. Prudent formal practice is to *choose* [not *opt for*] the less transitory term. (The family *chose* [not *opted*] to go to Mackinac Island for the weekend. At the age of fifty-five, my father *chose to retire* [not *opted out of the rat race*].)

SENTENCE FILL-IN

1. (*Above / More than*) _____ fifty percent of the engineering students at the university are foreign students.

2. My brother and (*I / myself*) _____ haven't seen much of each other since the Fourth of July, 1975.

3. They (*must of / must have*) _____ eaten five meals a day throughout the trip.

4. For forty years Charlotte's father worked the (*night / nite*) _____ shift at this mill. Now he is watching it being torn down.

5. Aunt Agnes is a bit of an (*old-fashion / old-fashioned*) _____ person; she prefers reading books to watching television.

6. Our progress was only (*miniscule / minuscule*) _____, hardly enough for anyone to notice.

7. Such a prompt (*negative / negatory*) _____ reply suggests that you had been thinking about the matter in advance.

8. The family doesn't usually (*open up / open*) _____ the cottage until the last weekend in May.

9. A regular diet of solid food is (*better / more better*) _____ for you than all this junk.

10. Last Sunday we had a (*nice / friendly*) _____ chat with the neighbors to the north about the upcoming elections.

11. Still convinced that he could fly, Blake jumped (*off / off of / off from*) _____ _____ the barn roof.

12. I think most people would agree that peace is (*more preferable than / preferable to*) _____ war.

13. Isoke tried to warn us that this place was located in the middle of (*nowhere / nowheres*) _____.

14. Gretchen could not continue in school (*because of / on account of*) _____ the increase in tuition.

15. I have been rich, and I have been poor; rich is (*more better / better*) _____.

16. Why do people with a (*negatory / negative*) _____ attitude seem surprised when others respond in a (*negatory / negative*) _____ manner to them?

17. Hubert thinks he can borrow the necessary equipment (*from / off of*) _____ _____ one of his uncles.

18. The injured child's brother (*must have / must of*) _____ run five miles to get a doctor.

19. Once again, the family had a (*nice / most enjoyable*) _____ autumn visit to New England.

20. After much discussion, Lucinda (*chose / opted for*) _____ the shorter of the two tours.

21. Such (*minuscule / miniscule*) _____ efforts to reclaim the environment amount to little more than a gesture.

22. We have always made our money the (*old-fashion / old-fashioned*) _____ way; we collect interest on our investments.

23. This lovely pair of pewter candlesticks was given to (*me / myself*) _____ by a retired leprechaun.

24. For the third (*nite / night*) _____ in a row, the neighbor's dog kept us awake by not barking.

25. The committee liked the last applicant (*more / more better*) _____ than any of the others.

26. We (*opted out of / quit*) _____ the investment scheme because it didn't offer a good return on our money.

27. I have been young, and I have been old; neither is (*more preferable / preferable*)

_____ .

28. The entire community searched for weeks, but the lost cattle were (*nowhere / nowheres*)

_____ to be found.

29. Here in Hinterland, Michigan, we had (*above / more than*) _____ two hundred inches of snow last winter.

30. The cat slipped (*off / off of*) _____ the freshly polished mantel and landed in the corncrib.

Nonstandard or Inappropriate Expressions (11)

orient/orientate: When you have an apparent choice between these two words, meaning "to adjust or adapt to conditions or surroundings," *orient* is better. (Several months will be required to *orient* [not *orientate*] yourself to life in Moscow. When Ellen was in college, she never really *oriented* [not *orientated*] herself to living in the dormitory.)

ourself: *Ourself* is a nonstandard form of *ourselves*. (We have only *ourselves* [not *ourself*] to thank for the situation we are in. The counselor said that we should get *ourselves* [not *ourself*] together and move on to the next issue.)

outside of: Avoid using *outside of* as a substitute for *except for*, meaning "excluding." (*Except for* [not *Outside of*] the last speaker, the conference was quite ordinary. The twins are doing well in college *except for* [not *outside of*] their composition courses.)

outstanding: Because this word has been overused as a substitute or synonym for so many other words—e.g., *important, creditable, impressive, significant, excellent, definitive, salient*— avoid it in favor of more exact choices. (Maryanne's performance on the cello was *moving* [not *outstanding*].)

over with: Either drop the *with* from this expression or use a synonym, such as *ended* or *finished*. (We thought the ceremony would never be *over* [not *over with*]. Because we thought the game would never *end* [not *be over with*], we left before it was decided.)

owing to the fact that: This is a pretentious and unnecessarily wordy substitute for *because*. (*Because* [not *Owing to the fact that*] the spring rains were several weeks late, the fields had to be replanted.) *Due to the fact that* is a fraternal twin of the construction and should similarly be avoided. (Mr. Owens refused to testify *because* [not *due to the fact that*] he was afraid for the safety of his family.)

paranoid: As an adjective, *paranoid* means "characterized by recurring delusions of grandeur and persecution caused by the mental disorder paranoia." Thus, it should not be used as a general substitute for such words as *uneasy, uncomfortable, suspicious, insecure, defensive, tense, displeased,* and the like. (Malcolm's cousin often feels quite *uneasy* [not *paranoid*] in large crowds. Edward becomes *defensive* [not *paranoid*] when anyone questions his opinions about anything. I am usually *very tense* [not *paranoid*] during a thunderstorm.)

partner/pardner: The second is a common misspelling of the first. (Alas, all my business *partners* [not *pardners*] have abandoned me.)

past history: Because all *history* is in the past, the redundancy of this expression is usually unnecessary. (The *history* [not *past history*] of relations between India and Pakistan has not been particularly cordial. The defendant's *past* [not *past history*] argued against his being entirely innocent of wrongdoing.)

phenomenon/phenomena: The first is singular. (A solar eclipse is always a slightly fearful *phenomenon* to watch. Frost is a *phenomenon* virtually unknown in the tropics.) The second is plural and thus should never be used with a singular verb. (Nature's *phenomena* [not *phenomenon*] provide the greater laboratory in which the scientist works. Such celestial *phenomena* [not *phenomenon*] are not likely to be seen twice in one lifetime.)

phony: Discretion suggests that *phony* be replaced by more specific terms, such as *counterfeit, false, fradulent, insincere, disingenuous, spurious, specious, pretentious.* (Everyone was offended by the speaker's obviously *insincere* [not *phony*] praise of the community. Such *specious* [not *phony*] logic will eventually reveal itself for what it really is. The scamp's *pretentious* [not *phony*] attempts at respectability should be viewed as an entertainment.)

plenty: *Plenty* is a noun meaning "enough" or "an abundance." (America has long been viewed as a land of *plenty*.) *Plenty* should not be used as an adverb meaning "very." (After working a ten-hour day, everyone was *very* [not *plenty*] tired.)

plus: *Plus* is a preposition meaning "added to" or "in addition to," or a noun meaning "an advantage." (Three *plus* six equals nine. Quickness is a real *plus* for a point guard.) *Plus* is not an appropriate substitute for the coordinating conjunction *and*. (The coach *and* [not *plus*] his starting players boarded the university bus.) Nor is it an appropriate substitute for such conjunctive adverbs as *moreover* and *furthermore*. (Janet enjoys her job; *moreover* [not *plus*], she is well paid. These students do not study; *furthermore* [not *plus*], they do not seem to care when they fail a class.)

SENTENCE FILL-IN

1. We heard nothing either (*outstanding* / *significant*) _____ or memorable in what the governor said.

2. What exactly is the (*history* / *past history*) _____ of race relations in this community?

3. Cadwallader can never be president (*because* / *owing to the fact that*) _____ he was not born in the United States.

4. The vehicle will not run; (*plus* / *furthermore*) _____, it will cost a fortune to repair the engine.

5. There was a time, and it wasn't so long ago, when husbands and wives assumed themselves (*partners* / *pardners*) _____ for life.

6. A (*phony* / *counterfeit*) _____ passport can cost several thousand dollars, as well as a jail sentence if you get caught.

7. Most colleges have a program to (*orient* / *orientate*) _____ first-year students to life on campus.

8. Because we had thought the crossing to France would never (*be over with* / *end*) _____, we decided to fly home.

9. The aurora borealis is a natural (*phenomenon* / *phenomena*) _____ that few cease to be amazed by.

10. The painting of the child gathering wildflowers wasn't an original; it was a (*phony* / *reproduction*) _____.

11. We kept telling (*ourself* / *ourselves*) _____ that everything would eventually work out, and it did.

12. (*Except for* / *Outside of*) _____ the first few games of the season, the team performed quite well.

13. The city did not get the franchise (*due to the fact that* / *because*) _____ it could not raise the necessary money.

14. Many tourists become progressively more (*paranoid* / *insecure*) _____ as they travel farther from home.

15. The discussion about who would represent the students to the administration was (*very* / *plenty*) _____ intense.

63

16. Who coined the expression "The opera isn't (*over with* / *over*) _____ until the fat lady sings"?

17. The work of an engineer requires intelligence (*plus* / *moreover*) _____ experience and common sense.

18. Marilyn isn't the only one who feels (*paranoid* / *tense*) _____ when forced to speak before a large audience.

19. When the workday was (*over* / *over with*) _____, most of the villagers went to the beach.

20. Some people have no difficulty at all becoming (*oriented* / *orientated*) _____ _____ to military life, but others do.

21. This man cannot be guilty of the charges (*due to the fact that* / *because*) _____ _____ he was out of the country when the crime occurred.

22. Byron admits that he had a (*plenty* / *very*) _____ tough time getting through second-year algebra.

23. These two fellows have been (*partners* / *pardners*) _____ in the candy business for half a century.

24. For years now we have devoted (*ourself* / *ourselves*) _____ to the task of restoring the old train station.

25. Gravity is the (*phenomenon* / *phenomena*) _____ that helps us keep our feet firmly planted on the ground.

26. The judges liked all the paintings (*outside of* / *except for*) _____ the ones done on compressed wood.

27. Most of the faculty members present recognized the (*phony* / *disingenuous*) _____ _____ praise for what it was.

28. The new coach did a(n) (*creditable* / *outstanding*) _____ job of developing a squad of inexperienced players.

29. The workers want higher wages; (*plus* / *moreover*) _____, they want better medical insurance.

30. The (*history* / *past history*) _____ of this organization does not tell a story consistent with enlightened management.

Nonstandard or Inappropriate
Expressions (12)

point in time: Avoid this silly and pretentious substitute for *time, when, now,* or *point*. (The exact *time* [not *point in time*] has not yet been determined. I can't remember *when* [not *the point in time*] I learned the truth about my parents. We should strike *now* [not *at this point in time*].)

poorly: Avoid using *poorly* to mean "ill" or "sick." (Carolyn has felt *ill* [not *poorly*] ever since taking her flu shots. After the team had lost five games in a row, the coach looked *sick* [not *poorly*].)

preceding/above: In constructions indicating something that has already been said, *above* is an inappropriate substitute for *preceding* or *foregoing*. (The *preceding* [not *above*] statements detail our position perfectly. The *foregoing* [not *above*] arguments notwithstanding, the case was poorly made.) Similarly, *below* is an inappropriate substitute for *following* in constructions indicating something that is going to be said. (The *following narrative* [not *narrative below*] suggests the gravity of the case.)

prejudiced/prejudice: A *prejudice* is an opinion held in disregard of facts that disprove it. (The judge admitted some small *prejudice* against people who speak English with a foreign accent.) *Prejudiced* means "having a prejudice or bias for or against something." (The speaker argued that racially *prejudiced* people should not be allowed to hold public office.) The common error is that *prejudice* is misused for *prejudiced*. (Sharon said that she had never before known such a *prejudiced* [not *prejudice*] person.)

presently: Because *presently* has two distinct meanings—"soon" or "in a little while" and "now" or "at present"—discretion would suggest that you avoid its use in favor of words that remove any risk of confusion. (Although the children are not *now* [not *presently*] at home, they should be along *in a little while* [not *presently*]. The factory is *currently* [not *presently*] operating at only fifty percent capacity; *soon* [not *presently*], however, new orders should improve the situation.)

pretty: *Pretty* means "pleasing" or "attractive" and should not be used in place of *moderately, quite, very, rather, somewhat,* and so on. (This is a *rather* [not *pretty*] serious situation. She seemed *quite* [not *pretty*] angry to me.)

preventive/preventative: *Preventative* is an unnecessary substitute for *preventive*. (Unfortunately, insufficient *preventive* [not *preventative*] measures were taken to stop the spread of the epidemic. A good school system is a *preventive* [not *preventative*] against ignorance.)

prior to: In most instances, *prior to* is a pretentious substitute for *before*. The same is true of *previous to*. (Edmund read most of the assignments *before* [not *prior to*] the beginning of

65

the term. *Before* [not *Prior to*] the invention of the telephone, neighbors typically visited one another more frequently. Three months *before* [not *previous to*] his death, President Kennedy is supposed to have had a premonition of being shot in an open car.)

prophesy/prophesize: *Prophesize* is an inappropriate substitute for the verb *prophesy,* meaning "to predict." (To *prophesy* [not *prophesize*] the end of the world can be a risky business, especially if one is not interested in becoming an object of ridicule.)

proven fact: Only a theory requires proof; a fact simply *is.* (It is a *fact* [not *proven fact*] that women live longer than men. The man's innocence *has been proven* [not *is a proven fact*].)

publicly/publically: *Publically* is a common misspelling of *publicly.* (The senator *publicly* [not *publically*] admitted his part in the conspiracy to reduce federal income taxes.)

rarely ever: *Rarely* and *ever* combined do not quite make sense. Better choices include *rarely* used alone, *rarely if ever, hardly ever, rarely or never,* or *almost never.* (Ted *rarely* [not *rarely ever*] swims at the public beach. We *hardly ever* [not *rarely ever*] ate at expensive restaurants. *Rarely if ever* [not *Rarely ever*] will you see an eagle take a fish on this lake. Stanley *almost never* [not *rarely ever*] beats Sharon at tennis.)

reason ... is because: This expression confuses *the reason ... is that* and *because.* The *reason* Susan moved to Europe *is that* [not *is because*] she wanted to learn languages from native speakers. The *reason* we lost the series *is that* [not *is because*] we were not in top physical condition. We lost the series *because* we were not in top physical condition.)

SENTENCE FILL-IN

1. The (*following sentences / sentences below*) _____ are intended to help you improve your word selection when you are writing.

2. Why do so many people (*publically / publicly*) _____ bare their souls on television talk shows?

3. You must be (*very / pretty*) _____ pleased with yourself at winning the super lottery.

4. Alas, we are all probably (*prejudice / prejudiced*) _____ to a greater or lesser degree.

5. Over time, (*preventative / preventive*) _____ medicine should be much more cost effective than traditional medical practice.

6. Can't this fellow (*prophesy / prophesize*) _____ anything other than doom and gloom?

7. The precise (*point in time / time*) _____ when the wall came down is still in dispute.

8. It is a (*fact / proven fact*) _____ that there are twenty-four time zones on earth.

9. Only a (*pretty / moderately*) _____ large crowd of demonstrators gathered outside the courthouse.

10. Since the mine closed, we (*almost never / rarely ever*) _____ see tourists in town.

11. Before the chemical leak was discovered, many people in the neighborhood had been feeling (*sick / poorly*) _____ .

12. The reason we moved here was (*because / that*) _____ we were tired of all the crime and violence in the city.

13. The Webster family does not (*now / presently*) _____ attend this church.

14. Everyone is waiting for Sebastian to (*publically / publicly*) _____ declare his candidacy for president of the student government.

15. (*Before / Prior to*) _____ going to college, I had never even heard of such things as existentialism and minimalist art.

16. If pressed, I'll have to admit some (*prejudice / prejudiced*) _____ in favor of life in a small midwestern town.

17. (*Rarely ever / Rarely if ever*) _____ will you see a moose north of the river during hunting season.

18. Anita has reached that (*point / point in time*) _____ in her life when public applause isn't as important as it once was.

19. The artist himself should arrive (*presently / soon*) _____ .

20. Actually, Baynard met Vivian (*previous to / before*) _____ either of them

    (*developing / had developed*) _____ an interest in Tibetan yodeling.

21. The primary reason Zachary has never married is (*that / because*) _____ solitude is the great love of his life.

22. To tell the truth, I can't remember (*the point in time / when*) _____ I learned to read.

23. If the investigation is conducted (*publicly / publically*) _____ , the truth will never be ferreted out.

24. Alas, there seems to be no sure (*preventive / preventative*) _____ against occasional outbursts of violence.

25. If you (*prophesy / prophesize*) _____ the end of the world often enough, you may eventually be right.

26. To say that the victims of the harrassment looked (*poorly / ill*) _____ would be an understatement.

27. Would you like dinner (*prior to / before*) _____ going to the meeting or after the meeting is over?

28. I thought the medicine was (*quite / pretty*) _____ potent.

29. Is it (*true / a proven fact*) _____ that modern birds are the descendants of dinosaurs?

30. The (*above / preceding*) _____ sentences were all structured to help you improve your word selection when you are writing.

Nonstandard or Inappropriate Expressions (13)

reason why: Avoid this expression in favor of *reason* used alone, *why* used alone, or *reason that*. (The *reason* [not *reason why*] John left the university remains a mystery to everyone who knew him. The pilot didn't know *why* [not *the reason why*] the starboard engine stopped. The *reason that* [not *reason why*] she left remains a matter of dispute.)

reckon: *Reckon* is an inappropriate substitute for *think, suppose,* or *presume.* (I *suppose* [not *reckon*] your father preferred hunting to churchgoing. I *think* [not *reckon*] that most of us will remain in the same social class where we began. Dr. Livingston, I *presume* [not *reckon*]?)

regardless/irregardless: *Irregardless,* which is an unfortunate blend of *irrespective* and *regardless,* is an inappropriate substitute for *regardless.* (The squad was determined to carry on, *regardless* [not *irregardless*] of the consequences. *Regardless* [not *Irregardless*] of what you may think, these are the facts.)

relate to: Avoid using *relate to* to mean "like," "enjoy," "appreciate," "sympathize with," "understand," and so on. (I can *appreciate* [not *relate to*] most classical music. Many people will *understand* [not *relate to*] the dilemma the defendant faced. Tess *likes* [not *relates to*] novels about women who have overcome great odds to be successful.)

relevant/revelant: *Relevant* is inappropriately used when it appears in constructions that do not make clear what relevancy is intended. (This course wasn't *relevant*.) *Relevant* to what? By following *relevant* with a *to* prepositional phrase, you can always answer the question. (This course wasn't *relevant to my curriculum*. There is little in this man's philosophy that is *relevant to my own experience*. How is a knowledge of eighteenth-century European history *relevant to your goal of becoming an attorney*?) *Revelant* is a nonstandard spelling (and pronunciation) of *relevant*.

remove/evacuate: Careful usage argues against *evacuate* as a synonym or substitute for *remove.* The root meaning of *evacuate* is "to make empty," not "to remove." Thus, we *evacuate* a village, a stadium, or a crime scene by *removing* the people who were there. The people were not *evacuated*—that is, emptied. (The *village* [not *villagers*] will be evacuated before the spraying begins.)

saving/savings: Avoid pluralizing the word *saving* when it is used to mean "any reduction in expense, time, effort, and the like." (By paying cash, we realized a *saving* [not *savings*] of almost a thousand dollars.) This proscription does not affect such expressions as *savings bank, savings account,* or *life savings*.

seldom ever: *Seldom* and *ever* combined do not quite make sense. Better choices include *seldom* used alone, *seldom if ever, hardly ever, seldom or never,* or *almost never.* (The family

69

seldom [not *seldom ever*] went to fancy restaurants. American cars *almost never* [not *seldom ever*] win this race.)

share: As a verb, *share* means "to use, occupy, enjoy, or have in common." (A husband and wife *share* the same bed. Joan and Mark *share* an interest in modern art.) Avoid the affected use of *share* to mean "to tell," "to have," "to give," or "to participate." (Susan has heard a story that she wants to *tell* [not *share with*] you. Liz and Angus *have* [not *share*] the same big blue eyes. Andrew often *gives* [not *shares . . . with*] his chemistry notes to me. Only a few members *participate* [not *share*] in the discussions.)

should have/should of: *Should of* is nonstandard for *should have.* (Taking into account the number of practices we had had, the team *should have* [not *should of*] performed better.)

simple reason: Reject using this condescending expression in favor of *because.* (The plan was rejected *because* [not *for the simple reason*] no one liked it.)

sneaked/snuck: *Snuck* is an inappropriate substitute for *sneaked,* the past tense form of *sneak.* (The children *sneaked* [not *snuck*] into the barn to look for Easter eggs.)

some/something: Avoid using either of these adverbially as a substitute for *somewhat, slightly, a bit, a little,* or the like. (The reporters were *somewhat* [not *some*] put off by the candidate's flippant responses to questions. John is *slightly* [not *something*] over six feet tall.) Do not use such an ambiguous statement as "Fred smells something awful" when you mean "Fred smells bad" or "Fred stinks."

somewhere/somewheres: *Somewheres* is nonstandard for *somewhere.* (The old hermit lives *somewhere* [not *somewheres*] deep in the ancient forest.)

SENTENCE FILL-IN

1. Your observations are not (*revelant / relevant*) _____ to what we have been discussing this morning.

2. These pictures are higher priced (*because / for the simple reason*) _____ they are much better.

3. Those old photographs must be (*somewhere / somewheres*) _____ in the attic of the house.

4. Old-fashioned sibling rivalry was the (*reason why / reason*) _____ Ignatius left home at the age of fifteen.

5. Brice (*snuck / sneaked*) _____ out of the house in the middle of the night and went fishing.

6. Campus security ordered the (*students / dormitories*) _____ to be evacuated within the hour.

7. This offer represents a (*saving / savings*) _____ to you and your family of about $25,000.

8. Although we didn't eat fancy food, the family (*seldom ever / almost never*) _____ _____ went hungry.

9. I (*presume / reckon*) _____ you know the type of business your cousin had been in for the last several years.

10. Everyone enjoyed (*sharing / participating*) _____ in such a lively exchange of ideas.

11. (*Regardless / Irregardless*) _____ of their grades, most students learn quite a lot during their freshman year.

12. The patient is (*some / somewhat*) _____ stronger than she was yesterday.

13. Few instructors can (*relate to / understand*) _____ all the pressures that today's college students experience.

14. We (*should have / should of*) _____ bought those old cars when we had the chance.

15. Thank you for (*showing / sharing with*) _____ me such an interesting magazine article.

16. I can (*relate to / appreciate*) _____ a good piece of elevator music as well as the next cliff dweller.

17. Meggan (*should have / should of*) _____ accepted the scholarship; she wouldn't have had to work two jobs.

18. The cottages right on the lake (*seldom ever* / *seldom if ever*) _____ change owners.

19. Burgess was told to leave the note (*somewhere* / *somewheres*) _____ on the patio behind the garage.

20. Lack of confidence in social situations was the (*reason that* / *reason why*) _____

_____ Austin would not apply for membership in the club.

21. Please present (*revelant* / *relevant*) _____ questions; otherwise, we will wander from the topic.

22. Every effort was made to (*evacuate* / *remove*) _____ the tenants from the burning buildings.

23. We (*sneaked* / *snuck*) _____ into the old orchard about dawn and made

(*ourself* / *ourselves*) _____ sick on green apples.

24. Do you (*reckon* / *think*) _____ the world will ever become a kinder, gentler place?

25. The old fellow was (*a little* / *something*) _____ beyond intoxication when the police found him.

26. I would bet that these five women will remain friends for life, (*irregardless* / *regardless*)

_____ of what path each one chooses.

27. Sean failed the test (*because* / *for the simple reason*) _____ he didn't take the time to study.

28. Fewer and fewer young people seem to (*enjoy* / *relate to*) _____ good food well prepared.

29. Melissa, a budding raconteur, can really (*share* / *tell*) _____ a great story.

30. By shopping with American money, we realized a (*saving* / *savings*) _____

_____ of between thirty and forty percent.

Nonstandard or Inappropriate Expressions (14)

still and all: Avoid this expression as a substitute for *still* used alone or *nevertheless*. (My grandfather wasn't a very well educated person; *nevertheless* [not *still and all*], he was successful in most of the things he did.)

such as/as: When indicating examples, do not omit *such* from the expression *such as*. (The instructor told the class many humorous anecdotes, *such as* [not just *as*] the one about the stuttering monkey.) Occasionally, the *such* and *as* may be separated by a few words. (None of us had ever seen *such* a boat *as* the one owned by the local yacht club.)

supposed to/suppose to: *Suppose to* is nonstandard for *supposed to*. (The juniors are *supposed to* [not *suppose to*] run the third race.)

thankfully: Avoid using *thankfully* as a sentence modifier meaning "I was thankful/grateful that," "we were thankful/grateful that," and other similar statements. (*We were thankful that* [not *Thankfully*] the weather was mild enough for the outing. *Everyone was grateful that* [not *Thankfully*] the speaker explained the delicate issue with such polite tact.)

themselves/theirselves: *Theirselves* is nonstandard for *themselves*. (Several of the skiers bought *themselves* [not *theirselves*] new equipment for the trip to Colorado.)

think/afraid: Avoid using *afraid* unless some clear indication of fear, fright, apprehension, or alarm is intended. In any event, do not use *afraid* to indicate ordinary thought. (The board *thinks* [not *is afraid*] that the proposal includes inaccurate data. Alas, *we think* [not *we're afraid*] you have taken leave of your senses.)

through/thru: Except on highway signs, *thru* is a nonstandard spelling of *through*. (Only an accomplished ghost can walk *through* [not *thru*] a wall as thick as this one. We will never be *through* [not *thru*] with this project.)

thus/thusly: Avoid misusing *thusly* as a substitute for *thus*. (We drove day and night for three days and *thus* [not *thusly*] arrived at our destination on time. The unit requires only four hundred square feet; *thus* [not *thusly*], it will fit into the old warehouse with little difficulty.)

true facts: *True* and *facts* combined form an awkward redundancy that can be corrected by using either *truth* or *facts*. (The *truth* [not *true facts*] about the treatment historically of dissidents held in Soviet prisons is now being told. The *facts* [not *true facts*] here are that the child was first abused by its parents and then abandoned.) Similar expressions to be avoided are *actual facts* and *real facts*.

try to/try and: *Try and* is an inappropriate substitute for *try to*. (Who will *try to* [not *try and*] persuade the board to take some action? *Try to* [not *Try and*] place the order over the telephone.)

up until: Prudent usage suggests that *up* be omitted. (*Until* [not *Up until*] his family moved to St. Paul and he started to high school, Baxter had no idea that he could learn a foreign language.)

use/utilize: In most instances, *utilize* is a pretentious substitute for *use*. *Users* [not *Utilizers*] apparently think that a preference for *utilize* sounds more sophisticated. (Last winter we *used* [not *utilized*] the snow-thrower no more than a dozen times. Everyone should learn to *use* [not *utilize*] a computer.)

viable/viable alternative: The precise, literal meaning of *viable* is "physically capable of living," as in *viable fetus* or *viable species*. Because the word is being overused to mean "workable," "practical," or "likely to produce continued success," try to confine your own use to the literal meaning. Above all, avoid the off-putting cliché *viable alternative*. (This plan is *workable* [not *viable*] in that we have sufficient money to put it in place. The company is looking for *practical* [not *viable*], nuts-and-bolts ideas, not fantasy. One *possible choice* [not *viable alternative*] might be for the university to switch from the quarter system to the semester system.)

what/what all: Do not substitute *what all* for *what*. (The investigators didn't know *what* [not *what all*] they might find. Liz was never quite sure *what* [not *what all*] her parents expected of her.)

who/who all: Do not substitute *who all* for *who*. (We didn't know *who* [not *who all*] might come to the party. *Who* [not *Who all*] is on your side?)

SENTENCE FILL-IN

1. The children ate green apples until they made (*theirselves / themselves*) _____

    _____ (*quite / pretty*) _____ ill.

2. Many of the (*facts / actual facts*) _____ surrounding this incident will probably never be known.

3. I (*think / am afraid*) _____ the good old days of obscene profits are over for good.

4. Ginger, a very good student, often reads a novel (*thru / through*) _____ in a single evening.

5. (*What all / What*) _____ do you think you might learn by questioning the old recluse again?

6. The state is looking for a (*workable / viable*) _____ plan to make college available to as many young people as possible.

7. An accident like this was never (*suppose to / supposed to*) _____ happen on such a job.

8. If you want to do well in college, you must learn to (*use / utilize*) _____ both your time and your mind.

9. Shall we (*try and / try to*) _____ find a new place to dump our grass clippings?

10. (*We were thankful that / Thankfully*) _____ the dam held, even after a week of heavy rain.

11. There are only seven or eight dancing parts; (*thus / thusly*) _____ we can hire several beautiful statues to complete the cast.

12. The weather remained warm and autumnal (*up until / until*) _____ Thanksgiving Day.

13. Thurston didn't know (*who / who all*) _____ might show up to file a claim against the estate.

14. The team has only a mediocre record; (*nevertheless / still and all*) _____, it matches up well against the other teams remaining in the tournament.

15. Margaret sometimes demonstrates her intelligence in unusual ways, (*as / such as*)

    _____ the time she extemporaneously recited the entire "Prologue" to *The Canterbury Tales*.

16. (*Until / Up until*) _____ a few people had had too much to drink, the party was quite enjoyable.

17. Victor graduated from an obscure private liberal arts college; (*still and all / nevertheless*)

_____, he has done quite well for himself in the business world.

18. (*Thankfully / Everyone was grateful that*) _____ the bank didn't call in its loans.

19. One (*viable alternative / possible choice*) _____ might be for the company to stop making so many variations of its products.

20. The (*facts / true facts*) _____ in this case are that the victim was shot by several people who were not working together.

21. In truth, you made several blunders, (*as / such as*) _____ wiping your mouth on the tablecloth, stirring your tea with a steak knife, and gargling the after dinner wine.

22. They had no idea (*what / what all*) _____ they might find stored at the old homestead.

23. Poor Ted (*thinks / is afraid*) _____ that all his school friends have abandoned him.

24. Virgil said he flew (*thru / through*) _____ some rough weather between St. Louis and Denver.

25. Estelle thinks you should (*try to / try and*) _____ improve your relationship with your father.

26. On Wednesday the weather is (*supposed to / suppose to*) _____ warm up to seventy degrees.

27. Delivery now needs only a dozen vehicles; (*thusly / thus*) _____, we can sell all the old clunkers.

28. The instructors (*themselves / theirselves*) _____ acknowledged that the standardized test included some dubious questions.

29. The company is now (*utilizing / using*) _____ conference calls to counter the rising cost of air travel.

30. Does anyone know (*who / who all*) _____ indicated an interest in taking the tour of Spain?

Nonstandard or Inappropriate Expressions (15)

take and: *Take and* is an unnecessary expression often used in front of a verb—e.g., "We decided to *take and* tell the neighbors what was happening" or "The old woman *took and* scolded the children thoroughly." Drop the expression. (We decided *to tell* the neighbors what was happening. The old woman *scolded* the children thoroughly.)

transpire: Avoid the pretentious substitution of *transpire* for such verbs as *happen, occur, come to pass,* and *take place.* (The murder *occurred* [not *transpired*] on the same night as the power failure.)

trigger: As a matter of discretion, avoid using *trigger* as a verb to substitute for such words as *activate, cause, initiate, produce, provoke,* and *signal.* (A single spark *ignited* [not *triggered*] the explosion that leveled the building. An inappropriate remark *provoked* [not *triggered*] the argument that split the party.)

typical of/like: *Typical of* should not be used as a substitute for *like.* (The artist's work is *much like* [not *typical of*] that of his contemporaries.) *Typical* used alone should be confined to such meanings as "characteristic," "distinctive," "emblematic," "representative," or "symbolic." (Douglas was reared in a *typical* mountain cabin, which had neither electricity nor indoor plumbing.)

unfrequent: *Unfrequent* is an incorrect substitute for *infrequent,* which means "happening seldom," "occurring only at long intervals," or "not regular." (Royce is an *infrequent* [not *unfrequent*] user of any type of over-the-counter medicine.)

unless and until: *Unless* means "except on the condition that," and *until* means "up to the time that." Thus, when used together in this phrase, the two terms overlap. Use one or the other, but not both. (I will not support you *unless* [not *unless and until*] you support me. The team will not improve *until* [not *unless and until*] a new coach can be recruited.)

very: Avoid the frequent use of *very* to try to strengthen weak adjectives and adverbs. Replace both words with a more precise or stronger word. (Most readers found the novel *absorbing* [not *very interesting*]. Hodge often has a *provocative* [not *very challenging*] way of putting things.)

why/how come: Avoid substituting *how come* for the interrogative adverb *why* to introduce a noun clause. (I cannot understand *why* [not *how come*] she would make such accusations.) Also avoid the substitution in a direct question. (*Why are you* [not *How come you are*] so filled with energy on Monday mornings?)

-wise: Although the use of the suffix *-wise* to mean "in the manner or direction of" (e.g., *clockwise, lengthwise*) is standard, avoid using it indiscriminately to mean "with respect to" and attaching it to nouns; such usage leads to awkward and jargonish words like *racewise, vacationwise, qualitywise, flavorwise, resolutionwise,* or *situationwise*. (We had a wonderful time *on our vacation* [not *vacationwise*].)

without: Avoid using *without* as a subordinating conjunction meaning "unless." Use *unless*. (We cannot continue to live as we do *unless* [not *without*] we can find a way to earn more money.)

woman/lady: Avoid the quaintly honorific use of *lady* to refer to any woman or a woman of unusual accomplishment, authority, or ability. (The *woman* [not *lady*] who lives in the corner house won the lottery. Margaret Thatcher is no longer a powerful *figure* [not *lady*] in British politics.) Avoid the unnecessary coupling of the word *lady* with gender-neutral words indicating the performance of some activity—e.g., *lady* golfer, *lady* plumber, *lady* pilot, *lady* letter carrier. Also avoid the currently ubiquitous expression *neat lady*, which is used to mean almost anything. (Alice is a *perceptive person* [not *neat lady*]; she can always tell when someone needs a friendly ear. Gretchen, *an engaging conversationalist* [not *a neat lady*], has a mind filled with anecdotes about famous people.)

wore out: This is an ungrammatical substitute for *tired, exhausted,* or *worn out*. (The troops were *exhausted* [not *wore out*] after the fifty-mile march. We had never before been so *tired* [not *wore out*].)

would have/would of: *Would of* is nonstandard for *would have*. (If you hadn't given us a ride, we *would have* [not *would of*] been late to class.

you/youse: *Youse* is the unacceptable consequence of trying to make something plural that is already plural. *You* is plural. (*You* [not *Youse*] people are a friendly group.)

SENTENCE FILL-IN

1. Glaring at the audience, Horatio delivered his soliloquy in a (*very loud / thunderous*) _____ voice.

2. I do not know (*why / how come*) _____ so many people today are suffering from stress.

3. Gertrude advised us not to buy the stock (*until / unless and until*) _____ it drops to thirty dollars a share.

4. The class (*took and researched / researched*) _____ the problem from every possible point of view.

5. It was one of those (*unfrequent / infrequent*) _____ occasions when all the stars lined up and everyone agreed.

6. Penny (*would have / would of*) _____ won the race if only she had not fallen.

7. These widgets are (*like / typical of*) _____ too many American products, manufactured at the lowest possible cost.

8. (*Qualitywise / In terms of quality*) _____, no one's seventy horsepower rotary comes close to the one made by Acme.

9. Who was the first (*woman / lady*) _____ driver to compete in the Indianapolis 500?

10. We were (*weary / wore out*) _____ from having to argue with every customer who returned one of the television sets.

11. What (*provoked / triggered*) _____ so many students to withdraw from school during the spring semester?

12. By the end of the tour, everyone was (*very hungry / starved*) _____ for a juicy hamburger and fries.

13. The team will not be the same (*without / unless*) _____ you agree to coach us.

14. (*You / Youse*) _____ people are never going to amount to anything (*unless / without*) _____ you become more responsible.

15. More than a week passed before anyone heard what had actually (*transpired / happened*) _____ at the board meeting.

16. Most of the group will not leave (*until / unless and until*) _____ the weather improves.

17. This paper is actually quite good (*vocabularywise / in terms of word selection*) _____

    _____.

18. These old strings of lights will not burn (*unless / without*) _____ every bulb
    is tight in its fixture.

19. The innocent verdicts on April 19, 1992, for the four Los Angeles policemen tried as a

    result of the beating of Rodney King (*triggered / caused*) _____ wide-
    spread rioting.

20. Constance is such a (*neat lady / competent artist*) _____; she can work in
    almost any medium.

21. Avery (*repaired / took and repaired*) _____ the car before anyone knew it
    had been in an accident.

22. With less rain and wind, the day (*would of / would have*) _____ gone much
    better.

23. Apparently the fight (*took place / transpired*) _____ by the light of a full
    moon on the beach north of town.

24. (*How come Stanley is / Why is Stanley*) _____ so opposed to the contin-
    uation of varsity athletics at the university?

25. Your workers were understandably (*wore out / exhausted*) _____ after ten
    hours with hardly a break.

26. How can (*you / youse*) _____ spend so much time lying around doing
    nothing?

27. Hilary's family hasn't yet decided what to do (*vacationwise / for a vacation*) _____

    _____ this year.

28. Duane's little sister is (*typical of / like*) _____ most kids her age, inquisi-
    tive but short on concentration.

29. The provost made one of his (*infrequent / unfrequent*) _____ attempts to
    tell the faculty what he intended to do.

30. Alas, the reputed sage's advice (*was void of / included very little*) _____
    wisdom.

REVIEW EXERCISE
Nonstandard or Inappropriate Expressions

1. We found ourselves in (*a lot / alot*) _____ more trouble than we expected.

2. The main valves were (*accidentally / accidently*) _____ left open for the night.

3. A fallen tree lay (*acrossed / acrost / across*) _____ the old logging trail.

4. Everything was (*alright / all right*) _____ once the heat came on.

5. Edmund had never before demonstrated (*all that / very*) _____ much interest in hog calling.

6. The campers (*almost / like to have*) _____ died from eating bad meat.

7. Even as a child, Brenda was not (*ascared / afraid*) _____ of the dark.

8. The park ranger said we could camp (*anywhere / anywheres*) _____ we chose to.

9. Forty miles is (*all the farther / as far as*) _____ we traveled in a single day.

10. A thorough (*analyzation / analysis*) _____ of the problem was long overdue.

11. Which (*feature / aspect*) _____ of the new model did you not like?

12. Shakespeare (*authored / wrote*) _____ thirty-seven plays during his lifetime.

13. You must (*be sure to / be sure and*) _____ take enough money with you.

14. (*Being that / Because*) _____ school was closed, few people were on campus.

15. We had never before (*boughten / bought*) _____ so much food at one time.

16. Scott's house was (*burgled / burglarized*) _____ sometime during the holidays.

17. No one doubt (*that / but that*) _____ your motives were honorable and aboveboard.

18. Sometimes I cannot help (*wondering / but wonder*) _____ what my great-grandparents would think of the world today.

19. Grandfather (*can't hardly / can hardly*) _____ find parts for his '57 Studebaker anymore.

20. The controversy (*centered on / centered around*) _____ whether Christopher Columbus was a hero or a villain.

21. Bittle never (*asserted / claimed*) _____ that he had been an honor student.

22. Such a delicately (*complected / complexioned*) _____ person might spend a small fortune on skin-care products.

23. We were anticipating a (*large / considerable*) _____ number of complaints from our regular customers.

24. No one doubts that Reginald (*could have / could of*) _____ finished the final round.

25. College is greatly (*different than / different from*) _____ high school.

26. What you have done is (*the direct opposite of / contrary to*) _____ what you have advised others to do.

27. Occasionally I even (*forget / disremember*) _____ what day it is.

28. The mayor (*doubts that / doubts if*) _____ the local mill will ever reopen.

29. Your kitten looked like a (*drownded / drowned*) _____ rat when we pulled it from the fish pond.

30. Just how (*enthusiastic / enthused*) _____ are workers expected to become at the prospect of a two percent pay raise?

31. The second test was (*equally as / just as*) _____ difficult as the first one.

32. In truth, none of us ever expected to (*excape / escape*) _____ from the island.

33. (*Even though / Eventhough*) _____ the second position paid more money, Leslie took the first offer.

34. The inspector's (*expertise / competence*) _____ at reading people's motives was well known.

35. Aunt Isabel was the first (*female / woman*) _____ in the family to graduate from college.

36. The deal was not (*concluded / finalized*) _____ by those who originally proposed it.

37. Alas, I remain (*flustrated / flustered / frustrated*) _____ in my efforts to become a member of the country club.

38. Everyone had a (*fun / good*) _____ time at the thirty-fifth class reunion.

39. What is the precise (*function / functionality*) _____ of the personnel department within our corporate structure?

40. Uncle Ned has had some (*funny / unusual*) _____ jobs, including washing elephants in the Moscow Zoo.

41. You (*must / have got to*) _____ exercise regularly if you want to become fit.

42. Carlos knew in his heart that he (*had ought to / should*) _____ study more.

43. Nothing is more (*heartrending / heartrendering*) _____ than a well-told story about good love gone bad.

44. These bushes grow to a (*height / heighth*) _____ of about four feet.

45. The greatest (*hinderance / hindrance*) _____ to improved productivity with this company is low worker morale.

46. We wanted the task force to (*hone in on / home in on / pinpoint*) _____ the source of the discontentment.

47. To what extent has foreign competition (*impacted / affected*) _____ our margin of profit?

48. The instructor did say something, although only (*incidentally / incidently*) _____

_____, about Roosevelt trying to stack the Supreme Court.

49. Once again, Morris demonstrated an (*extensive / in-depth*) _____ aquaintance with the economy of China.

50. Perhaps students and faculty should (*interact verbally / talk*) _____ with each other away from the classroom.

51. How long has Aubrey been (*into / interested in*) _____ phrenology?

52. Diabetes (*occurs when / is when*) _____ a person has an insulin deficiency and an inability to process carbohydrates.

53. Within three months the car had lost most of (*its / it's / its'*) _____ paint.

54. A fifth of bourbon is sufficient to (*liquorize / inebriate*) _____ more than one person.

55. Isn't it (*kind of / sort of / a bit*) _____ unusual for a monkey to be able to play the piano?

56. Quincy, an international business student, is equally (*loquacious / fluent*) _____

_____ in French, German, Spanish, Russian, and English.

57. By graduation, (*a majority / most*) _____ of the students in the class already had jobs.

58. Alas, only seven (*men / males*) _____ had registered for the ballroom dancing class.

59. Although you (*may have / may of*) _____ intended your remark as a compliment, it wasn't taken as a compliment.

60. Because my luggage was never recovered, my only (*momento / memento*) _____ _____ of the trip was a small bottle of Pepto Bismol.

61. Compared to yours, my accomplishments are indeed (*minuscule / miniscule*) _____ _____.

62. Experience has taught me that being rich is (*more preferable than / preferable to*) _____ being poor.

63. Why does Justin have such a (*negative / negatory*) _____ attitude about so many things?

64. Working the (*nite / night*) _____ shift can be hard on one's social life.

65. Yvonne insists that she is an (*old-fashion / old-fashioned*) _____ country girl at heart.

66. Margaret left home (*because of / on account of*) _____ the constant bickering among her brothers and sisters.

67. Julian (*chose / opted*) _____ to enlist in the army rather than go to college.

68. The company operates a program to (*orient / orientate*) _____ all new employees.

69. We decided not to go to Europe (*due to the fact that / because*) _____ the airplane fares were so high.

70. Howard has always been (*paranoid / uneasy*) _____ about meeting new people.

71. Patrick is still looking for a (*partner / pardner*) _____ to go into business with him.

72. The applicant presented (*phony / counterfeit*) _____ credentials during the screening interview.

73. We were mislead by the brochure; (*plus / moreover*) _____, we were bumped off the plane.

74. Can you recall (*when / the point in time*) _____ you learned the truth about your brother?

75. The most (*prejudiced / prejudice*) _____ position taken was not reported in the press.

76. The company will (*soon / presently*) _____ sell its frozen foods division.

77. All those arrested were placed in (*preventative / preventive*) _____ detention.

78. Only three months (*before / prior to*) _____ the accident, my grandfather had sold the family farm.

79. Hasn't this company been (*publicly / publically*) _____ owned for more than fifty years?

80. In recent times we (*rarely ever / almost never*)_____ visit any of our relatives.

81. Lack of opportunity for advancement was the (*reason that / reason why*) _____ _____ Neville left the organization.

82. (*Irregardless / Regardless*) _____ of the financial consequences, I am going to take a trip around the world.

83. Alas, I have never learned to (*relate to / enjoy*) _____ most country and western music.

84. All the injured students were quickly (*removed / evacuated*) _____ from the damaged building.

85. Both twins (*share / have*) _____ the same crooked little finger.

86. Edmund weighs (*slightly / something*) _____ more than three hundred pounds.

87. Wasn't this game (*suppose to / supposed to*) _____ become less painful over time.

88. The children have taught (*themselves / theirselves*) _____ how to survive in the wilderness.

89. We (*think / are afraid*) _____ that you sold all the end tables at below cost.

90. I walk back and forth (*through / thru*) _____ that park twice each day.

91. Shouldn't the school (*try and / try to*) _____ do something to attract better students?

92. You must learn to (*use / utilize*) _____ the skills of your staff people more fully.

93. Have we no (*viable / workable*) _____ procedure for disposing of the waste materials?

94. Does anyone really know when the murder (*transpired / occurred*) _____ _____?

95. Dr. Hobson is (*like / typical of*) _____ most scholars, not easily influenced by the madding crowd.

96. Although our trips to the city became (*infrequent / unfrequent*) _____, we nevertheless maintained a number of close friendships there.

97. I want to know (*how come / why*) _____ we never go to the movies anymore.

98. We haven't yet decided what to do (*Halloweenwise / for Halloween*) _____ _____.

99. Frederica is a bona fide (*world traveler / neat lady*) _____; indeed, she has been everywhere—several times.

100. If I had only finished school, I (*would of / would have*) _____ had a high-paying job by now.

Chapter 3
Words That Sound Alike

Properly speaking, words with the same pronunciation but differing in spelling, meaning, and origin are called homophones. Thus, in pairs, the words *aisle* and *isle, bridal* and *bridle, cellar* and *seller, discreet* and *discrete, flour* and *flower,* and *mail* and *male* are homophones. Although such word pairs as *adherence* and *adherents, adolescence* and *adolescents, assistance* and *assistants,* and *dependence* and *dependents* are not properly homophones—because they have related meanings and common origins—they can be considered homophones for our purposes. Other sound-alike words—which are not exactly homophones either—include such pairs as the following: *addition* and *edition, anecdote* and *antidote, complacence* and *complaisance, exercise* and *exorcise, feudal* and *futile, hardy* and *hearty, highbred* and *hybrid, hurdle* and *hurtle, ladder* and *latter, liable* and *libel, moot* and *mute, ordinance* and *ordnance, quiet* and *quite, shudder* and *shutter, veracious* and *voracious, viral* and *virile,* and *weather* and *whether.*

The purpose of this chapter is to acquaint you with diction errors that can occur when either of a pair of sound-alike words is incorrectly used in place of the other. And sometimes a set of three or more words may be involved rather than just a pair—for example, *allusion, elusion,* and *illusion; cite, sight,* and *site; for, fore,* and *four; grisly, gristly,* and *grizzly; medal, meddle, metal,* and *mettle;* and *pair, pare,* and *pear.*

The chapter contains twenty-one instructional sequences. Each sequence is composed of four pages, two pages that explain the usage errors under consideration one by one and two pages that allow you to check your understanding of the explanations by completing the sentence fill-in exercise. You simply write the correct response in the blank provided within each sentence. If your instructor is using the Instructor's Manual that accompanies the text, you will probably be asked to work the sequences in sets of three; the Instructor's Manual provides quizzes at intervals of every three sequences: 1–3, 4–6, 7–9, 10–12, 13–15, 16–18, and 19–21. At the conclusion of the chapter is a review exercise that includes 150 items. Your instructor may want to give this as a test.

Before beginning the first instructional sequence, don't forget to turn back to page 8 in Chapter 1 and work through the pretest exercise for the chapter. The specific instructions for doing the pretest are on page 3.

Words That Sound Alike (1)

acclamation/acclimation: An *acclamation* is an expression of approval, as by loud applause. (Although admittedly by something less than unanimous *acclamation,* the motion did pass.) *Acclimation* is the process of becoming acclimated, as to a geographical area. (The group's *acclimation* to such a frigid climate took many years.)

acetic/ascetic: That which is *acetic* contains or produces acid or vinegar. (The salad dressing had a pronounced *acetic* taste.) An *ascetic* individual is a person who lives a life of strict self-denial, contemplation, and severe spiritual discipline. (Today, the *ascetic* life is a little too severe for most people.)

addition/edition: An *addition* is anything added on, or the process of doing it. (The *addition* of two large rooms made the house much more comfortable.) An *edition* is a specific issue of a publication or one of the forms or models in which something is manufactured or presented. (The new *edition* of the text is longer than the old one.)

adherence/adherents: *Adherence* means "a strong and steady attachment." (Your *adherence* to the truth is admirable.) *Adherents* are followers or supporters, as of some cause. (The earliest *adherents* of the teachings of Jesus were called disciples.)

adolescence/adolescents: *Adolescence* is the stage or period of time between youth and adulthood. *Adolescents* are teenagers. (*Adolescence* can be a difficult time for *adolescents,* and for their parents and neighbors as well.)

aid/aide/-ade: *Aid* has several meanings—"help," "assistance," "a helper or assistant," or "a helpful device." *Aide* is an abbreviated form of *aide-de-camp,* meaning "an assistant army officer." Thus, *aide* means only "one who acts as an official assistant to another." (The presidential *aide* sought *aid* for the unlucky farmers hit by the drought.) The suffix *-ade* means "a sweetened drink." (The *limeade* was a bit tart for my taste.)

ail/ale: To *ail* is to feel sick or to cause pain or distress for others. *Ale* is a beer-like brew made from malt and hops. (What really *ails* us this morning is all the *ale* we drank last night at the bonfire.)

aisle/isle: An *aisle* is a passageway between rows of seats. An *isle* is a small island. (The missionary chapel on the tiny tropical *isle* had very narrow *aisles*.)

alley/ally: An *alley* is a narrow street. (The garbage truck always comes down the *alley* behind the row of houses.) An *ally* is a friend with a common purpose. (Traditionally, Great Britain has been an *ally* of the United States.)

allowed/aloud: *Allowed* means "permitted" or "not prohibited." *Aloud* means "with voice." (The political prisoners were not *allowed* to read their personal mail *aloud*.)

allusion/elusion/illusion: An *allusion* is an indirect reference to something. (The instructor's *allusion* to Cervantes' *Don Quixote* was quite clever.) An *elusion* is an evasion or avoidance, as by cleverness or quickness, of a possible difficulty. (By clever *elusion*, Roscoe avoided a confrontation with the police.) An *illusion* is a deceptively false notion or impression. (The highway presented the *illusion* of becoming narrower in the distance.)

altar/alter: An *altar* is a stand used for religious purposes. To *alter* means "to change." (Although he was retiring, the minister would not allow us to *alter* the *altar*.)

analyst/annalist: An *analyst* is a person who analyzes something, as a *systems analyst* or a *psychoanalyst*. An *annalist* is a person who writes annals, or a historian. (An *annalist* of World War II might also be an *analyst* of the period.)

anecdote/antidote: An *anecdote* is a brief entertaining story, often about the life of a well-known person. An *antidote* is a remedy to counteract something bad or harmful. (As an *antidote* against the blizzard, the snowed-in students exchanged *anecdotes* about their professors.)

annunciate/enunciate: To *annunciate* is to announce, as the beginning of an important event or the arrival of an important person. (A court page will *annunciate* the arrival of the queen.) To *enunciate* is to pronounce words, usually clearly and distinctly, or to express something in a very systematic way. (We need a spokesperson to *enunciate* our position clearly.)

SENTENCE FILL-IN

1. Even the staunchest (*adherence* / *adherents*) _____ of free enterprise would not remove all import tariffs.

2. Playing radios was not (*allowed* / *aloud*) _____ at any of the private beaches.

3. Few (*adolescence* / *adolescents*) _____ manage to escape the power of peer pressure altogether.

4. At the top of the mountain stands an ancient (*altar* / *alter*) _____ to an old Norse god.

5. Alice's brothers live just off the back (*alley* / *ally*) _____ with some school friends.

6. One old-fashioned (*anecdote* / *antidote*) _____ for boredom is to read a good book.

7. (*Acclamation* / *Acclimation*) _____ to living in a university dormitory can take more than a week or two.

8. What your children (*ail* / *ale*) _____ from is overindulgence in pepperoni pizza.

9. The teacher's (*aid* / *aide*) _____ taught both the beginning class and the advanced class.

10. Several of the (*aisles* / *isles*) _____ in the auditorium were blocked with ladders and other equipment.

11. Cumberland County has hired an experienced (*analyst* / *annalist*) _____ to write a popular history of the region.

12. Serious university students often live something of an (*acetic* / *ascetic*) _____ life.

13. Your obnoxious roommate constantly uses literary (*allusions* / *elusions* / *illusions*) _____ to put other people down.

14. Radio and television newscasters must always (*annunciate* / *enunciate*) _____ clearly and carefully.

15. The latest (*addition* / *edition*) _____ of the tax manual includes multiple copies of most filing forms.

16. At the class reunion the old school chums drank strong (*ail* / *ale*) _____ imported from Scotland.

17. The new track coach insists on strict (*adherence / adherents*) _____ to her training rules.

18. Historically, Moscow has not been an (*alley / ally*) _____ of either Washington or London.

19. The company plans to (*altar / alter*) _____ the new models only slightly.

20. To no one's surprise, Andrea was reelected by (*acclamation / acclimation*) _____ _____.

21. This clever fox is a master of (*allusion / elusion / illusion*) _____; the hounds will never catch him.

22. Everyone agrees that the federal government must provide (*aid / aide*) _____ _____ to the victims of the earthquake.

23. Rabbi Goldman always prayed (*allowed / aloud*) _____ with the younger soldiers.

24. If the solution is (*acetic / ascetic*) _____, it will have a bitter taste.

25. After a chat with his (*analyst / annalist*) _____, Bernard usually feels much better, but for only a while.

26. Alas, most of us harbor an (*allusion / elusion / illusion*) _____ or two about our own hidden abilities.

27. The new (*addition / edition*) _____ to the hospital was paid for almost entirely with private funds.

28. The little (*anecdotes / antidotes*) _____ about the eccentricities of famous people are the best parts of my history professor's lectures.

29. Sailing from one (*aisle / isle*) _____ to another, the adventurers searched for buried treasure.

30. During early (*adolescence / adolescents*) _____, Meredith thought the rest of his body would never catch up with his feet.

Words That Sound Alike (2)

ant/aunt: An *ant* is a wingless insect that lives in colonies. The sister of one's mother or father is one's aunt. (My eccentric *aunt* served chocolate covered *ants* as an *hors d'oeuvre*.)

ante-/anti-: *Ante-* is a Latin prefix meaning "before" or "in front of." (Many of the *antebellum* houses in Memphis have been broken up into small apartments. The speaker's *antediluvian* ideas did not go well with the liberal audience.) *Anti-* is a Greek prefix meaning "against" or "opposite." For clarity, it is sometimes followed by a hyphen when joined to a free-standing word. (Several university presidents accused the governor and his staff of *anti-intellectualism*. *Antisocial* behavior can be quite uncivil.)

arc/ark: An *arc* is a curved line or part of a curved line. (An *arc* of light shot across the night sky.) An *ark* is a large awkward boat, like the one built by Noah before the Biblical flood. (After two weeks of steady rain, several people in the neighborhood started building an *ark*.)

ascent/assent: An *ascent* is a going up or a way leading up. To *assent* is to agree or concur. (If you *assent* to the conditions of this one compromise, your *ascent* to the head of the company should be swift.)

assistance/assistants: *Assistance* is help. *Assistants* are subordinates who are supposed to help. (Alas, the *assistance* given me by my *assistants* is not always as helpful as it should be.)

attendance/attendants: To be in *attendance* is to be present. *Attendants* are people who wait on or serve others. (Not all of the duke's *attendants* were in *attendance* at the banquet.)

auger/augur: An *auger* is a tool with a spiral cutting edge used for boring holes into wood or even the earth. An *augur* is a prophet or fortune-teller. To *augur* is to predict the future, usually by means of signs or omens. (A blunt *auger* does not *augur* well for the carpenter's day.)

baal/bail/bale: *Baal* refers to any number of local fertility gods or false gods of the Old Testament. (According to the sermon on Sunday, the worshipers of *baal* may still be with us today.) To *bail* means "to dip water from a boat" or "to deliver someone from arrest by posting bond." (We could not *bail* fast enough to keep the boat from sinking. No one was willing to *bail out* the man accused of starting the fire.) A *bale* is a large bundle of goods, such as hay or cotton. *Bale* is also mental anguish, suffering, or woe. (At the prospect of loading the *bales* of hay onto the truck by myself, my heart was filled with *bale*.)

bald/balled/bawled: *Bald* means "having no hair on the head" as well as "bare," "plain," "frank," or "blunt." (No one wants to be fat, fifty, and *bald*. You should have known that such a *bald* lie would be found out.) *Balled* means "formed into a round mass." *Bawled* means "cried out loudly, as in weeping." (Jan almost broke down and *bawled* when she discovered that the dryer had *balled* up her new sweaters.)

balm/bomb: *Balm* is something that heals, as a fragrant and soothing ointment. (Sound sleep can be a *balm* to the problems of the day.) A *bomb* was recently defined by the military as a "vertically descending antipersonnel projectile with an explosive capacity." (The atom *bomb* long ago made all-out warfare absurd.)

band/banned: A *band* is an organized group of people or an item that confines or constricts movement. (All the members of the *band* wore *bands* of mourning on their left arm.) Anything that is *banned* is prohibited. (Alcohol has been *banned* from all housing buildings on campus.)

bard/barred: A *bard* is a poet or minstrel. (Shakespeare is sometimes called the *bard* of Avon.) To be *barred* is to be shut out or kept out. (Several frontline players were *barred* from the tournament.)

baron/barren: A *baron* is a nobleman of the lowest hereditary rank. The term also refers to any person of great power or influence. That which is *barren* is sterile, without vegetation, unproductive, and so on. (The *baron's* estate is located on a *barren* moor too desolate to describe.)

bazaar/bizarre: A *bazaar* is a street lined with small shops or a part of a larger store where miscellaneous articles are sold. (Our church holds its annual *bazaar* for the needy just after Thanksgiving.) That which is *bizarre* is odd, strange, weird, grotesque, eccentric, and the like. (In truth, the accident was the result of a *bizarre* chain of events.)

SENTENCE FILL-IN

1. The climbing team's (*ascent* / *assent*) _____ of the mountain took several days.

2. Most of the guests thought the (*attendance* / *attendants*) _____ were unusually well trained.

3. Your faithful love is always a (*balm* / *bomb*) _____ to my heart.

4. Robin Hood and his (*band* / *banned*) _____ of merry men lived in Sherwood Forest.

5. The gathering clouds in the west did not (*auger* / *augur*) _____ well for the scheduled afternoon picnic.

6. We (*bald* / *balled* / *bawled*) _____ like babies when we learned that our old high school would be torn down and replaced by a shopping mall.

7. At the local (*bazaar* / *bizarre*) _____, Eleanor insisted on buying a pair of shrunken heads—(*bazaar/bizarre*) _____ gifts, most people thought.

8. Although likable enough, Hamilton's (*ant* / *aunt*) _____ is such an eccentric old curmudgeon.

9. The local (*bard* / *barred*) _____ had composed another of his sentimental sonnets for the occasion.

10. Although she gave her (*ascent* / *assent*) _____, rumor has it that she did not give her heart.

11. Not surprisingly, the speaker's blatant (*ante-* / *anti-*) _____ Americanism was applauded by the Third World radicals.

12. He was a (*baron* / *barren*) _____ of so little consequence that his coat of arms was a vest.

13. We found a miniature (*arc* / *ark*) _____ floating in the neighbor's swimming pool.

14. Too much (*assistance* / *assistants*) _____ can sometimes be as unhandy as too little.

15. A soul sufficiently weakened by (*baal* / *bail* / *bale*) _____ may not be able to regenerate itself without help from another.

16. Almost half the class had perfect (*attendance* / *attendants*) _____ for the entire semester.

17. The refugees spent most of the night trying to (*baal* / *bail* / *bale*) _____ water from a leaking barge.

18. Too many (*assistance / assistants*) _____ can sometimes be as unhandy as too few.

19. The potato salad was covered with (*ants / aunts*) _____, not maggots.

20. Alas, it was a (*baron / barren*) _____ speech, productive of no solutions whatsoever.

21. Tracy found a very old carpenter's (*auger / augur*) _____ at the local antique shop.

22. The terrorists attempted to place a (*balm / bomb*) _____ in the luggage of an unsuspecting tourist.

23. A pronoun's (*antecedent / anticedent*) _____ is the word to which the pronoun refers.

24. Once again, Rufus has been (*bard / barred*) _____ from the local vets club for reciting his grim poetry.

25. The morning hoarfrost created (*bazaar / bizzare*) _____ figures on the windowpanes.

26. Thirty minutes or so later the missile (*arced / arked*) _____ across the heavens toward Baghdad.

27. No moral person would ever (*ascent / assent*) _____ to the use of such disinformation.

28. For generations there have been no (*bald / balled / bawled*) _____ men in the Douglas family.

29. Alas, we have been (*band / banned*) _____ from playing our music within six blocks of the hospital.

30. No fewer than three of the (*assistants / assistance*) _____ in this department have been promoted to management positions.

Words That Sound Alike (3)

beach/beech: The *beach* is a sandy place beside the sea. A *beech* is a tree that produces edible nuts. (Don't expect to find any *beech* trees on or near the *beach*.)

bear/bare: A *bear* is a shaggy, thickset mammal that likes honey. To *bear* means "to carry," "to bring forth," or "to tolerate." (The polar *bear* displays no fear of people. These trees *bear* fruit every third year. I cannot *bear* any more of your silly chatter.) That which is *bare* is exposed to view, or naked. To *bare* is to uncover or strip. (We cleaned the house down to the *bare* walls. The maniac *bared* his chest to the storm and dared the lightning to strike him.)

beat/beet: To *beat* is to strike repeatedly or to defeat. (Don't *beat* your head against the wall; try another strategy.) A *beet* is a biennial plant of the goosefoot family with an edible bulbous root. (Borscht is a creamy sour soup made from *beets*.)

been/bin: *Been* is the past participle of *be*. (After a three-year trip around the world, I knew I had *been* somewhere.) A *bin* is a box-like receptacle for storing things. (The cat hid in the toy *bin* for three days.)

beer/bier: *Beer* is a fermented beverage made from malted barley and flavored with hops. (The best *beer* I have ever tasted is a royal English brew called Worthington II.) A *bier* is a platform or framework on which a coffin or dead body is placed, as for a funeral service. (After the funeral was over, the *bier*, coffin, and all were set on fire.)

berry/bury: A *berry* is a small juicy edible fruit. (When I was a child, my sister and I went *berry* picking in the mountains.) To *bury* is to put into the ground, as a dead body, or to hide or conceal something. (After the battle, the captain said to *bury* the dead and let God sort them out.)

berth/birth: A *berth* is a built-in bed or a ship's place of anchorage. (Thomas slept in an upper *berth* throughout the cruise.) *Birth* refers to the act of bringing forth offspring or of being born. (The baby's *birth* occurred precisely at noon. The American Revolution gave *birth* to a new nation.)

blew/blue: *Blew* is the past tense of *blow*. (A steady wind *blew* all afternoon.) *Blue* is the color of the clear sky, or between green and violet. (Janet is the only member of her family without *blue* eyes.)

bloc/block: A *bloc* is an affiliation of people, groups, voters, legislators, nations, or the like with a common agenda. (The liberal *bloc* will never accept such a conservative candidate.) A *block* is a good sized solid piece of wood, stone, or metal. (A *block* of granite a third the size of our house fell out of the sky and landed in the back yard.)

boar/bore: A *boar* is an uncastrated male pig or a wild hog with a hairy coat and a long snout. (A *boar* hog can be a dangerous critter.) Among other things, the noun *bore* means "a dull, tiresome person." Similarly, to *bore* is to make weary by being dull, monotonous, or uninteresting. (Please, don't *bore* us by telling stories about yourselves.)

boarder/border: A *boarder* is someone who pays to live and take meals at another's house. A *border* is an edge or boundary, as between countries. (The *boarder* at our house in Vermont has a job across the Canadian *border*.)

bode/bowed: To *bode* is to presage or indicate by signs or omens of. (The thunder and lightning *bode* a storm.) That which is *bowed* is bent or curved. (From all the moisture and heat, the window frame had *bowed* out on both sides.)

bolder/boulder: One who is *bolder* than someone else is more fearless in meeting danger or difficulty. A *boulder* is a massive rock worn round and smooth from weather and water. (We decided that it would take a *bolder* group than we to move the huge *boulder* precariously suspended above the cabin.)

born/borne: *Born* means "brought into being," "from birth," or "natural." (This is a man *born* with the desire to entertain others.) *Borne* is the past participle of *bear* and is often used to mean "endured," "withstood," or "tolerated." (The hostages had *borne* all manner of mistreatment without complaint.)

bouillon/bullion: *Bouillon* is broth made by the slow boiling of meat in water. *Bullion* is gold or silver in bars or ingots. (The miser polished his gold *bullion* with steaming beef *bouillon*.)

SENTENCE FILL-IN

1. The (*berth / birth*) _____ of our second child occurred on our seventh wedding anniversary.

2. Balthazar (*blew / blue*) _____ into town on a fast train and later left the same way he had arrived.

3. The body of the revered king lay on the funeral (*beer / bier*) _____ like a stone statue.

4. Your argumentative manner doesn't (*bode / bowed*) _____ well for your future with this organization.

5. Several officers from the (*boarder / border*) _____ patrol were searching for a lost caravan of senior citizens.

6. The night patrol discovered that a group of (*beach / beech*) _____ bums had been sleeping in the lifeboats.

7. About a cup of chicken (*bouillon / bullion*) _____ would have greatly improved the casserole.

8. Jeannette likes nothing better than to (*berry / bury*) _____ herself in a thick book for three or four days at a time.

9. Hamilton is much (*bolder / boulder*) _____ as an adult than he was as a child.

10. Alas, you went to a lot of trouble to (*bear / bare*) _____ your soul to the neighborhood gossip.

11. The farm (*bloc / block*) _____ is insisting on free access to foreign markets for the American farmer.

12. Fresh (*beats / beets*) _____ have a much sweeter taste than do canned ones.

13. The old woman had (*borne / born*) _____ more pain in her life than should be required.

14. Today we use the old coal (*been / bin*) _____ as a playpen for our grandchildren.

15. What a cliché-spouting (*boar / bore*) _____ my once clever and witty cousin has become since earning a few million dollars and joining the country club.

16. No matter how long you cook it, (*bare / bear*) _____ meat is tough, quite hard to chew.

17. For several years, Timothy was a (*boarder / border*) _____ with a traditional Mormon family.

18. Millions of dollars worth of gold (*bouillon / bullion*) _____ is stored in the vault beneath the building.

19. No one wanted to sleep in the top (*berth / birth*) _____ on the return trip from Birmingham to Charleston.

20. During the earthquake, a huge (*bolder / boulder*) _____ toppled from the mountain and fell into the lake.

21. The Michigan (*berry / bury*) _____ crop has never been better than it is this year.

22. Does anyone know whether or not betel nuts grow on (*beach / beech*) _____ _____ trees?

23. Few places in the world have not refined the process of brewing (*beer / bier*) _____ _____ .

24. The defensive linemen thought of themselves as the equivalent of (*blocs / blocks*) _____ of granite.

25. Please (*bear / bare*) _____ with me while I go about the business of making a fool of myself in front of thousands of total strangers.

26. The old man's back was (*bode / bowed*) _____ from a lifetime of carrying heavy loads.

27. Was Davy Crockett really (*born / borne*) _____ on a mountaintop in Tennessee?

28. To (*beat / beet*) _____ swords into plowshares is not an easy task.

29. Putting (*blew / blue*) _____ carpet in every room seemed a bit redundant to me.

30. Vivian says that she has (*been / bin*) _____ to Australia and New Zealand no fewer than three times.

Words That Sound Alike (4)

borough/burro/burrow: A *borough* is an incorporated village or town. (Jackson lives in the quaint little *borough* of Hampton.) A *burro* is a small donkey. (A mule and a *burro* are not the same creature.) A *burrow* is a small hole or tunnel dug by an animal. To *burrow* is to make such a tunnel. (In the spring and fall, moles often *burrow* across the neighborhood lawns.)

brake/break: A *brake* is a mechanical device to slow a mechanism or vehicle. To *brake* is to cause to slow down. To *break* is to smash or split into pieces. (Unless there is something to *brake* your fall, you will *break* more than your neck if your parachute doesn't open.)

bread/bred: *Bread* is food made of flour dough or grain meal. (Many people eat *bread* with every meal.) *Bred,* the past tense and past participle form of *breed,* means "brought forth, as from the womb," "produced," "reared," or "trained." (Such people, *bred* by peasants to be peasants, will never learn to read and write.)

brewed/brood: *Brewed* means "mixed together and produced by steeping, boiling, or fermenting." (Leslie's aunt *brewed* the best tea in the community.) A *brood* is the collective offspring of animals or a group of animals born or hatched at the same time. To *brood* is to think about something in a troubled way. (The mother robin hatched her *brood* and then promptly flew away. Why *brood* about what you can't change?)

bridal/bridle: A *bridal* is a nuptial festival or ceremony. The word is also generally descriptive of a bride or wedding. (No one could locate the *bridal* veil.) A *bridle* is the headgear by which a rider controls a horse. (Old Paint accepted the *bridle* with quiet dignity.) To *bridle* is to pull back in a manner indicating anger, scorn, or offense. (The instructor *bridled* with anger at the student's crude remark.)

broach/brooch: To *broach* is to open a discussion or topic, to bring up or introduce something. (No one dared *broach* the subject of the old man's estranged children.) A *brooch* is a rather large ornamental pin with a clasp. (Stephen bought his mother a beautiful rhinestone *brooch* in a local antique shop.)

burley/burly: *Burley* is a thin-leaved air-cured tobacco grown mainly in Kentucky. (Over the years, Kentucky tobacco farmers have exported *burley* to all parts of the world.) A *burly* person is strong, muscular, and rough and hearty of manner. (No one expected such a *burly* fellow to be a lyric poet.)

buy/by/bye: To *buy* something is to purchase it. (We don't have enough money to *buy* an airplane.) *By* means "beside" or "near." (The old men stood *by* the stone sea wall and baked in the afternoon sun.) A *bye* is a position in a tournament wherein a participant has no opponent. The same spelling is also used as an abbreviated form of *good-bye,* an expression of farewell. (The team was lucky enough to draw a *bye* in the first round of the tournament.)

callous/callus: *Callous* is most often used to mean "unfeeling," "insensitive," or "lacking pity or mercy." (It takes a *callous* person to view the suffering of the poor and feel no sympathy.) A *callus* is a hardened and thickened place on the skin formed from constant pressure and friction. (Meg has a *callus* on her thumb from playing the guitar.)

canapé/canopy: A *canapé* is a small piece of bread (or toast) or a cracker spread with spicy meat, fish, cheeses, and the like. (The caviar *canapés* were the best of the hors d'oeuvres.) A *canopy* is a drapery covering over a bed or any other covering over a structure. (The night sky forms a starlit *canopy* above the earth.)

cannon/canon: A *cannon* is a large tubular weapon that fires projectiles. (The troops pointed the *cannons* at the enemy lines.) A *canon* is a law, decree, regulation, or formal code. (One of the *canons* of the good life is to treat others decently.)

can't/cant: *Can't* is the contraction of *cannot*. *Cant* is the social or occupational jargon used by a particular group of people. (Adults *can't* understand much of the adolescent *cant* used by teenagers.)

canter/cantor: A *canter* is the three-beat gait that is slower than a full gallop. To *canter* is to move or ride at a smooth, easy pace. (The joggers moved along together at a comfortable *canter*.) A *cantor* is a synagogue official who sings or chants liturgical solos. (The *cantor* led the congregation in a common prayer.)

SENTENCE FILL-IN

1. For years, Geoffrey's grandfather (*brewed / brood*) _____ beer in the basement at home.

2. Although a (*burley / burly*) _____ lad by local standards, Clive was no match for the professional wrestler.

3. Alas, the (*bridal / bridle*) _____ cake had too much icing between the layers.

4. Professional baseball pitchers often develop a (*callous / callus*) _____ on the thumb of their pitching hand.

5. Poor Jessica has lost a diamond (*broach / brooch*) _____ that had been in the family for five generations.

6. It was quite pleasing to see the horse (*canter / cantor*) _____ across the meadow on a spring morning.

7. On the third try, the (*borough / burro / burrow*) _____ voted to establish a public day-care center.

8. We stood (*buy / by / bye*) _____ the river and watched the boats passing silently in the twilight.

9. Aren't the (*cannons / canons*) _____ of good taste and proper manners less rigid than they once were?

10. During a (*brake / break*) _____ in the action, we went to the concession stand for a snack.

11. In spite of its international reputation, the consortium did not have enough capital to

    (*buy / by / bye*) _____ the island.

12. These dogs were (*bread / bred*) _____ by experts in the field to hunt anything that moves and has a scent.

13. We were served a delicious mushroom (*canapé / canopy*) _____ at the wedding reception.

14. Every one of this latest (*brewed / brood*) _____ has the same spotted ears and a short tail.

15. Because he has chronic diverticulosis, Constantine (*can't / cant*) _____ eat peanuts or popcorn.

16. Although the driver almost stood on the (*brake / break*) _____, the vehicle would not slow down.

17. No one gets a (*buy / by / bye*) _____ in this tournament; we have democracy in action here.

103

18. The intonations of the (canter / cantor) _____ sometimes suggest that he is not singing with his heart and soul.

19. Is there anything that smells better than fresh (bread / bred) _____ baking in the oven?

20. Your words are only so much (can't / cant) _____; you are not really telling us anything.

21. The old (bridal / bridle) _____ was much too small for the horse's head.

22. A rusted (cannon / canon) _____ is the only memento that marks the location of the once famous battle.

23. A gentleman would never (broach / brooch) _____ such a delicate subject with a lady.

24. Man shall not live by (bread / bred) _____ alone, but (buy / by / bye) _____ every word that flows from the mouth of God.

25. I like to (borough / burro / burrow) _____ under the covers for a short snooze after the alarm goes off.

26. Over time, once sensitive individuals may become (callous / callus) _____ as a result of life's disappointments.

27. Must you (brewed / brood) _____ about every little insult or injury that life sends your way?

28. (Burley / Burly) _____ tobacco is used in both cigarettes and mild cigars.

29. The new (canapé / canopy) _____ at the entrance to the hotel was torn during the storm.

30. When she was a child, Janice had her picture taken on a (borough / burro / burrow) _____ in Guadalajara.

Words That Sound Alike (5)

canvas/canvass: *Canvas* is a closely woven often coarse material used for sails, outdoor furniture, or tents. (The sale featured *canvas* covered deck chairs.) To *canvass* is to examine or discuss in detail, or to go among the people asking what they think about something. (All the candidates will *canvass* this neighborhood several times.)

capital/capitol: A *capital* is a city that serves as the seat of government. (Charleston is the *capital* of West Virginia.) *Capital* is also money. (Starting a new business requires substantial *capital*.) A *capitol* is the actual building in which the legislature meets. (Each year thousands of tourists visit the *capitol* in Charleston.)

carrot/caret/carat: A *carrot* is a biennial plant with fernlike leaves and an orange-red root enjoyed by rabbits. (Grandmother always puts *carrots* in her rabbit stew.) A *caret* is a mark (∧) used in written material to indicate where something is to be added. (The copy editor used so many *carets* on my manuscript that I was reminded of my grandmother's stew.) A *carat*, also spelled *karat*, is a unit of weight for precious stones and pearls, and a unit of fineness for gold. (A diamond weighing a full *carat* can cost $2,500. A twenty-four *karat* wedding ring is pure gold.)

cash/cache: *Cash* is ready money, the currency of the realm. A *cache* is a place to hide your money, or to store anything of value. Anything stored in a hidden place is also called a *cache*. (Several million dollars in *cash* was found in the smugglers' *cache*.)

cast/caste: A *cast* is a form or mold, or the group of characters in a play. To *cast* is to throw. (Far be it from me to *cast* aspersions on a *cast* of characters trying to do a dance number with *casts* on both legs.) A *caste* is a rigid and exclusive social class. (In America we speak of social classes rather than *castes*.)

cellar/seller: A *cellar* is a storage room under the house, and a *seller* is a person who sells something to a buyer. (Mr. Fogarty has long been a *seller* of fine wines, which he stores in his own private *cellar*.)

censor/sensor: A *censor* is a person or official with the authority to examine publications, movies, television shows, and the like to remove objectionable material. To *censor* is to engage in such activity. (From what I have seen of several recent movies, the *censors* must be on holiday.) A *sensor* is a device designed to measure, detect, record, or respond to physical phenomena. (Because the heat *sensor* failed, the engine overheated and then exploded.)

cent/scent/sent: A *cent* is a 1/100th part of a dollar. (The beggar didn't have a red *cent*.) A *scent* is a fragrance. (The *scent* of lilies was in the air.) *Sent* is the past tense and past participle form of the verb *send* and is used to mean "dispatched" or "transmitted." (That was the message *sent* about midnight.)

cereal/serial: *Cereal* is any grain used for food. (The Midwest is the *cereal* bowl of the United States.) As an adjective, *serial* means "arranged in or forming a series." (The police feared that a *serial* killer was on the loose.)

choral/coral: *Choral* means "sung, recited, or performed by a choir or chorus." (I enjoy good *choral* church music.) *Coral* is composed of the skeletal deposits of certain marine polyps, such as the sea anemone. (This *coral* reef was half a millennium in the making.)

chorale/corral: A *chorale* is a hymn or psalm sung by a choir or congregation, or a group of singers or the performance itself. (The *chorale* presented by the University Singers was wonderful.) A *corral* is an enclosure for capturing or holding livestock. To *corral* is to surround and capture. (The horses escaped from the *corral* during the storm.)

cite/sight/site: To *cite* means "to quote or refer to as an authority." (The lecturer will likely *cite* several authorities during the presentation.) *Sight* means "vision" or "something seen." (His *sight* isn't as keen as it used to be. The Golden Gate Bridge was a *sight* to see.) A *site* is a specific location. (The company has finally located a *site* for its new office building.)

clause/claws: A *clause* is a group of words containing a subject and a verb, or a specific article or provision in a formal document. (The final *clause* of this contract contradicts several of the earlier ones. This isn't a *clause;* it has no verb.) *Claws* are the sharp nails or talons on an animal's toes. (A cat's *claws* can be lethal weapons.)

SENTENCE FILL-IN

1. The gang's (*cache / cash*) _____ included millions of dollars worth of electronic equipment.

2. Dogs are able to track an animal by its (*cent / scent / sent*) _____.

3. Alas, this is the very (*cite / sight / site*) _____ where the massacre took place.

4. Take care not to (*cast / caste*) _____ pearls before swine.

5. The press will try to (*chorale / corral*) _____ the president and pose some questions on the matter.

6. Most of these (*canvas / canvass*) _____ bags were imported from either Korea or Taiwan.

7. Dogs do not have (*clause / claws*) _____; they have paws.

8. This laser (*censor / sensor*) _____ is designed to detect any movement in the gallery.

9. Do you intend to (*cast / caste*) _____ your lot with these unscrupulous characters?

10. The visitors from England did not know that Washington, D.C., was the (*capital / capitol*) _____ of the United States.

11. All you have to divulge is your name, rank, and (*cereal / serial*) _____ number.

12. Lydia belongs to a (*choral / coral*) _____ society that performs more than a dozen times a year.

13. The copy editor's penciled in (*carrots / carets / carats*) _____ did not photocopy clearly.

14. On more than one occasion my grandmother warned me: "Do not a buyer or a (*cellar / seller*) _____ be."

15. Vincent was (*cent / scent / sent*) _____ home from school because he went to philosophy class wearing a gorilla costume.

16. In today's money markets, Third World countries often have to pay too high a price for (*capital / capitol*) _____.

17. I think the strangest (*cite / sight / site*) _____ that I have ever seen was an elephant waterskiing.

18. Last night Edward gave Susan a half (*carrot / caret / carat*) _____ diamond engagement ring.

19. This famous (*chorale / corral*) _____ that we are about to listen to was composed more than a hundred years ago.

20. As usual, Roxanne maintains that she doesn't have a (*cent / scent / sent*) _____ _____ to her name.

21. The speaker's muddled attempt to (*cite / sight / site*) _____ a passage from Shakespeare was quite amusing.

22. If the president of the university would only (*canvas / canvass*) _____ the faculty, he would discover that he is completely out of touch with his constituency.

23. People who use foul language in public places should learn to (*censor / sensor*)_____ _____ their tongues.

24. Throughout the world, millions of people eat (*serial / cereal*) _____ each morning for breakfast.

25. The east wing of the (*capital / capitol*) _____ building was damaged by a bomb blast.

26. There is a (*clause / claws*) _____ in the lease that prohibits tenants from keeping an animal.

27. Beverly's glazed (*carrots / carets / carats*) _____ were a bit too sweet for my taste.

28. Historically in Western society, the monied (*cast / caste*) _____ has also been the most active politically and the most powerful.

29. Someone might point out to the young man that the (*choral / coral*) _____ _____ snake doesn't get its name from its singing voice.

30. When I was a lad, the family (*cellar / seller*) _____ ran full of water almost every spring.

Words That Sound Alike (6)

clench/clinch: To *clench* is to bring together tightly, to close the teeth rigidly or a fist firmly, to grip tightly. (The senator *clenched* his teeth in silence as he listened to the charges brought against him.) To *clinch* is to fasten firmly together, in the sense of winning an argument, completing a bargain, or achieving a victory. In boxing a *clinch* occurs when opponents grip each other's bodies with the arms so as to restrict punching. (We *clinched* the victory when the opposing quarterback was forced to leave the game.)

click/clique: A *click* is a slight sharp sound, as that of a light switch snapping. (The old man sat across the office *clicking* his teeth until the nurse called him in.) A *clique* is a small, exclusive, and often snobbish group of people. (The country club *clique* arrived at the meeting about an hour late.)

close/clothes/cloths: To *close* is to shut. (Please *close* the door.) *Clothes* are garments. (We usually donated our used *clothes* to the hospital thrift shop.) *Cloths* are pieces of material or fabric. (The *cloths* were saturated with oil.)

coarse/course: That which is *coarse* is common, inferior, unrefined, indelicate, rough, harsh, crude, vulgar, or tasteless. (Your *coarse* jokes were not much appreciated.) A *course* is a specific path between two points. (The *course* we played in Scotland was almost 7,000 yards long.)

colonel/kernel: A *colonel* is a military officer. A *kernel* is a grain or seed, the inner part of a nut or fruit, or the fundamental part or core of anything. (There wasn't a *kernel* of truth in anything the *colonel* said about the incident.)

complacence/complaisance: *Complacence* is a rather smug self-satisfaction. (Over time, this inclination toward a national *complacence* can turn the nation into a third-rate economic power.) *Complaisance* is a disposition always ready to please and oblige. (Such *complaisance* offends even those it is intended to please.)

complement/compliment: To *complement* means "to make more complete." (Education should *complement* one's natural abilities.) To *compliment* means "to praise or flatter." (The dean will *compliment* the honor students for their high grades.)

council/counsel: A *council* is an official group of people meeting to conduct business. (Margaret's cousin is the youngest person ever elected to the town *council*.) *Counsel* is advice. To *counsel* is to advise. (Never accept the *counsel* of a fool.)

councillor/counselor: A *councillor* is a member of a council. (Only one *councillor* showed up for the press conference.) A *counselor* is an adviser, especially a legal adviser or lawyer. (Alas, the school *counselor* gave me bad advice.)

courier/currier: A *courier* is a messenger. (We employ a *courier* service to handle our mail.) A *currier* is a person who works tanned animal hides into marketable form, or a person who combs a horse. (Years ago, no leather shop was without two or three expert *curriers.*)

coward/cowered: A *coward* is a person with little or no courage. *Cowered* is the past tense and past participle form of *cower,* which means "to cringe in total fear of something." (No one was surprised when the *coward,* upon hearing this feeble threat, *cowered* as if his life were in the balance.)

creak/creek/crick: A *creak* is a subdued rasping or grating noise. To *creak* is to make such a noise. (Many of the boards in the floors of the old house *creak* when one walks on them.) A *creek* is a small stream. (The *creek* bed was dry from lack of rain.) A *crick* is a muscle spasm or cramp. (Helen awoke with a *crick* in her neck.)

crevice/crevasse: A *crevice* is a narrow split or crack. (Tiny spring flowers grew in the *crevices* of the stone wall.) A *crevasse* is a deep, wide crack or split, as in the ice of a glacier or in the ground following an earthquake. (The *crevasse* was too broad for the climbers to cross safely.)

cubical/cubicle: A *cubical* is a geometric shape with six equal square sides. A *cubicle* is a small room or sleeping compartment. (The *cubicles* that most students live in here at the university are indeed *cubicals.*)

SENTENCE FILL-IN

1. Most college students take at least one (coarse / course) _____ in European history.

2. I heard this same (creak / creek / crick) _____ in these old stairs forty years ago when I was a child.

3. Alas, the (colonel / kernel)_____ was killed in his sleep by a faulty bedspring.

4. After being scolded, the puppy (coward / cowered) _____ under the kitchen table.

5. Town (councillors / counselors) _____ must now run for reelection every four years rather than every six years.

6. In Japan there are hotels that provide air-conditioned (cubicals / cubicles) _____ _____ only slightly larger than coffins for one to sleep in.

7. Please try not to (click / clique) _____ your heels as the vows are being repeated.

8. A wise son listens to the (council / counsel) _____ of his father—if his father is also wise.

9. Bicycling (couriers / curriers) _____ in Manhattan have been rendered obsolete by the development of fax machines.

10. In the spring this little (creak / creek / crick) _____ sometimes becomes the next thing to a small river.

11. Gideon (clenched / clinched) _____ a position on the team when the starting quarterback failed algebra.

12. Racing wheels (complement / compliment) _____ the design of a sports car quite nicely.

13. Into the broad (crevice / crevasse) _____ tumbled the humble village and all its occupants.

14. Almost all the family's new (close / clothes / cloths) _____ were lost in the move from California to Michigan.

15. Your apparent (complacence / complaisance) _____ contradicts the meager value of your accomplishments to this point.

16. If you (close / clothes / cloths) _____ all the outside doors, the room will become stuffy.

17. Nasty little weeds are growing up through the (crevices / crevasses)_____ in the driveway.

111

18. The students' (*coarse / course*) _____ behavior provoked the provost to say some things she later wished she had not said.

19. In parts of the world where horse racing is important, a good (*courier / currier*) _____ can still earn a decent living.

20. Both fighters stood with (*clenched / clinched*) _____ fists waiting for the bell to ring.

21. The coach wanted to (*complement / compliment*) _____ everyone who finished the race, not just the winners.

22. The president's fawning (*complacence / complaisance*) _____ toward every splinter group did not sit well with the party regulars.

23. There is no place for a (*coward / cowered*) _____ on an urban fire brigade.

24. A (*click / clique*) _____ of jocks came to the meeting armed with the usual menu of simpleminded ball-game metaphors.

25. The psychological (*councillors / counselors*) _____ at the university have too heavy a work load.

26. The painting consisted of progressively smaller (*cubicals / cubicles*) _____, each one within the next larger one.

27. This new brand of popcorn guarantees that every (*colonel / kernel*) _____ will pop.

28. From moving a houseful of furniture, Franklin had a painful (*creak / creek / crick*) _____ in his back for weeks.

29. The dorm (*council / counsel*) _____ voted to accept the dean's proposal, but only on the third try.

30. We used only the softest (*close / clothes / cloths*) _____ to buff the freshly waxed car.

Words That Sound Alike (7)

cue/queue: A *cue* is anything that serves as a signal to do something or a long, tapered rod used in billiards. To *cue* is to give a signal for action or to punch the *cue* ball toward another ball when playing billiards. A *queue* is a line of people, automobiles, or the like. To *queue* is to form such a line. (Each of the players, *cue* in hand, stood in the *queue* along the wall awaiting the *cue* for the billiards tournament to begin.)

currant/current: A *currant* is a seedless raisin or any of a variety of sour berries from hardy shrubs used in jellies and jams. (Most *currant* jam is a bit tart for my taste.) *Current* means "at the present time." It also refers to the continuously moving flow of a stream or any moving liquid or air mass. (The *current* of the river is *currently* more rapid than it usually is.)

dairy/diary: A *dairy* is a place where milk products are processed. A *diary* is a personal journal. (Several of the students had kept a *diary* during the year they worked in the *dairy* at the university's college of agriculture.)

dear/deer: That which is *dear* is fondly regarded, highly valued, or expensive. As a noun, *dear* means "a loved person." (Although cantaloupe are very *dear* this year, our *dear* cousin bought them for us all the same.) A *deer* is a swift, graceful, cud-chewing mammal with hoofs that is hunted for sport in the autumn. (Today, many *deer* hunters use a camera rather than a rifle.)

decent/descent: *Decent* means "honorable," "good," "fair," or "kind." (The evening news notwithstanding, most people are *decent*.) A *descent* is an act of coming down or going down. (The change in air pressure during the plane's *descent* caused my ears to pop.)

dependence/dependents: *Dependence* is the state or condition of relying on something for continued existence or upon others for aid or support. (Growing up includes ending our *dependence* on our parents.) *Dependents* are people who rely on others for support. (The king's *dependents* include the servants as well as the members of the royal family.)

depravation/deprivation: *Depravation* is a state (or an act) of extreme moral corruption. (Such wicked behavior suggests *depravation* beyond repair.) *Deprivation* is a condition or instance of having something taken away. (One cannot remain in a sensory *deprivation* tank for very long.)

descent/dissent: A *descent* is an act of coming down or going down, or a downward slope. (Once it started, Gorbachev's *descent* from power seemed immutable.) *Dissent* is disagreement, as with a larger body of opinion. To *dissent* is to differ with beliefs and opinions or to reject traditional doctrines, as of the church or a political party. (Chronic *dissent* among members of the congregation eventually destroyed the little church.)

desert/dessert: A *desert* is a hot, dry, sandy region or a reward or punishment earned and deserved. (The cruel captain got his just *deserts,* twenty years at a *desert* outpost.) To *desert* is to abandon one's post or responsibilities. (One should never *desert* one's friends.) A *dessert* is a sweet food that is eaten at the end of a meal. (Cherries jubilee is a very popular *dessert.*)

dew/do/due: *Dew* is moisture that condenses on grass and flowers. (On cool summer nights, we often have a heavy *dew.*) To *do* something is to perform a task. (You must *do* your home-work before watching television.) That which is *due* is owed, suitable, required, or expected. (The money is *due* you for your hard work. The train is *due* to arrive at noon.)

die/dye: To die means "to stop living." (Alas, it is possible to *die* of a broken heart.) To *dye* means "to change the color of." As a noun, *dye* indicates the coloring agent itself. (Marilyn intends to *dye* her hair green for the part in the play.)

discreet/discrete: *Discreet* means "careful," "tactful," or "prudent." (One must be *discreet* when dealing with such a touchy issue.) *Discrete* means "separate" or "distinct from." (We are discussing two entirely *discrete* issues here.)

dual/duel: *Dual* means "two," "double," or "having two parts." (This car has *dual* controls.) A *duel* is a fight. (The film ended with a bloody *duel* between the two gunslingers.)

earn/urn: To *earn* something is to receive it in return for one's efforts. (Many people *earn* their livelihood through hard work.) An *urn* is a vase, usually with a foot or pedestal. A coffee *urn* is a large metal container with a faucet. (In ancient Greece and Rome, *urns* were used to hold the ashes of the dead.)

SENTENCE FILL-IN

1. In our part of the county, the woods sound like a war in progress during (*dear / deer*)

   _____ season.

2. Each morning the children must (*dew / do / due*) _____ their chores before dressing for school.

3. Such (*discreet / discrete*) _____ handling of the indelicate situation was much appreciated by everyone involved.

4. The state of (*depravation / deprivation*) _____ of the people who did these horrible things goes far beyond ordinary immorality.

5. The (*die / dye*) _____ used to color the garment was a brilliant red.

6. Luckily for us, all the training vehicles had (*dual / duel*) _____ controls.

7. At fast-food restaurants Americans are being trained to stand in a (*cue / queue*)

   _____ to wait for food.

8. Where in this town can a person get a (*decent / descent*) _____ meal and a cup of hot coffee?

9. Alas, Uncle Neville has been permanently relegated to the (*earn / urn*) _____

   _____ located on the mantel in the living room.

10. What is the (*currant / current*) _____ situation at each of the construction sites?

11. Hector is leaving college and going to work so he can end his (*dependence / dependents*)

    _____ on his parents.

12. The president of the university will tolerate no (*descent / dissent*) _____ among the members of her cabinet.

13. While touring the (*desert / dessert*) _____, we were struck by the great difference between day and night temperatures.

14. Most people would call it (*indiscreet / indiscrete*) _____ to discuss intimate family matters with strangers.

15. Students in this composition class are asked to write in their (*dairy / diary*) _____

    _____ each evening.

16. A local (*dairy / diary*) _____ owned by one of the oldest families in the area still serves freshly made ice cream.

115

17. Even on film, the scientists' (*decent / descent*) _____ into the volcano was frightening.

18. The (*dew / do / due*) _____ was so heavy on the house that we could not begin painting until noon.

19. Fought with water pistols, the (*dual / duel*) _____ wasn't as dangerous as it might have been.

20. Oxygen (*depravation / deprivation*) _____ for any length of time can permanently damage the brain.

21. The old man didn't want to (*die / dye*) _____ without seeing the village of his birth one more time.

22. We patiently waited for our (*cue / queue*) _____ to enter, but it was never given.

23. The chaos committee, a loose group, specializes in (*descent / dissent*) _____ _____ of every possible variety.

24. My cynical aunt maintains that only fools (*earn / urn*) _____ their living by the sweat of their brow.

25. Most (*currants / currents*) _____ used in cooking are grown in the eastern Mediterranean region.

26. For (*desert / dessert*) _____, most of the children chose apple pie à la mode.

27. Although we like it well enough, the painting is a bit too (*dear / deer*) _____ _____ for our pocketbooks.

28. Please remember that your rent will be (*dew / do / due*) _____ on the fifteenth of each month.

29. The university is composed of more than a dozen (*discreet / discrete*) _____ _____ colleges, each with its own requirements for graduation.

30. Alas, I have too many (*dependence / dependents*) _____ ever to be able to save any money.

Words That Sound Alike (8)

eave/eve: An *eave* is the lower edge of a roof that projects out over the side of a building. (The snow had melted from the *eave* on the south end of the house.) *Eve* refers to the evening (or day) before a special day or the time just before something memorable happens. (On the *eve* of her wedding, Joyce decided that married life would be too confining.)

elicit/illicit: To *elicit* means "to draw forth" or "to evoke." (Angry words often *elicit* angry responses.) *Illicit* means "unlawful" or "improper." (*Illicit* trafficking in drugs can carry a stiff prison sentence.)

emigrate/immigrate: To *emigrate* is to leave one country with the intent of living elsewhere. ("My great-grandparents *emigrated* from Ireland during the potato famine of 1845," the old man said with no small pride in his voice.) To *immigrate* is to enter a country with the intent of taking up residence. (Millions of people still want to *immigrate* to the United States.) Similarly, an *emigrant* is one who leaves a country, and an *immigrant* is one who enters a country.

eminent/imminent: *Eminent* means "renowned," "distinguished," or "exalted." (An *eminent* scholar, Dr. Wellington delivered a knowledgeable lecture about gene cloning.) *Imminent* means "likely to happen very soon." (According to the weather service, a tornado was *imminent*.)

emit/omit: To *emit* is to send out or to give forth. (The sun *emits* both heat and light.) To *omit* is to leave out or to fail to do. (I sometimes *omit* the second *r* from the word *occurred*.)

ewe/yew: A *ewe* is a female sheep, goat, or small antelope. A *yew* is an evergreen bush, shrub, or tree of many varieties. (The shepherd found the lose *ewe* sleeping beneath an ancient *yew* bush.)

exercise/exorcise: *Exercise* means several things, including regular physical activity, the performance of one's duties or job, a problem to be studied or worked out. To *exercise* is to do any of these things. To *exorcise* is to drive a devil or evil spirit out or away by means of some ritual or prayers. (To *exorcise* a mean devil from a troubled soul is not a simple *exercise* of purgation.)

faint/feint: That which is *faint* is weak, feeble, without courage, timid, dizzy, or barely perceptible. To *faint* is to swoon or pass out. (There was no *faint* praise for the returning soldiers.) A *feint* is a false appearance or pretense, or a movement intended to deceive. (Alice made a *feint* of being interested in what the instructor was saying, but she wasn't really listening.) To *feint* is to pretend to deliver a blow or launch an attack in order to trick an opponent or enemy. (The fighter *feinted* a left, then threw a crushing right.)

fair/fare: As an adjective, *fair* means "attractive," "unblemished," "blond," "clear and sunny," "honest," "impartial," "promising," "reasonable," "favorable," or "average." As a noun, *fair* means "a gathering for the sale of goods," "a festival or carnival," or "an exposition." (All in all, it was a *fair* day for the annual county *fair*.) A *fare* is money that a person pays for being transported or the passenger himself. *Fare* also refers to a range or type of food. (Although the food was usual railroad *fare*, the *fare* for the entire excursion was *fair* enough.)

fate/fete: *Fate* is the power that is supposed to determine events before they happen. (It was a pillow sale at Pier 1 that brought us together, not *fate*.) A *fete* is a festival or party, especially an elaborate one held outdoors. (A community *fete* was held to honor my parents on the fiftieth anniversary of their wedding.)

faze/phase: To *faze* is to disconcert, to disrupt, or to bother. (Once my uncle fastens onto a task, nothing will *faze* him.) A *phase* is one part of a sequence, a stage. To *phase in* means "to introduce," and to *phase out* means "to eliminate." (Everyone in the family seems to be going through a *phase* of some sort, even my grandfather.)

feat/feet: A *feat* is an accomplishment, often both daring and unusual. (Swimming the English Channel is still not a *feat* to be sneezed at.) Our *feet* are what we walk on. (My brother's *feet* are more than a foot long.)

feudal/futile: *Feudal* means "related to the economic, political, and social system of medieval Europe." (*Feudal* philosophies are anything but democratic.) That which is *futile* serves no useful purpose. (It may be *futile* to try to teach those who do not want to learn.)

SENTENCE FILL-IN

1. In the 1950s, Jewish (*emigrants / immigrants*) _____ were flocking out of the Soviet Union.

2. It is usually necessary for one to (*exercise / exorcise*) _____ if one wishes to lose weight.

3. The Thompsons have planted a hedge of (*ewe / yew*) _____ bushes around the yard at their new house.

4. The (*fate / fete*) _____ of those charged with the crime is now in the hands of the jury.

5. It is (*feudal / futile*) _____ to try to perform nuclear fusion in a bottle.

6. On the (*eave / eve*) _____ of the election, most of the polls still had the race even.

7. Volcanoes often (*emit / omit*) _____ lava and ash during an eruption.

8. At the moment Justin is going through a particularly contrary (*faze / phase*) _____

   _____ of his adolescence sometimes called the "tweenager."

9. Such (*elicit / illicit*) _____ activities are hardly appropriate for an elected official.

10. The tea had a (*faint / feint*) _____ taste of either garlic or iodine; it was delightful.

11. Please repeat what you have said, and take care not to (*emit / omit*)_____ a single word.

12. For a time during the Kennedy-Khrushchev stare-down in 1962, many military experts

    thought that a nuclear war was (*eminent / imminent*) _____.

13. Just finishing a marathon is a (*feat / feet*) _____ of significant enough accomplishment to include on one's résumé.

14. After losing his business in the Los Angeles riots of 1992, Ted's uncle decided to (*emigrate / immigrate*) _____ to Australia.

15. Plane (*fare / fair*) _____ from New York to London has almost doubled in recent years.

16. When a (*ewe / yew*) _____ falls in love, it is with a ram, not a bull.

17. Although the weather was (*fair / fare*) _____ until late afternoon, rain fell for most of the evening.

119

18. The purpose of the (*fate / fete*) _____ was to honor the 1940 graduates of the old high school.

19. During the early years of the twentieth century, thousands of (*emigrants / immigrants*)

_____ came to the United States from every part of Europe.

20. The night was so cold that I thought my (*feet / feat*) _____ would freeze.

21. A steady diet of greasy fast-food (*fair / fare*) _____ is not good for one's well-being.

22. On the (*eave / eve*) _____ of the big battle, few of the soldiers could sleep.

23. It takes more than a punch in the nose and a kick in the pants to (*faze / phase*)

_____ my single-minded cousin.

24. Northrup, a self-styled macho-man, (*fainted / feinted*) _____ at the first sight of blood.

25. This grim little anecdote will hardly (*elicit / illicit*) _____ smiles from an audience less cynical than yourself.

26. The time has come for you to (*exercise / exorcise*) _____ all such evil thoughts from your mind.

27. For such an (*eminent / imminent*) _____ individual, the Nobel Prize winner exhibited a most humble demeanor.

28. Nimble on his feet, the halfback (*fainted / feinted*) _____ left, then ran to his right.

29. The (*feudal / futile*) _____ knight was equally devoted to his liege and to his lady.

30. Take particular care not to (*emit / omit*) _____ the final ingredient; otherwise, you may find yourself sleeping with the angels—or worse.

Words That Sound Alike (9)

fiancé/fiancée: A *fiancé* is a man engaged to be married, and a *fiancée* is a woman engaged to be married. (Ted's *fiancée* is Elinor, and Elinor's *fiancé* is Ted.)

filter/philter: A *filter* is a device for separating solid particles or impurities from a liquid or gas. To *filter* is to remove or separate particles, impurities, light rays, or electrical frequencies. (An automobile's oil *filter* should be changed from time to time.) A *philter* is a magic potion that arouses romantic feelings, usually for a specific person. (No *philter* strong enough could be found to awaken that woman's hard heart.)

flair/flare: A *flair* is a natural ability to do something. (Les has a *flair* for remembering the lyrics of obscure show tunes.) A *flare* is a bright, unsteady flame. To *flare* is to burst into flame, anger, or violence. (A sudden gust of wind made the torches *flare* brightly.)

flea/flee: A *flea* is a small, wingless, bloodsucking insect that lives on dogs. (That mutt is a walking *flea* colony.) To *flee* is to run away or escape. (Although the thieves tried to *flee*, the police caught them.)

floe/flow: A *floe* is a field or sheet of floating sea ice. (The ice *floe* is very heavy this season.) To *flow* is to move in a stream, like water. (All of these streams eventually *flow* into the same bay.)

florescence/fluorescence: *Florescence* is a condition or period of full bloom or a time of great success and achievement. (Not until mid-June does this forest achieve full *florescence*.) *Fluorescence* is the emission of or property of emitting electromagnetic radiation as visible light. (The *fluorescence* of these new lamps is painfully intense.)

flour/flower: *Flour* is a finely ground meal of wheat or other cereal grain. (The *flour* for this bread was ground at our local mill.) A *flower* is the blossom of a plant that produces seeds. (These *flowers* were planted by the wind and rain.)

for/fore/four: *For* is most often used as a preposition (with many meanings) and connects its own object to the rest of the sentence. (These men and women had fought *for* their country. The time *for* talk had come and gone.) *Fore* means "at the front," "forward," "toward the beginning or front," or "situated (conspicuously) in front of something else." (The sailors searched the ship *fore* and aft *for* the lost child. Sooner or later quality usually comes to the *fore*. Only the *fore* wall of the house survived the blast.) *Four* is the number between three and five. (All *four* wheels left the ground at the same time.)

foreword/forward: A *foreword* is an introduction, as at the beginning of a book. (The *foreword* was not written by the author.) *Forward* means "at the front," "advanced," "moving toward a point," "bold," or "pushy." (Let's move *forward* with our plans, but let's not be too *forward* in presenting them to others.)

121

forth/fourth: *Forth* is an adverb meaning "forward" or "out into view." *Fourth* is an ordinal number. (The *fourth* knight to go *forth* in search of the grail came home with gruel in his confusion.)

foul/fowl: As an adjective, *foul* means "offensive," "dirty," "stinking," or "indecent." (A *foul* odor came from the swamp.) As a noun, *foul* means "a misconduct." (Both referees called the *foul.*) A *fowl* is a bird. (The hunters enjoyed fresh *fowl* for dinner.)

friar/fryer: A *friar* is a brother in any one of several mendicant orders. (Medieval *friars* spent much more time out in the world than did cloistered monks.) A *fryer* is a tender young chicken suitable for frying. (This bird is too old and tough to be a *fryer.*)

gait/gate: One's *gait* is one's manner of moving along on foot. (Jason can jog along at a steady *gait* for hours at a time.) A *gate* is an opening or movable entrance to an enclosed area. (The horses kicked open the *gate* and ran away.)

gamble/gambol: To *gamble* is to play games of chance for money. (Don't *gamble* your fortune away.) To *gambol* is to run, jump, and frolic about. (The wee elfin creatures *gamboled* about in the bright moonlight.)

SENTENCE FILL-IN

1. Uncle Alonzo ran a successful (*flea / flee*) _____ circus for many years.

2. On the (*forth / fourth*) _____ attempt, the rocket finally lifted off the launchpad and fled into the heavens.

3. For hours after the storm, a strange (*florescence / fluorescence*) _____ remained in the night sky.

4. Alas, there wasn't enough (*flour / flower*) _____ in the tin to bake fresh bread.

5. Once again, the weather (*forcast / forecast / fourcast*) _____ was incorrect.

6. The (*foreword / forward*) _____ to the text was a bit too patronizing to students.

7. We bought an antique railroad (*flair / flare*) _____ at the auction sale to benefit the Special Olympics.

8. Why would you (*gamble / gambol*) _____ away your tuition money and risk having to leave school?

9. Percival insists that his (*fiancé / fiancée*) _____ lived on a Greek island for several years.

10. It wasn't obvious to me that the Bulls' forward deliberately committed the (*foul / fowl*)

    _____.

11. The question of whether or not there was a conspiracy will soon come to the (*for / fore /*

    four) _____.

12. Once again, Justin forgot to get a new (*filter / philter*) _____ for the neighbor's pool.

13. This is the time to move (*foreword / forward*) _____, not to wait to see the direction of the wind.

14. Alas, the words (*floe / flow*) _____ from Isabel's mouth almost totally unobstructed by thought.

15. Did you know that a canter is one of the (*gaits / gates*) _____ of a horse?

16. Rhoda has a (*flair / flare*) _____ for thinking of the most outlandish puns; she calls herself a pundette.

17. Have you ever seen a (*flour / flower*) _____ with as many petals as this one?

18. Because of the assassination, John Kennedy's New Frontier never came to full (*florescence* / *fluorescence*) _____.

19. The examination included (*for* / *fore* / *four*) _____ wrong answers (*for* / *fore* / *four*) _____ every correct answer.

20. In the spring the lambs often (*gamble* / *gambol*) _____ about the meadow.

21. My aunt's (*fiancé* / *fiancée*) _____ is from a family of eleven children.

22. From the oven came the aroma of baking (*foul* / *fowl*) _____, one of my favorite culinary delights.

23. Although not unpleasant to be around, Toko is a (*foreword* / *forward*) _____ and assertive individual.

24. It would take a (*filter* / *philter*) _____ of great power to warm and win your cold heart.

25. Cadwallader's parrot has such a (*foul* / *fowl*) _____ mouth that it frequently embarrasses everyone.

26. The rear (*gait* / *gate*) _____ to the stables is almost always locked at night.

27. Alban has spent most of his life trying to (*flea* / *flee*) _____ from responsibility.

28. Never try to bake a (*friar* / *fryer*) _____; the Order of Gourmet will hunt you down like a dog.

29. We passed the night on an ice (*floe* / *flow*) _____ in the middle of the bay, waiting to be rescued.

30. Each day Professor Trivialous goes (*forth* / *fourth*) _____ to protect young minds from dangling modifiers.

Words That Sound Alike (10)

gel/jell: A *gel* is a semisolid substance formed by the coagulation of colloidal material. (This new shaving *gel* has a pleasant fragrance.) To *jell* is to become jelly, to thicken, to take shape, or to achieve some distinctness. (What began as a hunch soon *jelled* into a comprehensive plan of action.)

gild/gilled/guild: To *gild* is to overlay with a thin covering of gold or gold coloring, or to make (something) appear bright and attractive. (The plan is to *gild* the capitol dome. Praise from a catalog of unsavory characters will not *gild* your reputation.) *Gilled* means "having gills." (Fish are *gilled* creatures.) A *guild* is an association of people engaged in the same occupation or craft. (My grandfather viewed the steelworkers *guild* as his extended family.)

gilt/guilt: *Gilt* is the thin layer of gold or similar material used to *gild* something. In fact, it may refer to any (false) glitter. (The old *gilt* is coming off the capitol dome.) As an adjective *gilt* means "gilded." (The *gilt* sword was used only for show.) *Guilt* is the feeling of having done something wrong or blameworthy.) (Poor Margaret is hounded by *guilt* at having forgotten to attend her sister's graduation.)

gored/gourd: Anything *gored* has been pierced with a sharp instrument, such as an animal horn or tusk. (The man fatally *gored* during the running of the bulls at the feast of San Fermin in Pamplona died convinced of his manhood.) A *gourd* is a hard-shelled inedible fruit of the squash family that is often used as an ornament or a kitchen vessel or utensil. (A collection of colorful *gourds* decorated the kitchen walls.)

gorilla/guerrilla: A *gorilla* is the largest and most powerful of the great apes. (Many people are surprised to learn that *gorillas* are usually vegetarians.) A *guerrilla* is a member of an independent band of fighters who harass the enemy with frequent raids during wartime. (*Guerrilla* warfare can be a nasty business.)

grisly/gristly/grizzly: *Grisly* means "terrifying" or "horrible." (The bikers witnessed a *grisly* accident.) Meat is *gristly* when it has too much gristle, or cartilage, in it. A *grizzly* is a large, ferocious, brownish-yellow bear found in western North America. (Where does a *grizzly* sleep? Anywhere it wants to.) *Grizzly* also means "grayish." (It was another *grizzly* morning.)

groan/grown: A *groan* is a deep, harsh sound indicating distress, pain, or disappointment. To *groan* is to make such a sound. (Some people *groan* and complain about everything.) *Grown* is the past participle form of *grow* and means "fully developed," "mature," or "cultivated." (Potatoes *grown* in the Thumb region of Michigan are the sweetest on earth.)

hail/hale: *Hail* is little round pieces of ice that sometimes fall during a thunderstorm, and by extension a forceful shower of anything. (A *hail* of bullets chased the saboteurs from the building.) To *hail* is to welcome, to salute, or to summon. (We *hailed* a taxi and went directly to the airport.) *Hale* means "sound of body," "healthy," or "vigorous." (These are *hale* and hearty lads.) To *hale* is to pull, drag, or haul forcibly. (The villain was *haled* into court, tried, and summarily executed.)

hair/hare: *Hair* grows on one's head. (Alas, my *hair* is thinning.) A *hare* is a swift, gnawing creature with long ears, soft fur, a cleft upper lip, and related to the rabbit. (Remember that the *hare* lost the race with the tortoise.)

hairy/harry: *Hairy* means "covered with hair." (A gorilla is a *hairy* ape.) To *harry* is to assault, ravage, pillage, plunder, torment, or harass. (The Moorish pirates *harried* the coastal towns in southern England. Why must you *harry* your neighbors?)

hall/haul: A *hall* is a long passageway, an assembly room, or a large building. (The banquet *hall* was aglow from the sconces of flickering candles around the walls.) To *haul* is to pull, drag, transport, or carry. (We *haul* this equipment in unmarked trucks.) As a noun, *haul* refers to the things hauled; an amount stolen, won, or earned; or the distance or route over which items are transported. (Huge trucks are used for the longer *hauls*.)

halve/have: To *halve* is to divide into two equal parts. (These new computers will allow us to *halve* the time required to assemble widgets.) To *have* means "to hold" or "to possess." (I *have* a Petosky stone that weighs almost twenty pounds.)

handmade/handmaid: *Handmade* objects are produced by hand rather than by machine. (Amanda inherited a *handmade* quilt stitched in the double wedding ring pattern.) A *handmaid* is a woman servant or attendant. (The queen's *handmaid* spoke seven languages.)

SENTENCE FILL-IN

1. Alas, the young knight was (*gored / gourd*) _____ by a misdirected thrust of his own sword.

2. These particular carriers are used only to (*hall / haul*) _____ coal and iron ore.

3. You can probably (*halve / have*) _____ your expenses by staying in youth hostels rather than regular hotels.

4. The speaker responded to the question from the audience with an impatient (*groan / grown*) _____.

5. This team hasn't yet played together long enough to (*gel / jell*) _____ into a cohesive unit.

6. Why do you insist on telling such (*grisly / gristly / grizzly*) _____ stories to small children?

7. As it turned out, the roaming bands of (*gorillas / guerrillas*) _____ were more than a match for the regular army.

8. (*Hail / Hale*) _____ six inches deep accumulated in the yard during the storm.

9. Among other things, the queen's (*handmade / handmaid*) _____ is responsible for the queen's wardrobe.

10. The infant was so (*hairy / harry*) _____ that it looked more like a miniature ape than a person.

11. The (*gild / gilled / guild*) _____ creatures of the deep are being killed by industrial waste dumped into the oceans.

12. Several students were unnecessarily (*hailed / haled*) _____ before the chief security officer and threatened with expulsion.

13. These wigs, understandably more expensive, are made of human (*hair / hare*) _____, not plastic fiber.

14. Don't you feel any (*gilt / guilt*) _____ for the people you have mistreated on the way to the top?

15. The roast was too (*grisly / gristly / grizzly*) _____ to be cut with an ordinary knife, much less to be eaten.

16. In late autumn, the days gradually become (*grisly / gristly / grizzly*) _____, damp, and cold.

17. What (*hairbrained / harebrained*) _____ scheme is the chaos committee working on now?

18. This dandruff shampoo comes only in a (*gel / jell*) _____ form, not powder or cream.

19. The delicate young man didn't look (*hail / hale*) _____ enough to swing an ax, much less wrestle an alligator.

20. (*Gorillas / Guerrillas*) _____ and chimpanzees are not able to breed with each other.

21. Strawberries (*groan / grown*) _____ in Michigan are better than those imported from Florida.

22. Do we (*have / halve*) _____ enough time to overhaul the engine before the race?

23. Jessica has been a member of the Writer's (*Gild / Gilled / Guild*) _____ for most of her professional life.

24. Why are these teenage gangs allowed to (*harry / hairy*) _____ the older members of the community?

25. (*Handmade / Handmaid*) _____ bullets can be as dangerous for the shooter as they are for the target.

26. This (*gored / gourd*) _____ is a decoration, not a weapon.

27. A central (*hall / haul*) _____ ran from one end of the house to the other.

28. Do the artisans you employ know how to (*gild / gilled / guild*) _____ wood carvings?

29. According to the encyclopedia, a (*hair / hare*) _____ is generally larger than a rabbit.

30. Alas, the (*gilt / guilt*) _____ is coming off the wood carvings.

Words That Sound Alike (11)

hangar/hanger: A *hangar* is an enclosure for housing and repairing aircraft. (Someone broke into the *hangar* and stole a few old propellers.) A *hanger* is a person who hangs things or something on which, or from which, items are hung. (These coat *hangers* are made of cheap plastic.)

hardy/hearty: *Hardy* means "strong," "courageous," "brazen," or "able to withstand or survive severe weather." (Oxen are *hardy* draft animals. The *hardy* climbers pushed on to the top of the mountain. Plants as *hardy* as these pay no attention to a blizzard now and then.) *Hearty* means "warm and friendly," "wholehearted," "plentiful and nourishing," "vigorously healthy," or "unequivocal." (We appreciated the *hearty* welcome from our old friends. A few *hearty* meals will fix what ails you. On this issue, the faculty have the *hearty* support of the student body.)

heal/heel: To *heal* is to restore to health, to cure, or to remedy. (How does one *heal* a broken heart?) The *heel* is the back part of the foot beneath the ankle and behind the instep. It is also anything that suggests the human heel, as the end of a loaf of bread or the end of the day. (How can one break a *heel* kicking an old football?) To *heel* is to supply, especially with money. Thus, a *well-heeled* person is (more than) adequately supplied with money.

hear/here: To *hear* is to perceive (sound) with the ears. (Although I can *hear* you, I don't understand what you are saying.) *Here* means "in or at this place." (It is wonderful each year to watch the ducks stop *here* for a little rest on their way north to Canada.)

heard/herd: *Heard* is the past tense and past participle form of *hear*. (That was another shot *heard* around the world.) A *herd* is a group of large animals. (A *herd* of buffalo now lives in the county park.)

heroin/heroine: *Heroin* is an addictive narcotic made from morphine. (The life of a *heroin* addict is anything but glamorous.) A *heroine* is the principal woman character in a dramatic work. (Lady Macbeth is one of Shakespeare's complex *heroines*.)

hew/hue: To *hew* is to chop or cut, as with an ax, sword, or knife. (With his gilt sword, the noble knight *hewed* down the evil infidel.) A *hue* is a color, shade, complexion, or tint. (My true love's hair is the *hue* of a flaxen sun setting over an emerald sea.) A *hue* is also a general outcry or clamor against something, now used as *hue and cry*. (The increasing *hue and cry* from the angry audience finally drove the speaker from the hall.)

highbred/hybrid: Persons *highbred* are of superior stock, demonstrate their good breeding, and are always cultivated and refined. (Although the lady is *highbred*, she enjoys an occasional repast of a hamburger and french fries.) A *hybrid* is a crossbreed—the offspring produced by crossing animals or plants of differing species. (A mule is a *hybrid*, the offspring of a donkey and a horse.)

hoard/horde: A *hoard* is a secret supply (stash) of something needed or desired. To *hoard* is to accumulate and hide such items. (A *hoard* of weapons was found in a cave beside the sea.) A *horde* is a loosely organized group—a multitude, crowd, or swarm. (A raging *horde* of adolescents rushed onto the university common demanding to be taught foreign languages.)

hoarse/horse: *Hoarse* means "harsh," "rough," "rasping," or "grating"—as in voice. (Bernie usually had a *hoarse* voice after a night on the town.) A *horse* is a four-legged mammal featured in hundreds of Hollywood westerns. (Uzi might be an appropriate name for the *horse* of a high-tech cowboy.)

holey/holy/wholly: *Holey* means "full of holes." (The blanket was *holey* from hungry moths.) *Holy* means "without sin," "religious," or "spiritual." (This shrine is a *holy* place.) *Wholly* is an adverb meaning "entirely." (These assumptions are *wholly* inaccurate.)

hostel/hostile: A *hostel* is an inn or a public house for entertaining. (We stayed in *hostels* throughout our European trip.) *Hostile* means "antagonistic," "unfriendly," or "adverse." (The host seemed to be a *hostile* person.)

hour/our: An *hour* is a measurement of time. *Our* means "belonging or related to us." (The *hour* between nine and ten is *our* quiet time together.)

SENTENCE FILL-IN

1. Because of the pollution, no one wants to live (*hear / here*) _____ in Chemical City anymore.

2. Alas, the (*hour / our*) _____ has finally come for us to part and go (*hour / our*) _____ separate ways.

3. Everyone agreed that we had (*heard / herd*) _____ enough elevator music for one day.

4. The candidate's promises were (*holey / holy / wholly*) _____ at odds with the party's official platform.

5. It was no small task for the pioneers to (*hew / hue*) _____ the logs to build their cabins.

6. Of course, these grapes are a (*highbred / hybrid*) _____; that's why they have no seeds.

7. At the county airport the old (*hangar / hanger*) _____ is being replaced by a new one.

8. Students, especially serious ones, are beginning to complain about the (*hostel / hostile*) _____ environment that now exists on the campus.

9. A national (*hew and cry / hue and cry*) _____ arose as a result of the videotaped beating of Rodney King by four Los Angeles policemen.

10. Vivian had never before seen a whole family of such (*hardy / hearty*) _____ eaters.

11. During the night we (*heard / herd*) _____ a large (*heard / herd*) _____ of elephants crossing the plain.

12. Wilhelmina insists that she has a (*hoard / horde*) _____ of ideas just waiting to be developed into new products.

13. Both pairs of these shoes are too tight around the (*heal / heel*) _____ and toe.

14. The children returned home from their hike with (*holey / holy / wholly*) _____ socks and sore feet.

15. Like most of the author's works, this is a play with neither a hero nor a (*heroin / heroine*) _____.

16. One (*hardy / hearty*) _____ cheer after another echoed around the stadium.

17. During the tour, we attended several (*highbred / hybrid*) _____ entertainments, such as an opera, a ballet, and a chess tournament.

18. A (*hoard / horde*) _____ of locusts descended upon the field and devoured every (*colonel / kernel*) _____ of corn.

19. This ointment will cause the wound to (*heal / heel*) _____ in less than half the time.

20. We lost (*hour / our*) _____ antique (*hourglass / ourglass*) _____ _____ in the move from Cleveland to Buffalo.

21. What is the glamor in being a slave to (*heroin / heroine*) _____ or some other addictive substance?

22. These plastic shirt (*hangars / hangers*) _____ that you brought home from Chernobyl seem to glow in the dark.

23. The (*hoarse / horse*) _____ croaking of bullfrogs could be heard throughout the marsh.

24. Occasionally we stayed at a youth (*hostel / hostile*) _____, but more often at farmhouses.

25. It takes a (*hardy / hearty*) _____ race of people to survive, much less prosper, in such a harsh climate.

26. Both Sandra's dress and Chauncey's new suit were of an unusual greenish (*hew / hue*) _____.

27. We (*hear / here*) _____ from several sources that the president of the university intends to downsize the institution.

28. Estelle maintains that she learned to ride a (*hoarse / horse*) _____ before she learned to walk.

29. Each evening a little before dusk, a (*heard / herd*) _____ of deer gathers on the runway of the local airport.

30. Connor Pass on the Dingle Peninsula in Western Ireland is such a beautiful spot that it seems almost (*holey / holy / wholly*) _____.

Words That Sound Alike (12)

hurdle/hurtle: A *hurdle* is a wood frame structure to be jumped over or any sort of obstacle to be overcome. To *hurdle* is to jump over a barrier. (The horse was unable to *hurdle* the fence.) To *hurtle* is to move with great speed, to go with violent intensity, or to throw, shoot, or hurl something. (The speeding train *hurtled* through the dark night.)

idle/idol/idyll: *Idle* means "not occupied" or "unemployed." (Because of the strike, the workers remain *idle*.) An *idol* is an image of a divine being or a person or thing greatly loved and admired. (The prehistoric ruins were filled with *idols* to ancient gods long forgotten.) An *idyll* is a brief literary work descriptive of peaceful rural scenes and pastoral life. (The author is a regional writer who specializes in colorful *idylls* of the Appalachian Mountain region.)

incite/insight: To *incite* is to stir up or urge on. (Such inflammatory rhetoric may *incite* a riot.) *Insight* is clear understanding or discernment. (We study history to gain some *insight* into human behavior over time.)

indiscreet/indiscrete: *Indiscreet* means "careless," "tactless," or "lacking prudence." (It was *indiscreet* of the candidate to tell such a private joke at a public gathering.) *Indiscrete* means "not separated into distinct parts." (The organization of this company was so *indiscrete* that it was not possible to tell where money was being lost and where it was being made.)

knave/nave: A tricky, dishonest, and scheming person is a *knave*. (Even in his sleep, this *knave* couldn't stop thinking about deceitful schemes.) The *nave* is the main part of the interior of a large church or cathedral. The word also refers to the hub of a wheel. (Both sides of the *nave* were lined with enchanting stained glass windows depicting incidents of local history.)

knead/kneed/need: To *knead* is to mix into a blended whole by working over and over with the hands. (We were required to *knead* the dough for what seemed like hours.) Anything *kneed* has been hit or touched by someone's knee. (The ball carrier was *kneed* in the ribs by one of the defensive linemen.) A *need* is a necessity or requirement. To *need* is to want, require, desire, or lack. (I don't *need* as much sleep as I once did.)

knight/night: In the Middle Ages, a *knight* was a military servant of a king or some other feudal superior. He might also be devoted to the service of a lady. *Night* is the period of time between dusk and dawn. (The young *knight* rode his horse through the *night* to bring the news to his lord.)

ladder/latter: A *ladder* is a structure with two sidepieces and several rungs used to climb above the floor or ground. (This *ladder* is too light to be used when the wind is blowing.) *Latter* is the opposite of *former*. (Of the two paintings, the *latter* was better than the former.)

133

Latter can also be used to mean "more recent" or "nearer the end." (The disaster occurred during the *latter* stages of the contest.)

leach/leech: To *leach* means "to run water through slowly," "to dissolve," or "to filter." (The ashes from burned wood can be *leached* to extract lye.) A *leech* is a bloodsucking worm once used by physicians to bleed people. (The partially dry swamp was filled with *leeches.*)

leak/leek: To *leak* is to escape through a small opening. As a noun, a *leak* is the opening itself. (A small *leak* can sink a great ship.) A *leek* is a garden vegetable similar to an onion. (Potatoes and *leeks* make a very tasty soup.)

lean/lien: *Lean* means "with little fat," "meager," "deficient," or "brief." To *lean* is to bend (tilt) from a vertical position. (This fellow's ideas were as *lean* as his appearance.) A *lien* is a claim on property as security for the payment of a debt. (The bank holds a *lien* on this new Mercedes.)

lessen/lesson: To *lessen* means "to make less." (How can you *lessen* your workload?) A *lesson* is an exercise in learning. (Alice takes a tennis *lesson* twice a week.)

levee/levy: A *levee* is an embankment built to keep a river from overflowing. It is also a landing place for boats. (Part of the *levee* was in danger of washing away.) To *levy* is to impose or collect a tax or fine. (If you want to be reelected, don't *levy* any new taxes.)

SENTENCE FILL-IN

1. The (*indiscreet / indiscrete*) _____ structure of the organization made it impossible to determine who was in charge of what.

2. In *Man of La Mancha,* Don Quixote is called the (*knight / night*) _____ of the doleful countenance.

3. The police found the (*knave / nave*) _____ sleeping in the (*knave / nave*) _____ of Winchester Cathedral.

4. For a practicing psychologist, Dr. Blinders seems to have little (*incite / insight*)_____ into human motivation.

5. Luckily, there was only one (*lean / lien*) _____ of any consequence against the property.

6. Burgess was (*knead / kneed / need*) _____ in the head twice during the third quarter.

7. It is the general consensus among critics that the artist's (*ladder / latter*) _____ works are more symbolic than were the former.

8. Racial prejudice, like many other prejudices, can be a difficult (*hurdle / hurtle*)_____ to get over.

9. All these old boats (*leak / leek*) _____ to some extent.

10. Alas, we have allowed ourselves the luxury of electing a (*knave / nave*) _____ to the highest office in the land.

11. Rainwater, especially in sandy areas, (*leaches / leeches*) _____ through the soil quite quickly.

12. President John Kennedy has become almost a national (*idle / idol / idyll*) _____ in retrospect.

13. Everyone always agrees that Congress should take steps to (*lessen / lesson*) _____ the trade deficit.

14. For a time the (*levee / levy*) _____ was in danger of being washed away by the high water.

15. Oswald always seems to (*knead / kneed / need*) _____ more money than he can earn.

16. The (*lessen / lesson*) _____ most students learned from the assignment was not the one the instructor had intended to teach.

17. The fire department didn't have a (*ladder / latter*) _____ tall enough to reach the tenth floor.

18. The annual renewal of the rivalry is all that is needed to (*incite / insight*) _____ _____ both teams to play their best.

19. Student assistants have the (*knightly / nightly*) _____ tasks of mopping the floors and cleaning the toilets.

20. All the pews had been removed from the (*knave / nave*) _____ of the church for the upcoming rock concert.

21. Lack of rain produced a (*lean / lien*) _____ year for most of the farms in the valley.

22. How (*indiscreet / indiscrete*) _____ it was of you not to keep the confidence that you had promised to keep.

23. It wasn't until his (*ladder / latter*) _____ years that Andrea's father became a pleasant person to be around.

24. Damaged satellites are often left to (*hurdle / hurtle*) _____ through space, headed in no particular direction.

25. A few (*leaks / leeks*) _____ would have greatly improved that stew.

26. It is Cadwallader's vast fortune that allows him to live such an (*idle / idol / idyll*) _____ and unproductive life.

27. If you are hungry enough, (*leaches / leeches*) _____ will become quite edible.

28. A trained masseuse can (*knead / kneed / need*) _____ tight muscles as if they were willing dough in her hands.

29. The township intends to (*levy / levee*) _____ a tax on all homeowners to pay for the new storm sewer.

30. What the author has done is compose a political (*idle / idol / idyll*) _____ _____ describing a perfect, or mythical, democracy run by simple peasants.

Words That Sound Alike (13)

liable/libel: *Liable* means "legally bound or obligated." (The company claims that it isn't *liable* for injuries suffered by employees on the job.) *Libel* is any written or printed statement that is likely to expose another to public ridicule. (Alas, the truth is not always an adequate defense against *libel*.)

lightening/lightning: *Lightening* means "making something less heavy, harsh, or burdensome." (By *lightening* their load, the men were able to make it across the desert safely.) *Lightning* is a flash of electricity during a storm. (Alex just hasn't been the same person after having been struck by *lightning*.)

load/lode: Among other things, *load* means "a mass or weight, as one that is being carried." To *load* is to fill with something. (The truck carried a *load* of beach sand.) A *lode* is a vein of metal ore. (After twenty years of digging, the old sourdough finally struck the mother *lode*.)

loan/lone: A *loan* is money lent to someone. (You have ten years to repay your government *loan*.) *Lone* means "solitary" or "the only one." (Shannon was the *lone* survivor of the feud.)

loot/lute: *Loot* is stolen goods. To *loot* is to steal, plunder, or despoil. A *lute* is a stringed musical instrument with a pear-shaped body and a bent neck. (Andy spent his share of the *loot* to purchase a four-hundred-year-old *lute* made in Italy.)

made/maid: *Made* is the past tense and past participle form of *make* and is used to mean such things as "produced," "manufactured," "contrived," "invented," or "prepared." A *maid* is a young unmarried woman or a woman employed to do domestic work. (In the cook's absence, the new *maid made* dinner for the family.)

magnate/magnet: A *magnate* is a person of rank, power, influence, or distinction. (Ted Turner is today a television *magnate*.) A *magnet* is a stone or piece of metal that has the property of attracting iron or steel. By extension, anything that attracts is also called a *magnet*. (Mackinac Island, which is located in the Straits of Mackinac between Michigan's upper and lower peninsulas, is a tourist *magnet* that annually draws people from all over the world.)

mail/male: *Mail* is material shipped and delivered by the postal service. (Often we receive no *mail* on Monday.) That which is *male* belongs to or is characteristic of the sex that can fertilize eggs and father offspring. (The *male* of this particular species is smaller than the female.)

main/mane: That which is *main* is most important or principal. Open sea is also called the *main*. (The *main* reason for going to college, according to Stanley, is to avoid having to take a job.) A *mane* is the long hair that grows from the top or sides of the neck of some animals. (The child held tightly to the horse's *mane* as the creature galloped away.)

maize/maze: *Maize* is yellow corn, more often called Indian corn. *Maize* also refers to the color of ripe corn. A *maze* is an intricate and confusing network of winding pathways. (Walking through the field of wandering rows of tall *maize* was like being lost in a *maze* created by the seasons.)

mall/maul: A *mall* is a completely enclosed and air-conditioned shopping center. To *maul* is to injure by handling roughly or clumsily. (After an evening of serious shopping at the local *mall,* I feel as if I have been *mauled* and mistreated.)

manner/manor: One's *manner* is one's normal or usual mode of behavior. (Elizabeth has a very disarming *manner* when meeting new people.) A *manor* is a mansion or a large estate. (The Biltmore estate, built near Asheville, North Carolina, by George W. Vanderbilt at the close of the nineteenth century, is a *manor* in the grand tradition.)

mantel/mantle: A *mantel* is a shelf above a fireplace. A *mantle* is a cloak or cape. (While leaning against the *mantel,* the slightly tipsy duke set his *mantle* on fire.)

marry/merry: To *marry* is to unite in wedlock. Those who are *merry* are generally cheerful, joyous, and agreeable. (It was a *merry* day among the villagers when the young prince announced that he intended to *marry* the daughter of a commoner.)

marshal/martial: A *marshal* is a military commander or a federal police officer. (It was the *marshal's* job to maintain law and order throughout the territory.) To *marshal* is to arrange, order, or array. (You should carefully *marshal* your thoughts before writing the examination.) *Martial* means "suitable for war" or "eager to fight." (Proficiency at *martial* arts has become almost a cult in some parts of the country.)

SENTENCE FILL-IN

1. It may take Bertram the rest of his life to repay this (*loan / lone*) _____.

2. The mountains in the area are laced with a (*maize / maze*) _____ of caves and natural tunnels.

3. You don't have to (*mall / maul*) _____ the poor guy just because he scored a touchdown.

4. Didn't you know that Frieda has been taking lessons on the (*loot / lute*) _____ _____ for several years now?

5. In England, the (*mail / male*) _____ is still delivered twice each day.

6. It takes a number of years for a male lion to grow a full (*main / mane*) _____ _____.

7. As always, the bronze Buddha sat stoically on the (*mantel / mantle*) _____ _____ in the den, paying no attention to anyone.

8. No matter what it claimed, the airline was indeed (*liable / libel*) _____ for everyone's lost or damaged luggage.

9. Today karate is one of the most popular (*marshal / martial*) _____ arts, even more popular than jousting.

10. Most of these products are now (*made / maid*) _____ in either Japan or Korea.

11. This kid grew up in a (*manner / manor*) _____ house, not a normal family dwelling.

12. A bolt of (*lightening / lightning*) _____ hit this flagpole twice within the span of one week.

13. The days of the filthy rich railroad (*magnate / magnet*) _____ are long gone, and almost forgotten.

14. Contrary to romantic belief, most people (*marry / merry*) _____ within their own social class.

15. When the (*load / lode*) _____ of lumber suddenly shifted, the truck overturned.

16. As far as the police know, no one has discovered where the bandits hid their (*loot / lute*) _____.

17. Did the instructor say that aggression is an exclusively (*male/mail*) _____ _____ characteristic?

18. Our upstairs (*made/maid*) _____ has been with the family for twenty years.

19. The watercolor of the sunflowers was greatly improved by the (*maize/maze*) _____ _____ mat and carved frame.

20. A (*mantel/mantle*) _____ of handwoven cashmere was worn by the young prince.

21. The (*liable/libel*) _____ suit ended with the plaintiff receiving a not-too-shabby judgment of $10 million.

22. The engineers were unable to locate the (*main/mane*) _____ source of power for the unit.

23. A small (*magnate/magnet*) _____ holds each of the metal soldiers in place.

24. Although we were not a wealthy family, we usually had a (*marry/merry*) _____ _____ time at Christmas.

25. An increased use of plastics is today substantially (*lightening/lightning*) _____ _____ automobile bodies.

26. In the short story "The Bride Comes to Yellow Sky," the town (*marshal/martial*) _____ commits a major social sin; he breaks the rule and gets married.

27. We settled our differences in the usual (*manner/manor*) _____ ; we waited around for a few days until we had forgotten what the beef was.

28. Only a week or so after beginning to work, the miners struck a rich (*load/lode*) _____ of copper.

29. Each morning Clarence goes to the local shopping (*mall/maul*) _____ to jog five or six miles.

30. A (*loan/lone*) _____ house is all that remains of the old neighborhood where we grew up.

Words That Sound Alike (14)

material/materiel: *Material* means "matter," "substance," "the stuff of which anything is made." (There wasn't enough *material* to complete the garment.) Materiel is the equipment, apparatus, and supplies used by a large organization, especially an army. (The retreating troops left behind large quantities of *materiel*.)

mean/mien: A *mean* person is selfish, petty, bad-tempered, and without dignity. One's *mien* is one's appearance, bearing, conduct, and manner. (Although a *mean* spirited lout, this villain sometimes has the *mien* of a saint.) *Mean* also means "medium" or "average." (The *mean* score on the examination was almost eighty percent.)

meat/meet/mete: *Meat* is animal tissue used for food. To *meet* others is to come face to face with them or to encounter them. To *mete* is to allot, distribute, or apportion. (Each night the villagers would *meet* secretly to *mete* out what fresh *meat* they had to those who needed it most.)

medal/meddle/metal/mettle: A *medal* is an inscribed flat piece of metal, usually given as an award. (The soldiers won several *medals* during the war.) To *meddle* means "to interfere in the affairs of others." (Don't *meddle* in things that don't concern you.) A *metal* is any of a class of chemical elements, such as iron or aluminum. (Many things that used to be made of *metal* are now made of plastic.) *Mettle* is one's character, spirit, or courage. (Climbing Mount Everest requires a person of no small *mettle*.)

mewl/mule: To *mewl* is to whine or whimper like a baby. (Stop *mewling* and do your work.) A *mule* is the hybrid offspring of a horse and a donkey. It is also a very stubborn person. (*Mules* are actually smarter than horses.)

might/mite: *Might* is power, strength, or vigor. (You will have to train with all your *might* to compete at this level.) *Might* is also the past tense form of *may*. (You *might* win, and you *might* not.) A *mite* is a very small amount. It is also a tiny insect or a very small child. (*Might* I have just a *mite* of bread?)

miner/minor: A *miner* is someone who works in a mine. As an adjective, *minor* refers to something of lesser rank or importance. (Fortunately, the accident was a *minor* one.) As a noun, *minor* means "a person who has not reached full legal age." (The law prohibits the coal company from hiring *minors* as *miners*.)

moan/mown: A *moan* is a low (vocal) sound suggesting mournfulness, sorrow, pain, complaint, disappointment, and the like. To *moan* is to make such a sound. (We sat in the dark cabin and listened to the wind *moan* through the trees.) *Mown* means "cut close to the ground." (The freshly *mown* meadow smelled very sweet.)

moose/mousse: The *moose* is the largest member of the deer family. (Our silly cousin went cow hunting only to shoot a *moose* by mistake.) *Mousse* is any of a variety of chilled foods or desserts made with egg whites, gelatin, whipped cream, and the like and combined with fruit, flavorings, meat, or fish. (Chocolate *mousse* is a dessert that ten out of every eight people like.)

moot/mute: *Moot* means "arguable at best," "debatable," "doubtful," or "of little practical significance." (Yours is a *moot* question because it cannot really be answered.) *Mute* means "silent" or "not speaking." To *mute* is to soften, muffle, or subdue. (The accused stood *mute* before the court.)

morn/mourn: The *morn* is the beginning of the day. To *mourn* is to grieve. (Few *mourn* the passing of the night at the arrival of a cheerful *morn*.)

muscle/mussel: A *muscle* is an organ that expands or contracts to move a bone. The word is also used to mean "strength" or "power." To *muscle* is to force oneself in where one is not wanted. (It takes a lot of *muscle* to do this job.) A *mussel* is an often edible mollusk resembling a clam. (These mother-of-pearl buttons were made from *mussel* shells.)

mustard/mustered: *Mustard* is a pungent yellow condiment. (Most people agree that *mustard* improves the taste of a hot dog.) *Mustered* means "gathered" or "assembled," as for inspection. (The men *mustered* at dawn were transported directly to the airport.)

nap/nape: A *nap* is a brief, light sleep. The short, soft, woolly threads or hairs raised above the surface of a piece of material are also the *nap*. The *nape* is the back of the neck. (Awakening from a pleasant *nap*, I heard a bloodcurdling scream that raised a *nap* of goose flesh on the *nape* of my neck.)

SENTENCE FILL-IN

1. Astronauts seem to be individuals, men and women, of no small (*medal / meddle / metal / mettle*) _____.

2. For thousands of retired coal (*miners / minors*) _____, black lung disease is more than a (*miner / minor*) _____ health problem.

3. The cat carries her kittens about by the (*nap / nape*) _____ of the neck.

4. After the guards were (*mustard / mustered*) _____, the search began in earnest.

5. Although Dr. Potter has the impressive (*mean / mien*) _____ of a full professor, when he speaks he doesn't really say much.

6. It was such a (*morn / mourn*) _____ as few of us had ever before seen in the desert.

7. There is no place on campus where we can (*meat / meet / mete*) _____ in sufficient privacy.

8. The (*moose / mousse*) _____ we saw in the road had been terribly mistreated by black flies.

9. These fields are usually (*moan / mown*) _____ three or four times during the season.

10. Alas, our lives are too much occupied with matters of the (*material / materiel*)_____ _____ world.

11. Although some of these charms appear to be made of (*medal / meddle / metal / mettle*) _____, they are actually plastic.

12. Sigmund calls (*meat / meet / mete*) _____ grass processed by a cow.

13. The newborn baby was hardly a (*might / mite*) _____ of a creature.

14. It takes a lot of (*muscle / mussel*) _____ to crush rocks all day, day after day.

15. Must you people (*mewl / mule*) _____ about every little setback you experience?

16. The (*might / mite*) _____ of what was once the Soviet Union is now greatly dissipated.

17. Grace maintains that when someone close to us dies, we really (*morn / mourn*)_____

_____ for ourselves, not for the dead.

18. Does everyone win a (*medal / meddle / metal / mettle*) _____ in the Special Olympics?

19. Most of the candidates chose to remain (*moot / mute*) _____ on the issue of one's right to die with dignity.

20. Do you prefer (*mustard / mustered*) _____ or mayonnaise on your ham sandwich?

21. After the Gulf war, Iraq was strewn with destroyed military (*material / materiel*)

_____ of every type.

22. The patient is in terrible pain; why shouldn't he (*moan / mown*) _____ ?

23. Professor Ludwig spent half the term lecturing about the (*miner / minor*) _____

_____ Romantic poets.

24. Elizabeth usually takes a (*nap / nape*) _____ about two o'clock in the afternoon.

25. Strawberry (*moose / mousse*) _____ was the best dessert on the menu.

26. It takes a (*mean / mien*) _____ spirited person to say the things you have said.

27. You make a (*moot / mute*) _____ point at best; the problem has no simple solution, no quick fix.

28. The military tribunal continued to (*meat / meet / mete*) _____ out its brand of justice with impunity.

29. At the buffet, I sampled many unusual items, the most unusual being (*muscle / mussel*)

_____ mousse.

30. Senator Bleak thinks that private citizens should not (*medal / meddle / metal / mettle*)

_____ in the affairs of the nation's foreign policy.

Words That Sound Alike (15)

naval/navel: *Naval* means "related to the navy and ships." (The *naval* officer retired after almost thirty years in the service.) The *navel* is the belly button. (After the stomach operation, the patient had no *navel*.)

nay/nee/neigh: *Nay* means "no" or "not only that, but also." (The troops are ready, *nay* eager, to engage the enemy.) *Nee* means "born" or "originally or formally known as." (Mrs. Ellen Ruffner, *nee* White, was elected to chair the planning committee. Cape Canaveral, *nee* Kennedy, *nee* Canaveral, was the setting of the demonstrations.) A *neigh* is the sound a horse makes. (This horse says *neigh* no matter what his opinion is.)

none/nun: *None* means "not one" or "not any." (I will hear *none* of your lies.) A *nun* is a woman belonging to a religious order who lives under the vows of poverty, chastity, and obedience. (Throughout elementary school, all of Angelo's teachers were *nuns*.)

oar/or/ore: An *oar* is a long pole with a broad, thin blade used to row a boat. (It is difficult to row a boat without putting both *oars* into the water.) *Or* is a coordinating conjunction used to indicate an alternative or choice. (Is he a rich man, beggar man, *or* thief?) An *ore* is an unrefined mineral mined from the earth. (Millions of tons of iron *ore* were taken from these mountains.)

ordinance/ordnance: An *ordinance* is a municipal statute or regulation. (The winter parking *ordinance* is in effect from the first part of November.) *Ordnance* is military supplies of all kinds, but especially weapons, vehicles, ammunition, and so on. (As a child, Arthur lived near an *ordnance* plant in South Charleston, West Virginia.)

outright/outwrite: *Outright* means "altogether," "entirely," or "without reservation." (They never received an *outright* refusal.) To *outwrite* is to write better or faster than someone else. (Several of the students in the creative writing class could *outwrite* the instructor.)

overate/overrate: If you *overate,* you ate too much. (Almost everyone at the banquet *overate.*) To *overrate* is to estimate or value too highly. (Don't *overrate* your ability to persuade others to do what you want them to do.)

overdo/overdue: To *overdo* is to do too much. (In the spring, the neighbors always *overdo* their yardwork and suffer the consequences with aches and pains.) Anything *overdue* is late or past due. (The plane is *overdue* by several hours.)

pain/pane: *Pain* is physical or mental discomfort, agony, or anxiety. (*Pain* may be one of nature's ways of reminding us that we are alive.) A *pane* is a single sheet of glass in a division of a window or door. (There was a small round hole in the upper left *pane* of glass.)

pair/pare/pear: A *pair* is two of something. To *pare* means "to cut," "to trim," or "to peel." A *pear* is a fruit high in soluble fiber. (I have a *pair* of *pears* that I would like to *pare*.)

parish/perish: A *parish* is an administrative district that has its own church and pastor or priest. (This is a poor *parish* composed mostly of unskilled laborers.) To *perish* is to die or to be destroyed. (Several expensive horses *perished* in the fire.)

parity/parody: *Parity* is a close equivalence in value, rank, power, and the like. (Wage *parity* is one of the goals of feminism.) A *parody* is a literary, musical, or artistic work that mimics other similar works for the purpose of ridicule. (A fine line sometimes separates serious imitation and *parody*.)

parlay/parley: To *parlay* is to bet repeatedly and successfully, to transform something of little value into something of great value, or to exploit (an ability) to one's advantage. To *parley* is to speak or have a conference with, especially with an enemy. (Your old college roommate has *parlayed* a natural ability to *parley* with almost anyone into a career as a diplomat.)

passed/past: *Passed* is the past tense and past participle form of the verb *pass*. (The winning driver *passed* four other cars on the last lap of the race.) *Past,* as a noun, means "a time gone by." (It isn't a good idea to live entirely in the *past*.) As an adjective, *past* means "gone by," "ended," "over," or "of a former time." (Our *past* experiences are always with us.) As a preposition, past means "beyond" or "farther than." (Your arguments have wandered *past* all reason.)

SENTENCE FILL-IN

1. This (*oar / or / ore*) _____ is barely of sufficient concentration to be mined profitably.

2. Georgiana's family has lived in this (*parish / perish*) _____ for five generations.

3. To a greater or lesser degree, most people live in the (*passed / past*)_____.

4. For a dozen years now, (*none / nun*) _____ of the company's profit has been reinvested in the enterprise.

5. Not a single (*pain / pane*) _____ of glass was broken during the storm.

6. Transporting (*ordinance / ordnance*) _____ to the front lines is always a difficult problem for an army.

7. Throughout the tour, I (*overate / overrate*) _____ at almost every meal.

8. Myrna has (*parlayed / parleyed*) _____ a very small singing voice into a very large career.

9. The (*naval / navel*) _____ is something of a universal birthmark.

10. Only one (*pair / pare / pear*) _____ of swans is now left at the lake.

11. Alas, my manuscript is already more than a month (*overdo / overdue*) _____ _____ to the publisher.

12. Not surprisingly, the provost maintains that there are too many (*nay / nee / neigh*) _____ sayers among the faculty.

13. Although tasty, a (*pair / pare / pear*) _____ from this tree is as crisp as an apple.

14. Generally speaking, Mexican laborers do not enjoy wage (*parity / parody*) _____ with American workers.

15. Jacqueline Kennedy, (*nay / nee / neigh*) _____ Bouvier, was as important to the Camelot mystique as was John Kennedy.

16. It takes more than one (*oar / or / ore*) _____ to row a scull in competition.

17. Why do you always (*overate / overrate*) _____ your contribution to everything you take part in?

18. The village has an (*ordinance / ordnance*) _____ prohibiting anyone under the age of thirty-five from uttering the expression "you know."

19. In a nuclear war, millions will (*parish / perish*) _____, not just thousands.

20. Not until we had (*passed / past*) _____ the same house three times did I realize we were lost.

21. Throughout history, Britain has been a great (*naval / navel*) _____ power.

22. It can be a dangerous business to (*parlay / parley*) _____ with the enemies of your friends.

23. Shall we dine at home (*oar / or / ore*) _____ go out for the evening?

24. Is it true that there is no pleasure without (*pain / pane*) _____ ?

25. Some horses (*nay / nee / neigh*) _____, while others whinny.

26. Take the trainer's advice and don't (*overdo / overdue*) _____ your exercise regimen.

27. When Professor Wattlehammer lectures, he always seems to be doing a (*parity / parody*)

    _____ of himself.

28. Believe it or not, a (*none / nun*) _____ taught the champ how to throw that left hook.

29. Widget Incorporated has no choice but to (*pair / pare / pear*) _____ its work force by thirty percent.

30. What the third witness did was tell the judge an (*outright / outwrite*) _____

    _____ lie.

Words That Sound Alike (16)

peace/piece: *Peace* means "tranquility," "calmness," or "an absence of hostility." A *piece* is a small part or portion. (Everyone had a *piece* of harmony cake during the *peace* demonstration at the United Nations.)

peak/peek/pique: A *peak* is the pointed top, as of a mountain. It is also the highest point. To *peak* is to reach the highest point. (Many tennis players seem to reach their *peak* at a very early age.) To *peek* is to glance at quickly or furtively. The glance itself is also a *peek*. (Although I did *peek* at the textbook, I didn't really study.) *Pique* is a fit of displeasure provoked by insult. To *pique* is to arouse resentment in someone by giving offense. (In a sudden *pique,* the instructor gathered up his materials and left the lecture hall.)

peal/peel: A *peal* is the loud ringing of a bell or chimes. It is also any loud and prolonged sound. To *peal* is to sound or ring. (We could hear the *peal* of thunder in the distance.) *Peel* is the rind or skin of fruit. To *peel* is to strip away bark, skin, rind, or any surface covering. (The lad was too weary even to *peel* a banana.)

pedal/peddle/petal: A *pedal* is a mechanical device operated with the feet. To *pedal* is to operate such a device. To *peddle* is to travel from place to place selling things. *Petals* are flowering leaves on plants. (As I traveled about the countryside trying to *peddle* magazines, flower *petals* kept getting stuck in the *pedals* of my bike.)

peer/pier: A *peer* is a person of the same rank and ability as another. (Becky and John, both sophomores at State U., are *peers.*) To *peer* is to look closely, as if to see more clearly, or to come out slowly or partway. (The morning sun *peered* through the fog at the still sleepy village.) A *pier* can be several things—a structure built out over water and supported by columns, a support between two bridge spans, any sort of vertical support structure, or a breakwater. (In the evenings we often went walking on the *pier* to feed the pigeons.)

penance/pennants: *Penance* is any act performed to demonstrate that one is sorry for some wrongdoing. (There is no adequate *penance* for the crimes you have committed.) *Pennants* are tapered or pointed flags used as an emblem or symbol of identification. (The *pennants* around the stadium flapped loudly in the strong wind.)

plain/plane: *Plain* means "simple," "evident," "unadorned," or "an expanse of level country." (The *plain* truth is that this rolling *plain* produces some of the best beef cattle on earth.) Any flat surface is a *plane*. To *plane* is to smooth wood with a tool called a *plane*. *Plane* is also short for *airplane*. (Alas, my troubles are lined up like *planes* over O'Hare.)

plastic/plastique: As an adjective, *plastic* means "easily molded or shaped," "adaptable," "pliable," or "hypocritically false or synthetic." (In the modern world, one needs to be more *plastic* and less rigid.) *Plastique* is a putty-like substance containing explosives that can be detonated by an electric signal. *Plastique* is also the technique of performing very slow dance movements, as in pantomime. (*Plastique* was used to blow up the ship.)

plodder/plotter: A *plodder* is a trudge, one who works slowly and unimaginatively. A *plotter* is a schemer. (This slug-footed *plodder* is too much of a drudge ever to be a successful *plotter* of anything.)

plum/plumb: A *plum* is an edible fruit. That which is *plumb* is straight up and down. To *plumb* is to make straight up and down or to get to the bottom of something, as a mystery. (We shall never *plumb* this case until we learn who left the half-eaten *plum* at the scene.)

pole/poll: A *pole* is a long slender piece of wood, metal, plastic, or the like. (Ted has lost his fishing *pole*.) A *poll* is a counting of persons or a canvassing of a selected or random group of people to gather information. (A *poll* was conducted to determine public opinion on the issue.)

pore/pour/poor: A *pore* is a tiny opening in the skin. To *pore* means "to read attentively" or "to think deeply." To *pour* means "to flow or cause to flow in a steady stream." *Poor* means "without money" or "lacking in some way." (Because of inflamed *pores* on her arm, Susan did a *poor* job of *pouring* the tea.)

SENTENCE FILL-IN

1. Madeleine broke a (pedal / peddle / petal) _____ or two off her corsage.

2. As a (penance / pennants) _____ for unrelenting arrogance, Steadman was required to compliment everyone he met for three weeks.

3. When we try to (peer / pier) _____ into the future, we sometimes see things we don't want to see.

4. I suppose we will never understand why Gabrielle retired at the (peak / peek / pique) _____ of her career.

5. Old Jake said that all he wanted was to be (plum / plumb) _____ with the world when he died.

6. The sun and wind (pealed / peeled) _____ the skin of the lost soldiers away like tissue paper.

7. Although they did their best to keep the debate on a high (plain / plane) _____ , the effort was not successful.

8. Because he desperately needed some (peace / piece) _____ and quiet, Ian went into the wilderness.

9. The union conducted a (pole / poll) _____ to determine whether or not the faculty favored switching from quarters to semesters.

10. I'll admit to being something of a (plodder / plotter) _____ when it comes to understanding calculus.

11. How many times can you (pedal / peddle / petal) _____ that old bike around the island?

12. The advantage of using (plastic / plastique) _____ is that a fuse will not be needed to set the bomb off.

13. One should never (pore / pour / poor) _____ a red wine immediately after uncorking the bottle.

14. The western (plains / planes) _____ of North America were once populated by millions of buffalo.

15. If you (peak / peek / pique) _____ before you're supposed to, the gift will not be a surprise.

16. After all these years, I can still hear those chimes (peal / peel) _____ in my dreams.

151

17. All of us agreed that the most sinister (*plodder* / *plotter*) _____ among the radicals was Cadwallader Tecumseh.

18. These children often (*pore* / *pour* / *poor*) _____ over their lessons for hours at a time.

19. Such a (*plastic* / *plastique*) _____ morality can be reshaped to accommodate almost any wrongheaded behavior.

20. During the winter months, the (*peer* / *pier*) _____ at the lake is impacted in ice.

21. Sarah sat eating a (*plum* / *plumb*) _____, while Tom (*pealed* / *peeled*) _____ a juicy peach.

22. What Ian got when he went into the wilderness was a (*peace* / *piece*) _____ of the park ranger's mind.

23. Insulted by what had been said to them, the couple left the party in an angry (*peak* / *peek* / *pique*) _____.

24. The (*penance* / *pennants*) _____ of both schools were carried into the stadium by cheering students.

25. Your meaning is (*plain* / *plane*) _____ enough; you want complete control of the family business.

26. If what you (*pedal* / *peddle* / *petal*) _____ is mean gossip, what will be your profit?

27. A squirrel has been sitting at the top of that light (*pole* / *poll*) _____ for three days.

28. When it comes to telling tall tales, Barnabas has no (*peer* / *pier*) _____ among the students.

29. The day when one can buy a (*plastic* / *plastique*) _____ automobile may not be far away.

30. The (*pore* / *pour* / *poor*) _____ fellow in Company D forgot to (*pore* / *pour* / *poor*) _____ water on the campfire.

Words That Sound Alike (17)

populace/populous: The *populace* is the (total number of) common people. (The *populace* is opposed to the new trade agreement with Japan.) *Populous* means "full of people" or "thickly populated." (Parts of the country are not as *populous* as they were fifty or seventy-five years ago.)

pray/prey: To *pray* is to talk to God or a god. As a noun, *prey* is an intended victim, as an animal to be killed for food. (The villagers *prayed* that they would not fall *prey* to the savagery of the warlord.) As a verb, *prey* means "to hunt," "to kill," or "to plunder." (In the wild, lions *prey* on wildebeests among other things.)

premier/premiere: *Premier* means "first in rank, importance, or time." (Shakespeare is the *premier* dramatist of any age.) A *premiere* is the first public performance of anything. (The *premiere* of the film was sparsely attended.)

presence/presents: *Presence* is the condition of being at hand or in view. *Presents* are gifts. (The best of my birthday *presents* was your *presence* at the party.)

principal/principle: As an adjective, *principal* means "chief," "foremost," or "main." (The *principal* reason for the disagreement was mutual distrust.) As a noun, *principal* means "chief official" or "leader" as well as "a capital sum of money." (The *principal* of my high school was very strict. These loan payments include substantial interest on the *principal*.) *Principle* is a noun meaning "a fundamental rule or teaching." (The *principle* of freedom of expression seems at present to be under attack in certain quarters.)

profit/prophet: *Profit* is the money a company has left over after all expenses have been met. (Big *profits* make happy stockholders.) A *prophet* is a person who predicts the future. (At the time, *prophets* of doom and gloom seemed to be everywhere.)

quiet/quite: *Quiet,* either as an adjective or noun, refers to the absence of noise or agitation. *Quite* is an adverb meaning "entirely" or "completely." (The library wasn't *quite quiet* enough for the head librarian.)

rain/reign/rein: *Rain* is water that falls from clouds. A *reign* is a period of rule. To *reign* is to rule. (The populace took it as a bad omen that *rain* fell steadily for the first forty days of the new king's *reign*.) A *rein* is a narrow strip of leather used with a bit to control a horse. To *rein* is to slow down or stop. (Please *rein* your tongue.)

raise/raze: To *raise* means "to put in an upright position," "to increase," or "to elevate." To *raze* means "to tear down" or "to flatten." (The demolition company *raised* its estimate for *razing* the building.)

rapport/report: *Rapport* is a close, sympathetic, or harmonious relationship. (My psychology instructor enjoys a good *rapport* with most of his students.) Among other things, a *report* is an account—often written—of an event. To *report* is to make such a presentation. (If early *reports* are accurate, the vaccine is effective.)

real/reel: That which is *real* is actual, true, genuine, or authentic. (We needed a *real* doctor, not a quack.) A *reel* is a frame or spool on which something is wound. To *reel* is to wind or pull in. It also means "to stagger" or "to lurch," as from dizziness. (Long movies were once called *four-reelers*.)

reek/wreak: To *reek* is to give off a strong and disagreeable odor. (Following storms, the beach sometimes *reeks* of dead fish.) To *wreak* is to give expression to, to inflict, or to cause. (These villains will try to *wreak* their wrath upon us.)

residence/residents: One's *residence* is the place where one lives, the act of residing there, or the time during which one lives there. *Residents* are people who live at a particular *residence*. (Today there are only two *residents* staying at the old family *residence* in Big Rapids.)

rest/wrest: To be at *rest* is to be in a state of quiet, ease, or repose. To *rest* is to be still, quiet, or inactive. (An hour's *rest* in the afternoon refreshes one for the affairs of the evening.) To *wrest* is to turn or twist, or to take by force. (The officer *wrested* the pistol away from the thief.) *Rest* can also mean "what is left" or "those that are left." (We didn't know what to do for the *rest* of the day.)

SENTENCE FILL-IN

1. Alas, our (*principal / principle*) _____ benefactors have withdrawn their support from the institution.

2. No one was able to (*rest / wrest*) _____ the secret from Simone's lips.

3. Without (*profits / prophets*) _____, there would be little reason for people to go into business.

4. The play was not of sufficient importance even to have a (*premier / premiere*) _____ _____.

5. This fellow is the (*real / reel*) _____ thing, not some actor playing a part.

6. Is California the most (*populace / populous*) _____ state in the United States?

7. Bertram and Roxanne have never lived at the same (*residence / residents*) _____ _____ for more than two years.

8. There are times when a parent has to give (*rain / reign / rein*) _____ to a growing child.

9. If you're going to (*pray / prey*) _____ for a high grade on the examination, do it after you study.

10. The bank (*raised / razed*) _____ every old building on the block in order to build a larger parking facility.

11. The (*principal / principle*) _____ that government is the servant of the people doesn't operate in all parts of the world.

12. We have already had (*quiet / quite*) _____ enough disharmony in this organization.

13. Apparently there is little (*rapport / report*) _____ among the members of the family living next door.

14. We could not help noticing the (*reek / wreak*) _____ of garlic as we entered the mess hall.

15. As in the past, most of the children's (*presence / presents*) _____ came from their grandparents.

16. Following a strenuous workout, we usually enjoy a (*quiet / quite*) _____ evening on the (*beach / beech*) _____.

17. The treasurer will make her (*rapport / report*) _____ at the July meeting.

18. For the fourth year in a row, the Wildcats (*rain / reign / rein*) _____ as champions of the league.

19. A kid will never be able to (*real / reel*) _____ in a fish of that size.

20. The former president's (*presence / presents*) _____ at the convention helped to unify the party.

21. These people are determined to (*reek / wreak*) _____ their revenge on their enemies and the enemies of their ancestors.

22. How many (*residence / residents*) _____ are there in each building?

23. What (*profit / prophet*) _____ is there if a man gains the whole world and loses his own soul?

24. There is little question now that the (*populace / populous*) _____ of the nation is ready for a national health system.

25. The first (*principal / principle*) _____ of life, according to my biology instructor, is to survive and procreate.

26. When property taxes go up, our landlord always (*raises / razes*) _____ our rent.

27. In truth, we human creatures (*pray / prey*) _____ on all the planet's resources.

28. Without adequate (*rest / wrest*) _____ few people will be able to do their best work.

29. Would you say that Michael Jordan was once the (*premier / premiere*) _____ player in the National Basketball Association?

30. The (*profits / prophets*) _____ of doom and gloom are always either at the door or on television talk shows.

Words That Sound Alike (18)

retch/wretch: To *retch* is to heave, as when vomiting. A *wretch* is a miserable and unhappy person, or a scoundrel. (I thought I would *retch* when I saw how this *wretch* had treated his parents and family.)

review/revue: To *review* something is to take another look at it, to reexamine it. A *review* is a general survey or reexamination. (The university has decided to *review* its entire budget process.) A *revue* is a light theatrical entertainment including skits, dances, parody, songs, and the like. (The group of tourists attended a musical *revue* that featured parodies of popular show tunes.)

right/rite/write: *Right* means "correct" among other things. (You didn't leave the message in the *right* place.) A *rite* is a ceremonial act. (The *rite* of baptism is older than Christianity.) To *write* is to put words on a page. (If you really want to know who you are, *write* your own life story.)

ring/wring: A *ring* is the sound of a bell. *Rings* are also worn on the fingers. To *wring* is to compress with the hands by squeezing and twisting. (While *wringing* out her bathing suit, Susan dropped her class *ring* down the shower drain.)

road/rode/rowed: A *road* is a way or course made for traveling from one place to another. *Rode* is the past tense form of *ride,* and *rowed* is the past tense of *row,* meaning "to propel a boat by using oars." (As we *rode* our bikes down the *road* toward the lake, I was reminded of the time we had *rowed* all the way across to Waverly.)

role/roll: A *role* is a part (character) that an actor plays during a performance. (In a single day, most people assume quite a variety of *roles.*) A *roll* is a list of items or names. To *roll* is to move by turning over and over. (Although Ian had paid his tuition, his name was not on the class *roll.*)

roomer/rumor: A *roomer* is a lodger. A *rumor* is an unconfirmed report. (*Rumor* has it that your new *roomer* is from the moon.)

root/route/rout: The *root* is the part of a plant that grows underground. (Cut the bush but leave the *root* in the ground.) A *route* is a road, highway, pathway, or regular course. (My paper *route* included more than two hundred houses.) A *rout* is an overwhelming defeat or a noisy mob of people. To *rout* is to soundly defeat. (The game turned into a *rout;* we lost by thirty points.)

rot/wrought: *Rot* is nonsense. (Don't talk such *rot.*) To *rot* is to decay. (Bananas sometimes *rot* very quickly.) *Wrought* means "fashioned," "formed," or "created," as with great care. (What God hath *wrought* let no man put asunder.)

157

saccharin/saccharine: *Saccharin* is an artificial sweetner. (Did you know that *saccharin* is five hundred times sweeter than sugar?) *Saccharine* means "affectedly pleasant" or "overly sweet." (It will take more than a *saccharine* smile to sweeten the heart of such an old prune.)

sail/sale: A *sail* catches the wind and moves a boat. To *sail* is to travel upon the water in a boat. We go to a *sale* to buy things. (Ted bought a new *sail* for his boat at a neighborhood garage *sale*.)

salon/saloon/solon: A *salon* is a large room where guests are received or entertained as well as a place where works of art are exhibited. It may also be a fashionable retail shop. (There is a very chic dress *salon* at the top of Water Tower Place.) A *saloon* is a tavern. A *solon* is a "wise" legislator. The term is often used with some sarcasm. (Alas, the *solons* of the state legislature conduct too much of their business in the *saloon* across the street from the state house.)

sane/seine: *Sane* means "mentally sound" or "rational." (Although the proposal is *sane,* the man who made it is not.) A *seine* is a narrow fishing net with floats at the top and sinkers at the bottom. (It is more efficient to fish with a *seine* than a pole.)

scene/seen: A *scene* is the place or setting where something occurs, or a view of a location or incident. *Seen* is the past participle form of *see* and means "perceived by sight." (Has anyone actually *seen* what the crime *scene* looked like?)

scull/skull: A *scull* is a light, narrow racing boat rowed by one or more people. It is also an oar used with a side twist from one end of a boat. (The *scull* races will be held on Saturday.) A *skull* is the entire bony framework of the head. (The *skull* of modern Europeans is larger than it was only 20,000 years ago.)

seam/seem: A *seam* is a line where two edges join together. (The pants were torn at the *seam*.) To *seem* is to appear or look like. As one ages, time *seems* to pass more quickly.)

SENTENCE FILL-IN

1. No one in the class had ever before (*scene / seen*) _____ a demonstration of signing.

2. The main (*root / route / rout*) _____ of the tree extended down to a subterranean stream.

3. The (*scull / skull*) _____ taken from the burial mound had several peculiar characteristics.

4. Jonathan works in a stylish hair (*salon / saloon / solon*) _____ on Fifth Avenue.

5. Have you heard the (*roomer / rumor*) _____ that the university is going to close the College of Ephemeral Studies?

6. I would love to (*sail / sale*) _____ if only I didn't get seasick.

7. It sometimes helps to have the (*right / rite / write*) _____ friends in high places.

8. Didn't the plan (*seam / seem*) _____ like such a good idea at the beginning?

9. I would hardly call a one-touchdown victory a (*root / route / rout*) _____.

10. This is the (*retch / wretch*) _____ who squandered his family's fortune on fast cars and slow horses.

11. NutraSweet has replaced (*saccharin / saccharine*) _____ as the artificial sweetener of choice.

12. If you win the lottery this week, you can (*right / rite / write*) _____ your own ticket.

13. Each morning the campers heard the bells (*ringing / wringing*) _____ in the church tower.

14. Too much rain will (*rot / wrought*) _____ the fruit before it ripens.

15. The new crew (*road / rode / rowed*) _____ the course in near record time.

16. These peasants (*road / rode / rowed*) _____ all the way to Dingle in a donkey cart.

17. In spite of all the evidence to the contrary, the jury found the man (*sane / seine*) _____ enough to stand trial.

18. As it turned out, many of the (*salons / saloons / solons*) _____ of Congress were unable to balance their checkbooks.

19. A (*seam / seem*) _____ of coal was visible along the face of the mountain for several miles.

20. We have a (*roomer / rumor*) _____ staying at our house who can speak six languages.

21. The evening began with the ceremonial (*right / rite / write*) _____ of initiation into the club.

22. I cannot stand to listen to someone speak in such a (*saccharin / saccharine*) _____ _____ tone of voice.

23. In the Old West, a (*salon / saloon / solon*) _____ was a place where tough men drank whiskey and ate lead.

24. This is indeed a cleverly (*rot / wrought*) _____ piece of pottery.

25. After we floundered through the first (*scene / seen*) _____, everyone calmed down and the production went well.

26. The new (*road / rode / rowed*) _____ to the top of the mountain was paved only last year.

27. Each member of the team played a different (*role / roll*) _____ in winning the championship.

28. The troop decided to take the northern (*root / route / rout*) _____ rather than the southern.

29. Each morning Professor Precise laboriously calls the (*role / roll*) _____ before beginning his lecture.

30. Be sure to (*review / revue*) _____ your lecture notes before taking the examination.

Words That Sound Alike (19)

sear/seer: To *sear* is to burn or char, to become callous or unfeeling, or to dry up or wither. (Although the steaks were *seared* on the outside, they were not cooked through.) A *seer* is a prophet. (It doesn't take a *seer* to know that this business is failing.)

seated/seeded: *Seated* means "positioned in a seat." (The people *seated* in the front row could not see very well.) *Seeded* means "planted with seeds" or "scheduled according to a previous won-loss record." (The Trojans, one of the top *seeded* teams in the tournament, lost by a rout.)

serf/surf: A *serf* is a slave bound to a specific parcel of land, or in modern times any person who is underpaid and mistreated. (Alas, we may all become *serfs* of the multinational corporations.) The *surf* is the sea swell that breaks upon the shore. (The *surf* here is usually calm in the early evening.)

shear/sheer: To *shear* is to cut, clip, trim, or sever something. (It is no easy task to *shear* a sheep.) *Sheer* means "thin to the point of transparency," "absolute," or "pure." (What you are saying is *sheer* balderdash.)

shone/shown: *Shone* is a past and past participle form of *shine* and means "gleamed" or "glimmered." (A strange blue light *shone* across the meadow for hours.) *Shown* is a past participle form of *show* and means "exhibited," "directed," or "explained." (The paintings *shown* to the public represented only a small part of the collection.)

shudder/shutter: To *shudder* means "to tremble with horror or disgust." A *shutter* is a movable device used to cover an opening, such as a window or the aperture of a camera lens. (I *shudder* at the thought of cleaning the *shutters* to the fourth-floor windows.)

slay/sleigh: To *slay* is to kill, slaughter, or amuse. (In war, one must *slay* the enemy.) A *sleigh* is a vehicle on runners used for transportation over snow and ice. (Alas, even in the wilds of Canada, the *sleigh* has been replaced by the snowmobile.)

sleight/slight: *Sleight* is cunning or craft used in tricking or deceiving. *Slight* means "slender," "frail," or "fragile." To *slight* is to treat with disrespect. A *slight* is an insult. (By clever *sleight* of hand, this *slight* fellow bested all the muscle heads in the room.)

soar/sore/sower: To *soar* is to rise up and fly aloft. (In my dream, I wanted to *soar* above the city.) *Sore* means "painful" or "tender." A *sore* is an infected place. (The runner had a *sore* spot on his thigh.) A *sower* is a planter of seeds. (A *sower* of bad acts becomes a reaper of bad habits.)

sole/soul: *Sole* means "only." (Ruth was the *sole* survivor.) *Sole* also refers to the bottom or undersurface of the foot or a shoe and to an edible flatfish. The *soul* is the spiritual (perhaps immortal) part of a person. *Soul* also means "the essential part." (Brevity is the *soul* of wit.)

stair/stare: A *stair* is a flight of steps or a single step. (We climbed a winding *stair* to the top of the tower.) To *stare* is to gaze at fixedly. (It is not polite to *stare* at strangers.)

stake/steak: A *stake* is a pointed rod designed to be pounded into the ground. A *steak* is a slice of meat carved from the fleshy part of an animal carcass. (When several *stakes* pulled out of the ground, the tent blew across the *steaks* that were cooking on the grill.)

stationery/stationary: *Stationery* is writing paper and envelopes. To be *stationary* is to be immobile or unchanging. (Alas, my wages at the *stationery* store have been *stationary* for three years.)

stayed/staid: *Stayed* is the past tense of the verb *stay.* (We *stayed* on campus during spring vacation.) *Staid* means "sober," "sedate," "settled," or "unchanging." (From such a *staid* person, no one expected such an outrageous remark.)

steal/steel: To *steal* is to take something that belongs to someone else or to move in a stealthy manner. *Steel* is a commercial metal composed of iron alloyed with various other metals. To *steel* is to harden or toughen. (We shall have to *steal* most of the *steel* needed to make the swords.)

stile/style: A *stile* is a set of steps going up and down over a wall or fence. *Stile* is also used as an abbreviated form of *turnstile.* (One side of the *stile* was missing.) *Style* means "manner," "fashion," "method," "mode," or "way." (The house was built in a pseudo-Victorian *style.*)

SENTENCE FILL-IN

1. A (*stationery* / *stationary*) _____ target is usually easier to hit than a moving one.

2. On clear nights the stars (*shone* / *shown*) _____ like millions of tiny diamonds in the sky.

3. The family always brings the Christmas tree to the house in the old (*slay* / *sleigh*) _____ .

4. We made the mistake of consulting a financial (*sear* / *seer*) _____ to tell us what stocks to (*by* / *buy* / *bye*) _____ .

5. This isn't just a bargain; it's a (*steal* / *steel*) _____ .

6. You must put a token into the (*stile* / *style*) _____ in order to enter the building.

7. Unfortunately, the (*shudder* / *shutter*) _____ on the camera did not work properly.

8. Vivian was the (*sole* / *soul*) _____ member of the family to show any interest in restoring the old house.

9. I did not expect such a (*sleight* / *slight*) _____ from people who had once been my friends.

10. Alas, we (*stayed* / *staid*) _____ in Europe until it was too late to register for the fall semester.

11. Listening to the distant (*serf* / *surf*) _____ in the night is quite relaxing.

12. These gulls can catch a thermal and (*soar* / *sore* / *sower*) _____ above the coastline for hours.

13. We needed a large bundle of (*stakes* / *steaks*) _____ to rid the neighborhood of vampires.

14. The instructor (*seated* / *seeded*) _____ the members of the class in alphabetical order.

15. These curtains are too (*shear* / *sheer*) _____ to provide you any protection from the sun.

16. Paula said that a good cook will (*sear* / *seer*) _____ the roast before putting it into the oven to bake.

17. I had never before been (*shone* / *shown*) _____ how to organize a process paper on a technical topic.

18. Although a radical hippie in the 1960s, my cousin is now a (*stayed / staid*) _____

    _____ and conventional individual.

19. I have become an economic (*serf / surf*) _____ bound to my job so I can keep life and limb together.

20. Somehow, a (*stake / steak*) _____ seems more to me than just a piece of a dead animal.

21. The corporate CEO intends to (*shear / sheer*) _____ this company of all unnecessary employees.

22. The wax figure in the museum seemed to (*stair / stare*) _____ directly through me.

23. I (*shudder / shutter*) _____ to think what living conditions will be like when the earth has a human population of fifteen or twenty billion.

24. Mercedes always puts her heart and (*sole / soul*) _____ into her work.

25. Nothing is gained by developing a writing (*stile / style*) _____ that is difficult for others to read.

26. Rita gave her parents a box of personalized (*stationery / stationary*)_____ for their anniversary.

27. There is far less (*steal / steel*) _____ in automobiles today than there used to be.

28. Twenty years later, the loss of the championship game was still a (*soar / sore / sower*)

    _____ subject with the members of the team.

29. You just (*slay / sleigh*) _____ me with such outrageous tales.

30. Once again, we have (*seated / seeded*) _____ the north fields too early in the season.

Words That Sound Alike (20)

straight/strait: *Straight* means "without curves" or "direct." (The shortest distance between two points is a *straight* line.) A *strait* is a narrow waterway connecting two large bodies of water. (The Bering *Strait* connects the Arctic Ocean and the Bering Sea.)

summary/summery: A *summary* is a recap of something longer. *Summery* means "summerlike." (On such a *summery* day, no one wants to hear a *summary* of all the world's problems.)

sweet/suite: *Sweet* means "sugary," "nice," or "pleasing to the taste." (Many people dislike *sweet* wines.) A *suite* is a group of connected rooms or a set of matching furniture. It is also an instrumental composition including several movements. (Our *suite* at the resort included no less than five rooms and two baths.)

tail/tale: A *tail* is what a monkey swings by. To *tail* is to follow. A *tale* is a story, whether true or fiction. (In medieval times there were often *tales* told of strange people in alien lands who had long *tails* and two heads.)

taught/taut: *Taught* means "instructed." *Taut* means "tense," "tightly stretched," "rigidly drawn," or "tidy." (Even when we were children, Father *taught* us the importance of running a *taut* ship.)

tea/tee: *Tea* is a beverage, whereas a *tee* is what one hits a golf ball off. (Elizabeth stores her golf *tees* in the drawer of a beautiful Victorian *tea* cart.)

team/teem: A *team* is composed of a group of players. (The *team* finished the regular season in second place.) To *teem* means "to swarm" or "to abound." (At Christmas, the stores *teem* with shoppers.)

their/there/they're: *Their* is a possessive form of *they*. (*Their* reasons for leaving school were many.) *There* is either an adverb indicating place or an expletive. (I can assure you that *there* was no one sitting *there* when we came in.) *They're* is a contraction of *they are*. (*They're* always complaining about the food.)

threw/through: *Threw* is the past tense form of *throw*. (She *threw* me a kiss, and she *threw* it softly.) *Through* is a preposition or adverb with a variety of meanings. (The explorers crawled *through* the tunnel. The children were wet *through* and *through*. Are you *through* with school?) In the third example, *through* is used as an adjective. (We no longer live on a *through* street.)

throne/thrown: A *throne* is what royalty sit on. *Thrown* means "tossed through the air." (The king was *thrown* unceremoniously from the royal *throne* by an explosion in the nursery.)

time/thyme: *Time* is what a clock keeps, whereas *thyme* is an aromatic herb of the mint family used as a seasoning. (I had so little *time* to prepare the soup that I forgot to add the *thyme*. The soup was thus short of *thyme*.)

tide/tied: The *tide* is the regular rise and fall of the surface of the oceans occurring approximately every twelve hours. (At high *tide* the water runs upstream in some coastal rivers.) *Tied* means "fastened," "attached," or "made an equal score." (The game was *tied* four times.)

timber/timbre: *Timber* is trees or forests collectively or wood suitable for the building of dwellings. *Timber* also means "value" or "worth," as of a person's character. (The *timber* business has always been important to the economy of Michigan.) *Timbre* refers to the characteristic quality of a (musical) sound independent of pitch and volume. (The *timbre* of a cello is quite different from that of a viola.)

to/too/two: *To* is a preposition. (Webster has recently been *to* Sweden.) *Too* is an adverb. (Margaret has been to Sweden, *too*. We stayed *too* long at the party.) *Two* is the whole number between one and three. (We attended *two* concerts over the weekend.)

told/tolled: *Told* means "narrated" or "recounted," as a story. (Juan has *told* that tale a dozen times.) *Tolled* means "sounded," as a bell. (Those bells are *tolled* each evening at sunset.)

trader/traitor: A *trader* is a person who buys and sells things. (The colonial *traders* often swindled the Indians.) A *traitor* is a person who violates a trust or commits treason against his or her country. (Benedict Arnold was an infamous *traitor* to the American cause during the Revolutionary War.)

SENTENCE FILL-IN

1. As far as we know, (*their / there / they're*) _____ are no other humanoid creatures living in our solar system.

2. The children go swimming at high (*tide / tied*) _____ and dig for clams at low (*tide / tied*) _____.

3. These low-lying areas (*team / teem*) _____ with bad-tempered insects during the warm summer months.

4. I think you (*told / tolled*) _____ me a story that was not altogether true.

5. And later on you put together a (*tail / tale*) _____ about ghosts that would have made a counterfeit medium blush.

6. It takes an experienced ghost to walk (*threw / through*) _____ concrete walls as thick as these.

7. As is usual for weekends, the (*straight / strait*) _____ was lined with pleasure boats making their way westward to the big lake.

8. The perfume had such a (*sweet / suite*) _____ aroma that it almost made me sick.

9. Benedict thought there were (*to / too / two*) _____ many car chases in the film.

10. Your (*summary / summery*) _____ was about a hundred words longer than the original article.

11. The rope had to be kept (*taught / taut*) _____ and steady to hold the crate in place.

12. Patrick's next-door neighbor has been accused of being a (*trader / traitor*) _____ in stolen goods.

13. Because the hotel was filled, we stayed in the bridal (*sweet / suite*) _____.

14. This victory was a (*team / teem*) _____ effort, not the work of one person.

15. We walked all the way from the first village (*to / too / two*) _____ the last.

16. Meg and Franklin paid for (*their / there / they're*) _____ parents' trip to Bermuda.

17. Incredibly, the infant had been (*tide / tied*) _____ to the dresser for three days.

18. All the (*timber* / *timbre*) _____ for these houses came from nearby forests, not from the Northwest.

19. Having (*to* / *too* / *two*) _____ wives or husbands at the same time is at least one (*to* / *too* / *two*) _____ many.

20. The village bell (*told* / *tolled*) _____ on the hour throughout the search for the trapped miners.

21. Is it true that babies are sometimes born with a (*tail* / *tale*) _____ and fangs?

22. There isn't (*time* / *thyme*) _____ enough in this stew for anyone to taste.

23. When we were children, our mother always told us to come (*straight* / *strait*) _____ _____ home from school.

24. Vidkun Quisling was a (*trader* / *traitor*) _____ executed by the Norwegian people at the close of World War II.

25. When we moved to California, we (*threw* / *through*) _____ most of our furniture away rather than transport it across the country.

26. It was indeed a (*summary* / *summery*) _____ sun that (*shone* / *shown*) _____ on our picnic.

27. Believe it or not, Dominic (*taught* / *taut*) _____ himself to read Latin.

28. Our (*tea* / *tee*) _____ time was shortly after sunrise, and four hours later we all enjoyed a tall glass of iced (*tea* / *tee*) _____ in the clubhouse restaurant.

29. The president of the United States occupies a hot seat rather than a (*throne* / *thrown*) _____ .

30. The authors of these articles say that (*their* / *there* / *they're*) _____ in agreement about the value of studying foreign languages.

Words That Sound Alike (21)

troop/troupe: A *troop* is a group or body of soldiers, whereas a *troupe* is a group or company of stage performers. (Strangely enough, the acting *troupe* was composed mostly of a *troop* of Welsh fusiliers.) To *troop* is to go (walk along) as a group.

undo/undue: To *undo* is to untie or unfasten, to cancel or annul, to put an end to, or to upset emotionally. (Public knowledge of this one document will *undo* all your careful plans.) *Undue* means "improper," "inappropriate," "excessive," or "unreasonable." (*Undue* emphasis on short-term profits will eventually leave the company unable to compete in the international market.)

vain/vane/vein: *Vain* means "worthless," "fruitless," "futile," or "showing an excessively high regard for oneself." (Alas, this has become a *vain* enterprise.) A *vane* is a movable device that indicates, or is driven by, wind direction. (The wind was in such a confusion that the weather *vane* spun round and round.) A *vein* is a blood vessel that carries blood from some part of the body toward the heart. It is also a streak, a stripe, or a quality. (There is a certain *vein* of truth in what the fellow is saying.)

vary/very: To *vary* is to change, to modify, or to make different. (One should *vary* one's style of writing from time to time.) *Very* is an adverb meaning "extremely" or "exceedingly." (If I weren't a gentleman, I would say that you were *very* ugly at the party.)

veracious/voracious: *Veracious* means "truthful" or "accurate." (The witness was absolutely *veracious* in everything she said.) *Voracious* means "greedy," "ravenous," or "insatiable." (Your little brother has a *voracious* appetite for mystery novels.)

vial/vile: A *vial* is a small glass or bottle for holding medicines. (A *vial* with traces of poison was found near the body.) *Vile* means "wicked," "repulsive," "worthless," "mean," or "very bad." (The weather has been *vile* all spring.)

vice/vise: *Vice* is evil or wicked behavior. A *vice* is a specific self-indulgence. (My one *vice* is addiction to cheesecake.) A *vise* is a two-jawed tool for holding objects to be worked on. (It takes a large *vise* to hold an engine block.)

viral/virile: A *viral* condition is caused by a virus. (The child died of *viral* pneumonia.) *Virile* means "manly," "masculine," "vigorous," or "potent." (King Henry VIII was considered *virile* because he excelled at hunting and jousting and had six wives.)

waist/waste: Your *waist* is located between your ribs and your hips. (My *waist* is not the same size it was ten years ago.) *Waste* is anything useless or discarded. (Nuclear *waste* may be very dangerous to future generations.) To *waste* is to destroy, to squander, or to use up. (Don't *waste* your time preaching to the church choir.)

169

wait/weight: To *wait* is to remain inactive until the appropriate time or until something happens. (I hate to *wait* for weeks to see what my final grades are.) *Weight* is how heavy something is. (My *weight* fluctuates a bit between winter and summer.)

waive/wave: To *waive* is to give up or forgo something voluntarily. (The accused may *waive* his right to a jury trial.) A *wave* is an undulation, as of the surface of the sea. To *wave* is to move up and down or to flutter. (The sailors *waved* goodbye as the ship left port.)

warn/worn: To *warn* is to caution, to admonish, or to give notice. (The police will *warn* you only once for such a violation.) *Worn* means "attached to the body or clothing" or "damaged through wear or use." (These garments, *worn* only on state occasions, are the property of the government.)

way/weigh: A *way* is a path or route. It is also a manner, style, or technique. (We went the wrong *way* home. They were trying to find a better *way* to make spaghetti.) To *weigh* is to determine the heaviness of something or to try to balance (consider) ideas in the mind. (Perhaps you should *weigh* your words more carefully before speaking.)

weak/week: *Weak* means "feeble," "infirm," "diluted," or "unconvincing." (*Weak* tea is worse than no tea at all.) A *week* is seven days in sequence. (My father never takes more than one *week* of vacation at a time.)

weather/whether: The *weather* is the atmospheric conditions at a specific time in a particular place. To *weather* is to survive or endure, or to become discolored over time by exposure to the elements. (Western Michigan experiences a lot of cold *weather* in January and February.) *Whether* is a conjunction indicating a choice between alternatives. (We didn't know *whether* to go to the beach or stay home.)

SENTENCE FILL-IN

1. There was more than a narrow (*vain / vane / vein*) _____ of hostility in the comedian's routine.

2. A small (*vial / vile*) _____ of a powerful love potion was found at the site of their meeting.

3. (*Viral / Virile*) _____ infections seem to be more and more common among infant children today.

4. The problems presented during the last three weeks of the term were (*vary / very*) _____ difficult to work.

5. Wasting time isn't a minor (*vice / vise*) _____; it's an addiction that runs through many generations of some families.

6. We are expecting a (*waive / wave*) _____ of cold weather about the end of next week.

7. Alas, we suddenly found ourselves (*waist / waste*) _____-deep in garbage.

8. Algernon has been working on a new (*vain / vane / vein*) _____ for the antique windmill located on his property.

9. Scholars have never been able to find a (*veracious / voracious*) _____ account of what happened during the trial.

10. A pocket billiards table of this vintage can (*way / weigh*) _____ more than a ton.

11. Ashley maintains that her (*wait / weight*) _____ today is the same that it was twenty years ago.

12. Shall we (*warn / worn*) _____ the new students about the parking problems in the dorm lots?

13. It takes about a (*weak / week*) _____ for a three-man team to paint a house of this size.

14. Why should you want to (*undo / undue*) _____ all the good that the organization has done in recent years?

15. As usual, we couldn't make up our minds (*weather / whether*) _____ we wanted to go or stay.

16. Opinions will (*vary / very*) _____ greatly from student to student on this issue; they are not in agreement.

17. This book is (*warn / worn*) _____ from use, not from neglect.

171

18. Imogene fixed the boards in the (*vice* / *vise*) _____; then she drilled a row of holes (*threw* / *through*) _____ them.

19. The travel club is looking for a (*way* / *weigh*) _____ to finance a trip to Russia.

20. It is true that Electra is a beautiful woman, but she is also terribly (*vain* / *vane* / *vein*)

    _____ .

21. I would classify as (*viral* / *virile*) _____ any man who can pick up the rear end of a mid-sized automobile *and* play croquet with his children while their mother takes a watercolor course.

22. Many people, including other faculty members, think Professor Wiggens puts (*undo* / *undue*) _____ pressure on her students to perform well.

23. When you enter a hospital, never (*waive* / *wave*) _____ your right to sue the place for medical malpractice.

24. Thaddeus is a (*veracious* / *voracious*) _____ consumer of war novels and crossword puzzles.

25. Why do we always have to (*wait* / *weight*) _____ for hours in the doctor's office?

26. The company's new liquid (*waist* / *waste*) _____ disposal system has malfunctioned again.

27. Everyone from both schools was (*weak* / *week*) _____ and weary from lack of sleep.

28. A (*troop* / *troupe*) _____ of angry scouts marched into the store and demanded to see the manager.

29. The (*weather* / *whether*) _____ has been in a state of confusion for weeks now.

30. On hot days an absolutely (*vial* / *vile*) _____ odor comes from the landfill.

REVIEW EXERCISE
Words That Sound Alike

1. Hannibal was named student of the year by (*acclamation / acclimation*) _____ _____.

2. Is the original (*addition / edition*) _____ of this novel still in print?

3. For some people, (*adolescence / adolescents*) _____ may extend into their early thirties.

4. When the family first visited the (*aisle / isle*) _____, it had neither electricity nor running water.

5. A mirage may be thought of as a type of optical (*allusion / elusion / illusion*) _____ _____.

6. The couple exchanged vows at the (*altar / alter*) _____ before they cut the cake at their wedding reception.

7. What is an effective (*anecdote / antidote*) _____ for a broken heart?

8. Our local Bible museum houses a replica of Noah's (*arc / ark*) _____.

9. The (*ascent / assent*) _____ of the hot-air balloons was quite spectacular.

10. When Malcolm asked for (*assistance / assistants*) _____, he wanted help, not helpers.

11. How long does it take, on average, for a horse to eat a (*baal / bail / bale*) _____ _____ of hay?

12. The lost calf (*bald / balled / bawled*) _____ for its mother.

13. Has cigarette advertising been (*band / banned*) _____ from television in Europe?

14. After returning from his trip abroad, Boris told (*bazaar / bizarre*) _____ tales about talking stones and singing plants.

15. How much heartbreak can one person (*bear / bare*) _____ before losing control?

16. Margo insists on trying to (*beat / beet*) _____ the devil at his own game.

17. During the night we heard a strange noise coming from the wood (*been* / *bin*) _____

_____ in the scullery.

18. Grandmother always baked a variety of (*berry* / *bury*) _____ pies at Thanksgiving.

19. The neighborhood has a (*bloc* / *block*) _____ party three or four times each year.

20. Surprisingly, only a small sign marked the Scottish (*boarder* / *border*) _____

_____ .

21. Who would you say is (*bolder* / *boulder*) _____ in these situations, Baldwin or Balthazar?

22. At one end of the meadow were several rabbit (*boroughs* / *burros* / *burrows*) _____

_____ .

23. These dogs were (*bread* / *bred*) _____ to hunt, not to lounge about the house and beg for food.

24. We did not (*broach* / *brooch*) _____ such subjects as sex or religion in family discussions.

25. Alas, the workers stood (*buy* / *by* / *bye*) _____ and watched as the two young men fought.

26. What a (*callous* / *callus*) _____ and unfeeling remark Glenna made to the old woman.

27. President Clinton says that he does not subscribe to all the liberal (*cannons* / *canons*)

_____ of the Democratic party.

28. In the afternoon, members of the local aristocracy often (*canter* / *cantor*) _____

_____ about the park to show off their best horses.

29. These tents are made of plastic, not (*canvas* / *canvass*) _____ .

30. The old (*capital* / *capitol*) _____ building is located in the mountains across the river.

31. Where was the first wine (*cellar* / *seller*) _____ in the village dug?

32. Godfrey insists that he was never (*cent* / *scent* / *sent*) _____ on such a mission.

33. Occasionally, a wild horse would jump the fence of the (chorale / corral) _____

 _____ and become a member of our herd.

34. The old man would often go out to the (cite / sight / site) _____ where his house had once been and stay for hours.

35. An introductory adverb (clause / claws) _____ is usually followed by a comma.

36. The deal was (clenched / clinched) _____ when the buyer laid his money on the table.

37. Mother never allowed us to wear our play (close / clothes / cloths) _____ to school.

38. At the time, I had never met another person as (coarse / course) _____ as Francine's cousin.

39. All five players on the starting team (complement / compliment) _____ one another quite nicely in their play.

40. The school (councillor / counselor) _____ advised me to work for a few years before trying college.

41. Were it not for a small (creek / crick / creak) _____ in the cabin floor, the thief would probably have gotten away.

42. The (cubicals / cubicles) _____ in which we lived during the experiments had very poor air circulation.

43. Your (cue / queue) _____ to enter will be a flashing blue light.

44. The (currant / current) _____ price of these cars puts them out of reach for most of their potential buyers.

45. In my opinion, Tristan has always been a (decent / descent) _____ person.

46. Such apparent moral (depravation / deprivation) _____ suggests that you have no conscience at all.

47. The train wasn't (dew / do / due) _____ to leave the station until noon.

48. We usually walked in the (desert / dessert) _____ after our evening meal.

49. How (discrete / discreet) _____ it was of you not to mention your host's recent difficulties with the law.

50. The police have been charged with the (elicit / illicit) _____ sale of confiscated goods.

51. Today, fewer Europeans (*emigrate / immigrate*) _____ to the United States than in the past.

52. From her work with chimpanzees of Grombe Stream National Park in Tanzania, Jane Goodall became an (*eminent / imminent*) _____ ethologist without ever having graduated from college.

53. Regular physical (*exercise / exorcise*) _____ is good for one's general well-being.

54. Don't I hear a (*feint / faint*) _____ hint of anger in your tone of voice?

55. Plane (*fair / fare*) _____ to Europe has almost doubled in recent years.

56. In (*feudal / futile*) _____ times, ordinary peasants had almost no civil rights.

57. We could not locate a replacement oil (*filter / philter*) _____ for the old car anywhere in town.

58. Only one (*flair / flare*) _____ continued to burn throughout the ceremony.

59. The veterinarian could not locate a single (*flea / flee*) _____ on the dog.

60. Which plants are the first to (*flour / flower*) _____ in the spring?

61. I am (*for / fore / four*) _____ generations removed from my immigrant ancestors.

62. The (*foreword / forward*) _____ greatly misrepresented the intent of the book.

63. As we mature, we learn that many things in life are a (*gamble / gambol*) _____; little is for certain.

64. The American Medical Association (AMA) is basically a physicians (*gild / gilled / guild*) _____.

65. How can you claim to have been (*gored / gourd*) _____ by a horse?

66. On the whole, (*gorillas / guerrillas*) _____ are more interested in automatic weapons than in bananas.

67. It was indeed a (*grisly / gristly / grizzly*) _____ gray morning when we marched off to meet the enemy.

68. At last, we heard a faint (*groan / grown*) _____ coming from the bottom of the pit.

69. We did not (*have* / *halve*) _____ all the melons; some were shipped to market whole.

70. This craft shop sells only (*handmade* / *handmaid*) _____ items.

71. All the pants (hangars/hangers) _____ were in use.

72. Only the (*hardy* / *hearty*) _____ among the young can hope to survive in such a hostile climate.

73. The moose (*heard* / *herd*) _____ is greatly diminished from what it once was.

74. Who played the part of the (*heroin* / *heroine*) _____ in the play?

75. Alas, judging by our recent behavior, there seem to be few (*highbred* / *hybrid*)_____ _____ people left among us.

76. A leaping (*hoard* / *horde*) _____ of grasshoppers descended upon our garden.

77. What is the most (*holey* / *holy* / *wholly*) _____ shrine that you visited?

78. The horse (*hurdled* / *hurtled*) _____ both the fence and the tractor beyond the ditch.

79. Money is the primary (*idle* / *idol* / *idyll*) _____ worshiped by these devoted entrepreneurs.

80. Over the years, Professor Whited has gained great (*incite* / *insight*)_____ into the causes of writing problems experienced by students.

81. Does the planet (*knead* / *kneed* / *need*) _____ a greater capacity to produce food or fewer people to feed?

82. Christmas is celebrated during the (*ladder* / *latter*) _____ part of December.

83. In clay soil a gas (*leak* / *leek*) _____ can result in a dangerous explosion.

84. The most important (*lessen* / *lesson*) _____ I learned in Professor Strait's class was not to miss class.

85. How can Susan be (*liable* / *libel*) _____ for damages caused by something she did not do?

86. We had only thirty minutes to (*load* / *lode*) _____ the plane.

87. Should we (*lute* / *loot*) _____ the house or the barn first?

88. This yard light has become a (*magnate* / *magnet*) _____ for every night-flying insect in the neighborhood.

89. What was the (*main* / *mane*) _____ reason for Glenna changing schools?

90. This old house is a (*maize* / *maze*) _____ of halls and secret passageways.

91. The (*mall* / *maul*) _____ at the north end of town has more than a hundred shops.

92. Although Christmas is supposed to be a (*marry* / *merry*) _____ time of year, many people have to fight off depression.

93. The (*mean* / *mien*) _____ score on the midterm examination was just above seventy percent.

94. Wasn't it the judge's responsibility to (*meat* / *meet* / *mete*) _____ out appropriate punishments to each of the convicted persons?

95. It takes no small (*medal* / *meddle* / *metal* / *mettle*) _____ for a scientist to go into the jungle alone to live with and study wild apes.

96. Sometimes just a (*might* / *mite*) _____ of kindness is all a person needs to perk up.

97. Why must you always (*moan* / *mown*) _____ so about having to cut the grass?

98. The young man accused of breaking into the cotton candy machine stood (*moot* / *mute*)

_____ before the judge.

99. When Andrew injured his favorite (*muscle* / *mussel*) _____, the poor little mollusk had to be put to sleep.

100. A hot dog without (*mustard* / *mustered*) _____ is like a day without sunshine.

101. The ship's captain always stocked a supply of (*naval* / *navel*) _____ oranges for the crew to eat during a voyage.

102. Are any of the Great Lakes (*oar* / *or* / *ore*) _____ carriers nuclear powered?

103. The town council has passed an (*ordinance* / *ordnance*) _____ making it illegal for unmarried students to rent local apartments together.

104. Everything the witness said was an (*outright* / *outwrite*) _____ fabrication.

105. Our order from the printer must be a week (*overdo* / *overdue*) _____ by now.

106. Wasn't the plaintiff awarded $5 million for (*pain / pane*) _____ and suffering?

107. I would suggest that you (*pair / pare / pear*) _____ your story by about half.

108. So long as there is hunger in the land, there will be no (*peace / piece*) _____

_____.

109. Give the monkeys an orange (*peal / peel*) _____ for dessert and they will be happy.

110. Each of these flowers has at least one off-color (*pedal / peddle / petal*) _____

_____.

111. Our new (*penance / pennants*) _____ include a silhouette of the school mascot.

112. The (*plain / plane*) _____ truth of the matter is that no one knows what happened.

113. Have any of the (*plodders / plotters*) _____ yet been punished for their black schemes?

114. What is the most (*populace / populous*) _____ city in China?

115. There is no question that Miriam has a very powerful stage (*presence / presents*)

_____.

116. What would you say is the first (*principal / principle*) _____ of a good life?

117. For three quarters in a row, the company has not earned a (*profit / prophet*) _____

_____.

118. Baxter hasn't yet (*quiet / quite*) _____ mastered the technique of teacher baiting.

119. (*Rain / Reign / Rein*) _____ your horses, lad, or they will carry you over a cliff.

120. Our new (*residence / residents*) _____ is located on Elm Street, next to the bowling alley.

121. Alas, what a (*retch / wretch*) _____ Oswald became later on in life.

122. If you do not (*right / rite / write*) _____ to your family, I shall.

123. Julia (*road* / *rode* / *rowed*) _____ the bucking horse longer than anyone else did.

124. Everyone on the team played an important (*role* / *roll*) _____ in the victory.

125. Stop talking such (*rot* / *wrought*) _____ and say something that makes sense.

126. In 1992, a good number of the (*salons* / *saloons* / *solons*) _____ in Washington were voted out of office.

127. I had begun to wonder whether or not there was a (*sane* / *seine*) _____ person left in my employ.

128. When I was a child, life did not (*seam* / *seem*) _____ as complicated as it did later on.

129. Make sure that you (*sear* / *seer*) _____ this meat thoroughly before baking it.

130. What these people are proposing is (*shear* / *sheer*) _____ nonsense.

131. I (*shudder* / *shutter*) _____ to think about what the world will be like in 2050 with ten billion people.

132. Avery seems too (*sleight* / *slight*) _____ a fellow to be a football star.

133. Yvonne is the (*soar* / *sore* / *sower*) _____ of more office gossip than anyone else.

134. Someone has moved the (*stationery* / *stationary*) _____ store where I buy my typing paper.

135. When it comes to a confrontation, Owen seems to have nerves of (*steal* / *steel*)

_____ .

136. Although Steadman is a (*straight* / *strait*) _____ shooter, he is sometimes a bit quick on the trigger.

137. The last week in November was almost (*summary* / *summery*) _____ .

138. Only one (*sweet* / *suite*) _____ had not been leased by the time we arrived.

139. Has anyone asked the children whether (*their* / *there* / *they're*) _____ going to go or stay?

140. The young king often lounges on the (*throne* / *thrown*) _____ and reads detective novels.

141. Of the (*to* / *too* / *two*) _____ brothers, Bernard seems a bit (*to* / *too* / *two*)

_____ self-important (*to* / *too* / *two*) _____ me.

142. Alas, you have finally (*told* / *tolled*) _____ everyone one tale too many.

143. Students sometimes put (*undo* / *undue*) _____ pressure upon themselves to do well.

144. There was more than a (*vain* / *vane* / *vein*) _____ of cruelty in Oliver's unswerving devotion to telling the truth.

145. In a long paper, one should take care to (*vary* / *very*) _____ paragraph length now and then.

146. Rosalind is the most (*veracious* / *voracious*) _____ reader of news magazines that I have ever known.

147. An epidemic of (*viral* / *virile*) _____ hepatitis has spread throughout the general population.

148. Try not to (*waist* / *waste*) _____ your energy arguing with fools.

149. This sign is intended to (*warn* / *worn*) _____ people against eating the fish they catch here.

150. Our geography instructor said that she wasn't sure (*weather* / *whether*) _____

_____ or not the climate was changing.

Chapter 4

Important Distinctions

The purpose of this chapter is to acquaint you with the importance of not being "word-sloppy" when you write. We want to convince you of the importance of verbal precision—of saying precisely what you mean and meaning precisely what you say when it comes to word selection.

The word *nuance* derives from the French verb *nuer,* meaning "to shade," and the Latin noun *nubes,* meaning "a cloud." Thus, *nuance* means "a slight, subtle, or shade (of) difference in meaning." In this chapter we feature important nuances of meaning that distinguish many words and expressions often mistakenly used one for the other. For example, one is *addicted* to something bad but *devoted* to something good. Similarly, one is *anxious* to learn his or her examination score but *eager* to begin a long summer vacation. *Childish* behavior is immature, whereas *childlike* trust is innocent. That which is *comprehensible* is understandable, whereas that which is *comprehensive* is thorough or all-inclusive. To be *disinterested* is to be impartial, whereas to be *uninterested* is to be indifferent. Likewise, to *dissemble* is to pretend, whereas to *disassemble* is to take apart. A person who is *exceedingly* friendly is nice to be around, but a person who is *excessively* friendly is not nice to be around.

The chapter contains twenty-two instructional sequences. Each sequence is composed of four pages, two pages that explain the usage items under consideration one by one and two pages that allow you to check your understanding of the explanations by completing the sentence fill-in exercise. You simply write the correct response in the blank provided within each sentence. If your instructor is using the Instructor's Manual that accompanies the text, you will probably be asked to work the sequences in sets of three; the Instructor's Manual provides quizzes at intervals of every three sequences (except for the final set): 1–3, 4–6, 7–9,

10–12, 13–15, 16–18, and 19–22. At the conclusion of the chapter is a review exercise that includes 150 items. Your instructor may want to give this as a test.

Before beginning the first instructional sequence, don't forget to turn back to page 13 in Chapter 1 and work through the pretest exercise for the chapter. The specific instructions for doing the pretest are on page 3.

Important Distinctions (1)

a/an: The indefinite article *a* should be used before words beginning with a consonant sound, even when the sound is spelled with a vowel (*a castle, a unicorn*). *An* should be used before words beginning with a vowel sound or a silent *h* (*an example, an honest man*).

abrogate/arrogate: To *abrogate* means "to abolish," "to cancel," "to annul," or "to put aside." (Should Congress *abrogate* our trade agreements with Japan?) To *arrogate* means "to claim or take without right," "to appropriate (to oneself)," or "to ascribe or assign." (You should not *arrogate* your own bad motives to the behavior of others.)

accede/exceed: To *accede* means "to give in or agree" or "to come into office or power." (I shall *accede* to your wishes because I think your motives are honorable. The prince cannot *accede* to the throne until the king is dead.) To *exceed* is to surpass or go beyond. (Take care not to *exceed* your authority.)

accept/except: *Accept* is a verb meaning "to receive" or "to take." (A lady can *accept* compliments gracefully.) *Except* is more often used as a preposition meaning "with the exclusion of." (The point was obvious to everyone *except* Nathan.) As a verb, *except* means "to leave out." (We may *except* certain groups from this new tax.)

access/excess: As a noun, *access* means "a way, means, or the action of approaching, reaching, or entering." (The club teams had *access* to the practice field only three days a week.) As a verb, *access* means "to gain entrance." (The computer would not *access* the records of the university's auxiliary budgets.) *Excess* means "an amount or quantity greater than is usual or normal." (Trying to shed *excess* weight isn't easy.)

accused of/charged with: One may be *accused of* some wrongdoing or *charged with* criminal behavior. However, one cannot be *accused with* breaking the law.

adapt/adopt: To *adapt* means "to make suitable by changing" or "to adjust to changed circumstances." (One cannot *adapt* to college life in only a week or two.) To *adopt* means "to take up or use" or "to take into one's immediate family." (Perhaps we should *adopt* a kinder attitude toward people different from ourselves.)

addicted/devoted: *Addicted* should always suggest an unfavorable or undesirable condition, whereas *devoted* implies a condition that is good, favorable, or beneficial. Thus, one is *addicted* to something bad, but *devoted* to something good. One is *addicted* to drugs, but *devoted* to good music.

adverse/averse: *Adverse* means "hostile," "antagonistic," or "unfavorable." (*Adverse* publicity forced the candidate to withdraw from the race.) *Averse* means "disinclined," "opposed to," or "reluctant." In a sentence, *averse* is usually followed by *to*. (Madge has always been *averse* to watching a movie in a crowded theater.)

185

advert/avert: To *advert* means "to call attention to" or "to refer." (You should not *advert* too openly to sex at polite gatherings.) To *avert* means "to turn away or aside," "to prevent," or "to ward off." (The driver swerved to *avert* an accident. The woman *averted* her eyes to avoid looking at the wounded bird.)

advice/advise: *Advice* is a noun meaning "an opinion given with the intention of assisting." (They sought the *advice* of experts on the matter.) *Advise* is a verb meaning "to give *advice* or counsel." (I *advise* you to stop drinking so much yak milk.)

affect/effect: *Affect* is usually used as a verb meaning "to influence." (Insufficient rainfall will seriously *affect* crop yield.) *Affect* is also used as a verb meaning "to pretend." (You may *affect* indifference, but I think you really care.) *Effect* is most commonly used as a noun meaning "result." (No one knows what the ultimate *effect* of acid rain might be.) *Effect* may also be used as a verb meaning "to bring about" or "to produce." (The new tax laws are intended to *effect* a fairer distribution of the wealth.)

aggravate/irritate: To *aggravate* means "to make worse or more troublesome." (The lotion *aggravated* an already painful skin condition.) To *irritate* means "to annoy" or "to provoke displeasure." (Your constant mumbling *irritates* everyone.)

agree to/agree with/agree on: *Agree to* means "to give consent." *Agree with* means "to concur" or "to be in harmony with." (I *agree with* your position on the issues; therefore, I shall *agree to* support your candidacy.) *Agree on,* or *agree about,* suggests a mutual coming to terms. (We must *agree on* each of these important issues. Will they never *agree about* what should be done?)

SENTENCE FILL-IN

1. Students now have (*access / excess*) _____ to the racquetball courts only on weekends.

2. The university has been (*accused of / charged with*) _____ lowering its academic standards over time.

3. The (*affect / effect*) _____ of a fleet of aliens openly landing on earth would be substantial.

4. We must (*agree to / agree with / agree on*) _____ the very important issue of which candidate to endorse.

5. The president of the university tried to (*abrogate / arrogate*) _____ the university's collective bargaining agreement with the faculty.

6. Both Alice and Norbert have (*a / an*) _____ uncle who lives in Moscow.

7. My (*advice / advise*) _____ to you is to get a second opinion before agreeing to have surgery.

8. Among other things, the Amish are (*adverse / averse*) _____ to fighting in wars.

9. Hot weather and high humidity almost always (*affect / effect*) _____ Benjamin's allergies.

10. If the president of the United States resigns, the vice president will (*accede / exceed*)

    _____ to the presidency.

11. Thurston liked everything about college (*accept / except*) _____ studying and going to class.

12. Gwendolyn, as always, tried to (*advert / avert*) _____ an argument by casually changing the subject.

13. Edwin was never able to (*adapt / adopt*) _____ himself to a regimen of reading books and writing papers.

14. You cannot (*abrogate / arrogate*) _____ such authority to yourself without approval by the board of directors.

15. The presence of a new dog in either household would have (*aggravated / irritated*)

    _____ the already tense relationship between the two families.

16. Don't bother to (*advice / advise*) _____ anyone who is only looking for flattery.

17. In recent years greater numbers of American women have become (*addicted / devoted*)

_____ to cigarette smoking.

18. The third applicant for the position was willing to (*accept / except*) _____ a salary of $30,000.

19. Even the candidate's oldest supporters were (*aggravated / irritated*) _____

_____ by her insensitive remarks.

20. Our next-door neighbors have legally (*adapted / adopted*) _____ a little girl from Botswana.

21. The bitterly cold weather has seriously (*affected / effected*) _____ the orange crop.

22. If I were you, I would not (*advert / avert*) _____ too openly to my past as a gangster.

23. Douglas usually eats half (*a / an*) _____ cantelope each morning for breakfast.

24. The committee can't (*agree to / agree with / agree about*) _____ your line of reasoning in this instance.

25. Actually, the university has (*a / an*) _____ (*access / excess*) _____

_____ of space to house married students.

26. Alas, Tobias has been (*accused of / charged with*) _____ taking himself too seriously.

27. How does one (*affect / effect*) _____ a change in such a long-standing company policy?

28. There is (*a / an*) _____ octopus in the fraternity swimming pool.

29. Try not to (*accede / exceed*) _____ the speed limit in this area; the police are quite strict.

30. Continual (*adverse / averse*) _____ statements in the press greatly damaged the organization's good name.

Important Distinctions (2)

aim/intend: It is best to confine your use of *aim*, as a verb, to mean "to point (as a weapon)" or "to direct (as a blow or remark)." Such usage is always followed by the preposition *at*. (The guns were *aimed* at the ancient fort. Elton's remarks were *aimed* at the heart.) Avoid using *aim* as a replacement for *intend, try,* or *hope.* (Jonathan *intends* [not *aims*] to be a good father. The thing to *try* [not *aim*] for is excellence. We *hope* [not *aim*] to break the old record.)

all/all of: Although either *all* or *all of* may be used in front of nouns that name countable items, such constructions are usually made tighter by the deletion of *of*. (*All* the apples were bad. *All* the pictures had been retouched.) When the noun following does not name countable items, *of* should always be deleted. (*All* her passion had vanished.) However, *of* should be retained before pronouns as well as before proper nouns. (*All of* us were weary of work. *All of* Michigan awaited the outcome of the game.)

allude/refer: To *allude* means "to refer to indirectly." (Must you always *allude* to the fact that your family has money?) To *refer* means "to make specific reference to" or "to direct someone's attention toward." (Father O'Hare *referred* specifically to the Biblical account of Creation. I would *refer* you to the most recent edition of *Newsweek*.)

already/all ready: *Already* is an adverb meaning "previously" or "by this time." (Alas, the fox had *already* eaten the chickens.) The phrase *all ready* means that everyone or everything is prepared and set to go. (By ten o'clock, everyone was *all ready* to leave.)

alternate/alternative: As an adjective, *alternate* means "by turns." (This class meets on *alternate* days.) As a noun, *alternate* means "a stand-in or substitute." Moss was an *alternate* on the nominating committee.) As an adjective, *alternative* means "offering a choice between two or more things." (The *alternative* plan was too complex for anyone to follow.) As a noun, *alternative* means "a choice between exclusive possibilities." (You offer me no real *alternative*.)

although/though: When you have an apparent choice between these two conjunctions, it is a good practice to use *although* at the beginning of sentences. (*Although* the day was a long one, everyone finished it in good spirits.) *Though* is more often used to connect words and phrases within sentences. (At the end of the trek, Ted was healthier *though* thinner.) *Though* is also used adverbally at the ends of statements. (Kevin hasn't yet recovered; he is better, *though*.)

altogether/all together: *Altogether* is an adverb meaning "wholly," "thoroughly," or "completely." (After a weekend in the wilderness, the twins were *altogether* exhausted.) *All together* means "in a group with none missing." (Seldom were we *all together* for either Christmas or Thanksgiving.)

always/all ways: *Always* is an adverb meaning "at all times," "forever," or "without exception." (Although Ellen isn't *always* right, she isn't *always* wrong either.) The phrase *all ways* means "in every way." (In *all ways,* Jonathan is a perfect gentleman.)

among/between: When you have an apparent choice between these two prepositions, understand that *among* is more effectively used to indicate a general relationship involving more than two, or one in which a single person or thing is part of a surrounding or common group. (There is no honor *among* thieves. We spent the afternoon searching *among* the ruins. The queen walked freely *among* her subjects. Winston Churchill was a man *among* men.) *Between* is used to indicate a relationship between two items or individuals or between a single individual or item and a group viewed collectively. (We found ourselves *between* a rock and a hard place. There was an implicit understanding *between* the coach and his players.) *Between* is used for more than two of anything when each is named or considered individually in relation to the others. (Despite a considerable range in age, there has always been a strong bond *between* my children. A new trade agreement *between* Great Britain, Canada, the United States, and Mexico was signed only recently.) *Between* is also used to refer to recurring intervals, no matter what the number. (How does one stop eating *between* meals? The fighters tried to catch their breath *between* rounds.)

SENTENCE FILL-IN

1. Although the lecturer did (*allude / refer*) _____ to the incident, she never mentioned it directly.

2. I love you in (*all ways / always*) _____, and I (*all ways / always*) _____ will.

3. The investors now think that (*all / all of*) _____ them may be affected to some degree.

4. Finally, the research team devised several (*alternative / alternate*)_____ methods of conducting the test.

5. Rebecca cannot be called a scholar; she is a clever person, (*although / though*)_____ _____.

6. Why must some people (*always / all ways*) _____ try to find fault with me?

7. One of Elizabeth's problems is that she (*aims / tries*) _____ to please everyone.

8. Marshall actually lived (*among / between*) _____ primitive tribesmen when he was in the Peace Corps.

9. The track of land was (*all ready / already*) _____ to have the streets laid out.

10. Conventional wisdom has it that Lucretius is (*all together / altogether*) _____ _____ too impressed with himself.

11. (*All / All of*) _____ your logic notwithstanding, you will not persuade those who choose not to be persuaded.

12. My political science instructor holds that ordinary American citizens are caught (*among / between*) _____ two equally incompetent political parties.

13. (*Although / Though*) _____ we were well paid for our work, conditions in the factory were terrible.

14. What a pity it was that summer was (*all ready / already*) _____ half gone when I met her.

15. With no small sense of self-importance, my philosophy professor often (*alludes / refers*) _____ to the fact that he graduated from Yale first in his class.

191

16. Dunstan sometimes (*alludes / refers*) _____ to his experiences in Vietnam, but never with any specific detail.

17. Just as it was last year, the Memorial Day service was (*all together / altogether*) _____ too long.

18. The afternoons (*always / all ways*) _____ become shorter and cooler during the autumn.

19. (*All / All of*) _____ America watched on television as the spaceship blasted off for the long trip to Mars.

20. During his internship, Byron will have to work on (*alternate / alternative*) _____ weekends.

21. Many years of experience as a diplomat made Gillian wiser (*although / though*) _____ not happier.

22. The chief moved (*among / between*) _____ his warriors, telling them that the coming battle would bring them a great victory.

23. You must understand that we did not (*aim / intend*) _____ to make anyone feel uncomfortable.

24. Although we were (*all together / altogether*) _____ when we left the dormitory, we became separated later on.

25. Bertram is convinced that Michelle is in (*always / all ways*) _____ a decent person.

26. Don't tell them what we have decided to do; don't even (*allude / refer*) _____ to it.

27. (*Among / Between*) _____ innings, the fans exercised themselves by doing the wave.

28. Most of the damage had (*already / all ready*) _____ occurred before the problem was discovered.

29. Unfortunately, we were left no (*alternate / alternative*) _____ but to continue with the same treatment.

30. These two farms (*aim / hope*) _____ to raise three times as much wheat as they did last year.

Important Distinctions (3)

amoral/immoral: *Amoral* means "without a moral code or set of principles." (Dogs and cats are *amoral* creatures.) *Immoral* means "not conforming to standard rules of behavior" or "wicked." An *amoral* person has no knowledge of proper behavior, whereas an *immoral* person knowingly violates the rules. (*Immoral* activities can result in a guilty conscience.)

amuse/bemuse: To *amuse* is to entertain pleasantly, humorously, or enjoyably. (The instructor's lectures *amuse* most of the students.) To *bemuse* is to muddle or stupefy, to bewilder or preoccupy. (The children were *bemused* by all the things they could do at the amusement park.)

angle/angel: An *angle* is the figure made by two straight lines extending from the same point. (The driveway enters the road at a sharp *angle*.) An *angel* is a supernatural, winged messenger of God. (The child dreamed that she was visited by an *angel*.)

angry/mad: *Mad* is best used to mean "insane," "frenzied," or "foolish." It should not be used as a synonym for *angry*, which means "upset," "stormy," or "inflamed." (A *mad* scene followed the explosion as people ran screaming in all directions. Jason went *mad* for a time after witnessing the airplane crash. I am *angry* with you because of the unpleasant things you said about my family. *Angry* clouds moved across the afternoon sky. An *angry* sore appeared on the child's forearm.)

ante-/anti-: *Ante-* is a Latin prefix meaning "before" or "in front of." (Many of the *antebellum* houses in Memphis have been broken up into small apartments. The speaker's *antediluvian* ideas didn't go well with the liberal audience.) *Anti-* is a Greek prefix meaning "against" or "opposite." For clarity, it is sometimes followed by a hyphen when joined to freestanding words. (*Antisocial* behavior can be quite uncivil. Several university presidents have accused the governor of *anti-intellectualism*.)

anxious/eager: *Anxious* means "nervous," "worried," or "full of anxiety." (We spent an *anxious* night waiting to hear how mother's operation had gone.) *Eager* means "impatient," "in a hurry," or "keenly desirous." (We were *eager* to begin our vacation.)

anybody/any body: *Anybody* denotes any unspecified person. (In America, almost *anybody* can run for elected office.) The phrase *any body* denotes a specified person, object, or group. It is usually followed by *of*. (*Any body* of information can be analyzed.)

anymore/any more: *Anymore*, an adverb meaning "any longer," or "now," is used exclusively in questions or negative contexts. (I don't play tennis *anymore*. Why doesn't the video store run specials *anymore*?) The two-word phrase *any more* is used to suggest a quantity or amount. (We couldn't find *any more* strawberries. Was there *any more* trouble at the station?)

anyone/any one: *Anyone* is an indefinite pronoun meaning "any person at all." (Some people will talk to *anyone* who will listen.) *Any one* is a phrase meaning "any individual person or thing." It is often followed by *of*. (Hilary was assigned more work than *any one* person could do. *Any one* of the graduates might have been selected for the position.)

appraise/apprise: To *appraise* means "to estimate the value or quality of" or "to judge." (Few would *appraise* the value of the painting to be more than a million dollars.) To *apprise* means "to inform" or "to notify." (The dean *apprised* the student body that exam week would be shortened by one day.)

arbiter/arbitrator: Current practice most often uses *arbiter* to mean "a final and absolute judge" and *arbitrator* to mean "a person selected by disputing parties to settle a disagreement." (Traditional Christianity views God as the ultimate *arbiter* of good and bad, right and wrong. An *arbitrator* was called in to settle the dispute between labor and management.)

assure/ensure/insure: To *assure* means "to state with confidence in a convincing manner." (I can *assure* you that we are on the right course.) To *ensure* means "to make certain or safe" or "to guarantee." (No publisher can *ensure* absolute accuracy in the printing of a book.) To *insure* means "to make a contract for repayment in the event of a specific loss." (Be sure to *insure* your house for its full market value.)

awful/very: *Awful* means "inspiring awe" or "fearsome." (In truth, the president of the United States has *awful* powers. The *awful* roar of the storm frightened everyone.) *Awful*, or *awfully*, should not be used as a general intensifier to mean "very" or "extremely." (We had a *very* [not *awful* or *awfully*] good time at the party.)

SENTENCE FILL-IN

1. I can tell by the expression on your face that you don't want (*any more* / *anymore*)

   _____ sushi.

2. Some of these new jets are able to take off at a very steep (*angle* / *angel*) _____

   _____.

3. A(n) (*angry* / *mad*) _____ frenzy seized the crowd after the air raid siren
   had sounded.

4. Compared to anything else that walks on four legs, elephants have (*awful* / *very*)

   _____ large appetites.

5. Didn't (*any body* / *anybody*) _____ with experience volunteer for the
   search party?

6. Tigers in the wild kill their prey with an (*amoral* / *immoral*) _____
   efficiency driven only by hunger.

7. In spite of a few imperfections, Edmund is a(n) (*awfully* / *very*) _____ nice
   fellow.

8. A vertically descending (*antepersonnel* / *antipersonnel*) _____ missile is a
   polite bomb.

9. To everyone's amazement, the house was (*appraised* / *apprised*) _____ at
   $500,000.

10. We can (*assure* / *ensure* / *insure*) _____ you that the problem will be taken
    care of immediately.

11. The children were greatly (*amused* / *bemused*) _____ by the antics of the
    clowns.

12. This university offers a doctorate in virtually (*any body* / *anybody*) _____
    of recognized knowledge.

13. I'll vote for almost (*any one* / *anyone*) _____ who favors a reduction in my
    property taxes.

14. The entire class spent an (*anxious* / *eager*) _____ afternoon waiting for
    the exam scores to be posted.

15. Eventually, all this confusion is going to drive large numbers of the staff (*angry* / *mad*)

    _____.

16. Although Artemas is no (*angle* / *angel*) _____, he is no monster either.

17. Both men grew (*angry / mad*) _____ as the discussion intensified.

18. Would someone please (*appraise / apprise*) _____ me of the particulars in this case?

19. Our parliamentarian is the final (*arbiter / arbitrator*) _____ in all matters pertaining to conducting a meeting.

20. It is (*amoral / immoral*) _____ to intentionally harm the name of a good person.

21. You would be wise to (*assure / ensure / insure*) _____ your house and property against tornadoes and earthquakes.

22. The American Revolution (*antedates / antidates*) _____ the Civil War by almost a century.

23. Heavy clothing will be required to (*assure / ensure / insure*) _____ us against the dangers of subzero temperatures.

24. Professor Amplitude occasionally (*amuses / bemuses*) _____ his students by lecturing over their heads.

25. Both sides requested an (*arbitrator / arbiter*) _____ even before negotiations got underway.

26. The blow caused a(n) (*angry / mad*) _____ bruise on Dominic's arm.

27. Hollis is (*anxious / eager*) _____ to graduate from college and find a good job.

28. (*Any one / Anyone*) _____ of these mechanical failures might have caused the crash.

29. We were told by the ambassador that Claire doesn't train gerbils (*any more / anymore*)

_____ .

30. In an (*amoral / immoral*) _____ world, there is no right and wrong, good and bad.

Important Distinctions (4)

awhile/a while: *Awhile* is an adverb meaning "for an interval of time." (We talked *awhile*, then went to bed.) *A while* is a two-word phrase consisting of an article and a noun. It usually functions as an object following the prepositions *for, in,* or *after*. (After *a while*, everyone grew tired of the game.) However, *a while* is also the correct choice before such words as *ago* and *longer* even when a preposition is not present. (It was *a while* ago that we won this trophy. We talked *a while* longer, then went to bed.)

bad/badly: *Bad* is an adjective. (Your cousin has a *bad* attitude. I felt *bad* about missing the service.) *Badly* is an adverb. (The team played *badly* in the second half.)

because/cause: *Because* is a subordinating conjunction that introduces a dependent clause. (The students volunteered *because* they wanted to help.) *Cause* is either a noun or a verb and should not be used in place of *because*. (The *cause* for which we are fighting is a good one. Chronic overeating will *cause* you to gain weight.)

belief/believe: A *belief* is an idea or opinion held to be true. (Dwight's *belief* in the free enterprise system remains strong.) To *believe* is to take on faith as true or real. (I *believe* in the power of positive thinking.)

benefactor/beneficiary: A *benefactor* is a person who provides help (benefits), especially financial help, to another. (An anonymous *benefactor* paid the student's bills.) A *beneficiary* is a person who receives benefits, such as income from a will or trust. (Andrew was one of the *beneficiaries* of his uncle's will.)

benign/malign: *Benign* is an adjective meaning "favorable," "gracious," or "not malignant." (Fortunately, the tumor was *benign*.) As a verb, *malign* means "to defame," "to slander," or "to speak evil of." (Why *malign* an honorable person when there are so many deserving scoundrels about?) As an adjective, *malign* means "hateful," "harmful," "sinister," "malicious," or "evil." (Managerial divisiveness has had a *malign* effect on the company.)

beside/besides: *Beside* is a preposition meaning "by the side of," "next to," "in comparison with," or "away from." (The trailer was parked *beside* the barn. *Beside* yours, my problems seem like small ones. The speaker's comments were *beside* the point.) *Besides* is a preposition meaning "except," "other than," or "in addition to." (There were others at the convocation *besides* our own class. Mother spoke of no one *besides* you.) *Besides* is also a conjunctive adverb meaning "moreover." (I don't like liver; *besides*, I have already eaten.)

better than/more than: *Better than* should not be used as a substitute for *more than* to indicate time, distance, or quantity. (Judy is *better than* Morris at tennis. My curriculum requires *more than* [not *better than*] four years to complete. Malcolm ate *more than* [not *better than*] his share of the pizza.)

197

biannual/biennial: *Biannual* should be used to mean "occurring twice a year," and *biennial* should be used to mean "happening every two years" or "lasting for two years." Unfortunately, many people confuse the issue by using the former to mean the latter. A sound solution is to drop *biannual* altogether in favor of either *semiannual* or *twice-yearly*. (The *biennial* [not *biannual*] elections for Congress always occur in even-numbered years. The *twice-yearly* [not *biannual*] royalties are paid in February and August.)

bisect/dissect: To *bisect* is to cut into two (equal) parts. (This is where the road *bisects* the county line.) To *dissect* is to cut apart piece by piece for the purpose of study. (I don't care if I never have to *dissect* another frog.)

bit/bitten: *Bit* is the past tense form of the verb *bite*. (During surgery, the patient *bit* through the tooth-hold.) *Bitten* is the most frequently used past participle form of *bite*. And it is the only proper passive form. (Ellen was *bitten* [not *bit*] by her own dog.)

breath/breathe: A *breath* is air taken into the lungs and then let out. (I needed a *breath* of fresh air.) To *breathe* is to draw air into the lungs and then release it. (It is easier for most people to *breathe* when the humidity is low.)

bring/take: Use *bring* to indicate movement toward you; use *take* to indicate movement away from you. (Please *take* these empty bottles to the store, and *bring* back a loaf of bread with you.)

SENTENCE FILL-IN

1. Francine works at Chrysler in the summer (*because / cause*) _____ she needs the money to stay in school.

2. Carol now lives (*better than / more than*) _____ five miles from campus.

3. The child expressed an unusually strong (*belief / believe*) _____ in ghosts.

4. I would be delighted if you could (*bring / take*) _____ me with you when you go to Europe.

5. One of the nicest things about Lucinda is her (*benign / malign*) _____ inclination to believe what you are telling her.

6. Everyone now admits that the project was timed (*bad / badly*) _____ from the beginning.

7. Let us (*bisect / dissect*) _____ the essay for a more thorough analysis of what the author has said.

8. I don't like to go shopping; (*beside / besides*) _____ , I have no money to spend.

9. There was not a single (*breath / breathe*) _____ of originality in the entire speech.

10. Congressional elections occur (*biennially / semiannually*) _____ , not every four years.

11. Because everyone was having such a good time, the choir decided to stay (*awhile / a while*) _____ longer in Bavaria.

12. The refrigerator worked (*awhile / a while*) _____ , then started making strange noises.

13. Benjamin has been (*bit / bitten*) _____ by the antique bug; he spends all his time shopping for old furniture.

14. There is nothing I can say; I felt (*bad / badly*) _____ about forgetting the memorial service.

15. Nicole maintains that everyone will be the (*benefactor / beneficiary*) _____ of a sound national health system.

16. When Andrew was in college, he worked for (*awhile / a while*) _____ in a printing shop.

17. (*Beside / Besides*) _____ yours, my financial investments seem penny ante.

199

18. The apartment was so poorly ventilated that the guests could hardly (*breath / breathe*)

_____ at night.

19. What you are calling a (*benefactor / beneficiary*) _____ some people might call a sugar daddy.

20. Today fewer and fewer people seem to (*belief / believe*) _____ in the importance of marital fidelity.

21. My sister and I go on our (*biannual / twice-yearly*) _____ shopping trip to Chicago in the spring and in the fall.

22. I would say that Marshall is (*better than / more than*) _____ average at Scrabble; no one has beaten him all semester.

23. You show bad judgment when you (*benign / malign*) _____ people with whom you were once in concert.

24. When I was a child, my parents always sat (*awhile / a while*) _____ after dinner and talked.

25. Bernard doesn't seem to understand that there are other things to do at college (*beside / besides*) _____ study.

26. The child was (*bit / bitten*) _____ on the arms and legs.

27. I can't tell you how (*bad / badly*) _____ I feel about your losing all your hair.

28. "Will you please (*bring / take*) _____ this package to the post office for me and bring back some stamps?" the student asked.

29. If you (*bisect / dissect*) _____ a 90-degree angle, you are left with two 45-degree angles.

30. I love you just (*because / cause*) _____ you are you.

Important Distinctions (5)

bunch/group: *Group* should be used to refer to a collection or gathering of people. (A large *group* of computer experts conducted the seminar on artificial intelligence.) A *bunch* is a cluster or number of things of the same kind. (We bought a *bunch* of grapes at the roadside stand.)

can/may: Strictly, *can* indicates the ability, capacity, or power to do something. (You *can* pass this course if you study. The president *can* veto any bill passed by Congress.) *May* indicates permission to do something. (*May* I study with you?) In negative constructions employing a contraction, however, *can't* is always a better choice than *mayn't*. (You *can't* [not *mayn't*] be excused from taking the final examination.)

carton/cartoon: A *carton* is a cardboard box used for shipping merchandise or any boxlike container. (In Canada, a *carton* of cigarettes costs almost fifty dollars.) A *cartoon* is a drawing, a sketch that precedes a painting, or a humorous animated film. (*Roger Rabbit* is a full-length *cartoon*.)

casual/causal: *Casual* means "happening by chance," "unplanned," "nonchalant," "informal," or "relaxed." (It is sometimes easy to mistake Edmund's *casual* behavior for rudeness.) *Causal* means "relating to cause and effect." (No one now doubts that there is a *causal* relationship between cigarette smoking and lung cancer.)

catholic/Catholic: With a lower case "c," *catholic* means "universal," "all-inclusive," "liberal," or "broad in outlook." (Professor Engles is a person of *catholic* tastes who has traveled about the world more than a little.) With a capital "C," *Catholic* means "Roman Catholic" or "connected in any way with the Roman Catholic church." (The *Catholic* mass is quite different from a Presbyterian church service.)

cause/reason: *Cause* and *reason* are never quite synonyms. A *cause* is what produces an effect. (Fire was the *cause* of most of the damage. Inexperience was the *cause* of my anxiety.) A *reason* is what one produces to account for or explain an effect. (I can't understand your *reason* for saying such a thing.)

censor/censure: To *censor* means "to examine for the purpose of removing objectionable material." (Many people think that movies with excessive violence should be *censored*.) To *censure* means "to reprimand formally." (For such questionable activities, the two congressional representatives were *censured* by their colleagues.)

celebrant/celebrator: Although both of these words refer to someone who is celebrating, the former should be used to indicate one who is participating in a religious rite or other solemn ceremony and the latter to indicate one who is celebrating something more festive. (While the *celebrants* within the cathedral attended a funeral mass, the *celebrators* outside enjoyed themselves at the annual parish picnic.)

ceremonial/ceremonious: *Ceremonial* is usually applied to things or events and *ceremonious* to people. (*Ceremonious* individuals receive great enjoyment from attending *ceremonial* events.)

cheap/inexpensive: *Cheap* suggests shoddiness or inferior craftsmanship in addition to low price. (I wasted my money on a pair of *cheap* shoes.) *Inexpensive* also means "low-priced," but there is no implication of inferior quality, rather the suggestion of quality in excess of price. (Although *inexpensive,* these jackets are very nicely made.)

childish/childlike: *Childish* is an uncomplimentary term meaning "immature," "silly," "temperamental," "self-centered," "foolish," and the like. (Your *childish* insistence on always getting your own way is very off-putting.) *Childlike,* never a term of rebuke, means "innocent," "trusting," "simple," "frank," "uncomplicated," and the like. (There is something almost *childlike* about my art instructor's appreciation of a good painting.)

class/category: Be sure to think of *categories* as the divisions of a *class,* rather than the other way around. (Human beings can be separated into an almost infinite number of *categories.*)

classical/classic: These two words are not exactly synonyms. *Classical* most often refers to the art, literature, and life of ancient Greece and Rome or to serious music such as symphonies, concertos, and operas. (Raymond is a student of *classical* languages.) *Classic* is most often used to mean "of the first or highest class," "a model of a particular type," or "precedent-setting." (Rochelle's cousin bought a *classic* 1956 Chevy hardtop. *A Tale of Two Cities,* by Charles Dickens, is considered a *classic* novel of its kind.)

SENTENCE FILL-IN

1. People who use foul language in public places should learn to (censor / censure) _____ their tongues.

2. Renting a good movie to watch on the VCR is a(n) (cheap / inexpensive) _____ way to entertain oneself of an evening.

3. Investigators indicated that there was no (casual / causal) _____ connection between the gas leak and the explosion.

4. One of the most interesting events of our tour of Britain was the (ceremonial / ceremonious) _____ opening of Parliament.

5. Everyone went to the costume party dressed as a (carton / cartoon)_____ character from the funny papers.

6. (Can / May) _____ we be allowed to remain at the cottage through August?

7. What (cause / reason) _____ can you give to explain the behavior of the rioters?

8. This novel is a murder mystery about (celebrants / celebrators) _____ of the Eucharist being poisoned by bad wine.

9. Dr. Wiggens is a (classical / classic) _____ scholar well versed in all matters related to ancient Greek and Roman society.

10. A (bunch / group) _____ of joggers went by the cottage every morning about daylight.

11. The milk (carton / cartoon) _____ leaked all over the inside of the refrigerator.

12. Avery went to a (catholic / Catholic) _____ school in Cleveland through the eighth grade.

13. Pouting when you don't get your way seems a bit (childish / childlike) _____ in an adult.

14. The characters in this play can be separated into three (classes / categories) _____: the good, the evil, and the innocent.

15. While searching the cottage, we found a (bunch / group) _____ of antique keys on a brass ring.

16. The invitation said that (casual / causal) _____ attire was appropriate for the occasion.

17. Political (*cartons / cartoons*) _____ appear on the editorial pages of many newspapers.

18. Hanging the trees in the yard of your physics professor full of toilet paper is a very

(*childish / childlike*) _____ prank for university students.

19. Your (*catholic / Catholic*) _____ opinions about a variety of topics suggest that you are well-read and well-traveled.

20. At three o'clock in the morning, the (*celebrants / celebrators*) _____ of the school's first championship were still going strong.

21. The fight provided a (*classical / classic*) _____ example of a boxer pitted against a slugger.

22. If I didn't know you better, I would tell you that what you are saying is a (*bunch / group*)

_____ of nonsense.

23. My grandfather has remained almost (*childish / childlike*) _____ in his belief that most people are basically good.

24. The speaker argued that middle-(*category / class*) _____ people pay a disproportionate amount of federal taxes.

25. Of course, you (*can't / mayn't*) _____ go into the wilderness alone; you don't even know how to use a knife.

26. Dr. January was (*censored / censured*) _____ by the local medical board for overcharging Medicare patients.

27. Alas, a broken heart was the (*cause of / reason for*) _____ the old man's death.

28. Antonia is a chronically (*ceremonial / ceremonious*) _____ individual, even to the way she sets the table for a meal.

29. We ate in this very (*cheap / inexpensive*) _____ restaurant and later paid a painful price in indigestion.

30. (*Can / May*) _____ I have this dance? The evening is almost over.

Important Distinctions (6)

client/customer: A *client* is a person who seeks the specialized advice and assistance of a lawyer or other professional person. (Professor Tuttle has long been a *client* of my father's law firm.) A *customer* is a person who purchases something from a retail establishment. (Baxter has been a *customer* of the local big-and-tall shop ever since it opened.) Calling a *customer* a *client* is pretentious, much like calling a clerk a sales associate.

climatic/climactic: *Climatic* refers to the weather. (There are many *climatic* differences between Texas and Alaska.) *Climactic* refers to a dramatic high point or a decisive turning point. (The most *climactic* scene in the film occurred when the long-separated sisters recognized each other.)

college/university: A *college* is an undergraduate school that grants mostly bachelor's degrees. (Before going into pharmacy, Baldwin was a student in the *college* of arts and sciences.) A *university* includes several undergraduate colleges as well as graduate and professional schools. (Ferris State University comprises seven *colleges*.)

comprehensible/comprehensive: *Comprehensible* means "intelligible" or "understandable." (Much of this material is not *comprehensible* to me.) *Comprehensive* is most often used to mean "in great detail," "thorough," or "inclusive." (Professor Winthrop's examinations are *comprehensive* if nothing else.)

comprise/compose: To *comprise* means "to include," "to contain," or "to consist of." (The United States *comprises* fifty states. The football team *comprises* more than a hundred players.) To *compose* means "to make up" or "to form." (This university is *composed* of several colleges.) Avoid the expression *comprised of*. (The continental United States *comprises* [not *is comprised of*] five time zones. All of these products are *composed* [not *comprised*] of recycled materials.) A further distinction, this between *comprise* and *include,* is that you should use *comprise* only when all parts of something are named or referred to and *include* when only some parts are referred to. (This list *comprises* all known criminals living in the area. That list *includes* both your name and mine.)

concave/convex: *Concave* means "curved inward, like the inside of a sphere," and *convex* means "curved outward, like the outside of a ball." (The palm of one's hand is *concave,* whereas the bulge of a mound is *convex.*)

confident/confidant: To be *confident* is to be self-assured. A *confidant* is a close and trusted friend. (I am *confident* that Gifford, my *confidant,* will never disclose anything told to him in confidence.)

confidently/confidentially: *Confidently* means "with confidence, self-assurance, or certainty." (Both fighters entered the ring *confidently.*) *Confidentially* means "in confidence,"

205

"intimately," or "in secret." (Are we speaking *confidentially,* or is this information for public consumption?)

conscience/conscious: *Conscience* is one's sense of right and wrong. To be *conscious* is to be awake and able to think and feel. (I am *conscious* of the fact that my *conscience* is bothering me.)

consistently/constantly: *Consistently* means "without change," "unwaveringly," or "steadfastly." (Ashley is *consistently* in arrears with his rent.) *Constantly* means "without interruption" or "unceasingly." (The president of the faculty union is *constantly* under attack from the more radical faculty members.) Both words are overused and may be effectively replaced by other words. (Ashley is *regularly* in arrears with his rent. The president of the faculty union is *always* under attack from the more radical faculty members.)

contemporary: Because the adjective *contemporary* has two meanings, it must be used precisely. First, it means "living, existing, or occurring at the same time" or "characteristic of the same age." (Thomas Jefferson and Thomas Paine were *contemporary* political thinkers of the eighteenth century. William Shakespeare and Christopher Marlowe were *contemporary* Elizabethan dramatists.) Second, *contemporary* means "modern," "current," "present-day," or "up-to-date." (Most of the members of my family are not very *contemporary;* in fact, they are downright old-fashioned.) Thus, the statement "We passed a pleasant evening listening to Mozart chamber music performed on *contemporary* instruments" is unclear. Were the instruments crafted in the eighteenth century? Or were they modern instruments? A sensible way to avoid this confusion is to confine your use of *contemporary* to the first meaning and use an appropriate synonym where the word might be used in its second sense. (Mozart and other composers *contemporary* to him might be amazed to hear their music performed on *present-day* [not *contemporary*] instruments.)

SENTENCE FILL-IN

1. This university is (*comprised of / composed of*) _____ more than a dozen (*discreet / discrete*) _____ colleges.

2. I realize that my ideas about marriage aren't (*contemporary / up-to-date*) _____; I think the vows should be permanent.

3. The only reason Emeline's (*conscience / conscious*) _____ is bothering her is that she didn't want anyone to know she made so much money.

4. Because this information was given to me (*confidently / confidentially*) _____, you should take care not to repeat it.

5. Esteban is (*usually / consistently*) _____ late for his nine-o'clock class on Friday morning.

6. The homecoming game had a (*climatic / climactic*) _____ conclusion, three touchdowns and a field goal within the last two minutes of play.

7. Generally, (*colleges / universities*) _____ are likely to have many comprehensive graduate programs.

8. The manager of Rickety Antiques always contacts her best (*customers / clients*) _____ when she returns from Europe.

9. As it turned out, the senator was a bit too (*confidant / confident*) _____ that he would be reelected.

10. Meggan (*consistently / constantly*) _____ overestimates how much work she can do in one day.

11. The thirty-volume work, which is meticulously researched, is the most (*comprehensible / comprehensive*) _____ history of England now in print.

12. Antonio Vivaldi would be amazed to hear his concerti performed on (*contemporary / modern*) _____ instruments.

13. The indentation where the boulder hit the side of the metal building was almost perfectly (*concave / convex*) _____.

14. Our Olympic basketball team (*comprises / composes*) _____ twelve players, all but one from the NBA.

15. Although Owen began the task (*confidently / confidentially*) _____ enough, he later admitted that he didn't know what he was doing.

16. (*Climatic / Climactic*) _____ changes usually occur over a long period of time, not all at once.

17. Basil admitted that he was always (*conscience / conscious*) _____ of the size of his feet.

18. The eyes of a dragonfly are (*concave / convex*) _____ bulges on the sides of its head.

19. The list (*comprised / included*) _____ only a few names familiar to me.

20. The American Bar Association holds the lawyer-(*client / customer*) _____ relationship to be almost sacred.

21. Duncan carries himself (*confidently / confidentially*) _____ even when he has butterflies in his stomach.

22. (*Contemporary / Current*) _____ medical practice favors keeping patients in the hospital as brief a period of time as possible.

23. Maria's lifelong (*confidant / confident*) _____, her sister, recently married and moved to New Zealand.

24. Jeffrey (*consistently / constantly*) _____ clears his throat when he tries to speak before a group.

25. Why do people sometimes have a guilty (*conscience / conscious*) _____ when they have done nothing wrong?

26. The material was not (*comprehensible / comprehensive*) _____ to Douglas; he could not understand it.

27. The (*climatic / climactic*) _____ event of the tour occurred when we met Prince Charles at an ordinary English pub.

28. Bruno has so much (*confidants / confidence*) _____ that he is a virtual one-man mutual admiration society.

29. The head waiter at the Lamplighter always saved the best tables for his regular (*customers / clients*) _____.

30. Adelaide, a talented person, (*comprises / composes*) _____ brief pieces for the piano as a hobby.

Important Distinctions (7)

contemptible/contemptuous: *Contemptible* means "deserving scorn." (This *contemptible* lout deserves whatever happens to him.) *Contemptuous* means "showing scorn." (I have never seen a more *contemptuous* look than the one she gave her ex-husband.)

continual/continuous: *Continual* means "often repeated." (Bridget could not study because of *continual* interruptions.) *Continuous* means "without interruption," "unceasing," or "constant." (The *continuous* patter of rain on the roof left me quite placid.)

controversial/contentious: *Controversial* means "debatable," "disputable," or "arguable." (Euthanasia remains a *controversial* topic in modern society.) *Contentious* means "quarrelsome" or "argumentative." (*Contentious* people will argue about almost anything.) Generally, topics are *controversial,* and people are *contentious.*

convince/persuade: To *convince* means "to satisfy a person's mind, as by proof or the power of reason." The word is often followed by *of* or *that.* (These arguments *convince* me of the validity of your position.) To *persuade* means "to talk someone into a course of action." The word is often followed by *to.* (The priest *persuaded* the youth to surrender to the police.)

covert/overt: *Covert* means "hidden," "secret," "concealed," or "surreptitious." (When information about the *covert* plan became known, the community was amazed and astounded.) *Overt* means "not hidden," "open to view," "apparent," "manifest," or "public." (The rift between the university president and provost was quite *overt,* public for all to witness.)

credible/creditable: *Credible* means "believable," "reliable," or "trustworthy." (Because the senator's explanation of his behavior was *credible,* most of the voters believed him.) *Creditable* means "deserving credit" or "praiseworthy." (Although the team gave a *creditable* performance, the competition was just too good.)

creditor/debtor: A *creditor* is a person who is owed money, whereas a *debtor* is a person who owes money. (In recent times, the United States has gone from being a *creditor* nation to being a *debtor* nation.) A *debtor* may also owe something other than money. (I am a *debtor* to my friends for all the good things they have said about me.)

criteria/criterion: *Criteria* is plural for *criterion,* which means "a standard by which something is judged." (The *criteria* for determining who is a good teacher are many, but the single most important *criterion* is difficult to judge.)

data/datum: Strictly speaking, *data* is the plural form of *datum,* which means "fact" or "something known." (The *data* gathered from the experiments are going to require careful analysis.) Except in the most formal situations, however, *data* may be either (collectively) singular or plural. (This *data* isn't complete.)

209

decisive/incisive: *Decisive* means "conclusive," "final," "bringing to an end," or "settling beyond question." (The victory was *decisive;* we won by thirty points.) *Incisive* means "sharp," "keen," "penetrating," "piercing," "acute," or "cutting." (Meggan's *incisive* wit is not always painless for its target.)

decriminalize/legalize: To *decriminalize* some action or form of behavior is to remove it from statutory criminality, thereby greatly reducing legal penalties while still maintaining some regulation. To *legalize* is to make legal and not to regulate in any major way. (The use of marijuana has been *decriminalized* in some places but not really *legalized*.)

deduce/deduct: To *deduce* means "to draw a conclusion." (From the audit, one must *deduce* that money has been mishandled.) To *deduct* means "to take away" or "to subtract." (May I *deduct* the price of the broken item from the bill?) The noun form of both words is the same: *deduction.*

defective/deficient: *Defective* means "imperfect," "faulty," or "flawed." (Most of the lamps had *defective* wiring.) *Deficient* means "lacking," "insufficient," or "inadequate." (Elston was denied admittance to the doctoral program because of his *deficient* writing skills in German.) Keep in mind that one may be *deficient* in some way without being *defective* generally.

definite/definitive: *Definite* is most often used to mean "clear," "exact," or "not vague." (Alas, the speaker wasn't very *definite* about solutions.) *Definitive* is most often used to mean "conclusive," "decisive," "final," or "comprehensive and accurate." (The most *definitive* biography of the author doesn't mention the matter at all.)

SENTENCE FILL-IN

1. Your (*criteria / criterion*) _____ for judging the winner differ from mine.

2. The critic's (*decisive / incisive*) _____ analysis of the film was painfully honest about all of its flaws.

3. Are you (*convinced / persuaded*) _____ that the public school system is a total failure?

4. The most (*covert / overt*) _____ attack against the mayor came on the front page of the local newspaper.

5. The diet of these children is (*defective / deficient*) _____ in both protein and complex carbohydrates.

6. To determine your net income, (*deduce / deduct*) _____ all expenses from your gross income.

7. Alas, all my (*creditors / debtors*) _____ are after me to pay them what I owe them.

8. This year's model represents a (*definite / definitive*) _____ improvement over last year's model.

9. The (*continual / continuous*) _____ hum of the air conditioner finally put the children to sleep.

10. One of the most (*controversial / contentious*) _____ questions of the day continues to be whether or not people have the right to end their own lives.

11. The courts have (*legalized / decriminalized*) _____ insider trading by giving the guilty such light sentences.

12. We are making bad decisions because we are suffering from a shortage of good (*data / datum*) _____.

13. Our food supplies are (*defective / deficient*) _____; we will not be able to feed the army through the winter.

14. The only thing I can (*deduce / deduct*) _____ from your remarks is that you are over-fond of the drone of your own voice.

15. For telling such (*contemptible / contemptuous*) _____ lies, you should expect the scorn of all who find you out.

16. Gretchen has a (*controversial / contentious*) _____ nature; she wants to argue about everything.

17. This is not a (*credible / creditable*) _____ witness; he has been convicted on three counts of perjury.

18. Most of the *data* you have given us (*is / are*) _____ too old to be of any use.

19. Would it be possible to (*convince / persuade*) _____ your parents to go to Europe for the summer?

20. These activities must remain (*covert / overt*) _____ because we don't want anyone to know about them.

21. What is (*credible / creditable*) _____ about the candidate's record of voting against affordable medical care for the poor?

22. (*Continual / Continuous*) _____ commercial interruptions make trying to watch a movie on television almost impossible.

23. Because of its foreign trade deficit, the United States has become a (*creditor / debtor*) _____ nation.

24. Why is Tobias always so (*contemptible / contemptuous*) _____ of well-meaning people?

25. The newspapers called the faculty's ninety percent no-confidence vote in the president of the university a (*decisive / incisive*) _____ indication of his incompetence.

26. The most important (*criteria / criterion*) _____ for success in almost anything is hard work.

27. Because of a (*defective / deficient*) _____ heart valve, the child must be operated on as soon as possible.

28. This isn't a (*definite / definitive*) _____ work on the author's life; it doesn't even mention her detective novels.

29. Because Casper's story was not (*credible / creditable*) _____, no one believed it.

30. Should I (*deduce / deduct*) _____ from what you are saying that you think the United States should never have invaded Iraq?

Important Distinctions (8)

denote/connote: To *denote* means "to indicate," "to signify," or "to mean." (With a dog, growling usually *denotes* anger.) To *connote* means "to suggest or imply in addition to explicit or literal meaning." (The word "home" *connotes* more than just a house where one lives.) The noun forms of these words are *denotation* and *connotation*. The *denotation* of a word is its exact, literal meaning, whereas the *connotation* of a word includes all of its implications or overtones. (It is more often the *connotations* of words that people object to than the *denotations*.)

deprecate/depreciate: *Deprecate* is most often used to mean "to express strong disapproval of" or "to disparage." (Do not *deprecate* the importance of traditional family values.) *Depreciate* is most often used to mean "to lessen in value." (Today a new automobile *depreciates* several thousand dollars the minute it is driven out of the showroom.)

device/devise: *Device* is a noun that usually refers to an object or scheme. (This clever little *device* peels apples.) To *devise* means "to work out," "to create," or "to plan." (Can you *devise* a computer program that will ignore wrong commands?)

diagnosis/prognosis: A *diagnosis* is the act or process of figuring out what disease a person has based on the symptoms. It is also a careful study of anything to determine essential characteristics. (The physician's original *diagnosis* of the patient's illness proved to be accurate.) A *prognosis* is a forecast or prediction of the probable course of a disease or illness, or an estimate of any future development. (The short-term *prognosis* for the economy remains grim.)

discover/invent: To *discover* something is to learn of its existence for the first time. (Pierre and Marie Curie, a famous husband and wife team, *discovered* both polonium and radium.) To *invent* is to make something up or to create something new. (Alexander Graham Bell *invented* the telephone, but my little brother *invents* tall tales.)

disinterested/uninterested: Disinterested means "impartial," "unbiased," or "objective." (A *disinterested* third party was called in to settle the argument.) *Uninterested* means "indifferent." (They were *uninterested* in anything requiring physical activity.)

displace/misplace: To *displace* means "to take the place of," "to replace," "to remove from a position of authority," or "to move anything from its usual place or position." (Word processors have *displaced* typewriters in the modern office. The president of the university *displaced* her vice president for academic affairs. A ship *displaces* its own weight of water when floating in the sea.) To *misplace* is to put in the wrong place and thus to lose. (Alas, Martha has once again *misplaced* her Lamborghini.)

dissemble/disassemble: To *dissemble* means "to disguise," "to feign," "to pretend," or "to simulate." (Although the students may *dissemble* interest in the lecture, they are not really listening.) To *disassemble* is to take apart. (It takes longer to *disassemble* this engine than it did to put it together in the first place.)

distinct/distinctive: *Distinct* means "not the same," "different," "separate," "well defined," or "clear." (Problem A is *distinct* from problem B. We were asked three *distinct* questions. The sound was quite *distinct*.) *Distinctive* means "characteristic," "special," or "distinguishing from all others." (The British have a *distinctive* way of pronouncing many words. Your manners are *distinctively* British.)

due to/because of: When you have an apparent choice between these two expressions, *due to,* meaning "the result of," is generally acceptable as a subject complement after a form of the linking verb *be.* (Our success was *due to* careful planning.) However, more careful usage might prefer "Our success was *the result of* careful planning." *Due to* should never be used as a substitute for *because of,* meaning "on account of," introducing an adverbial construction. (We lost the championship game *because of* [not *due to*] injuries to key players.)

each other/one another: When you have an apparent choice between these two expressions, use *each other* when only two persons are involved and *one another* when more than two are involved. (The two brothers have fought with *each other* all their lives. The English department faculty members do not socialize with *one another* very much.)

SENTENCE FILL-IN

1. The Clements insisted that they were (*disinterested / uninterested*) _____ in all things related to computers.

2. Greta (*dissembled / disassembled*) _____ her gratification at graduating first in her class by feigning surprise.

3. Ethan's reputation as a wit was (*due to / the result of*) _____ a single remark he had once made to the dean.

4. Apparently the Croatians and the Serbians are no fonder of (*each other / one another*) _____ today than they were a hundred years ago.

5. Tell us, old great one, whether or not you have (*discovered / invented*) _____ the secret of life.

6. Educated Brits luxuriate in their (*distinct / distinctive*) _____ way of saying almost nothing in the most erudite manner.

7. The automobile long ago (*displaced / misplaced*) _____ the horse and buggy as a means of domestic transportation.

8. The speaker's (*diagnosis / prognosis*) _____ for the new world order was a planet of two groups—the haves and the have-nots.

9. Alas, the game was lost (*due to / because of*) _____ sloppy play in the final quarter.

10. Do we have to completely (*disassemble / dissemble*) _____ society in order to improve it?

11. Johannes Gutenberg, a fifteenth-century German printer, is reputed to have (*discovered / invented*) _____ movable type.

12. What a clever (*device / devise*) _____ this is; you should have it patented.

13. The original (*denotation / connotation*) _____ of the word "euthanasia" had nothing to do with mercy killing.

14. Those who prefer a sedentary life sometimes (*deprecate / depreciate*) _____ the alleged joys of exercise.

15. Contrary to popular mythology, college students seldom form lasting relationships with (*each other / one another*) _____ as a result of common intellectual interests.

16. The witness maintained that she had no (*distinct / distinctive*) _____ recollection of the mugger's face.

17. (*Due to / Because of*) _____ a power failure, the computer workshop had to be postponed.

18. We bought a high-tech (*device / devise*) _____ guaranteed to improve our car's gas mileage.

19. A(n) (*disinterested / uninterested*) _____ witness came forward to present the details of the accident.

20. Once again, Fenwick seems to have (*displaced / misplaced*) _____ his pipe and slippers.

21. Franklin and Gabriel have been in love with (*each other / one another*) _____

    _____ since both were little more than children.

22. If we could (*deprecate / depreciate*) _____ the value of the American dollar by twenty-five percent, perhaps we would be able to export more goods to foreign countries.

23. Many students today seem (*disinterested / uninterested*) _____ in courses not directly related to their program major.

24. My unprofessional (*diagnosis / prognosis*) _____ of the malaise that ails us is an addiction to instant gratification and a chronic fear of failure.

25. Ever greater numbers of semiskilled workers are today being (*displaced / misplaced*)

    _____ by automated systems.

26. Most of the currently popular (*denotations / connotations*) _____ associated with the word "discrimination" are not very positive.

27. The time has come to (*device / devise*) _____ a scheme to protect the neighborhood from burglars.

28. Your tone of voice (*denotes / connotes*) _____ a message quite different from the words you are speaking.

29. Each of the tribal chieftans wore a (*distinct / distinctive*) _____ headdress.

30. Pluto, the outermost planet of the solar system, was not (*discovered / invented*)

    _____ until 1930.

Important Distinctions (9)

earthly/earthy: *Earthly* means "of the earth" or "possible." (The Dingle Peninsula in Western Ireland is indeed an *earthly* paradise. I can see no *earthly* good coming of all this scheming.) *Earthy* means "common," "coarse," "not refined," or "practical." (These are *earthy* people, given to coarse tales and plain speech.)

easy/easily: *Easy* is an adjective, *easily* an adverb. (This is an *easy* job. The job was *easily* done.) Take care not to use *easy* adverbally. (We worked *easily* [not *easy*] together.)

economic/economical: *Economic* means "having to do with the management of the income, expenses, and supplies of a household or organization." (The long and the short of it is that these are tough *economic* times in the state of Michigan.) *Economical* means "not wasteful," "thrifty," or "saving." (Small cars are more *economical* to operate than are large ones.)

e.g./i.e.: The abbreviation *e.g.* stands for the Latin phrase *exempli gratia,* meaning "for example." (Several university administrators are exorbitantly overpaid— *e.g.*, the dean of the evening school makes $90,000 a year.) The abbreviation *i.e.* stands for the Latin phrase *id est,* meaning "that is," "that is to say," or "namely." (The uneducated, *i.e.*, those who cannot read and write, have no chance to compete for today's high-tech jobs.)

elemental/elementary: When you have an apparent choice between these two words, understand that the first is usually applied to basic natural elements such as power, strength, size, the mind, the weather, fire, and so on. (The seasons exact an *elemental* deterioration even on structures of palatial magnificence.) *Elementary* is most often used to mean "simple," "introductory," or "easy." (Alas, I have only an *elementary* knowledge of art.)

elusive/illusive: *Elusive* means "hard to understand, grasp, or retain" or "baffling." (The concept was so *elusive* that I could keep it straight in my mind only for brief periods of time.) *Illusive* means "caused by an illusion," "deceptive," or "unreal." (For many people, real happiness is an *illusive* dream.)

endless/innumerable: *Endless* means "without end," "lasting forever," or "continuous." (This tropical island really does have an *endless* summer.) *Innumerable* means "too many to count," "countless," or "numberless." (At colleges and universities across the country, *innumerable* students are enrolling in remedial math and science courses.)

envelop/envelope: To *envelop* means "to surround" or "to conceal." (The clouds will soon *envelop* the mountain.) An *envelope* is what a letter is mailed in. (My Valentine's Day card came in a bright red *envelope*.)

envious/enviable: *Envious* is a negative term applied to a person who is experiencing some resentment or even jealousy toward another. (Emery is *envious* of his sister's accomplishments in the field of medical research.) *Enviable* is a praising term meaning "worthy," "desirable," or "exemplary." (Webster has compiled an *enviable* record in graduate school.)

epigram/epigraph/epithet/epitaph: An *epigram* is a terse, witty statement, often antithetical—e.g., Oscar Wilde's "I can resist everything except temptation." An *epigram* is also a short poem with a satirical point—e.g., Matthew Prior's "A Reply." *Sir, I admit your general rule / That every poet is a fool; / But you yourself may serve to show it, / That every fool is not a poet.* An *epigraph* is an inscription on a building or monument, or a quotation appearing at the beginning of a book. ("The greatest good for the greatest number" was the *epigraph* inscribed on the columns at the entrance to the 1964 New York World's Fair.) An *epithet* is a markedly descriptive word or phrase that characterizes a person, often negatively—e.g., "What do these *eggheads* know about the real world?" or "Just call me Andrew *the astonished*." An *epitaph* is a brief commemorative statement, as to the dead, or an inscription on a tombstone. One of the most famous *epitaphs* was written by English poet John Gay for his own tombstone. *Life is a jest, and all things show it; / I thought so once, but now I know it.*

epidemic/endemic/pandemic: *Endemic* means "peculiar or native to a particular region, climate, people, or culture." (Malaria is *endemic* to tropical climates. Religious animosity between Catholics and Protestants seems *endemic* to Northern Ireland.) *Epidemic* means "spreading rapidly among many individuals within a population." (The tiny island was suffering an *epidemic* of measles.) *Pandemic* means "prevalent over a large area," "general," "worldwide," or "universal." (Because of ever growing populations, hunger has become a *pandemic* problem in Third World countries.)

SENTENCE FILL-IN

1. Some agencies of the federal government are greatly feared by the citizenry—(*e.g.* / *i.e.*)

   _____, the Internal Revenue Service.

2. Glenna is in the (*envious* / *enviable*) _____ position of having buyers bid against one another for her paintings.

3. My grandfather often repeated his personal revision of an old (*epigram* / *epigraph* / *epithet* / *epitaph*) _____ : "Spare the rod, spare the child."

4. You must understand the (*elemental* / *elementary*) _____ principles of physics before mastering the whole universe.

5. Alas, my troubles seem to be (*endless* / *innumerable*) _____; they never stop.

6. Is it more (*economical* / *economic*) _____ to buy a new car or to lease one?

7. Although the (*envelop* / *envelope*) _____ was improperly addressed, the letter arrived safely.

8. A cure for cystic fibrosis has so far proved (*elusive* / *illusive*) _____ for medical researchers.

9. The (*epigram* / *epigraph* / *epithet* / *epitaph*) _____ on the crumbling tombstone read as follows: "Alonzo Thomas is doing what he always did best— / Leave the work for others and take for himself a rest."

10. The priest said that we have both an (*earthly* / *earthy*) _____ father and a heavenly Father.

11. This (*elusive* / *illusive*) _____ idea you have of secretly associating with aliens is nothing more than a fantasy.

12. It is not unusual for children to be (*envious* / *enviable*) _____ of the accomplishments of their siblings.

13. The man and woman talked (*easy* / *easily*) _____ together, as they had known each other for a long time.

14. There now seems to be little doubt that AIDS will be the planet's (*epidemic* / *endemic* / *pandemic*) _____ disease of the twenty-first century.

15. In most places, it is more (*economic* / *economical*) _____ to heat a house with natural gas than with electricity.

16. There are no two ways about it; these are tough (*economic* / *economical*) _____ times for many people.

17. Medical history amounts to a chronicle of (*endless / innumerable*) _____ diseases attacking the human race and then being either cured or controlled.

18. A three-day blizzard, displaying an (*elemental / elementary*) _____ fury, buried the village under several feet of snow.

19. "Pinheads" is the (*epigram / epigraph / epithet / epitaph*) _____ the townies use to refer to university students.

20. As night begins to (*envelop / envelope*) _____ the village, soft candlelight can be seen glowing from the windows of each cottage.

21. No matter how fast we drove, the (*elusive / illusive*) _____ image of a pirate ship retreated across the desert just ahead of us.

22. The (*epigram / epigraph / epithet / epitaph*) _____ following the title page of the vocabulary textbook read "A picture is worth a thousand words only if you know the thousand words."

23. A letter bomb may come in a small (*envelop / envelope*) _____.

24. The Swains, an (*earthly / earthy*) _____ clan, make no pretenses of refinement.

25. Why are some people so (*envious / enviable*) _____ of what other people have?

26. Alas, violence seems (*epidemic / endemic / pandemic*) _____ to the American way of life.

27. With this much money, we should be able to get by (*easy / easily*) _____ enough.

28. Last winter we had a flu (*epidemic / endemic / pandemic*) _____ in the Midwest.

29. The indigent—(*e.g. / i.e.*) _____, those who cannot feed and clothe themselves—represent a growing percentage of the population.

30. Earthquakes are (*elemental / elementary*) _____ occurrences over which we as yet have little control.

Important Distinctions (10)

equable/equitable: *Equable* means "not varying much," "steady," "uniform," "tranquil," or "serene." (An *equable* disposition is required to be a hall director on a university campus.) *Equitable* means "fair," "just," "right," or "reasonable." (Both parties agreed that the settlement was *equitable*—i.e., fair and just.)

especially/specially: *Especially* means "particularly," "unusually," or "to a marked degree." (We were *especially* happy to be invited to join the club.) *Specially* means "for a specific reason or purpose." (These dogs were bred *specially* for rabbit hunting.)

ever so often/every so often: The first of these phrases means "very frequently," whereas the second means "occasionally," or "now and then." (Bradley mispronounces this word *ever so often;* in fact, he almost never gets it right. *Every so often* I enjoy a good cup of mocha java.)

everyday/every day: *Everyday* is an adjective meaning "common," "ordinary," or "usual." (Most students wear their *everyday* clothes to class.) *Every day* is an adjective-noun combination. (Frances doesn't much like the idea of having to go to work *every day*.)

everyone/every one: *Everyone* is an indefinite pronoun meaning "every person." (In a perfect world, *everyone* would be happy and prosperous.) *Every one* is a phrase meaning "each individual person or thing." (*Every one* of the players on the high school team went on to play in college.)

evoke/invoke: To *evoke* means "to call forth," "to bring to mind," "to summon," or "to reawaken." (The sound of a helicopter passing overhead *evokes* unpleasant memories of a twenty-seven-month visit some years ago to Vietnam.) To *invoke* means "to call on, as in prayer," "to resort to," "to put into use," or "to cite approvingly." (Alas, the law that Godfrey tried to *invoke* in his defense existed only in his own mind.)

exceedingly/excessively: Exceedingly means "extremely," "extraordinarily," "to an unusual degree," or "very." (Last week the weather was *exceedingly* pleasant for this time of year.) *Excessively* means "too much," "more than enough," or "beyond sensible limits." (Many teenagers talk *excessively* on the telephone.)

exceptional/exceptionable: *Exceptional* means "much above average," "out of the ordinary," "uncommon," or "unusual." (Your performance in the decathlon was *exceptional,* the best I had ever seen.) *Exceptionable* means "open to objection," or "objectionable." (The judge ruled the plaintiff's outbursts *exceptionable* and had him gagged for the remainder of the trial.)

exhaustive/exhausting: *Exhaustive* means "leaving nothing out," "thorough," or "comprehensive." (I have just read an *exhaustive* study of the life of James Joyce; there is little else to learn about the man.) *Exhausting* means "totally fatiguing" or "draining the whole of." (Polishing stones by hand is *exhausting* work.)

exotic/erotic/esoteric: *Exotic* means "foreign," "strange," "unusual," "striking," or "exciting." (Is a plant that eats lizards and hums classical tunes *exotic* enough for your collection?) *Erotic* means "arousing sexual desires" or "responsive to sexual stimulation." (Are there fundamental differences between *erotic* literature and hard-core pornography?) *Esoteric* means "appreciated or understood by only a select few," "beyond the knowledge of most ordinary people," "private," or "secret." (This poet is so *esoteric* that he is understood only by himself, and then only part of the time.)

explicit/implicit: *Explicit* means "clearly stated." *Implicit* means "suggested" or "implied." (Contractual agreements tend to be *explicit,* personal ones *implicit.*)

extended/extensive: *Extended* means "made longer," "stretched out," or "outstretched." (Amanda took an *extended* leave of absence.) *Extensive* means "covering a large area," "vast," or "comprehensive." (The speaker possessed *extensive* experience at negotiating settlements between labor and management.)

false/fallacious: *False* is more often used to mean "untrue" or "not genuine." (The witness admitted making several *false* statements to the press.) *Fallacious* means "not logical." (*Fallacious* arguments convince only the unsophisticated.)

famous/notorious: *Famous* means "well-known," "much talked about," or "renowned." (The students were not accustomed to rubbing elbows with such *famous* people.) *Notorious* means "infamous"—i.e., "well-known for bad reasons." (John Dillinger, a *notorious* bank robber in the 1930s, was gunned down July 22, 1934, outside a Chicago movie theater.)

SENTENCE FILL-IN

1. (*Everyone / Every one*) _____ of these problems was brought up over a year ago and explained to the members of this board.

2. What you are saying is (*false / fallacious*) _____; the truth is quite another tale.

3. Your repeated association with known criminals is so (*exceptional / exceptionable*) _____ that you are requested to resign from this club forthwith.

4. A dissertation of this sort will require (*exhaustive / exhausting*) _____ research; no stone can be left unturned.

5. Genetic engineering is still an (*exotic / erotic / esoteric*) _____ field, understood by only a few scientists and specialists.

6. It's the little (*everyday / every day*) _____ problems that make this job so difficult, not the big emergencies.

7. The (*famous / notorious*) _____ gangster Al Capone was brought to his knees by the IRS, not the FBI.

8. We did not anticipate that such an (*extended / extensive*) _____ period of time would be required to do the research.

9. Frederica said that she was going to invite (*everyone / every one*) _____ who was (*anyone / any one*) _____.

10. These birds are quite (*exotic / erotic / esoteric*) _____; they come from unexplored islands off the west coast of Africa.

11. The accused could only (*evoke / invoke*) _____ the name of his beloved father to defend himself.

12. These clubs were (*especially / specially*) _____ designed for left-handed golfers.

13. It is not (*equable / equitable*) _____ to pay women less money for the same work than men are paid.

14. You must be quite (*explicit / implicit*) _____ when you explain the rules of the contest.

15. Many people do not know that the west of Ireland has such an (*equable / equitable*) _____ climate that palm trees grow there.

16. That alarm goes off (*everyday / every day*) _____ at noon and then again at midnight.

17. Thomas Edison is probably the most (*famous* / *notorious*) _____ American inventor.

18. Not frequently, but (*ever so often* / *every so often*) _____, Bertram drinks a glass of wine with dinner.

19. Her indication of consent was (*explicit* / *implicit*) _____ rather than clearly stated.

20. Margaret has become an (*exceptional* / *exceptionable*) _____ student; she is at the top of her class.

21. The film was (*exotic* / *erotic* / *esoteric*) _____ but not hardcore—i.e., it was sexy but not dirty.

22. Everyone had an (*excessively* / *exceedingly*) _____ good time at the annual church picnic.

23. The smaller children (*especially* / *specially*) _____ liked the clowns and the elephants.

24. Such (*false* / *fallacious*) _____ conclusions are based upon bad logic and wrongheaded reasoning.

25. The instructor's powerful ability to tell a story would sometimes (*evoke* / *invoke*)

_____ tears from the eyes of the students.

26. Professor Nebulous wears his (*everyday* / *every day*) _____ hair to school but not to church.

27. Almost (*everyone* / *every one*) _____ who attended the town meeting favored the building of a new high school.

28. I have had an (*exhaustive* / *exhausting*) _____ day trying to discover why we appear to have a cash flow problem.

29. These outfits, although nice enough, are (*exceedingly* / *excessively*) _____ priced.

30. Four years at a university will very likely result in (*extended* / *extensive*) _____

_____ changes in the way you think and the way you view the world.

Important Distinctions (11)

farther/further: *Farther* refers to distance. (Emeline lives *farther* from campus than she used to.) *Further* means "more," "additional," or "moreover." (This matter requires *further* study. Tim's advisor *further* said that Tim needed to reduce his social obligations.) As a verb, *further* means "to promote" or "to forward." (The committee will do anything within reason to *further* the cause of student rights.)

few/a few: Used alone, *few* has negative implications. (After the televised interview, the governor had *few* supporters.) The phrase *a few* is neutral or positive. (We still have *a few* tricks up our sleeve. Your instructors have said quite *a few* nice things about you.)

fewer/less: *Fewer* refers to individual countable items. (*Fewer* season tickets for the hockey team were sold this year than last.) *Less* refers to general amounts. (Americans eat *less* meat than they used to.)

flaunt/flout: To *flaunt* means "to show off defiantly." (The prisoners *flaunted* their guilt in front of the television cameras.) To *flout* means "to mock," "to scoff," or "to jeer." (The counselor said that only foolish children *flout* their parents' advice.)

forcible/forceful: *Forcible* is used to mean "involving the use of physical force or violence." (To rule by *forcible* means is the strategy of a tyrant.) *Forceful* is used to describe anything that is powerful, vigorous, effective, or cogent. (Such *forceful* arguments will not be easy to counter.)

foreword/preface: A *preface* is an introduction to a book written by the author of the book, whereas a *foreword* is written by someone other than the author—e.g., someone more famous and authoritative than the author of the book. (Publishers often employ well-known individuals to compose *forewords* for books written by young authors not yet known to the reading public.)

formally/formerly: *Formally* means "according to established forms, conventions, and rules." *Formerly* means "at an earlier time." (*Formerly*, these proceedings were conducted more *formally*.)

founder/flounder: To *founder* means "to fill with water and sink," "to stumble and fall," "to become stuck in soft mud," or "to collapse and fail." (The entire fleet *foundered* in rough waters off the Irish coast. If the family business *founders*, I shall go to live in Europe.) To *flounder* means "to move clumsily, as by stumbling about" or "to proceed confusedly and disjointedly." (The speaker *floundered* through his speech, lurching from topic to topic and never connecting one to another.)

funeral/funereal: A *funeral* is the rites and ceremonies connected with burial. (The *funeral* procession slowly made its way from the church to the cemetery.) *Funereal* means "like a

225

funeral"—i.e., "gloomy," "sad," "solemn," "dismal," or "doleful." (Heather wore a *funereal* face when she went to try to persuade her teacher to raise her grade.)

gamut/gauntlet: *Gamut* means "the entire range of anything." (Our conversation ran the *gamut,* beginning with the weather and ending with a scheme to overthrow the government.) A *gauntlet* is a heavy (protective) glove, as that worn by a medieval knight, or two lines of people who beat others forced to run between them. (Life itself can be viewed as something of a *gauntlet* that no one runs without sustaining some injury.)

gaseous/gassy: *Gaseous* means "in the form of gas." (Steam is water in a *gaseous* state caused by heat.) *Gassy* means "full of gas." (Garlic bread and chili in combination can have a *gassy* effect on the strongest digestive system.)

genus/genius: A *genus* is any group of related things, such as plants or animals. (In recent years a new *genus* of college student has evolved; it wants to be educated, or at least degreed, but doesn't want to expand its existing puddle of knowledge.) A *genius* is a person with superior mental powers. (Meg isn't really a *genius;* she simply works very hard.)

glance/glimpse: To *glance* is to look quickly. (I happened to *glance* out the window just as the two cars collided.) What one may see when one has a quick look is a *glimpse,* or "a fleeting view." (We caught only a *glimpse* of the satellite through the clouds.)

good/well: *Good* is an adjective. (Have a *good* time over term break.) *Well* is an adverb. (Janet performs *well* under pressure.) *Well* can also be used to refer to health. (Gilbert hasn't felt *well* all winter.)

SENTENCE FILL-IN

1. Dr. Judson was (*formally / formerly*) _____ a professor at the University of London in England.

2. Someone made a (*forcible / forceful*) _____ entry into the campus computer lab and stole a lot of equipment.

3. The young attorney (*foundered / floundered*) _____ through his opening argument, leaving everyone in the courtroom confused.

4. Bernard will himself admit that he has never been very (*good / well*) _____

    _____ at meeting new people.

5. If you want a (*foreword / preface*) _____ for the book you have written, you will have to write it yourself.

6. I (*glanced / glimpsed*) _____ up from my desk to see my old chum from high school enter the library.

7. (*Farther / Further*) _____ investigation of the matter proved all the allegations but one to be false.

8. Last semester Algernon's grades ran the (*gamut / gauntlet*) _____ from "A" to "F."

9. I suppose we're looking for a (*genus / genius*) _____ who is willing to work for the wages of a moron.

10. We all agreed that we had never before attended a (*funeral / funereal*) _____

    _____ that we enjoyed so much.

11. Your manuscript contained (*fewer / less*) _____ errors than the editor had expected.

12. Suddenly I realized that I had a (*gaseous / gassy*) _____ feeling in the pit of my stomach.

13. Sometimes the very rich seem to (*flaunt / flout*) _____ their wealth—e.g., by buying $100,000 automobiles.

14. Our employer acknowledged that Bertram and I worked (*good / well*) _____

    _____ together.

15. Because (*few / a few*) _____ students are still interested in acquiring a rounded education, many professors in their fifties are taking early retirement.

16. When among their peers, college students sometimes (*flaunt / flout*)_____ the religious beliefs of their parents.

17. While it rained at the lake, we occupied ourselves playing the (*genus / genius*)

_____ edition of Trivial Pursuit.

18. Going to college is a bit like running a (*gamut / gauntlet*) _____ with one's professors on one side and one's fellow students on the other side.

19. Elsa did (*good / well*) _____ on her first writing assignment in advanced composition.

20. I have been asked to write the (*foreword / preface*) _____ to a book written by one of my colleagues.

21. It was on just such a gloomy (*funeral / funereal*) _____ afternoon that Clay realized the innocence of his youth was gone.

22. Professor Resonant is one of the most (*forcible / forceful*) _____ and persuasive speakers I have ever heard.

23. Michelle has moved (*farther / further*) _____ away from home than any other member of the family.

24. We haven't given up; we have (*few / a few*) _____ logs yet to saw.

25. A stinking (*gaseous / gassy*) _____ mist drifted across the field, and then everyone started coughing.

26. The federal government is spending (*fewer / less*) _____ money on social programs than it did fifteen years ago.

27. What can be done to (*further / farther*) _____ the cause of lost causes?

28. Few people at the banquet were as (*formally / formerly*) _____ dressed as was the head football coach.

29. In my dream I caught just a (*glance / glimpse*) _____ of what I must have looked like as a child.

30. Alas, the family business has (*foundered / floundered*) _____ during the most recent recession and may well never recover.

Important Distinctions (12)

gourmet/gourmand: A *gourmet* is an expert in matters of food and drink. (No real *gourmet* would recommend leaving the skin on fried chicken.) A *gourmand* is an enthusiastic eater of large quantities of food. By implication, the *gourmand* also possesses a fair degree of knowledge about food. (A true *gourmand* can pass hours consuming a multicourse feast.)

grateful/gratified: *Grateful* is an adjective meaning "appreciative," "thankful," or "feeling gratitude." (The immigrants were *grateful* for the opportunities provided them.) *Gratified* is the past tense and past participle form of *gratify* and means "pleased," "satisfied," "indulged," or "humored." (We were *gratified* to learn that we were no longer judged uncivilized by our host.)

habitable/inhabitable: *Habitable* means "suitable (as a dwelling) to be lived in." (The house where I lived as a child now hardly seems *habitable*.) *Inhabitable* also means "suitable (or fit) to be lived in." But the word is used in reference to geographical areas, countries, or climates. (Much of Alaska is quite *inhabitable,* even by people accustomed to the amenities of a "softer" life.) The antonym of *habitable* is phrasal—*not habitable,* whereas the antonym of *inhabitable* is *uninhabitable.*

half/have: *Half* is one of two equal parts, but it also means "partly." (Is the glass *half* empty or *half* full?) To *have* is to possess, to control, to hold, to experience, and so on. (Alas, we no longer *have* more time than money.)

hanged/hung: Although both *hanged* and *hung* are past-tense forms of the verb *hang, hanged* refers to an execution. (The prisoner was to be *hanged* at sunrise. Thousands of bats *hung* from the trees like strange ornaments.)

hate/dislike: *Hate* is a much stronger word than *dislike* and thus should be used with some restraint. (I *dislike* people who use vulgar language in public places, but I *hate* the bean-counter mind-set that judges everything by its cost-effectiveness.)

he/him/himself: *He* is the nominative form of the personal pronoun and is used as a subject, subject complement, or an appositive of either. (*He* won the contest. The winner was *he.* They—Jan, Fran, and *he*—were the winners. They were the winners, Jan, Fran, and *he.*) *Him* is the objective form of the personal pronoun and is used in all object positions. (The principal sent *him* home. The teacher gave *him* an apple. This assignment wasn't for *him.* Confronting *him* took some courage. Exercise will make *him* strong in no time.) *Himself* is both the reflexive and intensive form of the personal pronoun. (Poor Harris shot *himself* in the foot; thus, he *himself* is responsible for the injury.)

healthy/healthful: *Healthy* means "possessing health," "full of health," "well," "vigorous," "sound," and so on. It is used to refer to people and animals, and sometimes institutions. (In

229

spite of a limited diet, the villagers seemed *healthy* enough.) *Healthful* means "contributing to good health." It is used in references to places, conditions, and foods. (A *healthful* diet and a *healthful* exercise program can help one become a *healthy* person.)

historic/historical: Although these two words are closely related, the first should be used to mean "important," "renowned," "influential," or "history-making." (The first moon landing, on July 20, 1969, was an *historic* event.) *Historical* means "established by history rather than by legend or fiction," "factual," "chronological," or "authentic." (The film presented an *historical* account of the early development of Williamsburg.)

house/home: A *house* is a (small) building where a person or persons—a family—live. (A new *house* was being built in the middle of the old baseball field.) A *home* is a house and all the family things that occur in and around the dwelling. (After two years adrift in the jungles of Southeast Asia, Clifton placed a greater value on hearth and *home*.)

human/humane: A *human* is a person. As an adjective, *human* means "typical of human-kind." *Humane* is an adjective meaning "having the best of human qualities." (Constance maintains that every *human* should strive to make *human* behavior more *humane*.)

hypercritical/hypocritical: *Hypercritical* means "too critical" or "overly critical." (Claudia is *hypercritical* of everything her sisters do.) *Hypocritical* means "insincere, in the sense of pretending to be virtuous when one is not." (Being *hypocritical* is an exercise in the pot calling the kettle black.)

SENTENCE FILL-IN

1. In March, Nigel and Erica were no more than (*half / have*) _____ certain that they were going to Iceland.

2. Such (*hypercritical / hypocritical*) _____ remarks are a bit like a hippo calling a rhino ugly.

3. There had always been a strong bond between Felicia and (*he / him / himself*) _____ _____, but no romance.

4. Charles Lindbergh's (*historic / historical*) _____ flight in 1927 from New York to Paris caught the attention of the civilized world.

5. Would you call an assisted suicide a (*human / humane*) _____ act?

6. The artist (*hanged / hung*) _____ the paintings on the wall and waited for everyone's reaction.

7. (*Hypercritical / Hypocritical*) _____ parents run the risk of destroying the self-confidence of their children.

8. There hasn't been a (*home / house*) _____ for sale in the neighborhood in many years.

9. Burgess said he was (*grateful / gratified*) _____ that his injuries were minor.

10. (*He / Him / Himself*) _____ and Fran spent the afternoon riding their dirt bikes on the dunes.

11. A (*healthy / healthful*) _____ diet must include as broad a variety of foods as possible.

12. The (*human / humane*) _____ body is nothing short of a universe of muscles, bones, and nerves.

13. Professor Snide was of course (*grateful / gratified*) _____ that his work was at last being recognized.

14. It would cost a small fortune to make this old house (*habitable / inhabitable*) _____ _____ again.

15. In some instances, a fine line separates the (*gourmet / gourmand*) _____ and the pig-out artist.

16. Most people (*dislike / hate*) _____ having to stand in line at the super-market checkout.

17. After the (*historic / historical*) _____ landing on the moon in 1969, most of the other space missions have seemed anticlimactic.

18. At the present time, it appears that the rest of our solar system is (*not habitable /
uninhabitable*) _____.

19. The family was (*grateful / gratified*) _____ to learn that Hilary had been
accepted at Harvard Medical School.

20. Professor Florid is (*hypercritical / hypocritical*) _____ when she critiques
student papers; she redlines every little peccadillo.

21. As strange as it may appear, the Johnsons have decided to trade (*homes / houses*)

_____ with the Goads.

22. In the Wild West, cattle rustlers were sometimes (*hanged / hung*) _____
from a convenient tree.

23. Would it be possible for us to (*half / have*) _____ you back at some time in
the near future?

24. Do we now have a (*healthy / healthful*) _____ economy, or are we just
between recessions?

25. The (*human / humane*) _____ thing to do would be to put the suffering
animal out of its misery.

26. Crispin is indeed a (*healthy / healthful*) _____ young man; he can run a
marathon and have energy enough left to wash and dry the dinner dishes.

27. After several weeks on the road, DeWitt was looking forward to a (*house / home*)

_____ cooked meal.

28. Many times a (*gourmet / gourmand*) _____ seems to take more pleasure in
preparing food than in eating it.

29. (*Historic / Historical*) _____ novels combine a little history and a lot of
fiction to entertain the reader.

30. We were so hungry that we didn't care whether or not the food was only (*have / half*)

_____ cooked.

Important Distinctions (13)

I/me/myself: *I* is the nominative form of the personal pronoun and is used as a subject, subject complement, or an appositive of either. (*I* was at the door. It was *I* at the door. We—Jan, Fran, and *I*—were at the door. We were the winners, Jan, Fran, and *I*.) *Me* is the objective form of the personal pronoun and is used in all object positions. (The principal sent *me* home. The teacher gave *me* an apple. This assignment wasn't for *me*. Her teasing *me* was unkind. Exercise will make *me* strong in no time.) *Myself* is both the reflexive and intensive form of the personal pronoun. (Alas, I shot *myself* in the foot; thus, I *myself* am responsible for my injury.)

ignorant/stupid: *Ignorant* means "uneducated" or "inexperienced." (Although the peasants were *ignorant* of life outside their village, they were quite clever and resourceful.) *Stupid* means "unable to learn" or "slow-witted." (It is unrealistic to expect a *stupid* person to become a brain surgeon.)

illegible/unreadable: Handwriting that is difficult or impossible to read is *illegible*, whereas a perfectly printed book that is boring, dull, tedious, trite, and sleep-causing is *unreadable*. An old book (or a manuscript) with faded print might also be called *unreadable*. (Although your handwriting is not *illegible*, what you have said is *unreadable*; I can make nothing of it.)

illustrative/illustrious: *Illustrative* means "serving as an example." (So far as I can tell, the incident is *illustrative* of nothing.) *Illustrious* means "distinguished," "eminent," "famous," or "outstanding." (Katherine Hepburn had a long and *illustrious* career as a motion picture actress.)

imaginary/imaginative: *Imaginary* means "existing only in the mind," "not real," or "fancied." (Children sometimes create *imaginary* worlds for themselves.) *Imaginative* means "showing imagination" or "creative." (Few people are *imaginative* enough to dream up so many *imaginary* characters.)

immature/premature: *Immature* means "not mature," "not developed," "not complete," or "childish." (These trees are too *immature* to transplant.) *Premature* means "too soon," "before the proper time," "too early," or "not yet ready." (The announcement of a complete victory turned out to be *premature*.)

imply/infer: To *imply* means "to suggest." (The speakers meant to *imply* that the senator wasn't doing a good job.) To *infer* means "to draw a conclusion." (One can *infer* from the speakers' remarks that they don't like the senator's policies.)

in/into: *In* indicates being inside of or enclosed within something. (There is a lynx living *in* the old barn.) *Into* indicates movement from the outside to the inside. (Burgess went *into* the barn to look for a rake.)

inability/disability: An *inability* is a fundamental lack of ability, capacity, or power. (Your *inability* to concentrate on your course work is hurting your grades.) A *disability* is a defect, often caused by injury. (The loss of a toe can be a permanent *disability* for a runner. Although humans have an *inability* to fly, the condition is not considered a *disability*.)

incapable/unable: *Incapable* is followed by *of* and usually refers to some long-standing or permanent inability. (Humans are *incapable* of hearing some of the sounds that dogs hear.) *Unable* is followed by *to* and usually refers to a temporary incapacity. (Early in the season, I was *unable* to remember all the plays and keep up with the game at the same time.)

incredible/incredulous: *Incredible* means "unbelievable." (Rufus told another of his *incredible* stories.) *Incredulous* means "skeptical," "doubting," or "unbelieving." (From your *incredulous* expression, I can see that you do not believe what you have been told.)

ingenious/ingenuous: *Ingenious* means "clever," "resourceful," or "inventive." (This *ingenious* little device may replace an entire occupation.) *Ingenuous* means "simple," "artless," "naive," "frank," or "sincere." (Such an *ingenuous* reaction smacked of a child's innocence.) An antonym of this word quite popular at the moment is *disingenuous*, which means "not frank or sincere but pretending to be so." (I think your English professor is being *disingenuous* when he pretends to have forgotten what it is like to be a student.)

inhuman/unhuman: *Inhuman* means "cruel," "unfeeling," "brutal," "heartless," or "without normal human kindness and compassion." (Hector often displays an *inhuman* disregard for the feelings of others.) *Unhuman* means "not human" or "supernatural." (It is *unhuman* how Giles can work at the computer for days at a time.)

SENTENCE FILL-IN

1. Are you (*implying / inferring*) _____ by what you have said that the United States is now a nation past its prime?

2. From working in a noisy factory for many years, Meredith has a severe hearing (*inability / disability*) _____.

3. Just between you and (*I / me / myself*) _____, I think this instructor is running on empty.

4. The governor-elect's (*ingenious / ingenuous*) _____ handling of such an insignificant situation suggested political inexperience.

5. It is a pity and a shame that such a long and (*illustrative / illustrious*) _____ career can be ruined by a single allegation of misconduct.

6. Do you realize that the time zones are (*imaginary / imaginative*) _____ ? They exist only in our minds.

7. Capable people are sometimes (*ignorant of / stupid about*) _____ events occurring distant from themselves.

8. These creatures are (*inhuman / unhuman*) _____; they come from outer space.

9. I would say that your handwriting is (*illegible / unreadable*) _____; I didn't even recognize it as handwriting.

10. Dudley is (*immature / premature*) _____; he insists that the dormitory hall director tuck him into bed each night.

11. Thaddeus can no longer fit (*in / into*) _____ his high school cheerleading costume.

12. A hundred times I have told (*I / me / myself*) _____ not to panic when the examination begins.

13. These people will always be (*incapable of / unable to*) _____ do(ing) the job they were hired to do; it is beyond their ability.

14. The announcement was a bit (*immature / premature*) _____; we haven't actually accomplished nuclear fusion in a bottle.

15. To most Americans who remember World War II, the recent collapse of the Soviet Union was an (*incredible / incredulous*) _____ event.

16. This little computer is so (*ingenious / ingenuous*) _____ that it can read the operator's mind.

17. Although my father listened to the neighbor's crazy story, the (*incredible / incredulous*)

_____ expression on his face told me that he didn't believe a word of it.

18. Viola was (*incapable of / unable to*) _____ play(ing) because she had pulled a hamstring the day before the game.

19. I may have cost (*I / me / myself*) _____ another chance to stay in school by giving the dean a piece of my mind.

20. Just because you have had one bad experience, you need not (*imply / infer*) _____

_____ that all chemistry teachers are heartless martinets.

21. Cadwallader's (*inability / disability*) _____ to see a project through to completion cost him his job.

22. Alas, there are those who are too (*ignorant / stupid*) _____ to be taught very much, even if it is considered bad manners to mention the fact.

23. My wife and (*I / me / myself*) _____ have been married—to someone or other—almost all of our lives.

24. Alas, my friend's new book is mostly silly, (*illegible / unreadable*) _____ nonsense, no doubt the product of burnout.

25. The demented fool walked straight (*in / into*) _____ the path of a speeding dune buggy.

26. What happened to this fellow is (*illustrative / illustrious*) _____ of what the press can do to a candidate if it wants to.

27. Cars look so much alike today because there are too few (*imaginary / imaginative*)

_____ designers.

28. The fellow's account of the incident was so (*ingenious / ingenuous*) _____ that he practically indicted himself.

29. Several of your friends and (*I / me / myself*) _____ decided to look for another place to stay.

30. It is (*inhuman / unhuman*) _____ to throw these old people out of their dwellings.

Important Distinctions (14)

initiate/instigate: To *initiate* means "to introduce," "to originate," "to start," "to set going." (Many people think that the government should *initiate* a national health system.) To *instigate* means "to incite," "to stir up," "to foment," or "to urge on." (How does one *instigate* a quarrel between the president of the university and the board of regents?)

insidious/invidious: *Insidious* means "working in a slow and unnoticed manner," "crafty," "sly," "wily," or "tricky." (The HIV virus works in an *insidious* manner on its victims.) *Invidious* means "exciting ill will or envy," "giving offense," or "promoting resentment." (The speaker's use of *invidious* comparisons was clearly intended to annoy the audience.)

integrate/segregate: These words are antonyms, opposites. To *integrate* means "to make whole by bringing all parts together," "to blend," or "to incorporate." (An *integrated* curriculum will include courses from a variety of disciplines.) To *segregate* means "to separate from others," "to set apart," or "to isolate." (Some private schools still *segregate* male and female students.)

inter-/intra-: *Inter-* is a prefix meaning "between," "among," "mutually," or "together." (*Intercollegiate* athletics have become big business.) *Intra-* is a prefix meaning "within" or "inside." (*Intramural* club sports have been allowed to languish on many college campuses.)

invigorating/enervating: *Invigorating* means "enlivening" or "animating." (A brisk walk through the woods at daybreak is an *invigorating* activity.) *Enervating* means "sapping the strength of," "weakening," "devitalizing," or "debilitating." (Endless days of sedentary studying can have an *enervating* effect on a young spirit.)

judicial/judicious: *Judicial* should be used to refer to judges, courts of law, and justice in general. (*Judicial* robes are no longer used in all courts.) *Judicious* means "showing sound judgment," "wise," "careful," or "sensible." (Through a *judicious* use of her time, Miriam was able to graduate a term early.)

ketchup/catsup/catchup: Although all three forms of this word may be found almost anywhere, careful usage prefers the first, *ketchup,* which derives from the Malay word *kechap,* a spiced fish sauce.

laboratory/lavatory: A *laboratory* is a room or building for scientific experimentation. (Boris left his bomb in the *laboratory* over Christmas break.) A *lavatory* is a bathroom or toilet. (Once again, there was no soap in the *lavatory.*)

later/latter: *Later* means "farther ahead in time." (The concert is planned for *later* in the evening.) *Latter* means "the more recent or last named of two items or events." (The *latter* proposal was better than the former.)

laudable/laudatory: *Laudable* means "praiseworthy" or "commendable." (Your putting yourself through college at no expense to your parents is indeed *laudable.*) *Laudatory* means "expressing praise," "containing praise," or "extolling." (As usual, the president directed his *laudatory* remarks at the wrong people.)

lay/lie: *Lay* is a transitive verb—i.e., it is followed by an object—meaning "to place" or "to put." Its principal parts are *lay, laid, laid,* and *laying.* (Please *lay* your books on the table. Don't try to *lay* the blame on someone else.) *Lie* is an intransitive verb—i.e., it is not followed by an object—meaning "to recline" or "to be situated." Its principal parts are *lie, lay, lain,* and *lying.* (I often *lie* awake at night. Last night, I *lay* awake until three o'clock.)

learn/teach: To *learn* means "to acquire knowledge or skill." (Most people can *learn* to play the piano.) To *teach* means "to instruct." (Will you *teach* me to play the piano?)

leave alone/let alone: Only when accompanied by *alone* can *leave* and *let* be interchangeable. (If you don't *leave* [or *let*] Isabel *alone,* she will never finish her work.) However, *let alone,* meaning "or even" or "much less," cannot be replaced by *leave alone.* (Fritz can't ride a bike, *let alone* [not *leave alone*] a unicycle.) Furthermore, *leave* by itself cannot be a substitute for *let* by itself, meaning "to allow," "to permit," or "to cause." (Vivian's parents will probably *let* [not *leave*] her go to Florida.)

SENTENCE FILL-IN

1. Please don't (*lay / lie*) _____ anything on the table until the varnish has dried.

2. The speech about you was entirely (*laudable / laudatory*) _____; you were praised to high heaven.

3. During the (*intermission / intramission*) _____ we ran into a few friends from the old neighborhood.

4. I can't program my VCR, (*let alone, leave alone*) _____ the personal computer.

5. Having to work under chronically stressful conditions can eventually have an (*invigorating / enervating*) _____ effect on one.

6. Sal was (*initiated / instigated*) _____ into the wonders of ballroom dancing by his next-door neighbor.

7. As far as we could tell, the (*later / latter*) _____ offer was very little different from the former.

8. All of the (*laboratory / lavatory*) _____ animals are protected from mis-treatment by a variety of federal statutes.

9. The patient is being maintained by several (*intervenous / intravenous*) _____ solutions.

10. We were (*laying / lying*) _____ on the chaises lounges in the backyard when the spaceship landed.

11. Many people think that our (*judicial / judicious*) _____ system has become quite self-serving in recent times.

12. Such (*insidious / invidious*) _____ remarks are clearly intended to pro-mote resentment, not provide reassurance.

13. It was not very (*judicial / judicious*) _____ of the dean to publicly abuse the most revered professor at the university.

14. I am looking for someone who can (*learn / teach*) _____ me to snorkel.

15. It has become very difficult for the Democratic party to (*integrate / segregate*) _____ the ideas of so many constituencies into a single and consistent political philosophy.

16. When Vernon was in elementary school, his parents would never (*let / leave*) _____

    _____ him go to the movies alone.

17. The students are urging the university to invest more money in (*intramural / intermural*)

    _____ activities of all types.

18. Only well-motivated people seem to be able to (*learn / teach*) _____
    themselves a foreign language.

19. Just how (*laudable / laudatory*) _____ a goal is it to want to legalize a vice
    for the single purpose of generating revenue?

20. In spite of all efforts to the contrary, in large cities many ethnic groups continue to

    (*integrate / segregate*) _____ themselves from one another.

21. According to the forecast, the weather should improve (*later / latter*) _____

    _____ in the week.

22. Through a (*judicial / judicious*) _____ use of her resources, Estelle has
    been able to build a successful business.

23. Alzheimer's is an (*insidious / invidious*) _____ disease, slowly destroying
    a person's mind and personality.

24. More than a few times I have (*laid / lain*) _____ awake all night thinking
    about the future and what it would bring.

25. A cold shower in the morning can provide an (*invigorating / enervating*) _____

    _____ beginning to the day.

26. Cynthia was greatly embarrassed when she went into the boys' (*laboratory / lavatory*)

    _____ by mistake.

27. From such an (*internecine / intranecine*) _____ struggle as this, there will
    be no winners.

28. You will not have to (*initiate / instigate*) _____ a disagreement between
    these two factions; they will be more than willing to do it on their own.

29. Last Thursday, Burgess (*lay / laid*) _____ his wallet right there on the
    dresser; everyone saw him do it.

30. Gisele insists that she wants both (*ketchup / catsup / catchup*) _____ and
    mustard on her hot dogs.

Important Distinctions (15)

lectern/podium: A *lectern* is a stand that holds the notes for, or text of, a lecturer's speech. (The speaker towered like a giant over the *lectern*.) A *podium* is the raised platform on which a speaker stands to face an audience. (The speaker left the *podium* when the audience began questioning his remarks.)

lend/loan: Careful writers distinguish between *lend,* which is a verb, and *loan,* which is a noun. We *lend* money, and the money we *lend* is a *loan.* The past tense and past participle forms of *lend* are *lent.* (How often have you *lent* [not *loaned*] someone money and never gotten it back?)

liable/apt/likely: *Liable* means "legally bound or obligated." (You are *liable* for the damages you caused.) *Apt* means "suitable," "appropriate," or "quick to learn." (What an *apt* response the mayor gave to the question. My roommate is an *apt* student.) *Likely* means "probable." (The volcano is *likely* to erupt at any moment.)

libel/slander: *Libel* is written (or published) material that damages another's good name through the use of false and malicious statements. *Slander,* by contrast, is an oral statement of falsehoods that damages another's reputation. (Although your opponents are attacking you with both pen and tongue, I can see no evidence of either *libel* or *slander.*)

lifelong/livelong: *Lifelong* means "continuing throughout one's life." (Konrad has been a *lifelong* Democrat.) *Livelong* means "tediously long in passing," "whole," or "entire." (We spent a *livelong* summer taking up crossties.)

like/as: When you have an apparent choice between *like* and *as,* use *like* before one or more naming words not part of an expressed dependent clause. (*Like* a giant toad, Ted hopped all about the room. The day looked *like* midwinter.) Use *as* (*as if, as though*) before a dependent clause. (Just *as* [not *like*] everyone thought, your motion was adopted. The child sang *as if* [not *like*] her heart were broken. You talk *as though* [not *like*] you have inside information.)

limp/limpid: *Limp* means "lacking firmness," "flaccid," "tired," or "weak." (Nothing is less reassuring than a *limp* handshake.) *Limpid* means "clear," "transparent," "simple," or "serene." (Her eyes were *limpid* orbs of innocence.)

loath/loathe: *Loath* is an adjective meaning "not willing," "reluctant," or "disinclined." (The children were *loath* to admit where they had been playing.) *Loathe* is a verb meaning "to dislike intensely," "to detest," or "to hate." (Don't you just *loathe* public displays of bad manners?)

lose/loose: *Lose* is a verb meaning "to mislay." (Did you *lose* your wallet again?) *Loose* is an adjective meaning "not tight." (The bumpers on my car rattle because they are *loose.*) *Loose*

241

can also function as a verb meaning "to set free." (At the call to the hunt, we shall *loose* the dogs and be on our way.)

lunch/luncheon: A *lunch* is a light meal eaten at midday. (Fewer and fewer students are eating *lunch* in the student union.) A *luncheon* is a more formal *lunch* scheduled for a special occasion and may include awards or short speeches. (The annual *luncheon* of the Chaos Committee is always held on April Fools' Day.)

lustful/lusty: *Lustful* means "lecherous" or "sexually desirous." (*Lustful* glances do not always please those at whom they are directed.) *Lusty* means "vigorous," "robust," "strong," "hearty," "sturdy," and so on. (It was a crew of *lusty* lads that rebuilt the farmer's barn.)

majority/plurality: A *majority* is more than half, as of those voting in an election. (Although those people who did not vote constituted a *majority,* they elected no one to office.) A *plurality* is the difference between the votes received by the person getting the greatest number and the person getting the second greatest number, this occurring only when there are more than two candidates and no one receives a majority of all votes cast. (Although he received only forty percent of the vote, Ernest won the election by a *plurality* of three hundred votes over the second-place candidate.)

malign/impugn: To *malign* is to speak evil of or to slander. (You *malign* only yourself by speaking evil of such a revered person.) To *impugn* is to call into question, to challenge as false, or to attack with words and arguments. (Quite imperiously, the president of the university *impugned* the instructor's right to criticize anything about the administration.)

man: As a matter of discretion, avoid using *man* (or any of its variations or combinations) as a generic designator for all human beings. *Postmen* can just as easily be *letter carriers,* *firemen* can be *fire fighters,* and *mankind* can be *humankind.* However, try to avoid silly-sounding words like *fisherperson, flagger,* or *gamestership.*

SENTENCE FILL-IN

1. Cadwallader's clothes are (*loose / lose*) _____ because he has lost so much weight.

2. Our pastor has been charged with (*libel / slander*) _____ as a result of statements he made during a sermon.

3. Please tell us the story exactly (*like / as*) _____ it happened; don't change a thing.

4. Baxter received seventy percent of the votes cast and thus won the election by a (*majority / plurality*) _____.

5. It will take a (*lustful / lusty*) _____ crew of hard workers to sail this ship around the world.

6. In spite of declarations to the contrary, the airline is (*liable / apt / likely*) _____ for all lost or damaged luggage.

7. As I grow older, I am often (*loath / loathe*) _____ to leave the comfortable confines of my own nest.

8. The speaker tumbled off the (*lectern / podium*) _____ and broke more than his train of thought.

9. Few people know that it has been Wyatt's (*lifelong / livelong*) _____ ambition to coach a women's volleyball team.

10. Each fall the faculty association holds its annual (*lunch / luncheon*) _____ to formally welcome new faculty members.

11. It isn't easy to (*lose / loose*) _____ something as conspicuous as a fire truck.

12. The poor child ate (*like / as if*) _____ he hadn't eaten in weeks.

13. From the front yard at the cottage we could watch the (*fishermen / fisherpersons / fishers / anglers*) _____ enjoying themselves on the lake.

14. On a night as (*limp / limpid*) _____ as this, there seem to be more stars than darkness.

15. If you set out to (*malign / impugn*) _____ another's good reputation, you should expect a little slander in return.

16. If you say something like that on television, you are (*liable / apt / likely*) _____ to hear from a number of viewers.

17. The speaker was so short that we could hardly seem him above the (*lectern / podium*)

_____ .

18. We (*maligned / impugned*) _____ the witness's testimony because it was false, and we knew we could prove as much.

19. (*Lose / Loose*) _____ the evil creatures, and we can watch them run.

20. I absolutely (*loath / loathe*) _____ these people who live for one cause and will never give it a rest.

21. The youthful candidate for mayor wasn't particularly (*liable / apt / likely*) _____

_____ at dealing with hecklers.

22. Elspeth was charged with (*libel / slander*) _____ as a result of statements she made in a letter to the editor of the local newspaper.

23. Although Nadine received fewer than half of the votes cast for president of her sorority,

she won the election by a comfortable (*majority / plurality*) _____ over the closest candidate.

24. Unfortunately, the (*garbage men / garbage collectors / garbagepersons*) _____

_____ arrived more than an hour late.

25. For (*lunch / luncheon*) _____ , I often have fish and chips at the student cafeteria.

26. If I hadn't (*lent / loaned*) _____ my nephew the money to move to the West Coast, he would still be living with me.

27. The crew spent a (*lifelong / livelong*) _____ month trying to move the huge Victorian house.

28. It was with (*lustful / lusty*) _____ eyes that King Henry VIII looked at his new queen.

29. Alas, Ross dances (*like / as*) _____ an elephant with four left feet.

30. After eight hours of crushing rocks, Oswald was as (*limp / limpid*) _____ as a damp rag.

Important Distinctions (16)

marital/martial: *Marital* means "related to marriage." (The couple took their *marital* vows in the chapel.) *Martial* means "suitable for war" or "eager to fight." (Proficiency at *martial* arts has become almost a cult among segments of the population.)

maybe/may be: *Maybe* is an adverb meaning "perhaps." (*Maybe* the school can do better against Division III teams.) *May be* is a verb phrase. (The suspect's story *may be* true and it *may* not *be* true.)

media/medium: *Media* is the plural of *medium,* which means "a means of transmitting information." (The news *media* include newspapers, radio, television, and magazines. Television is now our dominant entertainment *medium.*) When *medium* refers to a person who claims to be able to communicate with the dead, the plural is *mediums.* (My uncle employed a pair of *mediums* to get in touch with his late wife.)

median/meridian: The *median* is the middle number in a series. It is also a strip of land separating opposing lanes of a divided highway. (All of the damaged cars came to rest in the *median.*) A *meridian* is an imaginary circle passing through any point on the surface of the earth and through both poles. *Meridian* also means "highest point." (The *prime meridian* passes through Greenwich, England. The *meridian* of life for most people occurs between the ages of twenty-five to forty-five, when we are healthy and full of vigor.)

monologue/dialogue: A *monologue* is a speech by a single person. The term is often used disparagingly to refer to the performance of a person who insists on talking long without interruption. (Sidney delivered his daily *monologue* on the evils of communism.) A *dialogue* is a conversation between two or more parties. *Dialogue* is also popularly used to mean "discussion as a tool to achieving harmony and understanding." (The author is better at *dialogue* than narration.) Avoid using *dialogue* as a verb. (These people must be made to *talk* [not *dialogue*].)

morale/moral: *Morale* means "mental condition." (The patient's *morale* was high.) *Moral,* as an adjective, means "ethical." (The physician faced a *moral* dilemma.) As a noun, *moral* means "an ethical point or lesson." (The *moral* of the story was difficult to explain.)

morbid/sordid: *Morbid* means "unhealthy," "diseased," "gruesome," "grim," "grisly," or "pathological." (Let's try not to dwell on the *morbid* details of the killer's activities.) *Sordid* means "dirty," "filthy," "mean," "low," "base," "wretched," or "selfish." (Is this the *sordid* shack where the children grew up?)

most/almost: *Most* is an adjective meaning "the greatest number or part of." (Natalie spends *most* weekends in the library.) *Almost* is an adverb meaning "nearly." (Her roommate goes home *almost* every weekend.) Avoid the reverse combination of *almost*—i.e., *most all.* (*Almost all / Most* [not *Most all*] parakeets can be trained to talk.)

nauseous/nauseated: *Nauseous* should be used to mean "causing nausea"; that is, "sickening," "disgusting," or "loathsome." (A *nauseous* smell came from the laboratory.) *Nauseated* means "sick at the stomach" or "disgusted." (Everyone became *nauseated* from the smell in the laboratory.)

negligent/negligible: *Negligent* means "careless," "neglectful," or "indifferent." (One should never be *negligent* on the job.) *Negligible* means "able to be disregarded," "unimportant," "trifling," or "meager." (Our losses are *negligible,* but so are our profits.)

notable/notorious: *Notable* means "noteworthy," "remarkable," "outstanding," or "praiseworthy." (For a person of such *notable* accomplishments, the visiting lecturer appeared quite unassuming.) *Notorious* is a negative word and means "well-known for bad reasons." (John Dillinger was a *notorious* bank robber.)

number of/amount of: *Number of* is followed by a plural noun referring to countable items. (The *number of* guests exceeded our estimate by two hundred.) *Amount of* is followed by a singular noun indicating a quantity that cannot be counted. (The banquet committee misjudged the *amount of* food the guests would consume.) The use of *number of* sometimes results in wordy constructions that can be shortened through revision—e.g., " A large *number of* students left the room" can be revised to "*Many* students left the room" or "*several* students left the room."

obsolete/obsolescent: *Obsolete* means "no longer in use" or "out of date." *Obsolescent* means "passing out of use" or "becoming out of date." (Quill pens are *obsolete,* whereas ordinary electric typewriters are *obsolescent.*)

SENTENCE FILL-IN

1. The (*median / meridian*) _____ age of Americans is increasing, not decreasing; we are growing older.

2. Parents should always take the time to (*dialogue / talk*) _____ with their children.

3. Even in the fall, the family goes to the lake (*almost / most*) _____ every weekend.

4. I can't remember the (*number of / amount of*) _____ times we told the child not to fly the plane over the city.

5. Nathan's eccentric cousin hired two large (*media / mediums*) _____ to try to communicate with his late wives in the next world.

6. Margaret was her (*negligent / negligible*) _____ self, careless and indifferent about what she was doing.

7. The president of the company admitted that employee (*morale / moral*) _____

   _____ had never been lower.

8. Poor Leslie becomes (*nauseous / nauseated*) _____ every time she eats tropical grubs or calves' brains.

9. Of all musical instruments, the bagpipe is probably the most suited for (*marital / martial*)

   _____ music; its squealing drone makes even a coward want to take up arms.

10. Bertram's one (*notable / notorious*) _____ accomplishment while in college was breeding transparent spiders.

11. Although misinformed on several matters, the defendant was nonetheless a (*moral /*

    morale) _____ individual.

12. Aren't you distressed by seeing the (*morbid / sordid*) _____ living conditions of Third World countries as they are frequently shown on television news shows?

13. (*Maybe / May be*) _____ our problem is that too many people want white-collar jobs.

14. The futurist maintained that physical labor was (*obsolete / obsolescent*) _____

    _____ at the present time, and would disappear altogether in the next century.

15. The student newspaper is not a very reliable (*media / medium*) _____ through which to learn about the university.

247

16. The (*median / meridian*) _____ of my uncle's life occurred when he struck oil on the family farm.

17. It seems to me that one professional requirement for a coroner would be a (*morbid / sordid*) _____ dedication to grim detail.

18. The driver in the red hat is (*notable / notorious*) _____ for crashing his cars.

19. According to this article, most (*marital / martial*) _____ problems occur because of lack of communication between spouses.

20. This (*nauseous / nauseated*) _____ little man makes me sick every time I look at him.

21. Do you think Jay Leno's (*monologues / dialogues*) _____ are as entertaining as those Johnny Carson used to perform?

22. Bernard's actual contribution to the project was (*negligent / negligible*) _____ at best.

23. (*A number of / Several*) _____ people from the neighborhood wanted to withdraw from the township.

24. It (*maybe / may be*) _____ true that some animals can think and remember much as humans do.

25. We may be facing a (*moral / morale*) _____ dilemma—whether to promote abortion worldwide or vastly overpopulate the planet.

26. The (*monologue / dialogue*) _____ in the second act between the duke and the duchess was wonderful.

27. Is television now the (*media / medium*) _____ that most manipulates the news?

28. (*Almost all / Most all*) _____ the members of my class had jobs lined up months before graduation.

29. For cutting Christmas trees on the freeway (*meridian / median*) _____, Vera had to pay a fine.

30. Are fax machines going to make the traditional business letter (*obsolete / obsolescent*) _____ ?

Important Distinctions (17)

odd/oddly: *Odd* is an adjective meaning "peculiar," "strange," "eccentric," or "unusual." (Old Cadwallader is an *odd* character.) *Oddly* is an adverb, and so should not be used to modify a noun. (The dean laughed *oddly* and uncomfortably at the professor's remark.)

official/officious: *Official* means "authorized" or "having authority." (The student employees were given an *official* reprimand.) *Officious* means "more helpful than is needed," "too ready to assist," "meddlesome," or "overly obliging." (The assistant office manager was an *officious* little twit who seemed to be everywhere at once.)

on/onto/on to: The statements "He lived his whole life *on* the stage" and "He stepped *onto* the stage for the last time" demonstrate the distinction between the first two. *Onto* suggests more clearly movement toward something. In constructions where *on* is an adverb and *to* a preposition, the two are written separately. (The time had come for Susan to move *on to* bigger things.)

on/upon: When you have an apparent choice between these two, current usage prefers *on* except when it is awkward. (Austin spilled his drink *on* the carpet. The village fell *on* hard times. Once *upon* a time, there were leprechauns in Ireland.)

our/ours: *Our* is a possessive pronominal adjective meaning "belonging to us." (*Our* clothes had been put in the wrong room.) *Ours* is a possessive pronoun meaning "that or those belonging to us." (After 360 payments, this house will be *ours*.)

penance/penitence: A *penance* is any voluntary act of self-punishment performed to show that one is sorry for a wrongdoing. (Alastair maintains that there is no *penance* adequate for the taking of another's life.) *Penitence* is sorrow or remorse felt for having done wrong. (The young man's *penitence* for his actions was obvious.)

pendant/pendent: A *pendant* is an ornamental hanging object, such as a locket. (Alison wore a beautiful amber *pendant* to the party.) *Pendent* is an adjective meaning "hanging," "suspended," "dangling," "overhanging," or "undecided." (The *pendent* decorations were blowing in the wind. All the motions were left *pendent* for the next meeting.)

percent/percentage: *Percent* should be used only after a number. (At least thirty *percent* of the herd is infected.) Except in such expressions as "fifteen *percentage* points," *percentage* is not used with a specific number. (Fortunately, only a small *percentage* of the crop was damaged.)

perimeter/parameter: *Perimeter* means "the distance around the total outer boundary of an area." (The *perimeter* of my grandfather's ranch exceeds twenty-five miles.) A *parameter* is a constant factor or characteristic element. (Rapidly developing technology is one of the *parameters* of modern life.) Avoid using *parameter* as a substitute for *perimeter*. (One can no longer distinguish the *perimeter* [not *parameter*] of the battlefield.)

perpetrate/perpetuate: *Perpetrate* means "to commit," "to perform," or "to carry out." Anything *perpetrated* is usually bad. (The president has *perpetrated* a crime against the university by discontinuing successful programs.) To *perpetuate* is to cause to continue or to preserve from oblivion. (It is difficult to *perpetuate* the reputations of great writers in a land where so few people read.)

persecute/prosecute: *Persecute* means "to afflict," "to harass," "to oppress," "to trouble," "to torment," and the like. (Professor Demento doesn't teach students; he *persecutes* them.) To *prosecute* is to begin legal proceedings against someone. (The federal government will *prosecute* these people for making counterfeit money.) *Prosecute* also means "to carry out" or "to follow up." (President Truman *prosecuted* the war against Japan to its inevitable conclusion.)

personal/personnel: *Personal* means "private." *Personnel* are people employed to do work. (*Personal* problems may not be the responsibility of the *personnel* department.)

perspective/prospective: *Perspective* is usually a noun meaning "a view of things showing their proper relationship with one another." (The artist employed an unusual *perspective* in this drawing. The *perspective* of management is not the same as that of labor.) *Prospective* is an adjective meaning "looking toward the future," "likely to happen," "expected," or "potential." (Several *prospective* frontline players were unable to pass the university's entrance examination.)

SENTENCE FILL-IN

1. Overcoming such a serious injury to win the championship is indeed a (*personal /personnel*) _____ triumph.

2. Many people thought that President Bush did not (*persecute / prosecute*) _____ _____ the Gulf war to a satisfactory conclusion.

3. The speeding car crashed through the bridge and fell (*on / onto / on to*) _____ _____ the freeway ramp below.

4. It is now (*official / officious*) _____; Aubrey and Julia have won $20 million in the lottery.

5. Stress seems to be one of the (*perimeters / parameters*) _____ of a college student's life.

6. I can't even walk (*on / upon*) _____ ice, much less water.

7. All the motions introduced at the meeting remain (*pendant / pendent*) _____ _____; i.e., they are undecided, in limbo.

8. Ian's (*perspective / prospective*) _____ of many things is influenced by a view from fifty years' experience at life.

9. A substantial (*percent / percentage*) _____ of any class will likely leave school before graduating.

10. It would appear that the (*penance / penitence*) _____ for this behavior is going to be a long, slow death from an incurable disease.

11. Someone must save me from this (*official / officious*) _____ office manager; she is into everyone's business but her own.

12. Will you please stop (*persecuting / prosecuting*) _____ the instructor with all these silly questions.

13. We have been (*on / onto / on to*) _____ daylight savings time during the summer months for many years.

14. Our goal here is to (*perpetrate / perpetuate*) _____ the image of our community as a good place to rear a family.

15. I had never before seen such an (*odd / oddly*) _____ dressed wee person in the forest.

16. The (*official / officious*) _____ explanation of the incident was that the governor accidentally shot himself three times while cleaning his nephew's loaded revolver.

17. Profits are up no less than twenty-two (*percent* / *percentage*) _____ points over last year.

18. We had to construct a screen fence around the (*perimeter* / *parameter*) _____ _____ of the garden to keep the rabbits out.

19. First, the team went to Beckley, then (*onto* / *on to*) _____ Bluefield and White Sulphur Springs.

20. The judge wanted to see clear evidence that the young man felt (*penance* / *penitence*) _____ in his heart.

21. The robbery was (*perpetrated* / *perpetuated*) _____ by professionals who knew exactly what they were doing.

22. In the deepest, darkest part of the forest, we happened (*on* / *upon*) _____ a village no more substantial than a fleeting thought.

23. The (*perspective* / *prospective*) _____ from the top of the tower was one of a parking lot with flattened people walking about under large hats.

24. Old Cuthbert had an (*odd* / *oddly*) _____ way of blinking one eye after the other rather than both at the same time.

25. The market is absolutely flat; we haven't a single (*perspective* / *prospective*) _____ _____ buyer for the property.

26. About twenty (*percent* / *percentage*) _____ of the senior class graduated with honors.

27. The district attorney must (*persecute* / *prosecute*) _____ this man for what he did or face removal from office.

28. A crystal (*pendant* / *pendent*) _____ was supposed to be suspended from each of the sconces.

29. Professor Golden looks (*odd* / *oddly*) _____ and a little scary when she does dramatic readings in class.

30. The director of (*personal* / *personnel*) _____ isn't a particularly friendly individual.

Important Distinctions (18)

phenomenon/phenomena: A *phenomenon* is a fact, circumstance, or event—especially one with unusual characteristics. (A tornado is a fearsome natural *phenomenon*.) *Phenomena* is the plural form, and care should be taken to match it with plural verbs when necessary. (*Phenomena* [not *Phenomenons*] like telepathy and clairvoyance are not to be dismissed out of hand.)

physiology/physiognomy: *Physiology* is the (study of) bodily functions and processes of an organism. (Human *physiology* will not allow us to eat rocks and drink oil.) One's *physiognomy* is one's facial features. (Balthazar has a *physiognomy* suitable for a silver dollar.)

plaintiff/defendant: A *plaintiff* is anyone who brings a complaint (a suit) in a court of law. (The state was the *plaintiff* in this particular action.) A *defendant* is the party against whom the *plaintiff* has brought the complaint. (The *plaintiff* charged the *defendants* with stealing her idea for a screenplay.)

please/kindly: When you have an apparent choice between these two words as an indicator of courteousness, *please* is usually the better choice; *kindly* is often a bit demanding, imperious, or provoking. (Would you *please* [not *kindly*] call me at home this evening? Would you *kindly* [not *please*] close your mouth and give everyone's ears a rest.)

politics is/politics are: *Politics* is singular when used to mean "activities conducted for political purposes," "the art of government," or "maneuvering for power." (Campus *politics* controls most college-wide committee appointments.) *Politics* is plural when used to mean "one's political principles or beliefs." (My parents' *politics* are neither to the left nor the right.)

port/starboard: *Port* is the left-hand side of a boat, ship, or airplane as one faces the bow, or front. *Starboard* is the right-hand side. (The ship's *starboard* guns misfired, but those on the *port* did their job.)

possible/probable: That which is *possible* could happen, whereas that which is *probable* likely will happen. (Winning the lottery is *possible*—if one buys a ticket—but not *probable*.)

precede/proceed: To *precede* means "to come or go before." To *proceed* means "to move forward" or "to continue." (Youth *precedes* adulthood, which then *proceeds* into middle age.)

predominant/predominate: *Predominant* is an adjective meaning "superior," "controlling," "prevailing," or "authoritative." (Russia will hardly be the *predominant* voice of Eastern Europe that the Soviet Union once was.) *Predominate* is a verb meaning "to have ascendency over others," "to be stronger and more powerful," or "to be generally superior." (In Western Michigan, inclement weather can *predominate* during the winter months.) Avoid using *predominate* as an adjective. (River State has been the *predominant* [not *predominate*] team in the conference for many years.)

prerequisite/perquisite: A *prerequisite* is something required beforehand. (Organic chemistry is a *prerequisite* to inorganic chemistry.) A *perquisite* is an additional benefit (for work) other than standard wages. (One of the *perquisites* of this job is the private use of a company car.)

prescribe/proscribe: To *prescribe* is to construct a formula (rules) to be followed. (Common sense would *prescribe* a warm climate and several months of rest.) To *proscribe* means "to prohibit" or "to forbid.") (Alas, my responsibilities seem to *proscribe* sufficient time to rear my children properly.)

presumptuous/presumptive: *Presumptuous* means "arrogantly forward in taking too much for granted." (Miriam thought it *presumptuous* of her boyfriend to telephone his physics professor at home.) *Presumptive* means "based on probability but not evidence" or "possessing reasonable grounds for belief." (The fact that you lied provides *presumptive* evidence that you had something to hide.)

prevent/hinder: To *prevent* something is to keep it from happening. (Dry weather *prevented* the corn from reaching full size.) To *hinder* is to make the accomplishment of something more difficult, although not impossible. (Blaring stereos up and down the hall of the dormitory *hinder* my concentration.)

prophecy/prophesy: *Prophecy* is a noun meaning "a prediction of the future, usually with some divine assistance." (Fortunately, the *prophecy* that the world would end was inaccurate.) *Prophesy,* a verb, means "to predict a future event" or "to foretell." (To *prophesy* that the morning sun will again rise in the east doesn't require much foresight.) Avoid using the nonstandard *prophesize* as a substitute for *prophesy*.

SENTENCE FILL-IN

1. Doctors sometimes (*prescribe / proscribe*) _____ the smoking of marijuana for patients suffering from glaucoma.

2. Cadwallader's (*physiology / physiognomy*) _____ is not substantially different from the visage of Cro-Magnon man.

3. Below average reading skills may (*prevent / hinder*) _____ a student's progress in this class.

4. Your skipping the country was (*presumptive / presumptuous*) _____ evidence of your guilt.

5. In this case the (*plaintiff / defendant*) _____ has been charged with practicing medicine without a license.

6. Shouldn't we (*precede / proceed*) _____ with the business that called us together rather than wander into other topics?

7. The problem was that if the first (*prophecy / prophesy*) _____ came true, the other two would not be possible.

8. What we are looking at here are (*phenomenons / phenomena*) _____ that modern science, in all its wisdom, cannot explain.

9. The Smalleys' trip to Scotland will (*precede / proceed*) _____ their vacation to Monte Carlo.

10. Tourism is probably the (*predominant / predominate*) _____ industry in northern Michigan.

11. One of the (*prerequisites / perquisites*) _____ of being a commercial pilot is free tickets to fly almost anywhere.

12. The entry doors on an airliner are located on the (*port / starboard*) _____ side of the plane.

13. (*Please / Kindly*) _____ don't shout into the telephone; it is painful to the person on the other end of the line.

14. Your politics (*is / are*) _____ hardly what they were thirty years ago when we were roommates in college.

15. For many years now, the (*predominant / predominate*) _____ school in the Northern Lakes Conference has been Hinterland State University.

16. At most colleges, freshman composition is a (*prerequisite / perquisite*) _____ _____ for other composition classes.

17. It is always (*probable / possible*) _____ that one will win the lottery, but not very likely.

18. Alas, in the real world, might will often (*predominant / predominate*) _____ _____ over right.

19. Human (*physiology / physiognomy*) _____ allows us to be omnivorous rather than merely carnivorous or herbivorous.

20. The documentation should not (*precede / proceed*) _____ the body of the text; properly inserted, it follows the text.

21. (*Please / Kindly*) _____ stop talking with your mouth full; if I want background music, I'll turn on the radio.

22. When an ocean liner turns to the right, it turns to (*port / starboard*)_____.

23. Do you think the federal government will ever (*prescribe / proscribe*) _____ _____ the production and sale of tobacco products?

24. The aurora borealis is a celestial (*phenomenon / phenomena*) _____ occasionally seen in the northern night sky, particularly during the winter.

25. Montague is a (*defendant / plaintiff*) _____ in life as well as in court; he has a complaint about everything.

26. Your asking me to go away with you for the weekend after knowing me only a few days is extremely (*presumptuous / presumptive*) _____.

27. The old man had something to (*prophesize / prophesy*) _____ about almost every topic that came up.

28. Here at Tink-Tink Tech, office politics (*is / are*) _____ a complicated business.

29. I might live to be a hundred, but I don't think it is (*possible / probable*) _____ _____.

30. Not having taken the prerequisites (*prevented / hindered*) _____ Mavis from enrolling in the course.

Important Distinctions (19)

prostrate/prostate: *Prostrate* means "lying flat," "lying with the face downward," "helpless," or "humbled." To *prostrate* is to put in a flat position on the ground. (The prisoners lay *prostrate* before the king. The worshipers *prostrated* themselves before the high altar.) The *prostate* is an organ surrounding the neck of the urinary bladder and beginning of the urethra in males. (The occurrence of *prostate* cancer in middle-aged men has reached epidemic levels in recent years.)

questionable/questioning: *Questionable* means "doubtful," "dubious," "uncertain," or "open to question." (You begin your argument with several *questionable* assertions.) *Questioning* means "inquiring." (Scientific research requires both proper methodology and a *questioning* mind.)

quick/quickly: *Quick* is an adjective, *quickly* an adverb. (Rebecca has a *quick* mind and a sharp eye; she works both *quickly* and carefully.)

quotation/quote: *Quotation* is a noun, whereas *quote* is a verb. (If you *quote* someone in your paper, take care to get the *quotation* accurate word for word.)

raise/rise: *Raise* is a transitive verb and thus always takes an object. (Our neighbors to the west usually *raise* a hundred acres of corn.) *Rise* is an intransitive verb and thus never takes an object. (On this farm, everyone *rises* before dawn.)

rational/rationale: *Rational* means "able to reason," "of sound mind," "sensible," or "logical." (Why would a *rational* person suddenly leap off a tall building and try to fly?) *Rationale* means "a fundamental system of reasons" or "a logical basis." (No one understood the star's *rationale* for retiring at the peak of his career.)

real/really: *Real,* an adjective, should not be used in place of *really,* which is an adverb meaning "truly" or "genuinely." (These pendants are made of *real* amber by a craftsman who is *really* devoted to his craft.)

receipt/recipe: A *receipt* is a written acknowledgment that one has received goods, money, or services. *Receipt* also means "an act of receiving." (State law requires that retailers provide customers with a *receipt* including the name of the retailer prominently printed. We are in *receipt* of more suggestions than we know what to do with.) A *recipe* is a set of directions and ingredients for preparing something to eat—and by extension, a formula for preparing anything. (My mother has a *recipe* for Swiss steak that she won't reveal to anyone.)

recur/reoccur: *Recur,* and the noun *recurrence,* should be used in connection with something that happens again and again. (The summer solstice *recurs* every year on June 21 or 22.) *Reoccur,* or the noun *reoccurrence,* should be used in connection with a one-time repetition of an event. (If there is a *reoccurrence* of this reaction to the drug, you should go to the hospital at once.)

regretful/regrettable: *Regretful* means "filled with regret" or "sorrowful." (Bertram has always felt *regretful* about not attending his parents' fiftieth wedding anniversary.) *Regrettable* means "provoking regret" or "unfortunate." (The university's decision to drop varsity football is *regrettable* but not terminal.) Generally, *regretful* is applied to persons, *regrettable* to events or situations.

restful/restive: *Restful* means "peaceful and quiet." (I spent a *restful* day in the hammock listening to the birds.) *Restive* means "restless," "uneasy," "nervous," or "impatient." (The dogs were *restive* throughout the night in anticipation of the morning hunt.)

respectfully/respectively/respectably: *Respectfully* means "with respect." *Respectively* means "singly" or "each in the order given." (Each of the hall-of-famers, *respectively* introduced by the master of ceremonies, was *respectfully* applauded by the audience.) *Respectably* means "in a manner worthy of esteem" or "adequately or acceptably done." (After getting out of prison, Jason lived *respectably* in the community for many years. The team performed *respectably* in the second half.)

SENTENCE FILL-IN

1. The instructor became (*real / really*) _____ upset when no one responded to her questions.

2. Alas, my allergies (*recur / reoccur*) _____ every spring and every fall.

3. (*Prostrate / Prostate*) _____ cancer is one of the major killers of middle-aged men.

4. The (*receipt / recipe*) _____ we received when we bought the auto-biography of Shamu was for the wrong amount of money.

5. (*Quote / Quotation*) _____ marks are not supposed to be used to enclose indirect (*quotes / quotations*) _____.

6. What a (*quick / quickly*) _____-witted person your little brother has become since getting out into the world.

7. Your (*receipt / recipe*) _____ for four-alarm chili was almost identical to the one my grandmother used.

8. Jane dressed (*quick / quickly*) _____ and was ready to go.

9. The cottage was so (*restful / restive*) _____ that we slept for ten hours without waking.

10. Some of the farms in the area are now (*raising / rising*) _____ two crops a year in many fields.

11. Although the bombing of Pearl Harbor by the Japanese was (*regretful / regrettable*) _____, it did relieve America of the agony of deciding whether or not to enter the war.

12. Children should learn to speak (*respectfully / respectively*) _____ to every-one, including their elders.

13. The degrees submitted by the candidate with his application are of (*questionable / questioning*) _____ legitimacy.

14. Can you explain your (*rational / rationale*) _____ for holding such an unusual position on this issue?

15. Isn't it just a little vain to (*quote / quotation*) _____ yourself?

16. Although quite poor, the family was always (*respectfully / respectively / respectably*) _____ dressed.

17. Howard is of course (*regretful / regrettable*) _____ for any part he may have played in this unfortunate incident.

18. The first, second, and third prizes were awarded to Avis, Zachary, and Babette (*respectfully / respectively / respectably*) _____.

19. One of the qualities of the (*rational / rationale*) _____ mind is that it requires hard evidence to arrive at a conclusion.

20. Everyone spent a (*restful / restive*) _____ night waiting to hear whether or not Agnes had been on the plane lost at sea.

21. The (*quote / quotation*) _____ cited was most inappropriate for the occasion.

22. Shouting people seldom put forth (*rational / rationale*) _____ arguments.

23. There is something inherently (*restful / restive*) _____ about a commodious cottage surrounded by forest on three sides and facing a quiet lake.

24. American enterprise must always (*rise / raise*) _____ to the challenge of foreign competition.

25. None of us had ever seen a cornerback move so (*quick / quickly*) _____.

26. This is to let you know that we are in (*receipt / recipe*) _____ of your letter dated June 11.

27. In Oslo and Stockholm the days are (*real / really*) _____ short during December, January, and February.

28. The wounded knight lay (*prostrate / prostate*) _____ on the ground, dreaming of his lady with his last thoughts.

29. If there is a (*recurrence / reoccurrence*) _____ of such behavior by the groundskeeper, call the sheriff at once.

30. Bernice's (*questionable / questioning*) _____ approach to areas new to her is appropriate for her goal of becoming a research scientist.

Important Distinctions (20)

sank/sunk: As a matter of discretion, use *sank* as the past tense form of the verb *sink* and *sunk* as the past participle form. (The ferry *sank* [not *sunk*] in no more than ten feet of water about two hundred yards from port. The oil rig will have *sunk* [not *sank*] into the sea long before help arrives.)

sculpture/sculptor: *Sculpture* is the art of modeling clay or wax, carving wood, casting metal, or chiseling stone. A *sculpture* is a work produced by any of these activities. A *sculptor* is a person who creates *sculpture*. (A work of *sculpture* belongs to the *sculptor* only until it is finished; then it becomes the possession of all who view it.)

seasonable/seasonal: *Seasonable* means "appropriate to the time of year" or "at the right or proper time." (The weather has been *seasonable* but dry.) *Seasonal* means "related to the seasons" or "occurring at regular intervals." (The tourist business is *seasonal*.)

set/sit: *Set* is a transitive verb meaning "to put in place." (She was told to *set* the case on the top shelf.) *Sit* is an intransitive verb meaning "to occupy a seat." (Gwen can *sit* at her desk for hours studying.)

shall/will: Use *shall* when your intention is to indicate politeness or strong emphasis, or when *will* seems awkward. (We *shall* not be moved. We *shall* overcome. *Shall* we dance? You *shall* be home by nine!) *Will* is standard—on this side of the Atlantic—in all other future tense constructions.

she/her/herself: *She* is the nominative form of the personal pronoun and is used as a subject, subject complement, or an appositive of either. (*She* won the contest. The winner was *she*. They—Jan, Fran, and *she*—were the winners. They were the winners, Jan, Fran, and *she*.) *Her* is the objective form of the personal pronoun and is used in all object positions. (The principal sent *her* home. The teacher gave *her* a good grade. This assignment just wasn't for *her*. Confronting *her* required courage. Exercise will make *her* healthy in no time.) *Herself* is both the reflexive and intensive form of the personal pronoun. (Poor Harriet shot *herself* in the foot; thus, she *herself* is responsible for the injury.)

simplified/simplistic: When you have an apparent choice between these two words, use the first to mean "made less complicated and thus more understandable" and the second to mean "oversimplified and thus inadequate." (We need a *simplified* version of this bill to present to the populace. Such *simplistic* solutions to complex problems create more problems than they solve.)

since/because: *Since* is best used to indicate only time. (Alice has known Tom *since* they were in the fifth grade together.) *Because* indicates causation. (I love you *because* you're you.) Ambiguity often results if *since* is used to mean *because*—e.g., "*Since* you went away, I have been blue."

sludge/slush: *Sludge* is soft, thick mud, whereas *slush* is partly melted snow. (In the early spring, there are both *sludge* and *slush* in the back yard.)

solid/stolid: *Solid* means many things—"firm," "hard," "substantial," "sturdy," and so on. (This is a *solid* structure, made entirely of stone.) *Stolid* means "difficult to arouse," "showing little emotion," or "impassive." (It took a *stolid* group not to be moved by the speaker's performance.)

some/somewhat: *Some* is an adjective indicating an indefinite number or amount. (The children had *some* small amount of money when they appeared at our doorstep.) *Somewhat* is an adverb meaning "to some degree" or a noun meaning "some part." (We were *somewhat* skeptical of your motives. The loud explosion gave us *somewhat* of a start.) Avoid using *some* as a substitute for *somewhat*. (Everyone was *somewhat* [not *some*] weary after such a long day.)

someone/some one: *Someone* is an indefinite pronoun meaning "a person unknown or unnamed." (*Someone* slipped into the kitchen and ate the cold pizza.) *Some one* is a phrase meaning "some individual person or thing." (Is there *some one* plan that the entire membership can live with?)

sometime/some time: *Sometime* is an adverb meaning "at a time not known or specified." (The family hopes to visit *sometime* in the spring.) The phrase *some time* means "a period of time." (I would like to spend *some time* with you.)

spatial/spacious: *Spatial* means "of space" or "existing in space." (The *spatial* arrangement of the furniture was quite pleasing.) *Spacious* means "roomy" or "vast." (These *spacious* plains were once the home of millions of buffalo.)

SENTENCE FILL-IN

1. These houses should be completed (*sometime / some time*) _____ near the end of October.

2. What a (*spatial / spacious*) _____ house this is, so large and roomy.

3. The unpaved road at the construction site in the rain forest was almost always a quagmire of (*sludge / slush*) _____ and slippery rock.

4. Rather than (*set / sit*) _____ on your hands all day, try doing a little work.

5. Here in the north, fresh strawberries are a (*seasonable / seasonal*) _____ treat looked forward to each spring.

6. Between Kathlyn and (*she / her / herself*) _____ there had always been an unusual friendship.

7. Is there (*someone / some one*) _____ attribute the manager has that annoys employees the most?

8. About fifteen minutes after the collision, the tug (*sank / sunk*) _____ to the bottom of the bay.

9. More than a hundred times the lad had been told not to (*set / sit*) _____ the thermos on the hot stove.

10. The weather was only (*some / somewhat*) _____ better during the following weeks.

11. Wasn't the lass herself to blame for the difficulty (*she / her / herself*) _____ _____ was having?

12. Both political parties seem quite satisfied with offering the public only (*simplified / simplistic*) _____ formulas for correcting major social problems.

13. After major stomach surgery, the patient was able to eat (*solid / stolid*) _____ _____ food in only a week.

14. (*Since / Because*) _____ my sister had already explained fractions to me, I had no trouble with the assignment.

15. There are those who sometimes have difficulty seeing avant-garde (*sculpture / sculptor*) _____ as works of art.

16. The report is a very nicely (*simplified / simplistic*) _____ analysis of an extremely complex concept.

17. We should spend (*sometime* / *some time*) _____ together before I am transferred to Europe.

18. For (*she* / *her* / *herself*) _____ to take a job so far from home would be costly.

19. We were told that a well-known (*sculpture* / *sculptor*) _____ was living in the old Higgens place.

20. (*Because* / *Since*) _____ the day was going to be a long one, everyone ate a hearty breakfast.

21. Although the snow was soft and powdery up on the ski slopes, the valley road leading to

    the lodge was sloppy with melting (*sludge* / *slush*) _____.

22. When on holiday at the lake, I love to (*set* / *sit*) _____ in the afternoon sun and doze.

23. For the third year in a row, Alison and (*she* / *her* / *herself*) _____ were the winners of the golf tournament.

24. Something needs to be done about the (*spatial* / *spacious*) _____ organization of the office; everyone is on top of everyone else.

25. This was the most (*solid* / *stolid*) _____ group of people I had ever encountered; I could discern no emotion in any of them.

26. Trust me; the day (*will* / *shall*) _____ come when all this (*will* / *shall*)

    _____ be a faint memory.

27. The weather has been fairly (*seasonable* / *seasonal*) _____ most of the winter—i.e., terrible.

28. Alas, our enemies have (*sank* / *sunk*) _____ us almost before we knew they were enemies.

29. Thaddeus was looking for (*someone* / *some one*) _____ who liked dogs as much as children.

30. The little girl was still (*some* / *somewhat*) _____ hesitant about talking to anyone other than her parents.

Important Distinctions (21)

specie/species: *Specie* means "money in the form of coins." (Pennies, nickles, dimes, quarters, fifty-cent pieces, and silver dollars are all American *specie.*) *Species,* which is both singular and plural, means "a class of plants or animals that can interbreed." (There is only one *species* of human being.)

stank/stunk: As a matter of discretion, use *stank* as the past tense form of the verb *stink* and *stunk* as the past participle form. (The smoldering potpourri *stank* terribly. The contaminated meat should have *stunk,* but it didn't.)

suggestible/suggestive: *Suggestible* means "inclined to be influenced by suggestions." (The wise leader can be both *suggestible* and firm.) *Suggestive* means "hinting at something that is often improper," "risque," or "suggesting certain thoughts or ideas." (The speaker's *suggestive* remarks were not appreciated by some of the women in the audience.)

supernatural/unnatural: *Supernatural* means "beyond what is natural," whereas *unnatural* means "not natural" or "perverted." (It is *supernatural* for a person to be able to fly, but *unnatural* for a child to torture small animals.)

sure/surely: *Sure* is an adjective. (This horse is a *sure* winner. The turning leaves are a *sure* sign of autumn.) *Surely* is an adverb. (*Surely* we can do better than we did last year. That creature was *surely* nothing from this planet.)

suspect/suspicion: *Suspect,* as a verb, means "to be suspicious of." *Suspicion,* a noun meaning "the act or feeling of suspecting guilt in someone," should not be used as a substitute for *suspect.* (Most of the townspeople now *suspect* [not *suspicion*] the mayor's motives.)

tasteful/tasty: *Tasteful* means "having, displaying, or conforming to good taste," "refined," or "unaffected." (The memorial service turned out to be a very *tasteful* affair.) *Tasty* means "pleasing to the taste," "flavorful," or "palatable." (My sister makes very *tasty* dried apple pies.)

temporal/temporary: *Temporal* means "not eternal," "not spiritual," "worldly," or "limited by time." (My days are occupied mostly with *temporal* matters.) *Temporary* means "lasting only for a short time" or "impermanent." (This setback is only *temporary.*)

temperature/fever: When you have an apparent choice between these two words, remember that the body always has a *temperature*—98.6 degrees Fahrenheit. When it rises above this level, for any reason, a *fever* exists. Thus, avoid using *temperature* when you mean *fever.* (The child's *temperature* was 104 degrees; thus, she had a *fever.*)

than/then: *Than* is a subordinating conjunction used to make comparisons. (Michigan has shorter summers *than* does Alabama.) *Then* is an adverb indicating time. (It was only *then* that Robin realized she wanted to be a tank commander.)

that/which: *That,* as a relative pronoun, always introduces restrictive clauses. (This is the house *that* a million dollars built.) *Which* can introduce either restrictive or nonrestrictive clauses; in formal writing, however, it is a good practice—for consistency—to limit *which* to nonrestrictive clauses. (This ugly little car, *which* I bought last year in France, was made in Korea.)

they/them/themselves: They is the nominative (plural) form of the personal pronoun and is used as a subject or subject complement. (*They* were the winners of the contest. The winners of the contest were *they.*) *Them* is the objective (plural) form of the personal pronoun and is used in all object positions. (The principal sent *them* home. The teacher gave *them* a warning. This assignment wasn't for *them.* Confronting *them* took courage. Exercise will make *them* strong in no time.) *Themselves* is both the reflexive and intensive form of the personal pronoun. (Figuratively speaking, the poor lads shot *themselves* in the foot; thus, they *themselves* are responsible for their own difficulties.)

think/feel/believe: *Think* means "to consider with the mind." (After considering all the possibilities, we *think* bankruptcy is our only sensible move.) *Feel* usually refers to a physical or emotional sensation or reaction. (These pants *feel* like silk. The loss of a friend makes one *feel* sad.) *Believe* means "to accept as a matter of faith." (Muslims *believe* in Allah as the sole deity and in Muhammad as his prophet.)

SENTENCE FILL-IN

1. Many people are not aware of the fact that African elephants are much larger (*than / then*)

   _____ Asian elephants.

2. Our days on the ranch, (*that / which*) _____ began at four in the morning,
   were filled with hard work.

3. To be paid in (*specie / species*) _____ is to be paid in coins.

4. Although you might not think so, Montague is actually quite (*suggestible / suggestive*)

   _____; he listens very carefully to what others say to him.

5. By any standard, it is (*supernatural / unnatural*) _____ for a child of nine
   to crave raw meat.

6. Why would anyone (*suspect / suspicion*) _____ the motives of the provost?
   He will gain nothing by the decision.

7. The roast will (*sure / surely*) _____ be well enough cooked by this time.

8. For (*they / them / themselves*) _____ to invest a million dollars in an ostrich
   farm seems a bit extravagant.

9. As the doctor feared, the sick child seemed to be burning up with a (*temperature / fever*)

   _____.

10. Cheryl has always said that she would rather be a common laborer (*than / then*)

    _____ an office manager.

11. The edelweiss is a small flowering plant (*that / which*) _____ flourishes
    in the high mountains of Europe, especially the Alps.

12. Montague, who fancies himself a bit of a gourmet, does not make a very (*tasteful / tasty*)

    _____ spaghetti sauce.

13. I (*think / feel / believe*) _____ like taking a warm bath and going to bed
    early.

14. If Emily hadn't stopped them, the exterminators would have (*stank / stunk*) _____

    _____ up the whole house with their chemicals.

15. While there is only one (*specie / species*) _____ of human, there are

    hundreds of (*specie / species*) _____ of monkeys.

16. Gretchen and Burgess, who are now engineers, put (*they / them / themselves*) _____

_____ through school without assistance from anyone.

17. No one was surprised when (*they / them / themselves*) _____, Gretchen and Burgess, won this year's achievement award.

18. Charleston, (*that / which*) _____ is the capital of West Virginia, is neither a northern city nor a southern city.

19. Among the (*supernatural / unnatural*) _____ powers possessed by Superman are an ability to fly and a facility for looking through solid objects.

20. If the patient still has a (*temperature / fever*) _____, there is probably an infection of some type.

21. My political science instructor (*thinks / feels / believes*) _____ the Germans still want to be a dominant world power.

22. Until he finds a better one, Norbert has a (*temporal / temporary*) _____ job as a waiter.

23. On hot summer days, the landfill (*stank / stunk*) _____ so (*bad / badly*)

_____ that everyone became (*nauseous / nauseated*) _____.

24. The workmen (*sure / surely*) _____ did a professional job, considering the conditions under which they had to work.

25. We Presbyterians (*think / feel / believe*) _____ that God planned every detail of human history before creating the first snail.

26. Murdock has furnished his house throughout with only the most (*tasteful / tasty*)

_____ pieces of furniture.

27. The dress worn by the soloist was a bit (*suggestible / suggestive*) _____ for the occasion.

28. Is it still true that the hand (*that / which*) _____ rocks the cradle rules the world?

29. Everyone (*suspected / suspicioned*) _____ that the old man's young wife had run away with the gamekeeper.

30. First came the wind, (*than / then*) _____ the rain.

Important Distinctions (22)

thorough/through: *Thorough* means "careful," "complete," or "exact." *Through,* as a preposition, means "in one side and out the other," "from end to end," or "from start to finish." (The supervisors made a *thorough* inspection as they walked *through* the plant.)

thrash/thresh: To *thrash* means "to beat or flog" or "to toss about wildly." (Teachers are no longer allowed to *thrash* students who misbehave.) To *thresh* means "to separate grain (seeds) from the husk by beating." (Today huge machines are used to *thresh* grains.)

tortuous/torturous: *Tortuous* means "including many turns, twists, and curves," and thus "involved," "indirect," "devious," or "deceitful." (Such a *tortuous* tale would make anyone suspicious.) *Torturous* means "involving torture or pain." (These three-hour lecture classes are absolutely *torturous.*)

turgid/turbid: *Turgid* means "swollen," "inflated," "distended," "overblown," "pompous," or "pretentious." (The actress's behavior is as *turgid* offstage as it was in the play.) *Turbid* means "muddy or cloudy, as from having sediment stirred up" or "thick, dense, and confused." (I often get lost in the *turbid* explanations of the economy offered by my economics professor.)

unaware/unawares: *Unaware* is an adjective meaning "not aware or conscious." (The astronomers said that they were *unaware* of a second moon.) *Unawares* is an adverb meaning "unintentionally," "unexpectedly," "suddenly," or "by surprise." (The police snuck up on the burglars *unawares.*) *Unaware* is often followed by *of; unawares* should not be followed by *of.*

unique/unusual: *Unique* means "one of a kind" and thus should not be compared. Do not say *more unique, most unique,* or *very unique;* use *unusual. Unusual* means "not usual or common," "rare," or "exceptional." (Although the performance was very *unusual,* I would not call it *unique.*)

used to/use to: *Use to* should not be used in place of *used to* in affirmative past constructions. (We *used to* have great times when we went to our cottage on weekends. The southerners were not *used to* such cold winters.) However, *use to* is correct in constructions following the word *did.* (It didn't *use to* be so cold in March. Did Jarvis *use to* play professional baseball?)

voluntary/involuntary: Voluntary means "done of one's own free will." (The confession was *voluntary,* not forced.) *Involuntary* means "independent of one's free will," "unconscious," "accidental," or "automatic." (Sneezing is an *involuntary* response to any number of things.)

wait on/wait for: To *wait on* means "to serve" or "to attend." (Some parents *wait on* their children hand and foot.) To *wait for* means "to await the arrival of." (Everyone hates to *wait for* a bus.)

we/us: *We* is the nominative form of the personal pronoun. (*We* were the winners of the contest. The winners of the contest were *we*.) *Us* is the objective form. (The principal sent *us* to the doctor. The instructor gave *us* a makeup text. Because of *us*, the mystery was solved. The vitamins made *us* strong in no time.)

whether/if: When you have an apparent choice between these two subordinate conjunctions, use *whether* (or *whether or not*) to introduce alternative conditions. (*Whether* [not *if*] the weather was fair or foul, the grunts kept on working. Confused, the speaker didn't know *whether or not* [not *if*] he should continue. The instructor wasn't sure *whether* [not *if*] she was making progress with the class *or not*.) Use *if* to introduce a single (supposed) condition. (*If* we save our money, we can go to Europe. You must pay the piper *if* you would call the tune.)

who/whom: Use *who* (*whoever*) when the pronoun is used as a subject. (These are the people *who* designed the new boat. We will elect *whoever* promises to do the most for us.) Use *whom* (*whomever*) when the pronoun is used as an object. (He dances well to *whom* fortune pipes. Alas, Rosalind criticizes *whomever* she meets. *Whomever* you select is okay with us.)

who's/whose: *Who's* is a contraction of *who is*. (I wonder *who's* watching the children.) *Whose* is a possessive pronoun. (*Whose* child is this?)

wrestle/rustle: To *wrestle* is to struggle hand to hand with an opponent. (There is no harder task than to *wrestle* with a guilty conscience.) To *rustle* is to make a series of soft sounds, as when leaves are moved by the wind, or to steal cattle. (Someone has *rustled* the entire shipment of Ford Broncos.)

your/you're: *Your* is a possessive pronominal adjective. *You're* is the contraction of *you are*. (It is necessary to warn you that *you're* now on *your* third and final try.)

SENTENCE FILL-IN

1. The invention of the printing press was a(n) (*unique / unusual*) _____ occurrence in human history.

2. Ted's schedule last term was (*tortuous / torturous*) _____; he wondered what he had done to deserve such punishment.

3. Ian said that he spent half his childhood (*waiting on / waiting for*) _____ his sisters to get out of the bathroom.

4. Victoria didn't know (*whether / if*) _____ she should stay the night or go home.

5. The (*turgid / turbid*) _____ strutting about of the performers throughout the play smacked of inflated pomposity.

6. The painters did a very (*thorough / through*) _____ job on the interior of the house.

7. To tell the truth, my dear, (*your / you're*) _____ an easy person to pick on.

8. (*Unaware / Unawares*) _____ of the weather forecast, Edmund was caught (*unaware / unawares*) _____ when the rain came pouring down.

9. Will you dance with (*whoever / whomever*) _____ asks you?

10. (*Your / You're*) _____ absolutely right; we didn't (*used to / use to*) _____ watch as much television as we do now.

11. Is there (*anyone / any one*) _____ in the room who knows (*who's / whose*) _____ winning the game?

12. I love to listen to the wind (*wrestle / rustle*) _____ through the trees in the fall when the leaves have become brittle.

13. (*Whoever / Whomever*) _____ the search committee selects will become the next president of the university.

14. Carolyn said that taking physical education was a(n) (*voluntary / involuntary*)_____ part of her schooling; she had protested, but to no avail.

15. Alas, I will probably never become (*used to / use to*) _____ reading a novel on a computer screen.

16. In matters like these, the truth didn't (*used to / use to*) _____ be so complicated.

17. For (*awhile / a while*) _____, it wasn't clear (*whether / if*) _____ _____ the men or the women were going to win.

18. We knew that if we didn't finish (*thrashing / threshing*) _____ the wheat we might get a good (*thrashing / threshing*) _____ when we got home.

19. (*Waiting on / Waiting for*) _____ people who are seriously ill can become quite burdensome after a time.

20. The accused insisted that his actions had been (*voluntary / involuntary*) _____ _____; he had not intended to harm anyone.

21. Although we (*wrestled / rustled*) _____ with the problem for several days, we couldn't think of an equitable solution.

22. Wanda didn't know (*who / whom*) _____ had to make the cake or for (*who / whom*) _____ it was intended.

23. Can poltergeists walk (*thorough / through*) _____ walls as well as ordinary ghosts do?

24. For (*we / us*) _____ to arrive by noon, (*we / us*) _____ had to leave about four-thirty in the morning.

25. My economics professor's explanations are often so (*turgid / turbid*) _____ _____ and confused that I can make nothing of them.

26. Natalie has a most (*unique / unusual*) _____ sense of humor—*e.g.,* she thinks simply saying the word "aspidistra" is hilarious.

27. The (*tortuous / torturous*) _____ stream twisted itself in so many directions that it passed under the freeway more than a dozen times.

28. As I recall, there (*used to / use to*) _____ be only one radio station in this town; now (*their / there / they're*) _____ are five.

29. Is that the woman (*who's / whose*) _____ collie bitch had a litter of twelve pups?

30. You should have known that (*your / you're*) _____ willingness to cooperate with the opposition would be misunderstood.

REVIEW EXERCISE
Important Distinctions

1. It is against the law to shoot (*a / an*) _____ elephant in the game reserve.

2. The public will never (*accept / except*) _____ the design of this line of cars.

3. We still have an (*access / excess*) _____ of inventory on hand.

4. Often the office manager has been (*accused of / charged with*) _____ a lack of sensitivity for the feelings of some employees.

5. Lucian is (*addicted / devoted*) _____ to the welfare of the community.

6. What (*advice / advise*) _____ did the president of the college have for the class?

7. They might at least (*agree to / agree with / agree about*) _____ which drapes to buy.

8. Does your cousin (*aim / intend*) _____ to run for reelection?

9. Unfortunately, (*all / all of*) _____ the electricians have gone on strike.

10. One should never (*allude / refer*) _____ to one's spouse as one's meal ticket.

11. By nightfall everyone was (*already / all ready*) _____ gone.

12. In truth, we had no (*alternate / alternative*) _____ plan for recovering our money.

13. As usual, Steadman was (*altogether / all together*) _____ confused by the new material presented in the lecture.

14. (*Among / Between*) _____ Marmaduke, Esmerelda, and me there has always been a special camaraderie.

15. Nothing (*amuses / bemuses*) _____ the children more than a fuss between their aunts.

16. Why did the child have such an (*angry / mad*) _____ wound on his leg?

17. After four years of college, Eva was (*anxious / eager*) _____ to find a job and go to work.

18. Alas, we almost never visit our relatives (*anymore / any more*) _____.

19. The investigator thought that (*anyone / any one*) _____ of the neighbors present might have committed the crime.

20. Many people who live in large cities can no longer afford to (*assure / ensure / insure*) _____ their automobiles.

21. We had a(n) (*very / awfully*) _____ pleasant stay with our old neighbors who had moved to Ottawa.

22. The children talked for (*awhile / a while*) _____, getting reacquainted, and then went to the beach together.

23. Alden wants to be friends with these people only (*because / cause*) _____ they are wealthy.

24. An unknown (*benefactor / beneficiary*) _____ has given the school money to start a program in glassblowing.

25. No one would question that the drug culture has had a (*benign / malign*) _____ influence on public education.

26. Almost all the programs require (*better than / more than*) _____ four years to complete.

27. Angus took a deep (*breath / breathe*) _____ and then dove into the murky water.

28. When you go off to college, be sure to (*take / bring*) _____ your set of encyclopedias with you.

29. A (*bunch / group*) _____ of fifth graders had remained in the medieval room of the museum.

30. No doubt remains that there is a (*causal / casual*) _____ relationship between the HIV virus and AIDS.

31. The university board of control (*censured / censored*) _____ the vice president for academic affairs for making public remarks uncomplimentary to some of the senior faculty.

32. I find such (*ceremonial / ceremonious*) _____ individuals a bit stifling.

33. Throwing a temper tantrum seems quite (*childish / childlike*) _____ for a full professor.

34. Global warming is a (*climatic / climactic*) _____ change with possible grave consequences for the future.

35. Although brief, the explanation was sufficiently (*comprehensible / comprehensive*) _____ for everyone in the class to understand.

36. Wasn't the second symphony on the program (*comprised* / *composed*) _____ _____ of four movements?

37. Vivian has never been as (*confidant* / *confident*) _____ about herself as she is now.

38. How can you in good (*conscience* / *conscious*) _____ deny that these are your children?

39. When he is trying to think, Thurston (*consistently* / *constantly*) _____ pulls at his left ear; he never stops!

40. More than a few (*contemporary* / *modern*) _____ short story writers do not maintain traditional plot structure.

41. What is more (*contemptible* / *contemptuous*) _____ than a person who betrays a confidence?

42. It was the (*continual* / *continuous*) _____ roar of the waterfall that gave everyone a headache.

43. Do not try to (*convince* / *persuade*) _____ us to take the law into our own hands.

44. It is one of the goals of a(n) (*covert* / *overt*) _____ act not to have witnesses.

45. Providing medical care for one's parents is a (*credible* / *creditable*) _____ gesture.

46. If you (*deduce* / *deduct*) _____ the cost of all the new machinery, you can show a loss for the year.

47. One of the negative (*denotations* / *connotations*) _____ of the word *teacher* is a person who because of an inability to *do* chooses to instruct.

48. We agree that most of these watercolors are (*deficient* / *defective*) _____ in pigment.

49. This strange looking (*device* / *devise*) _____ can remove paint from furniture.

50. An engineering student at the university has (*discovered* / *invented*) _____ _____ a technique whereby food can be stored indefinitely at room temperature.

51. After playing basketball for four years in college, Imogene became (*uninterested* / *disinterested*) _____ in the game.

52. The bobwhite's call is even more (*distinct* / *distinctive*) _____ than its markings.

53. Our cause was lost (*because of* / *due to*) _____ insufficient long-range planning.

54. The twins have always been able to read (*one another's* / *each other's*) _____ _____ thoughts.

55. Of what (*earthly* / *earthy*) _____ use is a hairless cat?

56. Just how (*economic* / *economical*) _____ is it to heat one's house by burning wood?

57. It is difficult to tackle such an (*elusive* / *illusive*) _____ running back.

58. Over the years, we have encountered (*endless* / *innumerable*) _____ cases almost identical to this one.

59. You must know that many of your classmates are (*envious* / *enviable*) _____ _____ of your accomplishments.

60. We spent an enjoyable afternoon reading (*epigrams* / *epigraphs* / *epithets* / *epitaphs*) _____ in the antebellum cemetery west of town.

61. Starvation has become (*epidemic* / *endemic* / *pandemic*) _____ in the developing nations throughout the world.

62. These clubs were designed (*especially* / *specially*) _____ for tall golfers with short arms.

63. Ashley still plays tennis, but only (*ever so often* / *every so often*) _____.

64. (*Every day* / *Everyday*) _____ on this job becomes a life-and-death struggle.

65. For one so thin, Sylvia is an (*exceedingly* / *excessively*) _____ healthy person.

66. The dean of students ruled Vincent's behavior (*exceptional* / *exceptionable*) _____ _____ and had him removed from the class.

67. (*Erotic* / *Esoteric* / *Exotic*) _____ dancers are supposed to be sexually stimulating, not aesthetically offensive.

68. The story that you told was not true; it was (*fallacious* / *false*) _____.

69. More money is needed to finance (*farther* / *further*) _____ research of the disease.

70. (*Fewer* / *Less*) _____ people came to this year's party than to last year's.

71. To accommodate the court's unpopular ruling, the child had to be (*forcibly* / *forcefully*) _____ taken from his adoptive parents.

72. In the (*foreword* / *preface*) _____ the author of the book spoke of her own unhappy childhood.

73. The ship (*foundered* / *floundered*) _____ after running onto submerged rocks in the outer harbor.

74. Vincent caught just a (*glance* / *glimpse*) _____ of the eagle as it flew by.

75. Vivian and Sylvester have always worked (*well* / *good*) _____ together on jobs like this one.

76. One might say that the (*gourmand* / *gourmet*) _____ enjoys cooking as much as the (*gourmand* / *gourmet*) _____ enjoys eating.

77. It is the dwelling that is (*habitable* / *inhabitable*) _____ and the area where the dwelling is located that is (*habitable* / *inhabitable*) _____ .

78. Valentine (*hanged* / *hung*) _____ a picture on the wall of the recently (*hanged* / *hung*) _____ man.

79. From regularly eating a (*healthy* / *healthful*) _____ combination of foods, Jennifer has become a (*healthy* / *healthful*) _____ person.

80. The (*historic* / *historical*) _____ razing of the Berlin Wall began a series of events that is still in progress.

81. A twenty-foot wall of water washed the vacant (*home* / *house*) _____ into the sea.

82. These (*hypocritical* / *hypercritical*) _____ individuals have made an avocation of pretending to be what they are not.

83. How (*ignorant* / *stupid*) _____ it was of me not to see the connection between the cold weather and the slow movement of the oil.

84. The author's confused reasoning makes the book virtually (*unreadable* / *illegible*) _____ .

85. Although marginally entertaining, your observations were (*illustrative* / *illustrious*) _____ of nothing in particular.

86. Joyce has a very (*imaginary* / *imaginative*) _____ way of telling a story.

87. When you use the word *macho*, do you mean to (*imply / infer*) _____ something negative?

88. Russell seems to have a fundamental (*disability / inability*) _____ to think about anyone other than himself.

89. Most people will find your story too (*incredible / incredulous*) _____ to be believed.

90. Alzheimer's (*invidiously / insidiously*) _____ destroys the minds of its victims.

91. Few schools today (*segregate / integrate*) _____ students by gender.

92. Thurston always begins his day with an (*enervating / invigorating*) _____ _____ shower.

93. Incredibly, Solomon puts (*catsup / catchup / ketchup*) _____ on his scrambled eggs.

94. Jeanne maintains that there is a conspiracy among architects of public buildings to make women's (*laboratories / lavatories*) _____ too small.

95. Almost every afternoon Grace (*lies / lays*) _____ down for a little nap.

96. I can hardly fly a kite, (*leave alone / let alone*) _____ an airplane.

97. The audience could hardly see Timothy standing behind the tall (*lectern / podium*) _____ .

98. If you (*loan / lend*) _____ me a pound on Monday, I will repay you a guinea on Friday.

99. If you confront the instructor in the classroom, you are (*liable / apt / likely*) _____ _____ to pay a price for it later on.

100. This business of writing a comprehensive history of the local township can become a (*lifelong / livelong*) _____ project.

101. Just (*like / as*) _____ my parents once warned me it would be, the world has often turned out to be an unfriendly place.

102. In the final race Jerome ran (*as if / like*) _____ he was possessed.

103. No one believed the lad's (*limp / limpid*) _____ attempt at explaining his frequent absences.

104. Vivian (*maybe / may be*) _____ guilty, and she may not be guilty.

105. Television has become the most popular entertainment (*media / medium*) _____ _____ in the nation.

106. The (*median / meridian*) _____ score on the examination was seventy-four.

107. As usual, the (*moral / morale*) _____ of Umberto's tale was difficult to discern.

108. (*Most / Almost*) _____ everyone enrolled in the seminar had attended the year before.

109. A (*nauseous / nauseated*) _____ fog arose from the cavern.

110. The (*amount of / number of*) _____ students entering the program has remained constant for several years.

111. What an (*odd / oddly*) _____ shaped artifact Naomi found north of the excavation site.

112. The (*official / officious*) _____ reason for the troop withdrawal was not credible.

113. Your (*penance / penitence*) _____ seems more a reward than a punishment.

114. What (*percent / percentage*) _____ of the crop ripened in time to be sold?

115. The (*parameter / perimeter*) _____ of the burial ground was marked by a line of ancient stones.

116. It is the commander in chief's responsibility to (*prosecute / persecute*) _____ _____ the war against the nation's enemies.

117. What possible new (*prospective / perspective*) _____ can a person with no experience in the field bring to us?

118. Many of the (*phenomena / phenomenons*) _____ of nature are still a mystery to us.

119. Professor Key's politics (*is / are*) _____ more liberal than my own.

120. It is (*possible / probable*) _____ that the world will end next Friday, but not likely.

121. Drab was the (*predominate / predominant*) _____ hue of the winter landscape.

122. When I was in high school, algebra was a (*prerequisite / perquisite*) _____ _____ for plane geometry.

123. Today, few churches (*prescribe / proscribe*) _____ either card playing or dancing as sinful.

124. If your (*prophecy / prophesy*) _____ comes true, none of us will have to worry about the future.

125. Your behavior was both inappropriate and of (*questioning / questionable*) _____ _____ taste.

126. What was the (*quotation / quote*) _____ that you intended to use at the beginning of your presentation?

127. During June, the sun will (*raise / rise*) _____ before five o'clock.

128. Each spring there is a (*recurrence / reoccurrence*) _____ of interest in baseball among the young men in the neighborhood.

129. It is (*regretful / regrettable*) _____ that you so casually label the traditional behavior of little boys as mean and evil.

130. In times as (*restful / restive*) _____ as these, it is difficult for many people to relax and enjoy themselves.

131. Most of the students at Crash and Burn High School did (*respectfully / respectively / respectably*) _____ well on the competitive examinations.

132. Much of the (*sculpture / sculptor*) _____ in the show was done by amateurs.

133. So far, the weather in May has been (*seasonal / seasonable*) _____; that is, cold, cloudy, and damp.

134. If you (*set / sit*) _____ too long on your laurels, they will go flat.

135. The (*simplistic / simplified*) _____ mind-set tends to view the world in black and white.

136. (*Since / Because*) _____ I had lived in Germany for four years when my father was in the army, I had little difficulty with the introductory German course.

137. A few members of the audience were (*some / somewhat*) _____ put off by your remarks.

138. We should arrive (*sometime / some time*) _____ after the first of the year.

139. People who are (*suggestive / suggestible*) _____ to new ideas are less difficult to work with.

140. Does anyone (*suspect / suspicion*) _____ us of any wrongdoing?

141. We enjoyed a (*tasteful* / *tasty*) _____ serving of monkey brain soup.

142. Ian is two years older (*than* / *then*) _____ his sister.

143. This is the house (*that* / *which*) _____ two years of hard work built.

144. The child had been (*threshed* / *thrashed*) _____ with a long hickory stick.

145. After considering all the facts, I (*think* / *feel* / *believe*) _____ that both parties contributed to the accident.

146. We were (*unaware* / *unawares*) _____ of any problem with the hydraulic system.

147. Roland has the most (*unique* / *unusual*) _____ batting stance I have ever seen.

148. Did you (*use to* / *used to*) _____ own a house on Eagle's Nest Lake?

149. We didn't know (*if* / *whether*) _____ we should go or stay.

150. Everyone hates to (*wait for* / *wait on*) _____ a tardy instructor to arrive.

PART TWO

SENTENCE MECHANICS

Chapter 5

Introduction to Sentence Mechanics

Sentence mechanics includes the conventions of usage for all the marks of sentence punctuation (e.g., comma, semicolon, colon, period, question mark, exclamation point, dash, parentheses, apostrophe, quotations marks) as well as the conventions of usage for what might be called the "marks" of word punctuation—that is, capitals, abbreviations, numbers, italics (underlining), and hyphens.

Brackets, Slashes, and the Ellipsis Mark

To get an idea how punctuation marks perform specific and necessary tasks, let's look at three less frequently used ones: brackets, slashes, and the ellipsis mark.

Brackets

As marks of punctuation, brackets are used (1) within quoted material to enclose words or phrases that have been added or changed for the purpose of clarity, and (2) within parenthetical elements already enclosed by parentheses to set off other parenthetical or explanatory words or commentary.

1. "The local bike trails are perfect for [cross-country] skiing during the winter months."
2. "It was during his third year at school [1941] that Swain met his future wife."
3. One editorialist wrote, "She [President Grimsby] apparently has no idea what goes on in the classroom and no inclination to find out."
4. The report concluded with the following statement: "It is feudal [sic] to try to grow corn in so cool a climate." (*Sic* indicates that the word *feudal* is noted as an error.)
5. In 1952, Hinterland Institute (the name was later [1963] changed to Hinterland State College) was saved from certain ruin by being incorporated into the state's postsecondary educational system.

Slashes

The slash mark is used (1) to separate one option from another within the structure of an ordinary sentence, (2) to join word compounds and some number combinations, and (3) to separate (or join) lines of poetry presented in a prose setting.

1. Taking a course on a pass/fail basis is a little like trying to win a competition without keeping score.
2. Alas, we were not faced with an either/or choice; the situation was more complicated than that.
3. Genevieve grew up in the Minneapolis/St. Paul area.
4. Is *The MacNeil/Lehrer News Hour* your favorite television show?
5. The doctor says that 20/20 vision is possible with this correction.
6. Fiscal year 1992/93 was a disaster for the company.
7. If a person pays the piper, he/she is entitled to call the tune.
8. From the appearance of your attire, I presume that you agree with Robert Herrick's contention that "A sweet disorder in the dress / Kindles in clothes a wantonness."
9. The poem begins with a fairly good quatrain: "When I was a child, / My dreams were my flying times; / And daily my waking hours / Awaited those flights in wilder climes."

The Ellipsis Mark

Consisting of three spaced periods, the ellipsis mark is used to indicate an intentional omission of one or more words from a direct quotation.

original:	The text defines *folie à deux* as "a madness shared by two people who have been together for many years, such as a husband and wife."
with omission:	The text defines *folie à deux* as "a madness shared by . . . a husband and wife."
original:	The reviewer held that the film was "funny where it should have been funny, sad where it should have been sad, and bad where everyone wanted it to be bad."
with omission:	The reviewer held that the film was "funny . . . , sad . . . , and bad . . ." in all the right places.

The more commonly used marks of sentence punctuation are taken up in Chapter 6, "Current Conventions of Punctuation." Similarly, the conventions of "word punctuation" are covered in Chapter 7, "Additional Mechanical Conventions." To prepare yourself for these chapters, you should work through each of the following self-checking pretest exercises.

In the first pretest exercise (1) identify the mark of punctuation needed to correct each sentence by putting the appropriate letter in the blank in front of the sentence and (2) correct each sentence by inserting the needed mark of punctuation. In about half of the sentences the needed punctuation is simply missing; however, in the other half, incorrect punctuation must be deleted before the correct punctuation can be inserted. Although more than one instance of a mark of punctuation may be needed to correct some of the sentences, no sentence requires the addition of multiple *types* of punctuation.

In the second pretest exercise (1) identify the *two* incorrectly handled mechanical conventions in each sentence by putting the appropriate letters in the blanks in front of the sentence and (2) correct each sentence by editing it right there on the page. Although some of the sentences have more than two mistakes, they have only two *kinds* of mistakes. Thus, if the first error in the sentence involves italics, put a *D* in the first blank in front of the sentence. Don't put another *D* in the second blank even if there are other errors involving italics. Into the second blank put only the letter that indicates whatever the other error in the sentence is. And there may be more than one instance of this error as well. Finally, be sure to correct *all* instances of both errors when you edit the sentences.

SELF-CHECKING PRETEST EXERCISE 1
Current Conventions of Punctuation

A. Comma   D. Dash
B. Semicolon   E. Apostrophe
C. Question Mark

_____ 1. Timothy was late for class on the first day, as a result, he missed the assignments for the entire term.

_____ 2. "Your father-in-laws house is indeed a pleasant place," the architect admitted, continuing to take notes.

_____ 3. Few of the students, if any, were able to read the text, it was written at too high a level.

_____ 4. Even if we were to win $40 million in the lottery I wouldn't build a new house—only enlarge the old one.

_____ 5. My old VCR I bought the thing in 1983, if you remember has almost no cash value.

_____ 6. In what specific ways is this university different from the other fourteen state universities.

_____ 7. The foreign students; so happy to be going to school in America; did not complain about the size of their dorm rooms.

_____ 8. In this company, at least, the womens room has been relocated right next to the board room.

_____ 9. With anger in his eyes, the president turned to the reporters and said, "Who in this room was elected to office anyway."

_____ 10. Vivian the youngest member of our department in terms of seniority intends to resign and return to graduate school.

_____ 11. In truth, I cant tell you how long weve been at this—too long probably.

_____ 12. The long, sleek, powerful speedboat was tied to the dock, and Thurston, eyes sparkling, gazed at it longingly.

_____ 13. A glass of wine, a triangle of cheese, a slug of bread, and thou; these compose a small recipe for a pleasant evening.

_____ 14. Most of these units were produced using the new technology yet some of the same control problems still exist.

_____ 15. "How many ss are there in the word Mississippi?" Seymour asked.

_____ 16. Gretchen, my second cousin, won a full scholarship, otherwise, she would not have been able to go to college, much less the university.

_____ 17. Leslie said, "I only mean to quiet the" and was herself quieted before she could complete her thought.

_____ 18. Where did the villains come from? The old Thompson place. A passing freight train. The county jail. The local asylum.

_____ 19. As it turned out, Elizabeth was not the shy unassuming person we thought she was.

_____ 20. "We stole seven loaves of fresh bread, no, I suppose it was closer to seventy, from the poor baker over the summer," Valentine admitted.

_____ 21. If you can afford to invest a few hundred thousand in these new voice recognition systems.

_____ 22. Professor Duggan—wasn't she your biology instructor—seems to have either invented or discovered a new virus.

_____ 23. We went to the gourmet shop in the mall—Langley's, I think it was—to buy some fresh Columbian coffee not to hear a lecture about the dangers of consuming caffeine.

_____ 24. Is it true that the smallest kittens toy was laced with catnip?

_____ 25. Present at the gathering were Ian Thomas, the visiting artist, about seventy-five students, all members of the new program, and Dr. Morris, head of the art department.

F. Colon
G. Period
H. Exclamation Point
I. Parentheses
J. Quotation Marks

_____ 26. "When the coach instructs you to run," the assistant coach said, "you had better _run_."

_____ 27. "If you say you know one more time," the instructor said, "I am going to remove the batteries from my hearing aid."

_____ 28. First, great banks of dark clouds moved in from the southwest, then a cold wind began to howl a chilling tune.

_____ 29. According to this article, the guillotine was intended to be a (humane) instrument of execution.

_____ 30. According to several accounts, Angus Whited first came upon the unusual formation in the winter of 1691 ? during a driving snowstorm.

_____ 31. The opening couplet of Alexander Pope's _An Essay on Man_ reads as follows, "Know then thyself, presume not God to scan; / The proper study of mankind is man."

_____ 32. Did I take a few notes? No, I didn't take a _few_ notes; I took _forty pages_ of notes.

_____ 33. The HLFA Hinterland Faculty Association has decided to cooperate with the administration on this issue rather than file a grievance.

_____ 34. Professor Bile seems to have one great pleasure in life; humiliating students.

_____ 35. Belize—formerly British Honduras—is a Central American country with which this university was once intimately associated—and little to the credit of either in the eyes of some.

_____ 36. Tobias wants none of the following items for Christmas, a flowered necktie, an imported fruitcake, a motivational tape hawked on late-night television, or a partridge in a pear tree.

_____ 37. Isn't it John 3,16 that begins "For God so loved the world"?

_____ 38. After the final lecture, several students (freshmen) asked the instructor what would be on the examination?

_____ 39. As I recall, Dr P Dudley Pringle, Jr, and Prof Etienne Busybody, PhD, both ran for the county board.

_____ 40. The committee's findings, see Table 9, do not support the university's contention that our instructors work only from ten to fifteen hours per week.

_____ 41. The author's latest novel, _The Birth of Time; A Fable for Children,_ will no doubt become a classic in record time.

_____ 42. Horatio did not disappoint the crowd; he ran a four-minute mile all right—backwards.

_____ 43. According to the latest US government statistics, the number of millionaires is increasing more rapidly than it ever has, even during the eighties.

_____ 44. No student in that class would venture a question, Murdock said; everyone was fearful of the instructor's response.

_____ 45. "I said _unique_" the instructor thundered, his face reddening, "not _eunuch._"

_____ 46. I had never read Andrew Lang's little poem Scythe Song until the instructor pointed it out to the class.

_____ 47. The flight left Kennedy International at 7-30 on Monday evening and arrived in Stockholm at about 10-30 on Tuesday morning.

_____ 48. American novelist and short story writer Ernest Hemingway [1899-1961] won the Nobel Prize for Literature in 1954; he did not, however, attend the award ceremony in Stockholm.

_____ 49. Was the RJ Reynolds Tobacco Company established before or after the American Civil War?

_____ 50. Each time the speaker asked, Who are we? the audience replied, We are the children of our age.

Answers: 1. *B* [day; as], 2. *E* [father-in-law's], 3. *B* [text; it], 4. *A* [lottery, I], 5. *D* [VCR—I] [remember—has], 6. *C* [universities?], 7. *A* [students, so] [America, did], 8. *E* [women's], 9. *C* [anyway?"], 10. *A* [Vivian, the] [seniority, intends], 11. *E* [can't] [we've], 12. *B* [dock; and], 13. *D* [thou—these], 14. *A* [technology, yet], 15. *E* [s's], 16. *B* [scholarship; otherwise], 17. *D* [the—" and], 18. *C* [The old Thompson place? A passing freight train? The county jail? The local asylum?], 19. *A* [shy, unassuming], 20. *D* [bread—no] [seventy—from], 21. *A* [to, invest], 22. *C* [instructor?—seems], 23. *A* [coffee, not], 24. *E* [kitten's], 25. *B* [artist; about] [program; and], 26. *H* [*run!*"], 27. *J* ['you know'], 28. *G* [southwest. Then], 29. *J* ["humane"], 30. *I* [1691 (?) during], 31. *F* [follows: "Know], 32. *H* [*forty pages* of notes!], 33. *I* [(Hinterland Faculty Association)], 34. *F* [life: humiliating], 35. *I* [(formerly British Honduras)], 36. *F* [Christmas: a], 37. *F* [John 3:16], 38. *G* [examination.], 39. *G* [Dr. P. Dudley Pringle, Jr., and Prof. Etienne Busybody, Ph.D., both], 40. *I* [(see Table 9)], 41. *F* [*The Birth of Time: A Fable for Children*], 42. *H* [backwards!], 43. *G* [U.S. government], 44. *J* ["No . . . question,"] ["everyone . . . response."], 45. *H* [*unique!*"], 46. *J* ["Scythe Song"], 47. *F* [7:30] [10:30], 48. *I* [(1899-1961)], 49. *G* [R.J. Reynolds], 50. *J* ["Who are we?"] ["We . . . age."].

SELF-CHECKING PRETEST EXERCISE 2
Additional Mechanical Conventions

A. Capitals   D. Italics
B. Abbreviations   E. Hyphens
C. Numbers

__/__ 1. No less than 2/3 of the forget me nots were beyond their prime.

__/__ 2. The word bonhomie is french and means "an easygoing disposition."

__/__ 3. Each Spring my Uncle and Mister Pitts take a golfing vacation in North Carolina.

__/__ 4. The mean voiced receptionist glared at me and said, "just who do you think you are, young man?"

__/__ 5. The contest is scheduled to begin promptly at seven thirty p.m.

__/__ 6. A good description of rapid eye movement (rem) sleep is presented in the text The Processes of Regeneration.

__/__ 7. Twenty nine times out of thirty, Aspirin will stop my headache.

__/__ 8. More than a little american know how will be needed to do that job.

__/__ 9. We must have watched the film of the 1937 Hindenburg disaster more than 30 times.

__/__ 10. Was it Samuel Boston, Junior, or Samuel Boston, Senior, who won the Two for One Award?

__/__ 11. Eleanor smiled and said, "didn't you know that we were sailing on the Queen Elizabeth II in June?"

__/__ 12. We were instructed to memorize 4 verses from the bible each day.

__/__ 13. Was the film Citizen Kane produced by Metro-Goldwyn-Mayer or Radio-Keith-Orpheum?

__/__ 14. In the fall we intend to purchase 12 22 foot units just like this one.

__/__ 15. I think that 5:00 *ante meridiem* is a bit early to face the dog eat dog world.

__/__ 16. The ne plus ultra of luxury automobiles is still the jaguar sedan.

__/__ 17. 5 has always been my lucky number—*exempli gratia,* I was born on May 5, 1955, at 5:55 in the morning.

__/__ 18. A branch of the Federal Deposit Insurance Corporation (fdic) is located west of the city on I 96.

__/__ 19. Ingrid Littleton, Bachelor of Arts, Master of Science, Doctor of Philosophy, has invited 10 or 12 scholars on a weekend retreat.

__/__ 20. My instructor said that the word selfsufficient should always be hyphenated.

__/__ 21. There was an interesting article about short fused referees in last week's issue of Time.

__/__ 22. In professor Glaspell's class, we wrote 4 7-page reports.

__/__ 23. It was about 3:00 *post meridiem* when the swedish ambassador began his speech.

__/__ 24. In this class we read no fewer than 7 400-page books, the least interesting of which was John Pfeiffer's The Emergence of Man.

__/__ 25. Alas, my son in law almost always mispronounces the word sesquipedalian.

Answers: 1. *C/E* [two-thirds] [forget-me-nots], 2. *D/A* [*bonhomie*] [French], 3. *A/B* [spring] [uncle] [Mr. Pitts], 4. *E/A* [mean-voiced] ["Just], 5. *C/A* [7:30] [P.M.], 6. *B/D* [REM] [*The Processes of Regeneration*], 7. *E/A* [Twenty-nine] [aspirin], 8. *A/E* [American] [know-how], 9. *D/C* [*Hindenburg*] [thirty], 10. *B/E* [Samuel Boston, Jr., or Samuel Boston, Sr.,] [Two-for-One Award], 11. *A/D* ["Didn't] [*Queen Elizabeth II*], 12. *C/A* [four verses] [Bible], 13. *D/B* [*Citizen Kane*] [MGM or RKO], 14. *C/E* [twelve] [22-foot], 15. *B/E* [5:00 A.M.] [dog-eat-dog], 16. *D/A* [*ne plus ultra*] [Jaguar], 17. *C/B* [Five] [e.g.,], 18. *A/E* [(FDIC)] [I-96], 19. *B/C* [Ingrid Littleton, B.A., M.S., Ph.D.,] [ten or twelve], 20. *D/E* [*self-sufficient*], 21. *E/D* [short-fused] [*Time*.], 22. *A/C* [Professor Glaspell's] [four 7-page reports.], 23. *B/A* [3:00 P.M.] [Swedish], 24. *C/D* [seven 400-page books] [*The Emergence of Man*], 25. *E/D* [son-in-law] [*sesquipedalian*].

Chapter 6
Current Conventions of Punctuation

The Comma

The comma, the most frequently used mark of punctuation, functions in two fundamental ways: (1) to separate certain parts of the sentence from the rest of the sentence and (2) to enclose or set off words, phrases, or clauses that interrupt the normal or smooth word-flow of the sentence.

Commas to Separate

Compound sentence   In a compound sentence—that is, a sentence with two independent clauses joined by one of the coordinating conjunctions *and, but, or, nor, for, yet,* or *so*—the clauses are separated by a comma that precedes the coordinating conjunction.

1. Rufus ordered the duck, *but* Bruno preferred the liver.
2. Elizabeth went home on Thursday, *for* she was weary of all the turmoil on campus.
3. The ideas were original, *and* they were well presented.
4. Ginger had already seen the video, *so* she allowed Bennet to borrow it.
5. Jonathan is worth a million dollars, *yet* he says that he does not feel wealthy.

6. You must hand in your assignments on time, *or* the instructor will reduce the grade they receive.
7. I have not seen Cadwallader lately, *nor* has anyone else seen him.

Items in a series   Items (words, phrases, or clauses) occurring in a series of three or more are separated by commas.

1. Jennifer described the young man as *tall, dark,* and *handsome.*
2. The candidate's supporters included *college students, ordinary laborers, professional people,* and *retirees.*
3. Tirelessly, the posse chased the rustlers *out of town, across the border,* and *into the badlands of Mexico.*
4. Do you know *what you want to make of yourself, what field of study you might pursue,* or *what universities you like?*
5. At the cottage *Avery always unloads the car, Wendy takes the covers off the furniture, Rodney lights the pilots on the furnace and the water heater,* and *auntie quickly begins making familiar food noises in the kitchen.*
6. The unfortunate truth is that *we came, we saw,* and *we capitulated.*

Coordinate adjectives   Two or more adjectives that modify the same noun with equal force and can thus be reversed without changing the meaning of the sentence—coordinate adjectives—are separated by commas. A test to determine whether two adjectives are coordinate is to (mentally) insert an *and* between them. If the meaning is not altered, the adjectives are coordinate.

1. Ingrid has always been a *quiet, unassuming* person.
2. That was an *ugly, monstrous* thing to say.
3. The *hot, muggy* weather had done its worst on the audience.
4. My history instructor plays the role of *bumbling, confused, absentminded* professor flawlessly.
5. The old library building was once surmounted by a *tall, stately, ivy-covered* tower.

Contrasting coordinate elements   Commas are used to separate contrasting coordinate elements occurring at the ends of sentences, whether they are words, phrases, or clauses. Note that the final three examples that follow are sometimes called "tag" questions.

1. A hockey game has periods, *not quarters.*
2. The answer was incredible, *not incredulous.*
3. Your low grade is the result of laziness, *not stupidity.*
4. Francine's best pitch is a slider, *not a curve.*
5. Books should be read, *not put on the shelf as some sort of wall decoration.*
6. The harder we worked, *the more behind we got.*
7. The more sleep we got, *the more we seemed to need.*
8. Balthazar asked about his grade, *didn't he?*

9. Our presentation was the best one, *wasn't it?*

10. You had a good time, *didn't you?*

Elements that might be misread   As a matter of discretion, commas are used to separate any words or other sentence elements that might be misread without the comma. Each of the following sentences would likely be misread if the comma was omitted.

1. The day after, the book mysteriously appeared on the dining room table.
2. Several of the players came in, in an angry frame of mind.
3. Shortly after seven, forty-five more volunteers arrived at the gymnasium.
4. Rather than cod, perch was the fish of choice.
5. Stanley had the blues, and his girlfriend took good care of him.
6. In 1990, 684 freshmen dropped out of school.
7. Pilots who like to watch elephants, fly low over the game reserve.
8. To Alice, Carter was a mysterious character.
9. Those who can afford to, go to the beach every weekend.
10. If you can, tell me what your brother said about me.

A variety of introductory constructions are separated from the rest of the sentence by commas. They include (1) adverbs and conjunctive adverbs, (2) mild interjections, (3) adverbial clauses, (4) verbals and verbal phrase modifiers, (5) absolute phrases, (6) longer prepositional phrases, and (7) transitional expressions.

Adverbs and conjunctive adverbs   Many *-ly* adverbs appearing at the beginning of sentences are followed by a comma. Other introductory adverbs are followed by a comma when the omission of the comma would confuse the meaning of the sentence. Introductory conjunctive adverbs—words like *accordingly, also, consequently, furthermore, however, likewise, nevertheless, nonetheless, otherwise, therefore,* and *thus*—are followed by a comma; these adverbs modify the sentence in which they appear and connect the sentence to the one preceding it.

1. *Actually,* the game wasn't as close as the final score would suggest.
2. *Slowly,* Norbert became aware of his surroundings.
3. *Unfortunately,* the day did not end any better than it began.
4. *Before,* the lad had been a normal and optimistic young man.
5. *Below,* the turgid river roared beneath the fragile bridge with a scary intensity.
6. *Later,* that very issue was brought up again.
7. The pay was excellent; *however,* the working conditions were unacceptable.
8. We did not like the candidate's position on pay equity; *therefore,* we did not endorse her.
9. *Nevertheless,* people continue to invest substantial amounts of money in the bond market.
10. *Accordingly,* all the speakers limited themselves to fifteen minutes.

Mild interjections   Exclamatory words—mild interjections—that begin a sentence are separated from the rest of the sentence by a comma.

1. *Alas,* prospective employers were not standing in line on graduation day.

2. *Ah,* if people would put as much energy into their causes as they do their hobbies, they could move the world.

3. *Fie,* we have lost our vision and are not the people we once were.

4. *Tush, tush,* you tested the law and found it a good student.

5. *Whoops,* I misspoke myself.

Adverbial clauses An adverb clause is a clause that functions as an adverb; that is, it modifies the things that an adverb modifies. Adverb clauses are usually introduced by such subordinators as *after, although, as, as if, as though, because, before, even though, if, in order that, once, only, since, so that, than, unless, until, when, whenever, where, whereas, wherever, whether,* and *while.* When an adverb clause occurs at the beginning of a sentence, it is usually separated from the rest of the sentence by a comma.

1. *After Cadwallader swam the channel,* nothing intimidated him.

2. *When I became a man,* I began to invest in much more expensive toys.

3. *Whenever Ermengarde sees the mountains of West Virginia,* she is thrilled to the marrow.

4. *Before you grease the monkey,* you should buff the dog.

5. *Wherever Melinda goes,* Leopold will be close behind.

6. *If the tax is too high,* the revenue will be nothing.

7. *Once you have faced death as a regular part of your daily employment,* an occasional threat of personal injury seems a bit ordinary.

8. *Although I love you,* I do not love your faults.

Verbals and verbal phrase modifiers Introductory verbals and verbal phrases used as modifiers—in most instances those of the participle or infinitive variety—are followed by a comma to separate them from the rest of the sentence. Modifying phrases that begin with a preposition but contain a gerund—that is, an *-ing* noun—also fall into the category of verbal phrase modifiers. They, too, may occur at the beginning of the sentence and be followed by a comma.

1. *Undiscouraged,* the team fought back and tied the score.

2. *Laughing,* the children approached the monster with casual innocence.

3. *Frustrated yet smiling,* Dexter prepared for this third try at seventeen feet.

4. *To survive,* we learned to live off the land.

5. *Deserted for more than forty years,* the village looked like a geographical time capsule.

6. *Catching sight of the flag,* the soldiers fought on to victory.

7. *Standing at the top of the mountain,* the old man shouted a greeting across the valley.

8. *To get the most for your money,* you should shop at the government surplus outlet.

9. *By telling me your deepest secrets,* you have put yourself at my mercy forever.

10. *After pausing for applause and after receiving none,* the speaker left the podium.

Absolute phrases   An absolute phrase usually consists of a noun or pronoun followed by a present or past participle modifying the noun or pronoun. Although the participle is usually expressed, it may be understood. The expression is called "absolute" because it modifies no particular word in the main clause of the sentence, yet it is not able to stand alone as a sentence itself. Introductory absolute phrases are followed by a comma. Similarly, absolute phrases that conclude a sentence are preceded by a comma.

1. *The occasion being an important one,* no one wanted to miss it.
2. *It being midday,* the sun was almost directly overhead.
3. *Their time together having run its course,* they parted and never met again.
4. *Your party over,* there was nothing left to do for the rest of the week.
5. *Our hopes for instant wealth again shattered,* we tossed the worthless lottery tickets on the fire.
6. *Her nose in the air,* Candice walked past without speaking to any of her old friends.
7. Algernon sold his entire collection, *his interest in Elvis Presley memorabilia having died of natural causes.*
8. *All things considered,* most people would prefer wealth over poverty.
9. *To make a long story short,* the public education system cannot attract first-rate people to be teachers. (Note that this absolute phrase is an infinitive phrase.)
10. The farmhands worked frantically, *the storm almost upon them.*

Longer prepositional phrases   Prepositional phrases—except short ones that create no confusion—occurring at the beginning of sentences are usually followed by a comma to separate the phrase from the rest of the sentence. Often, these long prepositional phrases will have compound parts and are actually two or three phrases in succession.

1. *After a six-course dinner and a four-act play,* we were ready to collapse.
2. *With the possible exception of one or two figures,* the report was quite accurate.
3. *Because of a lifelong fear of being drowned in the sea,* Bork spent the afternoon sunning himself on the beach.
4. *As a result of his loss of face in recent weeks,* Cadwallader had become persona non grata on campus.
5. *After the final performance of the season,* the local drama society always throws a big party. (The comma may be borderline in this sentence.)

Transitional expressions   Finally, introductory transitional expressions are often separated by commas from the sentences they begin. For convenience, we here define the term *transitional expressions* in a general way to mean "any words or phrases, other than those already taken up under other headings, that serve to enhance writing coherence by assisting the smooth word-flow from sentence to sentence." Transitional expressions improve sentence coherence through indications of such things as time passage, spatial arrangement, addition, comparison, contrast, cause/effect, concession, enumeration, exemplification, or summarization.

1. *After a time,* a truce was called and the fighting ceased. (time indication)
2. *In the future,* no company should enter into such agreements. (time indication)

3. *To the north,* what was left of the village was still smoldering. (spatial indication)

4. *In the distance,* Edmund could just make out the silhouette of the monument. (spatial indication)

5. *In addition,* many of the better students began leaving the university to attend other schools. (indication of addition)

6. *In all,* this simpleminded experiment cost Acme three subsidiaries. (indication of addition)

7. *In like manner,* Bland Corporation reduced the quality of its products and went into the retail market. (indication of comparison)

8. *With similar motives,* Cadwallader began reading books about the safe use of high explosives. (indication of comparison)

9. *By contrast,* such a position will never be popular with the over-fifty voter. (indication of contrast)

10. *On the other hand,* we might move our operation to Central America and save a fortune on labor costs. (indication of contrast)

11. *As a result,* we have lost markets that we will never be able to recapture. (cause/effect)

12. *As a consequence,* there will be fewer competing companies in the domestic airline business. (cause/effect)

13. *Although marketable,* the line would be only marginally profitable. (indication of concession)

14. *Even though justifiable,* such actions are regrettable in the long run. (indication of concession)

15. *In the first place,* we no longer have suppliers on whom we can always depend. (indication of enumeration)

16. *Thirdly,* your so-called new ideas are really old ideas wrapped in plastic. (indication of enumeration)

17. *For example,* a seven percent increase in benefits will cost us tens of millions over three years. (indication of exemplification)

18. *For instance,* more than 40 million Americans are now without basic medical insurance. (indication of exemplification)

19. *In conclusion,* we need new and original ideas, not more clever sales gimmicks. (indication of summarization)

20. *On the whole,* the company is better off than it should be. (indication of summarization)

The following exercise quiz provides you the opportunity to insert any commas needed to separate items in each of the fifty sentences *and* to label the reasons for the commas by matching the appropriate letters with the appropriate sentences. Place the capital letters—from the list at the top—in the blanks in front of the sentences. All the sentences require one or more commas to separate; however, no sentence requires commas for more than one reason.

EXERCISE
Commas to Separate

A. Compound Sentence
B. Items In a Series
C. Coordinate Adjectives
D. Contrasting Coordinate Elements
E. Reading Clarification
F. Introductory Adverb

G. Mild Introductory Interjection
H. Introductory Adverb Clause
I. Introductory Verbal (Phrase) Modifier
J. Introductory Absolute Phrase
K. Long Introductory Prepositional Phrase(s)
L. Introductory Transitional Expression

_____ 1. The last traitor having been shot the villagers retired to their humble cottages for a meal of gruel and black bread.

_____ 2. Our first stop was either the Globe Theatre or Madame Tussaud's not the Tower of London.

_____ 3. My how bold we are when we are young and do not yet know what a hard place the world is.

_____ 4. Everyone feared that the building might cave in in the middle of the night.

_____ 5. In conclusion we think we are safe in saying that life in the Great Lakes region was not particularly lyrical during the 1700s.

_____ 6. The Brotherhood of the Bulging Biceps toasted the coach the mayor the governor the president and the makers of toast.

_____ 7. Many of the residents of Friendly Lake are quite famous but they prefer to be inconspicuous when they are on holiday.

_____ 8. Fortunately the Osgoods had invested their money in bonds unaffected by the stock market.

_____ 9. One does not expect to discover such a full-flavored robust wine in a screw-top bottle with a label that reads "Zippy."

_____ 10. If you put a chain around the neck of a slave the other end fastens itself firmly around your own.

_____ 11. After three weeks on the road and several bouts with mean-spirited mosquitoes most of the students were looking forward to sleeping in their own beds.

_____ 12. Turning her eyes toward the open window Marigold caught a glimpse of the fleeing Martians.

_____ 13. It is difficult not to respond to a person with such a friendly energetic forthright personality.

_____ 14. Gretchen has decided to become a professional volleyball player not a waste management engineer.

_____ 15. Laughing loudly with a mouthful of food Vernon embarrassed everyone at the table.

_____ 16. If I win the $40 million lottery prize on Saturday I think I'll take a brief holiday on Monday.

_____ 17. The day was a cold and rainy one yet our hearts were overflowing with optimism.

_____ 18. Customarily it is the bride who brings a dowry to the marriage.

_____ 19. Senators Flimflam Hayseed Doublespeak and Kickback are all opposed to the term-limitation bill.

_____ 20. Alas poor Roderick has lost his desire to master the fluegelhorn.

_____ 21. In almost total darkness and with no experience in the wilderness Balthazer inched his way along the narrow ledge.

_____ 22. Brumback said that once inside the cats began trashing the camper.

_____ 23. Helen was a bit of a grim person and she had no inclination toward personality modification.

_____ 24. Mercedes was a very sociable individual. By contrast her younger brother was an introvert.

_____ 25. Above the tribesmen observed the search party like vultures contemplating a wounded wildebeest.

_____ 26. Many of the students being ill the picnic was called off.

_____ 27. Ah what a beautiful day it is here among these glistening mountains of garbage.

_____ 28. Those who have the money to buy these items in large quantities and thus get a better price.

_____ 29. Testing the waters too soon after eating Miriam became nauseated as she swam across the lagoon.

_____ 30. No one could believe that Godfrey had committed the dastardly underhanded deed.

_____ 31. Because of the terrible storm and our own fatigue we had to stop for the night.

_____ 32. Not all suburbanites are stereotypical Republicans. For example my cousin, who lives outside East Grand Rapids, considers himself a liberal Democrat.

_____ 33. Although Aldo was pleased with his progress he knew he would have to work harder in the future.

_____ 34. My accomplishments last summer included painting the house planting a few trees in the yard reading several good books and making peace with my contrary neighbors.

_____ 35. The season over many of the players didn't know what to do with all their free time.

_____ 36. Professor Bergman is an exceptional lecturer isn't she?

_____ 37. Few students took the examination seriously; consequently many of them failed it.

_____ 38. Engrossed in her work Gwendolyn forgot to make an appointment with the veterinarian.

_____ 39. Behold young master Gilbert is now able to tie both of his shoes with a single string.

_____ 40. At the very site of my childhood home on top of Bloodhound Mountain the federal government has erected a radio telescope to communicate with aliens in outer space.

_____ 41. The truth was that for Rosemary Burgess seemed a sophisticated and erudite individual.

_____ 42. Stunned by the blow to the head the child wandered about the woods for several hours.

_____ 43. The soft soothing voice of the reader quickly put many of the children to sleep.

_____ 44. Most of the valley had been replanted. To the north one could already see a horizon of green foliage.

_____ 45. No one had put forward a proposal to deal with the problem nor was anyone likely to do so.

_____ 46. Monument would be a village without a future the railroad having gone elsewhere.

_____ 47. The more Marco studied the worse he seemed to do on the daily quizzes.

_____ 48. You might try the basement the shed the neighbor's garage or the repair shop in town.

_____ 49. In the twilight of a spectacular career in the field of education Professor Andresen admitted that if he were a young man today he would choose another occupation.

_____ 50. When my baby walks down the street the little birdies go tweet, tweet, tweet.

Commas to Enclose or Set Off

Nonrestrictive expressions   Commas are used to enclose, or set off, nonrestrictive expressions—that is, adjective clauses, adverb clauses, participial phrases, prepositional phrases, or appositives that provide additional but nonessential information about the items they describe. The descriptive detail provided by nonrestrictive structures is not necessary for _identification_ of the items being modified. Also note that nonrestrictive adverb clauses are sometimes elliptical—that is, the subject or verb, or both, will be omitted but understood.

1. Charleston, _which is neither a northern city nor a southern city,_ is the capital of West Virginia. (adjective clause)

2. Edmund's oldest sister, *who was a fighter pilot in the air force for ten years,* runs a bakery shop on Main Street. (adjective clause)

3. Cruncher Malone, *whose left hook is as good as anyone's in the fight game,* has a good shot at the middleweight title. (adjective clause)

4. Intelligence, *because it is such a difficult thing to define,* should not be used as the sole criterion for judging a person's worth. (adverb clause)

5. I shall leave the house at midnight, *when the clock strikes twelve,* and drive directly to the bank. (adverb clause)

6. Domestic cats, *although notorious for their independent dispositions,* are really very affectionate creatures. (elliptical adverb clause)

7. Your observations, *while both clever and amusing,* are not likely to change anyone's mind. (elliptical adverb clause)

8. The brighter students, *engrossed in their work,* did not hear the tornado warning. (participial phrase)

9. Vera's friend, *discovering the winning ticket in her purse,* began to jump up and down and scream. (participial phrase)

10. Bruno's manuscript, *rejected by all the publishers in New York and left on the shelf for years,* has become a best-selling novel. (participial phrase)

11. Angela, *at the top of her game,* was eager to take on all challengers. (prepositional phrase)

12. This team, *on its home field,* can give any other team in the conference a lesson in hard-nosed football. (prepositional phrase)

13. Estelle, *our newly elected chair,* will conduct her first meeting on Monday night. (appositive)

14. The birch, *a tree indigenous to the region,* is rapidly dying off. (appositive)

15. The two senators under investigation, *namely, Sweetbread and Lockstep,* are a bit past their prime. (appositive)

The following exercise quiz provides you the opportunity to insert any commas needed to enclose nonrestrictive elements in the twenty sentences *and* to label the reasons for the pairs of commas by matching the appropriate letters with the appropriate sentences. Place the capital letters—from the list at the top—in the blanks in front of the sentences. All the sentences require pairs of commas to enclose nonrestrictive elements.

EXERCISE
Commas to Enclose Nonrestrictive Elements

A. Adjective Clause   D. Prepositional Phrase
B. Adverb Clause   E. Appositive
C. Participial Phrase

_____ 1. Zoe's favorite ice cream Cornish vanilla isn't available here in Hinterland, Michigan.

_____ 2. These cars which have come to symbolize the poor quality of American craftsmanship cannot be marketed anywhere in Europe.

_____ 3. Poor Lindley at the end of his rope decided to go home to his parents.

_____ 4. Our night security guards diverted by their usual game of Trivial Pursuit did not notice that the store was being robbed.

_____ 5. The new football stadium once the city obtains sufficient funding will be completed within three years.

_____ 6. Legions of recreational runners enjoying themselves at the rear of the pack and chatting with one another as they went held no illusions about becoming "world-class" marathoners.

_____ 7. Two of our more difficult courses of study namely engineering and chemistry are begging for students.

_____ 8. The papers presented at the conference with one or two exceptions were not of the quality they should have been.

_____ 9. Ida Morris who coached for ten years at Hinterland High has now taken a job at a university.

_____ 10. Your children in a state of panic ran from house to house awakening the neighbors.

_____ 11. Father O'Hare encouraged by the congregation to preach shorter sermons adopted the strategy of talking faster.

_____ 12. A fellow like Lorenzo wherever he decides to settle will more than likely be successful.

_____ 13. Nelson's grand aim to compose a symphony in honor of poverty proved to be a costly mistake.

_____ 14. The old colonial house at 15 Elm Street where our first two children were born is for sale.

_____ 15. Mayor Simpleton hoping to encourage students to patronize local shops hung university pennants from the lampposts in town.

_____ 16. These plans for reorganizing the university while interesting enough theoretically could if implemented severely reduce the student population.

_____ 17. This young woman without assistance from anyone has put herself through medical school.

_____ 18. Mary Ryan whose mother taught her to sew has become a famous dress designer.

_____ 19. These things working from a hidden agenda and lying to the public will eventually chase you from office.

_____ 20. The word _discrimination_ because it is often used in negative contexts has gotten a bad reputation.

Commas are also used to enclose or set off (1) parenthetical expressions, (2) a direct address, (3) modifiers out of their usual position, (4) direct quotations, (5) degrees and titles, (6) dates, (7) addresses, and (8) to "punctuate" large numbers.

Parenthetical expressions Words, phrases, or clauses that interrupt the word-flow of a sentence to emphasize something, to qualify what has already been said, or to move thought in a particular direction are parenthetical expressions. Many of the same words or phrases that are used as ordinary introductory adverbs, conjunctive adverbs, or transitional expressions when they appear at the beginning of a sentence and connect the sentence to the previous sentence are considered parenthetical expressions when they occur within a sentence, or within the main clause of a sentence; that is, when they interrupt rather than connect.

1. Several studies, *incidentally,* have shown that on average professional athletes live shorter lives than the general population. (adverb)

2. The movie was, *nonetheless,* an improvement on the book. (adverb)

3. Those same board members have also indicated, *however,* that they do not intend to reappoint the president. (adverb)

4. Ann's point, *in brief,* was that even a healthy free market does not solve all of society's problems. (prepositional phrase)

5. Income and sales taxes, *on the other hand,* work from the broadest possible base. (prepositional phrase)

6. One might want to consider, *for example,* the higher costs of shipping such small quantities of goods. (prepositional phrase)

7. The experience of spending a month in the wilderness, *to tell the truth,* taught me several things I really didn't want to know. (infinitive phrase)

8. My opinion of this fellow, *to be blunt about it,* is that he is a scoop short of a cone. (infinitive phrase)

9. It is Ted's opinion, *if anyone wants to hear Ted's opinion,* that violence should be avoided when the opposition is so inclined to violence. (adverb clause)

10. The dean of students, *according to local gossips,* intends to resign his position and enter a Tibetan monastery. (prepositional phrase)

11. Better business practices, *i.e., prudence,* might have saved the college much of its current difficulty. (clause)

12. The university invited the governor, *not one of his subordinates,* to address the graduating class. (contrasting phrase)

A direct address Words or phrases in direct address name whatever or whomever is spoken to. Such expressions are enclosed or set off by commas.

1. You shall, *sir,* do precisely what your commanding officer orders you to do.

2. We are gathered here tonight, *ladies and gentlemen,* to discuss how to protect our children against a violent society.

3. We hope, *gentle readers,* that you will be better acquainted with the comma when you have completed this part of the book.

4. *O World,* I cannot hold thee close enough.

5. Awake, *old dreams,* and remind me how wonderful it was to be young and immortal.

Modifiers out of their usual position   In a sentence, modifiers occurring out of their normal position are usually enclosed by commas.

1. Maple trees, *tall and well-shaped,* lined the front of the property.
2. My father's farm equipment, *old and rusty,* was scattered about the unplowed fields.
3. The three-story house at 25 Elm Street, *Victorian,* was once owned by a wealthy lumber baron.
4. Your opinions, *thoroughly Midwestern,* are as monotonous as their namesake.
5. His mystery novels, *carefully plotted,* are much more compact than his better-known works.

Direct quotations   In most instances, commas are used to set off a direct quotation from the identifying tag—that is, the expression that identifies the speaker of the quotation.

1. Elizabeth said sadly, "I have seen all this before."
2. "I have seen all this before," Elizabeth said sadly.
3. "This will have to do," Elizabeth said sadly, "until the public realizes the seriousness of the situation."
4. "This will have to do," Elizabeth said sadly; "the public doesn't yet realize the seriousness of the situation."
5. "I had a wonderful time," Elizabeth said happily. "We shall have to come here again."

Notice that in example sentences 4 and 5 the identifying tag is *not* followed by a comma. The reason for this is that in these two sentences both parts of the (split) direct quotation are independent clauses; thus, a comma after the identifying tag would be a comma splice, a punctuation error covered later in the text. A semicolon (rather than a period) is the better choice in sentence 4 because the implication or suggestion of "because" exists between the two parts of the quotation. In sentence 3, a comma follows the word "sadly" in the identifying tag because the second part of the quotation is *not* an independent clause; it is an adverb clause.

Degrees and titles   Commas are used to enclose or set off academic degrees, titles, or initials (in alphabetization) when they follow a person's name.

1. Those who knew him considered Henry Wolf, *Ph.D.,* a pianist and musicologist extraordinaire.
2. Some people thought Martin Luther King, *Jr.,* was an orator the equal of Winston Churchill.
3. All manuscripts should be sent to Norbert Pennyworth, *Editor-in-Chief,* unless the author has been instructed otherwise.
4. In recent time, Charles, *Prince of Wales,* seems to have been experiencing a bit of trouble with hearth and home.
5. Artman, *M. R.,* Ashbury, *V. T.,* and Atkins, *W. C.,* are at the top of the revised list.

Dates   When a full date is given—including the day of the week—a comma follows the day of the week, the date of the month, and the year. When only the month and year are given

(September 1969), no commas are used. Similarly, when the sequence is date-month-year (28 November 1938), no commas are used.

1. The Japanese launched their surprise attack on Pearl Harbor on Sunday, December 7, 1941, at 7:55 A.M. local time.
2. Cadwallader lived in Chicago from February 1984 until October 1987.
3. We guarantee that on 26 November 1993 this will be the busiest store in Water Tower Place.
4. I still remember where I was and what I was doing on November 22, 1963, when the terrible news came; do you remember?
5. Eleanor's father was killed on June 8, 1944, during the Allied invasion of Western Europe; however, she didn't learn about it until February 1945.

Addresses   In addresses and place names, a comma is used after each major part, including the name of the state. However, if a ZIP code is included, no comma precedes or follows it. In most instances, the inclusion of ZIP codes should be confined to business type writing.

1. Malcolm Anthony Swain was born at 1492 Portage Place, Charleston, West Virginia, on December 10, 1938, as he often said, at a very early age.
2. We canvassed the voters in Hinterland, Michigan, and Stratford, Ontario, with surprisingly similar results.
3. All suggestions about this text should be forwarded by mail to the Department of Languages and Literature, Ferris State University, Big Rapids, Michigan 49307.
4. As far as I can tell, the only similarity between London, Ontario, and London, England, is the name.
5. The mailing address of the hotel you inquired about is 80 Ravenswood Avenue, Tunbridge Wells, Kent TN2 3SJ.

Large numbers   With large numbers (five digits or more), a comma is used between each set of three digits, counting right to left. Some people prefer to use the comma with four-digit numbers as well. The test, however, isn't the number of digits; it is pronunciation. If the four-digit number 1999 is intended to be read "nineteen hundred and ninety-nine" in the sentence context where it occurs, there should be no comma. However, if it is intended to be read "one thousand nine hundred and ninety-nine," there should be a comma. Also note that commas are never used in telephone numbers, street numbers, social security numbers, ZIP codes, or the year in ordinary dates.

1. Although we expected only about 25,000 responses to our advertisements, the number exceeded 250,000 in only a week.
2. The film made some $85,000,000 while playing before audiences totaling in excess of 20,000,000 people.
3. If the average price of a car is $22,500 and the average price of a house is $150,000, how can one survive on an average family income of $36,000?

In the following exercise quiz, insert all necessary commas in the twenty-five sentences *and* indicate the reason for the commas by placing the appropriate letters in the blanks in front of the sentences.

EXERCISE
Commas to Enclose or Set Off

A. Parenthetical Expression   E. Degree/Title/Initials
B. Direct Address   F. Date
C. Modifier in Unusual Position   G. Address/Place Name
D. Direct Quotation   H. Number

_____ 1. According to our records William Bobolink Sr. and William Bobolink Jr. have the same birth date.

_____ 2. On Saturday December 10 1938 American novelist Pearl Buck was presented the Nobel Prize for Literature in Stockholm.

_____ 3. Between 10000 B.C. and 1990 the population of the world increased from 10000000 to 5420000000 souls.

_____ 4. Professor Dillman did in fact announce that the class would have a test on Monday.

_____ 5. Denver Colorado will be the location of our home office by 15 March 1993.

_____ 6. Rain Rain go away and don't come back until another day.

_____ 7. "These units must be in Buffalo by noon Tuesday" the foreman said to the loading crew.

_____ 8. Brumback stood up and announced of all things that he intended to give his fortune to the London Society for the Prevention of Bad Manners.

_____ 9. Your positions in these matters typically liberal will not sell well in my part of the country.

_____ 10. Ashley Plimpton D.B.A. Ph.D. M.D. seems to be a fellow with time on his hands these days.

_____ 11. Gonzo's first shot although one could hardly call it a shot collided with a tree and finally came to rest thirty-five yards behind the tee.

_____ 12. Some 6000000 Jews were among the 9000000 people systematically exterminated by Hitler's Nazis during the Holocaust associated with World War II.

_____ 13. "A tax system that punishes people for working" Harriet said "will eventually have a regressive effect on the economy."

_____ 14. The instructions were to send all entries to 18075 Hemlock Boulevard Hinterland Michigan by 30 November 1993.

_____ 15. Sit Fido and show these wonderful people what a smart dog you are.

_____ 16. The committee might on the other hand choose someone from outside the organization.

307

_____ 17. The closet contained a hundred suits custom-made that had apparently never been worn.

_____ 18. Did Christopher Columbus really discover America on Monday October 12 1492?

_____ 19. Gibbs J. L. Giddings C. D. and Giffen J. V. have all been removed from the acceptance list.

_____ 20. O Lord how manifold are Thy mercies throughout the earth.

_____ 21. "Turn out the lights" Roxane yawned; "the party is over."

_____ 22. It was during the night of Tuesday April 18 1775 that Paul Revere made his famous ride through the Massachusetts countryside to warn the people that the British were coming.

_____ 23. Reason if anyone still cares about reason would suggest that we do a little more research before spending a few billion dollars.

_____ 24. Is it true that Canton Ohio is the birthplace of professional football in the United States?

_____ 25. The discussions very heated extended late into the night.

The Semicolon and the Colon

The Semicolon

The semicolon is a mark of punctuation (;) that separates sentence elements only. It indicates a greater break or longer pause than does the comma, but not an ending break like one of the terminal marks of punctuation: the period, the question mark, or the exclamation point.

The four specific uses of the semicolon are (1) to separate closely related independent clauses *not* joined by one of the coordinating conjunctions (*and, but, or, nor, for, yet,* and *so*); (2) to separate independent clauses joined by a coordinating conjunction when one (usually the first) or both clauses already contain commas or other internal punctuation; (3) to separate independent clauses joined by either conjunctive adverbs (e.g., *accordingly, also, anyway, besides, consequently, furthermore, hence, however, indeed, instead, likewise, moreover, nevertheless, nonetheless, notwithstanding, otherwise, similarly, still, then, therefore, thus*) or transitional expressions functioning like conjunctive adverbs; and (4) to separate items in a series when the items themselves contain commas. The following fifteen sentences demonstrate these uses.

1. The witnesses refused to testify; they were fearful for their lives.
2. Eight hours of hard labor in a day is enough; tired workers make mistakes and thus cost you money.
3. A week in the wilderness was sufficient; everyone was ready for running water and a soft bed.

4. Few students write as well as Kirsten; they are not willing to labor over the necessary revisions.

5. My first two years in college were a revelation; I discovered all the things that I knew absolutely nothing about.

6. We ordered a mat cutter, two picture frames, four brushes, and a video about watercolors; *but* the company sent us three sheets of Plexiglas, a miter box, a dozen tubes of oil paints, and a video about painting with acrylics.

7. Our days were quiet, peaceful, and rejuvenating; *and* our nights were, well, embellished by several tall, dark strangers.

8. Left-handed people think differently, perceive the world differently, even fall in love differently; *yet* most of them manage to get through life without overthrowing the government or setting fire to a cathedral.

9. We have been told a thousand times that computers are inanimate mechanical devices; *nevertheless,* they often display a number of human-like idiosyncrasies.

10. The plans were well made; *however,* their implementation was carried out by morons and maniacs.

11. Germany, East as well as West, seems to have recovered from World War II; *indeed,* the Fatherland will likely become the dominant economic power in Europe in the twenty-first century.

12. Each year the university publishes the names of programs that might be discontinued; this year, *for example,* ornamental horticulture and business economics were threatened with execution.

13. Carlotta spent a dozen years in the rain forest of Brazil working on her doctoral dissertation; *in like manner,* her brother Jules has passed ten years in the laboratory searching for a cure for AIDS.

14. Ginger concluded that the youth was tall, but not too tall; dark, but not too dark; and handsome, but not too handsome.

15. Present at the meeting were Augustus Hitzemann, mayor of the city; Trudy Lord, owner of the Long Branch Bar and Grill; Harley Crowley, the chief of police; Dudley Moorse and Cicely Wooten, the arresting officers; and the accused, three criminal justice students from the university.

Sentences 1 through 5 all demonstrate the first usage, to separate two closely related independent clauses *not* joined by a coordinating conjunction. Notice that the "closely related" characteristic of the pairs of sentences occurs in the notion of "because" at the point of the semicolon. This is not an absolute requirement for the use of a semicolon alone between independent clauses, but it is a sound practice. Sentences 6 through 8 are examples of the semicolon separating independent clauses joined by a coordinating conjunction with both clauses containing commas. Notice that if a comma were also used before the coordinating conjunction, some reading awkwardness might occur.

Sentences 9 through 11 are examples of the semicolon used to separate independent clauses joined by a conjunctive adverb. Notice that the conjunctive adverbs are also followed by a comma, as we have already seen in the previous section of the text. Sentences 12 and 13 provide examples of transitional expressions functioning exactly as conjunctive adverbs do in the joining of independent clauses. In sentence 12 the transitional expression *for example* does not follow the semicolon, but occurs within the second clause. This is a good usage and can also occur with conjunctive adverbs. The semicolon, however, remains at the point where the clauses come together, and the transitional expression or conjunctive adverb is enclosed by commas. Sentences 14 and 15 demonstrate how items in a series are separated by semicolons when the items themselves contain commas.

The Colon

The colon is a formal mark of punctuation (:) used to introduce or to separate. Colons typically introduce (1) appositives, (2) a list or a series, (3) formal quotations, or (4) an explanation. Colons separate (1) titles from subtitles, (2) minutes from hours in numerical expressions of time, and (3) chapter from verse in Biblical citations. The following sentences demonstrate these uses.

1. Everything Gwendolyn is doing at the present time is directed at a single goal: gainful employment.

2. There is one appeal that should not be overlooked: bribery.

3. Cadwallader had only one alternative left: to travel by magic carpet.

4. When it comes to reading for pleasure, Brice usually focuses on his favorite genre: the murder mystery.

5. It would appear that you want it all: money, power, position, praise, and a place in heaven.

6. When he was in high school, Emmett participated in the following extracurricular activities: varsity basketball and baseball, the chess club, newspaper reporting, the jazz ensemble, and the investment society.

7. If you are a student of American society, you might want to read the following: *Showing Off in America,* by John Brooks; *Class,* by Paul Fussell; *Trivializing America,* by Norman Corwin; *Illiberal Education,* by Dinesh D'Souza; and *The Closing of the American Mind,* by Allan Bloom.

8. To properly prepare this soup, the cook will need the following ingredients: two large baking potatoes, six or seven carrots, one large yellow onion, seventeen-ounce cans of "no salt added" sweet peas and "no salt added" cut green beans, a pound and a half cut from a sirloin roast, salt, pepper, parsley, thyme, bay leaves, barley, and a thirty-ounce can of "no salt added" tomato puree—fancy quality.

9. At the beginning of the press conference, the president made the following statement: "The first amendment was not intended to guarantee the press exclusive authority to choose our candidates for public office."

10. President Kennedy concluded his speech with the now famous declaration: *"Ich bin ein Berliner."*

11. After reading the remarks I had written on his paper, the young man articulated his credo of higher education: "Look, I came to college to get an education, not to have no one like you mess with my mind."

12. Globally, we are headed for a disaster: throughout the Third World, population is increasing much faster than food production.

13. Many of these students have come to college with a self-imposed handicap: they are barely able to read and write.

14. Professor Pedantic has a very irritating way of making a point: he always quotes someone else—someone we have never heard of—rather than saying what he has to say in his own words.

15. Common sense suggests that the following strategy is in order: (1) apologize for your recklessness, (2) swear on a stack of Bibles that it will never happen again, (3) pay for the damage to the car *and* the house, and (4) take your parents to the Hoof and Claw for Sunday dinner.

16. Bruce Catton's well-known essay "Grant and Lee: A Study in Contrasts" appears in virtually all freshman readers.

17. Lew Wallace's classic novel *Ben Hur: A Tale of the Christ* has been made into two four-star motion pictures, the first in 1926 by director Fred Niblo, and again in 1957 by William Wyler.

18. The unidentified flying objects finally disappeared from the screen at precisely 3:17 A.M. local time.

19. The title of this science fiction thriller is *11:59 P.M. and Counting: A Narrative of the Apocalypse*.

20. You can find the Ten Commandments in Exodus 20:1-17.

Sentences 1 through 5 all present examples of the colon introducing an appositive. Sentences 6 through 8 include examples of lists or series, and 9 through 11 demonstrate the colon introducing a formal quotation. Note with the lists that the word *following* precedes the colon in the sentence. Examples 12 through 15 demonstrate the colon introducing an explanation—that is, the material (sentence or sentences) following the colon explains more completely what is said in the sentence preceding the colon. Sentences 16 through 20 provide examples of the colon separating things: title from subtitle in books and essays, minutes from hours in numerical expressions of time, and chapter from verse in Biblical citations.

Each of the sentences in the following exercise quiz requires that a comma be removed from the sentence and replaced by either a semicolon or a colon. As a mental exercise, explain to yourself *why* each semicolon or colon is needed and, if you are game, why each comma that you remove was incorrectly used.

EXERCISE
Semicolon and Colon

1. The Sermon on the Mount, an important segment of the New Testament, can be found in Luke 6,20-49, not the Book of Revelation.

2. Among the most popular artists at the fair were Vivian Lewis, a watercolorist, Ian Holmes, a sculptor, Stephen Price, who specializes in family portraits, and Estelle Tice, who works in both oils and acrylics.

3. One attribute, equally unpleasant and unfortunate, dominates Florence's response to anyone, friend or foe, who has accomplished anything significant, jealousy.

4. Few of the workers, family men, favor the wage freeze, on the other hand, the company's offer to continue fully paid medical insurance is quite attractive.

311

5. A science fiction fanatic, Meta used to be infatuated by Ray Bradbury's novel *Fahrenheit 451;* now, however, she is obsessed with Arthur Clark's *2001, A Space Odyssey.*

6. Although they had had an interesting trip, especially in Ireland, Spain, and Norway, the students looked forward to the flight home, they wanted to see their friends.

7. To play major league baseball, you must be able to do the following things, run, throw, catch, hit, think, and stay out of trouble between games.

8. Reynard's brothers, sisters, aunts, and uncles went on the first plane, and his parents, grandparents, and cousins went on the second plane.

9. As was almost always the case, the night train, which was something of a mechanical monster to us, entered the station at precisely 11,48 P.M., took on passengers and water, then departed at 12,18 A.M. for places we couldn't even imagine.

10. Most people in the audience, quite conservative, didn't like what you said, moreover, they didn't like the way you said it.

11. After a life that had included four wives, many children, many more grandchildren, making and losing several fortunes, and being revered by most literate people on earth, the celebrated author said that there was only one thing he wanted but could not have, immortality.

12. The rescued pilot, stranded for seven years on a desert island, was amazed to be found, she had expected to spend the rest of her days alone.

13. The following people are instructed to report to the registrar, Burchett, D. G., Faller, A. F., Isanhart, C. K., and Schneider, R. H.

14. For these people, and millions of others like them, the American Dream has become a nightmare, for example, none of them, not one, can hope to save enough money to make a down payment on a decent house.

15. Having completed the address, Kennedy then made his great challenge to the American people, "Ask not what your country can do for you, but what you can do for your country."

16. Most days were long, tedious, hard, furthermore, the weather was bitter cold, life threatening.

17. I can never remember; is it John 3,16 that begins "For God so loved the world"?

18. When my English teacher casually instructed the class to read the personal essay "Okinawa, The Bloodiest Battle of All," written by William Manchester, the author of *Death of a President,* I had no idea what I was in for.

19. Now and then, everyone enjoys a fortnight in Europe, a week at the beach, a weekend on the slopes, an evening on the town, but for regular, everyday living, the nuts and bolts stuff, most people prefer their noses pretty close to the grindstone.

20. Whether anyone wants to hear about it or not, this company faces a major, and potentially fatal, problem, no one wants to buy our overpriced, shoddily constructed cars.

21. The lady was attractive, although not too attractive, intelligent, although not too intelligent, and ambitious, although not too ambitious.

22. On the morning of July 16, 1945, apparently unable to think of another strategy, we settled the disagreement about whether or not exploding an atomic bomb would also destroy the universe, we took a deep breath, closed our eyes, stuck our fingers into our ears, and set one off.

23. Incredibly, the flight made stops at Columbia, South Carolina, Asheville, North Carolina, Roanoke, Virginia, Charleston, West Virginia, and Columbus, Ohio, before going on to Chicago.

24. If it has tail feathers, waddles, and quacks, it is probably a duck, however, if it has tail feathers, waddles, and says things like "reconstructed deconstructionism," "dialectical epitome," or "semiotic ambiguity," it is probably a practicing rhetorician.

25. Satchel Paige, the legendary pitcher in the old Negro baseball leagues, and, toward the end of his career after the color barrier had fallen, in the major leagues, when asked about life, always offered the following advice, "Don't look back; someone might be gaining on you."

The Period, Question Mark, and Exclamation Point

Periods, question marks, and exclamation points are used primarily to mark the ends of sentences; thus, they are called *end marks*.

The Period

The period is used at the end of a declarative sentence (a statement), a mild command, or an indirect question.

1. All my classes this semester meet on Monday, Wednesday, and Friday.
2. The summers are much cooler in Michigan than they are in Georgia.
3. Please contact the members of the study group by next Wednesday.
4. Take the time to do your warm-up exercises before beginning the workout.
5. The children asked whether or not Santa Claus would be able to find our new house.
6. Several instructors inquired about the extent of your injuries.

Periods are also used within/after abbreviations, and three (spaced) periods used together indicate an ellipsis—that is, words omitted—in a quotation.

1. At precisely 3:09 P.M. Desiree Fizer, Ph.D., entered the classroom, introduced herself as Ms. Fizer, then began a lecture about the importance of promptness in the business world.
2. According to U.S. government statistics, caring for the indigent—i.e., those who do not feed, clothe, and house themselves—costs taxpayers billions of dollars each year.

3. The hospital director made the following statement: "When ten patients pay the bills for thirty patients, those ten . . . pay for three times the services they used."

4. Desmond Morris says, "The development of the pair-bond . . . will naturally favour monogamy, but it does not absolutely demand it."

The Question Mark

The question mark follows a direct question, which in English can be arranged in several ways. A question mark inside parentheses, for example, can be used to indicate doubt or uncertainty about the accuracy of something that is said.

1. Will someone please show me how to put this thing together?
2. You really do know the difference between a crow and a raven?
3. Why is everyone acting so silly?
4. Where is the race supposed to begin?
5. Which house is the one where the president slept?
6. We're going home next weekend, aren't we?
7. Who in the Bible asked, "Am I my brother's keeper?"
8. Who said, "The English know nothing about music, but they love the noise it makes"?
9. Malcolm Anthony Swain's great, great, great grandfather, who was born in County Kerry in 1818, came to America in 1834 (?) as a stowaway on a clipper ship.
10. Georgiana bought an expensive leather (?) bag on the reservation.
11. Some of the units (twenty dozen?) were accidentally shipped to California.
12. Someone—an angry employee?—may have put finely ground glass into one of the beef stew vats.
13. We were distressed: Whom should we call? Where could we go for help? Who was trying to kill us? What had we done to provoke such drastic behavior?
14. Where had the culprits hidden? In the house? In the barn? In one of the machine buildings? Somewhere on the property?
15. "Is this the silver bullet that killed Dracula?" an incredulous Cadwallader asked.

Note that sentence number 1 begins with an auxiliary verb. Number 2 would have an entirely different meaning without the question mark; in fact, it wouldn't even be a question. Sentences 3 through 5 demonstrate the types of interrogative markers that often begin questions: *why, where, which,* and so on. Number 6 includes a tag question, which we have already discussed in the comma section. The question mark goes inside the final quotation marks in sentence 7 because the quoted material is a question within the larger question of the sentence. By contrast, the question mark in sentence 8 goes after the final quotation marks because the quoted material is not a question; it is the statement of an opinion. Sentence number 9 indicates an uncertainty about the year 1834; number 10, an uncertainty about whether or not the bag was leather; number 11, an uncertainty about the number of units shipped; and number 12, an uncertainty about whether or not the perpetrator was an angry employee. Also note how dashes (rather than parens) can be employed in some of these constructions. Numbers 13 and 14 demonstrate the use of multiple questions, the former

314

being complete sentences and the latter being phrases. Finally, sentence 15 shows how a direct question can occur at the beginning of a declarative sentence.

The Exclamation Point

The exclamation point is used after words, phrases, or clauses (complete sentences) to indicate strong feeling—e.g., surprise, emphasis, fear, anger, happiness, warning, and so on. The most important caveat about the exclamation point is this: use it sparingly!

1. Ouch! I have once again been ridiculed on national television.
2. "Fire!" the usher shouted, running down the aisle waving his arms.
3. "Married!" Scratchy said, not at all comprehending.
4. Look out! The sky is falling!
5. All right, lads, brace yourselves for the ride of your lives!
6. Edwin didn't just run the hundred yard dash; he ran it in nine seconds flat!
7. When I tell you to jump—jump!

In the following exercise quiz, insert any needed periods, question marks, or exclamation points. You should also remove any incorrect punctuation and replace it with a period, question mark, or exclamation point if needed.

EXERCISE
Period, Question Mark, and Exclamation Point

1. The students were given a form that asked whether or not they planned to attend summer school? No one was interested!

2. Once again, the Tigers won, It was their fifty-third victory at home this season.

3. You're still a member of the chaos committee, aren't you. Or do I have you confused with someone else. Maybe your roommate.

4. Although Rolland has both a JD and a PhD, he works at MIT as a collective bargaining representative for the faculty.

5. Lt Gov Ian Blind, Rev Marcellus Valhalla, and Ms Lucy Mystic all claim to have known one another in Rome between 250 BC and 220 BC, or thereabouts.

6. Nigel asked, "Where did she shoot the bird"? / "In its plumage," Grace responded after some thought.

7. Hank Greenfeld—or was it Greenberg—was a standout player for the Detroit Tigers in the '30s and '40s.

8. Video, Inc, has stopped accepting cod orders for feature films, to place an order, you must have a national credit card—eg, Mastercard or American Express.

9. Was it Julius Caesar who said, "Give me liberty or give me death?" Or was it Caesar Augustus. Or was it neither.

10. "Stop," shouted the guard, "If you take one more step, you will be walking in a mine field."

The Dash and Parentheses

Both dashes and parentheses are used to set off asides, commentary, added information, definitions, explanations, examples, embellishments, and other parenthetical items that interrupt the smooth word-flow of the sentence. Generally, commas are used when parenthetical elements or other nonrestrictive structures are closely related to the main consideration of the sentence. However, dashes and parentheses may be used—sometimes as a matter of style—when the interruption is either abrupt or emphatically parenthetical, or when the use of commas would create an awkward (looking) sentence. When you have an apparent choice between dashes and parentheses, keep in mind that current practice tends to prefer dashes over parentheses to emphasize more strongly the element set off; dashes feature the element to a greater degree. Parentheses, by contrast, are used to enclose material of minor, secondary, or supplemental significance to the sentence, material that quietly clarifies, illustrates, comments upon, reiterates, or shades what is said before or after the interruption. Observe the following sentences.

1. Texas—more a state of mind than a political entity—was the place of their youth.
2. Stagflation is an unfortunate economic situation combining rising prices (inflation) and a downturn in production (stagnation).
3. Erotica—unlike everyday hard-core pornography—is literature that treats the subject of sexual love tastefully.
4. Humus is the dark (black or brown) material in soil produced from the incomplete decay of plant and animal matter.
5. There is no reason—no civilized reason, that is—for denying 40 million citizens the opportunity to obtain basic medical insurance.
6. In Jonathan Swift's satirical novel *Gulliver's Travels,* the giant Brobdingnagians (twelve times the size of ordinary humans) treat Lemuel Gulliver as a curious house pet.
7. So far—knock wood—every design that we have created has made money.
8. Imprinting, the process by which young animals (or humans) become firmly attached to the first creature(s) who care(s) for them, is a mysterious phenomenon.
9. My mother is not squeamish—she is, after all, a surgeon—when it comes to butchering a hog or castrating a bull.
10. The OPEC (Organization of Petroleum Exporting Countries) oil embargo of 1973–1974 permanently changed international alignments among the industrial nations.
11. Muhammad Ali was among the first to articulate the futility of the Vietnam War—was he the greatest, or not!—when he said, "I ain't got nothing against no Viet Cong."
12. Neologisms are new words (e.g., *glitch* or *glitz*) or old words used in a new way (e.g., *cosmetic* to mean "superficial" or *grunt* to mean "an unskilled laborer").

13. The gross national product—often abbreviated GNP— is the total value of a nation's (annual) output of goods and services.

14. *Bomfog*—one of the ugliest words I have ever heard—is that part of a (political) speech featuring all that brotherhood-of-man-under-the-fatherhood-of-God stuff.

15. An idiom is an expression whose (accepted) meaning cannot be determined from the words it contains—e.g., "plug away at" or "could care less."

A dash can also be used (1) before a sentence-ending afterthought, (2) to introduce a summary statement following a list or series, or (3) to show an interruption or hesitation in speech (dialogue).

1. We didn't have enough money for expensive clothes—not even for ordinary togs.

2. Your proposal was unfortunate—no, it was a bona fide, red-faced disaster.

3. The banquet turned out to be a feast—better than that, it was the culmination of a glorious four-month tour of parts of the world we had never seen before.

4. A Mercedes sedan, a seven-figure annual income, a monster house overlooking Lake Michigan, a husband who already had his 2.5 brilliant children—these were Miranda's immediate goals.

5. The meek, the kind, the gentle, the egalitarian—these are the people whom Cadwallader calls "whining liberals."

6. "The team comes first," "Play within yourself," "Respect the opposition," "Don't cry or crow"—Over four years Duncan had heard Coach Gray repeat these ground rules hundreds, if not thousands, of times.

7. "We lost seven—no, it was nine—planes in the raid," Simeon admitted.

8. Meaning to please, Justin said, "I only meant—" / "I'm quite aware of what you meant, young man," Sister Fawley snapped, not about to be moved.

Parentheses can also be used (1) to enclose letters or numbers labeling items in a list or series, (2) to enclose a question mark indicating uncertainty about the accuracy of something that is said, (3) to enclose the beginning and end year of an important event or lifespan, (4) to indicate a cross-reference in the body of a paper, or (5) to indicate a citation in documented writing.

1. The task force concluded that the university's problems resulted from (1) poor advertising of academic programs, (2) perennial underfunding by the state legislature, (3) indifferent recruiting of qualified faculty, (4) excessive expenditure of money on varsity athletic programs and other nonacademic endeavors, (5) an inflated administration in virtual gridlock, and (6) a board of regents completely uninformed about conditions at the institution.

2. When Jarvis left home to go to college, his father told him five things: (1) study three hours for every hour you're in class, (2) get eight hours of sleep every night, (3) eat three good meals a day, (4) take the hardest teachers the school has to offer, and (5) don't be a schmuck; you can be a schmuck without going to college.

3. This film, one of the president's all-time favorites, won four (?) Oscars.

4. During the Vietnam War (1961–1972) 50,000 (?) Americans were killed in action.

5. If Wolfgang Amadeus Mozart (1756–1791) were still alive today, he would be 236 years old!

6. For a well-known presentation of the opposing position, see Chapter 12 (pp. 290–331).

7. Although Nixon continued to maintain his innocence, few people—even in his own party—believed him (Smalley, "The Decline of Milhous" 88).

In the following exercise quiz, insert any needed dashes into the odd-numbered sentences and any needed parentheses into the even-numbered sentences.

EXERCISE
The Dash and Parentheses

1. Until that time as dumb luck would have it everything had gone according to plan.

2. Rhetoric is the art perhaps science of using words effectively, either in speech or writing.

3. Alden's new sports car long, low, and confidently engineered was quietly begging to be taken for a spin.

4. A zygote is a cell formed by the union of male and female gametes reproductive cells that can develop into a new individual.

5. Several members of this organization I don't have to call the roll have become a bit too confident about their importance to the rest of us.

6. This study the Smithson Study of 1991 offers some practical suggestions for dealing with starvation in Third World countries.

7. Lillian's grandfather who fought in World War I, World War II, and Korea says that if he were a young man today he would be a conscientious objector.

8. If John Kennedy 1917–1963 were alive today, he would be seventy-six years old.

9. Most of these books patronize their readers pat them on their stupid little heads.

10. The committee's conclusions see Table 9 supported no single candidate's position over that of another candidate.

11. Reading books and articles, revising classroom notes, writing papers, preparing for tests and quizzes these are the things that make up my days and nights at school.

12. Some movies for example, *The Silence of the Lambs* teach us things about human nature that we would just as soon not know.

13. "I warned him well, I meant my remarks to him to be taken as a warning."

14. By the fall of '89, the president of the union had no ? support among the rank and file.

15. Powerful people that is, those who daily buy and sell the rest of us have a completely different set of problems.

16. Today, there are only five apes remaining: 1 the gorilla, 2 the chimpanzee, 3 the orangutan, 4 the gibbon, and 5 the siamang.

The Apostrophe

The apostrophe is used in three ways: (1) to form the possessive case of nouns and indefinite pronouns, (2) to indicate the omitted material in contractions, and (3) to form a few plurals.

To form possessive case   Any noun, whether singular or plural, not ending in *s* and indefinite pronouns (e.g., *anyone, everybody, someone*) form the possessive by adding *'s*.

1. Your *friend's* cat has been found in the *neighbor's* garage.
2. The *lad's* coat was taken from your *father's* closet.
3. Please put the *children's* new toys under the tree.
4. Where did you say the *women's* department is?
5. *Anyone's* guess is as good as mine.
6. Alas, John insists on doing *everybody's* work but his own.

All plural nouns ending in *s* form the possessive by adding only an apostrophe after the *s*. However, current practice is divided with singular nouns ending in *s;* some style manuals say that only the apostrophe is necessary, while others indicate the addition of *'s* in most situations. Ease of pronunciation is probably the best test.

1. Several crates of the *players'* uniforms had been sent to the wrong stadium.
2. These *animals'* dining habits are less than refined.
3. Dean Littlefallow could no longer ignore the *students'* complaints.
4. No one could believe the *witness's* (*witness'*?) testimony.
5. You must understand that the *boss's* (*boss'*?) position is always a good one.
6. *Hastings'* (*Hastings's*?) new mayor wants to revise the city charter.
7. Did *Moses'* (*Moses's*?) staff have magical powers?

In compound or phrasal nouns, only the last word indicates possession. Similarly, in nouns of joint ownership, only the last noun indicates possession. However, if individual ownership is intended, both nouns must indicate possession.

1. As usual, the attorney *general's* position was confusing.
2. Your editor-in-*chief's* prose hasn't lost its edge after all these years.
3. My *in-laws'* peevishness is a bit distracting at family gatherings.
4. Many of Gilbert and *Sullivan's* operettas are as popular today as they ever were. (joint ownership)
5. Gifford and *Andrea's* apartment is on the third floor. (joint ownership)
6. *Gifford's* and *Andrea's* apartments are in different buildings. (individual ownership)
7. Aren't *Canada's* and *England's* health care systems about the same? (individual ownership)

To indicate omitted material in contractions   Apostrophes mark the omission of letters or numbers in contractions.

1. *I'll* never be able to stay awake until two *o'clock*.
2. "*Don't* you remember the blizzard of *'89*?" Murray asked.
3. *It's* been six months—give or take an evening—since *we've* won at this game; but *who's* counting?

To form plurals   For the sake of clarity more than anything else, the plurals of (1) letters, (2) numbers, (3) symbols, (4) some abbreviations, and (5) words referred to as words are formed by the addition of *'s*. Pluralized letters, numbers (except years), and words referred to as words are also usually italicized; the following *s*, however, is not italicized. The practice of using the apostrophe with the *s* to pluralize numbers is in transition and will probably disappear in time. Furthermore, when there is no danger of confusion, the apostrophe in all these plural constructions may be deleted. Prudence would suggest, however, that you use them (except to indicate years) at this point in the development of your writing skills.

1. "Are there four *i*'s in the word *Mississippi*?" Bruno asked.
2. "Yes," Gloria replied, "and there are four *s*'s as well."
3. During the 1980s the national debt ballooned.
4. Your *7*'s and *9*'s are indistinguishable from each other.
5. In formal papers your &'s should be spelled out as *and*'s.
6. Each discrete rule was marked by a series of three *'s.
7. There aren't many Btu's left in logs as rotten as these.
8. These are not CD's that you listen to; they are CD's that collect interest at the bank.
9. Alas, there are too many *somewhat*'s and *perhaps*'s in your writing.
10. With this group, the *no*'s always dominate the *yes*'s by about two to one.

In the following exercise quiz, insert any needed apostrophes into the sentences. For purposes of the quiz, if an apostrophe can be correctly used, use it—as practice.

EXERCISE
Apostrophe

1. Anthonys 79 Saab is on its last legs—or, rather, wheels.

2. Im at my wits end from having to watch my *p*s and *q*s so closely.

3. Alas, when everybodys somebody, nobodys anybody.

4. Youre rolling nothing but *6*s and *7*s.

5. The clubs monthly meetings are held at Franklin and Aviss place, not at a students house.

6. Professor Rawlings predilection for sesquipedalians doesnt compare with Dr. Hastings partiality for obfuscation.

7. There will be no *if*s, *and*s, or *but*s here; reproducing a painting of Roses thorns is not beyond the classs ability.

8. Weve never been asked to do anyones work other than our own.

9. As the poet says, "Well take a cup o kindness yet for auld lang syne."

10. Theyre leaving at six oclock and dont know when theyll return—maybe by days end on Friday.

11. As theyve already explained, the eyewitnesses testimony was all that was needed.

12. Its Edwins never-ending *thus*s and *notwithstanding*s that exhaust the childrens ears.

13. "The +s and −s denote positive and negative values, respectively," the instructor explained.

14. Thats what we dont know: whos going to defend the 20s and 30s during this grand debate?

15. Andrews and Amandas tickets, which were for the nine oclock show, were located somewhere up in the *X, Y, Z*s.

Quotation Marks

Quotation marks (" ") are used to set off (1) direct quotations, (2) the titles of shorter works or productions and the subdivisions of books, (3) the definitions of words or phrases, and (4) words or expressions used in a special sense.

Direct quotations   A direct quotation repeats, word for word, what someone has said or written. If a second quotation occurs within the quotation, single quotation marks (' ') are used to enclose the second one.

1. Given the opportunity, most Englishmen would probably become Ellen Wilkinson's "strong being who takes a cold bath in the morning and talks about it for the rest of the day."

2. Not one speaker at the Republican convention mentioned Lord Byron's contention that "the devil was the first democrat."

3. Hilary accurately described the course as "the blind leading the bland."

4. "I prefer not to" was Bartleby's repeated response to several suggestions.

5. "*Et tu, Brute!*" is an epiphany repeated by many who have occupied positions lesser than an emperor.

6. Jennifer grimaced at her ex-husband and said, "My goal in life is to pay my own fiddler and dance my own tune."

7. "My life is an open book," the accused said to the chair of the inquisition.

8. Chester smiled as if reminiscing and said, "When Constantine left the house for school each morning, he always said, 'Well, lads, here goes what in a perfect world would pass for almost nothing.'"

9. "If you say 'I told you so' one more time, I'm going to smother you with unkindness," Ursula said.

10. "I read Robert Frost's little poem 'Stopping by Woods on a Snowy Evening' when I was in the seventh grade," Lafayette said, attempting another of his infamous put-downs.

Sentences 1 through 5 all provide examples of "referred-to" quotations rather than quotations wherein people are speaking as the quotation occurs. Except for sentence number 3, all these quotations are identifiable in that they are attributable to known persons or literary characters. Sentence 6 demonstrates the identifying (quotation) tag at the beginning of the sentence and the actual quotation at the end. Sentence 7 does just the reverse, presenting the quotation at the beginning and the tag at the end. Numbers 8 and 9 show a quotation within a quotation, and number 10 shows the title of a poem within a quotation.

Structuring and punctuating direct quotations can become a little more intricate when the quotations are split and additional marks of punctuation come into play.

11. "When I was a student," Aunt Louise said, "we rode the city bus to school."

12. "I have observed," the new branch manager said, "that no one comes to work on time."

13. "The weather here is absolutely beautiful," Marion said. "We like it so much that we are contemplating a move."

14. "Happiness is my goal in life," Carmel said. "Do you have a better one?"

15. "We did not care much for the fellow's excessive bravado," Evelyn admitted; "moreover, we thought he was vulgar."

16. "Montague is a friend of mine," Julia said; "I haven't seen him recently, however."

17. "The eyewitnesses declined to testify," Vincent said; "they were not convinced that the police would protect them."

18. "This strange looking old hippie type came into the store this afternoon and bought the following items," Alden said: "a box of rat poison, two sacks of lime, an ax handle, a fifty-gallon drum, a shovel, and some grass seed."

19. "Evan really has only one passion in life," Estelle said: "reading murder mysteries."

20. "Good food, leisurely travel, a few close friends, interesting conversation, adequate currency," Uncle Bertram said—"these are the things that make life worthwhile."

21. In *The Naked Ape* Desmond Morris contends the following: "The wearing of spectacles and sunglasses makes the face appear more aggressive because it artificially and accidentally enlarges the pattern of the stare."

22. Reluctantly, I thought, the university president said, "I am required by law to tell you now that we shall drop football next year"; then she quietly left the podium.

23. Avery said that he had two reasons for rereading "The Wooing of Ariadne": Marko was a real man, and Ariadne was a real woman.

24. Was it not some famous person or other who said, "As a hawk flieth not high with one wing, even so a man reacheth not to excellence with one tongue"?

25. Professor Mund paused a moment and then asked, "What person in American military history said, 'Damn the torpedoes, full speed ahead'?"

Sentences 11 through 20 split the quotations in a variety of ways. Both 11 and 12 set off the identifying tags in the middle ("Aunt Louise said" and "the new branch manager said") with commas. This is appropriate usage because both parts of the quotation in the two sentences are *not* independent clauses. The first half of the quotation in number 11 is a dependent clause, and the second half of the quotation in number 12 is a dependent clause. By contrast, the identifying tags in sentences 13 and 14 are followed by periods. This is appropriate usage because both parts of the quotation in the two sentences *are* independent clauses.

In sentences 15 through 17, the identifying tags are followed by a semicolon. Conjunctive adverbs connect the two parts of the split quotations in 15 and 16, and the notion of "because" occurs between the two parts of the spit quotation in number 17. In all three sentences, both parts of the split quotation are independent clauses. A colon follows the identifying tag in sentences 18 and 19. The colon is needed in sentence 18 because the second part of the quotation is a list. It is needed in sentence 19 because the second part of the quotation is an appositive. A dash follows the identifying tag in sentence 20 because the second part of the quotation is a summary statement following the list that occurs in the first part of the quotation.

Except for sentence 23—which demonstrates the title of a short story within quotation marks followed by a colon that introduces a pair of appositives—sentences 21 through 25 begin with the identifying tag. Number 21 follows the tag with a colon to introduce the formal quotation. A semicolon follows the quotation in number 22 because the conjunctive adverb *then* introduces an independent clause. The question mark ending sentence 24 is outside the closing quotation mark because the quotation itself is not a question. In sentence 25 the question mark is outside the single quotation mark but inside the double mark. "Damn the torpedoes, full speed ahead" is not a question, but "What person in American military history said" is a question.

Titles of works   Quotation marks are used to enclose the titles of articles appearing in newspapers, magazines, and scholarly and professional journals as well as the titles of essays, short stories, songs, short poems, chapters or sections of books, speeches, and individual episodes of radio and television series. Do not, however, enclose in quotation marks the titles or names of books, magazines, newspapers, pamphlets, journals, movies, television or radio series, long poems, plays, musicals or operas, paintings and sculptures, ships, trains, aircraft, or spaceships. These items are italicized—that is, underlined in manuscript or typescript format.

1. Herbert Carson's poem "Thomas Beemer Ashburton" originally appeared in *Kansas Quarterly*.
2. "Here Comes Santa Claus" is my favorite selection from Ramsey Lewis's famous jazz album *Sound of Christmas*.
3. Chapter 8, "How To Make a Bomb at Home with Materials Purchased at Your Local Hardware Store," was quite a good example of process writing.
4. Although "The Monkey's Paw," written by W. W. Jacobs, is considered to be a powerful ghost story, it doesn't have a ghost.
5. "The Time for Term Limitation Legislation," the Tuesday editorial in the *Hinterland Times*, almost flirted with treating a timely topic in a rational manner.

Definitions of words   When words are specifically defined in the flow of prose writing, even when the definitions are created by the author of the piece rather than being taken from another source, the definitions are usually enclosed by quotation marks. Words so defined are italicized (underlined).

1. The word *cardiomyopathy*—which you may recall was featured in the motion picture *Beaches*—is created from *cardio*, meaning "heart," *myo*, meaning "muscle," and *pathy*, meaning "disease" or "suffering"; thus, it means "a disease (chronic and progressive) of the heart muscle."

2. *Chauvinism,* which means "a fanatical, militant, and unreasoning devotion to one's country," is not a characteristic peculiar to a particular ethnic community.

3. When Paul Fussell uses the word *class* in his book of the same title, he really means "caste."

4. Austin was surprised to learn that *quid pro quo* meant "something for something" or "this for that."

5. *Uninterested* means "indifferent" or "apathetic," whereas *disinterested* means "impartial," "unbiased," or "objective."

Special uses of words Words or expressions used in a special sense may be set off by quotation marks. This convention is used to indicate irony, doubt, disapproval, emphasis, and so on, and it sometimes makes use of coinages—that is, (recently) made up words or expressions.

1. George Steinbrenner's "lifetime" suspension from major league baseball lasted a year.

2. Alas, most of the dead were killed by "friendly fire."

3. Everyone agreed that it had been "indiscreet" of the chief accountant to embezzle $40 million from the bank.

4. Because of price "adjustments," construction of the house cost twice the original estimate.

5. Professor Simmer argues that the Christian "psyche" is still evolving.

6. How does one "speed shift" an economy?

7. The president's squad of "spinsters" is hardly composed of elderly, unmarried women looking for a husband.

8. Members of Congress seldom break the "beholden rule" and vote against legislation supported by major contributors of campaign funds.

9. These violent "tweenagers," who range from ten through twelve years of age, are becoming a scourge even to traditional adolescents.

10. Professor Goodman maintains that we are rapidly becoming a nation of "videots," that our only reality comes from the television screen.

In the following exercise quiz, properly position quotation marks—single or double—in each sentence. All the sentences require the addition of quotation marks.

EXERCISE
Quotation Marks

1. If you're going to run for office, Tim's sister cautioned, be prepared to hear the worst about yourself repeated throughout the community.

2. Is the ninth commandment Thou shalt not bear false witness against thy neighbor?

3. Alice, after studying the dean for a minute or two, said, I've never before met anyone who was born middle-aged; then she left the room.

4. After twenty-five years of rejections by editors and agents, the author became an overnight success.

5. We have noticed, the new dean said, that no one argues with the axiom if you can make it in New York, you can make it anywhere.

6. You went ping-ponging along? What does that mean?

7. Can one sensibly define *reality* as that which exists in fact?

8. If you say so it goes one more time, Leopold warned, I'm going to go myself.

9. Andrew Lang's poem Scythe Song contains the repeated refrain hush, ah hush.

10. Baynard's little brother says you know and awesome seven hundred times a day, and he means it every time.

11. Chapter 12, When We Are Immortal, of the book *Future* raises some interesting questions about population control.

12. By repeatedly calling your opponent a yellow-bellied sapsucker, Marsha said, are you suggesting that there is something avian about him?

13. Throughout the trip, they dined on burgers and fries.

14. I forgot my best line, Ambrose said: Modern cities can run no faster than their sewer pipes.

15. By defining the word *tory* as a male chauvinist pig, Vivian said, you alienated a substantial portion of your audience.

16. I never read Walt Whitman's poem There Was a Child Went Forth, Mercedes said, until I was in college and came across a copy of *Leaves of Grass*.

17. Who said, I have been both rich and poor, and rich is better?

18. That was one wedding ceremony that left out the love, honor, and obey stuff.

19. In the short story The Wooing of Ariadne, written by Harry Mark Petrakis, Ariadne indicates her acceptance of Marko's courting when she says to Marko, You may call on me tomorrow.

20. Contrary to what you may have heard, the word *logorrhea* means running off at the mouth.

21. We didn't care much for your cute use of the expression ask and it shall be given, Natalie said; moreover, we thought you had dressed yourself for a Halloween party.

22. The Simpsons' cottage at the north end of Clear Lake included seven bedrooms, nine baths, an elevator, an indoor swimming pool, and a four-car garage.

23. If you ask me, most politicians are interested in only one thing, Greta said: staying in office.

24. The word *disease* does not refer only to a contagious illness; it means . . . any harmful, destructive, or degenerative condition.

25. An annoyingly self-important young man took exception to Professor Haunt's evaluation of his paper. Do you know who I am? the young man asked. No, sir, I do not, the professor replied. But I shall make inquiries and inform you directly.

In the following review exercise, you should (1) identify the mark of punctuation needed to correct each sentence by putting the appropriate letter in the blank in front of the sentence and (2) correct each sentence by inserting the needed mark of punctuation. In thirty of the sentences, the needed punctuation is simply missing; in nineteen of the sentences, incorrect punctuation must be deleted before the correct punctuation can be inserted; and in 1 sentence both situations occur. Although more than one instance of a mark of punctuation may be needed to correct some of the sentences, no sentence requires the addition of multiple types of punctuation.

REVIEW EXERCISE
Current Conventions of Punctuation

A. Comma	F. Exclamation Point
B. Semicolon	G. Dash
C. Colon	H. Parentheses
D. Period	I. Apostrophe
E. Question Mark	J. Quotation Marks

_____ 1. Hodge's younger brother wanted the following items for Christmas; a CD player, a red Corvette, a two-bedroom condo, and a job that didn't require too much effort.

_____ 2. From all appearances, hed never felt the suns rays on his face nor heard the oceans soft swell at night.

_____ 3. The plan for Hinterland, Michigan, to annex New Village was a good one, moreover, both communities were in favor of it.

_____ 4. No one in the class could believe that the professor—who, after all, was a well-known scholar, the author of several books—didn't know that James Joyce's short story A Little Cloud was from *Dubliners*.

_____ 5. Was it a member of this class who said to the instructor, "I can't take notes until you say something noteworthy"

_____ 6. We tried every way we could think of to show Logan the errors in his argument but he wouldn't listen to us.

_____ 7. A ride around the neighborhood on his bike, a good video to watch, a chat with his friends, the evening news: these were the things that held the old man's day together.

_____ 8. According to US government statistics, caring for the indigent—i e, those who do not feed, clothe, and house themselves—costs taxpayers millions, if not billions, of dollars each year.

_____ 9. John Cheever 1912–1982, author of the short story "The Swimmer," which was made into a movie starring Burt Lancaster, wrote mostly about the affluent suburbs.

_____ 10. While working on a construction crew in Ashland, Kentucky; Burgess realized that he preferred a more leisurely more sedentary way of life.

_____ 11. The lawyer (narrator) in Herman Melville's story Bartleby, the Scrivener sums up his philosophy of life as follows: I am a man who, from his youth upwards, has been filled with the profound conviction that the easiest way of life is the best.

_____ 12. Personally, I care nothing for varsity athletics, nevertheless, I voted in favor of keeping women's volleyball.

_____ 13. In 428 ? Germanic tribes began an invasion of Britain that lasted for several hundred years.

_____ 14. "But where will you live" Jessica asked Bertram, fearful for his future as well as her own happiness. "How will you take care of yourself"

_____ 15. Why must you—in spite of all advice to the contrary, all friendly counsel—invite every Tom Dick and Harry to your party?

_____ 16. Derek and Graces new car (a Jaguar sedan) had been moved to an unknown location somewhere on the citys north side.

_____ 17. The speaker concluded her address with the following bit of advice; "Get the idea that the world owes you anything out of your head."

_____ 18. Bats which have unfairly gotten a bad reputation are not dangerous bloodsucking creatures of the night.

_____ 19. Intending to set the record straight, Montague began, "If you ask me" Then he realized what sort of person he was dealing with.

_____ 20. As I recall, Dr J William Meekly, Jr, and Prof Linda Hobson headed the task force.

_____ 21. Ellen's old television set—she bought it at a garage sale ten years ago, didn't she—finally gave up the ghost last night during a rerun of _Monty Python's Flying Circus._

_____ 22. Nelson's position in brief is that private schools are pricing themselves out of the market.

_____ 23. "You can't be serious" the instructor exclaimed, shards of fire erupting from her angry eyes.

_____ 24. Prudence might suggest the following steps, (1) go to class regularly, (2) read your assignments, (3) hand your papers in on time, and (4) don't antagonize the instructor.

_____ 25. The word _intrastate_ means within a state, whereas _interstate_ means between or among states.

_____ 26. "What a pleasant accommodating person Elizabeth has become in recent years" Alfred said.

_____ 27. About eight oclock, tired of the whole affair, Baxter made a comment about all his in-laws bad manners and then drove to Andreas place for dinner.

_____ 28. Three of the most outspoken opponents of the measure, Ian French, Walter Hinton, and Alexis Sanford, suddenly reversed themselves and came on board.

_____ 29. Rollo smoked, drank, consumed great quantities of junk food, and hardly slept at all, yet, on the whole, he seemed to be in good health.

_____ 30. Fortunately, the task force's analysis, see Table 16, was thorough and fairly done.

_____ 31. Richard Wright's "The Ethics of Living Jim Crow; An Autobiographical Sketch" was once published as an introduction to *Uncle Tom's Children*.

_____ 32. The students in my evening classes include secretaries, plumbers, nurses, electricians, carpenters, truck drivers, Elvis impersonators: all kinds of working people.

_____ 33. The fourth novel (the science fantasy) was better than the first three, wasn't it.

_____ 34. We lost for three reasons: 1 we were exhausted from the doubleheader the day before, 2 we were playing in the opposition's home park, and 3 we had never before faced the starting pitcher.

_____ 35. We spent the weekend studying for our chemistry exam; not working on the homecoming float.

_____ 36. There are four *ss* in *scissors,* three *es* in *tepee,* two *ps* in *supper,* and no *ks* in *cocoa.*

_____ 37. "These meetings begin promptly at 11:30 AM and conclude at 2:15 PM," Francine said, tired of repeating the information.

_____ 38. At the time, many people did not believe their eyes: men were actually walking on the moon.

_____ 39. Maximilian maintains that he was born on Friday December 13 1950 at seven-thirty in the morning in Columbus Ohio.

_____ 40. Moderation in all things, including moderation was my grandfather's often repeated formula for a long life.

_____ 41. The AAUP American Association of University Professors is dedicated to improving the quality of classroom instruction, isn't it?

_____ 42. Alas sir you have not comported yourself well nor have you provided a model for your charges.

_____ 43. How many accounts did Andrew manage to lose anyway. Two. Five. Seven. Or was it a dozen.

_____ 44. We know that an 88 Mercury collided with a 92 Dodge; we do not, however, know the *why*s and *wherefore*s of the accident.

_____ 45. If the dogs are not properly trained when they are young; they will not hunt when they are grown.

_____ 46. With more than a hint of irony in his voice, the guide explained that the newer houses in the village had been built between 1700 and 1740.

_____ 47. The final game of the '92 playoffs lasted seventeen innings, Tim was exhausted when it finally ended.

_____ 48. "Save yourselves, lads" the captain shouted; "the hounds of hell are upon us"

_____ 49. The applicant was qualified, although not too qualified, capable, although not too capable, and ambitious, although not too ambitious.

_____ 50. Our vacation (why we ever decided to go to Miami in the middle of August is still a mystery to me) was a total bust; we couldn't even breathe outside our motel room.

Chapter 7
Additional Mechanical Conventions

Capitals

The conventions for the use of capital letters can be quite intricate, and they have changed over the years. Generally, we capitalize fewer things today than we did in the past. The most important convention of capitalization—that is, the one that creates the most difficulty for student writers—has to do with what we call a *proper noun*.

All nouns (naming words) fall into one of two categories: common or proper. Common nouns are words that name any of a class of things, places, or people. Proper nouns, by contrast, are words that name a single, specific, particular person (or group of persons), place, or thing. Proper nouns are capitalized; common nouns are not capitalized. What is important, then, is to be able to distinguish between the two. For example, the word *athlete* is a common noun, whereas *Jennifer Capriati* is a proper noun; *ballplayer* is a common noun, whereas *Michael Jordan* is a proper noun; *organization* is a common noun, whereas *National Organization for Women* is a proper noun; *company* is a common noun, whereas *General Motors* is a proper noun; *city* is a common noun, whereas *Paris* is a proper noun; and *automobile* is a common noun, whereas *Volvo* is a proper noun.

As an exercise in distinguishing proper nouns from common nouns, supply appropriate examples of proper nouns in the following blanks. Be sure to capitalize your examples.

Common Noun	Proper Noun(s)
1. artist	_____
2. dramatist	_____
3. entrepreneur	_____
4. movie star	_____
5. poet	_____
6. politician	_____
7. institution	_____
8. association	_____
9. labor union	_____
10. ethnic group	_____
11. college	_____
12. region	_____
13. continent	_____
14. county	_____
15. country	_____
16. river	_____
17. park	_____
18. bay	_____
19. peninsula	_____
20. geyser	_____
21. building	_____
22. monument	_____
23. ship	_____
24. airplane	_____
25. language	_____
26. day	_____

Common Noun	Proper Noun(s)
27. month	_____
28. holiday	_____
29. trade name	_____
30. church	_____
31. religion	_____
32. divinity	_____
33. historical event	_____
34. title	_____
35. academic course	_____

Proper adjectives—that is, proper nouns used in a modifying position or adjectives derived (formed) from proper nouns—are also often capitalized. Thus, we have the following conventional usages:

American know-how	Hollywood bed
British understatement	Machiavellian scheme
Christmas cheer	Marxist ideology
Chrysler engineering	Ohio coal
Elizabethan drama	Shakespearean sonnet
Florida tan	Swedish angst
Freudian slip	Victorian morality

Not all proper nouns or proper adjectives are today capitalized, however. Some have been used so often and for so long that the capitalization has been dropped. Observe the following examples of words that were once proper nouns or proper adjectives; but today, as evidenced by the dropping of the capitalization, are considered common nouns or ordinary adjectives.

aspirin	frisbee	bogus	lilliputian
bedlam	jello	cherubic	macadamized
billingsgate	mackintosh	colossal	puritanical
blarney	martinet	cynical	quixotic
boycott	maverick	draconian	sadistic
cardigan	quisling	erotic	sardonic
chauvinism	solon	gargantuan	stentorian
chinaware	volt	herculean	titian
frankfurter	watt	jovial	utopian

Current convention also capitalizes (1) the first word in a sentence; (2) the first word of a direct quotation that is not grammatically incorporated into the sentence in which it occurs; (3) the first word of material occurring within brackets when that material is an independent clause; (4) abbreviations if the first letters of the words they represent would be capitalized—e.g., *FBI, OPEC, CIA;* (5) the pronoun *I* and the interjection *O* along with single letters that appear alone or as part of a naming expression—e.g., *Model A, D-Day, U-boat, an A grade, Vitamin C;* (6) personal titles, including those that indicate family relationships, that immediately precede a proper name or are used in place of the name—e.g., *Count Dracula, Princess Grace, Major General English, Uncle Jake, Aunt Bea;* (7) the first word and all other words (except articles and conjunctions or prepositions of fewer than five letters) occurring in the titles of books, magazines, journals, newspapers, plays, essays, poems, short stories, films, television programs, musical compositions, computer software, pictures, sculptures, and so on; and (8) the first word after a colon in a title—e.g., *"Flirting with Death: A Day in the Life of a Soldier."*

Current convention does *not* capitalize (1) the names of diseases, conditions, or medical tests unless a proper noun is part of the name—e.g., *pneumonia, cancer, mumps, Alzheimer's disease;* (2) points of the compass (*north, south, east, west*) except when they designate specific geographical locations—e.g., the *Northwest*, the *Old South;* (3) the seasons of the year—*spring, summer, fall, winter;* and (4) nouns indicating kinship when they are preceded by an article or a possessive—e.g., *my uncle, your cousin, the father.*

In the following exercise quiz, capitalize all words that should be capitalized in each sentence. All the sentences require additional capitalization.

EXERCISE
Capitalization

1. This article, "the me generation: a nation of spoiled brats," is a bit sardonic in its criticism of the '80s in america.

2. Does the federal deposit insurance corporation (fdic) insure this account, or am i on my own?

3. "Do we have enough k rations?" seargent major goofus asked, "or should we stop at wendy's for a hamburger?"

4. If she is not offered a commission in the united states army, glenna intends to study english literature at either the university of michigan or notre dame.

5. Early in the spring, probably march or april, we shall go to chicago and see for ourselves whether or not this bible-quoting miracle worker is really a man of god.

6. The house where andrew grew up was located at 734 cedar drive, hinterland, michigan, near the west end of lake waverly.

7. After living so long in the north, the samuelsons are having a difficult time adjusting to the warm winters in the south—particularly at thanksgiving and christmastime.

8. According to both mother and father, uncle nelson worked for either the cia or the fbi after leaving general motors.

9. Alas, it was elizabeth's innocence that made her think a freudian slip was a woman's undergarment.

10. Rumor has it that count mountebank is suffering from parkinson's disease, a family weakness possibly extending back to the middle ages.

11. Was it in *the glass menagerie* or *on the waterfront* that Marlon Brando said, "i coulda been a contender"? Or was it Robert De Niro in *raging bull?*

12. Young siegfried eats his wheaties every day; he hopes to compete in the olympic games in atlanta in 1996.

13. "In the film *a walk on the wild side: real animal behavior,*" the instructor said, "we get quite a different view of nature: it is a darwinian view."

14. Was it John Kennedy or Richard Nixon who won the pulitzer prize for writing the book *profiles in courage?*

15. Last thursday afternoon, professor bernard nadeau, who is a well-known scholar in european political history, addressed the grand rapids chapter of the american association of university women.

Abbreviations

The general rule is that formal college writing not intended for a specialized (technical) audience should avoid using abbreviations as much as possible. Conventional usage does, however, allow a few. They include abbreviations for (1) titles occurring before or after a proper name—e.g., *Mr., Ms., Mrs., Dr., Sr., Jr., Esq.;* (2) academic or professional degrees occurring after a proper name—e.g., *M.B.A., Ph.D., L.L.D., M.D., J.D., C.P.A., Th.D.;* (3) designations of specific dates, times of day, or units of measurement—e.g., *55 B.C., A.D. 313, 7:15 A.M., 4:30 P.M., 12° C, 450° F, $238.75, 65 mph;* (4) two Latin expressions: *e.g.* (*exempli gratia,* meaning "for example") and *i.e.* (*id est,* meaning "that is"); and (5) the names of a few well-known agencies, organizations, people, corporations, or technical phrases—e.g., *FBI, CIA, KGB, IRA, AMA, NCAA, ACLU, AT&T, BBC, CBS, IBM, 3M, JFK, FDR, Dr. J., LEM, REM, AIDS, VCR, CAD-CAM,* and *CD.*

Numbers

The key consideration with numbers is the determination of when numerals (figures) are used and when words are used—that is, when the numbers are written out as words. In nontechnical college writing, general numbers that can be expressed in one or two words are spelled out. Additionally, larger numbers are written out if they occur at the beginning of a sentence.

1. Between *six* and *ten* students were absent every class session.
2. By the time he was *twenty-one* years old, Rollo had collected *sixty-five* antique cars and restored *thirty-three* of them.
3. We ordered *twelve hundred* fliers for the campaign.
4. Rollo traveled more than *thirty-five thousand* miles last year alone. (Because *thirty-five* is a hyphenated word, this may be counted as a two-word number.)

5. *Nine hundred and forty-four* seniors participated in the graduation ceremony.

6. No fewer than 944 seniors participated in the graduation ceremony.

When two separate numbers are used next to each other (adjacent numbers), one of them—usually the first, but not always) may be written out for easy reading.

1. This year we have sold *fifteen* 22-foot units.

2. Last semester I wrote *seven* 12-page papers.

3. The league now has *nine* 7-foot players.

4. To complete the finishing work, the carpenters need about *thirty* ½-inch pieces of moulding.

5. We ordered 10,000 *two-dollar* watches.

6. Apparently, 5,500 *twenty-year* employees are being let go.

Although fractions are usually indicated with numerals, they are written out when they stand alone or are followed by *of a* or *of an*. Similarly, even though a time of day or a sum of money is usually indicated with numerals, when either is a round figure or a total sum it is written out. *O'clock* is used only with the hour.

1. As expected, the inclement weather reduced the crop by at least *two-thirds*.

2. Would *three-quarters* of the shares be of any assistance?

3. They still live about *one-third* of a mile from campus.

4. The family usually has dinner between *seven* and *eight* o'clock.

5. On the farm we were up by *five* every morning.

6. It costs me *five dollars* every time I change the policy.

7. Do you realize that this candy bar costs *seventy-five cents*?

8. A building like that might run *forty million* or more.

Large numbers, including those that indicate sums of money, can be written with words and figures in combination for easy reading or recognition. Such numbers are always round numbers, however.

1. How can anything be *875 trillion* light-years distant from earth, or from anything else?

2. Our trade deficit now exceeds *$600 billion* annually.

3. The Milky Way, our galaxy, is a collection of *100 billion* (?) stars.

Current conventions for most other writing situations wherein numbers are necessary require the use of numerals or figures. They include the following:

Addresses
18045 Hemlock Boulevard
424 Portage Place
175 Fifth Avenue, New York, New York 10010

Dates
February 4, 1992 or 4 February 1992

336

54 B.C.; A.D. 46
1558–1603; 1542 (?)–1577

Exact times of day
8:07
11:00 A.M. or 11 A.M. (but not 11:00 o'clock)
7:50 P.M.

Exact sums of money
$37.55
$7644.00 or $7,644.00
$36,448,000
$130 million

Exact measurements

75 mph	25 cc
10 K run	32-ounce bottle
238 pounds	6 feet 11 inches
44° or 44 degrees	40-watt bulb

Decimals/fractions/percentages
3.14
32¼
86 percent or 86%

Pages and other divisions of written material
pages 74–79
Chapter 9
As You Like It, Act 2, Scene 7, lines 139–166

Scores/statistics/ratios
an 8 to 7 victory or an 8–7 victory
median score of 84; mean age of 26
ratio of 7 to 1

Identification numbers
I-77; Route 66; M[ichigan]-37
Channel 33
SS 243-84-2796
Gate 5

The *rule of consistency* is often important in the overall determination of whether numerals or written numbers will be used in a given situation. This rule argues that when you have several numbers—particularly if they are connected with a series—in close proximity to one another, all of them should be treated the same way. Thus, if one or two of them must be numerals for some conventional reason, all of them should be numerals—even if making all of them numerals violates our earlier "two-word" rule for writing out general numbers. Observe the following examples of the rule of consistency at work.

1. Of the 450 students participating in the experiments, 175 were American, 144 were Canadian, 90 were European, 21 were Columbian, 12 were Iranian, and 8 were Ethiopian.

2. Although the complaint department received 1,283 calls on the matter, it got only 34 letters.

3. In only three years, our sales people on the road grew from 4 to 12 to 35 to 215.

4. On average, I would say that 18 sport coats, 27 suits, 85 shirts, and 127 ties amount to a full closet.

5. During the last three years or so, Allen has worked nine months in a shoe store, four months in a supermarket, three months in a car wash, and about forty-five minutes as a carpenter.

Finally, many times enumeration (numbering) is an important device in formal papers. When presenting examples or listing categories, you may want to number them—to give the paper, or that part of the paper, a firmer structure. Similarly, a cause-effect paper featuring either multiple causes producing a single effect or multiple effects arising from a single cause will almost certainly be strengthened by numbering the multiple causes or multiple effects. Likewise, a process paper is usually improved when the steps in the process are counted. Generally, it is better to count lists with numerals enclosed within parentheses: (1), (2), (3), (4), and (5). Steps in a process, individual divisions in an analysis, and multiple causes or effects—particularly when there is a substantial amount of information between the numbers—are more effectively counted with ordinal numbers written out: *first, second, third, fourth, fifth.* Always avoid adverbial ordinal numbers: *firstly, secondly, thirdly, fourthly, fifthly.*

Italics

Italics—the equivalent of underlining in either manuscript or typescript—are used to indicate the titles of such things as books, pamphlets, movies, long poetic works, plays, musicals, operas, and paintings or sculpture.

The Grapes of Wrath (novel)
The Naked Ape (nonfiction)
Fiction 100: An Anthology of Short Stories (collection)
Thomas Paine's *Common Sense* (pamphlet)
Citizen Kane (movie)
John Milton's *Paradise Lost* (long poem)
Arthur Miller's *A Memory of Two Mondays* (play)
South Pacific (musical)
Mozart's *The Marriage of Figaro* (opera)
Picasso's *Guernica* (painting)
Alexander Calder's *La Grande Vitesse* (sculpture)

Similarly, italics are used to indicate the names of such things as newspapers, magazines, journals, radio and television series (whose individual episodes have titles that are enclosed within double quotation marks), ships, trains, aircraft, and spacecraft.

the *Grand Rapids Press* (newspaper)
Mother Jones (magazine)
Journal of the American Medical Association (journal)
CBS Mystery Theater (radio series)
Perry Mason (television series)
Titanic (ship)
The Orient Express (train)
the *Hindenburg; Enola Gay* (aircraft)
Challenger (spacecraft)

Italics are also used to indicate or signify (1) foreign expressions not yet fully assimilated into Engligh; (2) words, letters, numbers, or phrases that refer to themselves; (3) words or phrases that are being defined; (4) emphasis; or (5) clarification.

1. A person with such a *carpe-diem* attitude toward life does not worry much about the future.

2. The Jaguar sedan is the *ne plus ultra* in luxury automobiles.

3. Felix has not yet discovered his *raison d'être;* he doesn't know what to do with himself.

4. The collapse of the Soviet Union is a *fait accompli,* not something that may or may not happen in the future.

5. It takes a bit of a *sans-coeur* to tell the young that they may not have the ability to accomplish their dreams.

6. Believe it or not, there is a *lie* in the middle of *believe.*

7. Thomas is opposed to the word *euthanasia* being used as a synonym for the expression *mercy killing.*

8. In some words the *sh* sound is spelled with a *ti* or a *ch,* as in *mention* and *machine.*

9. I can't remember the winning number, but there was no *7* in it.

10. Glibly, the speaker defined *heaven* as "pie in the sky by and by."

11. Cadwallader defines the old pejorative *bleeding heart* as "a liberal who never had to meet a payroll."

12. "This *is* my teacher," Benjamin said, answering his mother's angry question.

13. *Every* player from the '89 team won a college scholarship, not just the high scorers.

14. The thing is a *propane* heater, not a *profane* heater.

15. Andrew lost his *knife,* not his *wife.*

Hyphens

The most common conventional use of the hyphen is to divide multisyllabic words occurring at the ends of lines. Note that monosyllabic (one-syllable) words may not be divided at the ends of lines. The first rule for correct word division is to check a standard dictionary. The dictionary will not tell you everything you need to know, however. Following are a few important conventions for word division:

1. The hyphen dividing a word occurs at the end of the line on which the word starts, not at the beginning of the line on which the word concludes.

2. Words are divided only between syllables—e.g., *augmentation* (*aug-men-ta-tion*), *carnivorous* (*car-niv-o-rous*), *inanimate* (*in-an-i-mate*), *memento* (*me-men-to*), *obelisk* (*ob-e-lisk*), *locality* (*lo-cal-i-ty*), *bipartisan* (*bi-par-ti-san*).

3. A minimum of two letters must appear on each of the lines where the divided word occurs. Thus, such words as *abort* (*a-bort*), *enough* (*e-nough*), *irate* (*i-rate*), *leaky* (*leak-y*), and *sneaky* (*sneak-y*) cannot be divided at all; and a word like *anemia* (*a-ne-mi-a*) can be divided only between the second and third syllables.

4. Words of only four letters, even if they are composed of two syllables of two letters each—e.g., *into* (*in-to*), *only* (*on-ly*), *open* (*op-en*)—should not be divided.

339

5. In compound words the divisions should be made only between the main parts of the compound, not between syllables within the main parts. Thus, *microeconomics* should only be divided (*micro-economics*). Similarly, *aquamarine* should only be divided (*aqua-marine*).

6. Although in most instances words can be divided between double consonants—e.g., *common* (*com-mon*), *sullen* (*sul-len*), *fodder* (*fod-der*), *jigger* (*jig-ger*)—when a word that ends in a double consonant has a suffix added, the resulting word is usually divided after the double consonant—e.g., *dullness* (*dull-ness*), *stressful* (*stress-ful*), *pressing* (*press-ing*).

7. Words with prefixes or suffixes (or both) and a freestanding or identifiable central word part should be divided only after the prefix or before the suffix; they should not be divided within the prefix, within the suffix, or within the main part of the word. Thus, *nonconformist* can only be divided (*non-conformist*) or (*nonconform-ist*). Similarly, *disappearance* can be divided either (*dis-appearance*) or (*disappear-ance*).

8. Words that already have one or more hyphens should be divided only at an existing hyphen—e.g., *helter-skelter, anti-American, thirty-seven, all-conference, three-quarters, safe-conduct, neo-Platonic, son-in-law.*

9. Even though the pronunciation of numerals, contractions, and many abbreviations produces syllables that the ear can hear, these items are never divided from one line to the next.

As an exercise in word division, look up the following words in a standard dictionary. First, indicate the syllabication given for each word in the dictionary. Second, indicate the place(s) the words can be divided at the end of a line. Keep in mind that many words cannot be divided at every point where two syllables come together.

EXERCISE
Word Division

	Syllabication	Division(s)
1. encyclopedia	_____	_____
2. homecoming	_____	_____
3. impeachable	_____	_____
4. basketball	_____	_____
5. amorphous	_____	_____
6. father-in-law	_____	_____
7. simpleton	_____	_____
8. fullness	_____	_____
9. hummingbird	_____	_____
10. slinky	_____	_____

	Syllabication	**Division(s)**
11. allowance	_____	_____
12. topsy-turvy	_____	_____
13. correspondence	_____	_____
14. summarize	_____	_____
15. absenteeism	_____	_____

In addition to indicating where words may be divided at the ends of lines, hyphens are also used to connect pairs of words, groups of words, and words and word parts in a variety of ways for a variety of purposes. Observe the following conventions.

1. Hyphens join constructed two-word modifiers that describe nouns following the constructed modifier—e.g., "a _well-trained_ work force," "these _short-fused_ referees," "a _dirty-dog_ attitude," "a _close-cropped_ head of hair," "an _even-tempered_ instructor," "another _thirty-page_ report," "a _time-consuming_ job." Two cautions are important here: When the first word in a pair of words modifying a third word ends in _-ly_ (e.g., "_barely audible_ sound" or "_openly hostile_ attitude"), no hyphen should be used. Second, no hyphen is used when such two-word modifiers do not immediately precede the word they modify—e.g., "She was even tempered" or "He was well trained."

2. Hyphens connect the words in a coined phrase used in a modifying context—e.g., "_life-or-death_ situation," "_get-out-of-my-face_ expression," "_holier-than-thou_ attitude," "_money-in-his-pocket_ stride."

3. Hyphens connect the words of a phrasal noun—e.g., _editor-in-chief, man-about-town, lady-in-waiting, jack-of-all-trades, go-between, seventy-five-year-olds, make-believe._

4. Hyphens join the words in written-out numbers (between twenty-one and ninety-nine) or fractions, and they separate numerals followed by units of measurement—e.g., _twenty-eight,_ "_seventy-five_ thousand," _one-tenth, two-thirds,_ "_50-hour_ workweek," "_60-watt_ bulb."

5. Hyphens join prefixes to capitalized words or figures—e.g., _pre-Columbian, post-Ronald Reagan, anti-CIA, trans-Siberian, un-American, pseudo-1950s,_ "the _under-25_ age group."

6. Hyphens join the prefixes _all-, ex-, half-, quarter-, quasi-,_ and _self-,_ and the suffixes _-elect_ and _-odd_ to other words—e.g., _all-clear, ex-governor, half-moon, self-sufficient, governor-elect, thirty-odd._

7. Hyphens join single capital letters to nouns or to past participles—e.g., _A-frame, G-man, T-bar, L-shaped._

8. Hyphens prevent some words from being misread as other words or from being awkward looking and thus difficult to read—e.g., _co-op_ as distinguished from _coop, re-creation_ rather than _recreation, re-cover_ rather than _recover, re-treat_ rather than _retreat, re-ally_ rather than _really, co-workers_ as a clarification of _coworkers_ or _bell-like_ as a clarification of _belllike._

One other conventional use of the hyphen is important to student writers. It is called the _suspended hyphen._ The suspended hyphen occurs when two or more compound modifiers together have the same second word but that word is not used until the end of all the modifiers. In its place a hyphen (the suspended hyphen) is used. Observe the following sentence examples.

1. At the present time, *two-* and *four-year* colleges are experiencing equally painful fiscal difficulties.
2. Most of the *third-, fourth-,* and *fifth-floor* suites are being redecorated.
3. Are you interested in a *whole-* or *half-year* lease?
4. We could find no houses in the *seventy-, eighty-,* or *ninety-thousand-dollar* range.
5. Will these items be equally attractive to *low-, medium-,* and *high-income* buyers?

In the following exercise quiz, insert needed hyphens into each of the twenty-five sentences. All the sentences require the addition of more than one hyphen; many of them require several hyphens.

EXERCISE
Hyphens

1. What had been able bodied young men only weeks earlier were now battle weary veterans who dreamed of mom's apple pie.

2. Twenty five of the 160 gallon drums were the property of that fly by night operator Angus Kilroy.

3. Except for the V neck sweaters and autographed T shirts, the other ten and twenty dollar items were so much junk.

4. How unchristian it was of those self righteous people to ridicule the mayor elect in public.

5. The company has had enough of this johnny come lately; what it needs now is a hard nosed, no nonsense manager.

6. In general, do your teachers prefer hands on or hands off methods of instruction?

7. "One upmanship is the name of the game in this world of quasi scientific advertising," the editor in chief said glibly.

8. Our afternoon meal, a 90 minute affair attended by all 375 members of the organization, included homegrown vegetables, fresh baked bread, and a 16 ounce T bone steak.

9. Can one be proIrish without being antiBritish?

10. Although Lilian wore her lost little girl face at the hearing, the judge fined her ninety five dollars for making a U turn on Main Street.

11. After the double barreled tongue lashing delivered by the coach, most of the players remained tight lipped pupils for several weeks.

12. Few of your coworkers want to reuse the earlier discarded materials.

13. To operate a 1,650 acre farm as a profit making enterprise, you will need a good sized crew of self motivated hands who never heard of a 40 hour week.

14. Stirred from her peace imparting reverie by belllike sounds coming from the garden, Sister Stephanie knew that she must really herself with the more conservative members of the order.

15. The transCanadian pipeline is just one example of postWorld War II technology; the H bomb is another.

16. Three quarters of the owners of those A frames on Lost Lake north of the S curve on M 79 have decided to recover their roofs with materials from the local farm coop.

17. To understand why so many students performed equally well on the pre and posttest will require a recreation of the entire testing environment and procedure.

18. Those eighteenth century gentlemen who formulated the Constitution were, indeed, high powered thinkers, but hardly born again Christians.

19. Although the all clear was given before they could redress their wounds, the soldiers knew that the battle wasn't over.

20. For your run of the mill Japan bashing hard hat, this idea has a half life of about two boilermakers.

21. Alas, those flag waving, speech making, finger pointing conventioneers drove the local ne'er do wells crazy.

22. The first, second, and third place finishers were warmly greeted by seventy five odd well wishers, most of whom had never even run to catch a bus.

23. Although facing an openly hostile audience, the speaker went on attacking both the ex mayor and the state attorney general elect as if he were running for both offices.

24. At least two thirds of your so called clients are actually low minded mooches.

25. This self promoting would be man at the top handed the valet a C note for bringing his Volvo around to the front entrance.

In the following review exercise, you should (1) identify the *two* incorrectly handled mechanical conventions in each sentence by putting the appropriate letters in the blanks in front of the sentence and (2) correct each sentence by editing it right there on the page. Although many of the sentences have more than two mistakes, they have only two *kinds* of mistakes. Thus, if the first error in the sentence involves italics, put a *D* in the first blank in front of the sentence. Don't put another *D* in the second blank even if there are other errors involving italics. Into the second blank put only the letter that indicates whatever the other error in the sentence is. And there may be more than one instance of this error as well. Finally, be sure to correct *all* instances of both errors when you edit the sentences.

REVIEW EXERCISE
Additional Mechanical Conventions

A. Capitals   D. Italics
B. Abbreviations   E. Hyphens
C. Numbers

__/__ 1. The lifeguard said that the infants were red from the sun and the 100 degree heat, not dead.

__/__ 2. Each year in the Spring and Fall, my father and mother join Mister and Mistress Gingrich from the next block for a shopping trip to Pittsburgh.

__/__ 3. No one was surprised when Kevin came to the door wearing a silk robe-de-chambre and holding a well worn copy of The Other Victorians in his hand.

__/__ 4. Germaine Rushmore, Bachelor of Science, Master of Arts, Master of Business Administration, Doctor of Philosophy, has joined 12 of her colleagues in the English department at Hinterland Community College to offer a double-paced summer seminar on stress management.

__/__ 5. The university bookstore ordered 7,000 4-dollar copies of "Webster's Modern World Dictionary" but received 4,000 7-dollar copies of Westrum's "Modern World Discoveries."

__/__ 6. This is a dog eat dog world, father; there is little room for vegetarians.

__/__ 7. 7 has always been my lucky number; *exempli gratia,* I was born on July 7, 1957, at 7:07 o'clock in the morning.

__/__ 8. When professor Jensen said that princess Caroline had been photographed au naturel, did he mean she was naked or simply cooked?

__/__ 9. Aren't these two hundred watt bulbs too bright to read by?

__/__ 10. Claudia looked knowingly at Conrad and said, "of the 9 children in the Sherman family, little Fritz has always been my Auntie's favorite."

__/__ 11. Hannibal's c'est-la-vie approach to business problems drives the button down collar crowd up the walls.

__/__ 12. Rumor has it that two student coops will open next fall just South of town.

__/__ 13. Doctor Bumstead, normally a reliable surgeon, met this exotic woman at the Grand Old Party convention, and the two of them flew to Europe for a nostalgic ride on The Orient Express.

___/___ 14. "In this particular sentence," the instructor said, a bit weary of having to repeat herself, "egyptian is a proper adjective."

___/___ 15. Sooner or later, the have nots—*id est,* those people heretofore without money, land, homes, or political power—will rise up with a life threatening fury.

___/___ 16. We read 9 400-page novels in the class, the best of which was "All the King's Men."

___/___ 17. Few people today are familiar with the roman philosopher maximus acerbus, who lived from 75 before christ until *anno Domini* 43.

___/___ 18. The ninety-minute intervals of rapid-eye-movement sleep turned out to be consistent with 175 of the 250 subjects, or 70%.

___/___ 19. A bone chilling article in the latest edition of *Newsweek* entitled "life among the rich young politicos" will affirm your less than optimistic opinions about the future.

___/___ 20. According to this report, more than ninety percent of all people who test positive for the HIV-virus eventually develop Acquired Immune Deficiency Syndrome.

___/___ 21. "Do you wish to speak to Doctor Crispin Hollenbeck, Senior, or Doctor Crispin Hollenbeck, Junior?" the indignant voiced receptionist said.

___/___ 22. The expression "sub rosa" is latin and means literally "under the rose"; by extension, however, it also means "secretly" or "confidentially."

___/___ 23. When uncle Frederick gave his Niece the pendant made of swedish amber, she went into one of her I can't thank you enough routines.

___/___ 24. "The Last Picture Show," which runs exactly one hundred and eighteen minutes, was the last picture show that Aunt Miriam was able to sit through.

___/___ 25. On the farm we were at the breakfast table by 5:00 *ante meridiem,* worked a twelve to fourteen hour day, and were in our bunks again by 8:30 *post meridiem.*

PART THREE
SENTENCE EDITING

Chapter 8

Commonly Occurring Sentence Problems

Just as there are conventions of correctness for diction and usage, punctuation and mechanics, there are also conventions of correctness for sentence structure. To observe these conventions, you must be able to recognize and avoid a number of fundamental sentence errors. For the sake of efficiency, we are concentrating on the ten most commonly occurring sentence errors. They are (1) sentence fragment, (2) fused (run-on) sentence, (3) comma splice, (4) subject-verb agreement error, (5) pronoun case error, (6) pronoun-antecedent error, (7) misplaced modifier, (8) dangling modifier, (9) faulty parallelism, and (10) faulty verb form. The first five of these errors are taken up in this chapter, and the second five are covered in the next chapter.

To give yourself an idea of how well you can already recognize all ten of the sentence errors, work the following self-checking pretest exercise. Match the letters naming the errors from the list at the beginning of the exercise with the sentences in which the errors occur. There is one error in each sentence.

SELF-CHECKING PRETEST EXERCISE
Sentence Problems

A. Sentence Fragment   F. Pronoun-Antecedent Error
B. Fused (Run-on) Sentence   G. Misplaced Modifier
C. Comma Splice   H. Dangling Modifier
D. Subject-Verb Agreement Error   I. Faulty Parallelism
E. Pronoun Case Error   J. Faulty Verb Form

_____ 1. After watching three videos, our eyes felt like sacks of sand.

_____ 2. The administration will not publish their decision on the matter until after the fall semester.

_____ 3. Elton lost his best friend fortune, afterwards, was not very kind to him.

_____ 4. I don't think that Jay Leno's humor is as funny as Johnny Carson.

_____ 5. I can't guarantee that each of the linemen understand all the offensive plays; no one can.

_____ 6. Ashley stunned the bobcat that sprang at him with a four-battery flashlight.

_____ 7. First the wind started to blow, then the snow began to fall.

_____ 8. Although he didn't mean to, Grant throwed the ball onto a coal car of a passing train, and I suppose it rode all the way to Cincinnati.

_____ 9. Simply because Heather did not have an agent and had had nothing published.

_____ 10. Once again, you are wrong; I am not as old as him.

_____ 11. Ted's mother said very little, his father, however, delivered something close to a sermon.

_____ 12. Just between you and I and the gatepost, this year's team doesn't have a chance to make the playoffs.

_____ 13. Fortunately, the lad was revived after nearly being drowned by his brave Sunday school teacher.

_____ 14. An aging, overweight prizefighter, two bearded midgets in ballerina costumes, and a talking horse.

_____ 15. Vivian's mother was overjoyed when she was made captain of the seventh-grade team.

_____ 16. Not until three or four days after the ship sunk did bodies begin washing ashore.

348

_____ 17. Hamilton's favorite breakfast have always been bacon and eggs, not sausage and pancakes.

_____ 18. The substitute linebacker was tall, broad-shouldered, and could run 40 yards in 4.6 seconds.

_____ 19. After three long days in the jungle, we sat down and ate our new friends dined with us.

_____ 20. Approaching the campus from the west, the football stadium towers over Old Main.

_____ 21. Dean Moran was always sympathetic, tolerant, and taken advantage of by many students.

_____ 22. To everyone's great disappointment, more than half of the wines was bad.

_____ 23. What we discovered was that the gearbox had been broke before.

_____ 24. Anthony must have $75,000 by next Wednesday otherwise he will be a mark for the mob.

_____ 25. Once again, the time has come to take the gerbils out of the cages and wash them.

_____ 26. Frightened by the raging storm, my knees would hardly function.

_____ 27. As usual, the first day of practice was a disaster, no one was in condition.

_____ 28. While walking home from the annual boat races, Wanda found a diamond woman's necklace.

_____ 29. Carefully examining the paper—line by line—and pointing out each of its errors.

_____ 30. The truth is that my wife and myself have been married, off and on, for thirty years.

_____ 31. To possess real wisdom, several decades of experience are necessary.

_____ 32. We are certain that we know whom your choice for the new position will be.

_____ 33. When Ginger was a student in elementary school, she always done her work on time.

_____ 34. On the first day of our vacation the weather was beautiful; the kind of weather that is perfect for the beach.

_____ 35. Please tell us whether or not you plan to join the club on the enclosed computerized form.

_____ 36. Our family physician has assured us that mumps are not the dreaded disease it once was.

_____ 37. The students voted to strike the teachers, however, voted to go on teaching.

_____ 38. For the third weekend in a row, the weather was cold, storming, and snow was in the air.

_____ 39. Justin didn't prepare the defense carefully enough, consequently, his client is now doing hard time.

_____ 40. Almost every time Simeon tosses that old dog a bone, it barks at him.

_____ 41. You should try to if you can manage it take eighteen hours this semester.

_____ 42. "Cramming for an examination never helps me," Andrew said, "I have to study regularly throughout the term."

_____ 43. Connie told Millicent that she should never have flirted with Constantine.

_____ 44. By the time Bennett was in junior high school, all his brothers and sisters had went away to college.

_____ 45. Few students read for pleasure they prefer watching television.

_____ 46. The entire graduating class enjoyed you singing this evening.

_____ 47. Jan admitted that she liked to play volleyball as well as playing tennis.

_____ 48. Edwina, for instance, who spent seven years in Alaska and four years in Mexico.

_____ 49. When in the second grade, Elizabeth's mother had her fourth child.

_____ 50. A little tension and argumentation is sometimes good for the classroom.

Answers: 1. H, 2. F, 3. B, 4. I, 5. D, 6. G, 7. C, 8. J, 9. A, 10. E, 11. C, 12. E, 13. G, 14. A, 15. F, 16. J, 17. D, 18. I, 19. B, 20. H, 21. I, 22. D, 23. J, 24. B, 25. F, 26. H, 27. C, 28. G, 29. A, 30. E, 31. H, 32. E, 33. J, 34. A, 35. G, 36. D, 37. B, 38. I, 39. C, 40. F, 41. G, 42. C, 43. F, 44. J, 45. B, 46. E, 47. I, 48. A, 49. H, 50. D

Sentence Fragment

A sentence fragment is the error of writing and punctuating anything less than a sentence—a word, a phrase, a dependent clause—as if it _were_ a sentence. More often than not, a fragment is an incorrectly punctuated phrase or dependent (subordinate) clause preceding or following a sentence to which it is in some way linked. The error can usually be corrected either by adjoining the fragment to the sentence or by expanding the fragment into an independent clause or sentence. Other instances include fragments arising from compound-predicate constructions, fragments occurring as a result of the semicolon being incorrectly used where a comma should be used, and long dependent clauses unconnected with any sentence. Observe the following examples and note that each correction is marked by an asterisk (*).

1. Mona decided to leave college and go to work. For a variety of reasons.
   * For a variety of reasons, Mona decided to leave college and go to work.

2. Bertram completed the project on time. Without help or encouragement from anyone.
   * Without help or encouragement from anyone, Bertram completed the project on time.

3. Lydia completely revised the paper. Hoping to improve her grade in the class.

  * Hoping to improve her grade in the class, Lydia completely revised the paper.

4. Having worked in print shops throughout high school. Edmund tried to join the typesetters union.

  * Having worked in print shops throughout high school, Edmund tried to join the typesetters union.

5. As usual, they stayed the night in Hamilton. Not Toronto.

  * As usual, they stayed the night in Hamilton, not Toronto.

6. We ran into Stanley last Friday evening. At the mall on East Lake Boulevard.

  * We ran into Stanley last Friday evening at the mall on East Lake Boulevard.

7. Hilary's father, who was born in a village south of London, still speaks with an English accent. After living in the United States for almost thirty years.

  * Hilary's father, who was born in a village south of London, still speaks with an English accent after living in the United States for almost thirty years.

8. Alison grew up in the little town of Waverly. Which is located on Lake Michigan between Hinterland and Prudent.

  * Alison grew up in the little town of Waverly, which is located on Lake Michigan between Hinterland and Prudent.

9. With winter on the way. We knew that it was time to fill the larder.

  * With winter on the way, we knew that it was time to fill the larder.

10. Julian won first prize. Because he was the only one left standing when the final bell sounded.

  * Because he was the only one left standing when the final bell sounded, Julian won first prize.

11. We wanted to go to Europe. Although we didn't want to stay all summer.

  * We wanted to go to Europe; however, we didn't want to stay all summer.

12. Martin lost all his money. A fine fix.

  * Martin lost all his money. A fine fix that was.

13. The children were fascinated by the animals. Especially the elephants.

  * The children were fascinated by the animals. They especially liked the elephants.

14. After three days of rain, the river overflowed its banks. And flooded most of Old Town.

  * After three days of rain, the river overflowed its banks and flooded most of Old Town.

15. Harvey bought a camera for himself. And a CD player for his nephew.

  * Harvey bought a camera for himself and a CD player for his nephew.

16. If the first line of defense holds for an hour or so; everything should be all right.

  * If the first line of defense holds for an hour or so, everything should be all right.

17. As he looked upon the valley of his youth for the first time in fifty years; the old man could not hold back the tears.

    * As he looked upon the valley of his youth for the first time in fifty years, the old man could not hold back the tears.

18. Before trying to revise this paper; you should allow it to "age" for two or three days.

    * Before trying to revise this paper, you should allow it to "age" for two or three days.

19. If only we had enough money to do the job as it should be done.

    * If only we had enough money, we could do the job as it should be done.

20. In the event that nothing happens between now and midnight.

    * In the event that nothing happens between now and midnight, turn off the power and go home.

Fused (Run-on) Sentence

A fused sentence is the error of writing two independent clauses together—with no punctuation—as if they were a single sentence. Fused sentences are usually corrected (1) by separating the clauses into two sentences through the use of a period, (2) by separating the clauses and linking them with a semicolon and sometimes a conjunctive adverb, (3) by separating the clauses and linking them with a comma and a coordinating conjunction, (4) by recasting the clauses so that one of them is subordinate to the other, or (5) by recasting the clauses so that they are one independent clause. Keep in mind, however, that not all five options for correcting a fused sentence work equally well in every situation. Observe the following examples and note that each correction is marked by an asterisk.

1. Clarice read the novel then she watched the movie.
   * Clarice read the novel. Then she watched the movie.
   * Clarice read the novel; then she watched the movie.
   * Clarice read the novel, and then she watched the movie.
   * After she read the novel, Clarice watched the movie.
   * After Clarice read the novel, she watched the movie.
   * After reading the novel, Clarice watched the movie.
   * Before she watched the movie, Clarice read the novel.
   * Before Clarice watched the movie, she read the novel.
   * Before watching the movie, Clarice read the novel.
   * Clarice read the novel and then watched the movie.
   * Clarice read the novel, then watched the movie.

2. Coach Morgan looked at his championship team his heart was filled with pride.
   * Coach Morgan looked at his championship team. His heart was filled with pride.
   * Coach Morgan looked at his championship team; his heart was filled with pride.
   * Coach Morgan looked at his championship team, and his heart was filled with pride.
   * As Coach Morgan looked at his championship team, his heart was filled with pride.
   * Coach Morgan's heart was filled with pride as he looked at his championship team.

3. The birthrate must be reduced otherwise overpopulation will result in disaster.

* The birthrate must be reduced. Otherwise, overpopulation will result in disaster.

* The birthrate must be reduced; otherwise, overpopulation will result in disaster.

* Either the birthrate must be reduced, or overpopulation will result in disaster.

* Unless the birthrate is reduced, overpopulation will result in disaster.

* Overpopulation will result in disaster unless the birthrate is reduced.

Using the blank space provided, correct each of the following fused sentences in a variety of ways.

1. Ted and Agnes arrived late at the stadium they missed most of the first quarter.

* _____

_____.

* _____

_____.

* _____

_____.

* _____

_____.

* _____

_____.

2. The lecture halls in Old Main are too large students cannot hear their instructors.

* _____

_____.

* _____

_____.

* _____

_____.

* _____

_____.

* _____

_____.

3. These books were too long to read them took me several weeks.

* _____

_____ .

* _____

_____ .

* _____

_____ .

* _____

_____ .

* _____

_____ .

Comma Splice

A comma splice is the error of joining two independent clauses with only a comma. This error often occurs when a conjunctive adverb or a transitional expression that functions just like a conjunctive adverb—e.g., *accordingly, also, anyway, as a consequence, as a result, besides, consequently, finally, first, for example, furthermore, hence, however, indeed, in fact, in other words, instead, likewise, moreover, nevertheless, nonetheless, on the other hand, otherwise, regardless, similarly, still, then, therefore, thus*—appearing between independent clauses is treated as if it were a coordinating conjunction (*and, but, for, or, nor, so, yet*). This is to say that the conjunctive adverb is incorrectly preceded by a comma. Split direct quotations in which both parts of the quotation are independent statements also cause comma splices when both "halves" of the quotation are separated by only a comma.

Generally, comma splices are corrected (1) by substituting a period for the comma and thereby creating two separately punctuated sentences, (2) by including a coordinating conjunction with the comma, (3) by changing the comma to a semicolon if a conjunctive adverb introduces or occurs within the second clause, (4) by changing the comma to a semicolon even if there is no conjunctive adverb present but the notion of "because" exists between the first and second clauses, or (5) by subordinating one of the clauses to the other—usually the first to the second. Remember that not all five methods of correction are equally effective for every comma splice. Observe the following examples of comma splices and their "most appropriate" corrections.

1. I liked some of what the speaker said, most of the people in the room did.
* I liked some of what the speaker said. Most of the people in the room did.

2. Emery refused to attend the homecoming game, he said he hated football.
* Emery refused to attend the homecoming game; he said he hated football.

354

3. Ginger studied two hours every day for her physics class, still she received only a $C-$ grade at the end of the term.

* Ginger studied two hours every day for her physics class; still, she received only a $C-$ grade at the end of the term.

4. Ian forgot to bring his umbrella, he was drenched by the downpour after the concert.

* Because he forgot to bring his umbrella, Ian was drenched by the downpour after the concert.

5. Lloyd's uncle owns the largest motel in town, he is thinking about building another one in Waverly.

* Lloyd's uncle owns the largest motel in town, and he is thinking about building another one in Waverly.

6. Mildred wants to win an Olympic medal in gymnastics, she never misses practice.

* Because she wants to win an Olympic medal in gymnastics, Mildred never misses practice.

7. Jonah works eighty hours a week, he wants to be a millionaire before he is thirty.

* Jonah works eighty hours a week; he wants to be a millionaire before he is thirty.

8. A fellow like you will love living in Hinterland, there are absolutely no cultural or recreational activities.

* A fellow like you will love living in Hinterland; there are absolutely no cultural or recreational activities.

9. I think that computer science is an overcrowded field, many experts say the same thing.

* I think that computer science is an overcrowded field, and many experts say the same thing.

10. "We enjoy spending an evening watching a movie on our VCR," Millicent said, "besides going out at night can be risky."

* "We enjoy spending an evening watching a movie on our VCR," Millicent said; "besides, going out at night can be risky."

11. "Life is no Sunday afternoon picnic," Uncle Frank said, "A fellow with your experience should know that."

* "Life is no Sunday afternoon picnic," Uncle Frank said. "A fellow with your experience should know that."

12. I have never won a dime playing the lottery, nevertheless every week I squander another five or ten dollars.

* I have never won a dime playing the lottery; nevertheless, every week I squander another five or ten dollars.

13. This community has been growing smaller for the last twenty-five years, it is, nonetheless, a pleasant place to live.

* This community has been growing smaller for the last twenty-five years; it is, nonetheless, a pleasant place to live.

14. Carmel is a magician with small children, she can make them disappear into bed with only the raising of an eyebrow.

  * Carmel is a magician with small children, for she can make them disappear into bed with only the raising of an eyebrow.

15. I am not acquainted with Mr. Godheigh, as a matter of fact, I have never heard of him.

  * I am not acquainted with Mr. Godheigh. As a matter of fact, I have never heard of him.

Subject-Verb Agreement Error

The subject-verb agreement error occurs when the subject and verb of a sentence do not agree in number. The general rule is that singular subjects take singular verbs, and plural subjects take plural verbs. Most of the time the task of following this general rule is not particularly difficult. Occasionally, however, situations arise wherein you may be uncertain about how to match up the subject and verb. The following suggestions are intended to help you through such situations.

Subject-verb separation   When the subject and verb of a sentence are separated by a group of words that may include one or more nouns, be sure that the verb agrees in number with the subject of the sentence, not with one of these nouns in the intervening group of words.

1. As always, the contestant with the most points moves on to the second round of play.
2. Players with inadequate equipment are always at risk.
3. The school board, as well as the local citizens, was pleased with the plans for the new high school.
4. Litton, together with his usual entourage of supporters, was at the party.
5. My uncle, assisted by his sons and daughters, operates laundromats all over the city.
6. The protesters, accompanied by a single police officer, remain at the site of the spill.
7. The walls, as well as the ceiling, were in need of a fresh coat of paint.
8. The intelligence of many sea animals is indeed amazing.
9. Eleanor's cousins, not her brother, intend to spend the summer in Europe.
10. The principal cause of the disagreements was confused instructions.

Singular subjects joined by *and*   When two or more singular subjects are joined by the coordinating conjunction *and,* a plural verb should be used. An exception to this occurs when the parts of a compound subject refer to one thing or person or when *each* or *every* precedes the compound subject.

1. A cat and a canary are seldom confidants.
2. A little tension and argumentation are sometimes good for the classroom.
3. Freedom and justice were two cornerstones of the democracy from the beginning.
4. The sum and substance of the speaker's remarks has not gone unnoticed.

356

5. Vinegar and oil <u>was</u> the only salad dressing my grandfather ever used.
6. Each <u>car</u> and <u>truck</u> that passed us <u>was</u> exceeding the speed limit.
7. Every <u>man</u>, <u>woman</u>, and <u>child</u> <u>was</u> taken from the village.

Singular subjects joined by *or* and *nor*   When singular subjects are joined by *or* or by *either . . . or* or *neither . . . nor,* a singular verb should be used. However, if one of the subjects is singular and the other is plural, the plural one should be placed in the second position (closer to the verb) and the verb made plural.

1. An <u>apple</u> or an <u>orange</u> <u>was</u> the first choice.
2. At this hospital, a <u>doctor</u> or a <u>nurse</u> <u>is</u> always on call.
3. Either <u>psychology</u> or <u>sociology</u> <u>was</u> Isabel's favorite subject.
4. Either a certified <u>check</u> on deposit or a valid major credit <u>card</u> <u>is</u> required for one to bid on the merchandise.
5. Neither <u>John</u> nor <u>Mary</u> <u>makes</u> very good grades in chemistry.
6. Neither the liberal <u>candidate</u> nor the conservative <u>candidate</u> <u>supports</u> such a risky bill.
7. A good <u>book</u> or a few close <u>friends</u> <u>are</u> an antidote for a slow afternoon.
8. The <u>manager</u> or her <u>assistants</u> <u>were</u> usually available to give us direction.
9. Either Aunt <u>Agnes</u> or her <u>children</u> <u>were</u> left a small fortune by the local recluse.
10. Neither the <u>instructor</u> nor the <u>students</u> <u>want</u> to do another watercolor.

Indefinite pronouns (I)   Indefinite pronouns that end with *-body, -one,* or *-thing* (e.g., *somebody, someone, something*) always take a singular verb. In like manner, the indefinite pronouns *another, each, either, neither,* and *one* (used alone) take a singular verb. However, the indefinite pronouns *both, few, many, others,* and *several* always take a plural verb.

1. <u>Somebody</u> <u>has</u> been sleeping in my bed.
2. Not just <u>anyone</u> <u>is</u> capable of playing in the majors.
3. <u>Nobody</u> <u>knows</u> the trouble I've seen.
4. <u>Something</u> <u>is</u> rotten in the state of Denmark.
5. Alas, <u>another</u> of these detergents <u>has</u> proved to be harmful to the delicate skin of the househusband.
6. <u>Each</u> of these women <u>needs</u> a babysitter.
7. <u>Either</u> of the drawings <u>looks</u> nice in the family room.
8. As one might expect, <u>neither</u> of the films <u>was</u> available in the college collection.
9. <u>One</u> <u>does</u> what one can; <u>one</u> <u>isn't</u> always successful, however.
10. Although cleverly worded, <u>both</u> of the answers <u>were</u> incorrect.
11. <u>Many</u> <u>were</u> called, but <u>few</u> <u>were</u> chosen. <u>Others</u>, from all indications, <u>were</u> not paying attention to incoming messages.
12. <u>Several</u> in the audience <u>were</u> beside themselves with anger at what the speaker had said.

Indefinite pronouns (II)   The indefinite pronouns *all, any, more, most,* and *some* and other words that indicate a quantity, part, percentage, or fraction of something (e.g., *half,* *two-thirds, three-quarters*) may take either a singular verb or a plural verb, depending upon the number of the word they precede and refer to, which is the object of the prepositional phrase that follows the pronoun.

1. Virtually <u>all</u> of the wine <u>was</u> spoiled.
2. Almost <u>all</u> of the apples <u>were</u> frostbitten.
3. <u>Most</u> of the day <u>was</u> spent in court.
4. <u>Most</u> of the days <u>were</u> spent napping on the beach.
5. <u>Some</u> of the medicines <u>are</u> more effective than others.
6. <u>Some</u> of Herman's time <u>was</u> taken up settling disputes among the workers.
7. Sixty <u>percent</u> of the land <u>was</u> under water.
8. Forty percent of the trees <u>were</u> scheduled for harvest.
9. A <u>third</u> of the crop <u>was</u> left in the field.
10. A <u>third</u> of the Christmas orders <u>were</u> incorrectly mailed.

Indefinite pronouns (III)   The indefinite pronoun *none* poses peculiar problems. It always takes a singular verb when the object of the prepositional phrase following it is singular. It also takes a singular verb when used to mean "not one," even if the object of the following prepositional phrase is plural. However, *none* may take a plural verb when it is used to mean "not any" and the object of the following prepositional phrase is plural. Thus, when you use *none* in such constructions you must be sure of your meaning.

1. <u>None</u> of this food <u>was</u> easy to prepare.
2. <u>None</u> of our recent popularity <u>is</u> the result of our own efforts.
3. <u>None</u> [not one] of the melons <u>is</u> ready to pick.
4. <u>None</u> [not one] of the players <u>was</u> able to pass the physical fitness test.
5. We were surprised that <u>none</u> [not any] of the albums <u>were</u> sold out.
6. The dean was displeased to learn that <u>none</u> [not any] of the foreign students <u>are</u> majoring in education or sociology.

Collective nouns   Sometimes called group nouns, collective nouns are singular in form but denote a group of some sort. Examples include *committee, class, crew, family, staff, troop, jury, team, squad,* and *union.* A collective noun takes a singular verb when the group is regarded as a unit functioning as one. However, a collective noun takes a plural verb when individual members of the group are regarded as functioning separately.

1. Once again, the <u>team</u> <u>is</u> going to compete in the Christmas tournament.
2. Alas, the <u>team</u> <u>are</u> unable to agree on the selection of a captain.
3. The <u>family</u> <u>has</u> owned the cottage on Eagle Lake for thirty years.
4. The <u>family</u> <u>have</u> been arriving two or three at a time since last weekend.
5. For the third time this year, the <u>committee</u> <u>is</u> going to consider increasing the dues.
6. The <u>committee</u> <u>were</u> casually seated in armchairs about the room.

Inverted sentences   Sometimes sentences are structured in such a way (inverted) that the verb precedes the subject. Such sentences may begin with a modifying phrase or such words

358

as *here, there, how, what,* and *where.* When you write such sentences, take care to match the verb with the subject that follows.

1. Here <u>come</u> the <u>coaches</u> and the <u>players</u> for both teams.
2. There <u>have</u> been many exciting <u>games</u> this season.
3. How <u>are</u> the <u>children</u> after such an experience?
4. What <u>are</u> your <u>reasons</u> for taking such a position?
5. Where <u>have</u> those deep <u>snows</u> of my childhood gone?
6. In front of the auditorium <u>stands</u> a towering <u>oak</u> that was planted when my grandfather was a student here.
7. Beside the old gymnasium <u>stand</u> an <u>elm</u>, several <u>maples</u>, and a huge <u>linden</u>.
8. Fortunately, there <u>exist</u> <u>experts</u> who can advise us on these matters.

Relative pronouns   When the relative pronouns *who, which,* or *that* are used as subjects of dependent adjective clauses, the verb of the adjective clause must agree in number with the antecedent of the pronoun. If the antecedent is singular, the verb of the adjective clause must be singular; if the antecedent is plural, the verb of the adjective clause must be plural.

1. Each fraternity has its own elected <u>officers</u>, who <u>conduct</u> the business of the organization.
2. These are the <u>children</u> who <u>deserve</u> our help.
3. Where is the <u>man</u> you spoke of who <u>collects</u> medieval weapons of torture?
4. Those are the <u>houses</u> that <u>are</u> repainted every third year.
5. Our county has three excellent <u>parks</u>, which <u>attract</u> thousands of tourists throughout the year.
6. This reference book concludes with <u>pages</u> that <u>contain</u> lists of American colleges and universities.
7. Franklin happens to be one of those <u>people</u> who <u>like</u> to read.
8. Stephanie happens to be the <u>only</u> <u>member</u> of her family who <u>likes</u> to golf.
9. The ability to use language is one of the <u>things</u> that <u>set</u> humans apart from animals.
10. Estelle was the <u>only</u> <u>one</u> of Professor Hunt's children who <u>was</u> able to win a college scholarship.
11. Jarvis, I'm sorry to say, is one of these <u>individuals</u> who <u>seem</u> never to stop thinking about themselves.
12. The newspaper published the name of the <u>only</u> <u>one</u> of the conspirators who <u>was</u> acquainted with the ambassador's family.

Subjects with predicate nouns   When the subject and a predicate noun in the sentence differ in number, the verb—always a linking verb—should agree with the subject, not with the predicate noun.

1. To Clinton's way of thinking, fancy <u>dinners</u> <u>are</u> not a luxury.
2. We thought the <u>problem</u> <u>was</u> termites, but <u>it</u> <u>was</u> carpenter ants.
3. Even at the age of thirty, Quentin's favorite <u>food</u> <u>is</u> peanut butter and jelly sandwiches.

4. The <u>bride</u> and <u>groom</u> <u>were</u> the center of attention.
5. My favorite <u>brunch</u> <u>is</u> sausage, eggs, chips, and a green salad.

Verbal nouns and noun clauses   Verbal nouns—i.e., gerunds and gerund phrases, infinitives and infinitive phrases—and noun clauses used as subjects always take singular verbs.

1. <u>Swimming</u> <u>is</u> Gisele's favorite form of exercise.
2. <u>Swimming</u> <u>across</u> <u>the</u> <u>English</u> <u>Channel</u> <u>is</u> still a major accomplishment.
3. <u>To</u> <u>crash</u> <u>was</u> Newton's one great fear in night racing.
4. <u>To</u> <u>help</u> <u>a</u> <u>friend</u> <u>in</u> <u>need</u> <u>is</u> to give pleasure to oneself.
5. <u>To</u> <u>dance</u> <u>on</u> <u>the</u> <u>graves</u> <u>of</u> <u>their</u> <u>enemies</u> <u>was</u> the immediate goal of the young warriors.
6. <u>That</u> <u>the</u> <u>two</u> <u>men</u> <u>are</u> <u>not</u> <u>friends</u> <u>seems</u> obvious to me.
7. <u>Who</u> <u>is</u> <u>to</u> <u>go</u> <u>and</u> <u>who</u> <u>is</u> <u>to</u> <u>stay</u> <u>has</u> not yet been decided.
8. <u>Whether</u> <u>we</u> <u>were</u> great <u>leaders</u> <u>or</u> <u>ordinary</u> <u>citizens</u> really <u>makes</u> little difference later on.

Titles of works, names of businesses, and words as words   The title of a literary work, even if plural in form, always takes a singular verb. Similarly, the name of a business enterprise and words referred to as words take a singular verb.

1. *Great Expectations* <u>is</u> hardly one of Dickens's lighter works.
2. *Dubliners* <u>has</u> proved to be an even more important collection of short stories than its author thought it would be.
3. The local <u>Shakes 'n Suds</u> <u>is</u> a busy place on Saturday afternoon.
4. <u>Frames</u> <u>Unlimited</u> <u>does</u> most of the work for the gallery.
5. <u>Concerti</u> <u>is</u> the plural form of <u>concerto</u>.
6. <u>Grunts</u> <u>was</u> the term used for foot soldiers during the Vietnam War.

Plural forms with singular meanings   Some nouns are plural in form but singular in meaning, and thus take a singular verb. Examples include *aerobics, economics, headquarters, hives, mathematics, means, measles, mumps, news, physics, stamina, summons,* and *whereabouts.*

1. As usual, the evening <u>news</u> <u>was</u> mostly bad news.
2. <u>Economics</u> <u>has</u> never been exactly my cup of tea.
3. The witness claims that the <u>summons</u> <u>was</u> never delivered to her.
4. Alas, my <u>stamina</u> <u>is</u> not what it once was.
5. The <u>whereabouts</u> of the thieves <u>is</u> not known at this time.

Noun phrases   Subjects composed of noun phrases that indicate such things as a measured distance, a period of time, a specific quantity, or a sum of money, when considered as a single unit, take singular verbs.

1. <u>Fifty</u> <u>miles</u> <u>is</u> a long way to walk, much less run.
2. <u>Precisely</u> <u>thirty</u> <u>years</u> <u>was</u> his tenure of office.

3. Four hundred gallons of fuel was lost as a result of the accident.
4. Five million dollars is a lot to pay a baseball player for only one year.
5. Is forty seconds long enough for us to move the ball the length of the field?

To complete the following exercise quiz, read each sentence carefully and then write the correct verb—singular or plural—in the blank. If you need to, don't hesitate to recheck any of the instructional material in this section.

EXERCISE
Subject-Verb Agreement Error

1. In front of each of the buildings (*stands / stand*) _____ a plastic palm tree.

2. (*Do / Does*) _____ any of the spectators in the end-zone seats have season tickets?

3. Eating vegetables sprayed with toxic chemicals (*remains / remain*) _____ a risky dietary practice.

4. The captain, as well as several of his officers, (*was / were*) _____ experienced with such cases.

5. Half of the children in the third-grade class (*lives / live*) _____ in the government housing projects.

6. Over the years, this team (*has / have*) _____ enjoyed more success than any other team in the league.

7. The clock was reset to show that only twenty-six seconds (*was / were*) _____ left in the fourth quarter of the game.

8. Neither the coach nor the players (*has / have*) _____ an explanation for the team's poor performance.

9. More than a week had passed, and the whereabouts of the perpetrator (*was / were*) _____ still unknown.

10. What we are witnessing here is one of the more important events that (*has / have*) _____ ever occurred in Hinterland County.

11. Everyone who is a member of any of these organizations (*favors / favor*) _____ the reforestation of the area.

12. Yvonne is not one of these artists who (*produces / produce*) _____ five or six paintings in an afternoon.

13. That these problems are on the minds of most local citizens (*is / are*) _____

    _____ obvious to me.

14. When all was said and done, the main causes of the nasty disagreement (*was / were*)

    _____ financial.

15. None [not one] of the new faculty members (*cares / care*) _____ to teach
    this class.

16. There (*has / have*) _____ been so many complaints about the bookstore
    that the university has stopped responding to them.

17. Dr. Holmes is the only one of my professors who (*allows / allow*) _____
    students to record the lectures.

18. Bradley's computer and electronic typewriter (*was / were*) _____ stolen
    from the writing lab.

19. Meals on Wheels (*offers / offer*) _____ an important service to many
    elderly people in the community.

20. Insolent students (*has / have*) _____ become a major problem for teachers
    of first-year college students.

21. Several in the audience (*was / were*) _____ unable to hear at least two of
    the debaters.

22. Every boy and girl in the school (*has / have*) _____ the opportunity to learn
    to play a musical instrument.

23. Once again, the staff (*is / are*) _____ at odds about whether or not to form
    a union.

24. As you should know, United, Inc., is one of these companies that always (*makes / make*)

    _____ very low bids and then raise them later on.

25. Either geography or economics (*is / are*) _____ the course of study that
    Dwight intends to pursue.

26. Where (*has / have*) _____ all the protesters from the sixties and seventies
    gone?

27. Each and every student in my dormitory (*plans / plan*) _____ to attend the
    bonfire and pep rally.

28. Neither the engineer nor the technicians at the site (*was / were*) _____
    able to analyze the problem accurately.

29. After seventy-two hours without a verdict, the jury (*was*/*were*) _____ seated wearily in chairs about the room refusing even to look at one another.

30. Professor Girard is the only member of the faculty who (*has*/*have*) _____ _____ had a book published.

Pronoun Case Error

For the word *case* in this section of the text, read "form." Thus, when you make what is called a pronoun case error, what you have really done is used a wrong form of a pronoun. For example, you may have used *I* when you should have used *me, whom* when you should have used *who,* or *myself* when you should have used *I.* Using your general knowledge of pronoun case, correct the form of the incorrectly used pronoun in each of the following sentences. The correct answers appear at the end of the exercise.

1. My wife and *myself* (_____) have been visiting Crystal Beach every summer for twenty years.

2. A reluctant guide escorted *we* (_____) tourists through the entrance and into the castle.

3. Please tell me *whom* (_____) your favorite singer of sacred music is.

4. Rachael and *him* (_____) have known each other since they were in high school.

5. *Whoever* (_____) the committee selected will be okay with *we* (_____ _____).

6. Do you think that I can ever do as well as *them* (_____)?

7. As things turned out, *me* (_____) buying a foreign car was a big mistake.

8. Both finalists, Elizabeth and *her* (_____), were from Poughkeepsie, not Yonkers.

9. Just between you and *I* (_____), I wouldn't buy this house at any price.

10. I specifically recall that you were told several times that this was *me* (_____ _____) own house.

11. The Logans are the people *who* (_____) we met in Stockholm last year at Christmas time.

12. Wasn't that the Thanksgiving that I drove Alden, Greta, Inez, and *I* (_____ _____) to Tijuana?

13. Didn't anyone see *their* (_____) running away from the scene of the crime?

14. The association selected two new representatives, Glenna and *she* (_____

_____), to attend the national assembly.

15. As far as I know, no one objected to *you* (_____) leaving work an hour early.

16. For *he* (_____) to have spent so much money on a used stereo was unnecessary.

17. Does anyone know *who* (_____) all these gifts were intended for?

18. Everyone thought it was *us* (_____) who organized both the picnic and the dance.

19. We will buy the equipment from *whomever* (_____) will sell it to us.

20. The dean threatened Hiram and *I* (_____) with expulsion from school.

21. Although it wasn't true, Less was told that *him* (_____) coming forward persuaded others to do the same.

22. Once again, we have given *us* (_____) a black eye in the opinion of the local people.

23. This weekend may be the last chance for you and *I* (_____) to go to the beach.

24. Were all of *yours* (_____) houses designed and built by the same contractor?

25. It is simply untrue that Georgiana has less money than *us* (_____).

Answers: 1. I, 2. us, 3. who, 4. he, 5. Whomever, us, 6. they, 7. my, 8. she, 9. me, 10. my, 11. whom, 12. myself, 13. them, 14. her, 15. your, 16. him, 17. whom, 18. we, 19. whoever, 20. me, 21. his, 22. ourselves, 23. me, 24. your, 25. we

Although many texts present only three cases of pronouns, actual usage argues for six—as does thirty years of explaining pronoun case to students. They are (1) subjective, (2) objective, (3) noun-determiner possessive, (4) pure or absolute possessive, (5) reflexive, and (6) intensive or emphatic. Before reading on, take a few minutes to examine the *Pronoun Case Chart*. Perhaps your instructor will review it with you.

PRONOUN CASE CHART

	Subjective	Noun-Determiner Possessive	Pure Possessive	Intensive / Reflexive	Objective
Personal Pronouns					
Singular					
First person	I	my	mine	myself	me
Second person	you	your	yours	yourself	you
Third person	he/she/it	his/her/its	his/hers	himself/ herself/itself	him/her/it
Plural					
First person	we	our	ours	ourselves	us
Second person	you	your	yours	yourselves	you
Third person	they	their	their	themselves	them
Relative or Interrogative Pronoun					
Singular	who whoever	whose	whose		whom whomever
Plural	who whoever	whose	whose		whom whomever

Subjective case pronouns   Subjective case pronouns; that is, those pronouns down the left-hand column of the chart, whether they are singular or plural, should be used (1) as the subject of an independent clause, (2) as the subject of a dependent clause, (3) as the subject of an elliptical clause beginning with *than* or *as,* (4) as a subject complement after a linking (*be*) verb, and (5) as an appositive of either a subject or a subject complement.

1. You and *she* have always been honest with each other. [subject of an independent clause]

2. Albert and *I* have enrolled in a botany class. [subject of an independent clause]

3. These are the people *who* designed the new county park. [subject of a dependent clause]

4. Our instructions were to give the package to *whoever* answered the door. [subject of a dependent clause]

5. After *we* won the competition, orders came in from all around the country. [subject of a dependent clause]

6. That *he* is a worthy opponent in this event there can be little question. [subject of a dependent clause]

7. As usual, Ted and Ellen argued about whether *they* should make another effort to climb the mountain. [subject of a dependent clause]

8. Elizabeth has always been taller than *he.* [subject of an elliptical clause]

9. No one bought as much as *we* at the bazaar. [subject of an elliptical clause]

10. No one was more prepared for the tournament than *who?* [subject of an elliptical clause]

11. The champion of the court at the country club was *she.* [subject complement]

12. Our chief opposition during the meeting will most likely be *they.* [subject complement]

13. All three contestants—Frank, Orin, and *she*—had won in years past. [appositive of a subject]

14. We, you and *I*, are the only candidates from the north end of the county. [appositive of a subject]

15. They were the only beneficiaries, Kevin and *she*. [appositive of a subject complement]

Objective case pronouns   Those pronouns shown in the right-hand column of the chart—objective case pronouns—should be used as any type of object: (1) object of a preposition, (2) object of a verb, (3) indirect object of a verb, (4) object of a verbal, (5) indirect object of a verbal, (6) object of an elliptical clause beginning with *than* or *as*. Objective case pronouns are also used as appositives of other objects and as the subject of an infinitive.

1. Almost no one gets along with *him* very well. [object of a preposition]

2. The old man looked steadily at Ruth and *me,* then walked away. [object of a preposition]

3. Alas, the principal sent *us* home from school again. [object of a verb]

4. The principal sent *whom* home from school again? [object of a verb]

5. To our amazement, the hotel mailed Jody and *me* a refund for the days it rained. [indirect object of a verb]

6. Please give Susan and *him* time to finish their pictures. [indirect object of a verb]

7. Taunting *us* as they pleased, the soldiers did not comport themselves as gentlemen should. [object of a verbal—participle]

8. Teaching *her* about the outside world was not an easy task. [object of a verbal—gerund]

9. After telling *them* about the accident, we went to the hospital. [object of a verbal—gerund]

10. To beat *them* at their own game will require careful preparations. [object of a verbal—infinitive]

11. Handing *me* the letter and expelling a great sigh of relief, the postal clerk abruptly left the counter. [indirect object of a verbal—participle]

12. Awarding *us* first prize was not something the local officials really wanted to do. [indirect object of a verbal—gerund]

13. At the time, it cost Byron several hundred dollars to send *them* a Christmas gift from Romania. [indirect object of a verbal—infinitive]

14. The lecture confused my classmates as much as *me*. [object of an elliptical clause]

15. Although we like both Douglas and Madge, we like her more than *him*. [object of an elliptical clause]

16. The judge gave them, Philip and *her,* some sound advice. [appositive of an indirect object of a verb]

17. Hundreds of students stood in the courtyard calling for us—Alden, Helena, and *me*—in a tone of voice that did not bode well for our future. [appositive of an object of a preposition]

18. His history professor told *him* to study the last six chapters of the text. [subject of an infinitive]

19. For *them* to be elected to the city council will require more than a miracle. [subject of an infinitive]

20. Embarrassingly, we took *her* to be the office secretary. [subject of an infinitive]

Noun-determiner possessive pronouns and pure or absolute possessive pronouns
It is useful to distinguish between noun-determiner possessive pronouns and pure or absolute possessive pronouns because there are spelling and thus form differences (except for *his* and *whose*) between the two as well as differences between how the members of each case function. Incidentally, noun-determiners are (small) words that precede and mark the presence of nouns.

Noun-determiner possessive pronouns indicate possession with the assistance of nouns that follow them, whereas absolute possessive pronouns indicate possession alone or separate from nouns.

This is *my* shelter.	This shelter is *mine.*
This is *your* shelter.	This shelter is *yours.*
This is *his* shelter.	This shelter is *his.*
This is *her* shelter.	This shelter is *hers.*
This is *its* shelter.	This shelter is *its.*
This is *our* shelter.	This shelter is *ours.*
This is *your* shelter.	This shelter is *yours.*
This is *their* shelter.	This shelter is *theirs.*
This is *whose* shelter?	This shelter is *whose?*

Noun-determiner possessive pronouns (but not absolute possessive pronouns) also appear before gerunds—i.e., *-ing* verb forms functioning as nouns—for the purpose of placing emphasis on the action named by the gerund rather than upon the performer of the action.

1. Alas, *my* going to Texas in August was a meteorological mistake.
2. Surprisingly, *their* running away from home turned out to be a good move.
3. Really, there is no point in *your* going any farther.
4. Uncle Norman cannot be equaled in *his* shoeing of horses.
5. Alice said that *her* winning the scholarship was a complete surprise.
6. Did you know that *our* lighting the lamps prevented an accident?
7. We still do not know *whose* signaling it was that prevented the ships from running onto the rocks.

This usage of a noun-determiner possessive pronoun preceding a gerund should not be confused with an objective case pronoun preceding a participle or participle phrase that modifies the pronoun. In the following examples, you will notice that in this construction the emphasis is on the person rather than the action, just the opposite of the emphasis with the noun-determiner possessive pronoun and gerund construction.

1. Last Wednesday we met *him* coming out of his stockbroker's office.
2. My little friends in the neighborhood always watched *me* fixing my cars.
3. The rumor was that everyone saw *them* talking to the accused on the day after the robbery.

4. From the adjoining booth we heard *them* eating peanuts and laughing like crazy people.

5. The doctor felt *him* slipping into unconsciousness.

Sometimes, depending upon the point of emphasis, the same sentence can be written both ways.

The aging impresario said that he remembered *my* singing.
The aging impresario said that he remembered *me* singing.

In the first example, what the impresario most remembers is the *singing,* which (grammatically) is a gerund preceded by the noun-determiner possessive pronoun *my.* In the second example, what the impresario most remembers is *me,* which (grammatically) is an objective case pronoun functioning as the direct object of *remembered* and being modified by the participle *singing.*

Reflexive pronouns   Although both reflexive and intensive pronouns are formed by adding *-self* (for the singular) and *-selves* (for the plural) to other case forms, they do not function in the same ways. Reflexive pronouns refer directly back to the subject of the sentence or clause in which they occur. They usually—but not always—follow a verb, verbal, or preposition and "reflect" the action back to the subject.

1. The young woman accidentally shot *herself* in the foot. [object of a verb]

2. Most of the players behaved *themselves* quite nicely. [object of a verb]

3. That you praised *yourself* to excess did not go unnoticed. [object of a verb]

4. Alas, you cost *yourself* a second chance at the title. [indirect object of a verb]

5. Each Christmas I give *myself* a gift that I can use throughout the coming year. [indirect object of a verb]

6. When we were children, we taught *ourselves* French songs. [indirect object of a verb]

7. After crying *itself* to sleep, the infant did not awaken until almost dawn. [object of a verbal—gerund]

8. After making *myself* a new dress, I was ready for the dance. [indirect object of a verbal—gerund]

9. Andrew has not been *himself* for several days. [subject complement]

10. The season is *itself* only if we have snow on Christmas Eve. [subject complement]

11. We found the children playing by *themselves* in the landfill. [object of a preposition]

12. My English teacher is always telling me to think for *myself.* [object of a preposition]

Intensive or emphatic pronouns   Intensive or emphatic pronouns have a limited function; they rename or modify in an explanatory manner the nouns or other pronouns that they identify or make emphatic. When the word being intensified is a direct object, an object of a preposition, or a subjective complement, the intensive pronoun usually follows it. However, when the intensive pronoun refers to the subject of a sentence or the subject of a dependent clause, it may also be placed after the verb.

1. I *myself* am responsible for the mess this company is experiencing. [intensifies the subject of the sentence]

2. I am going to take care of this problem *myself.* [intensifies the subject of the sentence]

3. If you *yourself* had this information, why didn't you go to the police? [intensifies the subject of a dependent clause]

4. We asked the workers *themselves* about the safety problems in the plant. [intensifies a direct object]

5. The annual report was presented by the president *himself.* [intensifies the object of a preposition]

6. It was the citizens *themselves* who proposed the new ordinance. [intensifies a subjective complement]

In the following exercise quiz, select the correct pronoun for each sentence and write it in the blank *within* the sentence. In the smaller blank in front of each sentence, indicate the case of the correct answer as follows: S for subjective, O for objective, ND for noun-determiner possessive, PP for pure possessive, R for reflexive, and I for intensive.

EXERCISE
Pronoun Case Error

_____ 1. The money was supposed to be divided equally between you and (*I / me*) _____.

_____ 2. (*Their / Them*) _____ leaving school without a degree was a big mistake.

_____ 3. Every year I promise (*meself / myself*) _____ that I will stop watching so much television.

_____ 4. To our delight, the airline sent Alice and (*me / I*) _____ an extra fifty dollars for our inconvenience.

_____ 5. Edmund should be congratulated for teaching (*himself / hisself*) _____ Spanish.

_____ 6. Did you and (*her / she*) _____ visit the cathedrals at Winchester and Wells?

_____ 7. Is this the person (*who / whom*) _____ is going to teach us all about foreign investments?

_____ 8. In a democracy one may vote for (*whoever / whomever*) _____ one wishes to vote for.

_____ 9. Alas, what we need most is for someone to save us from (*us / ourselves*) _____.

369

_____ 10. Wasn't (*your* / *you*) _____ spending an entire summer in Europe a bit expensive?

_____ 11. The players (*themselves* / *theirselves*) _____ are responsible for staying in condition.

_____ 12. As usual, (*him* / *he*) _____ and Eleanor took a two-hour lunch.

_____ 13. The officer gave them, Felix and (*she* / *her*) _____, the benefit of the doubt.

_____ 14. Once again, the roof of (*my* / *mine*) _____ house is leaking.

_____ 15. We were instructed to give the money to (*whoever* / *whomever*) _____ _____ asked for it.

_____ 16. The school nurse told Ralph and (*I* / *me*) _____ that we should eat more vegetables.

_____ 17. Did no one see (*him* / *his*) _____ sneaking into the bank building?

_____ 18. I splurged and bought (*me* / *myself*) _____ a fifty-dollar tie for the wedding.

_____ 19. Rachel has always been more artistic than (*him* / *he*) _____, but not more discreet.

_____ 20. We were told that (*our* / *us*) _____ reporting the break-in was a great help to the police.

_____ 21. I do not dance as well with Jonathan as I do with (*he* / *him*) _____ .

_____ 22. Was it (*they* / *them*) _____ who rebuilt the old car?

_____ 23. For (*them* / *they*) _____ to run away and get married was more than anyone could believe.

_____ 24. Are these beautiful flowers from our garden or (*your* / *yours*) _____?

_____ 25. We, you and (*I* / *me*) _____, are probably going to have to face the enemy alone.

To complete the following five Sentence Problems Review Exercises, identify the error that occurs in each of the twenty sentences by placing the appropriate letter in the blanks in front of the sentences.

REVIEW EXERCISE
Sentence Problems (1)

A. Sentence Fragment   D. Subject-Verb Agreement Error
B. Fused Sentence   E. Pronoun Case Error
C. Comma Splice

_____ 1. I think that Inez is in love with me mother told me so.

_____ 2. Unfortunately, neither Joan nor Edwin were prepared for the examination.

_____ 3. I don't like fruit-flavored yogurt, does anyone?

_____ 4. Swimming is excellent exercise. For anyone who enjoys a good workout.

_____ 5. On Sunday afternoons, my friends and myself used to fly our model planes at the local airport.

_____ 6. Alas, we will never win this tournament is out of our class.

_____ 7. Only one of the papers were lost, the rest were saved.

_____ 8. A high-tech system with which the company is quite pleased.

_____ 9. We have heard enough pep talks, now we need some action.

_____ 10. According to this document, no one has asked she to judge the show.

_____ 11. The lights were far too bright to focus the cameras was impossible.

_____ 12. At least three, and maybe four, members of the staff was included in the disagreement with the manager.

_____ 13. Beryl won't let us down, she does her best work under pressure.

_____ 14. Margaret, not Alison, is still slimmer than me, but plumper than him.

_____ 15. With the game having just gotten underway and the stands about half filled.

_____ 16. John's brother, not his cousins, intend to spend the summer in Greenland.

_____ 17. The entire squad attended the meeting afterwards everyone went to the opening game of the tournament.

_____ 18. You enrolling during the summer session rather than during the fall was a smart move.

_____ 19. Hundreds turned out at the airport, everyone wanted to wish the team well.

_____ 20. In the unlikely event that no one shows up for the execution.

REVIEW EXERCISE
Sentence Problems (2)

A. Sentence Fragment   D. Subject-Verb Agreement Error
B. Fused Sentence   E. Pronoun Case Error
C. Comma Splice

_____ 1. We spent a month on poetry before Christmas we wrote some verses of our own.

_____ 2. If you or me cheated on a test, the instructor would be very angry.

_____ 3. Everyone agree that we should look for a new sponsor, perhaps one with deeper pockets.

_____ 4. The sum and substance of your position have still not changed.

_____ 5. After the basic research has been completed; we shall seek financing.

_____ 6. Him and me always got along, even when we disagreed about things.

_____ 7. College is a pain in my English class, we are expected to be able to read and write— and enjoy both.

_____ 8. This type of violence, now almost epidemic, is senseless, we must put a stop to it.

_____ 9. There was a time—not so long ago—when young people wanted to learn, they wanted to be taught by demanding instructors.

_____ 10. A good story well told, holding the children on the edge of their seats.

_____ 11. Except for two or three, the players behaved theirselves quite nicely.

_____ 12. We walked into the room with a loud bang, a shipping crate fell from the loft, crashing upon the hardwood floor.

_____ 13. Each man, woman, and child were carefully examined for injuries.

_____ 14. Listening carefully and trying to remember every word that was said.

_____ 15. Most of our days and nights was spent disarming land mines.

_____ 16. Indeed, love may be the answer, however we don't really know what the question is.

_____ 17. Who were the officers asking for, Neddy or Jake?

_____ 18. Most of these items are too expensive. Too expensive for our customers, at any rate.

_____ 19. Not surprisingly, Douglas was the hero of the afternoon, he ate two dozen hotdogs.

_____ 20. Once again, Scott came in last night racing is very difficult for him.

REVIEW EXERCISE
Sentence Problems (3)

A. Sentence Fragment
B. Fused Sentence
C. Comma Splice

D. Subject-Verb Agreement Error
E. Pronoun Case Error

_____ 1. None of the required items were on the shelf, not one.

_____ 2. Isabel went to flight school. Hoping to become an airline pilot.

_____ 3. Everyone in the class, as well as the parents, enjoyed you singing last evening.

_____ 4. Liz reads very rapidly, she can finish a novel in a single evening.

_____ 5. The instructor said that such errors are not uncommon here are some obvious examples.

_____ 6. By now, you should know—indeed, everyone should know—that there are no accounting for differing tastes.

_____ 7. We have already paid this bill must belong to someone else.

_____ 8. The time has come for some serious thinking, otherwise we are likely to make a big mistake.

_____ 9. I'm certain it was her who told us where to buy the tickets.

_____ 10. When we were in Chicago, we stayed at the Radisson. Not the Hilton.

_____ 11. There was too much salt in the beans now my mouth is dry.

_____ 12. Neither mathematics nor physics are required for this curriculum.

_____ 13. Winning seven matches in a row without losing a single set.

_____ 14. Students completing this program are very employable, for example, my roommate was hired the day after graduation.

_____ 15. The judge smiled grimly and said, "You may as well enjoy your dinner at daylight you die."

_____ 16. Whom, in your opinion, will be the next president of the faculty union?

_____ 17. These items were given to she and I by our great aunt, who lives in Malibu.

_____ 18. Finally attracting enough attention to get his picture in the national magazines.

_____ 19. We know what you did, moreover we have contacted the police.

_____ 20. The instructor, not to mention most of the students, were prepared to ask the dean some tough questions.

REVIEW EXERCISE
Sentence Problems (4)

A. Sentence Fragment   D. Subject-Verb Agreement Error
B. Fused Sentence   E. Pronoun Case Error
C. Comma Splice

_____ 1. Professor Waffle's new novel is thoroughly shocking everyone on campus is reading it.

_____ 2. Some people must always get their own way, no matter who they offend.

_____ 3. "Spring is a beautiful time of year," the visiting poet said, "it often brings out the romantic in each of us."

_____ 4. No one on the team, not even the seniors, can run faster than me.

_____ 5. Winston, still full of vigor and enthusiasm after more than two hours on the track.

_____ 6. Writing books and essays are no easy way to earn one's bread and water.

_____ 7. We cruised around town for a while then we went to the bar for a little refreshment.

_____ 8. Neither the fox nor the hounds has the energy for a hunt today.

_____ 9. Only because we were unable to afford advertising and the economy was flat.

_____ 10. You can't expect to win every tournament, situations vary from week to week.

_____ 11. Bob, Bryan, and Bruno all three broke the old record, however none of them won the race.

_____ 12. I asked for a cup of coffee. Not a lecture about the dangers of caffeine.

_____ 13. Does anyone know where Lucy and him were intending to go?

_____ 14. You must go directly to the dean's office at three o'clock you are expected there.

_____ 15. At least two-thirds of the land were acidic, not to mention submerged.

_____ 16. Bertram, for example, who had never been across the state line.

_____ 17. When we were children, little attention was given to my sister Jan and I.

_____ 18. The performance was first-rate, or even better, indeed some thought it was the best of the season.

_____ 19. I ran across this article in the city papers shouldn't print such unsubstantiated rumors.

_____ 20. Hiram, much like his older brothers, is one of these people who seems to care nothing for others.

REVIEW EXERCISE
Sentence Problems (5)

A. Sentence Fragment   D. Subject-Verb Agreement Error
B. Fused Sentence   E. Pronoun Case Error
C. Comma Splice

_____ 1. Don't eat your neighbors intend to invite you to dinner.

_____ 2. All in all, seventy-five years are not a lot of time to discover the secrets of the universe.

_____ 3. This is the person whom I think will be the next target of a letter bomb.

_____ 4. Early spring and early autumn can be risky times to visit Western Michigan, tornadoes are not uncommon.

_____ 5. We're asking a few friends, including yourselves, to spend the weekend with us.

_____ 6. With nothing to do and even less to look forward to. The youths were not very optimistic.

_____ 7. The desire to foretell the future is one of the things that sets humans apart from the animals.

_____ 8. Please say something nice just once I would like to hear a pleasantry.

_____ 9. As you might expect, the concert was too expensive for Ann and I to attend.

_____ 10. As was often the situation on Saturday mornings, the pool was overcrowded, consequently we decided to play tennis.

_____ 11. On the first leg of the race; almost half the runners dropped out.

_____ 12. As far as I know, the whereabouts of the hijackers are a mystery.

_____ 13. "Frank did study," the instructor admitted, "he earned only a _C_ grade, however."

_____ 14. Toward dawn, when the first glimmer of light was just visible on the horizon.

_____ 15. Please give me another chance, I promise to do better in the future.

_____ 16. Not just anyone can buy you have to be a member of the club.

_____ 17. To make millions have always been Goddard's first goal in life.

_____ 18. The day finally being over and everyone being weary of work.

_____ 19. Because Conrad's father did not approve of us smoking in the house, we went outside.

_____ 20. Alas, we have lost our way to the top has been blocked.

Chapter 9
Commonly Occurring Sentence Problems Continued

Pronoun-Antecedent Error

Pronouns should agree in number with their antecedents; that is, a singular pronoun should refer to a singular antecedent, and a plural pronoun should refer to a plural antecedent. Furthermore, a pronoun should refer clearly and unmistakably to only one antecedent. When either of these conventional prescriptions is ignored, a pronoun-antecedent error is the result. Thus, a pronoun-antecedent error occurs when there is *any* confusion between the pronoun and the word to which the pronoun refers. The following suggestions are intended to help you avoid the pronoun-antecedent error.

Indefinite pronouns as antecedents (I)   When the indefinite pronouns *another, anybody, anyone, anything, each, each one, either, either one, everybody, everyone, everything, neither, neither one, no one, nobody, nothing, person, somebody, someone,* and *something* are used as antecedents, conventional usage considers them singular; thus, the pronouns that refer to them should not be plural.

1. *Everyone* was asked to keep records of *his / her / his or her* [but not *their*] own travel expenses.
2. *Anyone* who has finished *his / her / his or her* [but not *their*] project should turn it in.
3. We knew that *neither* of the women was likely to change *her* [not *their*] position on the matter.

4. If *anybody* needs a ride to the conference center, *he / she / he or she* [but not *they*] should tell the coordinator.

5. It takes a bit of character for a *person* to admit that *he / she / he or she* [but not *they*] made a mistake.

6. *Each* of the runners took *his / her / his or her* [but not *their*] turn on the treadmill.

7. The medium insisted that *someone* in the house would lose *his / her / his or her* [but not *their*] life before morning.

8. *Each one* of the pictures was hung in *its* [not *their*] proper place.

9. *Nothing* was found where *it* had been left.

10. *Something* as valuable as a diamond necklace should have *its* own private hiding place.

Indefinite pronouns as antecedents (II)   To avoid the charge of sexism in your writing, try not to use either a generic masculine or a generic feminine pronoun to refer to an antecedent that is likely (in a given context) to include both women and men. Such usage can easily occur when indefinite pronouns are used as antecedents. It can also occur with many noun antecedents that may refer (in a specific context) just as easily to one sex as to the other. In either instance, the indiscretion can be corrected (1) by including both the masculine and feminine singular pronouns, (2) by pluralizing both the antecedent and the pronoun, (3) by eliminating the pronoun altogether, or (4) by completely recasting the sentence to say what you want to say. Because the first possible correction can produce very awkward sentences (e.g., *Anyone who thinks he or she knows the solution to the riddle should send his or her answer to the station as soon as he or she can*), the last three corrections are often used to avoid the first one.

1. *Everybody* in the class had *his* own ideas about what should be done.
   C1. *Everybody* in the class had *his or her* own ideas about what should be done.
   C2. *All* of the members of the class had *their* own ideas about what should be done.
   C3. *Everybody* in the class had different ideas about what should be done.
   C4. Nobody in the class could agree about what should be done.

2. *Each* of the candidates in turn presented *his* platform to the audience.
   C1. *Each* of the candidates in turn presented *his or her* platform to the audience.
   C2. *All* of the candidates in turn presented *their* platforms to the audience.
   C3. *Each* of the candidates in turn presented a platform to the audience.
   C4. The audience listened as the *candidates* took turns presenting *their* platforms.

3. *No one* wants to admit that *he* has been duped by a shyster.
   C1. *No one* wants to admit that *he or she* has been duped by a shyster.
   C2. *People* do not want to admit that *they* have been duped by a shyster.
   C3. *No one* wants to admit being duped by a shyster.
   C4. Being duped by a shyster isn't something anyone wants to admit.

4. As everyone knows, a college professor is not *someone* accustomed to having *her* authority questioned.
   C1. As everyone knows, a college professor is not *someone* accustomed to having *her or his* authority questioned.

378

C2. As everyone knows, college professors are not *people* accustomed to having *their* authority questioned.

C3. As everyone knows, a college *professor* is not accustomed to being questioned in matters of academic authority.

C4. As everyone knows, college *professors* are not accustomed to having *their* authority questioned.

5. One of the characteristics of a successful high school *coach* is that *he* makes *himself* into a necessary fixture in the local community.

C1. One of the characteristics of a successful high school *coach* is that *he or she* makes *himself or herself* into a necessary fixture in the local community.

C2. One of the characteristics of successful high school *coaches* is that *they* make *themselves* into necessary fixtures in the local community.

C3. One of the characteristics of a successful high school *coach* is the ability to become a necessary fixture in the local community.

C4. The ability to become a necessary fixture in the local community is one of the characteristics of a successful high school coach.

Indefinite pronouns as antecedents (III)   When the indefinite pronouns *both, few, many, others,* and *several* are used as antecedents, a plural pronoun should be used to refer to them. However, the indefinite pronouns *all, any, more, most,* and *some* and other words that indicate a quantity, part, percentage, or fraction of something (e.g., *half, two-thirds, three-quarters*) may take either a singular or a plural pronoun when they are used as an antecedent. The determination of whether the pronoun is singular or plural depends upon the number of the object of the prepositional phrase that follows the antecedent.

1. *Both* of the pitchers were off *their* game.
2. *Few* of the herds have returned to *their* historical migration routes.
3. *Many* of the students were frantic to learn *their* grades.
4. *Others* in the class had lost *their* notes as well.
5. Almost *all* of the wine was past *its* prime.
6. Almost *all* of the wines were past *their* prime.
7. By that time, *most* of the music had regained *its* popular appeal.
8. By that time, *most* of the songs had regained *their* popular appeal.
9. A *third* of the land had lost *its* earlier market value.
10. A *third* of the parcels had lost *their* earlier market value.

Singular antecedents in pairs (I)   When two or more singular antecedents are joined by the coordinating conjunction *and*, a plural pronoun is usually required. Two exceptions to this convention occur when the two antecedents refer to one thing or person and when the antecedents are preceded by *each* or *every*.

1. Weren't the *car and trailer* stored in *their* usual places?
2. Having gained entry into the house, *Alden and Milo* helped *themselves* to the contents of the refrigerator.
3. If anyone sees *Agnes and Greta,* please tell *them* to call the morgue.

4. The *pitcher and catcher* thought *they* had figured out how the players on the opposing team were stealing the signs.

5. Unfortunately, the *sum and substance* of the presentation lost much of *its* luster with the passage of time.

6. The *vinegar and oil* performed *its* usual magic on the salad.

7. Not surprisingly, the *secretary and treasurer* of the organization refused to budge from *her* original contention.

8. *Every car and truck* in the fleet needed *its* engine tuned up.

9. *Each supporter and opponent* of the bill explained *his or her* reasons for support or opposition.

10. *Every village and township* in the state must maintain *its* own solid waste facility.

Singular antecedents in pairs (II)   When two singular antecedents are joined by *either . . . or* or *neither . . . nor,* a singular pronoun is needed to refer to them. However, if one of the antecedents is singular and the other is plural, the pronoun should agree with the antecedent closer to it. As a matter of practice, always put the plural antecedent in the second position closer to the pronoun and make the pronoun plural.

1. *Neither Jud nor Heathcliff* has explained *his* relationship to the bank robbers.

2. Has *either Lilian or Beth* submitted *her* final paper to the department head?

3. We were told that *neither management nor the workers* wanted to have *their* proposal made public.

4. *Neither the coach nor the players* told the press how *they* really felt about the call that cost *them* the championship.

5. We must ask *either Professor Lamp or his students* what *they* think about the downsizing of the premed program.

Collective nouns as antecedents   When a collective noun is used as the antecedent of a pronoun, the pronoun should be singular if the collective noun is regarded as a unit functioning as one. However, the pronoun will be plural if the collective noun is regarded as a group of people acting separately.

1. Has the discipline *committee* submitted *its* report to the dean?

2. Once again the discipline *committee* are unable to agree on whom *they* should select to be the new chair.

3. After the race, the *crew* had *its* picture taken on deck.

4. One by one, the *crew* died in *their* tracks.

5. The *family* next door has been in *its* glory since winning the lottery.

6. The *family* were seated in *their* custom-made armchairs across the lawn.

Demonstrative pronouns as adjectives   When the demonstrative pronouns *this, that, these,* and *those* are used as adjectives, they should always agree in number with the words (nouns) they modify.

1. *This type* of problem usually crops up every fall.

2. Unfortunately, *these types* of allegations are becoming more and more common.

3. *That kind* of remark offends more people today than it did ten years ago.

4. *Those kinds* of remarks do little to help our cause.

Multiple antecedents Take care not to construct a sentence in which a pronoun has more than one possible antecedent. Each of the following examples is corrected in a second, and sometimes a third, sentence.

1. When *Nolan* talked to his *father, he* was in an angry mood.
* *Nolan* was in an angry mood when *he* talked to his father.
* Nolan's *father* was in an angry mood when Nolan talked to *him*.

2. My directions are to take the *books* off the *shelves* and dust *them.*
* My directions are to take the books off the shelves and dust the books.
* My directions are to take the books off the shelves and dust the shelves.

3. If the *children* fuss about eating their *vegetables,* slice *them* up and make a salad.
* If the children fuss about eating their vegetables, slice the vegetables up and make a salad.

4. After taking the *money* from the *safe,* Hannibal threw *it* into the river.
* After taking the money from the safe, Hannibal threw the money into the river.
* After taking the money from the safe, Hannibal threw the safe into the river.

5. When the old *women* had finished the *quilts, they* were promptly boxed and sent to stores on the East Coast.
* When the old women had finished the quilts, the quilts were promptly boxed and sent to stores on the East Coast.

Faulty referents (I) Avoid constructing sentences in which pronouns appear to refer to possessives or to nouns placed in a modifying position.

1. *Bernard's* mother is an astronaut, and *he* is very proud of her.
* Bernard is very proud of his *mother, who* is an astronaut.

2. I used to be a decent *poker* player, but I don't play *it* often these days.
* I used to be a decent poker player, but I don't play the game often these days.

3. In my *father's* private study, *he* has a large collection of impressionist paintings.
* My *father* has a large collection of impressionist paintings in *his* private study.

4. Charlotte's aunt had a slight *heart* attack, but *it* is much better now.
* Charlotte's *aunt* had a slight heart attack, but *she* is much better now.
* Charlotte's *aunt* had a slight heart attack, but *her* condition is much better now.

5. Estelle went to the *dean's* office at the appointed hour, but *he* was not there.
* Estelle went to the dean's office at the appointed hour, but the dean was not there.

Faulty referents (II) Avoid composing sentences in which the pronouns *this, that,* and *which* attempt to refer to an entire (preceding) clause or sentence rather than to a specific antecedent. Correcting such sentences often requires a substantial revision.

1. Professor Jipson lost our final examinations, *which* may have saved my grade in the class.

* Professor Jipson lost our final examinations, a *miscue that* may have saved my grade in the class. [Notice how the antecedent *miscue* is added, and the pronoun *which* is changed to *that.*]

2. We went to Canada for our vacation, *which* I enjoyed very much.
* We went to Canada for our vacation, a *trip that* I enjoyed very much.

3. Many illegal aliens are being exploited by their American employers. *This* should be dealt with by the government.

* Many illegal aliens are being exploited by their American employers. *This exploitation* should be dealt with by the government.

4. Many of the students did not really understand the laboratory experiments, and *that* made the examination difficult for them.

* Many of the students did not really understand the laboratory experiments, a *situation that* made the examination difficult for them.

5. Martin Luther King, Jr., was devoted to nonviolent methods of social change, *which* drew many people to him.

* Martin Luther King, Jr., was devoted to nonviolent methods of social change, a philosophical *position that* drew many people to him.

6. The counselor was quite abrupt with Joan, *which* hurt her feelings.
* The counselor was quite abrupt with Joan, an *occurrence that* hurt her feelings.

7. The nation's economy is in a terrible state, and *this* did not happen overnight.
* The nation's economy is in a terrible state, a *situation that* did not happen overnight.

No antecedents   Avoid constructing sentences in which pronouns have no antecedents at all.

1. During my four years at Hinterland State, *they* never painted my dormitory room even once.

* During my four years at Hinterland State, the university administration never painted my dormitory room even once.

* During my four years at Hinterland State, my dormitory room was never painted even once.

2. Even though I know *they* are harmful, I enjoy smoking now and then.
* Even though I know cigarettes are harmful, I enjoy smoking now and then.

3. Because there are not doctors in her family, *that* is what Elizabeth wants to study in college.

* Because there are not doctors in her family, medicine is what Elizabeth wants to study in college.

4. Although some people are able to retire comfortably in their fifties, for others *it* brings disappointment and hardship.

* Although some people are able to retire comfortably in their fifties, for others early retirement brings disappointment and hardship.

5. We had always wanted a spare room on the house, and last summer we did *it*.

   * We had always wanted a spare *room* on the house, and last summer we built *one*.

6. I called the local shoe store and told *them* what I thought about *their* substandard shoes.

   * I called the local shoe store and told the manager what I thought about her substandard shoes.

7. By ten o'clock Judith had become ill, and *it* grew steadily worse throughout the day.

   * By ten o'clock Judith had become ill, and she grew steadily worse throughout the day.

   * By ten o'clock Judith had become ill, and her condition grew steadily worse throughout the day.

In the following exercise quiz, edit (rewrite) each of the sentences to eliminate all pronoun-antecedent errors. Some of the sentences can be corrected by changing no more than a single word, whereas others require more substantial revision.

EXERCISE
Pronoun-Antecedent Error Editing

1. Every year on March 15, the finance committee submits their report to the membership.

   _____

   _____

2. When Alice spoke to her mother, she was in one of her giddy states.

   _____

   _____

3. By now you should know that those kind of remarks do not win friends and influence people.

   _____

   _____

4. As everybody knows, a person experiencing extreme stress may do things that are not in his own best interest.

   _____

   _____

5. After cooking the fish on a hot stone, the old trapper ate it.

   _____

   _____

6. Many of the students had not paid their tuition, and that resulted in their schedules being dropped.

_____

_____

7. The speaker charged that nowadays they allow everybody to graduate from high school.

_____

_____

8. Both of the speakers were a bit below his or her usual performance.

_____

_____

9. Had either Francine or Myrna returned to their regular place of employment?

_____

_____

10. Osgood called Geraldine's place half a dozen times before going to the party, but she never answered.

_____

_____

11. These kind of mistakes are simply inexcusable in a paper for an advanced composition class.

_____

_____

12. When we discovered that the garage had not repaired our car properly, we called them and asked what the problem was.

_____

_____

13. For the third time in as many weeks, Ruth told Doris that she should think about having her house refinanced.

_____

_____

14. Everyone in the research group recorded their thoughts in a daily journal.

_____

_____

15. Constantine had a brain hemorrhage about a month ago, but it is much improved now.

_____

_____

16. If the guests complain about the mosquitoes, kill them with the bug zapper.

_____

_____

17. Every man and woman in the community will now be asked their opinion on this matter.

_____

_____

18. We watched the crowd leaving the ballpark and scattering toward its cars.

_____

_____

19. We looked at every painting in the gallery, which took us all afternoon.

_____

_____

20. Neither the players nor the coach cared to say what they thought about the school's decision to drop varsity football.

_____

_____

21. Constance is studying journalism because that is what she wants to become.

_____

_____

22. Each of the scholarship applicants explained their reasons for wanting to go to college.

_____

_____

23. When the students had completed their papers, the instructor casually stuffed them into his briefcase.

_____

_____

24. Public education appears to be in a declining state, and this did not happen overnight.

_____

_____

25. As everyone who hasn't been living in a cave knows, they are not wearing animal fur this year.

_____

_____

Misplaced Modifier

The error of the misplaced modifier occurs when any type of modifying construction—an adjective, an adverb, a phrase, or a dependent clause—is inappropriately positioned in a sentence. Most of the time misplaced modifiers can be corrected by simply shifting them to a more sensible location, which is generally (but not always) next to the word they modify.

Misplaced Adjectives

1. Nicole asked Libby for a *hot* cup of cocoa.
* Nicole asked Libby for a cup of *hot* cocoa.

2. A *red* man's bathrobe was found at the scene of the crime.
* A man's *red* bathrobe was found at the scene of the crime.

3. Every morning, without fail, we ate a *cold* dish of cereal for breakfast.
* Every morning, without fail, we ate a dish of *cold* cereal for breakfast.

4. Vanessa purchased a *platinum* woman's watch at a local pawnshop.
* Vanessa purchased a woman's *platinum* watch at a local pawnshop.

5. Bradley, always a lucky fellow, won a *suede* student's backpack at the drawing.
* Bradley, always a lucky fellow, won a student's *suede* backpack at the drawing.

Misplaced Adverbs

1. Even when he is in training, Aubrey *only* runs seven miles each day.
* Even when he is in training, Aubrey runs *only* seven miles each day.

2. Last summer Rhea *only* waterskied three times.

* Last summer Rhea waterskied *only* three times.

3. After four games our team hadn't *even* scored one touchdown.

* After four games our team hadn't scored *even* one touchdown.

4. The hurricane victims in southern Florida needed medical volunteers to bandage their wounds *badly*.

* The hurricane victims in southern Florida *badly* needed medical volunteers to bandage their wounds.

5. Once again, the legislature has *scarcely* provided any funds for the transportation department.

* Once again, the legislature has provided *scarcely* any funds for the transportation department.

6. When Harley worked all summer for the railroad as a laborer, he *almost* saved $5,000.

* When Harley worked all summer for the railroad as a laborer, he saved *almost* $5,000.

7. Jules isn't *even* convincing when he tells the truth.

* Jules isn't convincing *even* when he tells the truth.

8. Last winter was quite mild; we *just* had one blizzard.

* Last winter was quite mild; we had *just* one blizzard.

9. Most of the students misunderstood what the instructor was trying to explain *completely*.

* Most of the students *completely* misunderstood what the instructor was trying to explain.

10. On the very top of the tree, Rosemary placed the red star *carefully*.

* On the very top of the tree, Rosemary *carefully* placed the red star.

Misplaced Phrases

1. When Morris was there, Carnarvon Castle was closed for repairs *to tourists*.

* When Morris was there, Carnarvon Castle was closed *to tourists* for repairs.

2. Fortunately, the blaze was brought under control before much damage had been done *by the volunteer fire brigade*.

* Fortunately, the blaze was brought under control *by the volunteer fire brigade* before much damage had been done.

3. There had once been a fence behind the old house *made of barbed wire*.

* There had once been a fence *made of barbed wire* behind the old house.

4. My youngest nephew dropped out of college after a year of struggling *between semesters*.

* My youngest nephew dropped out of college *between semesters* after a year of struggling.

5. We had a great time trimming a Christmas tree *with the family.*
   * We had a great time *with the family,* trimming a Christmas tree.

6. Neddy was revived after nearly being drowned *by his homeroom teacher.*
   * Neddy was revived *by his homeroom teacher* after nearly being drowned.

7. The authors allege that the coup d'état was caused by corruption *in the third chapter.*
   * The authors allege *in the third chapter* that the coup d'état was caused by corruption.
   * *In the third chapter,* the authors allege that the coup d'état was caused by corruption.

8. We discovered a great flock of gulls *looking out of our porthole on Friday morning.*
   * *Looking out of our porthole on Friday morning,* we discovered a great flock of gulls.

9. Nora and Alice liked to whistle to the dogs *on their way to school.*
   * *On their way to school,* Nora and Alice liked to whistle to the dogs.

10. *Buried in the back yard,* Fido couldn't find the bone.
    * Fido couldn't find the bone *buried in the back yard.*

Misplaced Dependent Clauses

1. We put the presents under the Christmas tree *that we had wrapped the night before.*
   * We put the presents *that we had wrapped the night before* under the Christmas tree.

2. I realized that I had left my wallet at home *after I reached the station.*
   * I realized *after I reached the station* that I had left my wallet at home.
   * *After I reached the station,* I realized that I had left my wallet at home.

3. The members of the task force knew that such a dramatic proposal would probably be rejected in an equally dramatic fashion *before they suggested it.*
   * The members of the task force knew *before they suggested it* that such a dramatic proposal would probably be rejected in an equally dramatic fashion.

4. The doctors recommended another test to determine whether or not the patient had multiple sclerosis, *which they said was painless.*
   * The doctors recommended another test, *which they said was painless,* to determine whether or not the patient had multiple sclerosis.

5. The student union was located next to the Timber River, *which was made of Michigan fieldstone.*
   * The student union, *which was made of Michigan fieldstone,* was located next to the Timber River.

6. One of the doves on the bird feeder had a cord around its neck *that was tightly twisted.*
   * One of the doves on the bird feeder had a cord *that was tightly twisted* around its neck.

388

7. We leased a condo in Malibu with a large courtyard and a double garage *that was nicely furnished.*

* We leased a *nicely furnished* condo in Malibu with a large courtyard and a double garage.

Three additional inappropriate usages also come under the general heading of misplaced modifiers. They are (1) the squinting modifier, (2) the split infinitive, and (3) the intrusive modifier.

Squinting Modifiers A squinting modifier is a type of misplaced modifier so positioned in a sentence that it may modify either what precedes it or what follows it; and because of this ambiguity, the squinting modifier sometimes seems to modify two things—in two directions—at once. You can usually correct the squinting modifier by moving it to a position that clarifies any ambiguity in the sentence.

1. My wife told me *on the way home* to stop at the supermarket.
* *On the way home,* my wife told me to stop at the supermarket.
* My wife told me to stop at the supermarket *on the way home.*

2. The woman who was watching Baxter *steadily* sipped a drink.
* The woman who was *steadily* watching Baxter sipped a drink.
* The woman who was watching Baxter sipped a drink *steadily.*

3. I promised Doreen *when the dust had settled* I would tell her everything she wanted to know.
* *When the dust had settled,* I promised Doreen I would tell her everything she wanted to know.
* I promised Doreen I would tell her everything she wanted to know *when the dust had settled.*
* I promised Doreen *that when the dust had settled* I would tell her everything she wanted to know.

4. We knew *in a matter of minutes* the championship was going to be ours.
* *In a matter of minutes,* we knew the championship was going to be ours.
* We knew the championship was going to be ours *in a matter of minutes.*
* We knew *that in a matter of minutes* the championship was going to be ours.
* We knew *in a matter of minutes that* the championship was going to be ours.

5. People who get high *often* make fools of themselves.
* *Often,* people who get high make fools of themselves.
* People who *often* get high make fools of themselves.
* People who get high make fools of themselves *often.*

6. The team that Meggan is with *now* practices on Monday and Thursday nights.
* The team that Meggan is *now* with practices on Monday and Thursday nights.
* The team that Meggan is with practices on Monday and Thursday nights *now.*

7. The members of the band were cautioned *routinely* to take care of their instruments.
* The members of the band were *routinely* cautioned to take care of their instruments.
* The members of the band were cautioned to take care of their instruments *routinely.*

8. They decided *that afternoon* to contact their old high school tennis coach.
* *That afternoon* they decided to contact their old high school tennis coach.
* They decided to contact their old high school tennis coach *that afternoon.*

Split Infinitives   An infinitive is the base form of the verb (e.g., *write, swim, join, submit, dissolve*) preceded by the marker word *to.* In sentences, infinitives may function as adjectives, adverbs, or nouns. The general convention is that the [*to* + base verb form] should not be interrupted by modifying words or constructions. Such words or constructions are said to "split" the infinitive, and they are thus the misplaced modifier in this situation. In fact, however, there is nothing ungrammatical about splitting an infinitive, and we here consider a split infinitive productive of a misplaced modifier only when the resulting sentence is awkward and can be improved—i.e., made more accurate—by moving the modifier to a more appropriate location.

1. Here at Hinterland State, we try not to *unnecessarily* tax our students.
* Here at Hinterland State, we try not to tax our students *unnecessarily.*

2. You should make an effort to, *if you can manage it,* take eighteen hours this semester.
* *If you can manage it,* you should make an effort to take eighteen hours this semester.
* You should make an effort to take eighteen hours this semester, *if you can manage it.*

3. The Townsends have agreed to *once and for all* dissolve their marriage.
* The Townsends have agreed *once and for all* to dissolve their marriage.
* *Once and for all,* the Townsends have agreed to dissolve their marriage.
* The Townsends have agreed to dissolve their marriage *once and for all.*

4. The winner of last year's race said that he expected to *just about* equal his previous best time. [This sentence is correct; the modifying construction that "splits" the infinitive cannot be moved.]

5. This seminar is designed to *better* prepare high school graduates to succeed in college. [This sentence is also correct; the modifier that "splits" the infinitive cannot be moved.]

6. We would like to *sometime in the spring* go to Chicago.
* *Sometime in the spring* we would like to go to Chicago.
* We would like to go to Chicago *sometime in the spring.*

Intrusive Modifiers   Intrusive modifiers occur when awkward and unnecessary interruptions are used in sentences, as between the subject and the verb, between the verb and its object or its complement, or between any of the words in a verb phrase.

1. Air pollution, *all but a few people seem to realize,* can sometimes be a product of nature itself.
* *All but a few people seem to realize* that air pollution can be a product of nature itself.

2. My errant cousin, *as soon as he had borrowed enough money from his indulgent friends,* gathered up his things and left town for the great unknown.

   * *As soon as he had borrowed enough money from his indulgent friends,* my errant cousin gathered up his things and left town for the great unknown.

3. In a tiny log cabin near Charleston, Edmund, *who was my neighbor for many years,* was born.

   * Edmund, *my neighbor for many years,* was born in a tiny log cabin near Charleston.

4. We found, *after an all-day search,* the money hidden in a coffee can.

   * *After an all-day search,* we found the money hidden in a coffee can.

5. Andrew wrote, *without giving the matter careful thought,* his letter of resignation.

   * *Without giving the matter careful thought,* Andrew wrote his letter of resignation.

6. The report concluded that the man was *by any moral standard* a villain.

   * The report concluded that *by any moral standard* the man was a villain.

7. Your committee appeared *to my way of thinking* silly and self-serving.

   * *To my way of thinking,* your committee appeared silly and self-serving.

8. Bertram forgot that we had *many years earlier* met the man.

   * Bertram forgot that we had met the man *many years earlier.*

9. I am, *despite your noisy objections,* going to apply for the position.

   * *Despite your noisy objections,* I am going to apply for the position.

10. You cannot hope *without careful planning* to win this competition.

    * *Without careful planning,* you cannot hope to win this competition.

    * You cannot hope to win this competition *without careful planning.*

In the following exercise quiz, edit (rewrite) each of the sentences to correct all misplaced modifiers. Some of the sentences can be corrected by moving no more than a single word, whereas others require a more substantial revision.

EXERCISE
Misplaced Modifier Editing

1. Bob and Marian chatted with each other while I read my assignment in whispers.

   _____

   _____

2. Although he didn't intend to, Marvin bought a black man's hunting jacket.

   _____

   _____

3. We shall, despite your efforts to squeeze us out of the market, continue to produce hummingbird feeders.

   _____

   _____

4. To almost everyone's delight, Professor English said on Friday we would take the day off.

   _____

   _____

5. Cyril remembered that he had left his laptop computer at home when he sat down at the board meeting.

   _____

   _____

6. In this family we only eat fish and chips on Fridays.

   _____

   _____

7. The university intends to within four or five years begin a doctoral program in genetic engineering.

   _____

   _____

8. Crispin bought his wife a cheap woman's negligee for her birthday.

   _____

   _____

9. The soccer field was located next to the hydroelectric dam, which was fertilized every spring.

   _____

   _____

10. I want to, so I can have a quiet place to study, go home on weekends.

   _____

   _____

11. For the good of all, students should not be allowed to enter a college without sufficient academic preparation.

_____

_____

12. We found, not more than twenty minutes after the police had gone, the money stolen from the local savings and loan.

_____

_____

13. My best advice is that you not buy a used car from a local dealer with high mileage.

_____

_____

14. The lad was wearing a cap on his head that came to a sharp point.

_____

_____

15. Thousands of voters misunderstood the differences between the two candidates completely.

_____

_____

16. Acme, Inc., has decided to once and for all terminate its partnerships with foreign suppliers.

_____

_____

17. The novel that Karen was reading slowly put her to sleep.

_____

_____

18. Summer is almost over, and we've just had three days with temperatures above ninety degrees.

_____

_____

19. Gretchen had planned without anyone's help to move the furniture into her apartment.

_____

_____

20. By running an ad in the classified, we were able to locate the lost child's pet.

_____

_____

21. On Mackinac Island we rented horses for tourists with adjustable saddles.

_____

_____

22. The company that Faustina is with now exports rice to China.

_____

_____

23. The psychedelic Volvo's paint job drew a large crowd of admiring spectators.

_____

_____

24. What these people need is for someone to explain the situation to them desperately.

_____

_____

25. Poor Clarence knew that his proposal of marriage would be rejected before he made it.

_____

_____

Dangling Modifier

A dangling modifier is a modifier appearing in a sentence so constructed that the modifier has nothing to modify. Thus, simply moving the modifier—which is usually sufficient to correct a misplaced modifier—will not repair the problem. Dangling modifiers are of two principal varieties: dangling verbal phrases or dangling elliptical clauses. Dangling verbal phrases may be (1) participle phrases, (2) prepositional-gerund phrases, or (3) infinitive phrases. Dangling modifiers are usually corrected in one of two ways: by leaving the modifier as it is and rewriting the rest of the sentence to include the term that the modifier actually modifies, or by expanding the dangling part of the sentence into a complete subordinate clause with a subject and verb. Sometimes, either method works equally well; other times, however, only one method will produce a clear sentence.

Dangling Participle Phrases   A participle is a word that can function both as a verb and as an adjective. In its *present* form the participle always ends in *-ing* (e.g., *driving, eating, speaking*). In its *past* form the participle ends in a variety of ways (e.g., *asked, beaten, begun, rung, sat*). In its *perfect* form the participle consists of *having* or *having been* followed by the past participle form (e.g., *having sold, having been fed*). A participle phrase consists of the participle and the words that complete it (e.g., *walking down the street, having been eaten by a bear*). The following examples include both the dangling participle phrase and the dangling participle phrase corrected.

1. *Running across the meadow,* my cap flew off.
  * As I was running across the meadow, my cap flew off.
  * Running across the meadow, I felt my cap fly off.

2. *Exhausted from so much exercise,* the lemonade was refreshing.
  * Because we were exhausted from so much exercise, the lemonade was refreshing.
  * Exhausted from so much exercise, we found the lemonade refreshing.

3. Many of the renovated Victorian houses can be seen *looking from the top of the carillon tower.*
  * Looking from the top of the carillon tower, one can see many of the renovated Victorian houses.
  * As one looks from the top of the carillon tower, many of the renovated Victorian houses can be seen.

4. *Having worked all summer on the railroad,* Bertram's stomach muscles were as hard as rocks.
  * Having worked all summer on the railroad, Bertram had stomach muscles as hard as rocks.
  * Because he had worked all summer on the railroad, Bertram had stomach muscles as hard as rocks.

5. *Lost in the wilderness,* no familiar landmarks presented themselves.
  * Lost in the wilderness, we were unable to find any familiar landmarks.
  * Because we were lost in the wilderness, no familiar landmarks presented themselves.

6. Registration seemed endless, *waiting in line at each check station.*
  * Because we had to wait in line at each check station, registration seemed endless.
  * Registration seemed endless because we had to wait in line at each check station.

7. *Driving up the west coast of the Dingle Peninsula,* the weather was terrible.
  * Driving up the west coast of the Dingle Peninsula, we experienced terrible weather.
  * As we were driving up the west coast of the Dingle Peninsula, the weather was terrible.

8. *Having been reared in a mountain village,* heavy traffic was quite unnerving.

   * Having been reared in a mountain village, I found heavy traffic quite unnerving.

   * Because I was reared in a mountain village, I found heavy traffic quite unnerving.

9. *Gazing out of the train window,* the forest could not be seen for the trees.

   * Gazing out of the train window, I could not see the forest for the trees.

   * As I was gazing out of the train window, I could not see the forest for the trees.

10. *Wanting to know more about English literature,* Hinterland State College seemed the place for her to go.

    * Wanting to know more about English literature, she thought Hinterland State College was the place to go.

    * Because she wanted to know more about English literature, she decided to go to Hinterland State College.

Dangling Prepositional-Gerund Phrases   A gerund is a verbal noun, or the *-ing* form of a verb used as a noun. Because a gerund is used as a noun, it may be used as the object of a preposition. When a gerund is used as the object of a preposition in a prepositional phrase appearing in a sentence so constructed that the phrase has nothing to modify, the result is a dangling prepositional-gerund phrase. The following examples also include revisions.

1. *After releasing the suspects,* new evidence was discovered.
   * After the suspects had been released, new evidence was discovered.
   * New evidence was discovered after the suspects had been released.

2. The hands should be carefully washed *before eating a meal.*
   * You should wash your hands carefully before eating a meal.
   * Before eating a meal, you should wash your hands carefully.

3. *By telling the truth,* other people will judge you to be more trustworthy.
   * By telling the truth, you will be judged more trustworthy by other people.
   * If you tell the truth, other people will judge you to be more trustworthy.
   * Other people will judge you to be more trustworthy if you tell the truth.

4. The mercury in the thermometer must be shaken down *before taking a patient's temperature.*
   * You must shake the mercury in the thermometer down before taking a patient's temperature.
   * Before taking a patient's temperature, you must shake the mercury in the thermometer down.

5. *After working for twelve long hours,* a hot meal feels good.
   * After one has worked for twelve long hours, a hot meal feels good.
   * A hot meal feels good after one has worked for twelve long hours.
   * I have discovered that after one has worked for twelve long hours a hot meal feels good.

Dangling Infinitive Phrases   An infinitive phrase consists of the infinitive (i.e., the marker word *to,* followed by the base form of the verb) and any modifiers, objects, or complements of the infinitive. An infinitive phrase dangles when there is nothing in the sentence for it to modify. Observe the following examples, which are followed by revised sentences that make the needed corrections.

1. *To be comfortable,* these insects must be disposed of.
   * For the guests to be comfortable, these insects must be disposed of.
   * These insects must be disposed of if you want the guests to be comfortable.

2. *To walk the mean streets of many American cities at night,* a certain amount of foolhardiness is required.
   * For a person to walk the mean streets of many American cities at night, a certain amount of foolhardiness is required.
   * A certain amount of foolhardiness is required for a person to walk the mean streets of many American cities at night.

3. Less food should be eaten at each meal *to lose weight.*
   * To lose weight, one should eat less food at each meal.
   * Less food should be eaten at each meal for one to lose weight.
   * If one wishes to lose weight, less food should be eaten at each meal.

4. *To enjoy a poem of this complexity,* it must be read several times.
   * To enjoy a poem of this complexity, you must read it several times.
   * One must read a poem of this complexity several times to enjoy it.

5. Your grade-point average must be above 3.25 *to apply for this scholarship.*
   * You must have a grade-point average above 3.25 to apply for this scholarship.
   * To apply for this scholarship, you must have a grade-point average above 3.25.

Dangling Elliptical Clauses   An elliptical clause is a dependent clause in which the subject or verb (or both) is understood or implied but not actually stated. An elliptical clause dangles when its implied or understood subject is different from the stated subject of the main clause. The following examples are edited, with needed additions being placed in brackets. You will notice that dangling elliptical clauses often begin with such subordinating conjunctions as *after, although, before, if, though, when,* and *while.*

1. *When only three years old,* my mother had my younger twin sisters.
   * When [I was] only three years old, my mother had my younger twin sisters.
   * My mother had my younger twin sisters when [I was] only three years old.

2. *Although struggling in the course,* the instructor kept giving me encouragement.
   * Although [I was] struggling in the course, the instructor kept giving me encouragement.
   * The instructor kept giving me encouragement although [I was] struggling in the course.

3. *While delivering what was actually a very clever speech,* the audience kept talking.

* While [the speaker was] delivering what was actually a very clever speech, the audience kept talking.
* The audience kept talking while [the speaker was] delivering what was actually a very clever speech.

4. A marlin stole my bait *while catching a nap in the back of the boat.*
* A marlin stole my bait while [I was] catching a nap in the back of the boat.
* While [I was] catching a nap in the back of the boat, a marlin stole my bait.

5. *If sufficiently ripened,* you may like these melons.
* If [they are] sufficiently ripened, you may like these melons.
* You may like these melons if [they are] sufficiently ripened.

6. Anyone might fall on this floor *if refinished recently.*
* Anyone might fall on this floor if [it has been] refinished recently.
* If [it has been] refinished recently, anyone might fall on this floor.

7. *While playing the harmonica,* her dogs began barking.
* While [she was] playing the harmonica, her dogs began barking.
* Her dogs began barking while [she was] playing the harmonica.

8. On the coast road, you should drive more carefully *when stormy.*
* On the coast road, you should drive more carefully when [the weather is] stormy.
* When [the weather is] stormy, you should drive more carefully on the coast road.

In the following exercise quiz, edit and rewrite each of the sentences, removing all dangling modifiers. You may also identify the specific type of dangling modifier in each sentence by placing the appropriate matching letter in the blank at the beginning of the sentence.

EXERCISE
Dangling Modifier Editing

A. Dangling Participle Phrase   C. Dangling Infinitive Phrase
B. Dangling Prepositional-Gerund Phrase   D. Dangling Elliptical Clause

_____ 1. To keep abreast of current developments in the field, frequent refresher courses are necessary.

_____

_____

_____ 2. Frightened by the constant thunder and lightning, our resolve to press on gradually diminished.

_____

_____

_____ 3. When working in a dusty place, a breathing mask should be worn.

_____

_____

_____ 4. A sense of the ridiculous is necessary to compose obvious examples of sentences with dangling modifiers.

_____

_____

_____ 5. After winning three championships in as many years, the fans began to buy season tickets by the thousands.

_____

_____

_____ 6. Under no circumstances should a motor vehicle be driven if under the influence of alcohol.

_____

_____

_____ 7. By lighting the oil lamps, the room became much cozier than it had been.

_____

_____

_____ 8. Flying high above the ancient oak trees, the rides in the amusement park looked like small toys.

_____

_____

_____ 9. My joints were so stiff after sleeping sixteen hours that I could hardly walk.

_____

_____

_____ 10. When just a kitten, I found that mangy cat.

_____

_____

_____ 11. The wind currents were unseasonable flying up from Asheville this morning.

_____

_____

_____ 12. The house and outbuildings should be secured before settling in for the night.

_____

_____

_____ 13. To succeed in this position, both ability and thorough training are needed.

_____

_____

_____ 14. If sufficiently inflated with hot air, several people can ride in this balloon.

_____

_____

_____ 15. Momentarily glancing up from my desk, a hideous monster was peering through the north window.

_____

_____

_____ 16. To join this club, deep pockets are a prerequisite.

_____

_____

_____ 17. The entire room should be kept free of distractions when typing the final draft of a research paper.

_____

_____

_____ 18. By setting the oven at 425 degrees, the turkey will cook in a third less time.

_____

_____

_____ 19. Although only eighteen years old, the judge sentenced the young man to life in prison.

_____

_____

_____ 20. To enjoy a novel as subtle as this one, it must be read two or three times.

_____

_____

_____ 21. Shaken by the news of the break-in, calling the police was our first move.

_____

_____

_____ 22. While studying for my algebra exam, the police burst into my room looking for stolen computer software.

_____

_____

_____ 23. To graduate summa cum laude at this university, an overall 3.75 grade-point average is required.

_____

_____

_____ 24. Fawns are born about six and a half months after mating.

_____

_____

_____ 25. More than two dozen hot-air balloons were visible looking north across Yellow Dog Valley.

_____

_____

Faulty Parallelism

The conventions of parallelism, or parallel construction, require that similar grammatical forms be used to express similar ideas. Said another way, items of equal importance within a sentence—or, sometimes, between sentences—should be stated in like grammatical constructions. Noun should be matched with noun, verb with verb, phrase with phrase,

401

clause with clause, and so on. Failure to observe this convention results in faulty parallelism. Observe the following specific examples of sentence parallelism. The early ones present (equal) items in a series, and the later ones present paired items.

1. Just as we expected, the presentation was specific, accurate, objective, and comprehensive. [a series of four adjectives]

2. Swimming, bicycling, and jogging are Ellen's three favorite ways of staying in condition. [a series of three -ing nouns]

3. My parents were forever telling me not to waste money, not to befriend scoundrels, and not to miss church. [a series of three phrases, each including an infinitive with an object]

4. We came, we saw, and we capitulated. [a series of three brief independent clauses]

5. One by one, the children ran wildly from the derelict house, across the front lawn, and into the dark woods. [a series of three prepositional phrases]

6. A delightful employee, Sybil performs her daily tasks quickly, willingly, and accurately. [a series of three adverbs]

7. She must be tall, but not too tall; attractive, but not too attractive; and ambitious, but not too ambitious. [a series of three adjectives, each followed by a qualifying phrase]

8. By the end of the day all I wanted to do was slip out of my damp clothes, sit in front of the purring air conditioner, and sip from a large stein of Guinness. [a series of three verbs, each followed by a prepositional phrase]

9. If college students attend class regularly, take careful lecture notes, read the required text materials, and submit all assignments on time, they generally do quite well. [a series of four verb-object constructions]

10. If we go east, we will be eaten by savage cannibals; if we go west, we will be torn to pieces by wild dogs; if we go south, we will be consumed by swamp fever; and if we go north, we will be degendered by politically correct university professors. [a series of four sentences, each beginning with an if adverb clause and concluding with a prepositional phrase at the end of the main clause]

11. These people are not gourmets; they come from meat and potato stock. [paired nouns modifying the word stock]

12. Just because you don't like cakes and ale, don't expect the rest of the world to be virtuous. [paired nouns used as direct objects in a dependent clause]

13. It is a bright and beautiful morning, lads. [paired adjectives modifying the word morning]

14. The purpose of the meeting was to review our position in the market and to outline future acquisitions. [paired infinitive phrases used as subject complements]

15. Winning the local conference title and winning the state championship are hardly the same thing. [paired gerund phrases used as the compound subject of the sentence]

16. On this occasion this body is supposed to be talking about who will lead the country, not about who will win the World Series. [paired prepositional phrases, each of which has a noun clause introduced by the word who used as the object of the preposition]

17. The sum and substance of your remarks offended many who were in the theater audience and many thousands who were in the television audience. [paired subject words as well as paired direct objects, each of which is followed by a who adjective clause]

18. First the wind started to blow, and then the snow began to fall. [paired independent clauses, each concluding with an infinitive]

19. Few people seem to realize that walking a brisk five miles is better for their overall well-being than racing up the side of a mountain. [paired gerunds, each used as the direct object of a clause]

20. Would you rather be a large frog in a small pond or a small frog in a large pond? [paired phrases, each consisting of a noun modified by both an adjective and a prepositional phrase]

21. Just as there is much money to be made off the collapse of a great nation, there is much money to be lost in the rise of a new nation. [paired antithetical clauses]

22. Ask not what your country can do for you; ask what you can do for your country. [paired antithetical statements]

In the following exercise quiz, do what has been done in the two models: correct the faulty parallelism by rewriting the sentence to include a series of parallel items (three or more) or a pair of parallel items.

EXERCISE
Faulty Parallelism Editing (1)

1. As usual, Murdock's workshop was dark, gloominess was everywhere, and covered with dust.

    As usual, Murdock's workshop was dark, gloomy,

    and dust covered.

2. Elizabeth's husband helps with the work around the house by washing his own clothes and cooking.

    Elizabeth's husband helps with the work around the house

    by washing his own clothes and cooking his own meals.

3. Alas, at the age of fifty Bradford remains what he has always been, a knave and foolish.

    _____

    _____

4. For as long as I knew him, Aldous liked reading old manuscripts, attending estate sales, and to rummage through out-of-the-way antique shops.

    _____

    _____

    _____

5. Germaine's fundamental problem wasn't that she earned too little money but spending it on frivolous purchases.

_____

_____

6. Professor Graham complimented Ingrid for writing such a well-ordered paper and because she had handed it in before the final due date.

_____

_____

_____

7. We have no time to reminisce about the good old days, to cry over spilt milk, or for second-guessing ourselves.

_____

_____

8. Although it is true that Anthony is tall, dark, and looks like a movie star, upstairs he may be a few shingles short of a roof.

_____

_____

9. The mayor's address was long, tedious, and it was filled with obscure political innuendo.

_____

_____

10. Dr. Munson is a woman with a sound academic track record and who will no doubt make a fine vice president for academic affairs.

_____

_____

_____

11. The family bakery, more successful today than it was ten years ago, is located in the old county jail building and which is hidden behind a stone wall with metal spikes on the top.

_____

_____

_____

12. Cleaning the house, preparing meals, and a good bit of work on the yard occupied my whole weekend.

_____

_____

13. No matter how hard we tried, we could not remember the applicant's name, where she lived, or her previous educational and work experience.

_____

_____

_____

14. After three months in the wilderness on our own, we were in need of rest and hungry.

_____

_____

15. It goes without saying that we look forward to hearing from our new partners and to have an opportunity to exchange ideas with them.

_____

_____

_____

Faulty parallelism can also occur when correlative conjunctions (*either . . . or, neither . . . nor, both . . . and, not . . . but,* and *not only . . . but also*) are followed by unlike or unequal grammatical elements. Observe the following examples of faulty parallelism involving correlative conjunctions *and* some acceptable corrections. Remember, the general rule for correctness is that whatever type of grammatical structure follows one of the correlatives must also follow the other.

1. The lads are *either* gifted *or* they are lucky.
* *Either* the lads are gifted *or* they are lucky. [a short clause after each correlative]
* The lads are *either* gifted *or* lucky. [an adjective after each correlative]

2. Although Rosalind lived in Europe for a year or two, she *neither* speaks French *nor* German.
* Although Rosalind lived in Europe for a year or two, she speaks *neither* French *nor* German. [the name of a language after each correlative]

3. Professor Demento is *both* infamous for his unusual anecdotes *and* eccentric behavior.
* Professor Demento is infamous *both* for his unusual anecdotes *and* for his eccentric behavior. [a prepositional phrase after each correlative]

* Professor Demento is infamous for *both* his unusual anecdotes *and* his eccentric behavior. [an object of the preposition *for* and modifiers after each correlative]

4. *Don't* tell us what we might lose *but* what we might gain.
* Tell us *not* what we might lose *but* what we might gain. [a noun clause after each correlative]

5. At the annual Labor Day art fair, Godfrey *not only* bought an expensive lithographic print *but also* an original watercolor caricature.
* At the annual Labor Day art fair, Godfrey bought *not only* an expensive lithographic print *but also* an original watercolor caricature. [a direct object after each correlative]
* At the annual Labor Day art fair, Godfrey *not only* bought an expensive lithographic print, *but* he *also* bought an original watercolor caricature. [a verb and a direct object after each correlative]

Finally, a variety of faulty comparisons may also be considered examples of faulty parallelism because they are corrected by being made grammatically parallel. These include (1) incomplete comparisons, (2) ambiguous comparisons, (3) comparisons of unlike items, (4) grammatically truncated comparisons, and (5) comparisons that omit a necessary *other* or *else*. Observe the following two examples of each of these problems of faulty parallelism *and* acceptable corrections of each.

1. A Maxitek is a better computer. (Better than what?)
* A Maxitek is a better computer than anything else in its price range.

2. Our new filing system is more complete. (More complete than what?)
* Our new filing system is more complete than our old one.

3. I cherish the memories of childhood more than you.
* I cherish the memories of childhood more than you [cherish them].
* I cherish the memories of childhood more than you [do].
* I cherish the memories of childhood more than [I cherish] you.

4. Professor Ambiguous teaches more about life than poetry.
* Professor Ambiguous teaches more about life than [she teaches about] poetry.
* Professor Ambiguous teaches more about life than poetry [does].
* Professor Ambiguous teaches more about life than [about] poetry.

5. It is one of the ironies of our society that a professional athlete's salary can be greater than the president.
* It is one of the ironies of our society that a professional athlete's salary can be greater than [that of] the president.
* It is one of the ironies of our society that a professional athlete's salary can be greater than the president['s].

6. The vice president for student affairs maintains that today employment opportunities for women are greater than men.
* The vice president for student affairs maintains that today employment opportunities for women are greater than [they are] for men.

8. The freedoms enjoyed by the citizens of Western European nations are as great, although not greater than, those enjoyed by American citizens.

* The freedoms enjoyed by the citizens of Western European nations are as great [as], although not greater than, those enjoyed by American citizens.

9. This guy is as good, if not better than, the old-time catchers.

* This guy is as good [as], if not better than, the old-time catchers.

10. Is the population of New York City greater than that of any American city?

* Is the population of New York City greater than that of any [other] American city?

11. In the end, Cadwallader did a better job than anyone on the city team. [Cadwallader was on the city team.]

* In the end, Cadwallader did a better job than anyone [else] on the city team.

In the following exercise quiz, edit and rewrite each sentence to remove all instances of faulty parallelism involving correlative conjunctions or faulty comparisons.

EXERCISE
Faulty Parallelism Editing (2)

1. The group of Swedish tourists found Montreal more intriguing than any Canadian city they had visited.

_____

_____

2. Luther, who is both a student of the game and knows how to motivate adolescent boys, will make a good coach.

_____

_____

3. Everyone agreed that the freshmen enjoyed their classes more than the seniors.

_____

_____

4. The new edition of the textbook for microbiology is much more comprehensive.

_____

_____

5. You simply cannot deny that Balthazar is as ambitious, if not more ambitious than, his brother Marmaduke.

_____

_____

6. Alas, my humanities instructor neither likes rock nor easy-listening music.

_____

_____

7. This elective course in logic beats anything I have taken during my three years at the university.

_____

_____

8. The game between Northern and Hinterland State was either the longest in the history of the league, or it was the second longest.

_____

_____

9. Emeline's watercolors have improved to the point that they are more marketable.

_____

_____

10. Not only did Ellen lose her taste for fried foods but also eating ice cream.

_____

_____

Faulty Verb Forms

Verbs have five fundamental forms. They are (1) the base form, (2) the -s form, (3) the present participle form, (4) the past tense form, and (5) the past participle form.

Base Form	-S Form	Present Participle	Past Tense	Past Participle
abridge	abridges	abridging	abridged	abridged
bite	bites	bitting	bit	bitten
come	comes	coming	came	come
jog	jogs	jogging	jogged	jogged
know	knows	knowing	knew	known
wish	wishes	wishing	wished	wished

Base form   The base form of the verb is the form listed in the dictionary and used with plural nouns as well as the pronouns *I, we, you,* and *they* to denote present time or some continuous action.

1. These people *laugh* at the strangest things.
2. Rivers *flow* to the sea because of the force of gravity.
3. We *go* to the supermarket at least three times a week.
4. They *teach* a class in conversational Russian on Wednesday evenings.
5. If you *drink* too much water, you will become chilled.

The -s form   The -s form of the verb is composed of the base form plus -*s* or -*es*. The form indicates the present tense and is used with all singular nouns, the third-person singular pronouns *he, she,* and *it,* and such indefinite pronouns as *another, each, either, neither, anything, someone,* and *everybody.*

1. This lamp *goes* perfectly with the drapes.
2. The Kanawha River *flows* into the Ohio River at Point Pleasant, West Virginia.
3. Elizabeth *knows* all about the bookkeeping system here.
4. He who *laughs* last *laughs* longest.
5. Each of these melons *tastes* bitter to me.
6. Almost every evening someone *pitches* a bag of grass clippings into the dumpster.
7. Neither of the brothers *boxes* professionally anymore.

Present participle form   The present participle form of the verb is constructed by adding -*ing* to the base form. When used alone, the present participle form may function either as an adjective or as a noun, but not as a predicate.

1. Outside, the *howling* wind rattled the shingles on the roof of the cabin. [an adjective]
2. The *developing* nations are harmed more by the recession than are the industrialized nations. [an adjective]
3. As time passes, the *reading* public represents a smaller and smaller percentage of the population. [an adjective]
4. *Studying* and *sleeping* occupied most of my weekend. [nouns or gerunds]
5. It is impossible to run a successful business without *advertising*. [a noun or gerund]
6. Shannon gave up *teaching* and took up *painting*. [nouns or gerunds]

Progressive tense   When the present participle form combines with such auxiliary verbs as *am, is, are, was,* and *were,* the progressive tense is created. The progressive tense indicates continuing action.

1. Does anyone know how many candidates *are running* for office in Backwoods County? [present progressive]
2. Alas, I *am losing* the battle against my bulging waistline. [present progressive]
3. Until we ran out of money, we *were improving* our share of the market. [past progressive]

4. Suddenly, Leopold *was winning* every match he played. [past progressive]

5. I promise absolutely that I *shall be seeing* you regularly in the spring. [future progressive]

6. For these last months, I *have been talking* to no one but you and your family. [present perfect progressive]

7. Before visiting Hinterland State, I *had been thinking* about going to college in Europe. [past perfect progressive]

Past tense form   The past tense form of the verb is used to indicate action that occurred at some time in the past. With most verbs, the past tense is formed by adding *-d* or *-ed* to the base form. Some verbs, however, form the past tense in irregular ways, and are thus called irregular verbs.

1. Edmund *completed* his course requirements last semester.

2. We *knew* the truth even before going into the house.

3. The instructor *gave* that assignment two weeks ago.

4. About dawn Curtis *threw* a few logs on the fire.

5. The doctor *cauterized* the wound to prevent infection.

Past participle form   With regular verbs, the past participle form is the same as that of the past tense. However, with some irregular verbs, the past participle form is different from that of the past tense (e.g., *bite / bit / bitten, come / came / come, know / knew / known, go / went / gone, drink / drank / drunk, give / gave / given, throw / threw / thrown*). When used alone, the past participle form may function as an adjective but not as a predicate.

1. The wreck was caused by a *blown* tire.

2. It takes a *driven* person to work eighty hours a week.

3. Lizzie prefers *frozen* yogurt to ice cream.

4. Were the *stolen* documents ever recovered?

5. Generally, the *written* language is more formal than the *spoken* language.

Perfect tenses   When the past participle form combines with certain auxiliary verbs, other tenses—called perfect tenses—are formed. These tenses are (1) the present perfect tense, (2) the past perfect tense, and (3) the future perfect tense. The present perfect tense combines *have* or *has* with the past participle; the past perfect tense combines *had* with the past participle; and the future perfect tense combines *shall have* or *will have* with the past participle.

1. We *have driven* four hundred miles and intend to drive four hundred more. [present perfect tense]

2. Professor Mumby *has been* a good lecturer in every class I *have taken* from him. [present perfect tense]

3. Actually, the lad *had chosen* Hinterland State even before the scholarship offer was forthcoming. [past perfect tense]

4. Even though Bernard *had eaten* only an hour earlier, he did a very good imitation of a starving man. [past perfect tense]

5. By going to summer school for three years, Carmel *will have completed* all of her requirements for graduation by the end of the fall semester. [future perfect tense]

6. By 1994, I *shall have completed* thirty-five years in the classroom. [future perfect tense]

The point of our explanation of the perfect tenses that arise as a result of the past participle form being combined with these auxiliary verbs is not to try to make you an expert on all possible verb tenses. What we want to impress upon you is the fact that when there is a difference between the past tense form and the past participle form of a verb—as there often is with irregular verbs—and one of these auxiliary verbs precedes the main verb, you *must* use the past participle form. Conversely, when no auxiliary verb is present, you *must not* use the past participle form. The following list includes about fifty irregular verbs that student writers sometimes find troublesome.

Base Form	Past Tense	Past Participle
become	became	become
begin	began	begun
bend	bent	bent
bet	bet	bet
bite	bit	bitten
blow	blew	blown
break	broke	broken
breed	bred	bred
bring	brought	brought
burst	burst	burst
buy	bought	bought
cast	cast	cast
choose	chose	chosen
come	came	come
cost	cost	cost
creep	crept	crept
deal	dealt	dealt
do	did	done
draw	drew	drawn
drink	drank	drunk
drive	drove	driven
eat	ate	eaten
fall	fell	fallen
forget	forgot	forgotten
freeze	froze	frozen
give	gave	given
go	went	gone
grind	ground	ground
grow	grew	grown
hide	hid	hidden
hit	hit	hit
hold	held	held
know	knew	known
lead	led	led

411

Base Form	Past Tense	Past Participle
lend	lent	lent
ride	rode	ridden
ring	rang	rung
rise	rose	risen
run	ran	run
see	saw	seen
sing	sang	sung
sink	sank	sunk
speak	spoke	spoken
steal	stole	stolen
swim	swam	swum
swing	swung	swung
take	took	taken
tear	tore	torn
throw	threw	thrown
wear	wore	worn
wring	wrung	wrung
write	wrote	written

In the following exercise quiz, select the correct verb form for each sentence. The incorrect choices are wrong for one of two reasons: they are the past tense form when they should be the past participle form (or the reverse of this) or they are a nonstandard form of either the past tense or past participle—e.g., *brung* rather than *brought* or *swang* rather than *swung*.

EXERCISE
Past Tense and Perfect Tense Verb Form Identification

1. Alas, the telephone has not (*rang / rung*) since midnight.

2. Antonia admitted that she (*saw / seen*) the children running from the barn.

3. The lad once known as Shagnasty has (*grown / growed*) into a handsome young man.

4. Once again, Bennet had (*tore / torn*) his trousers on the fence.

5. All things considered, we (*did / done*) the best job we could.

6. That old man has (*came / come*) into the station every evening for the last two weeks.

7. Between them, those two louts (*drank / drunk*) almost a gallon of cheap wine.

8. Amazingly, the second front (*blew / blowed*) half the pleasure boats out of the water.

9. In another three months, the thieves will have (*stole / stolen*) everything we own.

10. We (*began / begun*) to work exactly where we had left off after the previous season.

11. The patient had somehow (*bit / bitten*) through the leather belt.

412

12. Almost everyone in town (*knew / knowed*) the truth about the incident.

13. Since that Saturday afternoon, none of us has (*swam / swum*) across Deep Lake again.

14. That fellow (*ran / run*) up the hill as if the devil were after him.

15. Professor Drab has (*wore / worn*) that same brown jacket to class every day for the entire semester.

16. When it (*came / come*) to making a decision, Ashley was second to no one.

17. By the end of the summer, wear and tear will have (*broke / broken*) these pulleys again.

18. Incredibly, the ship (*sank / sunk*) in less than thirty feet of water.

19. There can be no good reason for what you (*did / done*).

20. My mother had never before (*gave / given*) me such an expensive gift.

21. Have you ever (*wrang / wrung*) a chicken's neck?

22. At the reunion everyone (*sang / sung*) the old songs as if they were an anthem for life itself.

23. We shall all have (*froze / frozen*) stiff by the time help arrives.

24. About two o'clock the graduating seniors (*rang / rung*) the bell in Hinter Tower, and then everyone went home to bed.

25. For the third Monday in a row, Jason had (*forgot / forgotten*) to go to physics class.

26. That mangy old cat has (*brought / brung*) another dead rabbit into the house.

27. After seven consecutive days of rain, the dam finally (*bursted / burst*) on Saturday afternoon.

28. By January 20, the president-elect will already have (*chose / chosen*) his cabinet.

29. If I had (*went / gone*) to college when I was younger, the work would not have seemed so difficult.

30. After a week in art class, Alice (*drew / drawed*) a huge chicken on the wall in the dinette.

To complete the following five Sentence Problems Review Exercises, follow the same procedure that you followed at the end of Chapter 8: identify the error that occurs in each of the twenty sentences by placing the appropriate letter in the blanks in front of the sentences. Each sentence demonstrates one particular error.

If your instructor is using materials provided by the Instructor's Manual that accompanies *Sentence Basics* to reinforce lessons taught in the text, you may have the opportunity to do as many as ten additional similar exercises called Sentence Error Identification Exercises. These exercises feature all ten of the sentence errors in each exercise, rather than one set of five in half the exercises and a second set of five in the other half. Otherwise, the instructions are the same, and each of the twenty sentences demonstrates only one error.

REVIEW EXERCISE
Sentence Problems (6)

F. Pronoun-Antecedent Error   I. Faulty Parallelism
G. Misplaced Modifier   J. Faulty Verb Form
H. Dangling Modifier

_____ 1. My new physics professor is an internationally known scholar and who has taught many famous students.

_____ 2. Our abiding goal was to whenever possible introduce new product lines.

_____ 3. To achieve just the right taste, you must apply the barbecue sauce while the burger is cooking.

_____ 4. Although years had passed since either had played, neither Giles nor Julius had lost their shooting eye.

_____ 5. During the years following his graduation from college, Hiram worked at several occupations: sales clerk, driving a truck, house painter, and repairing table lamps.

_____ 6. As it turned out, the company with the low bid done very good work.

_____ 7. Glenna gave her brother a gilded man's tie pin, but he didn't like it.

_____ 8. Before reading a book like this, the mind must be free of distractions.

_____ 9. When we tried to return the defective merchandise to the store, they would not accept it.

_____ 10. The crews usually begun work between six and seven o'clock.

_____ 11. As I recall, it was last Monday when I read the article in _Newsweek_ about euthanasia.

_____ 12. The instructor was angry because no one had did the homework assignment.

_____ 13. Although I have never seen a leprechaun, I have read about them in psychology class.

_____ 14. Chloe said that she would rather live in Chicago than any city in the United States.

_____ 15. Deeply shaken by the storm, returning home was out of the question.

_____ 16. Nathan has always wanted to be a movie star, which has cost him a fortune over the years.

_____ 17. After five years as an undergraduate, Wilma was in need of a job and broke.

_____ 18. When going through puberty, Mother had no patience with the children.

_____ 19. By the end of the season, the players will have went through dozens of pairs of shoes.

_____ 20. The hostesses served spicy hors d'oeuvres to the guests that were too hot to swallow.

REVIEW EXERCISE
Sentence Problems (7)

F. Pronoun-Antecedent Error   I. Faulty Parallelism
G. Misplaced Modifier   J. Faulty Verb Form
H. Dangling Modifier

_____ 1. The first thing I had to do every morning was take the gerbils out of the cages and wash them.

_____ 2. In reviewing the instructor's comments about the paper, it was obvious that further revision was necessary.

_____ 3. By June the workers will have tore down most of the old buildings.

_____ 4. Recently, American cars have become far less expensive to maintain.

_____ 5. Although she speaks several languages, Robin only reads English.

_____ 6. Why would anyone have stole such a worthless piece of junk?

_____ 7. One of the qualities of a good high school teacher is that he makes himself available to students seeking extra help.

_____ 8. Professor Kidney was neither a good lecturer nor did he care much about his students.

_____ 9. Jeffrey said, without taking sufficient time to think, some unnecessarily harsh things to his sisters.

_____ 10. Actually, the day went quite well after a nice little nap.

_____ 11. The receptionists convinced the typists that they should be earning more money than they had earned in the past.

_____ 12. To chase the dogs through the woods, a dress is inappropriate attire.

_____ 13. By the time school began, the twins had broke almost every toy that they took with them to the lake.

_____ 14. All the Volvos had been leased to local customers that had standard driver's-side air bags.

_____ 15. In the end I realized that I not only lacked the time needed to become a professional organist but also the talent.

_____ 16. Alas, some people do not have the ability to realize their dreams, and that can make their lives unhappy ones.

_____ 17. Having run the vacuum and changed the beds, the house was almost presentable.

_____ 18. We sunk a cool ten million into that project and got no return.

_____ 19. Maynard promised his mother after graduating from college he would clean up his act and become a normal human being.

_____ 20. After searching for weeks, we finally located a truck perfect for our needs and that we could afford to buy.

REVIEW EXERCISE
Sentence Problems (8)

F. Pronoun-Antecedent Error   I. Faulty Parallelism
G. Misplaced Modifier   J. Faulty Verb Form
H. Dangling Modifier

_____ 1. We were amazed to learn that every car and truck in the competition had had their engine overhauled.

_____ 2. When I was a child on the farm, we growed sweet corn for the birds.

_____ 3. Before applying the primer, all the exterior walls must be scraped and sanded.

_____ 4. Edmund's apartment, like most of the apartments in these buildings, was undersized, needed major repairs, and poorly lighted.

_____ 5. I can't think of anything I would rather not do than drink a warm glass of milk before going to bed.

_____ 6. The debris that blowed across the street came from the warehouse.

_____ 7. At the conclusion of the second act, the heroine relates the story of her marriage to one of her sisters.

_____ 8. As had been the case for many years, no one in the department except Bernice was willing to run for the faculty senate.

_____ 9. If the children leave any meat or vegetables, boil them into a stew.

_____ 10. Although carefully organized, few members of the audience enjoyed the concert.

_____ 11. Franklin says that he likes reading good books, listening to good music, viewing works of modern art, and winter trips to warm climates.

_____ 12. Jan realized in a more tranquil setting progress would be forthcoming.

_____ 13. Starved from weeks without food, the hamburgers tasted like a feast.

_____ 14. You might have wore something a little less flamboyant to a funeral.

_____ 15. The energy crisis will continue because we do not conserve it.

_____ 16. Please tell me about the martyred saints, the ancient philosophers, the famous teachers, and how to live a productive life.

_____ 17. Not surprisingly, the psychedelic Saab's paint job drew a large crowd of admiring spectators.

_____ 18. Ironically, the two brothers come to the same decision; they didn't want to go to college.

_____ 19. By twelve o'clock the party was over, and it became steadily colder throughout the night.

_____ 20. To photograph these birds in flight, complete concentration is required.

REVIEW EXERCISE
Sentence Problems (9)

F. Pronoun-Antecedent Error   I. Faulty Parallelism
G. Misplaced Modifier   J. Faulty Verb Form
H. Dangling Modifier

_____ 1. After sitting in the wrong class for two weeks, the instructor finally told me where to go.

_____ 2. So many of my old colleagues at the office have retired that I hardly recognized anyone at the Christmas party.

_____ 3. Few people seem to realize that walking is better for them than to jog.

_____ 4. It was just before dusk when we seen the deer on the runway.

_____ 5. The school insists on a three-point academic average to keep my scholarship.

_____ 6. If anyone requires assistance completing the project on time, they should contact the instructor.

_____ 7. Garvey said that he had never drank so much canned pop in his life as he did on the hunting trip.

_____ 8. When Ida tried to talk to her mother, she was in a grim mood.

_____ 9. After more than six weeks of testing, the task force reluctantly admitted that the foreign models were more carefully designed.

_____ 10. The old hermit lived in a hut on an island in the middle of a river that he built for himself.

_____ 11. Even though Ann has several orange trees in her yard, she doesn't eat them.

_____ 12. For ten years Phoebe has swam her laps in this pool each morning before breakfast.

_____ 13. Loren's youngest cousin had brain surgery about six months ago, and it has been improving ever since.

_____ 14. Gazing across the runway, three fighter planes suddenly came into view.

_____ 15. You are as well informed, if not more informed than, many of the contestants on _Jeopardy_.

_____ 16. How can this be winter when we have had just one freezing day all week?

_____ 17. Everyone in the class was surprised to learn that the industrial output of Germany was greater than Japan.

_____ 18. Once again, Carol's nephews have ran up a substantial bill at the local amusement center.

_____ 19. If planted too early in the season, freezing weather will kill the peas.

_____ 20. It is very important for us to if we can understand the fundamental structure of matter.

REVIEW EXERCISE
Sentence Problems (10)

F. Pronoun-Antecedent Error   I. Faulty Parallelism
G. Misplaced Modifier   J. Faulty Verb Form
H. Dangling Modifier

_____ 1. The exchange students were intelligent, possessors of pleasant personalities, and informed academically.

_____ 2. Ian's sister is a brain surgeon, and he is very envious of her.

_____ 3. That revered bell hasn't rang since August 7, 1982.

_____ 4. Although there were some objections, in the end everyone presented a report on their summer activities.

_____ 5. When sound to sleep, this medicine does its most effective work.

_____ 6. Alas, many of those things that I once thought would please me totally put me off.

_____ 7. When my father come home with too much venison, we always gave some to the neighbors.

_____ 8. Elizabeth had once met the man that her sister later married quite by accident.

_____ 9. Ted plays both tennis and soccer and very skillfully.

_____ 10. By brushing carefully each day, the teeth are less likely to develop cavities.

_____ 11. We fought this terrible war to, as they say, make the world safe for multinational corporations.

_____ 12. Standing precariously on the narrow ledge, the roaring wind didn't make things any less difficult.

_____ 13. Although the child had been bit by a poisonous snake, she was doing fine.

_____ 14. When the contract was ratified by the general membership, the bargaining team had completed their task and thus ceased to exist.

_____ 15. Alice is neither a student of Russian history nor does she speak the Russian language.

_____ 16. The police found, after a month-long search, the body of the victim.

_____ 17. We should have knowed that so old a car would need major repairs.

_____ 18. To be absolutely safe, at least $40 million should be put aside for a rainy day.

_____ 19. Only a Neanderthal wouldn't understand that those kind of pranks wound civilized people.

_____ 20. I must admit that I enjoyed the dean's stories of his undergraduate days at Ohio State more than you.

PART FOUR
THE WRITING PROCESS

Chapter 10

Introduction to the Writing Process

The ability to write well is not inherited from one's ancestors, distant or immediate; nor is it a magical, mystical power awarded to some of us and denied the rest of us. Writing is a craft. Thus, to be able to write well, you need to understand how the writing process works *and* how to customize or personalize the writing process so that it will work for you. For convenience, we can begin by dividing this process into three large parts or phases: (1) pre-writing, (2) drafting, and (3) revising.

As we discuss each of these general phases of the writing process, we must also keep in mind two important considerations: *purpose* and *audience*. Whatever you may be writing, you will need to have in mind a purpose; that is, a clear goal or specific intention. For example, your goal in writing a letter home to your parents may be to entertain them—to make them smile or even laugh aloud—by telling them about funny events on campus. In class, your purpose in writing a personal essay about growing up on a potato farm in Michigan might be to inform students, and the instructor as well, about all the sophisticated business practices used today to operate a successful farm. Our purpose in composing a piece of written material—short or long—may in fact be many things: to convince readers of the necessity of a national health system, to persuade the president of the university to discontinue several varsity athletic programs rather than increase student tuition, to teach people how to build something or follow a technical process, or simply to express ourselves—as in diaries, journals, stories, novels, or poetry. In every step of the writing process, you should keep your purpose in mind. Furthermore, take care not to confuse purpose with various outside motives that sometimes force us to write: because we owe our rich Aunt Isabel a letter, because we want to impress our history professor, or because the English course we are taking requires four 1500-word compositions.

Just as everything you write should have a specific purpose, it should also be aimed at some specific audience; that is, a person or group of persons you wish to reach. Because the ultimate purpose of almost all writing is to have an effect on readers, audience and purpose are closely related. Think how different two chapters entitled "The Structure of the Universe," one appearing in a textbook for fifth-grade students and the other appearing in a text for graduate students in astrophysics, would be. And why would they be so different? Primarily because of the vast differences between the intended audiences for the two texts. Age and level of education, however, are not the only items important to audience considerations. Others might include occupation, gender, ethnicity, sexual orientation, income level, religious preferences, political ideals, philosophical leanings, avocations—in short, almost anything that can contribute to common attitudes among a group of people. Thus, throughout the writing process, you should keep in mind the audience you are targeting. And doing this can influence virtually every decision you make about what is or is not appropriate for a paper intended for that audience—e.g., the topic, the thoroughness of the treatment of the topic, vocabulary level and diction, personal references, humor, style, and so on.

Pre-Writing

We have all known individuals who think that all there is to painting a house is to grab a bucket and a brush and start splashing paint around. We also know what the house looks like when they finish—if they finish. Painting a house properly requires some forethought, some planning, a bit of additional work, and not a few decisions before the first brush is dipped into the first bucket of paint.

You may also know a few people who think that all there is to writing a good short paper is to grab a pen or pencil and several pieces of paper and start splashing words around. Alas, it doesn't work that way. Pre-writing is that part of the writing process wherein you make initial or preliminary decisions about such things as the topic of the paper, your purpose for writing the paper, your intended audience (readers), the stylistic level appropriate for the purpose and audience, what sources of information are to be used, and what organizational strategies you intend to employ.

Suppose you have been given an assignment to write a paper of between 500 and 1,000 words about some specific person who has greatly influenced your life. The rest is entirely up to you. Where might you begin?

Simply stated, you begin by thinking. Two methods of thinking that often work in such situations are *free association* and *brainstorming*. The former involves allowing your mind to range freely over memories and past experiences, in this instance guided only by the motive of recalling those individuals who have influenced your life in some way. Dozens of people— e.g., teachers, preachers, coaches, childhood friends, sweethearts, family acquaintances, relatives, and the like—and perhaps hundreds of almost-forgotten occurrences may pass through your mind. The exercise can become a sort of nostalgic reverie. Eventually, though, you will arrive at the name of one person, and this person will become the focus of your paper.

Brainstorming, although a little more structured than free association, also involves spontaneous thought. For this exercise, you would scribble down on paper in no particular order all the things this person has done to influence your life or all the reasons that have led you to conclude that he or she has influenced your life in a major way. If you are a particularly visual person, you might want to add what is called *mapping* to this exercise. (Mapping may also be called *clustering, webbing,* or *charting.*)

To construct a brainstorming map, begin with a clean sheet of paper. Write your topic (the name of the person who has greatly influenced your life) in the center of the page and circle it. Next, in abbreviated form, write down each of the main items from your brainstorming list as sort of satellites to the topic; that is, they surround the topic. Circle these main items individually and connect them to the topic with lines. Then add any pertinent ideas, observations, details, facts, or examples that you can think of which relate to the main items. Then connect each of these supporting items to the main item to which it is related. In this way you can continue to generate supporting material until you run out of ideas on your chosen topic. Your map will probably look something like the following model.

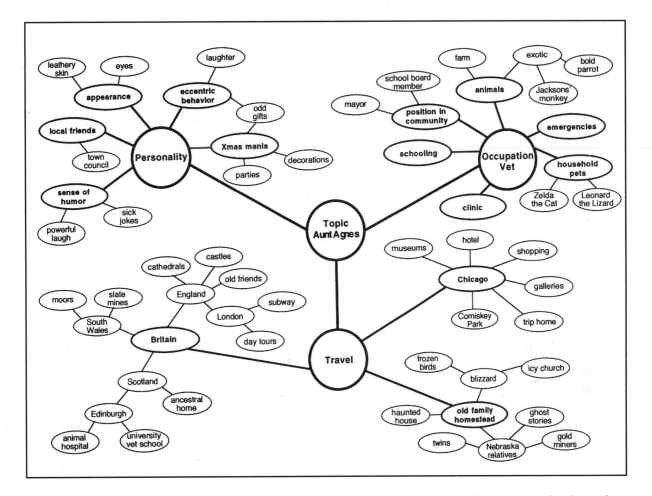

After you decide on the topic of your assigned paper and have at least a rough idea what its main items or considerations will be—along with some supporting ideas, details, facts, examples, occurrences, and observations—you must take the time to think about the other important decisions that have to be made before you actually start writing a draft.

First of all, you will want to decide what your purpose is in writing the paper; that is, what it is you hope to accomplish—your goal. More than likely, your purpose will be to demonstrate to your readers how the person whom you have chosen to feature has come to influence your life in a major way. If you actually write your purpose down in a statement intended to guide you later on in the drafting stage of the writing process, the statement is called a *working thesis;* and the form of this statement that finally appears in the finished paper is called the *thesis statement.*

Because this assignment appears in a freshman composition text, it is not unreasonable for you to assume that your primary audience for the paper will be your fellow students. The instructor might be considered a secondary audience. So, it is for your peers that you are writing, and you should take care not to misjudge, offend, confuse, or alienate individual members of this group. Generally, you misjudge an audience—even of your peers—when you assume that all its members think alike or think exactly as you do. Even in a college class of only twenty-five or thirty students, there will almost certainly be a substantial diversity of opinion on almost any topic.

You risk offending members of your audience by carelessly using words or expressions that others may find painful, insulting, inappropriate, or even indecent. Such expressions may involve an inappropriate reference to ethnicity, gender, age, physical appearance, education, religion, disabilities, social class, occupation, sexual orientation, or level of intelligence. You also risk confusing your audience by not beginning the paper with a clear thesis statement and then carrying through with what the statement suggests is to follow.

In addition to making sure that you begin your paper with a thesis statement that both informs your readers of the paper's main idea *and* suggests the direction the paper is going to take, you also need to have an organizational strategy in mind. The most commonly used organizational strategies are (1) narration, (2) description, (3) exemplification, (4) comparison, (5) analogy, (6) classification, (7) analysis, (8) process, (9) cause/effect, and (10) definition. We shall consider each of these in the section on "Drafting."

Drafting

Drafting is that part of the writing process in which you actually begin putting your thoughts on paper according to some organized plan. Most short papers include an introduction, a paragraph or two featuring the thesis statement; several body paragraphs, the number depending upon the intended length or complexity of the paper; and a conclusion, usually quite brief. More often than not, the drafting stage will result in the production of more than one draft of a paper. You will likely have a first draft, several working or rough drafts, and a final draft. And sometimes what you had thought was the final draft becomes a rough draft after the instructor or other students critique it and suggest additional revisions and refinements.

You can use the organizational strategies already mentioned in the pre-writing section as methods of development in your own compositions. We'll now look at each of the organizational strategies in more detail. You should keep in mind that your own papers are not often likely to be composed entirely of one strategy; rather, they will more often feature one strategy while using others to support the featured strategy. And sometimes several strategies will be featured together in combination.

Narration

A paper that features the narrative strategy details a sequence of events to tell a story. Usually, these events will be arranged in chronological order. The story itself may be either fiction or nonfiction, and the author's purpose for telling the story—as with all the organizational strategies—may be virtually anything: to inform, to explain, to persuade, to entertain, to amuse, and so on.

Carefully structured narratives make sure that readers know (1) what happens, (2) how it happens, (3) when it happens, (4) where it happens, and (5) who is involved. The teller of the story is called the *narrator,* and the place or position from which the story is told is called the *narrative point of view.* If the narrator refers to himself or herself as "I," the story is told from the *first-person point of view.* Otherwise, it will probably be told from the *third-person point of view,* in which case the narrator is not actually identified. With first-person narratives, the narrator may be the main character in the story, a secondary or minor character, or simply an observer of the events presented.

Because of a narrative's chronological pattern of development, make sure that your own narratives include an adequate number of time-indicating transitional words and phrases: "about the same time," "after a while," "as soon as," "in the meantime," "later on," "only moments later," "soon thereafter," "subsequently," and so on. When writing short narratives or narrative passages in longer papers, observe the following: (1) Focus on a single incident rather than try to summarize a large number of events. (2) Begin with a statement that clearly indicates a narrative incident is to follow—e.g., "When I was in the third grade, I learned—the hard way—that there are some things you just don't mess around with." (3) Even when the purpose of your narrative is to make an important point, don't belabor the point. (4) Don't try to mystify, trick, or surprise your audience; choose an incident that is in itself interesting enough to be simply and clearly told. (5) Consciously select one narrative point of view and then stick to it. Don't shift between first-person and third-person. (6) If you use dialogue (conversation between or among characters), be sure to begin a new paragraph each time the speaker changes. (7) Keep your conclusion brief.

Description

In contrast to narration, description presents a spatial (space) arrangement rather than a chronological one. In a sense, time is "frozen" in a description.

There are two fundamental types of description: *interpretive* and *technical,* which may also be called *subjective* and *objective.* Technical or objective description may be thought of as photographic description—that is, it confines itself to that which can be seen through a camera, under a microscope, or in the mind's eye. Such description is most often used in technical manuals, textbooks, and objective reportage. Interpretive or subjective description, on the other hand, explains or gives personal impressions as it describes. For example, a paper that describes a famous painting *and* presents the author's impressions of what the artist was trying to say when composing the picture would be interpretive. Similarly, a paper that describes an old farm house *and* explains what the place means to the author is also interpretive. Readers learn more from the description than they could from simply viewing the structure.

Effective descriptive papers, whether they are interpretive, technical, or a combination of the two, seek to leave the reader with a *dominant impression* of what is being described. This dominant impression is the equivalent of the point of the story told in a narrative paper. For example, a description of the destruction left by a tornado, whether it is written by an ordinary person who survived the storm or by a meteorologist who has a professional interest in weather phenomena, will likely leave the reader with the dominant impression of the awesome destructive power possessed by a tornado.

If the goal of the narrative strategy is to tell a story with words, the goal of the descriptive strategy is to paint a picture with words.

When composing descriptive papers of your own or descriptive passages in other papers, keep in mind that one of your most important sources of raw material is the senses: sight, hearing, taste, touch, and smell. Likewise, deliberate appeals to the appropriate senses in the reader can greatly enhance the impact of your work on your audience. Similarly, because of description's spatial pattern of development, be sure to include an adequate number of space-indicating transitional expressions: "adjacent to," "nearby," "in the distance," "farther on," "on the left," "separated from," "within in view of," and so on.

Exemplification

A paper featuring the strategy of exemplification, also called *illustration,* presents specific examples of something, and the "something" being illustrated will usually be indicated by the thesis statement. For example, an exemplification paper containing the thesis statement "Many Americans consume excessive amounts of sodium in their daily diets" will likely go on to give specific examples of "typical" American meals, pointing out how much sodium each item contains. Similarly, another exemplification paper including the thesis statement "The average middle-class home in America has become a virtual chemical warehouse" will go on to present specific examples of the many (dangerous) chemicals that are today used or found in middle-class American homes. Specific examples are used to support, amplify, or even prove the thesis statement they follow.

Sometimes an exemplification paper will present a single elaborate example. Other times, however, such papers will present many examples. Often, an exemplification paper presenting multiple examples will save the best example for last—as a sort of clincher or climax. Be sure to use transitional expressions to remind the reader of the paper's fundamental strategy: "for example," "for instance," "to illustrate," and so on.

Comparison

The comparison strategy may be employed in three distinct ways: (1) to show similarities, (2) to present differences, or (3) to show both similarities and differences. A comparison that features the thesis statement "Although African and Asian elephants are much alike, the two creatures differ in many ways" will likely go on to concentrate on the differences between the two animals. In fact, that will probably be the point of the paper. On the other hand, a comparison with the thesis statement "Even though elephants and human beings are not likely to be confused one for the other, there is a surprising number of similarities in elephant and human behavior" will go on to focus on the similarities between human and elephant behavior. A comparison paper that intends to show both similarities and differences should include a thesis statement that makes this intent clear to readers: "Going to high school and going to college are alike in many ways, but different in others."

Just as transitional expressions indicating time are important to the narrative strategy, those indicating space important to the descriptive strategy, and those indicating example to exemplification, transitional expressions such as "also," "in like manner," "likewise," "similarly," "correspondingly," "by contrast," "on the contrary," "on the other hand," "although true," "however," and "whereas" are important to the strategy of comparison.

Analogy

The strategy of analogy may be thought of as a type of creative comparison, comparison that concentrates on similarities. The "creative" element in analogy arises from the fact that the two things being compared might not at first glance be considered very much alike, perhaps not alike at all. Thus, the writer must "discover" similarities that other people may never have noticed. Often, although not always, analogy is used to explain or describe that which is unfamiliar by comparing it to something that is familiar. The comparisons are presented in an *extended analogy;* that is, an analogy controlling an entire paper or substantial portion of a longer piece of writing should be as detailed as possible.

A thesis statement featuring the strategy of analogy will frequently contain a simile, metaphor, or personification to establish the fundamental comparison that the paper is going to develop. (1) *Simile:* "Going to college is sometimes like living in a zoo that is surrounded by a jungle." (2) *Metaphor:* "Adolescence is a disease requiring more than two aspirins and a good night's sleep to recover from." (3) *Personification:* "Nature seems to be marshaling her forces for a counteroffensive against two hundred years of mistreatment by industrial societies." A paper with the first thesis statement (assuming the author is employing the strategy of analogy) will go on to draw as many comparisons as possible between a college campus and a zoo, as well as a few between the world outside the campus and a jungle. Similarly, a paper with the second thesis statement will go on to draw specific comparisons between adolescence and a lingering medical disability, as well as between the cure for such a condition and the experiences of life that lead one beyond adolescence. A paper featuring the third thesis statement will go on to draw comparisons between nature and a military commander who is organizing various (natural) forces for deployment against an enemy— i.e., the industrial societies who for two hundred years have been damaging the planet.

When using the strategy of analogy in papers of your own, make sure to (1) establish a valid connection between the two things being compared, (2) present specific details that both items being compared have in common, and (3) select an ample number of key (double-duty) words that relate equally to both items being compared. Suppose, for example, that you are developing an analogy detailing the similarities between the passage of the seasons of the year and the passage of an individual's life: *spring* (birth, infancy, youth, and adolescence); *summer* (young adulthood through full adulthood); *autumn* (middle age through the onset of physical decline); and *winter* (old age and death). For each season and its corresponding parts of a person's life, carefully select words that apply to both and thus reinforce the paper's intended comparisons.

Classification

A paper featuring the strategy of classification begins by establishing a class of some sort and then breaks the class down into separate categories. Usually, the body of the paper will deal more with the individual categories than with the inclusive classification. For example, a classification paper about the five types of apes will talk more about each of the apes than it will about apes in general. The thesis statement of such a paper might read "Although all gorillas are apes, not all apes are gorillas; in fact, there are five distinct types of apes: the gorilla, chimpanzee, orangutan, gibbon, and siamang." The paper will then go on to talk about each of the apes in turn.

When using the classification strategy, take care to do the following: (1) Narrow the (definition of the) inclusive class so that all possible categories can be included. You must have three categories, but anything over seven is probably too many. In any event, don't make the mistake of treating only a few "sample" categories. (2) Make sure that each of your categories is exclusive; that is, it should never be possible for any specific examples of the categories to fit into more than a single category—e.g., it makes no sense to subdivide the human race (the classification) into the categories of men, women, and artists; some people will fit into more than one of the three categories. (3) To the extent that you can, give each of the categories equal as well as parallel treatment. This means that items presented about one category should be presented about all categories *and* in the same order or sequence. (4) Check to make sure that what you have intended to be categories are indeed categories rather than necessary parts of a system or stages (steps) in a process. For example, it is a mistake to think of REM sleep as a category of sleep; REM is one step in the sleep process. The test here is one of exclusion or removal. If all the gibbons suddenly died or were carried away by aliens from outer space, gorillas, chimpanzees, orangutans, and siamangs would remain as they were—the other four types of apes. However, without REM sleep, sleep wouldn't be sleep. Everyone would have insomnia.

Analysis

The word *analysis* is derived from the Greek roots *ana,* meaning "throughout," and *lysis,* meaning "a loosening." Thus, a paper developed by the organizational strategy of analysis breaks (or loosens) a topic into necessary parts and examines each part by itself to provide a better understanding of the whole. Because it is fundamentally different from the strategy of classification, analysis makes no attempt to establish categories. A paper that discusses the five types of great roaring cats (the lion, tiger, jaguar, leopard, and snow leopard) uses the strategy of classification, whereas a paper that discusses the intricate pattern of relationships among all the cats in a lion pride uses the strategy of analysis.

You can analyze almost anything—chemical compounds, blood, an ecosystem, a movie, a beehive, the earth's atmosphere, a human personality, a word, the eleven o'clock news, an ant colony, a sentence, a short story, the National Football League, the structure of the United Nations, and so on.

Process

There are two fundamental varieties of the process strategy. One may be called *instructional* (how to do it) and the other *informational* (how something works). After reading a well-structured process paper entitled "How To Make Your Own Terrarium," you should indeed be able to make your own terrarium. However, after reading an equally well-structured process paper entitled "The Miracle of Photosynthesis," you are not expected to be able to stand in the sun and produce oxygen. However, you should understand how trees and green plants do it.

When using the process strategy in papers of your own, first decide which process you intend to use. More often than not, combining the two confuses the reader about the intent of the paper. Both types may be either *technical* or *nontechnical*. Papers entitled "How To Make Your Own Terrarium" and "The Miracle of Photosynthesis" would both be technical, whereas a process paper entitled "How To Spend a Three-Day Weekend in Chicago" will most likely be nontechnical. Similarly, a paper entitled "How To Mat and Frame a Watercolor" will be technical, whereas a paper entitled "How Hitler Rose to Power" will be nontechnical.

Because the process strategy, much like the narrative strategy, operates in a chronological pattern, make sure that your own process papers include an adequate number of time-indicating transitions: "first," "next," "after a while," "later on," "when ready," and so on. It is also a good practice to include a thesis statement that clearly shows a process will follow: "Making a terrarium is not as difficult as you may think." Following the thesis statement, list all the equipment, material, or ingredients needed to do the job—in sentence form—and then get on with telling your readers how to make the terrarium.

Cause/Effect

The cause/effect strategy seeks to show a link between events or situations, between forces or influences, and results or consequences. More often than not, papers featuring this strategy will focus on multiple causes producing a single effect or multiple effects resulting from a single cause. For example, a paper beginning with the thesis statement "Stress, an ailment that more and more people seem to be suffering from, can be caused by many things" will go on to discuss the many possible causes of stress. By contrast, a paper beginning with the thesis statement "Medical experts have now clearly established that cigarette smoking is harmful in more ways than one" will go on to discuss many of the harmful effects of cigarette smoking. Thus, a cause/effect paper presenting multiple causes will likely begin with the statement of a single effect. Conversely, a cause/effect paper presenting multiple effects will likely begin with the statement of a single cause.

Another way to distinguish between these two varieties of the cause/effect strategy is to understand that the question *why?* provokes a single effect and *what if?* a single cause. For example, to answer the question "*Why* do fools fall in love?" you would present all the reasons (multiple causes) that fools do indeed fall in love (the single effect). Conversely, to answer the question "*What* would happen *if* we lived on bread and water for a month?" you would present all the results (multiple effects) of living on such a diet (the single cause).

Definition

A paper developed by the strategy of definition explains what something means. Usually, the "something" is a difficult or complex word or expression: *autism, underclass, parapsychology, CAD, political correctness, deconstructionism, charisma, pogrom, plate tectonics, carcinogen,* and so on. However, it is usually a waste of time to use definition to explain such items as a *street,* a *rainy day,* or a *shower curtain;* most people will already know what the items mean. There is no question or confusion about them.

The briefest type of definition is the *synonym.* A synonym is a word with nearly the same meaning as another word. For example, *large* is a synonym for *big.* But because synonyms seldom have exactly the same meaning, they are of limited value to the strategy of definition. To call New York City the "*Large* Apple" isn't quite the same as calling it the "*Big* Apple."

The dictionary-type of definition is called a *formal definition.* Such a definition begins by placing the term being defined into a class of some sort and then differentiating the term from all other possible members of that class. For example, a formal definition of the word *cathedral* might read as follows: "A cathedral is a church that contains the official throne of a bishop." Thus, the word *cathedral* is first placed into a class called a church. Then it is differentiated from all churches that do not house "the official throne of a bishop." Similarly, the word *church* might be formally defined as "a building of public worship among Christians." First, it is placed into a class of "building[s] of public worship." Then the phrase "among Christians" differentiates *church* from, say, *synagogue* or *mosque.*

Although both synonyms and formal definitions may contribute to the structure of a definition paper, it is what we call *extended definition* that is at the heart of the strategy of definition. Of all the strategies discussed (excluding analogy), extended definition is probably the most complex, although not necessarily the most difficult to use. The main reason for this complexity is that extended definition must make use of one or more, and sometimes several, of the other organizational strategies. Unlike the other strategies, definition does not have its own pattern of development. Thus, if you are writing an extended definition of the word *kitsch,* you might begin with a formal definition, apply synonyms wherever possible, establish several separate categories, and list a variety of specific examples of each.

Also useful to the strategy of extended definition is the *etymological definition.* An etymological definition defines a word by explaining its origin and structural parts. Here is a combined formal and etymological definition of the word *pathogen:*

> Pathogens are organisms, usually microscopic, that produce diseases. The word *pathogen* comes from the Greek root *pathos,* meaning "suffering," and the combining form *gen,* which means "something that produces." Putting these parts together tells us that pathogens are something that produces suffering, the "something" being parasitic microorganisms.

Revising

At the beginning of our discussion of the writing process, we said that "for convenience" we were going to divide the process into three phrases: (1) pre-writing, (2) drafting, and (3) revising. This was done for convenience because the truth is that revision occurs throughout the writing process, even during the pre-writing phase when we are scribbling notes down during brainstorming activities, or writing topics and arranging them visually in mapping exercises. Even then, we are unable to keep ourselves from erasing things and changing them. The fact that erasers wear out much faster than pencils is evidence that revision is a constant part of writing. In fact, the word processor was developed specifically to allow people to revise *as* they write.

The word *revise* is composed of the Latin prefix *re-*, meaning "back" or "again," and the Latin root *vis,* meaning "to see" or "to survey." Quite literally, then, to revise is to look again (with a critical eye) at what you have already written—whether it is a few sentences, several paragraphs, or a draft of an entire paper. In fact, you may do several drafts of the same paper and revise every one of them. And the intention each time is to improve what has gone before. Ernest Hemingway (1899–1961), an American novelist, short-story writer, and winner of the Nobel prize for literature, is supposed to have revised the short story "A Clean, Well-Lighted Place" more than a hundred times before it was published.

The Revision Process

What is the first step in the process of revising a draft? As with most things, the first step is in the mind. It involves realizing that your paper could be improved upon in some way.

The second step involves rereading the paper, but this is not a casual reading—you have specific goals in mind. For example, you want to identify what is good about what you have already written and what could be improved. Identifying the strengths of your paper is important because revision that discards or dilutes good material is not helpful. On the other hand, being unwilling to admit that certain parts or qualities of your paper are not as effective as they should be is also not helpful. Sometimes it takes a certain amount of courage to admit (even to yourself) that something you have worked very hard on is not all it might be.

Other goals of your reading include an evaluation of how well you have handled the two important considerations discussed in the introduction to the writing process: *purpose* and *audience.*

Purpose

Purpose, as you will recall, is your personal goal in writing a particular piece. It is what you hope to accomplish, the overall design governing everything you do throughout the writing process. It may be to entertain or amuse, to inform or explain, or to convince or persuade. It may also be a combination of these. As you reread the piece—with as objective an eye as possible—you will want to note whether or not your purpose is clearly stated by the thesis statement. If it isn't, the purpose is likely to be vague and indistinct, left for the reader to ponder or guess at. You will also want to note whether or not your paper presents a clear and recognizable organizational strategy that works to support your purpose. We have studied ten of these strategies; keep in mind that when they are applied in combinations an almost infinite variety of prose patterns becomes available to you.

Audience

One good technique for reading your paper to evaluate its effectiveness for an intended audience is to pretend that you are a member of that audience yourself. You may also want to read aloud. Some writers even record their reading and then listen to the tape several times as a member of an audience would hear the presentation. Of course, you might ask a member of your intended audience either to read your paper or to listen to you read it and then give you some reactions and suggestions.

Perhaps the most important reading check of your paper in connection with audience has to do with manners. The question is whether or not your paper has good manners or bad manners. A paper that offends its intended audience has bad manners. Some people would even argue that a paper that offends any audience has bad manners. Trying to accommodate this latter standard, I fear, would render all of us mute on any topic of substance. But you really must accommodate the former; it simply makes no sense to offend the very readers you wish to reach. Going to all the trouble of writing a paper that offends its intended audience is much like a big corporation spending tens of millions of dollars to open, say, a huge retail furniture store and then insulting the customers when they show up to buy things. What student writers need to understand here is that offense does not have to be given to be taken. Reader are sometimes offended when we had no intention of offending. We had no idea that our words might be read in such a way as to perceive insult. Thus, to some extent at least, it is necessary to be able to imagine ourselves as members of our audience when we write. We must be careful with expressions associated with ethnicity, gender, age, physical appearance, education, religion, disabilities, social class, occupation, sexual orientation, level of intelligence, and so on. We should try to be civil when we write.

The third step in the revision process is actually a return to the drafting phase of the writing process. Having carefully read your paper through for all the reasons we have now described, you then incorporate the necessary changes into the paper. This is necessary if your paper is to be all that it can be. Finally, you must perform the last step in the revision process: editing.

Editing

The goal of editing is to make your paper correct in terms of diction and usage, mechanical conventions, and commonly occurring sentence problems. These items, of course, are the topics of instruction in Part One, Part Two, and Part Three of *Sentence Basics*. The more thoroughly you understand the material covered in the nine chapters that make up these three parts, the better job of editing you will be able to do. This time your rereading of the paper is called *proofreading*. When you proofread, you look for errors. When you edit a sentence, you change it in such a way that the errors it contained are removed. You must proofread and edit every sentence in your paper; that is, if you want it to be as good as it can be.

Appendix

The Parts of Speech

The "parts of speech" are the eight grammatical categories into which words are placed primarily according to their functions in sentences.

Nouns

A noun is a word that names something, such as a person, place, thing, idea, or quality. Types of nouns include ***proper nouns,*** which name particular people, places, or things (*Angela, Chicago, Big Ben*); ***collective nouns,*** which name groups of some sort (*committee, squad, congregation*); ***mass nouns,*** which name things that do not usually have plural forms (*courage, peace, dust*); and ***compound nouns,*** which are made up of two or more words func-
noun (*thunderstorm, man-of-war, sunflower, go-between*). Nouns are often
ences by noun determiners (*a/an, the, my, our, your, their*) and display char-
ndings, such as *-ary* (*missionary*), *-ation* (*starvation*), *-ment* (*government*),
and *-ship* (*citizenship*).

Pronouns

A pronoun is a word that substitutes for a noun. ***Personal pronouns***—all forms of *I, you, he, she, it, we,* and *they*—substitute for specific persons or things. (*They* are the players on the visiting team.) **Demonstrative pronouns**—*this, that, these,* and *those*—are used as substitutes for things being pointed out. (Doesn't everyone prefer *these* to *those*?) **Indefinite pronouns**—e.g., *all, another, anybody, both, each, everyone, few, most, none, nothing*—are used to substitute for unspecified things. (Has *anyone* found the buried treasure yet?) **Relative pronouns**—*who, whom, whose, whoever, whomever, which, whichever, that, what, whatever*—introduce dependent adjective clauses and substitute for the word to which they refer in the main part of the sentence. (This is the house *that* thirty years of saving my money built.) **Interrogative pronouns**—*who, whom, whose, which, what*—ask questions. (*Who* was the first man to walk on the moon?)

Verbs

A verb is a word that expresses an action (*jump, run, walk*), a state of being (*is, am, are, was, were*), or an occurrence (*become, evolve, suffer*). Verbs have five fundamental forms:

Base Form	-S Form	Present Participle	Past Tense	Past Participle
abridge	abridges	abridging	abridged	abridged
bite	bites	biting	bit	bitten
come	comes	coming	came	come

The **base form** is listed in the dictionary and used with plural nouns as well as the pronouns *I, we, you,* and *they* to denote present time or some continuous action. Accompanied by the marker *to*, the base form of the verb may also function as a noun, an adjective, or an adverb. (*To win* was her goal. Ted's attempt *to fly* was a disaster. The prisoners struggled *to escape*.)

The **-s form** is composed of the base form plus *-s* or *-es*. It indicates the present tense and is used with all singular nouns, the third-person singular pronouns *he, she,* and *it*, and such indefinite pronouns as *another, each, either, neither, anything, someone,* and *everybody*. (This picture *does* nothing for me. He who *pays* the piper *calls* the tune. Neither of the teams *shoots* well.)

The **present participle form** is constructed by adding *-ing* to the base form. When used alone, it may function as an adjective or a noun. When combined with such auxiliary verbs as *am, is, are, was,* or *were*, it forms what are called progressive tenses. (Alas, the *failing* economy is no better. *Eating* is one of John's passions. Isabel *is losing* her battle with the Internal Revenue Service.)

The **past tense form** is used to indicate action that occurred at some time in the past. With most verbs, the past tense is formed by adding *-d* or *-ed* to the base form. Some verbs, however, form the past tense in irregular ways, and are thus called irregular verbs. (Nolan *completed* the task in record time. I *knew* Ann when she was in high school. We *began* by blessing the boat.)

With regular verbs, the **past participle form** is the same as that of the past tense. However, with some irregular verbs, the form is different from that of the past tense—e.g., *bite/bit/bitten, come/came/come, go/went/gone, drink/drank/drunk*. When used alone, the past participle form may function as an adjective. (Life is filled with *blown* opportunities. The *stolen* items were never recovered.) The past participle form combines with certain auxiliary verbs to form what are called perfect tenses: (1) present perfect, (2) past perfect, and (3) future perfect. The present perfect tense combines *have* or *has* with the past participle; the past perfect tense combines *had* with the past participle; and the future perfect tense combines *shall have* or *will have* with the past participle. (We *have driven* this road many times. By the third inning, we *had lost* the game. By the time I am fifty, I *shall have been* on this job for thirty years.)

Adjectives

An adjective is a word that modifies (restricts the meaning of) a noun or pronoun, usually by describing it, defining it, or quantifying it. (*Red* cars attract *angry* bulls. Only a *few* times did I enjoy the *stressful* work. Only the *strongest* climbers made it to the top.)

Adverbs

An adverb is a word that modifies any type of word other than a noun, but most often verbs, adjectives, or other adverbs. (Tim *frequently* studies at the kitchen table. You made a *pointedly* unpleasant remark. Make these decisions *very* carefully.)

Conjunctions

A conjunction is a word that joins other words, phrases, or clauses. ***Coordinating conjunctions***—*and, but, or, nor, for, yet,* and *so*—join items of equivalent grammatical construction; that is, nouns and nouns, prepositions and prepositions, clauses and clauses. (He was tough *yet* gentle. We went to the mountains *and* the seashore. His ideas were easy to parody, *but* they were difficult to improve upon.) ***Correlative conjunctions***—*neither . . . nor, either . . . or, not only . . . but also, both . . . and, not . . . but*—are much like coordinating conjunctions, except that they are used in pairs. (*Both* hill *and* dale resounded. She was *neither* tall *nor* thin. He was *not* of an age, *but* for all times.) ***Subordinating conjunctions***—e.g., *after, although, as, as if, as though, because, before, even though, if, in order that, rather than, since, so that, unless, until, when, while*—join clauses that are not of equal rank in the sentence. The clause introduced by the subordinating conjunction is called a dependent or subordinate clause. (*Since* you went away, I have been lonesome. *If* I were you, I would study more. We won the tournament *because* we were better prepared.) ***Conjunctive adverbs***—e.g., *accordingly, consequently, finally, furthermore, however, moreover, nevertheless, otherwise, therefore*—join independent clauses not joined by one of the coordinating conjunctions. (You overstated your case; *moreover*, some of your data was suspect. Ian's picture won first prize; *however*, it did not bring the highest bid.)

Prepositions

A preposition is a word—e.g., *about, across, around, before, below, during, for, in, into, on, through, toward, under, upon, with, without*—that forms a phrase with a noun or pronoun. The entire phrase usually functions as an adjective or adverb, modifying the word that the preposition connects its own object to. (Your friendship *with* the best people has been noted. The boy has gone *on* an errand *for* his mother. The scent *of* lilies was *in* the air. Bombs fell *in* our vicinity *for* several days. What did you decide *upon*?)

Interjections

An interjection is a word (or group of words) that is grammatically independent of its surroundings and used to denote feelings or sudden emotion. Mild interjections that occur at the beginning of a sentence are followed by a comma. Otherwise, most interjections are followed by an exclamation point. (*Alas*, we have eaten our last melon of the season. *Oh*, we are very late. At last came the order—*Charge*!)

Index of Diction and Usage

ask a question, 25–26
aspect, 26
assistance/assistants, 93
assure/ensure/insure, 194
attendance/attendants, 93
auger/augur, 93
author, 26
awesome, 26
awful/very, 194
awhile/a while, 197

baal/bail/bale, 93
bad/badly, 197
balance, 29
bald/balled/bawled, 93
balm/bomb, 94
band/banned, 94
bard/barred, 94
baron/barren, 94
bazaar/bizarre, 94
beach/beech, 97
bear/bare, 97
beat/beet, 97
because/cause, 197
been/bin, 97
beer/bier, 97
being as/being that, 29
belief/believe, 197
benefactor/beneficiary, 197
benign/malign, 197
berry/bury, 97
berth/birth, 97
beside/besides, 197
be sure to/be sure and, 29
better had, 29
better than/more than, 197
biannual/biennial, 198
bisect/dissect, 198
bit/bitten, 190
blew/blue, 97
bloc/block, 97
boar/bore, 98
boarder/border, 98
bode/bowed, 98
bolder/boulder, 98
bored, 29
born/borne, 98
borough/burro/burrow, 101
boughten, 29
bouillon/bullion, 98
brake/break, 101
bread/bred, 101
breath/breathe, 198
brewed/brood, 101
bridal/bridle, 101
bring/take, 198
broach/brooch, 101

broke, 29
bunch/group, 201
burglarize/burgle, 29
burley/burly, 101
burst/bust, 30
but that/but what, 30
but yet/still yet, 30
buy/by/bye, 101

callous/callus, 102
canapé/canopy, 102
can/may, 201
cannon/canon, 102
cannot (can't) help but, 30
can't/cant, 102
can't hardly, 33
canter/cantor, 102
canvas/canvass, 105
capital/capitol, 105
carrot/caret/carat, 105
carton/cartoon, 201
cash/cache, 105
cast/caste, 105
casual/causal, 201
catholic/Catholic, 201
cause . . . is (was) due to, 33
cause/reason, 201
celebrant/celebrator, 201
cellar/seller, 105
censor/censure, 201
censor/sensor, 105
center on/center around, 33
cent/scent/sent, 105
cereal/serial, 106
ceremonial/ceremonious, 202
cheap/inexpensive, 202
childish/childlike, 202
choral/coral, 106
chorale/corral, 106
cite/sight/site, 106
claim, 33
class, 33
class/category, 202
classical/classic, 202
clause/claws, 106
clench/clinch, 109
click/clique, 109
client/customer, 205
climatic/climactic, 205
close/clothes/cloths, 109
coarse/course, 109
coleslaw/cold slaw, 33
college/university, 205
colonel/kernel, 109
commemorate, 33
complacence/complaisance, 109

complement/compliment, 109
complexioned/complected, 33
comprehensible/comprehensive, 205
comprise/compose, 205
concave/convex, 205
conference, 33–34
confident/confidant, 205
confidently/confidentially, 205–6
conscience/conscious, 206
considerable, 34
consistently/constantly, 206
contemporary, 206
contemptible/contemptuous, 209
continual/continuous, 209
controversial/contentious, 209
convince/persuade, 209
could have/could of, 34
council/counsel, 109
councillor/counselor, 109
couple of, 34
courier/currier, 110
covert/overt, 209
coward/cowered, 110
creak/creek/crick, 110
credible/creditable, 209
creditor/debtor, 209
crevice/crevasse, 110
criteria/criterion, 209
cubical/cubicle, 110
cue/queue, 113
currant/current, 113
cute, 34

dairy/diary, 113
date/datum, 209
dear/deer, 113
decent/descent, 113
decisive/incisive, 210
decriminalize/legalize, 210
deduce/deduct, 210
defective/deficient, 210
definite/definitive, 210
denote/connote, 213
dependence/dependents, 113
depravation/deprivation, 113
deprecate/depreciate, 213
descent/dissent, 113
desert/dessert, 114
device/devise, 213
dew/do/due, 114
diagnosis/prognosis, 213
die/dye, 114
different from/different than, 37

Index

449

Instructor's Manual to Accompany

ELLIOTT L. SMITH

BLYTHE M. SMITH

SENTENCE BASICS

DICTION, USAGE, AND MECHANICS

INSTRUCTOR'S MANUAL
to accompany

SENTENCE BASICS
Diction, Usage,
and Mechanics

Elliott L. Smith
Ferris State University

Blythe M. Smith

St. Martin's Press   New York

For information, write:
St. Martin's Press, Inc.
175 Fifth Avenue
New York, NY 10010

ISBN: 0-312-09563-5

Preface

The intent of this manual is to help make the instructor's use of *Sentence Basics: Diction, Usage, and Mechanics* as profitable as possible. To this end, the manual is organized into two main parts. Part One presents the answers to all exercises whose answers do not appear in the text. These exercises include (1) the fifty-seven instructional sequences treating diction and usage in Chapters 2, 3, and 4; (2) the review exercises appearing at the conclusion of Chapters 2, 3, 4, 6, 7, 8, and 9; (3) the eleven punctuation and mechanics exercises positioned throughout Chapters 6 and 7; and (4) the nine sentence error and sentence editing exercises appearing in Chapters 8 and 9.

Part Two presents additional exercises—they may be used as quizzes or tests—to accompany the text. These include five exercises treating "Nonstandard or Inappropriate Expressions" for Chapter 2, seven exercises treating "Words That Sound Alike" for Chapter 3, seven exercises treating "Important Distinctions" for Chapter 4, and ten Sentence Error Identification Exercises for Chapters 8 and 9. Answers to all these exercises appear at the end of the manual.

New books become better books as a result of suggestions made by instructors who use them in the classroom. Likewise, new instructor's manuals become better instructor's manuals as a result of suggestions made by instructors who regularly test their materials on diverse student groups. If, as you are using either *Sentence Basics* or this manual that accompanies *Sentence Basics*, you have suggestions about how either might be improved in future editions, please communicate your suggestions to me:

Elliott L. Smith, Professor
Department of Languages and Literature
Ferris State University
Big Rapids, MI 49307-2295
Telephone: (616) 592-2522

Contents

PART ONE
ANSWERS TO TEXT EXERCISES

Chapter 2 Nonstandard or Inappropriate Expressions

Nonstandard or Inappropriate Expressions (1)   [pages 23–24]

FILL-IN: 1. about, 2. isn't, 3. particularly, 4. man accused of rape, 5. a lot, 6, across, 7. nearly, 8. about, 9. admit, 10. accidentally, 11. Achilles' heel, 12. all right, 13. a number of, 14. apologize, 15. about, 16. woman accused of arson, 17. very, 18. across, 19. almost, 20. often, 21. aren't, 22. accidentally, 23. about, 24. Achilles tendon, 25. particularly, 26. excuse, 27. all right, 28. a lot, 29. contend, 30. about

Nonstandard or Inappropriate Expressions (2)   [pages 27–28]

FILL-IN: 1. somewhere, 2. afraid, 3. anyway, 4. written, 5. as far as, 6. impressive, 7. in the morning, 8. posed, 9. anywhere, 10. as happy as, 11. trait, 12. analysis, 13. scared, 14. and, 15. any way, 16. or, 17. compose, 18. any way, 19. feature, 20. as far as, 21. anywhere, 22. inquire, 23. exciting, 24. in the evening, 25. anywhere, 26. as fast as, 27. steps, 28. analysis, 29. fearful, 30. somewhere

Nonstandard or Inappropriate Expressions (3)   [pages 31–32]

FILL-IN: 1. because, 2. burst, 3. bored with, 4. yet, 5. bought, 6. laughing, 7. rest, 8. burglarize, 9. broken, 10. that, 11. be sure to, 12. but, 13. Because, 14. be sure to, 15. had better, 16. Because, 17. broken, 18. be sure to, 19. realizing, 20. should, 21. that, 22. bored from, 23. burglarized, 24. remainder, 25. still, 26. because, 27. burst, 28. store-bought, 29. thinking, 30. must

Nonstandard or Inappropriate Expressions (4)   [pages 35–36]

FILL-IN: 1. centered on, 2. complexioned, 3. could have, 4. coleslaw, 5. two, 6. can hardly, 7. smart, 8. described, 9. talked, 10. was, 11. can hardly, 12. asserts, 13. complexioned, 14. many, 15. quality, 16. in conferences, 17. revolved around, 18. clever, 19. innovative, 20. coleslaw, 21. can hardly, 22. could have, 23. says, 24. talk, 25. was, 26. several, 27. quite a few, 28. centered on, 29. insisted, 30. comment

Nonstandard or Inappropriate Expressions (5)   [pages 39–40]

FILL-IN: 1. has decided not, 2. equally, 3. doubtful whether, 4. enthusiastic, 5. cannot remember, 6. drowned, 7. escape, 8. different from, 9. Even though, 10. just as, 11. contrary to, 12. same, 13. different from what, 14. were it not that, 15. doubts that, 16. drowned, 17. same, 18. but, 19. don't recommend, 20 opposite, 21. escaping, 22. different from, 23. even though, 24. forget, 25. as, 26. doubt whether, 27. enthusiastic, 28. different from how, 29. everywhere, 30. doubted that

Nonstandard or Inappropriate Expressions (6) [pages 43–44]

FILL-IN: 1. carefree, 2. woman, 3. gratis, 4. concluded, 5. skill, 6. for nothing, 7. function, 8. woman, 9. elements, 10. free, 11. fantasy, 12. bizarre, 13. thought, 14. invigorating, 15. flustered, 16. judge, 17. gift, 18. complete, 19. gratis, 20. Competence, 21. circumstance, 22. frustrated, 23. at no cost, 24. component, 25. unusual, 26. fantasy, 27. nostalgic, 28. woman, 29. function, 30. expected

Nonstandard or Inappropriate Expressions (7) [pages 47–48]

FILL-IN: 1. raise, 2. had better, 3. himself, 4. many, 5. heartrending, 6. hold, 7. have to, 8. himself, 9. women, 10. home in on, 11. suppose, 12. height, 13. We hope, 14. should, 15. hindrance, 16. himself, 17. person, 18. hold, 19. had better, 20. I hope, 21. greatly, 22. height, 23. hindrance, 24. must, 25. increases, 26. described, 27. suppose; humorous, 28. himself, 29. heartrending, 30. should

Nonstandard or Inappropriate Expressions (8) [pages 51–52]

FILL-IN: 1. its, 2. communicating, 3. thorough, 4. concerned about, 5. diminish, 6. work together, 7. is the phenomenon wherein, 8. orange, 9. it's, 10. talk to, 11. hit, 12. incidentally, 13. become interested in, 14. If, 15. occurs when, 16. It's, 17. concerned about, 18. if, 19. hurt, 20. detailed, 21. communicate with, 22. occurs when, 23. green, 24. in the event, 25. broadens, 26. incidentally, 27. its, 2 8. get along with, 29. is created when, 30. affect

Nonstandard or Inappropriate Expressions (9) [pages 55–56]

FILL-IN: 1. knots, 2. like, 3. may have, 4. man, 5. almost, 6. serious, 7. most, 8. motivate, 9. memento, 10. fluent, 11. boys; girls, 12. may have, 13. rather, 14. might have, 15. most, 16. in a manner of speaking, 17. could have, 18. muffle, 19. most, 20. persuasive, 21. like, 22. mementos, 23. eloquent, 24. install fountains in, 25. man, 26. may have, 27. mildly, 28. symbolic, 29. nautical miles, 30. fellow

Nonstandard or Inappropriate Expressions (10) [pages 59–60]

FILL-IN: 1. More than, 2. I, 3. must have, 4. might, 5. old-fashioned, 6. minuscule, 7. negative, 8. open, 9. better, 10. friendly, 11. off, 12. preferable to, 13. nowhere, 14. because of, 15. better, 16. negative, 17. from, 18. must have, 19. most enjoyable, 20. chose, 21. minuscule, 22. old-fashioned, 23. me, 24. might, 25. more, 26. quit, 27. preferable, 28. nowhere, 29. more than, 30. off

Nonstandard or Inappropriate Expressions (11) [pages 63–64]

FILL-IN: 1. significant, 2. history, 3. because, 4. furthermore, 5. partners, 6. counterfeit, 7. orient, 8. end, 9. phenomenon, 10. reproduction, 11. ourselves, 12. Except for, 13. because, 14. insecure, 15. very, 16. over, 17. plus, 18. tense, 19. over, 20. oriented, 21. because, 22. very, 23. partners, 24. ourselves, 25. phenomenon, 26. except for, 27. disingenuous, 28. creditable, 29. moreover, 30. history

Nonstandard or Inappropriate Expressions (12)   [pages 67–68]

FILL-IN: 1. following sentence, 2. publicly, 3. very, 4. prejudiced, 5. preventive, 6. prophesy, 7. time, 8. fact, 9. moderately, 10. almost never, 11. sick, 12. that, 13. now, 14. publicly, 15. Before, 16. prejudice, 17. Rarely if ever, 18. point, 19. soon, 20. before; had developed, 21. that, 22. when, 23. publicly, 24. preventive, 25. prophesy, 26. ill, 27. before, 28. quite, 29. true, 30. preceding

Nonstandard or Inappropriate Expressions (13)   [pages 71–72]

FILL-IN: 1. relevant, 2. because, 3. somewhere, 4. reason, 5. sneaked, 6. dormitories, 7. saving, 8. almost never, 9. presume, 10. participating, 11. Regardless, 12. somewhat, 13. understand, 14. should have, 15. showing, 16. appreciate, 17. should have, 18. seldom if ever, 19. somewhere, 20. reason that, 21. relevant, 22. remove, 23. sneaked; ourselves, 24. think, 25. a little, 26. regardless, 27. because, 28. enjoy, 29. tell, 30. saving

Nonstandard or Inappropriate Expressions (14)   [pages 75–76]

FILL-IN: 1. themselves; quite, 2. facts, 3. think, 4. through, 5. What, 6. workable, 7. supposed to, 8. use, 9. try to, 10. We were thankful that, 11. thus, 12. until, 13. who, 14. nevertheless, 15. such as, 16. Until, 17. nevertheless, 18. Everyone was grateful that, 19. possible choice, 20. facts, 21. such as, 22. what, 23. thinks, 24. through, 25. try to, 26. supposed to, 27. thus, 28. themselves, 29. using, 30. who

Nonstandard or Inappropriate Expressions (15)   [pages 79–80]

FILL-IN: 1. thunderous, 2. why, 3. until, 4. researched, 5. infrequent, 6. would have, 7. like, 8. In terms of quality, 9. woman, 10. weary, 11. provoked, 12. starved, 13. unless, 14. You; unless, 15. happened, 16. until, 17. in terms of word selection, 18. unless, 19. caused, 20. competent artist, 21. repaired, 22. would have, 23. took place, 24. Why is Stanley, 25. exhausted, 26. you, 27. for a vacation, 28. like, 29. infrequent, 30. was void of

Review for Nonstandard or Inappropriate Expressions   [pages 81–86]

FILL-IN: 1. a lot, 2. accidentally, 3. across, 4. all right, 5. very, 6. almost, 7. afraid, 8. anywhere, 9. as far as, 10. analysis, 11. feature, 12. wrote, 13. be sure to, 14. Because, 15. bought, 16. burglarized, 17. that, 18. wondering, 19. can hardly, 20. centered on, 21. asserted, 22. complexioned, 23. large, 24. could have, 25. different from, 26. contrary to, 27. forget, 28. doubts that, 29. drowned, 30. enthusiastic, 31. just as, 32. escape, 33. Even though, 34. competence, 35. woman, 36. concluded, 37. frustrated, 38. good, 39. function, 40. unusual, 41. must, 42. should, 43. heartrending, 44. height, 45. hindrance, 46. pinpoint, 47. affected, 48. incidentally, 49. extensive, 50. talk, 51. interested in, 52. occurs when, 53. its, 54. inebriate, 55. a bit, 56. fluent, 57. most, 58. men, 59. may have, 60. memento, 61. minuscule, 62. preferable to, 63. negative, 64. might, 65. old-fashioned, 66. because of, 67. chose, 68. orient, 69. because, 70. uneasy, 71. partner, 72. counterfeit, 73. moreover, 74. when, 75. prejudiced, 76. soon, 77. preventive, 78. before, 79. publicly, 80. almost never, 81. reason that, 82. Regardless, 83. enjoy, 84. removed, 85. have, 86. slightly, 87. supposed to, 88. themselves, 89. think, 90. through, 91. try to, 92. use, 93. workable, 94. occurred, 95. like, 96. infrequent, 97. why, 98. for Halloween, 99. world traveler, 100. would have

Chapter 3 Words That Sound Alike

Words That Sound Alike (1) [pages 91–92]

FILL-IN: 1. adherents, 2. allowed, 3. adolescents, 4. altar, 5. alley, 6. antidote, 7. Acclimation, 8. ail, 9. aide, 10. aides, 11. annalist, 12. ascetic, 13. allusions, 14. enunciate, 15. edition, 16. ale, 17. adherence, 18. ally, 19. alter, 20 acclamation, 21. elusion, 22. aid, 23. aloud, 24. acetic, 25. analyst, 26. illusion, 27. addition, 28. anecdotes, 29. isle, 30. adolescence

Words That Sound Alike (2) [pages 95–96]

FILL-IN: 1. ascent, 2. attendants, 3. balm, 4. band, 5. augur, 6. bawled, 7. bazaar; bizarre, 8. aunt, 9. bard, 10. assent, 11. anti-, 12. baron, 13. ark, 14. assistance, 15. bale, 16. attendance, 17. bail, 18. assistants, 19. ants, 20. barren, 21. auger, 22. bomb, 23. antecedent, 24. barred, 25. bizarre, 26. arced, 27. assent, 28. bald, 29. banned, 30. assistants

Words That Sound Alike (3) [pages 99–100]

FILL-IN: 1. birth, 2. blew, 3. bier, 4. bode, 5. border, 6. beach, 7. bouillon, 8. bury, 9. bolder, 10. bare, 11. bloc, 12. beets, 13. borne, 14. bin, 15. bore, 16. bear, 17. boarder, 18. bullion, 19. berth, 20. boulder, 21. berry, 22. beech, 23. beer, 24. blocks, 25. bear, 26. bowed, 27. born, 28. beat, 29. blue, 30. been

Words That Sound Alike (4) [pages 103–104]

FILL-IN: 1. brewed, 2. burly, 3. bridal, 4. callus, 5. brooch, 6. canter, 7. borough, 8. by, 9. canons, 10. break, 11. buy, 12. bred, 13. canapé, 14. brood, 15. can't, 16. brake, 17. bye, 18. cantor, 19. bread, 20. cant, 21. bridle, 22. cannon, 23. broach, 24. bread; by, 25. burrow, 26. callous, 27. brood, 28. Burley, 29. canopy, 30. burro

Words That Sound Alike (5) [pages 107–108]

FILL-IN: 1. cache, 2. scent, 3. site, 4. cast, 5. corral, 6. canvas, 7. claws, 8. sensor, 9. cast, 10. capital, 11. serial, 12. choral, 13. carets, 14. seller, 15. sent, 16. capital, 17. sight, 18. carat, 19. chorale, 20. cent, 21. cite, 22. canvass, 23. censor, 24. cereal, 25. capitol, 26. clause, 27. carrots, 28. caste, 29. coral, 30. cellar

Words That Sound Alike (6) [pages 111–112]

FILL-IN: 1 course, 2. creak, 3. colonel, 4. cowered, 5. councillors, 6. cubicles, 7. click, 8. counsel, 9. couriers, 10. creek, 11. clinched, 12. complement, 13. crevasse, 14. clothes, 15. complacence, 16. close, 17. crevices, 18. coarse, 19. currier, 20. clenched, 21. compliment, 22. complaisance, 23. coward, 24. clique, 25. counselors, 26. cubicals, 27. kernel, 28. crick, 29. council, 30. cloths

Words That Sound Alike (7)   [pages 115–116]

FILL-IN: 1. deer, 2. do, 3. discreet, 4. depravation, 5. dye, 6. dual, 7. queue, 8. decent, 9. urn, 10. current, 11. dependence, 12. dissent, 13. desert, 14. indiscreet, 15. diary, 16. dairy, 17. descent, 18. dew, 19. duel, 20. deprivation, 21. die, 22. cue, 23. dissent, 24. earn, 25, currants, 26. dessert, 27. dear, 28. due, 29. discrete, 30. dependents

Words That Sound Alike (8)   [pages 119–120]

FILL-IN: 1. emigrants, 2. exercise, 3. yew, 4. fate, 5. futile, 6. eve, 7. emit, 8. phase, 9. illicit, 10. faint, 11. omit, 12. imminent, 13. feat, 14. immigrate, 15. fare, 16. ewe, 17. fair, 18. fete, 19. immigrants, 20. feet, 21. fare, 22. eve, 23. faze, 24. fainted, 25. elicit, 26. exorcise, 27. eminent, 28. feinted, 29. feudal, 30. omit

Words That Sound Alike (9)   [pages 123–124]

FILL-IN: 1. flea, 2. fourth, 3. flourescence, 4. flour, 5. forecast, 6. foreword, 7. flare, 8. gamble, 9. fiancée, 10. foul, 11. fore, 12. filter, 13. forward, 14. flow, 15. gaits, 16. flair, 17. flower, 18. florescence, 19. four; for, 20. gambol, 2 1. fiancé, 22. fowl, 23. forward, 24. philter, 25. foul, 26. gate, 27. flee, 28. fryer, 29. floe, 30. forth

Words That Sound Alike (10)   [pages 127–128]

FILL-IN: 1. gored, 2. haul, 3. halve, 4. groan, 5. jell, 6. grisly, 7. guerrillas, 8. Hail, 9. handmaid, 10. hairy, 11. gilled, 12. haled, 13. hair, 14. guilt, 15. gristly, 16. grizzly, 17. harebrained, 18. gel, 19. hale, 20. Gorillas, 21. grown, 22. have, 23. Guild, 24. harry, 25. Handmade, 26. gourd, 27. hall, 28. gild, 29. hare, 30. gilt

Words That Sound Alike (11)   [pages 131–132]

FILL-IN: 1. here, 2. hour; our, 3. heard, 4. wholly, 5. hew, 6. hybrid, 7. hangar, 8. hostile, 9. hue, 10. hearty, 11. heard; herd, 12. hoard, 13. heel, 14. holey, 15. heroine, 16. hearty, 17. highbred, 18. horde; kernel, 19. heal, 20. our; hourglass, 21. heroin, 22. hangers, 23. hoarse, 24. hostel, 25. hardy, 26. hue, 27. hear, 28. horse, 29. herd, 30. holy

Words That Sound Alike (12)   [pages 135–136]

FILL-IN: 1. indiscrete, 2. knight, 3. knave; nave, 4. insight, 5. lien, 6. kneed, 7. lather, 8. hurdle, 9. leak, 10. knave, 11. leaches, 12. idol, 13. lessen, 14. levee, 15. need, 16. lesson, 17. ladder, 18. incite, 19. nightly, 20. nave, 21. lean, 22. indiscreet, 23. latter, 24. hurtle, 25. leeks, 26. idle, 27. leeches, 28. knead, 29. levy, 30. idyll

Words That Sound Alike (13)   [pages 139–140]

FILL-IN: 1. loan, 2. maze, 3. maul, 4. lute, 5. mail, 6. mane, 7. mantel, 8. liable, 9. martial, 10. made, 11. manor, 12. lightning, 13. magnate, 14. marry, 15. load, 16. loot, 17. male, 18. maid, 19. maize, 20. mantle, 21. libel, 22. main, 23. magnet, 24. merry, 25. lightening, 26. marshal, 27. manner, 28. lode, 29. mall, 30. mall

Words That Sound Alike (14)   [pages 143–144]

FILL-IN: 1. mettle, 2. miners; minor, 3. nape, 4. mustered, 5. mien, 6. morn, 7. meet, 8. moose, 9. mown, 10. material, 11. metal, 12. meat, 13. mite, 14. muscle, 15. mewl, 16. might, 17. mourn, 18. medal, 19. mute, 20. mustard, 21. materiel, 22. moan, 23. minor, 24. nap, 25. mousse, 26. mean, 27. moot, 28. mete, 29. mussel, 30. meddle

Words That Sound Alike (15)   [pages 147–148]

FILL-IN: 1. ore, 2. parish, 3. past, 4. none, 5. pane, 6. ordnance, 7. overate, 8. parlayed, 9. navel, 10. pair, 11. overdue, 12. nay, 13. pear, 14. parity, 15. nee, 16. oar, 17. overrate, 18. ordinance, 19. perish, 20. passed, 21. naval, 22. parley, 23. or, 24. pain, 25. neigh, 26. overdo, 27. parody, 28. nun, 29. pare, 30. outright

Words That Sound Alike (16)   [pages 151–152]

FILL-IN: 1. pedal, 2. penance, 3. peer, 4. peak, 5. plumb, 6. peeled, 7. plane, 8. peace, 9. poll, 10. plodder, 11. pedal, 12. plastique, 13. pour, 14. plains, 15. peek, 16. peal, 17. plotter, 18. pore, 19. plastic, 20. pier, 21. plum; peeled, 22. piece, 23. pique, 24. pennants, 25. plain, 26. peddle, 27. pole, 28. peer, 29. plastic, 30. poor; pour

Words That Sound Alike (17)   [pages 155–156]

FILL-IN: 1. principal, 2. wrest, 3. profits, 4. premiere, 5. real, 6. populous, 7. residence, 8. rein, 9. pray, 10. razed, 11. principle, 12. quite, 13. rapport, 14. reek, 15. presents, 16. beach, 17. report, 18. reign, 19. reel, 20. presence, 21. wreak, 22. residents, 23. profit, 24. populace, 25. principle, 26. raises, 27. prey, 28. rest, 29. premier, 30. prophets

Words That Sound Alike (18)   [pages 159–160]

FILL-IN: 1. seen, 2. root, 3. skull, 4. salon, 5. rumor, 6. sail, 7. right, 8. seem, 9. rout, 10. wretch, 11. saccharin, 12. write, 13. ringing, 14. rot, 15. rowed, 16. rode, 17. sane, 18. solons, 19. seam, 20. roomer, 21. rite, 22. saccharine, 23. saloon, 24. wrought, 25. scene, 26. road, 27. role, 28. route, 29. roll, 30. review

Words That Sound Alike (19)   [pages 163–164]

FILL-IN: 1. stationary, 2. shone, 3. sleigh, 4. seer; buy, 5. steal, 6. stile, 7. shutter, 8. sole, 9. slight, 10. stayed, 11. surf, 12. soar, 13. stakes, 14. seated, 15. sheer, 16. sear, 17. shown, 18. staid, 19. serf, 20. steak, 21. shear, 22. stare, 23. shudder, 24. soul, 25. style, 26. stationery, 27. steel, 28. sore, 29, slay, 30. seeded

Words That Sound Alike (20)   [pages 167–168]

FILL-IN: 1. there, 2. tide; tide, 3. teem, 4. told, 5. tale, 6. through, 7. strait, 8. sweet, 9. too, 10. summary, 11. taut, 12. trader, 13. suite, 14. team, 15. to, 16. their, 17. tied, 18. timber, 19. two; to, 20. tolled, 21. tail, 22. thyme, 23. straight, 24. traitor, 25. threw. 26. summery; shone, 27. taught, 28. tee; tea, 29. throne, 30. they're

Words That Sound Alike (21)   [pages 171–172]

FILL-IN: 1. vein, 2. vial, 3. Viral, 4. very, 5. vice, 6. wave, 7. waist, 8. vane, 9. veracious, 10. weigh, 11. weight, 12. warn, 13. week, 14. undo, 15. whether, 16. vary, 17. worn, 18. vise; through, 19. way, 20, vain, 21. virile, 22. undue, 23. waive, 24. voracious, 25. wait, 26. waste, 27. weak, 28. troop, 29. weather, 30. vile

Review for Words That Sound Alike   [pages 173–181]

FILL-IN: 1. acclamation, 2. edition, 3. adolescence, 4. isle, 5. illusion, 6. altar, 7. antidote, 8. ark, 9. ascent, 10. assistance, 11. bale, 12. bawled, 13. banned, 14. bizarre, 15. bear, 16. beat, 17. bin, 18. berry, 19. block, 20. border, 21. bolder, 22. burrows, 23. bred, 24. broach, 25. by, 26. callous, 27. canons, 28. canter, 29. canvas, 30. capitol, 31. cellar, 32. sent, 33. corral, 34. site, 35. clause, 36. clinched, 37. clothes, 38. coarse, 39. complement, 40. counselor, 41. creak, 42. cubicles, 43. cue, 44. current, 45. decent, 46. depravation, 47. due, 48. desert, 49. discreet, 50. illicit, 51. immigrate, 52. eminent, 53. exercise, 54. faint, 55. fare, 56. feudal, 57. filter, 58. flare, 59. flea, 60. flower, 61. four, 62. foreword, 63. gamble, 64. guild, 65. gored, 66. guerrillas, 67. grizzly, 68. groan, 69. halve, 70. handmade, 71. hangers, 72. hardy, 73. herd, 74. heroine, 75 highbred, 76. horde, 77. holy, 78. hurdled, 79. idol, 80. insight, 81. need, 82. latter, 83. leak, 84. lesson, 85. liable, 86. load, 87. loot, 88. magnet, 89. main, 90. maze, 91. mall, 92. merry, 93. mean, 94. mete, 95. mettle, 96. mite, 97. moan, 98. mute, 99. mussel, 100. mustard, 101. navel, 102. ore, 103. ordinance, 104. outright, 105. overdue, 106. pain, 107. pare, 108. peace, 109. peel, 110. petal, 111. pennants, 112. plain, 113. plotters, 114. populous, 115. presence, 116. principle, 117. profit, 118. quite, 119. Rein, 120. residence, 121. wretch, 122. write, 123. rode, 124. role, 125. rot, 126. solons, 127. sane, 128. seem, 129. sear, 130. sheer, 131. shudder, 132. slight, 133. sower, 134. stationery, 135. steel, 136. straight, 137. summery, 138. suite, 139. they're, 140. throne, 141. two; too; to, 142. told, 143. undue, 144. vein, 145. vary, 146. voracious, 147. viral, 148. waste, 149. warm, 150. whether

9

Chapter 4   Important Distinctions

Important Distinctions (1)   [pages 187-188]

FILL-IN: 1. access, 2. accused of, 3. effect, 4. agree to, 5. abrogate, 6. an, 7. advice, 8. averse, 9. affect, 10. accede, 11. except, 12. avert, 13. adapt, 14. arrogate, 15. aggravated, 16. advise, 17. addicted, 18. accept, 19. irritated, 20. adopted, 21. affected, 22. advert, 23. a, 24. agree with, 25. an; excess, 26. accused of, 27. effect, 28. an, 29. exceed, 30. adverse

Important Distinctions (2)   [pages 191–192]

FILL-IN: 1. allude, 2. all ways; always, 3. all of, 4. alternative, 5. though, 6. always, 7. tries, 8. among, 9. all ready, 10. altogether, 11. All, 12. between, 13. Although, 14. already, 15. refers, 16. alludes, 17. altogether, 18. always, 19. All of, 20. alternate, 21. though, 22. among, 23. intend, 24. all together, 25. all ways, 26. allude, 27. Between, 28. already, 29. alternative, 30. hope

Important Distinctions (3)   [pages 195–186]

FILL-IN: 1. any more, 2. angle, 3. mad, 4. very, 5. anybody, 6. amoral, 7. very, 8. antipersonnel, 9. appraised, 10. assure, 11. amused, 12. any body, 13. anyone, 14. anxious, 15. mad, 16. angel, 17. angry, 18. apprise, 19. arbiter, 20. immoral, 21. insure, 22. antedates, 23. ensure, 24. bemuses, 25. arbitrator, 26. angry, 27. eager, 28. Any one, 29. anymore, 30. amoral

Important Distinctions (4)   [pages 199–200]

FILL-IN: 1. because, 2. more than, 3. belief, 4. take, 5. benign, 6. badly, 7. dissect, 8. besides, 9. breath, 10. biennially, 11. a while, 12. awhile, 13. bitten, 14. bad, 15. beneficiary, 16. a while, 17. Beside, 18. breathe, 19. benefactor, 20. believe, 21. twice-yearly, 22. better than, 23. malign, 24. awhile, 25. besides, 26. bitten, 27. bad, 28. take, 29. bisect, 30. because

Important Distinctions (5)   [pages 203–204]

FILL-IN: 1. censor, 2. inexpensive, 3. causal, 4. ceremonial, 5. cartoon, 6. May, 7. reason, 8. celebrants, 9. classical, 10. group, 11. carton, 12. Catholic, 13. childish, 14. categories, 15. bunch, 16. casual, 17. cartoons, 18. childish, 19. catholic, 20. celebrators, 21. classic, 22. bunch, 23. childlike, 24. class, 25. can't, 26. censured, 27. cause of, 28. ceremonious, 29. cheap, 30. May

Important Distinctions (6)   [pages 207–208]

FILL-IN: 1. composed of; discrete, 2. up-to-date, 3. conscience, 4. confidentially, 5. usually, 6. climactic, 7. universities, 8. customers, 9. confident, 10. consistently, 11. comprehensive, 12. modern, 13. concave, 14. comprises, 15. confidently, 16. climatic, 17. conscious, 18. convex, 19. included, 20. client, 21. confidently, 22. Current, 23. confidant, 24. constantly, 25. conscience, 26. comprehensive, 27. climactic, 28. confidence, 29. customers, 30. composes

Important Distinctions (7)   [pages 211–212]

FILL-IN: 1. criteria, 2. incisive, 3. convinced, 4. overt, 5. deficient, 6. deduct, 7. creditors, 8. definite, 9. continuous, 10. controversial, 11. decriminalized, 12. data, 13. deficient, 14. deduce, 15. contemptible, 16. contentious, 17. credible, 18. are, 19. persuade, 20. covert, 21. creditable, 22. Continual, 23. debtor, 24. contemptuous, 25. decisive, 26. criterion, 27. defective, 28. definitive, 29. credible, 30. deduce

Important Distinctions (8)   [pages 215–216]

FILL-IN: 1. uninterested, 2. dissemble, 3. the result of, 4. each other, 5. discovered, 6. distinctive, 7. displaced, 8. prognosis, 9. because of, 10. dissemble, 11. invented, 12. device, 13. denotation, 14. deprecate, 15. one another, 16. distinct, 17. Because of, 18. device, 19. disinterested, 20. misplaced, 21. each other, 22. depreciate, 23. uninterested, 24. diagnosis, 25. displaced, 26. connotations, 27. devise, 28. connotes, 29. distinctive, 30. discovered

Important Distinctions (9)   [pages 219–220]

FILL-IN: 1. e.g., 2. enviable, 3. epigram, 4. elementary, 5. endless, 6. economical, 7. envelope, 8. elusive, 9. epitaph, 10. earthly, 11. illusive, 12. envious, 13. easily, 14. pandemic, 15. economical, 16. economic, 17. innumerable, 18. elemental, 19. epithet, 20. envelop, 21. illusive, 22. epigraph, 23. envelope, 24. earthy, 25. envious, 26. endemic, 27. easily, 28. epidemic, 29. i.e., 30. elemental

Important Distinctions (10)   [pages 223–224]

FILL-IN: 1. Every one, 2. false, 3. exceptionable, 4. exhaustive, 5. esoteric, 6. everyday, 7. notorious, 8. extended, 9. everyone; anyone, 10. exotic, 11. invoke, 12. specially, 13. equitable, 14. explicit, 15. equable, 16. every day, 17. famous, 18. every so often, 19. implicit, 20. exceptional, 21. erotic, 22. exceedingly, 23. especially, 24. fallacious, 25. evoke, 26. everyday, 27. everyone, 28. exhausting, 29. excessively, 30. extensive

Important Distinctions (11)   [pages 227–228]

FILL-IN: 1. formerly, 2. forcible, 3. floundered, 4. good, 5. preface, 6. glanced, 7. Further, 8. gamut, 9. genius, 10. funeral, 11. fewer, 12. gassy, 13. flaunt, 14. well, 15. few, 16. flout, 17. genus, 18. gauntlet, 19. well, 20. foreword, 21. funeral, 22, forceful, 23. farther, 24. a few, 25. gaseous, 26. less, 27. further, 28. formally, 29. glimpse, 30. foundered

Important Distinctions (12)   [pages 231–232]

FILL-IN: 1. half, 2. hypocritical, 3. him, 4. historic, 5. humane, 6. hung, 7. Hypercritical, 8. house, 9. grateful, 10. He, 11. healthful, 12. human, 13. gratified, 14. habitable, 15. gourmand, 16. dislike, 17. historic, 18. unthinkable, 19. gratified, 20. hypercritical, 21. houses, 22. hanged, 23. have, 24. healthy, 25. humane, 26. healthy, 27. home, 28. gourmet, 29. Historical, 30. half

Important Distinctions (13)   [pages 235–236]

FILL-IN: 1. implying, 2. disability, 3. me, 4. ingenuous, 5. illustrative, 6. imaginary, 7. ignorant, 8. unhuman, 9. illegible, 10. immature, 11. into, 12. myself, 13. incapable, 14. premature, 15. incredible, 16. ingenious, 17. incredulous, 18. unable to, 19. myself, 20. infer, 21. inability, 22. stupid, 23. I, 24. unreadable, 25. into, 26. illustrative, 27. imaginative, 28. ingenuous, 29. I, 30. inhuman

Important Distinctions (14)   [pages 239–240]

FILL-IN: 1. lay, 2. laudatory, 3. intermission, 4. let alone, 5. enervating, 6. initiated, 7. latter, 8. laboratory, 9. intravenous, 10. lying, 11. judicial, 12. invidious, 13. judicious, 14. teach, 15. integrate, 16. let, 17. intramural, 18. teach, 19. laudable, 20. segregate, 21. later, 22. judicious, 23. insidious, 24. lain, 25. invigorating, 26. lavatory, 27. internecine, 28. instigate, 29. laid, 30. ketchup

Important Distinctions (15)   [pages 243–244]

FILL-IN: 1. loose, 2. slander, 3. as, 4. majority, 5. lusty, 6. liable, 7. loath, 8. podium, 9. lifelong, 10. luncheon, 11. lose, 12. as if, 13. anglers, 14. limpid, 15. malign, 16. likely, 17. lectern, 18. impugned, 19. Loose, 20. loathe, 21. apt, 22. liable, 23. plurality, 24. garbage collectors, 25. lunch, 26. lent, 27. livelong, 28. lustful, 29. like, 30. limp

Important Distinctions (16)   [pages 247–248]

FILL-IN: 1. median, 2. talk, 3. almost, 4 . number of, 5. mediums, 6. negligent, 7. morale, 8. nauseated, 9. martial, 10. notable, 11. moral, 12. sordid, 13. Maybe, 14. obsolescent, 15. medium, 16. meridian, 17. morbid, 18. notorious, 19. marital, 20. nauseous, 21. monologues, 22. negligible, 23. Several, 24. may be, 25. moral, 26. dialogue, 27. medium, 28. Almost all, 29. median, 30. obsolete

Important Distinctions (17)   [pages 251–252]

FILL-IN: 1. personal, 2. prosecute, 3. onto, 4. official, 5. parameters, 6. on, 7. pendant, 8. perspective, 9. percentage, 10. penance, 11. officious, 12. persecuting, 13. on, 14. perpetuate, 15. oddly, 16. official, 17. percentage, 18. perimeter, 19. on to, 20. penitence, 21. perpetrated, 22. upon, 23. perspective, 24. odd, 25. prospective, 26. percent, 27. prosecute, 28. pendant, 29. odd, 30. personnel

Important Distinctions (18)   [pages 255–256]

FILL-IN: 1. prescribe, 2. physiognomy, 3. hinder, 4. presumptive, 5. defendant, 6. proceed, 7. prophecy, 8. phenomena, 9. precede, 10. predominant, 11. perquisites, 12. port, 13. Please, 14. are, 15. predominant, 16. prerequisite, 17. possible, 18. predominate, 19. physiology, 20. precede, 21. Kindly, 22. starboard, 23. proscribe, 24. phenomenon, 25. plaintiff, 26. presumptuous, 27. prophesy, 28. is, 29. probable, 30. prevented

Important Distinctions (19)   [pages 259–260]

FILL-IN: 1. really, 2. recur, 3. Prostate, 4. receipt, 5. Quotation; quotations, 6. quick, 7. recipe, 8. quickly, 9. restful, 10. raising, 11. regrettable, 12. respectfully, 13. questionable, 14. rationale, 15. quote, 16. respectably, 17. regretful, 18. respectively, 19. rationale, 20. restive, 21. quotation, 22. rational, 23. restful, 24. rise, 25. quickly, 26. receipt, 27. really, 28. prostrate, 29. reoccurrence, 30. questioning

Important Distinctions (20)   [pages 263–264]

FILL-IN: 1. sometime, 2. spacious, 3. sludge, 4. sit, 5. seasonal, 6. her, 7. some one, 8. sank, 9. set, 10. somewhat, 11. she, 12. simplistic, 13. solid, 14. Because, 15. sculpture, 16. simplified, 17. some time, 18. her, 19. sculpture, 20. Because, 21. slush, 22. sit, 23. she, 24. spatial, 25. stolid, 26. will; will, 27. seasonable, 28. sunk, 29. someone, 30. somewhat

Important Distinctions (21)   [pages 267–268]

FILL-IN: 1. than, 2. which, 3. specie, 4. suggestible, 5. unnatural, 6. suspect, 7. surely, 8. them, 9. fever, 10. than, 11. that, 12 tasty, 13. feel, 14. stunk, 15. species; species, 16. themselves, 17. they, 18. which, 19. supernatural, 20. fever, 21. thinks, 22. temporary, 23. stank; badly; nauseated, 24. surely, 25. believe, 26. tasteful, 27. suggestive, 28. that, 29. suspected, 30. then

Important Distinctions (22)   [pages 271–272]

FILL-IN: 1. unique, 2. torturous, 3. waiting for, 4. whether, 5. turgid, 6. thorough, 7. you're, 8. Unaware; unawares, 9. whoever, 10. you're; use to, 11. anyone, 12. rustle, 13. Whomever, 14. involuntary, 15. used to, 16. use to, 17. a while; whether, 18. threshing; thrashing, 19. Waiting on, 20. involuntary, 21 wrested, 22. who; whom, 23. through, 24. us; we, 25. turbid, 26. unusual, 27. tortuous, 28. used to; there, 29. whose, 30. your

Review for Important Distinctions   [pages 273–281]

FILL-IN: 1. an, 2. accept, 3. excess, 4. accused of, 5. devoted, 6. advice, 7. agree about, 8. intend, 9. all, 10. refer, 11. already, 12. alternative, 13. altogether, 14. Between, 15. amuses, 16. angry, 17. eager, 18. anymore, 19. any one, 20. insure, 21. very, 22. a while, 23. because, 24. benefactor, 25. malign, 26. more than, 27. breath, 28. take, 29. group, 30. causal, 31. censured, 32. ceremonial, 33. childish, 34. climatic, 35. comprehensible, 36. composed, 37. confident, 38. conscience, 39. constantly, 40. modern, 41. contemptible, 42. continuous, 43. persuade, 44. covert, 45. creditable, 46. deduct, 47. connotations, 48. deficient, 49. device, 50. invented, 51. uninterested, 52. distinctive, 53. because of, 54. each other's, 55. earthly, 56. economical, 57. elusive, 58. innumerable, 59. envious, 60. epitaphs, 61. pandemic, 62. specially, 63. every so often, 64. Every day, 65. exceedingly, 66. exceptionable, 67. Erotic, 68. false, 69. further, 70. Fewer, 71. forcibly, 72. preface, 73. foundered, 74. glimpse, 75. well, 76. gourmet; gourmand, 77. habitable; inhabitable, 78. hung; hanged, 79. healthful; healthy, 80. historic, 81. house, 82. hypocritical, 83. stupid, 84. unreadable, 85. illustrative, 86. imaginative, 87. imply, 88. inability, 89. incredible, 90. insidiously, 91. segregate, 92. invigorating, 93. ketchup, 94. lavatories, 95. lies, 96. let alone, 97. lectern, 98. lend, 99. likely, 100. lifelong, 101. as, 102. as if, 103. limp, 104. may be, 105. medium, 106. median, 107. moral, 108. Almost, 109. nauseous, 110. number of, 111. oddly, 112. official, 113. penance, 114. percentage, 115. perimeter, 116. prosecute, 117. perspective, 118. phenomena, 119. are, 120. possible, 121. predominant, 122. prerequisite, 123. proscribe, 124. prophecy, 125. questionable, 126. quotation, 127. rise, 128. recurrence, 129 regrettable, 130. restive, 131. respectably, 132. sculpture, 133. seasonable, 134. sit, 135. simplistic, 136. Because, 137. somewhat, 138. sometime, 139. suggestible, 140. suspect, 141. tasty, 142. than, 143. that, 144. thrashed, 145. think, 146. unaware, 147. unusual, 148. use to, 149. whether, 150. wait for

Chapter 6 Current Conventions of Punctuation

Commas to Separate [pages 299–301]

J   1. The last traitor having been shot, the villagers retired to their humble cottages for a meal of gruel and black bread.

D   2. Our first stop was either the Globe Theatre or Madame Tussaud's, not the Tower of London.

G   3. My, how bold we are when we are young and do not yet know what a hard place the world is.

E   4. Everyone feared that the building might cave in, in the middle of the night.

L   5. In conclusion, we think we are safe in saying that life in the Great Lakes region was not particularly lyrical during the 1700s.

B   6. The Brotherhood of the Bulging Biceps toasted the coach, the mayor, the governor, the president, and the makers of toast.

A   7. Many of the residents of Friendly Lake are quite famous, but they prefer to be inconspicuous when they are on holiday.

F   8. Fortunately, the Osgoods had invested their money in bonds unaffected by the stock market.

C   9. One does not expect to discover such a full-flavored, robust wine in a screw-top bottle with a label that reads "Zippy."

H 10. If you put a chain around the neck of a slave, the other end fastens itself firmly around your own.

K 11. After three weeks on the road and several bouts with mean-spirited mosquitoes, most of the students were looking forward to sleeping in their own beds.

I 12. Turning her eyes toward the open window, Marigold caught a glimpse of the fleeing Martians.

C 13. It is difficult not to respond to a person with such a friendly, energetic, forthright personality.

D 14. Gretchen has decided to become a professional volleyball player, not a waste management engineer.

I 15. Laughing loudly with a mouthful of food, Vernon embarrassed everyone at the table.

H 16. If I win the $40 million lottery prize on Saturday, I think I'll take a brief holiday on Monday.

A 17. The day was a cold and rainy one, yet our hearts were overflowing with optimism.

F 18. Customarily, it is the bride who brings a dowry to the marriage.

B 19. Senators Flimflam, Hayseed, Doublespeak, and Kickback are all opposed to the term-limitation bill.

G 20. Alas, poor Roderick has lost his desire to master the fleugelhorn.

K   21.   In almost total darkness and with no experience in the wilderness, Balthazer inched his way along the narrow ledge.

E   22.   Brumback said that once inside, the cats began trashing the camper.

A   23.   Helen was a bit of a grim person, and she had no inclination toward personality modification.

L   24.   Mercedes was a very sociable individual. By contrast, her younger brother was an introvert.

F   25.   Above, the tribesmen observed the search party like vultures contemplating a wounded wildebeest.

J   26.   Many of the students being ill, the picnic was called off.

G   27.   Ah, what a beautiful day it is here among these glistening mountains of garbage.

E   28.   Those who have the money to, buy these items in large quantities and thus get a better price.

I   29.   Testing the waters too soon after eating, Miriam became nauseated as she swam across the lagoon.

C   30.   No one could believe that Godfrey had committed the dastardly, underhanded deed.

K   31.   Because of the terrible storm and our own fatigue, we had to stop for the night.

L   32.   Not all suburbanites are stereotypical Republicans. For example, my cousin, who lives outside East Grand Rapids, considers himself a liberal Democrat.

H   33.   Although Aldo was pleased with his progress, he knew he would have to work harder in the future.

B   34.   My accomplishments last summer included painting the house, planting a few trees in the yard, reading several good books, and making peace with my contrary neighbors.

J   35.   The season over, many of the players didn't know what to do with all their free time.

D   36.   Professor Bergman is an exceptional lecturer, isn't she?

F   37.   Few students took the examination seriously; consequently, many of them failed it.

I   38.   Engrossed in her work, Gwendolyn forgot to make an appointment with the veterinarian.

G   39.   Behold, young master Gilbert is now able to tie both of his shoes with a single string.

K   40.   At the very site of my childhood home on top of Bloodhound Mountain, the federal government has erected a radio telescope to communicate with aliens in outer space.

E   41.   The truth was that for Rosemary, Burgess seemed a sophisticated and erudite individual.

H   42.   Stunned by the blow to the head, the child wandered about the woods for several hours.

C   43.   The soft, soothing voice of the reader quickly put many of the children to sleep.

L   44.   Most of the valley had been replanted. To the north, one could already see a horizon of green foliage.

<u>A</u> 45. No one had put forward a proposal to deal with the problem, nor was anyone likely to do so.

<u>J</u> 46. Monument would be a village without a future, the railroad having gone elsewhere.

<u>D</u> 47. The more Marco studied, the worse he seemed to do on the daily quizzes.

<u>B</u> 48. You might try the basement, the shed, the neighbor's garage, or the repair shop in town.

<u>K</u> 49. In the twilight of a spectacular career in the field of education, Professor Andresen admitted that if he were a young man today he would choose another occupation.

<u>H</u> 50. When my baby walks down the street, the little birdies go tweet, tweet, tweet.

Commas to Enclose Nonrestrictive Elements   [pages 302–303]

<u>E</u> 1. Zoe's favorite ice cream, Cornish vanilla, isn't available here in Hinterland, Michigan.

<u>A</u> 2. These cars, which have come to symbolize the poor quality of American craftsmanship, cannot be marketed anywhere in Europe.

<u>D</u> 3. Poor Lindley, at the end of his rope, decided to go home to his parents.

<u>C</u> 4. Our night security guards, diverted by their usual game of Trivial Pursuit, did not notice that the store was being robbed.

<u>B</u> 5. The new football stadium, once the city obtains sufficient funding, will be completed within three years.

<u>C</u> 6. Legions of recreational runners, enjoying themselves at the rear of the pack and chatting with one another as they went, held no illusions about becoming "world-class" marathoners.

<u>E</u> 7. Two or our more difficult courses of study, namely engineering and chemistry, are begging for students.

<u>D</u> 8. The papers presented at the conference, with one or two exceptions, were not of the quality they should have been.

<u>A</u> 9. Ida Morris, who coached for ten years at Hinterland High, has now taken a job at a university.

<u>D</u> 10. Your children, in a state of panic, ran from house to house awakening the neighbors.

<u>C</u> 11. Father O'Hare, encouraged by the congregation to preach shorter sermons, adopted the strategy of talking faster.

<u>B</u> 12. A fellow like Lorenzo, wherever he decides to settle, will more than likely be successful.

<u>E</u> 13. Nelson's grand aim, to compose a symphony in honor of poverty, proved to be a costly mistake.

<u>A</u> 14. The old colonial house at 15 Elm Street, where our first two children were born, is for sale.

<u>C</u> 15. Mayor Simpleton, hoping to encourage students to patronize local shops, hung university pennants from the lampposts in town.

B 16. These plans for reorganizing the university, while interesting enough theoretically, could, if implemented, severely reduce the student population.

D 17. This young woman, without assistance from anyone, has put herself through medical school.

A 18. Mary Ryan, whose mother taught her to sew, has become a famous dress designer.

E 19. These things, working from a hidden agenda and lying to the public, will eventually chase you from office.

B 20. The word *discrimination*, because it is often used in negative contexts, has gotten a bad reputation.

Commas to Enclose or Set Off [pages 307–308]

E 1. According to our records William Bobolink, Sr., and William Bobolink, Jr., have the same birth date.

F 2. On Saturday, December 10, 1938, American novelist Pearl Buck was presented the Nobel Prize for Literature in Stockholm.

H 3. Between 10,000 B.C. and 1990 the population of the world increased from 10,000,000 to 5,420,000,000 souls.

A 4. Professor Dillman did, in fact, announce that the class would have a test on Monday.

G 5. Denver, Colorado, will be the location of our home office by 15 March 1993.

B 6. Rain, Rain, go away and don't come back until another day.

D 7. "These units must be in Buffalo by noon Tuesday," the foreman said to the loading crew.

A 8. Brumback stood up and announced, of all things, that he intended to give his fortune to the London Society for the Prevention of Bad Manners.

C 9. Your positions in these matters, typically liberal, will not sell well in my part of the country.

E 10. Ashley Plimpton, D.B.A., Ph.D., M.D., seems to be a fellow with time on his hands these days.

A 11. Gonzo's first shot, although one could hardly call it a shot, collided with a tree and finally came to rest thirty-five yards behind the tee.

H 12. Some 6,000,000 Jews were among the 9,000,000 people systematically exterminated by Hitler's Nazis during the Holocaust associated with World War II.

D 13. "A tax system that punishes people for working," Harriet said, "will eventually have a regressive effect on the economy."

C 14. The instructions were to send all entries to 18075 Hemlock Boulevard, Hinterland, Michigan, by 30 November 1993.

B 15. Sit, Fido, and show these wonderful people what a smart dog you are.

A 16. The committee might, on the other hand, choose someone from outside the organization.

C 17. The closet contained a hundred suits, custom-made, that had apparently never been worn.

F 18. Did Christopher Columbus really discover America on Monday, October 12, 1492?

E 19. Gibbs, J.L., Giddings, C.D., and Giffen, J.V., have all been removed from the acceptance list.

B 20. O Lord, how manifold are Thy mercies throughout the earth.

D 21. "Turn out the lights," Roxane yawned; "the party is over."

F 22. It was during the night of Tuesday, April 18, 1775, that Paul Revere made his famous ride through the Massachusetts countryside to warn the people that the British were coming.

A 23. ˙ Reason, if anyone still cares about reason, would suggest that we do a little more research before spending a few billion dollars.

G 24. Is it true that Canton, Ohio, is the birthplace of professional football in the United States?

C 25. The discussions, very heated, extended late into the night.

Semicolon and Colon   [pages 311–313]

1. Luke 6:20–49, 2. watercolorist; Ian / sculptor; Stephen / portraits; and, 3. significant: jealousy, 4. freeze; on, 5. *2001: A Space Odyssey*, 6. home; they, 7. things: run, 8. plane; and, 9. 11:48 P.M. / 12:18 A.M., 10. said; moreover, 11. have: immortality, 12. found; she, 3. registrar: Burchett, 14. nightmare; for, 15. people: "Ask, 16. hard; furthermore, 17. John 3:16, 18. "Okinawa: The Bloodiest Battle of All," 19. town; but, 20. problem: no one, 21. attractive; intelligent / intelligent; and, 22. universe: we, 23. Carolina; Asheville / Carolina; Roanoke / Virginia; Charleston / Virginia; and, 24. duck; however, 25. advice: "Don't

The Period, Question Mark, and Exclamation Point   [pages 315–316]

1. The students were given a form that asked whether or not they planned to attend summer school. No one was interested.

2. Once again, the Tigers won. It was their fifty-third victory at home this season.

3. You're still a member of the chaos committee, aren't you? Or do I have you confused with someone else? Maybe your roommate?

4. Although Rolland has both a J.D. and a Ph.D., he works at M.I.T. as a collective bargaining representative for the faculty.

5. Lt. Gov. Ian Blind, Rev. Marcellus Valhalla, and Ms. Lucy Mystic all claim to have known one another in Rome between 250 B.C. and 220 B.C., or thereabouts.

6. Nigel asked, "Where did she shoot the bird?" / "In its plumage," Grace responded after some thought.

7. Hank Greenfeld—or was it Greenberg?—was a standout player for the Detroit Tigers in the '30s and '40s.

8. Video, Inc., has stopped accepting c.o.d. orders for feature films. To place an order, you must have a national credit card—e.g., Mastercard or American Express.

9. Was it Julius Caesar who said, "Give me liberty or give me death"? Or was it Caesar Augustus? Or was it neither?

10. "Stop!" shouted the guard. "If you take one more step, you will be walking in a mine field."

The Dash and Parentheses [page 318]

1. Until that time—as dumb luck would have it—everything had gone according to plan.

2. Rhetoric is the art (perhaps science) of using words effectively, either in speech or writing.

3. Alden's new sports car—long, low, and confidently engineered—was quietly begging to be taken for a spin.

4. A zygote is a cell formed by the union of male and female gametes (reproductive cells than can develop into a new individual).

5. Several members of this organization—I don't have to call the roll—have become a bit too confident about their importance to the rest of us.

6. This study (the Smithson Study of 1991) offers some practical suggestions for dealing with starvation in Third World countries.

7. Lillian's grandfather—who fought in World War I, World War II, and Korea—says that if he were a young man today he would be a conscientious objector.

8. If John Kennedy (1917–1963) were alive today, he would be seventy-six years old.

9. Most of these books patronize their readers—pat them on their stupid little heads.

10. The committee's conclusions (see Table 9) supported no single candidate's position over that of another candidate.

11. Reading books and articles, revising classroom notes, writing papers, preparing for tests and quizzes—these are the things that make up my days and nights at school.

12. Some movies (for example, *The Silence of the Lambs*) teach us things about human nature that we would just as soon not know.

13. "I warned him—well, I meant my remarks to him to be taken as a warning."

14. By the fall of '89, the president of the union had no (?) support among the rank and file.

15. Powerful people—that is, those who daily buy and sell the rest of us—have a completely different set of problems.

16. Today, there are only five apes remaining: (1) the gorilla, (2) the chimpanzee, (3) the orangutan, (4) the gibbon, and (5) the siamang.

Apostrophe [pages 320–321]

1. Anthony's '79 Saab is on its last legs—or, rather, wheels.

2. I'm at my wit's end from having to watch my p's and q's so closely.

3. Alas, when everybody's somebody, nobody's anybody.

4. You're rolling nothing but *6*'s and *7*'s.

5. The club's monthly meetings are held at Franklin and Avis's place, not at a student's house.

6. Professor Rawlings' predilection for sesquipedalians doesn't compare with Dr. Hastings' partiality for obfuscation.

7. There will be no *if*'s, *and*'s, or *but*'s here; reproducing a painting of Rose's thorns is not beyond the class's ability.

8. We've never been asked to do anyone's work other than our own.

9. As the poet says, "We'll take a cup o' kindness yet for auld lang syne."

10. They're leaving at six o'clock and don't know when they'll return—maybe by day's end on Friday.

11. As they've already explained, the eyewitnesses' testimony was all that was needed.

12. It's Edwin's never-ending *thus*'s and *notwithstanding*'s that exhaust the children's ears.

13. "The +'s and -'s denote positive and negative values respectively," the instructor explained.

14. That's what we don't know: who's going to defend the '20s and '30s during this grand debate?

15. Andrew's and Amanda's tickets, which were for the nine o'clock show, were located somewhere up in the *X, Y, Z*'s.

Quotation Marks   [pages 324–326]

1. "If you're going to run for office," Tim's sister cautioned, "be prepared to hear the worst about yourself repeated throughout the community."

2. Is the ninth commandment "Thou shalt not bear false witness against they neighbor"?

3. Alice, after studying the dean for a minute or two, said, "I've never before met anyone who was born middle-aged"; then she left the room.

4. After twenty-five years of rejections by editors and agents, the author became an "overnight success."

5. "We have noticed," the new dean said, "that no one argues with the axiom 'if you can make it in New York, you can make it anywhere.'"

6. You went "ping-ponging" along? What does that mean?

7. Can one sensibly define *reality* as "that which exists in fact"?

8. "If you say 'so it goes' one more time," Leopold warned, "I'm going to 'go' myself."

9. Andrew Lang's poem "Scythe Song" contains the repeated refrain "hush, ah hush."

10. Baynard's little brother says "you know" and "awesome" seven hundred times a day, and he means it every time.

11. Chapter 12, "When We Are Immortal," of the book *Future* raises some interesting questions about population control.

12. "By repeatedly calling your opponent a 'yellow-bellied sapsucker,'" Marsha said, "are you suggesting that there is something avian about him?"

13. Throughout the trip, we "dined" on burgers and fries.

14. "I forgot my best line," Ambrose said: "Modern cities can run no faster than their sewer pipes."

15. By defining the word *tory* as a 'male chauvinist pig,'" Vivian said, "you alienated a substantial portion of your audience."

16. "I never read Walt Whitman's poem 'There Was a Child Went Forth,'" Mercedes said, "until I was in college and came across it in a copy of *Leaves of Grass.*"

17. Who said, "I have been both rich and poor, and rich is better"?

18. That was one wedding ceremony that left out the "love, honor, and obey" stuff.

19. In the short story "The Wooing of Ariadne," written by Harry Mark Petrakis, Ariadne indicates her acceptance of Marko's courting when she says to Marko, "You may call on me tomorrow."

20. Contrary to what you may have heard, the word *logorrhea* means "running off at the mouth."

21. "We didn't care much for your 'cute' use of the expression 'ask and it shall be given,'" Natalie said; "moreover, we thought you had dressed yourself for a Halloween party."

22. The Simpsons' "cottage" at the north end of Clear Lake included seven bedrooms, nine baths, an elevator, an indoor swimming pool, and a four-car garage.

23. "If you ask me, most politicians are interested in only one thing," Greta said: "staying in office."

24. The word *disease* does not refer only to a contagious illness; it means " . . . any harmful, destructive, or degenerative condition."

25. An annoyingly self-important young man took exception to Professor Haunt's evaluation of his paper. "Do you know who I am?" the young man asked. "No, sir, I do not," the professor replied. "But I shall make inquiries and inform you directly."

Review for Current Conventions of Punctuation   [pages 327–330]

C 1. Christmas: a CD player   I 2. he'd / sun's / ocean's   B 3. one; moreover   J 4. "A Little Cloud"
E 5. noteworthy"?   A 6. argument, but   G 7. news—these   D 8. U.S. / i.e.   H 9. (1912–1983)
A 10. Kentucky, Burgess / leisurely, more   J 11. "Bartleby, the Scrivener" / "I am . . . the best."
B 12. athletics; nevertheless   H 13. (?)   E 14. live?" / yourself?"   A 15. Tom, Dick, and Harry
I 16. Grace's / city's   C 17. advice: "Get   A 18. Bats, which / reputation, are   G 19. me—"
D 20. Dr. J. William Meekly, Jr., / Prof. Linda Hobson   E 21. she?—   A 22. position, in / brief, is
F 23. serious!"   C 24. steps: (1)   J 25. "within a state" / "between or among states."
A 26. pleasant, accommodating / years,"   I 27. o'clock / in-laws' / Andrea's   G 28. measure—Ian /
Sanford—suddenly   B 29. all; yet   H 30. (see Table 16)   C 31. Crow: An   G 32. impersonators—
all   E 33. it?   H 34. (1) / (2) / (3)   A 35. exam; not   I 36. s's / e's / p's / k's   D 37. A.M. / P.M.
F 38. moon!   A 39. Friday, December 13, 1950, at / Columbus, Ohio.   J 40. "Moderation . . .
moderation"   H 41. (American Association of University Professors)   A 42. Alas, sir, you / well, nor
E 43. anyway? Two? Five? Seven? Or was it a dozen?   I 44. '88 / '92 / *why*'s / *wherefore*'s
A 45. young, they   J 46. "newer"   D 47. innings. Tim   F 48. lads!" / us!"   B 49. qualified;
capable / capable; and   G 50. vacation—why / me—was

21

Chapter 7 Additional Mechanical Conventions

Capitalization [pages 334–335]

1. This article, "The Me Generation: A Nation of Spoiled Brats," is a bit sardonic in its criticism of the '80s in America.

2. Does the Federal Deposit Insurance Corporation (FDIC) insure this account, or am I on my own?

3. "Do we have enough K rations?" Seargent Major Goofus asked, "or should we stop at Wendy's for a hamburger?"

4. If she is not offered a commission in the United States Army, Glenna intends to study English literature at either the University of Michigan or Notre Dame.

5. Early in the spring, probably March or April, we shall go to Chicago and see for ourselves whether or not this Bible-quoting miracle worker is really a man of God.

6. The house where Andrew grew up was located at 734 Cedar Drive, Hinterland, Michigan, near the west end of Lake Waverly.

7. After living so long in the North, the Samuelsons are having a difficult time adjusting to the warm winters in the South—particularly at Thanksgiving and Christmastime.

8. According to both Mother and Father, Uncle Nelson worked for either the CIA or the FBI after leaving General Motors.

9. Alas, it was Elizabeth's innocence that made her think a Freudian slip was a woman's undergarment.

10. Rumor has it that Count Mountebank is suffering from Parkinson's disease, a family weakness possibly extending back to the Middle Ages.

11. Was it in *The Glass Menagerie* or *On the Waterfront* that Marlon Brando said, "I coulda been a contender"? Or was it Robert De Niro in *Raging Bull*?

12. Young Siegfried eats his Wheaties every day; he hopes to compete in the Olympic Games in Atlanta in 1996.

13. "In the film *A Walk on the Wild Side: Real Animal Behavior*," the instructor said, "we get quite a different view of nature: it is a Darwinian view."

14. Was it John Kennedy or Richard Nixon who won the Pulitzer Prize for writing the book *Profiles in Courage*?

15. Last Thursday afternoon, Professor Bernard Nadeau, who is a well-known scholar in European political history, addressed the Grand Rapids chapter of the American Association of University Women.

Word Division   [pages 340–341]

		Syllabication	Division(s)
1.	encyclopedia	en-cy-clo-pe-di-a	en-cyclo-pe-dia
2.	homecoming	home-com-ing	home-coming
3.	impeachable	im-peach-a-ble	im-peach-able
4.	basketball	bas-ket-ball	basket-ball
5.	amorphous	a-mor-phous	amor-phous
6.	father-in-law	fa-ther-in-law	father-in-law
7.	simpleton	sim-ple-ton	simple-ton
8.	fullness	full-ness	full-ness
9.	hummingbird	hum-ming-bird	humming-bird
10.	slinky	slink-y	slinky
11.	allowance	al-low-ance	allow-ance
12.	topsy-turvy	top-sy-tur-vy	topsy-turvy
13.	correspondence	cor-re-spon-dence	cor-re-spon-dence
14.	summarize	sum-ma-rize	sum-ma-rize
15.	absenteeism	ab-sen-tee-ism	ab-sen-tee-ism

Hyphens   [pages 342–343]

1. able-bodied / battle-weary,   2. Twenty-five / 160-gallon / fly-by-night,   3. V-neck / T-shirts / ten- / twenty-dollar,   4. self-righteous / mayor-elect,   5. johnny-come-lately / hard-nosed / no-nonsense, 6. hands-on / hands-off,   7. One-upmanship / quasi-scientific / editor-in-chief,   8. 90-minute / fresh-baked / 16-ounce / T-bone,   9. pro-Irish / anti-British,   10. lost-little-girl / ninety-five / U-turn, 11. double-barreled / tight-lipped,   12. co-workers / re-use,   13. 1,650-acre / profit-making / good-sized / self-motivated / 40-hour,   14. peace-imparting / bell-like / re-ally,   15. trans-Canadian / post-World War II / H-bomb,   16. Three-quarters / A-frames / S-curve / M-79 / re-cover / co-op, 17. pre- / post-test / re-creation,   18. eighteenth-century / high-powered / born-again,   19. all-clear / re-dress,   20. run-of-the-mill / Japan-bashing / half-life,   21. flag-waving / speech-making / finger-pointing/ ne'er-do-wells,   22. first- / second- / third-place / seventy-five-odd / well-wishers,   23. ex-mayor / attorney general-elect,   24. two-thirds / so-called / low-minded,   25. self-promoting / would-be / man-at-the-top / C-note

Review Exercise for Additional Mechanical Conventions   [pages 345–346]

<u>D / E</u> 1. The lifeguard said that the infants were *red* from the sun and the 100-degree heat, not *dead*.

<u>A / B</u> 2. Each year in the spring and fall, my father and mother join Mr. and Mrs. Gingrich from the next block for a shopping trip to Pittsburgh.

<u>D / E</u> 3. No one was surprised when Kevin came to the door wearing a silk *robe-de-chambre* and holding a well-worn copy of *The Other Victorians* in his hand.

<u>B / C</u> 4. Germaine Rushmore, B.S., M.A., M.B.A., Ph.D., has joined twelve of her colleagues in the English department at Hinterland Community College to offer a double-paced summer seminar on stress management.

<u>C / D</u> 5. The university bookstore ordered 7,000 four-dollar copies of *Webster's Modern World Dictionary*, but received 4,000 seven-dollar copies of Westrum's *Modern World Discoveries*.

<u>E / A</u> 6. This is a dog-eat-dog world, father; there is little room for vegetarians.

<u>C / B</u> 7. Seven has always been my lucky number; e.g., I was born on July 7, 1957, at 7:07 in the morning.

<u>A / D</u> 8. When Professor Jensen said that Princess Caroline had been photographed *au naturel*, did he mean she was naked or simply cooked?

<u>C / E</u> 9. Aren't those 200-watt bulbs too bright to read by?

<u>A / C</u> 10. Claudia looked knowingly at Conrad and said, "Of the nine children in the Sherman family, little Fritz has always been my Auntie's favorite."

<u>D / E</u> 11. Hannibal's *c'est-la-vie* approach to business problems drives the button-down-collar crowd up the walls.

<u>E / A</u> 12. Rumor has it that two student co-ops will open next fall just south of town.

<u>B / D</u> 13. Dr. Bumstead, normally a reliable surgeon, met this exotic woman at the GOP convention, and the two of them flew to Europe for a nostalgic ride on *The Orient Express*.

<u>A / D</u> 14. "In this particular sentence," the instructor said, a bit weary of having to repeat herself, "*Egyptian* is a proper adjective."

<u>E / B</u> 15. Sooner or later, the have-nots—i.e., those people heretofore without money, land, homes, or political power—will rise up with a life-threatening fury.

<u>C / D</u> 16. We read nine 400-page novels in the class, the best of which was *All the King's Men*.

<u>A / B</u> 17. Few people today are familiar with the Roman philosopher Maximus Acerbus, who lived from 75 B.C. until A.D. 43.

<u>C / B</u> 18. The 90-minute intervals of REM sleep turned out to be consistent with 175 or the 250 subjects, or 70%.

<u>E / A</u> 19. A bone-chilling article in the latest edition of *Newsweek* entitled "Life Among the Rich Young Politicos" will affirm your less-than-optimistic opinions about the future.

<u>C</u> / <u>B</u> 20. According to this report, more than 90 percent of all people who test positive for the HIV-virus eventually develop AIDS.

<u>B</u> / <u>E</u> 21. "Do you wish to speak to Dr. Crispin Hollenbeck, Sr., or Dr. Crispin Hollenbeck, Jr.?" the indignant-voiced receptionist said.

<u>D</u> / <u>A</u> 22. The expression *sub rosa* is Latin and means literally "under the rose"; by extension, however, it also means "secretly" or "confidentially."

<u>A</u> / <u>E</u> 23. When Uncle Frederick gave his niece the pendant made of Swedish amber, she went into one of her I-can't-thank-you-enough routines.

<u>D</u> / <u>C</u> 24. *The Last Picture Show*, which runs exactly 118 minutes, was the last picture show that Aunt Miriam was able to sit through.

<u>B</u> / <u>E</u> 25. On the farm we were at the breakfast table by 5:00 A.M., worked a twelve-to-fourteen-hour day, and were in our bunks again by 8:30 P.M.

Chapter 8   Commonly Occurring Sentence Problems

Corrections of Fused Sentences   [pages 353–354]

1. Ted and Alice arrived late at the stadium they missed most of the first quarter.
* Ted and Alice arrived late at the stadium. They missed most of the first quarter.
* Ted and Alice arrived late at the stadium; they missed most of the first quarter.
* Because Ted and Alice arrived late at the stadium, they missed most of the first quarter.
* Because they arrived late at the stadium, Ted and Alice missed most of the first quarter.
* Ted and Alice missed most of the first quarter because they arrived late at the stadium.
* Arriving late at the stadium, Ted and Alice missed most of the first quarter.
* Ted and Alice arrived late at the stadium and missed most of the first quarter.

2. The lecture halls in Old Main are too large students cannot hear their instructors.
* The lecture halls in Old Main are too large. Students cannot hear their instructors.
* The lecture halls in Old Main are too large; students cannot hear their instructors.
* Because the lecture halls in Old Main are too large, students cannot hear their instructors.
* In Old Main, students cannot hear their instructors because the lecture halls are too large.
* In Old Main, students cannot hear their instructors; the lecture halls are too large.
* The lecture halls in Old Main being too large, students cannot hear their instructors.
* Students in Old Main cannot hear their instructors; the lecture halls are too large.

3. These books were too long to read them took me several weeks.
* These books were too long. To read them took me several weeks.
* These books were too long; to read them took me several weeks.
* Because these books were too long, it took me several weeks to read them.
* To read these books took me several weeks; they were too long.
* These books were too long. Reading them took me several weeks.
* Because these books were too long, reading them took me several weeks.
* Reading these books took me several weeks; they were too long.

Subject-Verb Agreement Error   [pages 361–363]

1. stands, 2. Do, 3. remains, 4. was, 5. live, 6. has, 7. was, 8. have, 9. was, 10. have, 11. favors, 12. produce, 13. is, 14. were, 15. care, 16. have, 17. allows, 18. were, 19. offers, 20. have, 21. were, 22. has, 23. are, 24. make, 25. is, 26. have, 27. plans, 28. were, 29. were, 30. has.

Pronoun Case Error   [pages 369-370]

<u>O</u> 1. me,   <u>ND</u> 2. Their,   <u>R</u> 3. myself,   <u>O</u> 4. me,   <u>R</u> 5. himself,   <u>S</u> 6. she,   <u>S</u> 7. who,
<u>O</u> 8. whomever,   <u>R</u> 9. ourselves,   <u>ND</u> 10. your,   <u>I</u> 11. themselves,   <u>S</u> 12. he,   <u>O</u> 13. her,
<u>ND</u> 14. my,   <u>S</u> 15. whoever,   <u>O</u> 16. me,   <u>O</u> 17. him,   <u>R</u> 18. myself,   <u>S</u> 19. he,   <u>ND</u> 20. our,
<u>O</u> 21. him,   <u>S</u> 22. they,   <u>O</u> 23. them,   <u>PP</u> 24. yours,   <u>S</u> 25. I

Sentence Problems Review Exercises (1–5)   [pages 371–375]

Exercise 1:   B D C A E B D A C E B D C E A D B E C A

Exercise 2:   B E D D A E B C C A E B D A D C E A C B

Exercise 3:   D A E C B D B C E A B D A C B E E A C D

Exercise 4:   B E C E A D B D A C C A E B D A E C B D

Exercise 5:   B D E C E A D B E C A D C A C B D A E B

27

Chapter 9   Commonly Occurring
Sentence Problems Continued

Pronoun-Antecedent Error Editing   [pages 383–386]

1. Every year on March 15, the finance committee submits its report to the membership.

2. Alice was in one of her giddy states when she spoke to her mother.
Alice's mother was in one of her giddy states when Alice spoke to her.

3. By now you should know that those kinds of remarks do not win friends and influence people.

4. As everybody knows, people experiencing extreme stress may do things that are not in their own best interest.

5. After cooking the fish on a hot stone, the old trapper ate his dinner.

6. Many of the students had not paid their tuition, a mistake that resulted in their schedules being dropped.

7. The speaker charged that nowadays the public school system allows everybody to graduate from high school.

8. Both speakers were a bit below their usual performance.

9. Had either Francine or Myrna returned to her regular place of employment?

10. Osgood called Geraldine's place half a dozen times before going to the party, but Geraldine never answered.

11. These kinds of mistakes are simply inexcusable in a paper for an advanced composition class.

12. When we discovered that the garage had not repaired our car properly, we called the mechanics and asked what the problem was.

13. For the third time in as many weeks, Ruth told Doris to think about having her house refinanced.

14. Everyone in the research group recorded his or her thoughts in a daily journal.
All the participants in the research group recorded their thoughts in a daily journal.

15. Constantine had a brain hemorrhage about a month ago, but he is much improved now.

16. If there are complaints about the mosquitoes, kill them with the bug zapper.

17. Every man and woman in the community will now be asked his or her opinion on this matter.
All men and women in the community will now be asked their opinion on this matter.

18. We watched the crowd leaving the ballpark and scattering toward their cars.

19. We looked at every painting in the gallery, an exercise that took us all afternoon.

20. Neither the coach nor the players cared to say what they thought about the school's decision to drop varsity football.

21. Constance is studying journalism because she wants to become a journalist.

22. All of the scholarship applicants explained their reasons for wanting to go to college.

23. When the students had completed their papers, the instructor casually stuffed the papers into his briefcase.

24. Public education appears to be in a declining state, and this situation did not happen overnight.

25. As everyone who hasn't been living in a cave knows, people—especially the politically correct—are not wearing animal fur this year.

Misplaced Modifier Editing   [pages 391–394]

1. Bob and Marian chatted with each other in whispers while I read my assignment.

2. Although he didn't intend to, Marvin bought a man's black hunting jacket.

3. Despite your efforts to squeeze us out of the market, we shall continue to produce hummingbird feeders.

4. To almost everyone's delight, Professor English said we would take Friday off.

5. When he sat down at the board meeting, Cyril remembered that he had left his laptop computer at home.

6. In this family we eat only fish and chips on Fridays.

7. Within four or five years, the university intends to begin a doctoral program in genetic engineering.

8. Crispin bought his wife an inexpensive negligee for her birthday.

9. The soccer field, which was fertilized every spring, was located next to the hydroelectric dam.

10. I want to go home on weekends so I can have a quiet place to study.

11. For the good of all, students without sufficient academic preparation should not be allowed to enter a college.

12. Not more than twenty minutes after the police had gone, we found the money stolen from the local savings and loan.

13. My best advice is that you not buy a used car with high mileage from a local dealer.

14. On his head, the lad was wearing a cap that came to a sharp point.

15. Thousands of voters completely misunderstood the differences between the two candidates.

16. Acme, Inc., has decided once and for all to terminate its partnerships with foreign suppliers.

17. Karen was slowly put to sleep by the novel she was reading.

18. Summer is almost over, and we've had just three days with temperatures above ninety degrees.

19. Gretchen's plan was to move the furniture into her apartment without help from anyone.

20. By running an ad in the classified, we were able to locate the child's lost pet.

21. When we were tourists on Mackinac Island, we rented horses with adjustable saddles.

22. The company that Faustina is now with exports rice to China.

23. The Volvo's psychedelic paint job drew a large crowd of admiring spectators.

24. What these people desperately need is for someone to explain the situation to them.

25. Poor Clarence knew before he made it that his proposal of marriage would be rejected.

Dangling Modifier Editing   [pages 398–401]

C 1. To keep abreast of current developments in the field, one must take frequent refresher courses.
For one to keep abreast of current developments in the field, frequent refresher courses are necessary.

A 2. Frightened by the constant thunder and lightning, we saw our resolve to press on gradually diminished.
Because we were frightened by the constant thunder and lightning, our resolve to press on gradually diminished.

D 3. When one is working in a dusty place, a breathing mask should be worn.
You should wear a breathing mask when working in a dusty place.

C 4. A sense of the ridiculous is necessary for one to compose obvious examples of sentences with dangling modifiers.
One must possess a sense of the ridiculous to compose obvious examples of sentences with dangling modifiers.

B 5. After the team had won three championships in as many years, the fans began to buy season tickets by the thousands.
The fans began to buy season tickets by the thousands after the team had won three championships in as many years.

D 6. If under the influence of alcohol, you should not drive a motor vehicle under any circumstances.
Under no circumstances should a motor vehicle be driven by a person under the influence of alcohol.

B 7. By lighting the oil lamps, you made the room much cozier than it had been.
Your lighting the oil lamps made the room much cozier than it had been.

A 8. As we were flying high above the ancient oak trees, the rides in the amusement park looked like small toys.

B 9. After I had slept sixteen hours, my joints were so stiff that I could hardly walk.

D 10. I found that mangy cat when it was just a kitten.

A 11. As I was flying up from Asheville this morning, the wind currents were unseasonable.
The wind currents were unseasonable as I was flying up from Asheville this morning.

<u>B</u> 12. The house and outbuildings should be secured before we settle in for the night.
Before we settle in for the night, we should secure the house and outbuildings.

<u>C</u> 13. To succeed in this position, you need both ability and thorough training.
For anyone to succeed in this position, both ability and thorough training are needed.

<u>D</u> 14. If this balloon is sufficiently inflated with hot air, several people can ride in it.
Several people can ride in this balloon if it is sufficiently inflated with hot air.

<u>A</u> 15. When I glanced up momentarily from my desk, a hideous monster was peering through the north window.
As I glanced up momentarily from my desk, I saw a hideous monster peering through the north window.

<u>C</u> 16. You will find that deep pockets are a prerequisite to join this club.
To join this club, you will find deep pockets a prerequisite.

<u>D</u> 17. When typing the final draft of a research paper, you should keep the entire room free of distractions.
You should keep the entire room free of distractions when you are typing the final draft of a research paper.

<u>B</u> 18. By setting the oven at 425 degrees, you will cook the turkey in a third less time.
If you set the oven at 425 degrees, the turkey will cook in a third less time.

<u>D</u> 19. Although the young man was only eighteen years old, the judge sentenced him to life in prison.

<u>C</u> 20. To enjoy as novel as subtle as this one, you must read it two or three times.
If you want to enjoy as novel as subtle as this one, you must read it two or three times.

<u>A</u> 21. Shaken by the news of the break-in, we called the police as our first move.

<u>C</u> 22. While I was studying for my algebra exam, the police burst into my room looking for stolen computer software.

<u>C</u> 23. To graduate summa cum laude at this university, you are required to have an overall 3.75 grade-point average.
For anyone to graduate summa cum laude at this university, an overall 3.75 grade-point average is required.

<u>B</u> 24. Fawns are born about six and a half months after they are conceived.
After mating, a female deer can have a fawn in about six and a half months.

<u>A</u> 25. As we looked north across Yellow Dog Valley, more than two dozen hot-air balloons were visible.
Looking north across Yellow Dog Valley, we could see more than two dozen hot-air balloons.

Faulty Parallelism Editing (1)   [pages 403–405]

3. Alas, at the age of fifty Bradford remains what he has always been, a knave and a fool.

4. For as long as I knew him, Aldous liked reading old manuscripts, attending estate sales, and rummaging through out-of-the-way antique shops.

5. Germaine's fundamental problem wasn't that she earned too little money but that she spent too much of it on frivolous purchases.

6. Professor Graham complimented Ingrid for writing such a well-ordered paper and for handing it in before the final due date.

7. We have no time to reminisce about the good old days, to cry over spilt milk, or to second-guess ourselves.

8. Although it is true that Anthony is tall, dark, and handsome, upstairs he may be a few shingles short of a roof.

9. The mayor's address, long and tedious, was filled with obscure political innuendo.

10. Dr. Munson is a woman with a sound academic track record who will no doubt make a fine vice president for academic affairs.

11. The family bakery, more successful today that it was ten years ago, is located in the old county jail building, which is hidden behind a stone wall with metal spikes on the top.

12. Cleaning the house, preparing meals, and working on the yard occupied my whole weekend.

13. No matter how hard we tried, we could not remember the applicant's name, address, or previous experience.

14. After three months in the wilderness on our own, we were in need of rest and food.

15. It goes without saying that we look forward to hearing from our new partners and to having an opportunity to exchange ideas with them.

Faulty Parallelism Editing (2)   [pages 407–408]

1. The group of Swedish tourists found Montreal more intriguing than any other Canadian city they had visited.

2. Luther, who is a student both of the game and of motivating adolescent boys, will make a good coach.

3. Everyone agreed that the freshmen enjoyed their classes more than the seniors did.

4. The new edition of the textbook for microbiology is much more comprehensive than the old edition was.

5. You simply cannot deny that Balthazar is as ambitious as, if not more ambitious than, his brother Marmaduke.

6. Alas, my humanities instructor likes neither rock nor easy-listening music.

7. This elective course in logic beats anything else I have taken during my three years at the university.

8. The game between Northern and Hinterland State was either the longest or the second longest in the history of the league.

9. Emeline's watercolors have improved to the point that they are more marketable than her acrylics.

10. Not only did Ellen lose her taste for fried foods, but she also stopped eating ice cream.

Past Tense and Perfect Tense Verb Form Identification [pages 412–413]

1. rung, 2. saw, 3. grown, 4. torn, 5. did, 6. come, 7. drank, 8. blew, 9. stolen, 10. began, 11. bitten, 12. knew, 13. swum, 14. ran, 15. worn, 16. came, 17. broken, 18. sank, 19. did, 20. given, 21. wrung, 22. sang, 23. frozen, 24. rang, 25. forgotten, 26. brought, 27. burst, 28. chosen, 29. gone, 30. drew

Sentence Problems Review Exercises (6–10) [pages 415–424]

Exercise 6:	I	G	H	F	I	J	G	H	F	J	G	J	F	I	H	F	I	H	J	G
Exercise 7:	F	H	J	I	G	J	F	I	G	H	F	H	J	G	I	F	H	J	G	I
Exercise 8:	F	J	H	I	G	J	G	I	F	H	I	G	H	J	F	I	G	J	F	H
Exercise 9:	H	G	I	J	H	F	J	F	I	G	F	J	F	H	I	G	I	J	H	G
Exercise 10:	I	F	J	F	H	G	J	G	I	H	G	H	J	F	I	G	J	H	F	I

PART TWO

EXERCISE QUIZZES
TO ACCOMPANY TEXT MATERIALS

Nonstandard or Inappropriate Expressions (Sequences 1–3)

_____ 1-1. Haven't you lost (*a lot / alot*) of weight since last semester?

_____ 1-2. Clifton (*accidently / accidentally*) locked his keys in the car.

_____ 1-3. Several trees had fallen (*acrost / acrossed / across*) the old road.

_____ 1-4. I didn't think the game was (*all that / very*) exciting, except perhaps at the end.

_____ 1-5. The senators were questioned (*about / as to*) their personal wealth.

_____ 1-6. We arrived home (*around / around about / about*) four in the morning.

_____ 2-1. After the lecture, several students (*posed / asked*) interesting questions.

_____ 2-2. It isn't unusual for children to be (*ascared / afraid*) of the dark.

_____ 2-3. Your (*analysis / analyzation*) of the situation was quite good.

_____ 2-4. How many books had the visiting lecturer (*authored / written*)?

_____ 2-5. This is (*as far as / all the farther*) I feel like walking tonight.

_____ 2-6. The most intimidating (*aspect / feature*) of the dominant male gorilla is his size.

_____ 2-7. We are willing to go almost (*anywhere / anywheres*) you would like to go.

_____ 3-1. (*Be sure and / Be sure to*) wash your hands before eating dinner.

_____ 3-2. The store was (*burglarized / burgled*) sometime over the weekend.

_____ 3-3. (*Being as / Because*) we hadn't eaten for hours, everyone was very hungry.

_____ 3-4. I can't help (*thinking / but think*) we may have gone wrong somewhere.

_____ 3-5. In the future, you (*better had / should*) be more careful what you say.

_____ 3-6. Is there a chance that the dam will (*burst / bust*) from all this water?

_____ 3-7. You may enjoy the (*balance / rest*) of the afternoon doing what you please.

Nonstandard or Inappropriate Expressions (Sequences 4–6)

_____ 4-1. There was a time when we (*could have / could of*) won this battle with ease.

_____ 4-2. Historically, fair (*complected / complexioned*) people lived in northern climates.

_____ 4-3. After this little blunder, you (*can't hardly / can hardly*) expect people to trust you completely.

_____ 4-4. Do you like (*coleslaw / cold slaw*) on your hot dogs?

_____ 4-5. The two groups (*conferenced / talked*) over lunch.

_____ 4-6. As always, the discussion (*centered around / centered on*) management misbehavior.

_____ 4-7. Dr. Dodge (*asserts / claims*) that Shakespeare did not write all the plays attributed to him.

_____ 5-1. What you are saying is (*different from / different than*) what you have said before.

_____ 5-2. (*Eventhough / Even though*) it was only her first try, Ivy did well.

_____ 5-3. Are you still (*enthusiastic / enthused*) about our chances for success?

_____ 5-4. We (*doubt if / doubt that*) Windowwell, Inc., can raise the money.

_____ 5-5. Alas, they did not (*escape / excape*) in time to avoid being caught.

_____ 5-6. Your position is the (*direct opposite / opposite*) of what we had anticipated.

_____ 5-7. The old man is (*just as / equally as*) alert as he ever was.

_____ 6-1. Did you have a/an (*fun / enjoyable*) time at your class reunion?

_____ 6-2. Not one (*female / woman*) applied for the position.

_____ 6-3. The instructor's (*skill / expertise*) at teaching slow children is amazing.

_____ 6-4. No one (*thought / figured*) that you had a chance of winning over the boss.

_____ 6-5. What was the most important (*factor / consideration*) in your taking the position?

_____ 6-6. Those who work (*for nothing / for free*) may reduce the value of all labor.

Nonstandard or Inappropriate Expressions (Sequences 7–9)

_____ 7-1. Although (*heartrendering* / *heartrending*), the tale was entirely false.

_____ 7-2. I (*guess* / *suppose*) you remember our position on free trade?

_____ 7-3. It is time to (*home in on* / *hone in on* / *focus on*) the real causes of violence in our streets.

_____ 7-4. (*Hopefully* / *We hope*) they will do just as well in the second round.

_____ 7-5. The faculty has requested a wage (*increase* / *hike*) at the beginning of the spring semester.

_____ 7-6. Racial prejudice seems to be a great (*hindrance* / *hinderance*) to the nation's domestic tranquillity.

_____ 7-7. It pleases us (*heaps* / *greatly*) that you are doing well in school.

_____ 8-1. Hypocrisy (*is when* / *occurs when*) one pretends to be what one is not.

_____ 8-2. That dog has been chasing (*it's* / *its'* / *its*) tail since breakfast.

_____ 8-3. Will we ever be able to (*communicate* / *interface*) comfortably with people so different from ourselves?

_____ 8-4. These words will (*impact* / *affect*) virtually all who hear them.

_____ 8-5. The class has completed an (*exhaustive* / *in-depth*) study of elephant behavior.

_____ 8-6. This company is only (*incidently* / *incidentally*) interested in the business furniture market.

_____ 8-7. (*If* / *In case*) our service is not adequate, we will refund your money.

_____ 9-1. We (*might of* / *might have*) bitten off more than we can digest.

_____ 9-2. (*Most* / *A majority*) of the vegetables had been trucked in from either Florida or California.

_____ 9-3. We give you this dinosaur egg as a (*momento* / *memento*) of your many years at Acme, Inc.

_____ 9-4. Jan presented her case with a (*persuasive* / *meaningful*) personal narrative.

_____ 9-5. (*Motivated* / *Incentivized*) students are a pleasure to teach.

_____ 9-6. Margaret was (*kind of* / *somewhat*) bewildered by her brother's anger.

Nonstandard or Inappropriate Expressions (Sequences 10–12)

____10-1.   Don't (*opt for* / *choose*) the easy life; you will be bored out of your mind.

____10-2.   Ted dove (*off* / *off of*) the highest cliff overlooking Squid Bay.

____10-3.   The crew (*must of* / *must have*) redone that job a dozen times.

____10-4.   By morning, the talking chickens were (*nowhere* / *nowheres*) to be found.

____10-5.   There were only (*miniscule* / *minuscule*) traces of radioactivity in your fillings.

____10-6.   The children spent most of the (*nite* / *night*) telling ghost stories.

____10-7.   We lost the contract (*because of* / *on account of*) poor management practices.

____11-1.   I often feel (*paranoid* / *uneasy*) among strangers, especially on their turf.

____11-2.   Your (*partner* / *pardner*) in crime turned out to be not trustworthy.

____11-3.   After working all day, everyone was (*plenty* / *very*) tired and hungry.

____11-4.   The metamorphosis of a butterfly is a strange (*phenomenon* / *phenomena*) of nature.

____11-5.   We keep telling (*ourselves* / *ourself*) not to believe such incredible stories.

____11-6.   Alas, much of our lives is spent trying to (*orientate* / *orient*) ourselves to our surroundings.

____12-1.   We have (*publicly* / *publically*) stated our position in many forums.

____12-2.   Mark said some (*pretty* / *rather*) silly things toward the end of the evening.

____12-3.   This company (*almost never* / *rarely ever*) advertises on radio or television.

____12-4.   It is a (*proven fact* / *fact*) that on average men live shorter lives than women.

____12-5.   (*At present* / *Presently*) the student body numbers almost 15,000.

____12-6.   (*Prior to* / *Before*) coming to college, I was in the meat packing business.

____12-7.   Take care what you (*prophesy* / *prophesize*); it may come true and make you famous.

Nonstandard or Inappropriate Expressions (Sequences 13–15)

____ 13-1. The stricken children were (*transported* / *evacuated*) to a metropolitan hospital.

____ 13-2. (*Irregardless* / *Regardless*) of the odds, the troop carried on.

____ 13-3. The only (*relevant* / *revelant*) issue here is who has the necessary capital.

____ 13-4. Aunt Wilma is very accomplished a (*sharing* / *telling*) bedtime stories.

____ 13-5. The truth is probably (*somewhere* / *somewheres*) between these two lies.

____ 13-6. Now we know that we (*should of* / *should have*) taken the earlier flight.

____ 13-7. Inexperience is the primary (*reason that* / *reason why*) they agreed to such a bad contract.

____ 14-1. Why don't you (*try and* / *try to*) dance to the music?

____ 14-2. You should (*use* / *utilize*) your common sense in such matters.

____ 14-3. The (*true facts* / *actual facts* / *truth*) about the charges of embezzlement never came to light.

____ 14-4. Aren't we (*supposed to* / *suppose to*) eat at noon—every day?

____ 14-5. I (*am afraid* / *think*) the election of new officers will have to be postponed.

____ 14-6. (*Who* / *Who all*) was scheduled to speak at the afternoon session?

____ 14-7. Although your plan is (*viable* / *workable*), we don't like it.

____ 15-1. Nelson (*would have* / *would of*) stayed if he had only been asked.

____ 15-2. Does anyone know what (*triggered* / *provoked*) the latest run on the bank?

____ 15-3. The (*lady* / *woman*) who lives next door wrestles alligators for a living.

____ 15-4. These strange events are (*happening* / *transpiring*) even as we speak.

____ 15-5. Thaddeus is an (*infrequent* / *unfrequent*) patron of the local restaurants.

____ 15-6. Please explain to me (*how come* / *why*) so many people are angry at the public school system.

Words That Sound Alike (Sequences 1–3)

_____ 1-1. Many of the (*adherence* / *adherents*) of this sect are retired garment workers.

_____ 1-2. Norbert lives under the (*allusion* / *elusion* / *illusion*) that he is a clever fellow.

_____ 1-3. Your spouse is supposed to be an (*alley* / *ally*), not an enemy.

_____ 1-4. The marinade was too (*acetic* / *ascetic*) for my inexperienced palate.

_____ 1-5. Few (*adolescents* / *adolescence*) are prepared to assume the role of parent.

_____ 1-6. The current (*addition* / *edition*) of the text is printed in three colors.

_____ 1-7. Alison told a very funny (*anecdote* / *antidote*) from her first year in college.

_____ 2-1. Good (*attendance* / *attendants*) are difficult to find, no matter what wages you are willing to pay.

_____ 2-2. Your (*ascent* / *assent*) up the corporate ladder seems to have flattened out at bit.

_____ 2-3. Hogarth has been (*bard* / *barred*) from reading his terrible poetry in the park.

_____ 2-4. We could not (*baal* / *bail* / *bale*) fast enough to keep the boat from sinking.

_____ 2-5. Alas, it was a (*barren* / *baron*) book that I read, virtually devoid of ideas.

_____ 2-6. Jan (*bald* / *balled* / *bawled*) like a baby when she learned that her kitten had died.

_____ 2-7. Nan bought an antique magic carpet at the street (*bazaar* / *bizarre*).

_____ 3-1. When Margaret crossed the (*boarder* / *border*), he shot her dead.

_____ 3-2   Please don't (*berry* / *bury*) me on the lone prairie.

_____ 3-3   Although I was not (*born* / *borne*) in a log cabin, I would still like to be president.

_____ 3-4. The (*berth* / *birth*) of the child occurred between Denver and midnight on the prairie.

_____ 3-5. Must you (*boar* / *bore*) us to death with your dreadful tales?

_____ 3-6. These (*beach* / *beech*) nuts play volleyball in the scorching sun all day.

Name _____ Class _____ Section _____

Words That Sound Alike (Sequences 4–6)

____ 4-1. The wind tore a hole in the (*canapé* / *canopy*) at the south entrance to the building.

____ 4-2. These little creatures inhabit a narrow (*borough* / *burro* / *burrow*) west of the barn.

____ 4-3. Alas, we have forgotten that "man does not live by (*bred* / *bread*) alone."

____ 4-4. That is a subject we do not (*broach* / *brooch*) in polite society.

____ 4-5. Take care not to (*brake* / *break*) stride as you approach the finish line.

____ 4-6. What a (*callous* / *callus*) attitude my philosophy professor has about everything.

____ 4-7. How can I (*by* / *bye* / *buy*) some time to prepare for my examinations?

____ 5-1. The (*cent* / *scent* / *sent*) of morning glories drifted in the window.

____ 5-2. The canopy at the south entrance to the building was made of heavy (*canvas* / *canvass*).

____ 5-3. Have you decided on a (*cite* / *sight* / *site*) for the new county building?

____ 5-4. How many years ago was it that the old (*capital* / *capitol*) building burned?

____ 5-5. A (*carrot* / *carat* / *karat* / *caret*) marked the spot where the new paragraphs were to be inserted.

____ 5-6. Ellen eats a bowl of (*cereal* / *serial*) for breakfast each morning.

____ 5-7. The wine (*cellar* / *seller*) is kept at a constant temperature throughout the year.

____ 6-1. Don't pay me a (*complement* / *compliment*) unless you mean it.

____ 6-2. It was difficult to distinguish the (*coward* / *cowered*) from the hero.

____ 6-3. Esteban has been dreading this (*coarse* / *course*) for three years.

____ 6-4. Dolph has had a (*creak* / *creek* / *crick*) in his neck for weeks now.

____ 6-5. A (*courier* / *currier*) with hives tracked me down to deliver the message.

____ 6-6. A wise daughter listens to the (*council* / *counsel*) of her mother.

43

Words That Sound Alike (Sequences 7–9)

_____ 7-1. Without a sweet (*desert / dessert*), a meal isn't a meal.

_____ 7-2. The morning (*dew / do / due*) didn't dry until almost noon.

_____ 7-3. Alas, the (*current / currant*) crop of college graduates is shopping for a market.

_____ 7-4. The (*duel / dual*) was scheduled to be fought at dawn.

_____ 7-5. I so dislike to (*cue / queue*) up for a bus, much less a hamburger.

_____ 7-6. Edmund is a polite and (*discreet / discrete*) person.

_____ 7-7. If you must (*die / dye*) your hair, please choose a color other than green.

_____ 8-1. Caserta felt a little (*faint / feint*) after running fifteen miles.

_____ 8-2. If the employment picture doesn't improve, perhaps you should (*emigrate / immigrate*) to Australia.

_____ 8-3. Seven hundred dollars is a (*fare / fair*) price for the painting.

_____ 8-4. Everyone fears that the state treasury is in (*eminent / imminent*) danger of bankruptcy.

_____ 8-5. Why do the sheep keep eating these (*yew / ewe*) bushes?

_____ 8-6. You might (*exercise / exorcise*) your brain by reading a book now and then.

_____ 8-7. By any standard, the selling of drugs on the street is an (*elicit / illicit*) activity.

_____ 9-1. Walking across an ice (*floe / flow*) can be very dangerous.

_____ 9-2. By its (*gait / gate*), you could tell that the horse was pleased to be home.

_____ 9-3. The truth came to the (*for / four / fore*) quite by accident.

_____ 9-4. It requires a bit of culinary courage to bake a (*friar / fryer*).

_____ 9-5. Agnes has a (*flair / flare*) for saying the right thing at the right time.

_____ 9-6. Every step (*foreword / forward*) seemed to cost us two steps back.

Words That Sound Alike (Sequences 10–12)

_____ 10-1. Alice bought two (*handmade / handmaid*) quilts at the arts and crafts fair.

_____ 10-2. Your pet (*hair / hare*) departed this life in an abbreviated confrontation with a bobcat.

_____ 10-3. We have many (*grisly / gristly / grizzly*) gray days as fall moves into winter.

_____ 10-4. Isn't the (*gorilla / guerrilla*) the largest of the great apes?

_____ 10-5. Today, the premier teachers (*gild / gilled / guild*) is called the National Education Association.

_____ 10-6. It takes a (*groan / grown*) man, and a good one, to wrestle an alligator.

_____ 11-1. The story that you have just (*heard / herd*) is wholly untrue.

_____ 11-2. A (*hardy / hearty*) meal or two and the warriors will be on their way.

_____ 11-3. (*Hoarse / Horse*) from a throat infection, the speaker could hardly be heard.

_____ 11-4. The story that you have just listened to is (*holey / holy / wholly*) untrue.

_____ 11-5. The Lawsons live (*hear / here*) on the south side of the lake.

_____ 11-6. We stayed at the provincial (*hostel / hostile*) for almost a month.

_____ 11-7. The sunset was of an amber (*hew / hue*) indigenous to the Far North.

_____ 12-1. Does (*lean / lien*) meat come from cows that exercise regularly and watch their diet?

_____ 12-2. When the (*levee / levy*) broke, the entire town was in danger of washing away.

_____ 12-3. The (*lessen / lesson*) we have learned today is not one we would often want to teach.

_____ 12-4. For a stew, a (*leak / leek*) is as good as, if not better than, an onion.

_____ 12-5. I want to read a pleasant (*idle / idol / idyll*) set in plodding, uncomplicated times.

_____ 12-6. It is the (*ladder / latter*) of success that we most want to mount.

_____ 12-7. These starving villagers (*knead / kneed / need*) more bread and less rhetoric.

Words That Sound Alike (Sequences 13–15)

____13-1. Everyone had a (*marry* / *merry*) old time at the family reunion.

____13-2. Giant (*magnates* / *magnets*) are used to pick up this stuff.

____13-3. If you need a (*loan* / *lone*), try the bank.

____13-4. You are (*liable* / *libel*) for the damage you have caused.

____13-5. Alas, we have become lost in a (*maize* / *maze*) of paperwork.

____13-6. Alice has a pleasant (*manner* / *manor*) that puts everyone at ease.

____13-7. A bolt of (*lightening* / *lightning*) struck the barn about noon.

____14-1. It was indeed a (*moot* / *mute*) point whether the man was shot or hanged.

____14-2. We (*morn* / *mourn*) for ourselves, not for the dead.

____14-3. Plastic has today replaced (*medal* / *meddle* / *metal* / *mettle*) in the manufacture of thousands of items.

____14-4. Americans are now being told that (*mustard* / *mustered*) gas was used on our troops during the Gulf War.

____14-5. Is it now going to be government officials who (*meat* / *meet* / *mete*) out medical care to the people?

____14-6. The youth escaped going to prison only because he was a (*miner* / *minor*).

____14-7. It takes a person of some (*medal* / *meddle* / *metal* / *mettle*) to prosecute these drug lords.

____15-1. Although horses may (*nay* / *nee* / *neigh*), they are not naysayers.

____15-2. Edmund (*passed* / *past*) the examination with points to spare.

____15-3. Poor Norbert has spent his whole life with only one (*oar* / *or* / *ore*) in the water.

____15-4. Remember, a (*pair* / *pare* / *pear*) a day keeps the gastroenterologist away.

____15-5. The house payment is (*overdo* / *overdue*) by at least two weeks.

____15-6. Our court system seems to have become a (*parity* / *parody*) of itself.

Name _____ **Class** _____ **Section** _____

Words That Sound Alike (Sequences 16–18)

____ 16-1. About midday we reached the highest (*pique / peek / peak*) in the range.

____ 16-2. Is there a seafood restaurant at the end of the (*peer / pier*)?

____ 16-3. It is a (*pore / pour / poor*) soldier who cannot keep a rifle clean.

____ 16-4. Please tell the truth, (*plain / plane*) and simple.

____ 16-5. Stanley bought some (*pole / poll*) tacks to put up the posters with.

____ 16-6. The racers had to (*petal / peddle / pedal*) like mad to make it to the top of the last hill.

____ 16-7. Let's (*peal / peel*) a few bells and wake up the neighbors.

____ 17-1. Our next-door neighbor used to be the (*principal / principle*) of the local high school.

____ 17-2. Isn't China the most (*populace / populous*) nation in the world?

____ 17-3. Be careful what you (*pray / prey*) for; you may get it.

____ 17-4. It is time to (*rain / reign / rein*) in your ambition and take a little time to smell the roses.

____ 17-5. Without the children, the house was as (*quiet / quite*) as a tomb.

____ 17-6. Most of the (*residence / residents*) of this apartment complex are millionaires.

____ 18-1. In recent years, the religious (*right / rite / write*) is becoming more active politically.

____ 18-2. Everyone agrees that it is time for many of the old (*salons / saloons / solons*) in Washington to be replaced.

____ 18-3. Deirdre (*road / rode / rowed*) her custom Harley from coast to coast.

____ 18-4. The game became a (*root / route / rout*) almost before the fans were settled in their seats.

____ 18-5. What a lot of (*rot / wrought*) you try to include in your arguments.

____ 18-6. Even the (*sail / sale*) prices were too high for my budget.

____ 18-7. The ancient ships flew flags with a (*scull / skull*) and crossbones.

Words That Sound Alike (Sequences 19–21)

____19-1.   Somebody should put a (*stake* / *steak*) through that vampire's heart.

____19-2.   Don't (*stair* / *stare*) at me unless you have climbing on your mind.

____19-3.   The old man is a (*soar* / *sore* / *sower*) of seeds, not stitches.

____19-4.   Nothing in the universe seems to remain (*stationery* / *stationary*) for very long.

____19-5.   When I told you to (*sear* / *seer*) a ham, I didn't mean for you to torch a comedian.

____19-6.   On Sunday, we (*stayed* / *staid*) home most of the afternoon and watched television.

____20-1.   The king was (*throne* / *thrown*) from his horse and lost his crown.

____20-2.   (*Tea* / *Tee*) time at the manor house does not involve golf clubs.

____20-3.   They met on a (*summary* / *summery*) day and were married only weeks later.

____20-4.   "Listen," Montague said; "(*their* / *there* / *they're*) playing our song."

____20-5.   I have (*told* / *tolled*) you a hundred times not to play with the bells.

____20-6.   Experience has taught us that (*to* / *too* / *two*) houses to run are too many.

____20-7.   The (*trader* / *traitor*) was shot for cheating the trappers out of a few pelts.

____21-1.   Alice is a (*veracious* / *voracious*) reader of science fiction.

____21-2.   We found an empty medicine (*vial* / *vile*) on the sink in the bathroom.

____21-3.   There is a (*vain* / *vane* / *vein*) of flippancy in almost everything Ingrid says.

____21-4.   Don't spend an (*undo* / *undue*) amount of time on such a minor issue.

____21-5.   We didn't know (*weather* / *whether*) to go or stay.

____21-6.   Jerome says that dieting is an exercise in (*waist* / *waste*) management.

____21-7.   These were the boots (*warn* / *worn*) by the general who died with his epaulets on.

Important Distinctions (Sequences 1–3)

_____ 1-1. Perhaps you could (*adapt / adopt*) a more polite manner of behavior.

_____ 1-2. Dunstan is (*adverse / averse*) to eating red meat and other animal products.

_____ 1-3. That was the couple who couldn't even (*agree to / agree with / agree on*) the time of day to have dinner.

_____ 1-4. Try to avoid taking (*access / excess*) luggage on a European trip.

_____ 1-5. How will all this (*affect / effect*) the general membership?

_____ 1-6. Such questions will only (*aggravate / irritate*) an already tense situation.

_____ 1-7. Edgar has long been (*addicted / devoted*) to cigarettes and cigars.

_____ 2-1. Derek often (*alludes / refers*) to his older brother as Mr. Money Bags.

_____ 2-2. These explanations are (*altogether / all together*) too complicated for their intended audience.

_____ 2-3. This year we (*aim / intend*) to improve sales by 40 percent.

_____ 2-4. (*Although / Though*) he talks a good game, Franklin is no athlete.

_____ 2-5. You promised that you would (*all ways / always*) love me.

_____ 2-6. (*All / All of*) her anger suddenly vanished, and she smiled at me.

_____ 2-7. (*Among / Between*) quarters, the fans entertained themselves by throwing water balloons at one another.

_____ 3-1. We don't play golf (*anymore / any more*) because the greens fees are too high.

_____ 3-2. The police must (*appraise / apprise*) you of your rights before arresting you.

_____ 3-3. The state requires that you (*assure / ensure / insure*) yourself against other drivers.

_____ 3-4. With a little bad luck, (*anyone / any one*) of us could end up in debt.

_____ 3-5. The fellow was (*angry / mad*) enough to eat a rather expensive straw hat.

_____ 3-6. We had a(n) (*awfully / very*) good time at the family wake.

Important Distinctions (Sequences 4–6)

_____ 4-1. Don't (*breath* / *breathe*) with your mouth open.

_____ 4-2. The stipend comes from a wealthy (*benefactor* / *beneficiary*).

_____ 4-3. Everyone felt (*bad* / *badly*) about the outcome of the game.

_____ 4-4. After (*awhile* / *a while*), most people lost interest in the fight.

_____ 4-5. (*Beside* / *Besides*) yours, our troubles should have training wheels.

_____ 4-6. Edmund still runs (*better than* / *more than*) five miles each day.

_____ 4-7. We voted for you (*because* / *cause*) you didn't promise us anything.

_____ 5-1. Although (*cheap* / *inexpensive*), the suit was nicely tailored from beautiful material.

_____ 5-2. (*Can* / *May*) I borrow your Rolls Royce for a few days to go to Cleveland?

_____ 5-3. A (*bunch* / *group*) of carolers from the church stopped by the house for a cup of kindness.

_____ 5-4. Pouting is a bit (*childish* / *childlike*), even for a full professor.

_____ 5-5. We saw the film of the (*classic* / *classical*) English novel *Tom Jones*.

_____ 5-6. There is a clear (*causal* / *casual*) relationship between diet and colon cancer.

_____ 6-1. I am quite (*conscience* / *conscious*) of the magnitude of my blunder.

_____ 6-2. Shannon has (*consistently* / *constantly*) scored at the top of her class in math and science.

_____ 6-3. Who, may I ask, is your most trusted (*confident* / *confidant*)?

_____ 6-4. There are enormous (*climatic* / *climactic*) differences between Stockholm and Moscow.

_____ 6-5. A basketball team is (*comprised* / *composed*) of five players.

_____ 6-6. Although the book is quite (*comprehensible* / *comprehensive*), it is very difficult to understand.

_____ 6-7. (*Present-day* / *Contemporary*) musical instruments are not necessarily better than those of the past.

Important Distinctions (Sequences 7–9)

____ 7-1. An important (*criteria* / *criterion*) for judging good teaching is patience.

____ 7-2. By reputation, the CIA specializes in (*covert* / *overt*) intelligence activities.

____ 7-3. The noise was (*continual* / *continuous*); it never stopped.

____ 7-4. I owe my (*creditors* / *debtors*) a small fortune.

____ 7-5. The third contestant had a (*definite* / *definitive*) lisp when she spoke.

____ 7-6. You have (*convinced* / *persuaded*) me to enroll in graduate school.

____ 8-1. These two have been in love with (*each other* / *one another*) since elementary school.

____ 8-2. Recently, my brother has become (*disinterested* / *uninterested*) in televised football games.

____ 8-3. You lost your scholarship (*because of* / *due to*) old-fashioned laziness.

____ 8-4. Do we have to (*dissemble* / *disassemble*) the old system before creating the new one?

____ 8-5. Problem one is (*distinct* / *distinctive*) from problem two; they are not connected.

____ 8-6 A car (*deprecates* / *depreciates*) in value from the moment you purchase it.

____ 8-7. At what age does an infant (*discover* / *invent*) its toes?

____ 9-1. The (*epigram* / *epigraph* / *epithet* / *epitaph*) on the third tombstone had several spelling errors.

____ 9-2. At present, (*endless* / *innumerable*) people are trying to cross the border.

____ 9-3. I am no longer (*envious* / *enviable*) of people who have high-intensity jobs.

____ 9-4. The (*envelop* / *envelope*) had no glue on the flap.

____ 9-5. Alas, we are an (*earthly* / *earthy*) clan, not very sophisticated.

____ 9-6. We are looking for a more (*economical* / *economic*) way to heat the house.

____ 9-7. Fear of strangers seems to be (*endemic* / *epidemic* / *pandemic*) to the human species.

Important Distinctions (Sequences 10–12)

_____ 10-1.   I have spent an (*exhaustive / exhausting*) day trying to sell what no one wants to buy.

_____ 10-2.   These tales are (*false / fallacious*); they are filled with inconsistencies.

_____ 10-3.   (*Everyone / Every one*) of the problems has several possible answers.

_____ 10-4.   Isadore is an (*exceedingly / excessively*) gracious person.

_____ 10-5.   For such (*exceptional / exceptionable*) behavior, you are being dropped from the class.

_____ 10-6.   Louden is (*famous / notorious*) for giving people nice presents at Christmas.

_____ 10-7.   You did a(n) (*especially / specially*) nice job on the set design.

_____ 11-1.   Meta is a (*genus / genius*); she knows something about everything.

_____ 11-2.   From here, is it (*farther / further*) to Buffalo or Denver?

_____ 11-3.   Jeanne did very (*good / well*) on the second round of questions.

_____ 11-4.   (*Fewer / Less*) people attended this year than last.

_____ 11-5.   The ship (*floundered / foundered*) on a sandbar in the middle of the lake.

_____ 11-6.   Steam is water in a (*gaseous / gassy*) state.

_____ 11-7.   Don't (*flaunt / flout*) your parents; they have given you life and sustenance.

_____ 12-1.   This is the most (*historic / historical*) site of the entire war.

_____ 12-2.   Generally, fresh fruit and vegetables are more (*healthy / healthful*) than meat.

_____ 12-3.   We intend to build the new (*house / home*) on this very spot.

_____ 12-4.   The thief is scheduled to be (*hanged / hung*) at dawn.

_____ 12-5.   I am (*gratified / grateful*) that the damage was so minor.

_____ 12-6.   Muriel (*hates / dislikes*) this climate of perpetual sunshine and cool breezes.

Important Distinctions (Sequences 13–15)

____ 13-1.   This (*ingenious / ingenuous*) little machine corrects my spelling errors.

____ 13-2.   Such an (*illustrative / illustrious*) career cannot be praised too highly.

____ 13-3.   No one can see your (*imaginary / imaginative*) friends but you.

____ 13-4.   I fear that we have walked (*in / into*) yet another hornet's nest.

____ 13-5.   A monkey is (*incapable of / unable to*) learn(ing) to read.

____ 13-6.   Your (*incredible / incredulous*) expression tells me that you do not believe me.

____ 14-1.   Please don't (*lay / lie*) your head in the salad dish.

____ 14-2.   Will you (*learn / teach*) me the truth about departmental politics?

____ 14-3.   The former proposal was longer, but the (*later / latter*) was wiser.

____ 14-4.   Because of her (*judicious / judicial*) use of company funds, Stephanie has saved us tens of thousands of dollars.

____ 14-5.   Stanley still eats (*catsup / catchup / ketchup*) on his scrambled eggs.

____ 14-6.   The speaker said several (*laudable / laudatory*) things about the university.

____ 14-7.   Fritz can't ride a bike, (*let alone / leave alone*) a unicycle.

____ 15-1.   We have worked the (*lifelong / livelong*) day and accomplished almost nothing.

____ 15-2.   The state is (*liable / apt / likely*) to raise our property taxes again soon.

____ 15-3.   Please (*lend / loan*) me a dollar for a cup of coffee.

____ 15-4.   Don't you just (*loath / loathe*) such arrogant behavior?

____ 15-5.   Try not to (*lose / loose*) your glasses again.

____ 15-6.   These (*lustful / lusty*) lads can work a ten-hour day and still look forward to some exercise after dinner.

____ 15-7.   Just (*as / like*) I thought, you were the masked one.

Important Distinctions (Sequences 16–18)

____16-1. The time (*maybe* / *may be*) right to suggest a change at the top.

____16-2. (*Most* / *Almost*) all of our friends went to the fair.

____16-3. What is the current (*morale* / *moral*) of the line workers?

____16-4. We became (*nauseated* / *nauseous*) from the smell of burning rubber.

____16-5. Television is today our dominant entertainment (*media* / *medium*).

____16-6. Manual typewriters are (*obsolete* / *obsolescent*) in today's electronic office.

____16-7. The (*amount of* / *number of*) students who showed up surprised me.

____17-1. The (*official* / *officious*) word from the boss is that we make a bid.

____17-2. A substantial (*percent* / *percentage*) of our business is export.

____17-3. You shouldn't bring your (*personal* / *personnel*) problems to the office.

____17-4. Alas, intense competition seems to be one of the (*perimeters* / *parameters*) of a market-driven economy.

____17-5. What (*odd* / *oddly*) shaped heads these aliens have.

____17-6. Isn't it time to move (*on* / *onto* / *on to*) bigger and better things?

____17-7. Where do we look for (*prospective* / *perspective*) leaders for the future?

____18-1. In the end, the stronger species will (*predominant* / *predominate*).

____18-2. English I is a (*prerequisite* / *perquisite*) for English II.

____18-3. (*Please* / *Kindly*) be quiet; you have already convinced us that you are a lout.

____18-4. In this case, the (*plaintiff* / *defendant*) is suing the university.

____18-5. If this (*prophesy* / *prophecy*) comes true, were are all in for "interesting times."

____18-6. In this parade, the marching bands will (*precede* / *proceed*) the horses.

Important Distinctions (Sequences 19–22)

____ 19-1. Will the price of corn (*raise / rise*) in the fall?

____ 19-2. The group performed (*respectfully / respectively / respectably*) and then left the stage amid warm applause.

____ 19-3. The wounded man lay (*prostrate / prostate*) on the floor.

____ 19-4. You must offer some sort of (*rational / rationale*) for your proposal.

____ 19-5. Take care to get the (*quotation / quote*) right.

____ 20-1. Please don't (*set / sit*) in these chairs wearing your weapons.

____ 20-2. It was weeks before the patient could eat (*solid / stolid*) food.

____ 20-3. Does a (*sculpture / sculptor*) usually work from a live model?

____ 20-4. (*Some time / Sometime*) will be needed to plan the project.

____ 20-5. (*Since / Because*) we won't see each other again, I will say good-bye now.

____ 21-1. The first course is less demanding (*than / then*) the second one.

____ 21-2. Those fellows (*sure / surely*) know how to occupy a chair.

____ 21-3. After a careful study, we (*believe / feel / think*) we have uncovered the truth.

____ 21-4. (*Suggestible / Suggestive*) individuals are inclined to be influenced by others.

____ 21-5. This is the house (*which / that*) the high school construction class built.

____ 22-1. We (*used to / use to*) practice three times a week, but no more.

____ 22-2. I don't know (*if / whether*) we should enter the competition or just watch.

____ 22-3. Don't you just hate to (*wait on / wait for*) someone who is always late?

____ 22-4. The mechanic did a very (*thorough / through*) job of checking the car.

____ 22-5. Educated in China and Japan, Ramona is a very (*unique / unusual*) person.

Sentence Error Identification Exercise (1)

A. Sentence Fragment   F. Pronoun-Antecedent Error
B. Fused Sentence   G. Misplaced Modifier
C. Comma Splice   H. Dangling Modifier
D. Subject-Verb Agreement Error   I. Faulty Parallelism
E. Pronoun Case Error   J. Faulty Verb Form

_____ 1. None of the required items were on the shelf, not one.

_____ 2. When I was a child on the farm, we growed sweet corn for the birds.

_____ 3. Everyone in the class, as well as the parents, enjoyed you singing last evening.

_____ 4. Jan realized in a more tranquil setting progress would be forthcoming.

_____ 5. The instructor said that such errors are not uncommon here are some obvious examples.

_____ 6. As had been the case for many years, no one in the department except Bernice was willing to run for the faculty senate.

_____ 7. By twelve o'clock the party was over, and it became steadily colder throughout the night.

_____ 8. By now, you should know—indeed, everyone should know—that there are no accounting for differing tastes.

_____ 9. Not surprisingly, the psychedelic Saab's paint job drew a large crowd of admiring spectators.

_____10. I'm certain it was her who told us where to buy the tickets.

_____11. Starved from weeks without food, the hamburgers tasted like a feast.

_____12. Winning seven matches in a row without losing a single set.

_____13. Edmund's apartment, like most apartments in these buildings, was undersized, needed major repairs, and poorly lighted.

_____14. Students completing this program are very employable, for example, my roommate was hired the day after graduation.

_____15. To photograph these birds in flight, complete concentration is required.

_____16. We have already paid this bill must belong to someone else.

_____17. You might have wore something a little less flamboyant to a funeral.

_____18. Finally attracting enough attention to get his picture in the national magazines.

_____19. The energy crisis will continue because we do not conserve it.

_____20. We know what you did, moreover we have contacted the police.

Sentence Error Identification Exercise (2)

A. Sentence Fragment   F. Pronoun-Antecedent Error
B. Fused Sentence   G. Misplaced Modifier
C. Comma Splice   H. Dangling Modifier
D. Subject-Verb Agreement Error   I. Faulty Parallelism
E. Pronoun Case Error   J. Faulty Verb Form

____ 1. These items were given to she and I by our great aunt, who lives in Malibu.

____ 2. Before applying the primer, all the exterior walls must be scraped and sanded.

____ 3. Neither mathematics nor physics are required for this curriculum.

____ 4. Franklin says that he likes reading good books, listening to good music, viewing works of modern art, and winter trips to warm climates.

____ 5. We were amazed to learn that every car and truck in the competition had had their engine overhauled.

____ 6. Isabel went to flight school. Hoping to become an airline pilot.

____ 7. At the conclusion of the second act, the heroine relates the story of her marriage to one of her sisters.

____ 8. Liz reads rapidly, she can finish a novel in a single evening.

____ 9. Ironically, the two brothers come to the same decision; they didn't want to go to college.

____ 10. The judge smiled grimly and said, "You may as well enjoy your dinner at daylight you die."

____ 11. Although carefully organized, few members of the audience enjoyed the concert.

____ 12. If the children leave any meat or vegetables, boil them into a stew.

____ 13. The time has come for some serious thinking, otherwise we are likely to make a mistake.

____ 14. Please tell me about the martyred saints, the ancient philosophers, the famous teachers, and how to live a productive life.

____ 15. There was too much salt in the beans now my mouth is dry.

____ 16. I can't think of anything I would rather not do than drink a warm glass of milk before going to bed.

____ 17. The instructor, not to mention most of the students, were prepared to ask the dean some tough questions.

____ 18. Whom, in your opinion, will be the next president of the faculty union?

____ 19. The debris that blowed across the street came from the warehouse.

____ 20. When we were in Chicago, we stayed at the Radisson. Not the Hilton.

Sentence Error Identification Exercise (3)

A. Sentence Fragment   F. Pronoun-Antecedent Error
B. Fused Sentence   G. Misplaced Modifier
C. Comma Splice   H. Dangling Modifier
D. Subject-Verb Agreement Error   I. Faulty Parallelism
E. Pronoun Case Error   J. Faulty Verb Form

____ 1. If you or me cheated on a test, the instructor would be very angry.

____ 2. Having run the vacuum and changed the beds, the house was almost presentable.

____ 3. Each man, woman, and child were carefully examined for injuries.

____ 4. By June the workers will have tore down most of the old buildings.

____ 5. A good story well told, holding the children on the edge of their seats.

____ 6. The first thing I had to do every morning was take the gerbils out of their cages and wash them.

____ 7. After searching for weeks, we finally located a truck perfect for our needs and that we could afford to buy.

____ 8. Once again, Scott came in last night racing is very difficult for him.

____ 9. Jeffrey said, without taking sufficient time to think, some unnecessarily harsh things to his sisters.

____10. Him and me always got along, even when we disagreed about things.

____11. We sunk a cool ten million into that project and got no return.

____12. Most of our days and nights was spent disarming land mines.

____13. Not surprisingly, Douglas was the hero of the afternoon, he ate two dozen hot dogs.

____14. One of the qualities of a good high school teacher is that he makes himself available to students seeking extra help.

____15. Indeed, love may be the answer, however we don't really know what the question is.

____16. Although she speaks several languages, Robin only reads English.

____17. After the basic research has been completed; we shall seek financing.

____18. To chase the dogs through the woods, a dress is inappropriate attire.

____19. We walked into the room with a loud bang, a shipping crate fell from the loft, crashing upon the hardwood floor.

____20. In the end I realized that I not only lacked the time needed to become a professional organist but also the talent.

Name _____ Class _____ Section _____

Sentence Error Identification Exercise (4)

A. Sentence Fragment   F. Pronoun-Antecedent Error
B. Fused Sentence   G. Misplaced Modifier
C. Comma Splice   H. Dangling Modifier
D. Subject-Verb Agreement Error   I. Faulty Parallelism
E. Pronoun Case Error   J. Faulty Verb Form

_____ 1. "Spring is a beautiful time of year," the visiting poet said, "it often brings out the romantic in each of us."

_____ 2. Gazing across the runway, three fighter planes suddenly came into view.

_____ 3. Writing books and essays are no easy way to earn one's bread and water.

_____ 4. Professor Waffle's new novel is thoroughly shocking everyone on campus is reading it.

_____ 5. The old hermit lived in a hut on an island in the middle of a river that he built for himself.

_____ 6. I asked for a cup of coffee. Not a lecture about the dangers of caffeine.

_____ 7. Everyone in the class was surprised to learn that the industrial output of Germany was greater than Japan.

_____ 8. When we were children, little attention was given to my sister Jan and I.

_____ 9. Garvey said that he had never drank so much canned pop in his life as he did on the hunting trip.

_____ 10. You can't expect to win every tournament, situations vary from week to week.

_____ 11. After more than six weeks of testing, the task force reluctantly admitted that the foreign models were more carefully designed.

_____ 12. If planted too early in the season, freezing weather will kill the peas.

_____ 13. We cruised around town for a while then we went to the bar for a little refreshment.

_____ 14. Even though Ann has several orange trees in her yard, she doesn't eat them.

_____ 15. It was just before dusk when we seen the deer on the runway.

_____ 16. Bertram, for example, who had never been across the state line.

_____ 17. Loren's youngest cousin had brain surgery about six months ago, and it has been improving ever since.

_____ 18. No one on the team, not even the seniors, can run faster than me.

_____ 19. So many of my old colleagues have retired at the office that I hardly recognized anyone at the Christmas party.

_____ 20. Neither the fox nor the hounds has the energy for a hunt today.

Sentence Error Identification Exercise (5)

A. Sentence Fragment   F. Pronoun-Antecedent Error
B. Fused Sentence   G. Misplaced Modifier
C. Comma Splice   H. Dangling Modifier
D. Subject-Verb Agreement Error   I. Faulty Parallelism
E. Pronoun Case Error   J. Faulty Verb Form

____ 1. Everyone agree that we should look for a new sponsor, perhaps one with deeper pockets.

____ 2. In reviewing the instructor's comments about the paper, it was obvious that further revision was necessary.

____ 3. By the time school began, the twins had broke almost every toy that they took to the lake.

____ 4. Who were the officers asking for, Neddy or Jake?

____ 5. Maynard promised his mother after graduating from college he would clean up his act and become a normal human being.

____ 6. We spent a month on poetry before Christmas we wrote some verses of our own.

____ 7. Alas, some people do not have the ability to realize their dreams, and that can make their lives unhappy ones.

____ 8. This type of violence, now almost an epidemic, is senseless, we must put a stop to it.

____ 9. Professor Kidney was neither a good lecturer nor did he care much about his students.

____10. Listening carefully and trying to remember every word that was said.

____11. Actually, the day went quite well after a nice little nap.

____12. College is a pain in my English class, we are expected to be able to read and write—and enjoy both.

____13. Recently, American cars have become far less expensive to maintain.

____14. The sum and substance of your position have not changed.

____15. Why would anyone have stole such a worthless piece of junk?

____16. Most of these items are too expensive. Too expensive for our customers, at any rate.

____17. All the Volvos had been leased to local customers that had standard driver's-side air bags.

____18. There was a time—not so long ago—when young people wanted to learn, they wanted to be taught by demanding instructors.

____19. The receptionists convinced the typists that they should be earning more money than they had earned in the past.

____20. Except for two or three, the players behaved theirselves quite nicely.

Sentence Error Identification Exercise (6)

A. Sentence Fragment
B. Fused Sentence
C. Comma Splice
D. Subject-Verb Agreement Error
E. Pronoun Case Error

F. Pronoun-Antecedent Error
G. Misplaced Modifier
H. Dangling Modifier
I. Faulty Parallelism
J. Faulty Verb Form

____ 1. Some people must always get their own way, no matter who they offend.

____ 2. For ten years, Phoebe has swam her laps in this pool each morning before breakfast.

____ 3. It is very important for us to if we can understand the fundamental structure of matter.

____ 4. The performance was first rate, or even better, indeed some thought it was the best of the season.

____ 5. Only because we were unable to afford advertising and the economy was flat.

____ 6. The school insists on a three-point academic average to keep my scholarship.

____ 7. Does anyone know where Lucy and him were intending to go?

____ 8. Hiram, much like his older brothers, is one of these people who seems to care nothing for others.

____ 9. When Ida tried to talk to her mother, she was in a grim mood.

____ 10. I ran across this article in the city papers shouldn't print such unsubstantiated rumors.

____ 11. Few people seem to realize that walking is better for them than to jog.

____ 12. At least two-thirds of the land were acidic, not to mention submerged.

____ 13. Once again, Carol's nephews have ran up a substantial bill at the local amusement center.

____ 14. Bob, Bryan, and Bruno all three broke the old record, however none of them won the race.

____ 15. You are as well informed, if not more informed than, many of the contestants on *Jeopardy*.

____ 16. How can this be winter when we have had just one freezing day all week?

____ 17. Winston, still full of vigor and enthusiasm after more than two hours on the track.

____ 18. After sitting in the wrong class for two weeks, the instructor finally told me where to go.

____ 19. You must go directly to the dean's office at three o'clock you are expected there.

____ 20. If anyone requires assistance completing the project on time, they should contact the instructor.

Sentence Error Identification Exercise (7)

A. Sentence Fragment	F. Pronoun-Antecedent Error
B. Fused Sentence	G. Misplaced Modifier
C. Comma Splice	H. Dangling Modifier
D. Subject-Verb Agreement Error	I. Faulty Parallelism
E. Pronoun Case Error	J. Faulty Verb Form

____ 1. Unfortunately, neither Joan nor Edwin was prepared for the examination.

____ 2. Before reading a book like this, the mind must be free of distractions.

____ 3. Margaret, not Alison, is still slimmer than me, but plumper than him.

____ 4. As it turned out, the company with the low bid done very good work.

____ 5. Hundreds turned out at the airport, everyone wanted to wish the team well.

____ 6. Although I have never seen a leprechaun, I have read about them in psychology class.

____ 7. Swimming is excellent exercise. For anyone who enjoys a good workout.

____ 8. As I recall, it was last Monday when I read the article in *Newsweek* about euthanasia.

____ 9. Alas, we will never win this tournament is out of our class.

____10. Nathan has always wanted to be a movie star, which has cost him a fortune over the years.

____11. My new physics professor is an internationally known scholar and who has taught many famous students.

____12. Only one of the papers were lost; the rest were saved.

____13. The crews usually begun work between six and seven o'clock.

____14. The hostesses served spicy hors d'oeuvres to the guests that were too hot to swallow.

____15. Beryl won't let us down, she does her best work under pressure.

____16. You enrolling during the summer session rather than during the fall was a smart move.

____17. During the years following his graduation from college, Hiram worked at several occupations: salesclerk, driving a truck, house painter, and repairing table lamps.

____18. The lights were far too bright to focus the camera was impossible.

____19. To achieve the right taste, you must apply the barbecue sauce while the burger is cooking.

____20. A high-tech system with which the company is quite pleased.

Sentence Error Identification Exercise (8)

A. Sentence Fragment
B. Fused Sentence
C. Comma Splice
D. Subject-Verb Agreement Error
E. Pronoun Case Error

F. Pronoun-Antecedent Error
G. Misplaced Modifier
H. Dangling Modifier
I. Faulty Parallelism
J. Faulty Verb Form

____ 1. As far as I know, the whereabouts of the hijackers are a mystery.

____ 2. Although the child had been bit by a poisonous snake, she was doing fine.

____ 3. This is the person whom I think will be the next target of a letter bomb.

____ 4. The police found, after a month-long search, the body of the victim.

____ 5. Alice is neither a student of Russian history nor does she speak the Russian language.

____ 6. Don't eat your neighbors intend to invite you to dinner.

____ 7. Although there were some objections, in the end everyone presented a report on their summer activities.

____ 8. On the first leg of the race; almost half the runners dropped out.

____ 9. Please give me another chance, I promise to do better in the future.

____ 10. When sound to sleep, this medicine does its best work.

____ 11. Alas, many of those things that I once thought would please me totally put me off.

____ 12. To make millions have always been Goddard's first goal in life.

____ 13. By brushing carefully each day, the teeth are less likely to develop cavities.

____ 14. I must admit that I enjoyed the dean's stories of his undergraduate days at Ohio State more than you.

____ 15. We're asking a few friends, including yourselves, to spend the weekend with us.

____ 16. We should have knowed that so old a car would need major repairs.

____ 17. "Frank did study," the instructor admitted, "he earned only a C grade, however."

____ 18. With nothing to do and even less to look forward to. The youths were not very optimistic.

____ 19. Ian's sister is a brain surgeon, and he is very envious of her.

____ 20. Not just anyone can buy you have to be a member of the club.

Sentence Error Identification Exercise (9)

A. Sentence Fragment
B. Fused Sentence
C. Comma Splice
D. Subject-Verb Agreement Error
E. Pronoun Case Error

F. Pronoun-Antecedent Error
G. Misplaced Modifier
H. Dangling Modifier
I. Faulty Parallelism
J. Faulty Verb Form

_____ 1. On Sunday afternoons, my friends and myself used to fly our model planes at the local airport.

_____ 2. By the end of the season, the players will have went through dozens of pairs of shoes.

_____ 3. In the unlikely event that no one shows up for the execution.

_____ 4. Glenna gave her brother a gilded man's tiepin, but he didn't like it.

_____ 5. I think that Inez is in love with me mother told me so.

_____ 6. After five years as an undergraduate, Wilma was in need of a job and broke.

_____ 7. Although years had passed since either had played, neither Giles nor Julius had lost their shooting eye.

_____ 8. I don't like fruit-flavored yogurt, does anyone?

_____ 9. Deeply shaken by the storm, returning home was out of the question.

_____10. With the game having just gotten underway and the stands about half filled.

_____11. Chloe said that she would rather live in Chicago than any city in the United States.

_____12. At least three, and maybe four, members of the staff was included in the disagreement with the manager.

_____13. The instructor was angry because no one had did the homework assignment.

_____14. According to this document, no one has asked she to judge the show.

_____15. When going through puberty, Mother had no patience with the children.

_____16. When we tried to return the defective merchandise to the store, they would not accept it.

_____17. John's brother, not his cousins, intend to spend the summer in Greenland.

_____18. We have heard enough pep talks, now we need some action.

_____19. Our abiding goal was to whenever possible introduce new product lines.

_____20. The entire squad attended the meeting afterwards everyone went to the opening game of the tournament.

Sentence Error Identification Exercise (10)

A. Sentence Fragment
B. Fused Sentence
C. Comma Splice
D. Subject-Verb Agreement Error
E. Pronoun Case Error

F. Pronoun-Antecedent Error
G. Misplaced Modifier
H. Dangling Modifier
I. Faulty Parallelism
J. Faulty Verb Form

_____ 1. Please say something nice just once I would like to hear a pleasantry.

_____ 2. Ted plays both tennis and soccer and very skillfully.

_____ 3. Early spring and early autumn can be risky times to visit Western Michigan, tornadoes are not uncommon.

_____ 4. The day finally being over and everyone being weary of work.

_____ 5. All in all, seventy-five years are not a lot of time to discover the secrets of the universe.

_____ 6. Only a Neanderthal wouldn't understand that those kind of pranks wound civilized people.

_____ 7. Elizabeth had once met the man that her sister later married quite by accident.

_____ 8. As you might expect, the concert was too expensive for Ann and I to attend.

_____ 9. When Father come home with too much venison, we always gave some to the neighbors.

_____ 10. Toward dawn, when the first glimmer of light was just visible on the horizon.

_____ 11. To be absolutely safe, at least $40 million should be put aside for a rainy day.

_____ 12. Alas, we have lost our way to the top has been blocked.

_____ 13. That revered bell hasn't rang since August 7, 1982.

_____ 14. Because Conrad's father did not approve of us smoking in the house, we went outside.

_____ 15. We fought the war to, as they say, make the world safe for multinational corporations.

_____ 16. As was often the situation on Saturday mornings, the pool was overcrowded, consequently we decided to play tennis.

_____ 17. Standing precariously on the narrow ledge, the roaring wind didn't make things any less difficult.

_____ 18. When the contract was ratified by the general membership, the bargaining team had completed their task and thus ceased to exist.

_____ 19. The desire to foretell the future is one of the things that sets humans apart from the animals.

_____ 20. The exchange students were intelligent, possessors of pleasant personalities, and informed academically.

Chapter 2 Nonstandard or Inappropriate Expressions

Sequence 1–3:   A B C B A C A B A B A B A B A B A B A B

Sequence 4–6:   A B B A B B A A B A B A B A B A B B A A B A

Sequence 7–9:   B B C B A A B B C A B A B A B A B A B A A B

Sequence 10–12:   B A B A B B A B A B A A B A B A B A B A B A

Sequence 13–15:   A B A B A B A B A C A B A B A B B A A B

Chapter 3 Words That Sound Alike

Sequence 1–3:   B C B A A B A B A B B A C A A B A B B A

Sequence 4–6:   B C B A B A C B A C B D A A B A B C A B

Sequence 7–9:   B A A A B A B A B B B A A B A A C B A B

Sequence 10–12:   A B C A C B A B A C B A B A A B B C A C

Sequence 13–15:   B B A A B A B A B C A C B D C A A C B B

Sequence 16–18:   C B C A A C B A B A C A B A C B C A B B

Sequence 19–21:   A B C B A A B A A C A C A B A C B B A B

Chapter 4 Important Distinctions

Sequence 1–3:   B B C B A A A B A B A B A B A B A B C B A B

Sequence 4–6:   B A A B A B A B B B A A A B A B A B B A

Sequence 7–9:   B A B A A B A B A B A B A D B A B B A A

Sequence 10–12:   B A B A B A A B A B A B A B A B A A B B

Sequence 13–15:   A B A B A B A B B A C B A B C A B A B A

Sequence 16–18:   B B A A B A B A B A B B C A B A B A B A

Sequence 19–22:   B C A B A B A B A B A B C A B A B B A B

Chapter 8 and Chapter 9   Commonly Occurring Sentence Problems (Continued)

Sentence Error Identification Exercises

Exercise 1:	D	J	E	G	B	I	F	D	G	E	H	A	I	C	H	B	J	A	F	C
Exercise 2:	E	H	D	I	F	A	G	C	J	B	H	F	C	I	B	G	D	E	J	A
Exercise 3:	E	H	D	J	A	F	I	B	G	E	J	D	C	F	C	G	A	H	B	I
Exercise 4:	C	H	D	B	G	A	I	E	J	C	I	H	B	F	J	A	F	E	G	D
Exercise 5:	D	H	J	E	G	B	F	C	I	A	H	B	I	D	J	A	G	C	F	E
Exercise 6:	E	J	G	C	A	H	E	D	F	B	I	D	J	C	I	G	A	H	B	F
Exercise 7:	D	H	E	J	C	F	A	G	B	F	I	D	J	G	C	E	I	B	H	A
Exercise 8:	D	J	E	G	I	B	F	A	C	H	G	D	H	I	E	J	C	A	F	B
Exercise 9:	E	J	A	G	B	I	F	C	H	A	I	D	J	E	H	F	D	C	G	B
Exercise 10:	B	I	C	A	D	F	G	E	J	A	H	B	J	E	G	C	H	F	D	I

St. Martin's